THE ESSENTIAL
ENGLISH–GAELIC DICTIONARY

The Essential English–Gaelic Dictionary

A Dictionary for Students and Learners of Scottish Gaelic

Compiled by
ANGUS WATSON

Birlinn

First published in 2005 by
Birlinn Limited
West Newington House
10 Newington Road
Edinburgh EH9 1QS

www.birlinn.co.uk

ISBN 10: 1 84158106 2
ISBN 13: 978 1 84158106 4

British Library Cataloguing-in-Publication Data
A catalogue record for this book is available from the British Library

Thug Comhairle nan Leabhraichean tabhartas barantais dhan
fhoillsichear airson obair deasachaidh air an leabhar seo, agus chuidich
a' Chomhairle le cosgaisean an leabhair

Typeset by Edderston Book Design, Peebles
Printed and bound by Creative Print and Design, Ebbw Vale, Wales

Contents

❧

do Sheònaid, a-rithist

Introduction

This volume complements the same compiler's *Essential Gaelic–English Dictionary*, published by Birlinn in 2001. The intention has been to make available, in a format that is pleasant to handle, a generous proportion of "essential" or core Gaelic. For this reason much of the material given is common to the two volumes, and can thus be accessed from the starting point of either English or Gaelic.

Though dictionaries are not learning tools in the way that grammars or course books are, anyone who was to absorb a reasonable proportion of the content of these volumes would be well equipped to function in a Gaelic-speaking environment, and from then on to learn by using the language – which is, after all, the best way!

A key feature of both volumes has been, where appropriate, to present headwords in terms of the different senses and nuances they may have – something not seriously attempted for Gaelic since Dwelly's monumental *Illustrated Gaelic–English Dictionary* of 1901 and subsequent reprints. Dwelly's volume remains a very impressive work of lexicography, but Gaelic has evolved so much since he gathered his material that it is not to be put into the hands of the unwary.

Among English–Gaelic dictionaries, *An Stòr-Dàta Briathrachais Gàidhlig / The Gaelic Terminology Database*, Clò Ostaig, 1993, does not attempt to make clear distinctions between the different senses and shades of meaning a headword might have. Nonetheless, it gives a hefty range of Gaelic equivalents for a large number of English items, and is a valuable tool if used with discrimination. The number of equivalents given can be confusing or off-putting, but the principle followed by the compilers was generally to put the most commonly used Gaelic equivalents at the head of the entry. The wise learner, if unsure of an item, will always try to confirm in a Gaelic–English dictionary the precise sense of the Gaelic word or words found.

Among other sources for equivalents for words and phrases are the English–Gaelic *Faclan Ùra Gàidhlig*, produced for the Highland Council in 1993, and the much more nuanced *Faclair na Pàrlamaid/Dictionary of Terms*, published under the auspices of the Scottish Parliament in 2001. The first of these has a mix of technical and more everyday items. The second, which has both English–Gaelic and Gaelic–English sections, deals mainly with political and administrative vocabulary, but at the same time has words and expressions that are useful in other contexts.

* * * * *

In compiling the *Essential* dictionaries I have not knowingly favoured any particular Gaelic dialect, but have endeavoured to include words and expressions that can be used in most, if not all, Scottish Gaelic environments.

The Layout of the Entries

❦

Within the entries, all English material for translation into Gaelic is given in bold type. Italics are used for all other text in English, ie for abbreviations, instructions such as *see* and *Cf*, and all notes, comments, explanatory material and grammatical information. The Gaelic translation equivalents given for the English headwords, phrases and expressions, represent current Gaelic usage except where marked *trad* (*traditional*), *occas* (*occasionally*), &c. Gaelic spelling used corresponds to up-to-date norms. Occasionally two acceptable spellings are given for the same Gaelic word.

The examples given below show how in a typical entry the English headword is followed by its part of speech, which is abbreviated (see list of abbreviations pp. xiii to xv).

abrupt *adj* **1** (*sudden &c*) grad; **2** (*of persons: terse, short-tempered*) cas, aithghearr; **3** (*of slope &c*) cas
elder[1] *n* **1** (*church ~*) èildear *m*, (*more trad*) foirfeach *m*; **2** (*older of two*) am fear/an tè (*&c*) as sine, **John is the** ~ is e Iain am fear *m* as sine

These examples also show how synonyms or other indications, such as (*older of two*), are given in brackets, and often in numbered subsections, to distinguish between the senses or contexts for which a given Gaelic translation equivalent applies. In the case of **elder**[1], a superscript numeral is being used to make the distinction between English homonyms, that is words with the same form but different meanings – the entry **elder**[2] *n* refers to the elder tree.

Gaelic nouns are given in the nominative singular (radical) case, followed by the abbreviated gender of the noun, as follows:

safety *n* tèarainteachd *f invar*, sàbhailteachd *f invar*, **in** ~ an tèarainteachd, ~ **equipment** uidheam *f sing coll* sàbhailteachd

Some Gaelic nouns have both genders and this is shown by the abbreviation *mf*. In the example above *invar* (*invariable*) also shows that the nouns in question have only the one form, ie do not decline. It was also thought helpful, especially to learners, to give the gender of every noun used in the examples throughout the dictionary (*Cf* uidheam *f sing coll* above), except where the gender is shown by a definite article or a following adjective.

The Gaelic equivalents for many headwords are followed by common expressions involving that headword. Each repetition of the English headword is represented by the symbol ~, as in ~ **equipment** (for **safety equipment**) above. The abbreviation *in expr* (*in the expression*) is used to signal that in certain expressions, often idiomatic ones, the Gaelic equivalent for a particular English headword or phrase is different from the standard ones given earlier in the entry. This is illustrated by:

milk *n* bainne *m*, *in expr* ~ **cows** crodh-eadraidh *m*

Verbs are given in the second person singular imperative form. The abbreviation *vt* (*transitive verb*) indicates that, *in the sense concerned in the entry*, a given verb is used with a direct object, while *vi* (*intransitive verb*) shows that it is used without a direct object. The following example illustrates the difference between a transitive use of 'capsize', **they capsized her/the boat**, and an intransitive use, **the boat capsized**.

capsize *v* **1** (*as vt*) cuir *vt* thairis, **they ~d her** chuir iad thairis i; **2** (*as vi*) rach *vi* thairis, **the boat ~d** chaidh am bàta thairis, *also* chaidh car *m* dhen bhàta *m*

A verb that can be used in either of these ways is labelled *vti*, as follows:

gather *v* cruinnich *vti*, **they ~ed in the barn** chruinnich iad san t-sabhal, **he ~ed them (together) in the barn** chruinnich e iad san t-sabhal

Where a Gaelic verb takes a particular preposition, this is shown in brackets after the verb, as follows:

accentuate *v* cuir stràc *m*, leig cudthrom *m*, (*with prep* air)

In this particular case the comma after 'cudthrom *m*' indicates that both the verbs listed take the same preposition, air, whereas in the entry below the verbs concerned take different prepositions.

advise *v* comhairlich *vi* (*with prep* do), thoir comhairle (*with preps* air *or* do) . . .

At the end of the dictionary will be found a table of the forms of the Gaelic article, and much additional grammatical information is given within the individual entries. In particular, the forms of the prepositional pronouns are given in full, and readers should consult the entry for the corresponding English preposition.

The genitive and nominative plural forms of many Gaelic nouns, and the present participles of many verbs, are to be found within the relevant entries in the companion volume, *The Essential Gaelic–English Dictionary*. Tables giving the forms of the irregular verbs likely to be encountered in mainstream Gaelic are also to be found, at the end of the same volume.

Acknowledgements

෫

Warm thanks are due to the Gaelic Books Council for a grant towards the cost of compiling this dictionary.

Ailean Boyd was once again meticulous in his reading of the typescript, and I am very grateful for his many suggestions and emendations. Any errors remaining are, of course, mine entirely.

I wish especially to thank my wife for her financial support – and for her patience, encouragement and good humour – during the long gestation of this dictionary and its earlier Gaelic–English counterpart, when her man was so often incommunicado in front of the word processor!

List of Abbreviations

❧

abbrev	*abbreviation*
abstr	*abstract*
acc	*accusative*
adj	*adjective, adjectival*
adv	*adverb, adverbial*
agric	*agriculture, agricultural*
alt	*alternative*
anat	*anatomy*
approx	*approximate, approximately*
art	*article*
Bibl	*Bible, Biblical*
biol	*biology*
bot	*botany, botanical*
Cf	*compare*
chem	*chemistry, chemical*
coll	*collective*
comp	*comparative*
con	*concrete*
conj	*conjunction*
cons	*consonant*
corres	*correspondence, corresponding*
dat	*dative*
def	*defective*
derog	*derogatory*
dimin	*diminutive*
ed	*education, educational*
elec	*electric, electrical*
emph	*emphasis, emphatic*
Eng	*English*
engin	*engineering*
esp	*especially*
excl(s)	*exclamation(s)*
expr(s)	*expression(s)*

f	*feminine*
fam	*familiar*
fig	*figurative, figuratively*
fin	*financial, financially*
freq	*frequent, frequently*
fut	*future*
geog	*geography, geographical*
gen	*genitive*
gov	*government*
gram	*grammar, grammatical*
hist	*history, historical*
imper	*imperative*
incl	*including*
infin	*infinitive*
inter	*interrogative*
invar	*invariable*
irreg	*irregular*
IT	*information technology, computing*
lang	*language*
lit	*literally*
Lit	*literature, literary*
m	*masculine*
med	*medical*
misc	*miscellaneous*
mus	*music, musical*
n	*noun*
nec	*necessary, necessarily*
neg	*negative*
nf	*noun, feminine*
nm	*noun, masculine*
nmf	*noun, masculine & feminine*
nom	*nominative*
num(s)	*numeral(s), numerical*
obs	*obsolete*
occas	*occasionally*
past part	*past participle*
PC	*politically correct*
pej	*pejorative*
pers pron	*personal pronoun*
philo	*philosophy*
phys	*physical, physically*
pl	*plural*
poet	*poetical*
pol	*politics, political*

poss	*possessive*
prep pron	*prepositional pronoun*
pres part	*present participle*
pron	*pronoun*
prov	*proverb*
psych	*psychology, psychological*
pt	*part*
rel	*relative*
relig	*religion, religious*
Sc	*Scots (language)*
sing	*singular*
sing coll	*singular collective*
sp	*spelling*
sup	*superlative*
topog	*topography*
trad	*traditional, traditionally*
typog	*typography*
usu	*usual, usually*
v	*verb, verbal*
veg	*vegetable*
vi	*verb, intransitive*
vt	*verb, transitive*
vti	*verb, transitive & intransitive*
voc	*vocative*
vulg	*vulgar*

A

a.m. *adv* sa mhadainn *f*, **six ~** sia uairean *fpl* sa mhadainn

a, an *indefinite art, not expressed in Gaelic*, **I saw ~ man** chunnaic mi duine *m*, **I ate an apple** dh'ith mi ubhal *m*

abandon *v* trèig *vt*, **he ~ed his family** thrèig e a theaghlach *m*, **the people ~ed the island** thrèig na daoine *mpl* an t-eilean, **~ the faith of your forefathers** trèig creideamh *m* ur sinnsirean *mpl*

abandonment *n* trèigsinn *m invar*

abasement *n* ìsleachadh *m*, **self-~** fèin-ìsleachadh *m*

abash *v* nàraich *vt*

abashed *adj & past part* nàraichte, air a (*&c*) nàrachadh

abate *v* lùghdaich *vi*, rach *vi* sìos, **the storm ~d** lùghdaich an stoirm *mf*, chaidh an stoirm sìos

abatement *n* lùghdachadh *m*

abattoir *n* taigh-spadaidh *m*

abbess *n* ban-aba *f*

abbey *n* abaid *f*

abbot *n* aba *m*

abbreviate *v* giorraich *vt*

abbreviation *n* giorrachadh *m*

abdicate *v* leig dheth (*&c*) an crùn, **the queen ~d** leig a' bhanrigh dhith an crùn

abdication *n* leigeil *mf* dheth (*&c*) a' chrùin, **after their ~** an dèidh dhaibh an crùn a leigeil dhiubh

abduct *v* thoir *vt* air falbh

abduction *n* toirt *f invar* air falbh

abet *v* cuidich *vti*

abettor *n* pàirtiche *m*, neach-cuideachaidh *m* (*pl* luchd-cuideachaidh *m sing coll*)

abeyance *n* stad *m*, **the scheme is in ~** tha an sgeama *m* na stad

abhor *v*, **I ~ him/it** tha gràin *f* agam air

abhorrence *n* gràin *f*

abhorrent *adj* gràineil

abide *v* **1** (*stand, tolerate*) fuiling *vti*, **I can't ~ him/it** chan fhuiling mi e, (*also*) chan urrainn dhomh fhulang; **2** (*Lit: dwell, Sc stay*) fuirich *vi*, còmhnaich *vi*

abiding *adj* (*enduring*) maireannach

ability *n* comas *m*, **~ to speak** comas bruidhne *f*, **intellectual ~** comas inntinn *f*, **that's beyond my ~** tha sin thar mo chomais, (*ed*) **mixed ~** comasan measgaichte

abject *adj* truagh, (*more pej*) suarach, **~ poverty** bochdainn thruagh

able *adj* **1** (*skilled, highly competent*) comasach, **an ~ man** duine comasach, mentally ~ comasach na (&c) inntinn, glic; **2** (*capable of particular activity*) is *v irreg* urrainn (*with prep* do), **I am not ~ to write** chan urrainn dhomh sgrìobhadh, *also* chan eil sgrìobhadh *m* agam; **3** (*idiom: of invalid &c, fit for a particular activity*) **~ to go out** air chothrom *m* a dhol a-mach

-able *suffix* ion- *prefix* (*with past part of verb*), *eg* **eatable** ion-ithe, **practicable** ion-dhèanta

able-bodied *adj* corp-làidir, fallain

ablutions *n* (*the act*) ionnlad *m*

abnormal *adj* **1** (*unusual*) neo-chumanta, às a' chumantas; **2** (*phys ~*) meangach

abnormality *n* **1** (*state of being unusual*) neo-chumantas *m*; **2** (*phys ~*) meang *f*

aboard *adj* air bòrd *m* (*with gen*), **~ the aircraft** air bòrd na plèana

aboard *adv* air bòrd *m*, **come ~** thig *vi* air bòrd

abode *n* àite-còmhnaidh *m*, àite-fuirich *m*, **of no fixed ~** gun àite-còmhnaidh seasmhach

abolish *v* cuir *vi* às (*with prep* do), **they ~ed the monarchy** chuir iad às don mhonarcachd *f invar*

abolition *n* cur *m* às (**of** do)

abominate *v* gràinich *vt*

abomination *n* **1** (*the emotion*) mòr-ghràin *f*; **2** (*a source or cause of ~*) cùis-ghràin *f*, **it's an ~!** 's e cùis-ghràin a th' ann!

aborigene *n* tùsanach *m*, dùthchasach *m*

aboriginal *adj* dùthchasach, **~ culture** cultar dùthchasach

abortion *n* casg-breith *m invar*, casg-leatruim *m*, breith *f* an-abaich, **she had an ~** bha casg-breith aice

abortive *adj* (*fruitless*) gun toradh *m*, neo-tharbhach

abound *v* bi *vi irreg* pailt, bi lìonmhor, cuir *vi* thairis, **a land ~ing in game** tìr *mf* a' cur thairis le sitheann *f*

about *adv* **1** (*around*) mun cuairt, **the flu's going ~** tha an cnatan mòr a' dol mun cuairt; **2** *misc exprs* **up and ~** air a (&c) c(h)ois (*dat of* cas *f*), **we're (just) ~ to go/leave** tha sinn gu bhith a' falbh, **I'm just ~ ready** tha mi gu bhith deiseil, (*up to*) **what's she ~?** dè a tha i ris?

about *prep* **1** (*around*) mun cuairt & mu chuairt (*with prep* air), **fine views all ~ her** seallaidhean *mpl* brèagha fada mun cuairt oirre; **2** (*concerning*) mu dheidhinn *prep* (*takes the gen*), **~ me** mum dheidhinn, **they're saying dreadful/shocking things ~ the minister** tha iad ag ràdh rudan *mpl* oillteil mu dheidhinn a' mhinisteir *m*; **3** (*concerning and around*) mu (*takes the dat*), **~ me** umam(sa), **~ you** (*sing*) umad(sa), **~ him/it** (*m*) uime(-san), **~ her/it** (*f*) uimpe(se), **~ us** umainn(e), **~ you** (*pl*) umaibh(se), **~ them** umpa(san), **a story ~ the war** sgeulachd *f* mun chogadh (*also* sgeulachd mu dheidhinn a' chogaidh *and* sgeulachd air a' chogadh), **she put her coat ~ her** chuir i uimpe a còta *m*; **4** (*approximately*) timcheall air, mu (*takes dat & lenites following consonant*), **there'll be ~ ten people there** bidh timcheall air deichnear *mf invar* ann, bidh mu dheichnear ann

above *prep* **1** (*position*) os cionn (*with gen*), **clouds ~ the ocean** neòil *mpl* os cionn a' chuain, **~ me** os mo chionn; **2** (*misc exprs*) **~ all** (*ie especially*) gu h-àraidh *adv*, **~ board** follaiseach

abrasive *adj* sgrìobach

abridge *v* giorraich *vt*

abridged *adj & past part* giorraichte

abridgement *n* giorrachadh *m*

abroad *adv* **1** (*expr movement*) a-null thairis, **they went ~** chaidh iad a-null thairis; **2** (*expr position*) thall thairis, **they are ~** tha iad thall thairis; **3** (*circulating, current*) *in expr* (*formal*) **a rumour is ~** tha fathann *m* a' dol mun cuairt

abrupt *adj* **1** (*sudden &c*) grad; **2** (*of persons: terse, short-tempered*) cas, aithghearr; **3** (*of slope &c*) cas

abscess *n* niosgaid *f*

abscond *v* teich (air falbh) *vi*

absence *n* neo-làthaireachd *f invar*

absent *adj* neo-làthaireach, (*less formal*) **he's ~ today** chan eil e ann an-diugh, tha e dheth an-diugh

absent *v*, **~ oneself** (*fail to be present or to attend*) cùm *vi* às an làthair *f*, cùm *vi* air falbh

absentee *n* neach *m* (*&c*) neo-làthaireach

absent-minded *adj* dìochuimhneach

absolute *adj* **1** iomlan, **~ majority** mòr-chuid *f* iomlan; **2** làn- *prefix*, **~ power** làn-chumhachd *m*; **3** (*utter, complete, through & through*) dearg (*precedes the noun*), gu chùl (*follows the noun*), **an ~ fool** dearg amadan *m*, amadan gu chùl

absolutely *adv* gu h-iomlan, uile-gu-lèir

absolution *n* saoradh *m* (o pheacadh *m*)

absolve *v* saor *vt* (o pheacadh *m*)

absorb *v* **1** (*liquids &c*) sùigh *vt*; **2** (*information*) gabh *vt* a-steach

absorbent *adj* sùighteach

absorption *n* sùghadh *m*

abstain *v* **1** (*refrain from, avoid*) cùm *vi* (*with prep* o), seachain *vt*, **~ from drink** cùm on deoch-làidir *f*; **2** (*at election*) seachain bhòtadh *m*, **they ~ed** sheachain iad bhòtadh

abstemious *adj* stuama

abstention *n* seachnadh *m* (bhòtaidh *m gen*)

abstinence *n* stuamachd *f invar*

abstinent *adj* stuama

abstract *adj* **1** (*art, noun &c*) eas-cruthach; **2** *in expr* **~ idea** cùis-bheachd *f*

abstract *n* (*of document &c*) geàrr-chunntas *m*

abstraction *n* (*philo &c: an absract idea or concept*) cùis-bheachd *f*

abstruse *adj* deacair, iomadh-fhillte

absurd *adj* **1** (*philo &c*) mì-reusanta; **2** (*ridiculous*) gòrach, amaideach

absurdity *n* **1** (*philo &c*) mì-reusantachd *f invar*; **2** (*ridiculousness*) gòraiche *f invar*, amaideas *m*

abundance *n* pailteas *m*, lìonmhorachd *f*

abundant *adj* **1** (*numerous*) lìonmhor; **2** (*plentiful*) pailt

abuse *n* **1** (*verbal*) càineadh *m*, màbadh *m*; **2** (*phys*) droch-làimhseachadh *m*; **3** (*sexual*) truailleadh drùiseach

abuse *v* **1** (*persons, verbally*) màb *vt*, dèan ana-cainnt *f* (*with prep* air); **2** (*persons, phys*) droch-làimhsich *vt*; **3** (*persons, sexually*) truaill *vt*; **4** (~ *substances, position of authority &c*) mì-ghnàthaich *vt*, ~ **drugs** mì-ghnàthaich drogaichean *fpl*

abyss *n* àibheis *f invar*, dubh-aigeann *m invar* (*used with art*), **the** ~ an dubh-aigeann

academic *adj* sgoilearach, acadaimigeach

academic *n* **1** sgoilear *m*; **2** (*University teacher*) neach-teagaisg *m* oilthigh *m gen*

academy *n* **1** (*secondary school*) àrd-sgoil *f*, acadamaidh *m*; **2** (*learned institution &c*) acadamh *mf*, **The Royal Scottish Academy** Acadamh Rìoghail na h-Alba

accelerate *v* luathaich *vti*

acceleration *n* luathachadh *m*

accent *n* **1** (*mode of speech*) blas *m*, **he speaks Gaelic with an English** ~ tha blas na Beurla air a chuid Gàidhlig *f*; **2** (*stress, accentuation*) stràc *m*, **the** ~ **is on the first syllable** tha an stràc air a' chiad lide *m*, **acute** ~ stràc geur, **grave** ~ stràc trom

accent *v* (*lang*) cuir stràc *m* (*with prep* air)

accentuate *v* cuir stràc *m*, leig cudthrom *m*, (*with prep* air)

accept *v* gabh *vi* (*with prep* ri), **they ~ed the situation** ghabh iad ris an t-suidheachadh

acceptable *adj* iomchaidh, **an** ~ **solution** fuasgladh *m* iomchaidh, **an agreement** ~ **to all** còrdadh *m* ris an urrainn na h-uile gabhail

access *n* **1** (*way in*) inntrigeadh *m*, **right of** ~ còir *f* inntrigidh, ~ **road/door** rathad/doras *m* inntrigidh, *also* rathad/doras a-steach; **2** (*opening, opportunity*) cothrom *m* (**to** air), ~ **to higher education** cothrom air foghlam *m* àrd-ìre

accessible *adj* **1** (*of a place*) ruigsinneach; **2** (*of a person*) fosgarra, fosgailte

accessibility *n* (*esp of a place*) ruigsinneachd *f invar*

accident *n* **1** (*usu unpleasant*) tubaist *f*, **road** ~ tubaist-rathaid *f*; **2** (*not nec unpleasant*) tuiteamas *m*, **by** ~ le tuiteamas

accidental *adj* tuiteamach

acclaim, acclamation *n* **1** (*applause, approbation*) caithream (*gen* caithreim) *mf*; **2** (*more abstr: renown &c*) cliù *m invar*

accommodation *n* **1** (*dwelling*) àite-fuirich *m*, lòistinn *m*, *in expr* **a night's** ~ cuid *f* oidhche; **2** (*arrangement, agreement*) rèite *f*, còrdadh *m*, **they came to an** ~ thàinig iad gu rèite/còrdadh

accompaniment *n* (*mus &c*) com-pàirt *f*, (*esp mus*) taic *f*

accompanist *n* (*mus*) neach-taice (*pl* luchd-taice *m sing coll*), compàirtiche *m*

accompany *v* **1** rach *vi* còmhla (*with prep* ri), **I'll** ~ **you (there)** thèid mi (ann) còmhla riut; **2** (*mus*) com-pàirtich *vti*, thoir taic *f* (*with prep* do)

accompanying *adj* (*associated with*) an cois *prep*, an lùib *prep* (*both with gen*), **a report and its** ~ **documents** aithisg *f* agus na pàipearan *mpl* a tha na cois/na lùib

accomplice *n* pàirtiche *m*

accomplish *v* thoir *vt* gu buil *f*, coilean *vt*, **I ~ed nothing** cha tug mi càil *f* *invar* gu buil

accomplished *adj & past part* **1** (*task &c: completed, achieved*) coileanta; **2** (*of person: expert, skilled*) ealanta, **an** ~ **linguist** cànanaiche *m* ealanta

accord *n* co-aontachadh *m*, co-chòrdadh *m*

accordeon *n* bogsa-ciùil *m*, (*more fam*) bogsa *m*

accordance *n*, *in expr* **in** ~ **with** ann an co-rèir *f* ri

according *adj* a rèir (*with gen*), ~ **to your orders** a rèir nan òrduighean *mpl* agaibh, **The Gospel** ~ **to Matthew** An Soisgeul a rèir Mhata

accordingly *adv* **1** (*as a result*) o chionn sin, air sgàth sin; **2** (*proportionately, consistently*) a rèir, **they gave five pounds to Mary, and to the others** ~ thug iad còig notaichean do Mhàiri, agus dhan fheadhainn eile a rèir

account *n* **1** (*fin*) cunntas *m*, **bank** ~ cunntas banca, **I've an** ~ **at the Royal Bank** tha cunntas agam aig a' Bhanca *m* Rìoghail, **investment** ~ cunntas-tasgaidh, **savings** ~ cunntas-sàbhalaidh; **2** (*bill, invoice*) **an** ~ **to pay/settle** cunntas ri dhìoladh; **3** (*narrative, description &c*) cunntas *m*, (*in newspaper &c*) iomradh *m*, **an** ~ **of his life** cunntas a bheatha, **an** ~ **of the strike** iomradh air an stailc *f*

accountability *n* cunntachalachd *f invar*

accountable *adj* cunntachail

accountancy *n* cunntasachd *f invar*

accountant *n* cunntasair *m*

accounting *n* cunntasachd *f invar*

accoutrements uidheam *f sing coll*, acainn *f sing coll*

accredited *adj* barrantaichte

accumulate *v* càrn *vt*, cruinnich *vti*

accumulation *n* **1** (*the action*) càrnadh *m*; **2** (*the things accumulated*) co-chruinneachadh *m*

accurate *adj* **1** (*statements*) ceart, **what she said is** ~ tha na thubhairt i ceart; **2** (*sums, calculations*) cruinn, grinn; **3** (*aim*) amaiseach, cuimseach

accursed *adj* mallaichte

accusation *n* casaid *f*, **make an** ~ dèan casaid *f* (**against** an aghaidh *followed by gen*)

accusative *adj* (*gram*) cuspaireach

accuse *v* 1 (*esp legal*) dèan casaid *f* (*with prep* an aghaidh *followed by gen*), **he ~d me** rinn e casaid nam aghaidh; 2 (*more general*) cuir *vi*, tilg *vi*, fàg *vi*, (*all with prep* air), cuir *vi* às a (*&c*) leth, **they ~d me of not being honest** chuir iad orm/chuir iad às mo leth nach robh mi onarach, **they ~d me of not being conscientious** thilg iad orm nach robh mi dìcheallach

accused *adj & past part* fo chasaid *f* (*with gen*), **he is ~ of murder** tha e fo chasaid-mhuirt *f*

accused *n* neach *m* fo chasaid *f*

accuser *n* neach-casaid *m*

accustom *v* cleachd *vt*, (*less usu*) gnàthaich *vt*, (**to** ri), **~ yourself to it!** cleachd thu fhèin ris!

accustomed *adj & past part* cleachdte (**to** ri)

ace *n* (*cards &c*), **the ~** an t-aon

acerbic *adj* 1 (*of tastes &c*) geur; 2 (*of remarks, character &c*) guineach

ache *n* goirteas *m*

ache *v* bi *vi irreg* goirt, **her head ~d** bha a ceann *m* goirt, **my back ~s** tha mo dhruim *m* goirt

achieve *v* thoir *vt* gu buil *f*, coilean *vt*, **you never ~d anything** cha tug thu càil *f invar* gu buil a-riamh

achieved *adj & past part* coileanta

achievement *n* euchd *m*, **that's a great ~** 's e euchd mòr a tha sin

acid *n* searbhag *f*

acid *adj* searbhagach, **~ rain** uisge searbhagach

acidity *n* searbhachd *f invar*

acknowledge *v* aithnich *vti*, **he ~d his error** dh'aithnich e a mhearachd *f*, **he ~d that he was wrong** dh'aithnich e gun robh e ceàrr

acknowledged *adj* (*of expert, authority &c*) aithnichte

acne *n* cnàimhseagan *fpl*

acquaintance *n* 1 (*abstr*) eòlas *m* (**with** air); 2 (*persons*) **an ~** neach-eòlais *m*, **~s** luchd-eòlais *m sing coll*

acquainted *adj* 1 (*with persons*) eòlach (**with** air), **they're ~** tha iad eòlach air a chèile; 2 *in expr* **get ~ with someone** cuir eòlas *m* air cuideigin *mf invar*; 3 (*~ with objects, ideas &c*) eòlach (**with** air), fiosrach (**with** mu), **~ with technology** eòlach air teicneolas *m*

acquire *v* faigh *vt*, tog *vt*, (*by purchase*) ceannaich *vt*, **he ~d a house** fhuair/cheannaich e taigh *m*; **I ~d my Gaelic in Skye** 's ann san Eilean Sgitheanach a thog mi mo chuid *f* Gàidhlig *f*

acquit *v* fuasgail *vt*

acronym *n* acranaim (*pl* acranaimean) *m*

acre *n* acair *mf*

acrid *adj* searbh

acrimonious *adj* guineach

acrimony *n* guineachas *m*

across *adv* (*usu expr movement*) tarsainn, thairis, **they went** ~ chaidh iad tarsainn/thairis

across *prep* (*expr position or movement*) tarsainn (*with gen*), thar (*with gen*), thairis (*with prep* air), **a great tree was** ~ **the road** bha craobh mhòr tarsainn an rathaid *m*, **they went** ~ **the bridge/the mountains** chaidh iad tarsainn na drochaid *f*/nam beanntan *fpl*, **they are/they went** ~ **the ocean** tha iad/chaidh iad thar a' chuain, tha iad/chaidh iad thairis air a' chuan; **2** (*prep prons formed with* thar) ~ **me** tharam(sa), ~ **you** (*sing*) tharad(sa), ~ **him/it** (*m*) thairis(-san), ~ **her/it** (*f*) thairt(se), ~ **us** tharainn(e), ~ **you** tharaibh(se), ~ **them** tharta(san)

act *n* **1** (*deed, action*) gnìomh *m*; **2** (*parliament*) achd *f*, **an** ~ **of Parliament** achd pàrlamaid *f*; **3** (*in play*) earrann *f*

act *v* **1** gnìomhaich *vi*; **2** (*in play, film &c*) cluich *vti*

acting *adj* (*ie temporary*) an gnìomh *m*, ~ **chair** cathraiche *m* an gnìomh

action *n* **1** gnìomh *m*, **man of** ~ fear *m* gnìomha *m*, ~ **group** buidheann-ghnìomha *mf*; **2** (*law*) cùis-lagha *f*

active *adj* (*of persons: lively, energetic*) beòthail, èasgaidh, tapaidh, deas; **2** (*industrious*) dèanadach, gnìomhach, dìcheallach; **3** (*busy, involved*) an sàs, ~ **in politics** an sàs ann am poileataics; **4** (*gram*) spreigeach, ~ **verb** gnìomhair *m* spreigeach; **5** *in expr* ~ **volcano** bholcàno beò

activeness *n* beòthalachd *f invar*, tapachd *f invar*

activist *n* gnìomhaiche *m*

activity *n* **1** (*abstr*) gnìomhachd *f invar*; **2** (*professional* ~) dreuchd *f*; **3** (*spare time* ~) cur-seachad *m*

actor *n* actair *m*, (*more trad*) cluicheadair *m*, cleasaiche *m*

actress *n* ban-actair *f*

actual *adj* **1** (*not abstract*) nitheil, rudail; **2** (*real, true, genuine*) fìor (*precedes the n, which it lenites where possible*), ~ **temperature** fìor theodhachd *f*, ~ **costs** fìor chosgaisean *fpl*

acute *adj* **1** (*of faculties*) geur; **2** (*of illness*) dian; **3** *in expr* ~ **angle** ceàrn caol; **4** *in expr* ~ **accent** stràc geur

adage *n* ràdh *m invar*

Adam's apple, the *n* meall *m* an sgòrnain

add *v* cuir *vt* (*with prep* ri), ~ **some sugar (to it)** cuir siùcar *m* ris

adder *n* nathair *f*

addict *n* tràill *mf*

addicted *adj & past part* na (*&c*) t(h)ràill *mf* (*with prep* do), an urra (*with prep* ri), **he's** ~ **to drugs** tha e na thràill do dhrogaichean *fpl*, tha e an urra ri drogaichean

addiction *n* tràilleachd *f invar* (**to** do)

addition *n* **1** (*numerical*) meudachadh *m*; **2** *in expr* **in** ~ **to** a thuilleadh air, **we have two flats in** ~ **to the house** tha dà lobhta againn a thuilleadh air an taigh; **3** *in expr* **an** ~ **to the family** pàiste *m* a bharrachd san teaghlach *m*

additional *adj* (an) tuilleadh (*with gen*), a bharrachd, ~ **information** (an) tuilleadh fiosrachaidh *m*, **an ~ worker** obraiche *m* a bharrachd

address *n* **1** (*speech, talk*) òraid *f*, **give an ~** thoir seachad òraid, dèan òraid; **2** (*postal ~*) seòladh *m*

address *v* **1** (*speak/talk to*) bruidhinn (*with prep* ri); **2** (*give talk*) thoir seachad òraid *f* (**to** do), dèan òraid (*with prep* ri), **she ~ed the local history society** thug i seachad òraid do chomann *m* na h-eachdraidh ionadail; **3** (*~ letter &c*) cuir seòladh *m* (*with prep* air); **4** (*face up to*) cuir aghaidh *f* (*with prep* ri), **he ~ed the problem** chuir e aghaidh ris an duilgheadas *m*

adept *adj* sgileil, deas, tapaidh, teòma, ealanta

adhesive *adj* leanailteach

adjacent *adj* faisg (**to** air), dlùth (**to** do *or* air)

adjective *n* buadhair *m*

adjourn *v* **1** (*as vt*) cuir *vt* an dàil *f*, **the chair ~ed the meeting** chuir an cathraiche *m* a' choinneamh an dàil; **2** (*as vi*) sgaoil *vi*, **the meeting adjourned** sgaoil a' choinneamh

adjournment *n* cur *m* an dàil *f*, sgaoileadh *m*

adjust *v* **1** (*machine &c*) gleus *vt*, rèitich *vt*; **2** (*clothing*) socraich *vt*

adjustment *n* **1** (*of machine &c*) gleusadh *m*, rèiteachadh *m*; **2** (*of clothing*) socrachadh *m*

administer *v* **1** (*~ organisation &c*) riaghail *vt*, rianaich *vt*, seòl *vt*, stiùir *vt*; **2** (*put into effect*) cuir *vt* an gnìomh *m*

administration 1 (*abstr*) riaghladh *m*, rianachd *f invar*; **2** (*con*) **the ~** an luchd-riaghlaidh *m sing coll*

administrative *adj* rianachail

administrator *n* rianaire *m*, neach-riaghlaidh *m* (*pl* luchd-riaghlaidh *m sing coll*)

admissible *adj* (*acceptable, permissible*) ceadaichte

adolescence *n* òigeachd *f invar*

adolescent *n* (*male*) òganach *m*, òigear *m*, (*of either sex*) deugaire *m*

adopt *v* **1** (*child*) uchd-mhacaich *vt*; **2** (*a course of action, plan &c*) cuir *vt* an gnìomh *m*

adopted *adj* uchd- *prefix*, **an ~ child** uchd-leanabh *m*

adoption *n* **1** (*of child*) uchd-mhacachd *f invar*; **2** (*of course of action, plan &c*) cur *m* an gnìomh *m*

adorn *v* sgeadaich *vt*, sgèimhich *vt*

adroit *adj* **1** (*intellectually*) innleachdach, luath na (*&c*) inntinn *f*; **2** (*phys*) deas, làmhach

adult *adj* inbhidh, **~ education** foghlam *m* inbhidh

adult *n* inbheach *m*

adulthood *n* inbhe *f*, **reach ~** thig *vi* gu inbhe

advance *adj* **1** (*in time*) ro-làimh, **~ payment** dìoladh *m* ro-làimh; **2** (*of army &c*) toisich (*gen sing of* toiseach *m*), **~ party** buidheann *mf* toisich

advance *n* **1** (*progress, improvement*) adhartas *m*, piseach *m*, leasachadh *m*; **2** (*fin*) eàrlas *m*, **the publisher gave him an** ~ thug am foillsichear *m* eàrlas dha; **3** *in expr* **in** ~, ron là *m*, ron àm *m*, ro-làimh *f*, **do something in** ~ dèan rudeigin ron là/ron àm/ro-làimh

advance *v* **1** (*of troops &c*) rach *vi* air adhart; **2** (*foster, improve*) thoir *vt* air adhart, adhairtich *vt*, ~ **the cause of freedom** thoir air adhart/ adhairtich adhbhar *m* na saorsa

advantage *n* **1** (*benefit*) buannachd *f*, tairbhe *f invar*, **it would be of great** ~ **to you** bhiodh e na bhuannachd mhòr dhuibh; **2** *in expr* **take** ~ **of someone** (*unfairly*) gabh bràth *m* air cuideigin, (*not nec unfairly*) gabh cothrom *m* air cuideigin

advantageous *adj* buannachdail, tairbheach & tarbhach

adverb *n* co-ghnìomhair *m*

adverbial *adj* co-ghnìomhaireil

adversary *n* **1** (*enemy*) nàmhaid *m*; **2** (*opponent in argument, debate &c*) co-chòmhragaiche *m*

adversity *n* cruadal *m*

advertise *v* sanasaich *vti*

advertisement *n* sanas *m*, sanas-reic *m*

advice *n* comhairle *f*, **give** ~ thoir comhairle (**to** air *or* do), **take/get** ~ gabh comhairle

advisable *adj* iomchaidh, glic

advisability *n* iomchaidheachd *f invar*

advise *v* comhairlich *vt*, comhairlich *vi* (*with prep* do), thoir comhairle (*with preps* air *or* do)

adviser *n* neach-comhairle *m* (*pl* luchd-comhairle *m sing coll*), comhairleach *m*, **financial** ~ comhairleach ionmhais *m gen*

advocate *n* neach-tagraidh *m* (*pl* luchd-tagraidh *m sing coll*)

adze *n* tàl *m*

aeroplane *n* plèana *mf*, (*more trad*) itealan *m*

aerospace *n* adhar-fhànas (*gen* adhar-fhànais) *m*

aesthetics *n* feallsanachd-maise *f invar*

affair *n* **1** (*matter, situation*) cùis *f*, rud *m*, nì *m*, gnothach *m*, **how did the** ~ **go/turn out?** ciamar a chaidh a' chùis?, **it was a bad** ~ 's e droch nì a bh' ann, **their divorce was a bad** ~ 's e droch rud a bh' anns an sgaradh-pòsaidh *m* aca

affect *v* drùidh *vt* (*with prep* air), **the news didn't** ~ **her** cha do dhrùidh an naidheachd *f* oirre, (*more fam*) **it didn't** ~ **me in the least** cha do chuir e suas no sìos mi

affectation *n* leòm *f*

affection *n* gràdh *m*, rùn *m*, (*less strong*) tlachd *f invar*

affectionate *adj* gaolach, gràdhach, maoth

afforestation *n* coillteachadh *m*

afloat *adj*, air flod *m*, air fleòdradh *m*, air bhog *m*

afraid *adj* **1** fo eagal *m*, **a man ~** duine fo eagal; **2** (*after verb* **to be**) bi *vi irreg* an t-eagal (*with the prep* air), **she was ~ (of me)** bha an t-eagal oirre (romham); **3** *in expr* **become ~** gabh eagal; **4** (*expr polite regret*) **I don't know, I'm ~** chan eil fhios (*for* a fhios *m*, 'knowledge of it') agam, tha eagal orm

afresh *adv* às ùr, **start ~** tòisich *vti* às ùr

Africa *n* Afraga *f invar*

after *conj* an dèidh (*with prep* do), **~ I closed/had closed my eyes** an dèidh dhomh mo shùilean *fpl* a dhùnadh, **~ the pub opened** an dèidh dhan taigh-seinnse *m* fhosgladh

after *prep* **1** (*expr sequence*) an dèidh, às dèidh, (*followed by the gen*), **~ the storm** an dèidh na stoirme, **she came ~ him** thàinig i às a dhèidh; **2** (*expr interval of time*) an ceann (*with gen*), **~ a little while** an ceann greiseig *f*; **3** *in expr* **one ~ the other** fear *m* an dèidh fir, tè *f* an dèidh tè, **the policemen left, one ~ the other** dh'fhalbh na poileasmain *mpl*, fear an dèidh fir; **4** (*in pursuit or search of*) an tòir (*with prep* air), **the police are ~ him** tha am poileas an tòir air, **he went to town ~ a new car** chaidh e dhan bhaile *m* an tòir air càr *f* ùr; **5** *in expr* (*in family &c*) **take ~ someone** rach *vi* ri taobh *m* cuideigin *m*

afternoon *n* feasgar *m*, **yesterday ~** feasgar an-dè, **good ~!** feasgar math!, **we'll be in in the ~** bidh sinn a-staigh feasgar (*adv*)

afterthought *n* **1** ath-smuain *f*; **2** (*revised opinion &c*) ath-bheachd *m*

again *adv* **1** a-rithist, fhathast, **say it ~** can a-rithist e, can fhathast e, **I'll see you ~** chì mi fhathast sibh, **do it ~!** dèan fhathast/a-rithist e!; **2** *in exprs* **I told him time and ~/over and over ~** dh'innis mi dha uair *f* is uair; **3** (*after v in the neg*) tuilleadh, **don't do that (ever) ~** na dèan sin tuilleadh; **4** (*afresh*) *in expr* **start ~** tòisich *vti* às ùr

against *prep* **1** (*contrary to, opposed to*) an aghaidh (*with gen*), **~ the law** an aghaidh an lagha, **dead/completely/totally ~ the government** calg-dhìreach an aghaidh an riaghaltais, **he turned ~ me** thionndaidh *vi* e nam aghaidh; **2** (*expr struggle*) ri (*with dat*), **~ the current** ris an t-sruth; **3** (*expr proximity, leaning*) ri (*with dat*), **~ the wall** ris a' bhalla *m*

age *n* **1** aois *f*, **(old) age is a great hindrance** is mòr am bacadh an aois, **what age is he?** dè an aois a tha e?; **2** (*period*) linn *mf*, (*hist*) **the dark ~s** na linntean dorcha, **the space ~** linn an fhanais; **3** *in expr* (*fam*) **I've been here for ~s (and ~s)!** tha mi ann an seo bho chionn ùineachan *fpl* (is ùineachan)!; **4** (*contemporary*) *in expr* **they're ~s with one another** tha iad co-aoiseach *adj*, tha iad nan co-aoisean *mpl*

agency *n* **1** (*esp public service &c*) ionad *m*, **employment ~** ionad-cosnaidh *m*; **2** *in expr* **travel ~** bùth-siubhail *f*

agenda *n* clàr-gnothaich *m*

agent *n* **1** (*one's representative*) neach-ionaid (*pl* luchd-ionaid *m sing coll*); **2** (*one who takes action*) fear-gnìomha *m*

aggravate *v* **1** (*make worse*) dèan *vt* nas miosa; **2** (*annoy*) cuir dragh *m* (*with prep* air)

aggravating *adj* draghail, frionasach

aggravation (*annoyance*) dragh *m*, frionas *m*

agile *adj* **1** (*esp phys*) clis, grad, ~ **movements** gluasadan *mpl* grada; **2** (*mentally*) luath na (*&c*) inntinn *f*

agility *n* cliseachd *f invar*, luas *m*, lùth *m*

agitate *v* **1** (*shake*) crath *vt*; **2** (*stir up*) gluais *vt*; **3** (*incite, provoke*) brod *vt*, spreig *vt*, stuig *vt*; **4** (*upset*) cuir *vt* troimh-a-chèile

agitated *adj & past part* (*upset*) troimh-a-chèile

agitation *n* **1** (*stir, excitement*) gluasad *m*; **2** (*emotional confusion*) buaireas *m*

ago *adv* **1** o chionn & bho chionn (*with gen*), **a short time** ~ o chionn ghoirid, **long/a long time** ~ o chionn fhada, **a while** ~ o chionn greis; **2** (*in fairy stories &c*) **long long** ~ o chionn fada nan cian, fada fada ron a seo

agree *v* **1** (*be in or come to ~ment*) co-aontaich *vi*, co-chòrd *vi*; **2** *in expr* ~ **to** gabh *vi* (*with prep* ri), **we** ~ **to those proposals** gabhaidh sinn ris na molaidhean *mpl* sin

agreeable *adj* **1** (*esp people*) ciatach; **2** (*people, also things, situations*) taitneach (**to** ri); **3** (*acceptable*) iomchaidh; **4** *in exprs* **that is** ~ **to me, I find that** ~ tha sin a' còrdadh rium

agreeableness *n* taitneachd *f invar*, taitneas *m*

agreed *adj & past part* aontaichte

agreement *n* **1** (*abstr & con*) còrdadh *m*, aonta *m*, co-aontachadh *m*, co-chòrdadh *m*, **reach/come to an** ~ thig *vi* gu còrdadh, **be in** ~ co-aontaich *vi*; **2** (*business* ~, *contractual* ~) cùnnradh *m*, cùmhnant *m*

agriculture *n* **1** (*the subject*) àiteachas *m*; **2** (*the activity*) tuathanachas *m*, àiteach *m*

ahead *prep* air thoiseach (**of** air), **far** ~ **of us** fada air thoiseach oirnn, ~ **of other countries in technology** air thoiseach air dùthchannan *fpl* eile a-thaobh teicneòlais *m gen*

aid *n* **1** (*help*) cuideachadh *m*, cobhair *f*; **2** *in expr* (*med*) **first** ~ ciad-fhuasgladh *m*; **3** (*support*) taic *f*, **financial** ~ taic-airgid *f*; **4** (*tool, facilitator &c*) uidheam-cuideachaidh *f*, ~**s for the disabled** uidheaman-cuideachaidh do na ciorramaich *mpl*

aid *v* cuidich *vti*, thoir taic *f* (*with prep* do)

aide *n* neach-cuideachaidh (*pl* luchd-cuideachaidh *m sing coll*)

aide-mémoire *n* nota *f*

ail *v* bi *vi* ceàrr (*with prep* air), **what** ~**s you?** dè a tha ceàrr ort?, *also* dè a tha thu a' gearan?

ailing *adj* tinn, (*more fam*) bochd, meadhanach

aim *n* **1** (*of weapon*) amas *m*; **2** (*intention, ambition*) amas *m*, rùn *m*

aim *v* **1** (*weapon &c*) cuimsich *vti*, amais *vti*, (**at** air); **2** (*intend*) bi *vi irreg* am beachd *m* (*with infin or pres part*), **I'm** ~**ing to go to college** tha mi am beachd a dhol don cholaiste *mf*

air *n* **1** adhar *m*, **up in the** ~ shuas san adhar, **the Air Force** Feachd *f* an Adhair; **2** (*tune*) fonn *m*

aircraft, airliner *n* plèana *mf*, (*more trad*) itealan *m*

airfield *n* raon-adhair *m*

airport *n* port-adhair *m*

airstrip *n* raon-adhair *m*

alarm *n* rabhadh *m*, ~ **bell** clag-rabhaidh *m*

alas! *excl* (*trad*) och!, mo thruaighe! *f*, ~ **and alack** och nan och!

alcohol *n* **1** (*as drink*) deoch-làidir *f*; **2** (*the chemical substance*) alcol *m invar*

alcoholic *adj* **1** alcolach; **2** *in expr* ~ **drink** deoch-làidir *f*

alcoholic *n* tràill *mf* don deoch(-làidir) *f*, **he is an** ~ tha e na thràill don deoch(-làidir), *also* tha e an urra ri alcol *m invar*

alcoholism *n* tinneas *m* na dighe

alder *n* feàrna *f invar*

ale *n* leann *m*

alert *adj* **1** (*mentally*) ~ grad/geur na (*&c*) inntinn *f*; **2** (*of sentry &c*) furachail; **3** (*aware*) mothachail (**to** air), ~ **to the danger** mothachail air a' chunnart *m*

alert *n* (*signal*) comharradh *m* rabhaidh *m*

alert *v* thoir rabhadh *m* (*with prep* do), earalaich *vt*, **they ~ed me** thug iad rabhadh dhomh

alien *n* **1** neach *m*/creutair *m* à planaid *f* eile; **2** (*foreigner*) coigreach *m*

alienate *v* cuir *vt* na (*&c*) aghaidh fhèin, **you'll** ~ **all your colleagues** cuiridh tu do cho-obraichean *mpl* air fad nad aghaidh fhèin

alight *v* teirinn *&* teàrn *vi*

alike *adj* ionann (*with v* is), coltach ri chèile, **you and I are not** ~ chan ionann thusa agus mise, **all the buildings were** ~ bha na togalaichean *mpl* air fad coltach ri chèile

all *adj & adv* **1** (*without exception*) uile, air fad, gu lèir, **the soldiers** ~ **left**, ~ **the soldiers left** dh'fhalbh na saighdearan *mpl* uile/air fad, ~ **that's over** tha sin uile seachad, ~ **the houses were burned** chaidh na taighean *mpl* air fad/gu lèir a losgadh; **2** (*esp with periods of time*) fad (*plus gen*), ~ **the time** fad na h-ùine, **I was poor** ~ **my life** bha mi bochd fad mo bheatha *f*, **I'll be awake** ~ **night** bidh mi nam dhùsgadh *m* fad na h-oidhche; **3** (*the whole*) an t-iomlan *m*, air fad, **do you want** ~ **of it?**, **do you want it** ~**?** a bheil thu ag iarraidh an iomlain (dheth)?, **they ravaged** ~ **the country** sgrios iad an dùthaich *f* air fad; **4** (*idiom*) **that's** ~ **there is to it** chan eil an còrr ann ach sin

all- *prefix* uile- (*lenites following consonant where possible*), (*eg*) **all-powerful** uile-chumhachdach, **all-knowing** uile-fhiosrach

alleviate *v* (*pain, suffering*) faothaich *vti*

alleviation *n* (*of pain, suffering*) faothachadh *&* faochadh *m*, **he experienced some** ~ thàinig faothachadh air

alley *n* caol-shràid *f*

alliance *n* caidreabhas *m*

alliteration *n* uaim *f*

allocate *v* (*resources &c*) riaraich *vt*, sònraich *vt*

allocation *n* **1** (*abstr*) riarachadh *m*; **2** (*con*) cuibhreann *mf*, **we received our ~ of food** fhuair sinn ar cuibhreann de bhiadh *m*

allot *v* (*resources &c*) riaraich *vt*, sònraich *vt*

allow *v* leig *vi* (*with prep* do *or* le), ceadaich *vti*, **he ~ed me to buy it** leig e dhomh/leam a cheannach

allowable *adj* ceadaichte

allowance *n* (*fin &c*) cuibhreann *mf*, **disability ~** cuibhreann-ciorraim

allowed *adj & past part* **1** ceadaichte; **2** (*on notices &c*) (**smoking &c**) **not ~** chan fhaodar (smocadh *m &c*)

alloy *n* coimheatailt *f*, laghd-mheatailt *f*

allude *v* thoir tarraing *f*, thoir iomradh *m*, thoir guth *m*, (*all with prep* air), **you didn't ~ to my promotion** cha tug sibh tarraing/iomradh/guth air an àrdachadh *m* agam

allure *v* tàlaidh *vt*, meall *vt*

allurement *n* tàladh *m*, mealladh *m*

alluring *adj* meallach

allusion *n* iomradh *m*, tarraing *f*, guth *m*, (**to** air), **he made no ~ to it** cha tug e iomradh/tarraing/guth air

ally *n* caidreabhach *m*

almost *adv* **1** cha mhòr, **we see her ~ every day** bidh sinn ga faicinn a h-uile là, cha mhòr; **2** cha mhòr nach *conj*, gu ìre bhig *adv*, **I ~ lost my purse** cha mhòr nach do chaill mi mo sporan *m*, **we ~ missed the bus** chaill sinn am bus gu ìre bhig; **3** (*nearly completed action or process*) gu bhith (*plus adj*), **I'm ~ ready** tha mi gu bhith deiseil; **4** (*narrowly avoided action in the past*) theab *vi def*, **I ~ fell** theab mi tuiteam, **they ~ ruined me** theab iad mo sgriosadh

alms *n* dèirc *f*

alone *adj & adv* **1** nam (*&c*) aonar, leam (*&c*) fhìn/fhèin, **she was ~** bha i na h-aonar, bha i leatha fhèin, **when I'm ~** an uair a bhios mi leam fhìn; **2** (*idiom*) **let/leave them ~!** Leig *vi* leotha!

along *adv* **1** air adhart, air aghaidh, **how are you getting ~** ciamar a tha thu a' faighinn air adhart?, **that's coming ~ well** tha sin a' tighinn air adhart gu math; **2** (*idiom*) **we walked ~** choisich *vi* sinn romhainn

along *prep* **1** (*expr movement*) fad (*with gen*), **~ the house/road** fad an taighe/an rathaid; **2** (*expr position*) shuas, shìos, **a short distance ~ the road** pìos beag shuas/shìos an rathad; **3** (*accompanying*) ~ **with** còmhla ri, (*less usu*) maille ri, **~ with the others** còmhla ri càch *pron*

alongside *prep* ri taobh (*with gen*), **a boat ~ the quay** bàta ri taobh a' chidhe; **2** (*compared to*) an taca ri, **she's clever ~ her brother** tha i glic an taca ri a bràthair *m*

alphabet *n* aibidil *f*

alphabetical *adj* aibidileach, ~ **order** òrdugh *m* aibidileach, *also* òrdugh na h-aibidil

already *adv* mu thràth, *also found as* mar a tha *&* mar-thà, (*less usu*) (a) cheana, **as I said** ~ mar a thubhairt mi mu thràth/a cheana

also *adv* cuideachd, (*less usu*) mar an ceudna, **has Ewan left? yes, and Iain** ~ an do dh'fhalbh Eòghann? dh'fhalbh, agus Iain cuideachd/mar an ceudna

alter *v* atharraich *vti*, mùth *vti*

alteration *n* atharrachadh *m*, mùthadh *m*

alternate *v*, **the two of them** ~**d as spokesperson** bha an dithis *f* aca nan neach-labhairt *m* fear *m* mu seach

alternative *adj* eile, eadar-dhealaichte, eadar-roghnach, **an** ~ **plan** plana *m* eile, ~ **medicine** eòlas-leighis *m* eadar-dhealaichte

alternative *n* roghainn *f*, **we had no** ~ cha robh roghainn (eile) againn

alternatively *adv* an àite sin, air mhodh eile, ~ **we could take the bus** an àite sin b' urrainn dhuinn am bus a ghabhail

although *conj* ged, ~ **he wasn't ill** ged nach robh e tinn, **she didn't stop** ~ **she was exhausted** cha do sguir i ged a bha i claoidhte

altitude *n* àirde *f invar*

altogether *adv* uile-gu-lèir, gu tur, **she gave it up** ~ sguir i dheth uile-gu-lèir, **the two things are** ~ **different** tha an dà rud *m* gu tur eadar-dhealaichte

always *adv* daonnan, gun sgur, an còmhnaidh, **she's** ~ **on my mind** tha i daonnan air m' aire *f invar*, **she's** ~ **on at me!** tha i an sàs annam gun sgur/an còmhnidh!

Alzheimer's disease *n* tinneas *m* Alzheimer

amalgamate *v* **1** (*companies &c*) co-aonaich *vi*; **2** (*substances: fuse*) co-leagh *vti*, (*mix*) co-mheasgaich *vti*

amalgamation *n* (*of companies &c*) co-aonachadh *m*

amaze *v* cuir mòr-iongnadh *m* (*with prep* air), **it** ~**d me** chuir e mòr-iongnadh orm

amazed *adj & past part*, **I was** ~ ghabh mi mòr-iongnadh *m*

amazement *n* mòr-iongnadh *m*

amazing *adj* a chuireas/a chuireadh mòr-iongnadh *m* air duine *m*

ambassador *n* tosgaire *m*

amber *n* òmar *m*

ambiguity *n* dà-sheaghachd *f invar*

ambiguous *adj* dà-sheaghach

ambition *n* **1** (*for self-advancement*) miann-adhartais *m*, gionaiche *m invar*; **2** (*wish, aim*) glòir-mhiann *mf*, **it's my** ~ **to be a singer** 's e a' ghlòir-mhiann a th' agam a bhith nam sheinneadair *m*

ambitious *adj* gionach, glòir-mhiannach

ambivalence *n* **1** (*ambiguity*) dà-sheaghachd *f invar*; **2** (*state of being in two minds*) dà-bharaileachd *f invar*

ambivalent *adj* **1** (*ambiguous*) dà-sheaghach; **2** (*in two minds*) dà-bharaileach, ann an ioma-chomhairle *f*

ambulance *n* carbad-eiridinn *m*

ambush *n* feall-fhalach *m*

amenable *adj* fosgailte (**to** ri, do)

amend *v* **1** (*change*) atharraich *vt*; **2** (*improve*) leasaich *vt*

amendment *n* **1** (*change*) atharrachadh *m*; **2** (*improvement*) leasachadh *m*

amenity *n* goireas *m*, **the club has lots of amenities** tha goireasan gu leòr aig a' chlub *m*

amiss *adj* ceàrr, air iomrall, **something is ~** tha rudeigin *pron* ceàrr, chaidh rudeigin air iomrall

ammunition *n* connadh-làmhaich *m sing coll*

amorous *adj* leannanach

amount *n* uimhir *f invar*, uiread *f invar*, **a certain ~ of something** na h-uimhir/na h-uiread de rudeigin *pron*, **give me the same ~ as Iain (has)** thoir dhomh uiread 's a tha aig Iain

amphibian *n* muir-thìreach *m*

amphibious *adj* dà-bheathach, muir-thìreach

ample *adj* **1** (*of quantity*) pailt, **~ food** biadh pailt; **2** (*of person's build*) tomadach & tomaltach

amusement *n* **1** (*abstr*) àbhachd *f invar*; **2** (*fun &c*) spòrs *f*, dibhearsan *m*; **3** (*distraction, pastime, esp trivial*) caitheamh-aimsir *m*; **4** (*in ~ arcade*) **~s** faoin-chleasan *mpl*

amusing *adj* èibhinn

anachronism *n* às-aimsireachd *f invar*

anachronistic *adj* às-aimsireil

anaemia *n* cion-fala *m invar*

analyse *v* sgrùd *vt*, (*more rigorous*) mion-sgrùd *vt*

analysis *n* sgrùdadh *m*, (*more rigorous*) mion-sgrùdadh *m*

anatomical *adj* **1** (*abstr: pertainng to the subject of anatomy*) corp-eòlach; **2** (*pertaining to the actual body*) corporra

anatomist *n* corp-eòlaiche *m*

anatomy *n* **1** (*abstr: the science*) corp-eòlas *m*; **2** (*con: an actual body*) corp *m*, bodhaig *f*

anchor *n* **1** acair(e) *mf*; **2** *in expr* **at ~** aig acarsaid *f*, air an acair(e)

anchorage *n* acarsaid *f*

anchored *adj & past part* aig acarsaid *f*

and *conj* **1** agus, (*esp in common pairings of words*) is, **he came in ~ sat down** thàinig e a-steach agus shuidh e sìos, **bread ~ butter** aran is ìm; **2** (*other exprs*) **open the door ~ see if it's still raining** fosgail an doras feuch *imperative* a bheil an t-uisge ann fhathast, **come ~ see me** thig *vi* gam (*for* gu mo) fhaicinn

androgynous *adj* fireann-boireann

anecdote *n* **1** sgeul *m*, (*esp piece of gossip*) seanchas *m*; **2** (*~ told at ceilidh &c*) stòiridh *m*, naidheachd *f*

anew *adv* às ùr, **start** ~ tòisich *vti* às ùr

anger *n* fearg *f*, (*extreme*) cuthach *m*

angle *n* 1 (*geometry*) uileann & uilinn *f*, ceàrn *m*, **a right** ~ ceart-uilinn *f*, ceart-cheàrn *m*, **acute** ~ ceàrn caol; 2 (*more loosely*) *in expr* **at an** ~ air fhiaradh *m*

angler *n* iasgair *m*

angling *n* breacach *m*, iasgach-slaite *m*

angry *adj* 1 feargach, (*fam*) fiadhaich, **an** ~ **man** duine feargach, **I was** ~ **after what he said to me** bha mi fiadhaich an dèidh na thuirt e rium; 2 (*other exprs*) **she grew** ~ thàinig fearg/an fhearg oirre, ghabh i an fhearg, **she made him** ~ chuir i fearg/an fhearg air

anguish *n* 1 (*emotional*) dòrainn *f*; 2 (*mental or phys*) cràdh *m*

anguished *adj* dòrainneach

animate *adj* beò

animate *v* 1 (*bring to life*) beothaich *vt*; 2 (*stir up*) brosnaich *vt*, brod *vt*

animated *adj* 1 (*lively*) beothail; 2 (*excited, in high spirits*) mear

animation *n* 1 (*liveliness*) beothalachd *f invar*; 2 (*bustle*) drip *f*; 3 (*high spirits*) mearachas *m*

ankle *n* caol *m* na coise, adhbrann *m*, **my/her** ~ caol mo choise/a coise

annihilate *v* cuir *vi* às (*with prep* do), (*more formal*) neonithich *vt*

annotate *v* cuir notaichean (*with prep* ri)

annoy *v* cuir dragh *m* (*with prep* air), **the noise of that music is** ~**ing me** tha fuaim *mf* a' chiùil (*gen of* ceòl *m*) sin a' cur dragh orm

annoyance *n* dragh *m*, leamhadas *m*

annoying *adj* 1 (*of person, situation*) draghail; 2 (*irritating, niggling*) frionasach, leamh, **they're constantly asking me** ~ **questions** bidh iad a' cur cheistean *fpl* frionasach orm fad na h-ùine

annual *adj* bliadhnail

annual *n* 1 (*book*) bliadhnachan *m*; 2 (*flower*) flùr *m* aon-bhliadhnach *adj*

annul *v* cuir *vt* an neoni *f invar*

anonymous *adj* gun urra *f invar*, **an** ~ **letter** litir *f* gun urra, *also* litir gun ainm *m* rithe

anonymously *adv*, **the book came out** ~ nochd an leabhar *m* (an clò *m*) gun ainm *m* ùghdair *m*

another *adj* 1 (*different*) eile, **I'd prefer** ~ **book** b' fheàrr leam leabhar *m* eile; 2 (*additional*) eile, **I won't take** ~ **pint** cha ghabh mi pinnt *m* eile, **I don't want** ~ **thing** chan eil mi ag iarraidh càil *f invar* eile

answer *n* freagairt *f*, **I didn't get an** ~ cha d'fhuair mi freagairt, **we'll give you an** ~ **soon** bheir sinn freagairt dhuibh a dh'aithghearr

answer *v* freagair *vti*, **won't you** ~ **me?** nach freagair thu mi?, **he hasn't** ~**ed yet** cha do fhreagair e fhathast

Antarctic *n*, *used with art*, an Antartaig *f*

anthem *n* laoidh *mf*

anthology *n* cruinneachadh *m*, co-chruinneachadh *m*, (*esp of poetry*) duanaire *m*

anti-clockwise *adj* tuathal

antidote *n* urchasg *m*

antler *n* crò(i)c *f*, cabar *m*, **deer's** ~**s** cabair *mpl* fèidh (*gen of* fiadh *m*)

anus *n* tòn *f*, (*vulg*) toll *m*, toll-tòine *m*

anvil *n* innean *m*

anxiety *n* **1** cùram *m*, dragh *m*, imcheist *f*, iomagain *f*, **lack of money is causing me** ~ tha dìth airgid a' dèanamh dragh dhomh; **2** *in expr* **prone to** ~ iomagaineach, cùramach

anxious *adj* cùramach, fo chùram, fo imcheist, fo iomagain, imcheisteach, iomagaineach

any *adj & pron* **1** gin *pron*, **have we** ~ **envelopes?** a bheil gin chèisean-litreach *fpl* againn?, **he was wanting nails but I hadn't** ~ bha e ag iarraidh thairngean (*gen pl of* tarraing *f*) ach cha robh gin agam; **2** (*no matter which*) sam bith, ~ **book will do** nì leabhar *m* sam bith an gnothach *m*; **3** (*in neg sentence*) sam bith, **there wasn't** ~ **food (at all) in the shops** cha robh biadh *m* sam bith sna bùithtean *mfpl*; **4** *in expr* ~ **more** tuilleadh, **do you want** ~ **more?** a bheil thu ag iarraidh tuilleadh?, **don't do that** ~ **more** na dèan sin tuilleadh

anybody, anyone *pron* **1** duine *m*, **is there** ~ **there/in?** a bheil duine ann?; **2** (*no matter who*) duine sam bith, ~ **could do it** bhiodh duine sam bith comasach air, dhèanadh duine sam bith e; **3** (*in neg sentence*) duine, (*stronger*) duine sam bith, **there wasn't** ~ **(at all) in the church** cha robh duine (sam bith) san eaglais *f*

anything *n* **1** càil *f invar*, dad *f invar*, sìon *m*, rudeigin *pron*, **is there** ~ **in the cupboard?** a bheil càil/dad/sìon sa phreasa?, **I don't want** ~ **else** chan eil mi ag iarraidh càil eile, **I don't know** ~ **about it** chan eil càil a (*for* de) dh'fhios agam, **is** ~ **wrong?** a bheil rudeigin/càil ceàrr?; **2** (*no matter what*) rud *m* sam bith, nì *m* sam bith, **what do you want?** ~ **at all** dè a tha thu ag iarraidh? nì/rud sam bith; **3** (*idioms*) **don't have** ~ **to do with him/it!** na gabh gnothach *m* ris!, **she didn't say** ~ **else** cha tuirt i an còrr

anyway *adv* co-dhiù, **I'm leaving** ~! tha mise a' falbh co-dhiù!

aorta *n*, *used with art*, a' chuisle-chinn

apart *adj* **1** (*special*) air leth, **a man** ~ duine *m* air leth; **2** *in expr* ~ **from** ach a-mhàin, **the family left,** ~ **from the son** dh'fhalbh an teaghlach, ach a-mhàin am mac

apathy *n* cion-ùidhe *m*

aperture *n* fosgladh *m*

apolitical *adj* neo-phoileataigeach

apologise *v* **1** dèan leisgeul *m*, **I want to** ~ tha mi airson leisgeul a dhèanamh, **he** ~**d** rinn e leisgeul, *also* dh'iarr e a leisgeul a ghabhail; **2** *in expr* **I** ~! gabh(aidh) (*imperative*) mo leisgeul!

apology *n* leisgeul *m*

apostrophe *n* (*orthography*) asgair *m*

apparatus *n* uidheam *f*, acainn *f*

apparent *adj* **1** (*evident, obvious*) follaiseach, **it's ~ that he's not guilty** tha e follaiseach nach eil e ciontach; **2** (*idiom*) **become ~** thig *vi* am follais *f invar*

apparently *adv* a rèir c(h)oltais *m*, **he was a scoundrel, ~ 's** e slaoightear *m* a bh' ann dheth, a rèir choltais

appeal *n* **1** (*attractiveness*) tàladh *m*; **2** (*request, entreaty*) iarrtas (dian) *m*, guidhe *mf*; **3** (*law &c*) tagradh *m*, **an ~ against a sentence** tagradh an aghaidh binne *f gen*

appeal *v* **1** (*attract*) tarraing *vt*, tàlaidh *vt*; **2** (*request*) iarr *vt* (gu dian); **3** (*law &c*) tagair *vt*, **~ against a sentence** tagair an aghaidh binne *f gen*

appear *v* **1** (*come into sight, arrive*) nochd *vi*, **where did you ~ from?** cò às a nochd thu(sa)?, (*book*) **~ (in print)** nochd (an clò *m*), *also* thig *vi* am follais *f invar*; **2** (*seem*) bi coltach gu, **it ~s that she was married** tha e coltach gun robh i pòsta, *also* bha i pòsta, a rèir choltais; **3** (*look, have the appearance of*) **he ~s tired** tha coltas *m* na sgìths air

appearance *n* **1** (*abstr: act of appearing*) nochdadh *m*; **2** (*aspect*) cruth *m*; **3** (*of person's features, not nec permanent*) tuar *m*; **4** (*resemblance*) coltas *m*, **you have the ~ of a soldier** tha coltas saighdeir *m* ort; **5** *in expr* **judging by ~s** a rèir choltais, **judging by ~s, he's guilty** a rèir choltais, tha e ciontach

appease *v* (*opposing parties &c*) rèitich *vt*

appetite *n* càil *f*, càil-bidhe (*gen of* biadh *m*)

apple *n* **1** ubhal *m*; **2** *in expr* **the ~ of the eye** clach *f* na sùla

appliance *n* uidheam *f*, **heating ~** uidheam-teasachaidh

applicant *n* neach-iarraidh (*pl* luchd-iarraidh *m sing coll*), neach-tagraidh *m* (*pl* luchd-tagraidh *m sing coll*)

application *n* **1** (*for job &c*) iarrtas *m*, **~ form** foirm *m* iarrtais; **2** (*diligence &c*) dìcheall *m*; **3** (*putting into practice or effect*) cur *m* an gnìomh *m*, **the ~ of new rules** cur an gnìomh riaghailtean *fpl* ùra; **4** (*IT*) cleachdadh *m*, **~s programme** prògram *m* chleachdaidhean

apply *v* **1** (*for job &c*) cuir a-steach iarrtas *m* (**for** airson); **2** (*put into practice or effect*) cuir *vt* an gnìomh *m*; **3** (*be relevant, affect*) buin *vi* (**to** do), **this applies to you** buinidh seo dhut(sa)/dhuibh(se)

appoint *v* **1** (*select*) tagh *vt*, cuir *vt* an dreuchd *f*, **the best applicant was ~ed** chaidh an neach-iarraidh *m* a b' fheàrr a thaghadh; **2** (*set up*) suidhich *vt*, **~ a committee** suidhich comataidh *f*

appointed *adj & past part* **1** (*selected*) air a (*&c*) t(h)aghadh; **2** *in expr* **before the ~ time** ron mhithich *f invar*

apporti on *v* roinn *vt*, riaraich *vt*, pàirtich *vt*

apportionment *n* **1** (*abstr: the action*) roinneadh *m*; **2** (*con: a share*) cuibhreann *mf*, roinn *f*

appraisal *n* measadh *m*

appraise *v* meas *vt*, dèan measadh *m* (*with prep* air)

appreciate *v* **1** (*understand, sympathise with*) fidir *vt*, tuig *vt*, **you don't ~ the state I'm in for love of you** chan fhidir thu/cha tuig thu mar tha mise led ghaol *m*; **2** (*be grateful*) bi *vi irreg* taingeil (*with prep* airson), cuir luach *m invar* (*with prep* air), **I ~ what you did for me** tha mi taingeil airson na rinn thu dhomh

appreciation *n* **1** (*gratitude*) taingealachd *f invar*; **2** (*understanding, awareness*) tuigse *f invar*, mothachadh *m*

appreciative *adj* **1** (*grateful*) taingeil (**of** airson, *with gen*), **~ of what you did** taingeil airson na rinn sibh; **2** (*of audience &c: valuing, enjoying, aware*) mothachail, tuigseach

apprehend *v* glac *vt*, **the police ~ed him** ghlac am poileas e

apprentice *n* preantas *m*

approach *v* **1** (*phys*) dlùthaich *vi* (*with prep* ri), **we were ~ing the sea** bha sinn a' dlùthachadh ris a' mhuir *mf*; **2** (*fig*) teann *vi* (*with prep* ri), **it was ~ing midnight** bha e a' teannadh ris a' mheadhan-oidhche *m*

approachable *adj* (*person*) fosgarra, fosgailte

apron *n* aparan *m*

appropriate *adj* freagarrach, iomchaidh

appropriate *v* gabh seilbh *f* (*with prep* air)

approval *n* **1** (*agreement*) aonta *m*; **2** (*consent*) cead *m*

approve *v* **1** (*allow*) ceadaich *vt*, ùghdarraich *vt*; **2** (*consent, agree*) bi *vi irreg* airson (*with gen*), **I ~ of that!** tha mi airson sin!

approved *adj & past part* ceadaichte, ùghdarraichte

approximately *adv* timcheall air, **there'll be ~ ten people there** bidh timcheall air deichnear *mf invar* ann

April *n* Giblean *m*, Giblinn *f*, *used with art*, an Giblean, a' Ghiblinn

apt *adj* **1** (*appropriate*) freagarrach, iomchaidh; **2** (*liable, prone*) buailteach, dualtach, **~ to spend money** buailteach airgead *m* a chosg, **~ to be stingy** dualtach a bhidh spìocach

aquaculture *n* tuathanachas *m* uisge

Arab *n* Arabach *m*

Arabic *adj* Arabach, **~ numerals** figearan *mpl* Arabach

arable *adj* àitich, **~ land** talamh *m* àitich

arbiter *n* neach-rèiteachaidh *m* (*pl* luchd-rèiteachaidh *m sing coll*)

arbitrary *adj* **1** (*chance*) tuaireamach; **2** (*unreasonable &c*) neo-riaghailteach

arbitrate *v* (*between opposing parties &c*) rèitich *vi*

arbitration *n* rèiteachadh *m*

arch *n* stuagh *f*, bogha *m*

archbishop *n* àrd-easbaig *m*

archaeological *adj* àrsaidheil

archaeologist *n* àrsair *m*, arc-eòlaiche *m*

archaeology *n* àrsaidheachd *f invar*, arc-eòlas *m*

archaic *adj* àrsaidh

archer *n* boghadair *m*

archetypal *adj* prìomh-shamhlach

archetype *n* prìomh-shamhla *m*

architect *n* ailtire *m*

architectural *adj* ailtireach

architecture *n* ailtireachd *f invar*

archive *n* tasglann *f*

archivist *n* tasglannaiche *m*

Arctic, the *n* an Artaig *f*, **the ~ Circle** Cearcall *m* na h-Artaig, *also* An Cearcall Artach

ardent *adj* (*of persons, emotions, deeds*) dian

ardour *n* dèine *f invar*

area *n* **1** (*abstr*) farsaingeachd *f invar*; **2** (*district, locality &c*) ceàrn *m*, **a remote ~** ceàrn iomallach; **3** (*topic, field*) raon *m*, **expert in this ~** fìor eòlach san raon seo

argue *v* **1** (*discuss, also squabble*) connsaich *vi*, (*less trad*) argamaidich *vi*; **2** (*legal &c: ~ a case &c*) tagair *vti*

argument *n* **1** (*disagreement*) connsachadh *m*, (*less trad*) argamaid *f*; **2** (*discussion*) deasbad *m*; **3** (*sequence of ideas, points &c*) argamaid *f*

argumentative *adj* connsachail, aimhreiteach

arid *adj* **1** (*of landscape &c*) tioram, (*stronger*) loisgte, ana-thioram, ro-thioram; **2** (*uninteresting*) tioram

arise *v* èirich *vi*

aristocracy *n* **1** (*abstr quality*) uaisle *f invar*; **2** (*con*) **the ~** na h-uaislean *mpl*

aristocrat *n* mòr-uasal *m*, duin'-uasal *m*

aristocratic *adj* uasal

arithmetic *n* cunntas *m*, àireamhachd *f invar*

arm[1] *n* **1** (*part of body*) gàirdean *m*; **2** (*idiom*) **come to my ~s** thig *vi* nam chom *m*, thig nam achlais *f*

arm[2] *n* (*weapon*) ball-airm *m*

armchair *n* cathair-ghàirdeanach *f*

armful *n* achlasan *m*, ultach *m*

armour *n* **1** armachd *f invar*; **2** *in expr* **suit of ~** deise-airm *f*

armoury *n* armlann *f*

armpit *n* achlais *f*, lag *mf* na h-achlaise

armrest *n* taic-uilne *f*

army *n* arm *m*, **when I was in the ~** nuair a bha mi san arm

around *adv* **1** timcheall, mun cuairt *&* mu chuairt, **a rumour/the flu's going ~** tha fathann *m*/an cnatan mòr a' dol timcheall/a' dol mun cuairt

around *prep* **1** timcheall (*with gen*), timcheall air, mun cuairt air, **all ~ her** fada mun cuairt oirre, **we'll go ~ the loch** thèid sinn timcheall an locha, **they built houses ~ his garden** thog iad taighean *mpl* timcheall air a' ghàrradh *m* aige, **are there any shops ~ here?** a bheil bùithtean *mfpl* timcheall air an seo?; **2** (*approximately*) timcheall air, mu (*lenites following cons, takes dat*) **~ a hundred** timcheall air ceud, mu cheud;

3 (*of garment &c*) mu, **put your coat ~ you** cuir umad do chota *m*, **a bandage ~ his head** bann *m* mu cheann *m*; **4** *prep prons formed with* mu, **~ me** umam(sa), **~ you** (*sing*) umad(sa), **~ him/it** (*m*) uime(san), **~ her/it** (*f*) uimpe(se), **~ us** umainn(e), **~ you** (*pl*) umaibh(se), **~ them** umpa(san)

arrange *v* **1** (*organise, set up*) cuir *vt* air chois (*dat of* cas *f*), **~ a meeting** cuir coinneamh *f* air chois; **2** (*put in order*) sgioblaich *vt*, cuir *vt* an òrdugh *m*, cuir *vt* air dòigh *f*, **~ the furniture** sgioblaich an àirneis, **~ documents** cuir pàipearan *mpl* an òrdugh

arrangement *n* **1** (*state of affairs &c*) suidheachadh *m*, **she didn't like this ~ at all** cha robh an suidheachadh seo a' còrdadh rithe idir; **2** (*agreement, settlement*) còrdadh *m*, rèite *f*, **they reached an ~** thàinig *vi* iad gu còrdadh/rèite; **3** (*mus*) rian *m*

arranger *n* (*music*) rianadair *m*

arrest *v* cuir *vt* an làimh (*dat of* làmh *f*), cuir *vt* an sàs *m*

arrival *n* teachd *m invar*, **the ~ of spring** teachd an earraich

arrive *v* thig *vi*, ruig *vti*, **they haven't ~d yet** cha tàinig iad fhathast, cha do ràinig iad fhathast, **~ at Perth at 8 o'clock** ruig Peairt/thig gu Peairt aig ochd uairean *fpl*

arrogance *n* dànadas *m*, uaibhreas *m*, àrdan *m*

arrogant *adj* dàna, àrdanach

arrow *n* saighead *f*

arse *n* (*fam*) màs *m*, (*fam*) tòn *f*

arsehole *n* (*vulg in this sense*) toll *m*, (*vulg*) toll-tòine (*gen of* tòn *f*)

art *n* ealain *f*, **the Scottish Arts Council** Comhairle *f* nan Ealain an Albainn (*dat of* Alba *f*), **~ gallery** ealain-lann *f*, *also* taisbean-lann *f*

artery *n* cuisle *f*, **main ~** cuisle-mhòr *f*

artful *adj* innleachdach, carach

artfulness *n* innleachd *f*

arthritis *n* tinneas *m* nan alt *m*

article *n* **1** (*object, thing*) rud *m*; **2** (*journalism &c*) aiste *f*, alt *m*; **3** (*gram*) alt *m*; **4** *in expr* **an ~ of clothing** ball *m* aodaich *m gen*

articulate *adj* fileanta, pongail

articulate *v* (*express*) cuir *vt* an cèill (*dat of* ciall *f*)

artificial *adj* fuadain, brèige (*gen of* breug *f, used as adj*)

artisan *n* fear-ceàirde *m*

artist *n* neach-ealain (*pl* luchd-ealain *m sing coll*)

artistic *adj* ealanta

artistry *n* ealantas *m*

as *adv* **1** (*in comparisons*) cho, **it wasn't ~ good ~ (all) that** cha robh e cho math sin, **~ big ~ a house** cho mòr ri taigh *m*; **2** *in expr* **~ much ~** uiread agus/is, (*esp in neg sentences*) fiù agus/is, **give me ~ much ~ Iain (has)** thoir dhomh uiread agus a tha aig Iain, **there wasn't ~ much ~ a piece of bread left** cha robh fiù agus pìos *m* arain *m* air fhàgail;

3 (*distance*) ~ **far** ~ gu ruige (*with nom*), ~ **far** ~ **the ridge** gu ruige an druim *m*; **4** *in expr* ~ **for** (*ie concerning*) (a-)thaobh (*with gen*), ~ **for the election** . . . a-thaobh/thaobh an taghaidh . . .

as *conj* **1** mar, ~ **they say** mar a chanas iad, **he carried on** ~ **if/though it didn't matter** lean e air mar nach robh e gu difir, **be that** ~ **it may** biodh sin mar a bhitheas; **2** (*because*) on a & bhon a, **they put the stock on the hill** ~ **the grazing was good up there** chuir iad an sprèidh *f* dhan mhonadh *m* on a bha an t-ionaltradh math shuas an sin; **3** *in expr* ~ **well** (*ie also*) cuideachd, mar an ceudna, **has Ewan left? yes, and Iain** ~ **well** an do dh'fhalbh Eòghann? dh'fhalbh, agus Iain cuideachd/mar an ceudna; **4** *in expr* ~ **well** ~ (*ie in addition to*) cho math ri, a bharrachd air, **he had a dram** ~ **well** ~ **a pint** ghabh e drama *m* cho math ri pinnt *m*

ascertain *v* faigh *vt* a-mach

ascribe *v* cuir *vt* (*with prep* as leth), ~ **something to someone** cuir rudeigin às leth cuideigin *mf invar*

ash *n* **1** (*tree & wood*) uinnseann *m*, **mountain** ~ caorann *fm*; **2** (*fire residue*) luaithre *f invar*, luath *f*

ashamed *adj* fo nàire, nàraichte, air a (*&c*) nàrachadh *m*, **I'm** ~ tha mi fo nàire *f invar*, *also* tha nàire orm; **2** (*become* ~) gabh nàire, **I was** ~ **when she heard about it** ghabh mi nàire (*also* chaidh mo nàrachadh) nuair a chuala i mu dheidhinn

ashen *adj* bàn-ghlas

ashore *adv* **1** (*position*) air tìr *mf*; **2** (*movement*) gu tìr, air tìr, **they're coming** ~ tha iad a' tighinn *vi* gu tìr/air tìr

aside *adv* air leth, an dara taobh *m*, **put/set** ~ cuir *vt* air leth, cuir *vt* an dara taobh

ask *v* **1** (*enquire, question*) faighnich *vi* (*with prep* de *or* do), ~ **Morag** faighnich de Mhòrag, **she** ~**ed whether there was life on Mars** dh'fhaighnich i an robh beatha air Màrt *m*; **2** (*request*) iarr *vti* (*with prep* air), **they** ~**ed for a pay rise** dh'iarr iad àrdachadh-pàighidh *m*, **she** ~**ed me to close the door** dh'iarr i orm an doras a dhùnadh; **3** (*invite*) iarr *vt*, **they** ~**d me to a party** dh'iarr iad mi (tighinn) gu pàrtaidh; **4** *in expr* ~ **a question** faighnich ceist *f*, cuir ceist (*with prep* air), **she's always** ~**ing questions** bidh i a' faighneachd ceistean gun sgur, **they** ~**ed me questions** chuir iad ceistean orm; **5** (*idiom*) **Iain was** ~**ing after you** bha Iain a' gabhail do naidheachd *f*, bha Iain gad fhaighneachd

askew *adj* claon

aslant *adj* fiar

asleep *adj* na (*&c*) c(h)adal *m*, **we were** ~ bha sinn nar cadal

aspect *n* **1** (*appearance*) dreach *m*, cruth *m*; **2** (*facet &c*) taobh *m*, **it's that** ~ **of the matter that worries me** 'se an taobh sin den chùis a tha a' cur dragh *m* orm; **3** (*geographical exposure*) sealladh-aghaidh *m*

aspiration *n* (*ie desire, ambition*) miann *m*, mòr-mhiann *m*, rùn *m*

aspire *v* bi *vi irreg* miannach (**to** air), ~ **to fame/wealth** bi miannach air cliù *m invar*/beartas *m*

assailant *n* neach-ionnsaigh (*pl* luchd-ionnsaigh *m sing coll*)

assassin *n* murtair *m*

assassinate *v* murt *vt*

assassination *n* murt *m*

assault *n* **1** ionnsaigh *mf*; **2** (*as legal term*) droch-ionnsaigh *mf*

assault *v* thoir ionnsaigh *mf* (*with prep* air)

assemble *v* **1** (*gather, collect: of people*) cruinnich *vti*, thig *vi* còmhla; **2** (*of people & things*) co-chruinnich *vti*; **3** (~ *machinery, kit &c*) cuir *vt* ri chèile

assembled *adj & past part* **1** (*of things: put together*) co-dhèanta, air an (*&c*) c(h)ur ri chèile; **2** (*of people: gathered*) cruinn, **the congregation was ~ in the church** bha an coitheanal cruinn san eaglais *f*

assembly *n* **1** (*of people*) cruinneachadh *m*, tional *m*; **2** (*of people or things*) co-chruinneachadh *m*; **3** (*abstr: putting together*) cur *m* ri chèile

assent *n* **1** aonta *m*; **2** (*permission*) cead *m invar*

assent *v* thoir aonta *m* (**to** do)

assert *v* **1** (*state, argue*) cùm a-mach *vi*, **they were ~ing that the world wasn't round** bha iad a' cumail a-mach nach robh an cruinne cruinn; **2** *in expr* ~ **authority** gabh smachd *m invar* (**over** air), **he ~ed his authority over the country** ghabh e smachd air an dùthaich *f*

assess *v* meas *vt*

assessment *n* **1** (*abstr: the action*) measadh *m*; **2** (*con: an* ~) meas *m*

assessor *n* neach-meas *m* (*pl* luchd-meas *m sing coll*)

assets *n* maoin *f*, so-mhaoin *f*, **freeze** ~ reoth so-mhaoin

assign *n* (*resources, person to post*) sònraich *vt*

assist *v* cuidich *vti*, dèan cobhair *f* (*with prep* air) ~ **them** cuidich *vt* iad, (*more trad*) cuidich *vi* leotha

assistance *n* **1** cuideachadh *m*, cobhair *f*; **2** (*financial*) taic *f* (airgid)

assistant *n* neach-cuideachaidh *m* (*pl* luchd-cuideachaidh *m sing coll*)

associate *n* **1** companach *m*; **2** (*esp in business, crime &c*) (com)pàirtiche *m*

associated *adj & past part* an cois (*dat of* cas *f*), an lùib (*dat of* lùb *f*), (*both with gen*), **poverty and its ~ difficulties** bochdainn *f* agus na duilgheadasan *mpl* a thig na cois, *also* bochdainn agus a cuid *f* duilgheadasan, **there is a story ~ with each building** tha sgeul *m* an lùib gach togalaich *m*

association *n* **1** (*abstr*) cruinneachadh *m*, tighinn *f* còmhla, **freedom of** ~ còir *f* chruinneachaidh; **2** *in expr* **in** ~ **with** an co-bhann/co-bhuinn ri; **3** (*more con: club &c*) comann *m*

assortment *n* measgachadh *m*, taghadh *m*, (**of** de)

assume *v* **1** (*take as fact*) gabh *vi* ris, **I ~ he won't do it again** tha mi a gabhail ris nach dèan e tuilleadh e; **2** (*take on*) gabh *vt* os làimh (*gen of* làmh *f*), gabh *vt* air fhèin, **he ~d responsibility for the company** ghabh e os làimh/air fhèin uallach *m* a' chompanaidh

assumption *n* **1** (*hypothesis*) tuaiream *m*; **2** (*opinion, supposition*) barail *f*

assurance *n* **1** bar(r)antas *m*, (*less formal*) gealladh *m*, **we accepted the ~ he gave us** ghabh sinn ris a' bharrantas a thug e dhuinn; **2** (*insurance*) àrachas *m*, urras *m*, **an ~ policy** poileasaidh *m* àrachais/urrais *gen*

assure *v* rach an urras *m* (*with prep* do), **he ~d me that it was true** chaidh e an urras dhomh gun robh e fìor

asterisk *n* (*orthography*) reultag *f*

asthma *n* (*used with art*) a' chuing *f*, an sac *m*

astonish *v* cuir mòr-iongnadh *m* (*with prep* air), **it ~ed me** chuir e mòr-iongnadh orm

astonishment *n* mòr-iongnadh *m*

astray *adj & adv* **1** (*phys*) air fhuadan; **2** (*phys, morally*) air seachran air iomrall; **3** *in exprs* **go ~** (*phys, morally*) rach *vi* air seachran/air iomrall, **lead/go ~** (*esp morally*) claon *vti*

astride *adj & adv* casa-gòbhlach (*with prep* air), **~ the chair** casa-gòbhlach air a' chathair *f*, **riding ~** a' marcachd casa-gòbhlach

astrology *n* speuradaireachd *f invar*

astronaut *n* speur-sheòladair *m*

astronomer *n* reuladair *m*

astronomy *n* reul-eòlas *m*

asylum *n* (*abstr*) tèarmann *m*, **political ~** tèarmann poileataigeach

at *prep* **1** (*position & time*) aig, **~ home** aig an taigh *m*, **~ the door** aig an doras *m*, **~ sea** aig muir *mf*, **~ six o'clock** aig sia uairean, **~ dinner-time** aig àm *m* dìnnearach, **~ best** aig a' char *m* as fheàrr, **~ worst** aig a' char as miosa; **2** (*misc exprs & idioms*) **~ Perth** ann am Peart, **~ that, he went home** leis a sin chaidh e dhachaigh, (*work, a task &c*) **keep/stick ~ it!** cùm *vi* ris!, **~ (long) last** mu dheireadh (thall), **~ all** idir (*usu with neg verb*), **are you tired? not at all!** a bheil thu sgìth? chan eil idir!, **~ first** an toiseach, **I didn't like him ~ first** cha bu toigh leam an toiseach e

athletic *adj* lùthmhor

Atlantic *n*, **the** *used with art*, An Cuan *m* Siar

atom *n* dadam *m*

atomic *adj* atamach

atone *v*, **1** (*make reparation*) dèan èirig *f* (**for** airson), **you'll ~ for it** nì sibh èirig air a shon; **2** (*relig: with reference to Christ's atonement*) dèan rèite *f*

atonement *n* **1** (*reparation &c*) èirig *f*, **as ~ for his mistakes** an èirig a mhearachdan *mpl*; **2** (*relig: with reference to Christ's atonement*) rèite *f*

atrocious *adj* uabhasach, oillteil, eagalach

atrocity *n* uabhas *m*, **atrocities in time of war** uabhasan an àm *m* cogaidh *m*

attached *adj past part* **1** (*phys*) ceangailte (**to** ri), **~ to the wall** ceangailte ris a' bhalla; **2** (*emotionally or in friendship*) measail, dèidheil (**to** air), ceangailte (**to** ri), **I became quite ~ to them** dh'fhàs mi gu math measail/dèidheil orra, dh'fhàs mi gu math ceangailte riutha

attachment *n* **1** (*phys*) ceangal *m*; **2** (*liking, friendship*) tlachd *f invar*, dèidh *f*, spèis *f*

attack *n* **1** ionnsaigh *mf*, **make/mount/launch an ~** thoir ionnsaigh (**on** air); **2** (*verbal*) càineadh *m*, màbadh *m*; **3** *in expr* **heart ~** grèim-cridhe *m*, clisgeadh *m* cridhe *m*

attack *v* thoir ionnsaigh (*with prep* air)

attacker *n* neach-ionnsaigh *m* (*pl* luchd-ionnsaigh *m sing coll*)

attain *v* (*an aim &c*) faigh *vt*, ruig *vt*, **he ~ed his wish/ambition** fhuair e a mhiann *mf*/a rùn *m*

attempt *n* oidhirp *f*, **make an ~ at something** dèan oidhirp air rudeigin

attempt *v* feuch *vti* (*with prep* ri), dèan oidhirp *f* (*with prep* air), **I'll ~ to open the door** feuchaidh mi ris an doras fhosgladh, **they ~ed to lift us** dh'fheuch iad ri ar togail, **we have to ~ it** feumaidh sinn oidhirp a dhèanamh air

attend *v* **1** (*serve &c*) freastail *vi*, fritheil *vi*, (**on** air); **2** (*be present*) bi *vi* an làthair *f*, bi *vi* ann, fritheil *vt*, rach *vi* (*with prep* do), **they didn't ~** cha robh iad an làthair, **~ a meeting** rach do choinneimh; **3** (*pay attention*) thoir (an) àire *f invar* (**to** do); **4** *in expr* **~ to a matter** gabh cùis *f* os làimh (*dat of* làmh *f*)

attendance *n* **1** (*service &c*) freastal *m*, **~ at table** freastal don bhòrd; **2** (*~ on someone: at an event &c*) frithealadh *m*; **3** (*audience &c*) **there was a good ~** bha sluagh mòr ann, bha luchd-èisdeachd gu leòr ann

attendant *adj* na c(h)ois (*dat of* cas *f*), na lùib (*dat of* lùb *f*), **poverty and its ~ difficulties** bochdainn *f* agus na duilgheadasan *m* a thig *vi* na cois

attendant *n* neach-frithealaidh *m* (*pl* luchd-frithealaidh *m sing coll*)

attention *n* aire *f invar*, **pay ~** thoir (an) aire (**to** do)

attentive *adj* **1** (*alert*) aireachail, furachail; **2** (*~ to task, someone's needs &c*) furachail; **3** **~ to detail** mion-chùiseach, mionaideach

attestation *n* teisteanas *m*

attitude *n* **1** (*phys*) seasamh *m*; **2** (*mental*) gleus *mf* inntinn *f*

attract *v* **1** (*person, magnet &c*) tarraing *vt*; **2** (*charm, entice*) tàlaidh *vt*, **~ the customers back** tàlaidh an luchd-ceannaich *m sing coll* air ais

attraction *n* tàladh *m*, tarraing *f*

attractive *adj* **1** tàlaidheach, tarraingeach; **2** (*esp in personality*) tlachdmhor

attribute *n* (*esp inherent*) feart *m*, **we get many ~s from our forebears/ ancestors** gheibh sinn mòran fheartan bhor sinnsirean *mpl*

attribute *v* (*esp with implication of guilt, blame*) cuir *vt* às leth (*with gen*), **don't ~ the rumour to me** (*emph*) na cuir am fathann às mo leth-sa

attrition *n* bleith *f*

auctioneer *n* reiceadair *m*

audacious *adj* ladarna, dàna

audience *n* **1** (*radio, concert &c*) luchd-èisteachd *m sing coll*, **there was a good ~** bha luchd-èisteachd gu leòr ann; **2** (*meeting with important person*) coinneamh (phrìobhaideach), agallamh (prìobhaideach)

audio-visual *adj* lèir-chlaistinneach
audit *n* sgrùdadh *m* (chunntasan *mpl gen*)
audit *v* dèan sgrùdadh *m* (air cunntasan *mpl*)
auditor *n* neach-sgrùdaidh *m* (chunntasan *mpl gen*)
auger *n* drile *f*, snìomhaire *m*
augment *v* meudaich *vt*
augmentation *n* meudachadh *m*
August *n* (*used with art*) an Lùnastal *m*
aunt *n*, **my ~** (*on mother's side*) piuthar *f* mo mhàthar, (*on father's side*)
   piuthar *f* m' athar
au revoir *excl* chì mi fhathast sibh/thu
Aurora Borealis *n* (*used with art*) Na Fir Chlis *mpl*
auspices *npl*, *in expr* **under the ~** fo sgèith (*dat of* sgiath *f*) (*with gen*), **under
   the ~ of the Scottish Arts Council** fo sgèith Chomhairle Ealain na
   h-Alba
auspicious *adj* rathail, gealltanach
Austria *n* (*used with art*) an Ostair *f*
Austrian *n & adj* Ostaireach
author *n* ùghdar *m*
authorisation *n* ùghdarras *m*, cead *m*
authorise *v* ùghdarraich *vt*, ceadaich *vt*
authorised *adj & past part* ùghdarraichte, ceadaichte
authoritarian *adj* ceannsalach
authoritative *adj* ùghdarrasail
authority *n* **1** (*control, domination*) ceannsal *m*, smachd *m invar*, **under
   his enemy's ~** fo cheannsal a nàmhad *m*, **she maintained ~ over the
   class** chùm i smachd air a' chlas *m*; **2** (*council &c*) ùghdarras *m*, **local
   authorities** ùghdarrasan ionadail
autobiography *n* fèin-eachdraidh *f*
automatic *n* fèin-ghluaiseach
autonomous *adj* neo-eisimeileach, fèin-riaghlach
autumn *n* foghar *m*, **in ~** as t-fhoghar
auxiliary *adj* taiceil
auxiliary *n* cuidiche *m*, taicear *m*
avail *n* èifeachd *f invar*, buannachd *f*, tairbhe *f invar*, **of no ~** gun èifeachd
avail *v* **1** (*profit, be of use, usu in neg exprs*), **it will ~ you nothing to complain**
   cha leig thu a leas/cha dèan e feum (sam bith) dhut a bhith a' gearan;
   2 (*make use of, take advantage of*), **~ oneself of** cleachd *vt*, gabh cothrom
   m air, **~ oneself of the facilities** cleachd na goireasan *mpl*
available *adj* **1** (*to hand*) deiseil, ullamh; **2** (*to be had*) ri f(h)aighinn, **there
   is no beer ~** chan eil leann *m* ri fhaighinn *m* idir; **3** *in expr* **make ~**
   cuir *vt* an tairgse *f* (*with gen*), **make something ~ to other people** cuir
   rudeigin an tairgse dhaoine *mpl*/muinntir *f* eile
average *adj* **1** meadhanach, cumanta; **2** (*maths*) cuibheasach

average *n* **1** meadhan *m*; **2** (*maths*) cuibheas *m*

awake *adj* nam (*&c*) d(h)ùsgadh *m*, nam (*&c*) d(h)ùisg *m*, **she is** ~ tha i na dùsgadh, tha i na dùisg

awake, awaken *v* dùisg *vti*, **I awoke at six** dhùisg mi aig a sia

awakening *n*, dùsgadh *m*, (*less usu*) mosgladh *m*

award *n* duais *f*

aware *adj* mothachail (**of** air), ~ **of the problem** mothachail air an duilgheadas

awareness *n* mothachadh *m* (**of** air)

away *adv* (*misc exprs*), ~ **from home** on taigh, **right! I'm** ~ ceart! tha mi a' falbh, **she's** ~ (*ie gone*) tha i air falbh, **she's** ~ (*ie absent*) tha i às an làthair *f*, *also* chan eil i (ann) an seo, ~ **you go to the shop for me** thalla don bhùth *mf* dhomh, (*to dog &c*) ~ **home!** falbh/thalla dhachaigh!, **a long way** ~, **far** ~ fad' air falbh, **fade** ~ crìon *vi*, **keep** (*ie stay*) ~ cùm *vi* air falbh, cùm *vi* às an làthair, **keep her** ~ **from me!** cùm bhuam i!

awful *adj* uabhasach, eagalach, sgriosail, **that's** ~! tha sin uabhasach!

awfully *adv* **1** gu h-uabhasach, **how did you get on?** ~! ciamar a chaidh dhut? gu h-uabhasach!; **2** (*as intensifier*) uabhasach, (*stronger*) uabhasach fhèin, **that was** ~ **good!** bha sin uabhasach (fhèin) math!

awkward *adj* (*person, action*) cearbach, *in expr* **an** ~ **person** cearbair *m*

awry *adj* **1** (*slanting &c*) claon; **2** (*wrong, not as it should be*) tuathal

axe *n* tuagh *f*, **Lochaber** ~ tuagh-chatha *f*

axle *n* aiseal *mf*

B

baa, **baaing** *n* mèilich *f invar*

baa *v* dèan mèilich *f invar*

babble, **babbling** *n* gobaireachd *f invar*

baby *n* leanabh *m*, pàiste *m*, leanaban *m*, naoidhean *m*, **she had a ~** bha pàiste aice

babysitter *n* freiceadan *m* cloinne

bachelor *n* fleasgach *m*, (*usu middle-aged or elderly*) seana-ghille *m*, **old ~** seann fhleasgach

back *adj* **1** (*rear*) cùil (*gen of* cùl *m, used adjectivally*), **~ door** doras *m* cùil, **~ room** seòmar *m* cùil, **~ stroke** buille-chùil *f*; **2** (*of the anatomical ~*) droma (*gen of* druim *m used adjectivally*), **a ~ support** taic *f* droma, **~ pain** cràdh *m* droma

back *adv* air ais, **keep/hold ~** cùm *vt* air ais, (*more formal*) cuir maille *f invar* air/ann an , **I won't keep/hold you ~** cha chùm mi air ais sibh, **come/go ~** till *vi* (air ais), (*of time*) **a month ~** mìos *mf* air ais

back *n* **1** (*the phys ~*) druim *m*, **my ~'s sore** tha mo dhruim goirt, **the small of the ~** caol *m* an droma *m*; **2** (*rear part of human, animal, object &c*) cùl *m*, **I turned my ~ to/on him** chuir mi mo chùl ris, **the back of the hand/neck** cùl na làimh/na h-amhaich, **he shoved it in the ~ of the lorry** shad e an cùl na làraidh e, **chair ~** cùl cathrach *f*; **3** (*esp of an animal*) muin *f invar*, **he leapt on the donkey's ~** leum *vi* e air muin na h-asail; **4** (*~ part or section of something*) tòn *f*, **the ~ of the house/of the hall** tòn an taighe *m*/an talla *m*; **5** (*of book*) còmhdach *m*, **hard/soft ~** còmhdach cruaidh/bog; **6** *in expr* **~ to front** cùlaibh air beulaibh

back *v* **1** (*support*) cùm taic ri; **2** (*reverse vehicle &c*) rach *vi* an comhair a (*&c*) c(h)ùil; **3** (*bet*) cuir geall *m*/airgead *m* (**on** air)

back-biting *n* **1** (*the action*) cùl-chàineadh *m*; **2** (*the remarks &c*) cùl-chainnt *f*

backbone *n* cnà(i)mh-droma *m*, **the ~** cnà(i)mh an droma

backer *n* (*fin &c*) neach-taice (*pl* luchd-taice *m sing coll*)

backing *n* taic(e) *f*, **financial ~** taic-airgid *f*

backpack *n* màileid-droma *f*

backside *n* (*buttocks*) màs *m*, (*fam*) tòn *f*

backup *n* **1** (*support*) taic(e) *f*; **2** (*IT, to disc &c*) cùl-ghlèidheadh *m*

backward *adj* deireannach

backwards *adv* an comhair a (*&c*) c(h)ùil, **she fell ~** thuit *vi* i an comhair a cùil

bad *adj*, **1** droch (*cannot be used as a complement and always precedes the noun, which it lenites, except in the case of c*), **~ weather** droch aimsir *f*, droch shìde *f*, **~ language** droch-cainnt *f*, **~ luck** droch shealbh *m*, droch fhortan *m*, **in a ~ state/condition** ann an droch staid *f*, **that's a ~ sign!** is e droch comharradh *m* a tha sin!; **2** dona, **a ~ boy** gille dona, (*used as* *a complement, unlike* droch), **that was** ~ bha sin dona, **drink is** ~ **for you** tha deoch-làidir *f* dona dhut; 3 (*of food &c*, off, *rotten*) lobhte, grod, **go** ~ lobh *vi*; 4 *in expr* **in a** ~ **mood/temper** diombach, crost(a)

badge *n* suaicheantas *m*, bràiste *f*

badger broc *m*

badly *adv* 1 gu dona, **how did you get on?** ~! ciamar a chaidh dhut? chaidh gu dona!; 2 *in expr* ~ **behaved** mì-mhodhail, mìomhail, (*usu of child*) crost(a)

bad-natured *adj* droch nàdarrach

badness *n* donas *m*, (*stronger*) olc *m*

baffle *v* fairtlich *vi* (*with prep* air), **it** ~**d me** dh'fhairtlich e orm

bag *n* 1 poca *m*, baga *m*, **sleeping-**~ poca-cadail; 2 (*large* ~, *luggage &c*) màileid *f*, (*abbrev for* **handbag**) màileid-làimh *f*

baggage *n* treal(l)aichean *fpl*

bagpipe *n* pìob *f*, (*Highland* ~) pìob mhòr, *frequently used with art*, a' phìob, a' phìob mhòr, ~ **music** ceòl *m* na pìoba, *in expr* ~ **chanter** feadan *m*

bail *n* urras *m*, **release on** ~ fuasgail *vt* air urras

bailiff *n* maor *m*

baillie *n* bàillidh *m*

bait *n* (*for fishing*) maghar *m*, biathadh *m*

bake *v* fuin *vt*

baker *n* fuineadair *m*

bakery *n* taigh-fuine *m*

baking *n* (*the action and the product*) fuineadh *m*, fuine *f*, ~ **powder** pùdar-fuine *m*

balance *n* 1 (*equilibrium*) co-chothrom *m*, cothrom *m*, meidh *f*, (*fig*) ~ **of power** co-chothrom cumhachd *m gen*; 2 (*set of scales &c*) cothrom *m*, meidh *f*; 3 (*fin, abstr*) cothromachadh *m*, ~ **sheet** cunntas *m* cothromachaidh; 4 *in expr* **on** ~ air chothrom *m*; 5 (*fin, actual sum left in hand*) còrr *m*

balance *v* 1 cuir *vt* air mheidh *f*, cothromaich *vt*, **she** ~**ed the load/burden on her head** chuir i an t-uallach air mheidh air a ceann *m*; 2 (*fin*) cothromaich *vt*, ~ **a budget** cothromaich buidseat *m*

balanced *adj & past part* 1 (*in equilibrium*) air mheidh; 2 (*fair, even-handed*) cothromach, **a** ~ **discussion** deasbad cothromach; 3 (*fin*) cothromaichte

bald *adj* maol, *in expr* ~ **patch** sgall *m*

baldness *n* maoile *f invar*, maoilead *m*

bale *n* (*of hay &c*) bèile *m*

bale *v* (*boat &c*) taom *vti*

baler *n* taoman *m*

ball[1] *n* (*dance*) bàl *m*

ball[2] (*for games &c*) bàla *m*, ball *m*, **foot**~ ball-coise *m*

ballad *n* bailead *m*

ballast *n* balaiste *f invar*

ballot *n* **1** baileat *m*, taghadh *m*, **hold a ~ on a particular question** cùm baileat air ceist shònraichte; **2** *in expr* ~ **paper** pàipear *m* bhòtaidh

balmy *adj* (*evening &c*) tlàth

bamboo *n* cuilc *f* Innseanach

ban *n* toirmeasg *m*

ban *v* toirmisg *vt*

band[1] *n* **1** (*of people*) còmhlan *m*, buidheann *mf*, (*pej*) treud *m*; **2** (*music*) còmhlan(-ciùil) *m*

band[2] *n* (*loop of material*) crios *m*, bann *m*, **rubber ~** crios-rubair *m*

bandage *n* bann *m*

bandy-legged *adj* cama-chasach, crom-chasach

bang *n* cnag *f*, brag *m*

bang *v* cnag *vti*

banish *v* fuadaich *vt*, fògair *vt*, **the people were ~ed from the glen** dh'fhògradh an sluagh às a' ghleann *m*

banishment *n* fuadach *m*, fuadachadh *m*, fògradh *m*

bank[1] *n* (*fin*) banca *m*, **I've an account at the Royal ~** tha cunntas *m* agam aig a' Bhanca Rìoghail, **~ loan** iasad *m* banca

bank[2] *n* **1** (*of river &c*) bruach *f*; **2** (*hillside, slope*) bruthach *mf*; **3** *in expr* **peat ~** poll-mòna *m* (*also* poll-mònach *&* poll-mònadh)

bank *v* **1** (*money*) cuir *vt* sa bhanca; **2** (*idiom*) **don't ~ on it!** na cuir earbsa *f invar* ann!

banker *n* bancair *m*

banking *n* bancaireachd *f invar*

banknote *n* nota *f* (banca)

bankrupt *adj* briste

banned *adj & past part* toirmisgte

banner *n* bratach *f*

bannock *n* bonnach *m*

banquet *n* fèis *f*, cuirm *f*

baptise *v* baist *vt*

baptism *n* baisteadh *m*

Baptist *n & adj* Baisteach *m*

bar *n* **1** (*of wood, metal*) crann *m*; **2** (*obstacle, impediment*) bacadh *m*, **a ~ to promotion** bacadh air àrdachadh *m*, **colour ~** dath-bhacadh *m*; **3** (*in pub &c*) bàr *m*; **4** (*music*) car *m*; **5** (*IT &c*) **~ chart** clàr *m* colbh *m*

bar *v* **1** (*prevent, obstruct*) bac *vt*, cuir bacadh *m* (*with prep* air); **2** *in expr* **~ the door** cuir (an) crann *m* air an doras *m*

barb *n* gath *m*

barbaric, barbarous *adj* borb

barbed *adj & past part* gathach

barber *n* borbair *m*, (*more trad*) bearradair *m*

bard *n* bàrd *m*

bare *adj* **1** (*naked*) lomnochd; **2** (*uncovered*) rùisgte, **his back was ~** bha a dhruim *m* rùisgte; **3** (*landscape &c*) lom, **a ~ hillside** bruthach *mf* lom

bare *v* **1** (*esp body &c: strip*) rùisg *vt*, lom *vt*, **he ~d his forearm** rùisg e a ruighe *mf*; **2** (*sword*) rùisg *vt*

bared *adj & past part* **1** (*esp of body &c: naked, stripped*) rùisgte; **2** (*showing*) ris *prep pron*, **her forearm was ~** bha a ruighe *mf* ris

bare-faced *adj* ladarna, dàna

barefoot *adj* casruisgte

bare-headed *adj* ceannruisgte

barelegged *adj* casruisgte

barely *adv* **1** (*to a small extent, rarely, with difficulty*) is gann (*with conj* a), **we ~ saw him** is gann a chunnaic sinn e, **he ~ uttered two words** is gann a leig e às dà fhacal, **we ~ made out what she was saying** is gann a rinn sinn a-mach dè a bha i ag ràdh; **2** (*hardly, scarcely*) cha mhòr (*with conj* gun), **he ~ uttered two words** cha mhòr gun do leig e às dà fhacal *m*; **3** (*esp expr difficulty*) is ann air èiginn (*with conj* a), **we ~ made out what she was saying** is ann air èiginn a rinn sinn a-mach dè a bha i ag ràdh, **he ~ opened his eye** is ann air èiginn a dh'fhosgail e a shùil *f*

bareness *n* luime *f*, lomnochd *f invar*

bargain *n* **1** (*legal, official, fin &c*) cùmhnant *m*, cunnradh *m*; **2** (*good buy &c*) bargan *m*

bark[1] *n* (*of dog*) comhart *m*

bark[2] *n* (*of tree*) rùsg *m*, cairt *f*

bark *v* dèan comhart *m*, tabhannaich *vi*, (**at** ri)

barking *n* comhartaich *f*, tabhannaich *f*

barley *n* eòrna *m invar*

barn *n* sabhal *m*, *in expr* **~ owl** comhachag *f*

barnacle *n* giùran *m*, bàirneach *f*

barometer *n* glainne-sìde *f*

baron *n* baran *m*

barrel *n* baraille *m*, (*large ~, can be of metal*) tocasaid (*also* togsaid & tosgaid) *f*, **~ of oil** baraille ola *f*, **~ of gun** baraille *m*

barren *adj* **1** (*land*) fàs; **2** (*woman*) neo-thorrach; **3** (*livestock &c*) seasg

barrenness *n* **1** (*land*) fàsachd *f invar*; **2** (*woman*) neo-thorrachd *f invar*, neo-thorraichead *f invar*; **3** (*livestock &c*) seasgachd *f invar*

barrier *n* (*lit & fig*) bacadh *m*, cnap-starra *m*

barrister *n* neach-tagraidh *m* (*pl* luchd-tagraidh *m sing coll*), tagarair *m*

barter *n* malairt *f*

barter *v* malairtich *vi*, dèan malairt *f*

base *adj* suarach, tàireil

base *n* (*bottom, foundation*) bonn *m*, bun *m*

bash *v* (*fam, in fight &c*) pronn *vt*

bashful *adj* diùid, nàrach

bashfulness *n* diùideachd *f invar*, diùide *f invar*, nàire *f invar*

basic *adj* bunaiteach, **~ rights** còraichean *fpl* bunaiteach, **~ Gaelic** Gàidhlig bhunaiteach

basin *n* mias *f*

basis *n* **1** (*more usu phys*) stèidh *f*; **2** (*more usu abstr*) bunait *f*, **the ~ of his philosophy** bunait na feallsanachd aige

basket *n* basgaid *f*

basketball *n* ball-basgaid *m*

bass *n* (*music*) beus (*gen* beusa) *m*

bastard *n* duine/neach *m* dìolain

bastard *adj* dìolain

bat[1] *n* (*the animal*) ialtag *f*

bat[2] (*for games*) slacan *m*, bat *m*

batch *n* dòrlach *m*

bath *n* **1** amar *m*, ionnaltair *f*; **2** *in expr* ~ **towel** tubhailte mhòr, searbhadair mòr

bathe *v* ionnlaid *vti*, failc *vti*

bathing *n* ionnlad *m*

bathroom *n* seòmar-ionnlaid *m*, rùm-ionnlaid *m*

battalion *n* cath-bhuidheann *f*

batter *v* pronn *vt*, dochainn *vt*

battery *n* bataraidh *mf*

battle *n* cath *m*, blàr *m*, batail *m*, **the ~ of Culloden** Blàr Chùil Lodair

battle-axe *n* tuagh-chatha *f*

battlefield *n* blàr *m*, àr *m*

battleship *n* long-chogaidh *f*

bawdy *adj* drabasta, draosta

bawl *v* glaodh *vi*

bay *n* bàgh *m*, camas *m*, òb *m*

bayonet *n* bèigleid *f*

be *v* **1** bi *v irreg* (*cannot be used with a noun complement, cf 2 a) below*), **a)** *with adj complement*, **it's cold, isn't it?** tha i fuar, nach eil?, **~ quiet!** bi (*imperative*) sàmhach!, **that's good** tha sin math; **b)** *with adv complement*, **Ian was there** bha Iain ann; **c)** *with present participle*, **is he coming?** a bheil e a' tighinn?, **they weren't singing** cha robh iad a' seinn; **d)** *expr existence*, bi *with third pers prep pron* ann, **there are no fairies** (*ie fairies don't exist*) chan eil sìthichean *mpl* ann; **e)** *expr state, position, occupation &c, temporary or permanent*, bi *with prep & poss pron* nam, nad (*&c*), **he was alone** bha e na aonar, **they are asleep** tha iad nan cadal *m*, **she's a nurse** tha i na banaltram *f*/na nurs *f*, **I'm a part-time chef just now** tha mi nam chòcaire *m* pàirt-ùine an dràsta; **f)** (*in past tenses only: visit, spend time in*) **have you (ever) been to Lewis?** an robh sibh (riamh/a-riamh) ann an Leòdhas?; **2** is *v irreg & def, past tense* bu, *inter* an (am *before* b, f, m, p), *past inter* am bu, *neg* cha (*before vowel, or f followed by vowel*, chan), *past neg* cha bu, *neg inter* nach, *past neg inter* nach bu, **a)** *as a copula, linking or equating two nouns/pronouns*, **I am a man** is duine *m* mi, **is she Isabel?** an ise Iseabail?, **they were the**

ones who did it b' iadsan an fheadhainn *f* a rinn e; **b)** *expr professions, occupations, character &c*, **he's a surgeon** is e lannsair *m* a tha ann, **Fiona is a midwife** is e/i bean-ghlùine a th' ann am Fiona, **they are fools** is e amadain a tha annta (*Note: this construction, with* is, *can express more permanence than* bi *with* nam, nad *&c, cf examples under* **1 e)** *above*); **c)** *with adj complement (often in set exprs in Gaelic)* **that's good** is math sin, **that's a shame!** is truagh sin!, **it's good that it's finished/over** 's math seachad e; **d)** *with an emph or 'highlighted' adj or adv complement,* is *followed by* ann *prep pron,* **she's not young, she's ancient!** chan eil i òg, is ann a tha i aosta!, **is it tomorrow we'll see her?** no an ann a-màireach a chì sinn i? chan ann; **e)** *with an emph or 'highlighted' noun or pron complement,* is *followed by prep & noun/pron,* **he wouldn't do that, he's a minister** (*emph*)! cha dèanadh esan sin, 's e ministear *m* a tha ann!, **is/was it your bag** (*emph*) **that you lost?** an e do mhàileid a chaill thu?; **f)** *introducing a relative clause,* is *followed by noun or pron,* **was it you who wrote it? no!** an tusa a sgrìobh e? cha mhì!, **isn't it they who'll go (there)?** nach iadsan a thèid ann?, **it's the old man who lost it** is e am bodach *m* a chaill e, **isn't/wasn't it her husband who died?** nach e an duine aice a chaochail?

beach *n* tràigh *f*, (*often stony*) cladach *m*, (*shingly or pebbly*) mol *m*

bead *n* (*on necklace &c*) grìogag *f*

beak *n* gob *m*

beam *n* **1** (*ray*) gath *m*, **~ of light** gath solais *m gen*; **2** (*of timber*) sail *f*, spàrr *m*

beam *v* (*facial expr*) dèan fàite-gàire mhòr

bean, beans *n* pònair *f sing & coll*, **broad ~** pònair leathann, **French ~** pònair Fhrangach

bear *n* (*brown ~*) mathan *m*, **polar ~** mathan bàn

bear *v* **1** (*suffer, tolerate*) fuiling *vt*, **I couldn't ~ to do it** chan fhuilinginn a dhèanamh, **they had to ~ cold and hunger** b' fheudar dhaibh fuachd *mf* is acras *m* fhulang, **I can't ~ her** chan fhuiling mi i; **2** (*carry*) giùlain *vt*, iomchair *vt*; **3** (*give birth to*) beir *vt irreg*, **she bore a son** rug i mac *m*, *also* rugadh mac dhi; **4** *in expr* **~ in mind** cùm na (*&c*) c(h)uimhne *f invar*

beard *n* feusag *f*

bearded *adj* feusagach, ròmach

bearer *n* neach-giùlain *m*, neach-iomchair *m* (*pl* luchd-giùlain/iomchair *m sing coll*), (*less trad*) portair *m*

bearing[1] *n* (*compass ~*) gabhail *mf*, (*esp nautical*) àird *f*

bearing[2] (*posture*) giùlan *m*

bearing[3] (*engineering &c*) giùlan *m*, **ball ~** giùlan bhàla *m*, *also* gràn *m*

beast *n* **1** (*animal*) ainmhidh *m*; **2** (*esp farm animal*) beathach *m*; **3** (*term of abuse*) biast *f*, brùid *m*, bèist *f*

beat *n* (*music: rhythm*) buille *mf*

beat *v* **1** (*defeat*) fairtlich *vi*, dèan a' chùis, dèan an gnothach, (*all with* *prep* air), **it was the bad weather that ~ us** is e an droch aimsir *f* a dh'fhairtlich/rinn a' chùis oirnn, **they ~ the other team** rinn iad a' chùis/an gnothach air an sgioba *mf* eile ; **2** (*strike*) buail *vt*, slac *vt*; **3** *in expr* **~ up** (*fam, in fight &c*) pronn *vt*, dochainnich *vt*

beating *n* (*thrashing, beating up*) slacadh *m*, pronnadh *m*

beautiful *adj* rìomhach, (*esp of a place, a woman, or other living being*) bòidheach, brèagha, (*esp of a woman*) maiseach

beautify *v* maisich *vt*, sgèimhich *vt*

beauty *n* **1** maise *f invar*, bòidhchead *f invar*, àilleachd *f invar*; **2** *in expr* **~ spot** (*on face*) ball-seirce *m*, (*attractive place*) àite *m* brèagha

beaver *n* biobhar *m*

becalm *v*, **the boat was ~ed** thàinig fèath *mf* air a' bhàta *m*

because *conj* a chionn is gu, (*in neg exprs* a chionn is nach), a thaobh is gu (*in neg exprs* a thaobh is nach), **~ he was old** a chionn 's gu robh e sean, **~ there isn't a strike** a chionn 's nach eil stailc *f* ann

because of *prep* a chionn, a-thaobh, air sgàth, (*all with gen*), **~ of that** a chionn sin

beckon *v* smèid *vi* (*with prep* air *or* ri), **she ~ed to me** smèid i orm/rium

become *v* **1** (*followed by adj*) fàs *vi*, **they became old/rich** dh'fhàs iad sean/ beartach; **2** (*onset of emotion, sensation &c*) thig *vi* (*with n, & prep* air), **I became sorrowful/afraid/hungry** thàinig mulad *f*/(an t-)eagal *m*/(an t-)acras *m* orm; **3** (*adopt profession &c*) rach *vi* na (*&c*) *followed by n*, **he became a policeman** chaidh e na phoileas *m*; **4** (*befall*) tachair *vi*, èirich *vi*, (*with prep* do), **what became of James?** dè a thachair do Sheumas?, dè a dh'èirich do Sheumas?; **5** (*suit*) thig *vi* (*with prep* do), freagair *vi* (*with prep* air), **mourning ~s Electra** thig am bròn do Electra

bed *n* **1** leabaidh *f*; **2** *in exprs* **I was in ~** bha mi san leabaidh, *also* bha mi nam laighe, **go to ~** rach a laighe, rach a chadal *m*, **we're going to ~** tha sinn a' dol a laighe, **she took to her ~** ghabh i ris an leabaidh; **3** (*~ of sea*) grunnd *m*

bedclothes, bedding *n* aodach *m sing coll* leapa *f*

bedfellow *n* coimhleapach *mf*

bedroom *n* seòmar-cadail *m*

bee *n* seillean *m*

beef *n* mairtfheoil *f*

beehive *n* sgeap *f*

beer *n* leann *m*

beet *n* biotais *m invar*

beetle *n* daolag *f*

befall *v* tachair *vi*, èirich *vi*, tuit *vi*, (*all with prep* do)

befit *v* **1** (*suit*) thig (*with prep* do); **2** (*be incumbent on*) is *v irreg def* cubhaidh (*with prep* do), **as ~s a gentleman** mar as cubhaidh do dhuine-uasal *m*

befitting *adj* cubhaidh, iomchaidh, (**to do:** *used with v* is), **an action ~ a hero** gnìamh *m* as cubhaidh (*in past* a bu chubhaidh) do ghaisgeach *m*

before *adv* roimhe, **a man we never saw** ~ duine *m* nach fhaca sinn a-riamh roimhe

before *conj* mus & mun, ~ **the winter comes** mus/mun tig an geamhradh, **he didn't pay** ~ **he left** cha do phàigh e mus do dh'fhalbh e, **the night** ~ **she died** an oidhche *f* mus do chaochail i

before *prep* **1** (*space*) ro (*with dat*), fa chomhair (*with gen*), **standing** ~ **me** na stad romham, na stad fa mo chomhair, ~ **the door** fa chomhair an dorais; **2** (*time*) ro (*with the dat*), ~ **(the due) time** ron àm *m*, ron mhithich *f invar*; **3** *prep prons* ~ **me** romham(sa), ~ **you** (*sing*) romhad(sa), ~ **him/ it** (*m*) roimhe(san), ~ **her/it** (*f*) roimhpe(se), ~ **us** romhainn(e), ~ **you** (*pl*) romhaibh(se), ~ **them** romhpa(san)

beforehand *adv* ro-làimh

beg *v* **1** dèan faoighe *f invar*; **2** (*plead with*) guidh *vi* (*with prep* air), **I'm** ~**ging you to stay!** tha mi a' guidhe ort fuireachd!, **he** ~**ged us to let him go/set him free** ghuidh e oirnn a leigeil ma sgaoil

beget *v* gin *vt*, **Noah begat three sons** ghin Noah triùir mhac *mpl gen*

beggar *n* dìol-dèirce *m*, dèirceach *m*

begging *n* (*for gifts of food &c*) faoighe *f invar*

begin *v* tòisich *vi* (*with prep* air *or* ri), teann *vi* (*with prep* ri), ~ **singing** tòisich a' seinn, ~ **to sing** tòisich air/ri seinn, **he began climbing** theann e ri streap

beginning *n* **1** (*in time*) toiseach *m*, **the** ~ **of summer** toiseach an t-samhraidh, **at the** ~ an toiseach, **at the very** ~, **right at the** ~ aig an fhìor thoiseach, an toiseach tòiseachaidh *m*; **2** (~ *of a process &c*) tòiseachadh *m*, **a new** ~ tòiseachadh às ùr, (*saying*) ~ **is a day's work** is e obair *f* latha *m* tòiseachadh; **3** (*first or earliest stage*) tùs *m*, (*prov*) **the fear of God is the** ~ **of wisdom** 's e tùs a' ghliocais eagal *m* Dhè, **he's been working here from/since the (very)** ~ tha e ag obair an seo o thùs

beguile *v* meall *vt*

beguiling *adj* meallach

beguiling *n* mealladh *m*

behalf *n*, *in expr* **on** ~ **of** às leth (*with the gen*), **he did it on my** ~ rinn e às mo leth e

behave *v* **1** giùlain fhèin (*&c*), **I wasn't behaving too well** cha robh mi gam ghiùlan fhìn ro mhath; **2** (~ *towards, treat*) làimhsich *vt*, gnàthaich *vt*

behaviour *n* **1** (*conduct*) dol-a-mach *m invar*, giùlan *m*; **2** (*treatment*, ~ *towards someone*) làimhseachadh *m*, gnàthachadh *m*

behead *v* dì-cheannaich *vt*

beheading *n* dì-cheannachadh *m*

behind *adv* **1** (*position*) air dheireadh, air chùl, **the journey was hard and the old folks were far** ~ bha an turas cruaidh agus bha na seann daoine fada air dheireadh; **2** (*less advanced &c*) air dheireadh, ~ **in technology** air dheireadh a-thaobh teicneolais *m gen*

behind *prep* air cùlaibh, air cùl, (*with gen*), ~ **the church** air cùlaibh na h-eaglaise, (*also fig*) **I left/put it ~ me** dh'fhàg mi/chuir mi air mo chùlaibh e

being *n* **1** (*abstr*) bith *f invar*, **bring into ~** thoir *vt* gu/am bith; **2** (*living thing*) creutair *m*; **3** *in expr* **human ~** duine *m*

belch *n* rùchd *m*, brùchd *m*

belch *v* rùchd *vi*, brùchd *vi*, dèan brùchd *m*

belief *n* **1** (*abstr*) creideas *m*; **2** (*esp relig*) creideamh *m*

believe *v* creid *vti* (**in** ann an), thoir creideas (*with prep* do), **I don't ~ you** chan eil mi gad chreidsinn, chan eil mi a' toirt creideas dhut, **I don't ~ in fairies** chan eil mi a' creidsinn anns na sìthichean *mpl*

belittle *v* cuir *vt* an suarachas *m*

bell *n* clag *m*, **warning ~, alarm ~** clag-rabhaidh *m*

belling *n* (*of red deer stags*) langanaich *f*

bellow *n* (*humans, cattle &c*) geum *m*, beuc *m*, **he let out a ~** leig e geum às

bellow *v* **1** beuc *vi*, geum *vi*, ràn *vi*; **2** (*usu of animals*) nuallaich *vi*; **3** (*cattle & esp deer*) langanaich *vi*

bellowing *n* **1** (*humans, cattle &c*) beucadh *m*; **2** (*red deer stags*) langanaich *f*

belly *n* **1** (*abdomen*) balg *m*; **2** (*paunch*) brù *f*, maodal *f*, mionach *m*

belly-button *n* imleag *f*

bellyful *n* làn *m* broinne *f gen*, **I got a ~ of it** fhuair mi làn mo bhroinne dheth

belong *v* buin *vi* (**to** do), is *v irreg & def* (*with prep* le), **does it ~ to you?** am buin e dhutsa?, *or* an ann leatsa a tha e?, **who does this ~ to?** cò dha a bhuineas seo? *or* cò leis a tha seo?, **it ~s to me** 's ann leamsa a tha e

belongings *n* treal(l)aichean *fpl*

beloved *adj* gaolach, ionmhainn

below *adv* fodha (*&c*) *prep pron*, shìos bhuaithe (*&c*), **a room with a cellar ~** seòmar *m*, agus seilear *m* fodha, **we saw the river ~** chunnaic sinn an àbhainn shìos bhuainn, **the rocks down ~** na creagan shìos fodha

below *prep* **1** fo, *lenites following noun & takes the dat*, **~ the surface** fon uachdar *m*, (*prep prons*) **~ me** fodham(sa), **~ you** (*sing fam*) fodhad(sa), **~ him/it** (*m*) fodha(san), **~ her/it** (*f*) foidhpe(se) *or* foipe(se), **~ us** fodhainn(e), **~ you** (*pl or sing formal*) fodhaibh(se), **~ them** fòdhpa(san) *or* fòpa(san); **2** (*idiom*) **down ~ him** (*&c*) shìos bhuaithe (*&c*), **I saw the soldiers down ~ me** chunnaic mi na saighdearan *mpl* shìos bhuam

belt *n* crios *m*

bench *n* being(e) *f*

bend *n* **1** lùb *f*, **the stick has a big ~ in it** tha lùb mhòr air/anns a' bhata *m*; **2** (*~ in a river*) camas *m*

bend *v* **1** (*an object*) fiar *& fiaraich vti*, lùb *vti*; **2** (*the body*) crom *vti*, lùb *vti*, **she bent her head** chrom i a ceann *m*, **~ the knee** lùb a' ghlùin

bending, bendy *adj* lùbach

beneath *prep* fo, *lenites following noun & takes the dat*, ~ **the surface** fon uachdar *m*, ~ **a tree** fo chraoibh *f*, *(prep prons)* ~ **me** fodham(sa), ~ **you** *(sing fam)* fodhad(sa), ~ **him/it** *(m)* fodha(san), ~ **her/it** *(f)* foidhpe(se) *or* foipe(se), ~ **us** fodhainn(e), ~ **you** *(pl or sing formal)* fodhaibh(se), ~ **them** fòdhpa(san) *or* fòpa(san)

benediction *n* beannachadh *m*

benefactor *n* tabhartaiche *m*, tabhairteach *m*

beneficial *adj* tairbheach & tarbhach

benefit *n* **1** *(abstr: advantage &c)* tairbhe *f invar*; **2** *(usu fin)* prothaid *f*; **3** *(social security &c)* sochair *f*, **unemployment** ~ sochair cion-obrach *m*, *(fam)* dòil *m invar*

benefit *v* buannaich *vi*, *(less usu)* tairbhich *vi*

bent *adj* crom, lùbte, **a** ~ **stick** bata crom *m*, **with their heads** ~ crom an ceann *m*

bent[1] *n (natural ability)* tàlann *m*

bent[2] *(grass)* muran *m*

bequeathe *v* tiomnaich *vt* (**to do**)

bequest *n* tiomnadh *m*, dìleab *f*

berry *n* dearc *f*, dearcag *f*

beseech *v* guidh *vi (with prep* air), **I'm ~ing you to stay!** tha mi a' guidhe ort fuireach!

beside *prep* ri taobh *(with gen)*, ~ **the quay** ri taobh a' chidhe, ~ **me** rim thaobh; **2** *(idiom)* **I was** ~ **myself (with rage)** bha mi air bhoile *f invar /* air bhàinidh *f invar*

besides *prep* a bharrachd air, a thuilleadh air, **he has two flats,** ~ **a house** tha dà lobht aige, a bharrachd air taigh, *(adverbial use)* **I'm tired, and** ~**, I'm broke** tha mi sgìth, agus a thuilleadh air sin, chan eil sgillinn ruadh agam

best *sup adj* **1** feàrr *used in the exprs* as fheàrr *(with pres & fut tense)* & a b' fheàrr *(with past & conditional tense)*, **the** ~ **one/man** am fear *m* as fheàrr, **he was the** ~ **one/man** b' esan am fear a b' fheàrr, **Alan will be** ~ 's e Ailean as fheàrr a bhios (ann), **the** ~ **pen I had** am peann a b' fheàrr a bh' agam; **2** *in corres &c* **with** ~ **wishes** leis gach deagh dhùrachd *f*; **3** *in expr (at wedding)* ~ **man** fleasgach *m*, fear comhailteach

best *sup adv* feàrr, *with v irreg & def* is & *prep* do, **you'd** ~ **stay/you'd be** ~ **staying** b' fheàrr dhut fuireach, **you'd** ~ **be going** b' fheàrr dhuibh a bhith a' falbh, **as** ~ **I can** mar as fheàrr as urrainn dhomh, mar as fheàrr a thèid agam air

best *n* **1** dìcheall *m*, **I did my** ~ rinn mi mo dhìcheall; **2** *in expr* **at** ~ aig a' char *m* as fheàrr *(in past tense* a b' fheàrr*)*, **she'll be third, at** ~ bidh i san treas àite *m*, aig a' char *m* as fheàrr; **3** *(the* ~ *part or example of something)* brod *m*, smior *m (followed by gen sing of noun)*, **the** ~ **of the seed** smior/ brod an t-sìl *m*, **the** ~ **of school-masters** smior a' mhaighstir-sgoile, **the** ~ **of crofts** brod na croite

best *v* (*fam*) dèan an gnothach, dèan a' chùis, (*with prep* air), **we ~ed them** rinn sinn an gnothach/a' chùis orra, *also* ghabh sinn orra

bet *n* geall *m*, **put/lay/place a ~** cuir geall (**on** air)

bet *v* **1** (*put forward as probable*) cuir geall *m*, rach *vi* an geall, **I ~ he won't come** cuiridh mi geall nach tig e, thèid mi an geall nach tig e; **2** (*wager*) cuir geall *m* (**on** air), **~ on a horse** cuir geall air each *m*

betray *v* (*person, secret*) brath *vt*

betrayal *n* brathadh *m*

betrothal *n* **1** gealladh-pòsaidh *m*; **2** (*trad: involving family discussion, agreement and associated celebrations*) rèiteach *m*

better *comp adj* **1** feàrr, *used in the exprs* as fheàrr & nas fheàrr (*with pres & fut tense*) *and* a b' fheàrr & na b' fheàrr (*with past & conditional tense*), **A is ~ than B** tha A nas fheàrr na B, **that would be ~** bhiodh sin na b' fheàrr, **who's ~?** cò as fheàrr?; **2** (*better in health or quality*), **make ~** cuir *vt* am feabhas, **get ~** rach *vi* am feabhas, **the invalid got ~** chaidh an t-euslainteach am feabhas, **the local services are getting ~** tha na seirbheisean ionadail a' dol am feabhas; **3** (*idioms*) **we'd be (the) ~ for a wee stroll** b' fheàirrde sinn cuairt bheag, (*in a skill, activity &c*) **we're getting ~** tha (am) piseach a' tighinn oirnn

better *comp adv*, feàrr, *with v irreg & def* is & *prep* do, **you'd ~ stay** 's fheàrr/b' fheàrr dhut fuireach, **you'd ~ be going** 's fheàrr dhuibh/b' fheàrr dhuibh a bhith a' falbh

better *n, in expr* **get the ~ of** fairtlich *vi*, faillich *vi*, (*fam*) dèan an gnothach, dèan a' chùis, (*all with prep* air), **I wanted to climb the mountain but it got the ~ of me** bha mi airson a' bheinn a dhìreadh ach dh'fhairtlich/dh'fhaillich i orm

betting *n* **1** gealladh *m*; **2** *in expr* **~ shop** bùth *mf* gheall *mpl gen*

between *prep* eadar (*takes the nom*), **~ us** eadarainn, **~ you** eadaraibh, **~ them** eatarra

bevvy *n* **1** (*fam: drinking spree*) daorach *f*, **on the ~** air an daoraich *dat*; **2** (*fam: booze, drink*) deoch *f*, deoch-làidir *f*, **fond of the ~** dèidheil air (an) deoch(-làidir)

bevvying *n* daorach *f*, pòitearachd *f invar*

bewitch *v* cuir *vt* fo gheasaibh (*obs dat pl of* geas *f*)

bewitched *adj & past part* fo gheasaibh (*obs dat pl of* geas *f*), seunta

bewitching *adj* (*without magical association*) meallach

beyond *prep* thairis air, seachad air, (*more trad*) thar (*with gen*), **~ the ocean** thairis air a' chuan *m*, thar a' chuain, **you went ~ what I required** chaidh thu thairis air/seachad air na bha mi ag iarraidh, **that's ~ my capabilities** tha sin thar mo chomasan *mpl gen*

bi- *prefix* dà-, *eg* **bilingual** dà-chànanach, **bilateral** dà-thaobhach

bias *n* claon-bhàidh *f*, taobh *m*

Bible *n* Bìoball *m*

biblical *adj* bìoballach

bibliography *n* leabhar-chlàr *m*

bicycle *n* baidhsagal *m*, (*more trad*) rothar *m*

bid *n* **1** (*at sale &c*) tairgse *f*, **make a ~** thoir tairgse (**for** air); **2** *in expr* **a ~ for freedom** oidhirp *f* air saorsa *f invar*

bid *v* **1** (*at sale &c*) tairg *vti*, thoir tairgse *f*, (**for** air); **2** (*request*) iarr *vt* (*with prep* air), **we bade them stay** dh'iarr sinn orra fuireachd; **3** (*greetings &c*) *in exprs* **~ them welcome** cuir fàilte *f* orra, **we bade them farewell** ghabh sinn ar cead *m invar* dhiubh, *also* dh'fhàg sinn slàn aca

bidie-in (*Sc*) *n* coimhleapach *mf*

big *adj* **1** (*lit & fig*) mòr, **a ~ house** taigh mòr, **a ~ day** latha mòr, (*fam*) **~ money** airgead mòr *m*, (*ironic*) **the ~ shots** na daoine mòra *mpl*; **2** (*of person's build*) mòr, tomadach, calma

bigger *comp adj* **1** mò & motha, **the bigger** fish an t-iasg as mò, **this one's bigger** tha am fear seo nas mò; **2** *in exprs* **grow/get ~** rach *vi* am meud *m invar*, meudaich *vi*, **make ~** meudaich *vt*

big-wig *n* (*ironic*) duine mòr cudromach *m*, **~wigs** na daoine mòra *mpl*, na h-urracha (*pl of* urra *f*) mòra

bilateral *adj* dà-thaobhach

bilingual *adj* dà-chànanach

bilingualism *n* dà-chànanas *m*

bill[1] *n* **1** (*fin, household*) cunntas *m*, (*fam*) bileag *f*; **2** (*parliament*) bile *m*

bill[2] *n* (*of bird*) gob *m*

binary *adj* (*IT*) dà-fhillte

bind *v* ceangail *vt*

binding *adj* (*promise &c*) ceangaltach

binoculars *n* prosbaig *f*

biodegradable *adj* so-chnàmhach

biographer *n* beatha-eachdraiche *m*

biographical *adj* beatha-eachdraidheil

biography *n* eachdraidh-beatha *f*

biology *n* bith-eòlas *m*

biped *n* dà-chasach *m*

bird *n* eun *m*, **~s of prey** eòin-àir, eòin-seilge

birth *n* **1** breith *f invar*, **~ certificate** teisteanas *m* breith, **premature ~** breith an-abaich; **2** (*esp the actual delivery*) asaid *f*, **a difficult ~** asaid dhoirbh

birthday *n* ceann-bliadhna *m*, co-là-breith *m*, **it's my ~ today** tha ceann-bliadhna/co-là-breith agam an-diugh

birthright *n* (*trad*) dual *m*, **that was his ~** bu dual dha sin

bishop *n* easbaig *m*

bit *adv* car, caran, rudeigin, rud beag, **a ~ late** car anmoch, **a (little) ~ tired** caran/rudeigin/rud beag sgìth

bit *n* **1** mìr *m*, criomag *f*, **falling/dropping to ~s** a' dol na (*&c*) c(h)riomagan, a' tuiteam às a chèile, **~s and pieces** *n* criomagan *fpl*, *also* treal(l)aich *f sing coll*; **2** (*misc exprs*) **a ~ of bread** pìos *m* arain *m*, **a ~ of conversation**

còmhradh beag, ~ **by** ~ uidh *f* air n-uidh, **every** ~ **a Gael/Highlander** Gàidheal *m* gu chùl *m*, **every** ~ **as good as X** a cheart cho math ri X; **3** (*IT*) bìdeag *f*; **4** (*horse's* ~) cabstair *m*

bitch *n* **1** (*female dog*) galla *f*; **2** (*vulg: of a woman*) galla *f*, (*less trad*) bidse *f*

bite *n* **1** bìdeadh *m*; **2** (*of food*) grèim *m* bìdh *m*, **I fancy getting/having a ~ to eat** tha mi airson grèim bìdh a ghabhail

bite *v* bìd *vti*

biting *adj* **1** geur, ~ **wind** gaoth gheur, ~ **tongue** teanga gheur; **2** (*remarks, character &c*) guineach

bitter *adj* searbh geur, goirt, ~ **taste** blas searbh/geur, ~ **wind** gaoth gheur, ~ **distress** àmhghar ghoirt

bitterness *n* **1** (*the emotion; also* ~ *of taste*) gèire *f invar*; **2** (~ *directed at another person*) nimh & neimh *m*

bivouac *n* teanta bheag

bivouac *v* campaich *vi* (ann an teanta bheag)

black *adj* dubh, **the night was as** ~ **as coal** bha an oidhche cho dubh ri gual *m*, **a** ~ **woman** boireannach *m* dubh

black *n* dubh *m*, ~ **and white** an dubh 's an geal

blackberry *n* **1** (*the plant*) dris ; **2** (*the fruit*) smeur *f*

blackbird *n* lon-dubh *m*

blackboard *n* bòrd-dubh *m*

blackcock *n* (*male of black grouse*) coileach dubh

blacken *v* dubh *vti*

black-haired *adj* dubh, dorcha, **a** ~ **woman** boireannach *m* dubh

blackhead *n* cnàimhseag *f*, guirean dubh

blackout *n* dubhadh *m*

black out *v* dubh *vt* às

blacksmith *n* gobha *m*; *in expr* ~**'s shop** ceàrdach *f*

bladder *n* aotraman *m*

blade *n* lann *f*, **knife** ~ lann-sgeine *f*

blame *n* coire *f*, cron *m*, **lay** ~ **on someone** cuir coire air cuideigin, **it's with you that the** ~ **for it lies** 's ann ortsa a tha a chron

blame *v* **1**, coirich *vt*, cuir a' choire (*with prep* air), faigh cron *m* (*with prep* do); **2** (*idioms*) **it's you who are to** ~ **for it** 's ann ortsa a tha a chron, *also* is tusa as coireach ris, **the parents are to be** ~**d** tha na pàrantan rin coireachadh

bland *adj* **1** (*food, drink*) neo-bhlasmhor, gun bhlas *m*; **2** (*character, personality*) gun smior *m*, gun bhrìgh *f invar*

blank *adj* (*paper &c*) bàn

blanket *n* plaide *f*, (*less trad*) plangaid *f*

blarney *n* cabadaich *f*, goileam *m*

blasphemy *n* (*abstr & con*) toibheum *m*, (*abstr*) dia-mhaslachadh *m*

blast *n* **1** (*of wind*) sìon *m*, sgal *m*; **2** (*of noise*) toirm *f*, (*esp of noise made by people*) lasgan *m*, iorghail *f*; **3** (*explosion*) spreadhadh *m*; **4** (*mild oath*) ~**!** an donas!

blast *v* **1** (*blight*) searg *vt*, crìon *vt*; **2** (*give fierce row to*) càin/cronaich *vt* gu dian

blatant *adj* ladarna, dalma, **a ~ lie** breug *f* ladarna

blaze *n* lasair *f*

blaze *v* las *vi*

blazing *adj* lasrach, **a ~ fire** teine *m* lasrach

bleach *v* gealaich *vti*

bleaching *n* gealachadh *m*

bleak *adj* **1** (*landscape*) lom, **a ~ moor** sliabh *m* lom; **2** (*situation, prospects &c*) gun dòchas *m*

bleakness *n* (*landscape*) luime *f*, dìthreabhachd *f invar*

bleary-eyed *adj* prab-shùileach

bleat, bleating *n* (*esp of sheep*) mèilich *f invar*, (*esp of goats*) miogadaich *f invar*, meigeall *m*

bleat *v* (*esp sheep*) dèan mèilich *f invar*, (*esp goats*) dèan miogadaich *f invar*

bleed *v* **1** (*general*) caill fuil *f*, **he was ~ing** bha e a' call fala; **2** (*of specific part of body*) **my finger's ~ing** tha an fhuil a' tighinn às mo chorraig *f*, (*of nose only*) **my nose is ~ing** tha mo shròn *f* a' leum; **3** (*draw blood*) leig fuil (*with prep* à), **the nurse bled me** leig an nurs *f* fuil asam

blemish *n* (*moral, of character, personality*) fàillinn *f*, (*moral or physical*) meang *f*, gaoid *f*

blend *n* coimeasgachadh *&* co-mheasgachadh *m*

blend *v* coimeasgaich *&* co-mheasgaich *vti*

bless *v* **1** beannaich *vt*; **2** *in excl* (*to someone who has sneezed*) **~ you!** Dia leat!

blessed *adj & past part* **1** beannaichte, naomh; **2** (*mild oath*) **the ~ car!** càr *f* na croiche!

blessing *n* **1** beannachadh *m*, beannachd *f invar*, **God's ~** beannachadh Dhè, **my ~ on you!** mo bheannachd ort!; **2** (*boon, fortunate occurrence*) beannachd *f invar*, **good health is a ~** is e/i beannachd a th' ann an deagh shlàinte *f invar*

blether *n* **1** cabadaich *f*, cabaireachd *f invar*, goileam *m*; **2** (*person who ~s*) duine *m* cabach

blight *n* **1** (*disaster &c*) sgrios *m*; **2** *in expr* **potato ~** cnàmh *m*, (*used with art*) an gaiseadh *m*

blight *v* searg *vt*, crìon *vt*

blighted *adj & past part* **1** crìon; **2** (*fig: life, career &c*) air (a *&c*) sgrios(adh)

blind *adj* dall, **~ spot** spot dall, **a ~ person** dall *m*

blind *v* dall *vt*

blinding *adj* (*dazzling*) boillsgeach

blinding *n* dalladh *m*

blindness *n* doille *f invar*

blink *n* priobadh *m*

blink *v* priob *vi*, caog *vi*

blister *n* leus *m*, balg *m*, builgean *m*

blizzard *n* cathadh-sneachda *m*

block *n* **1** ceap *m*, cnap *m*, ~ **of wood/peat** ceap fiodha *m*/mòna *f*; **2** *in expr* (*usu fig*) **stumbling-~** cnap-starra *m*

block *v* **1** (~ *an aperture &c*) tachd *vt*; **2** (*stop, prevent*) caisg *vt*

blockage *n* tachdadh *m*

blockhead *n* bumailear *m*, ùmaidh *m*, stalcaire *m*

blond(e) *adj* bàn, **blond hair** falt bàn, **a blond man** duine/fear bàn, **a blonde woman** tè bhàn, boireannach bàn

blonde *n* tè bhàn, boireannach *m* bàn

blood *n* fuil *f*, ~ **relationship** càirdeas-fala *m*, ~ **is thicker than water** is tighe fuil na bùrn *m*, ~ **pressure** bruthadh *m* fala, ~ **vessel** caochan *m* fala, **shed** ~ dòirt fuil

bloodshed *n* dòrtadh-fala *m*

bloodstream *n* ruith *f* na fala

bloody *adj* **1** (*lit*) fuil(t)each, ~ **battle** cath fuilteach; **2** (*fig, as excl, swear*) *n followed by* na croiche *or* na galla, **the ~ hammer!** òrd *m* na croiche!, òrd na galla!

bloom *n* blàth *m*, flùr *m*

blot *n* **1** (*of ink*) smal *m* duibh *m*, smal inc *mf invar*; **2** (*fig: blemish &c*) smal *m*, **a ~ on his reputation** smal air a chliù *m*

blot *v* **1** leig *vt* inc *mf invar* (air pàipear *m*); **2** (*soak up*) sùgh *vt*; **3** ~ **out** dubh *vt* às

blotting-paper *n* pàipear-sùghaidh *m*

blow *n* **1** (*with fist &c*) buille *f*; **2** (*disappointment, setback*) bristeadh-dùil *m*

blow *v* **1** sèid *vt*, **the wind blew** shèid a' ghaoth, **blow (up) the pipes** sèid a' phìob, ~ **up a football** sèid suas ball-coise *m*; **2** *in expr* ~ **up** (*ie explode*) spreadh *vti*; **3** *in expr* ~ **up** (*ie enlarge photo, image &c*) meudaich *vt*

blowout *n* **1** (*tyre*) spreadhadh *m*; **2** (*food*) làn *m* broinne *f gen* (de bhiadh *m*)

blubber *n* saill *f* (na) muice-mhara

blubber *v* (*fam: cry, weep*) ràn *vi*

bludgeon *n* cuaille *m*

blue *adj* gorm, ~ **sky** adhar gorm, ~ **eyes** sùilean *fpl* gorma

blue *n* gorm *m*

bluff *n* (*relief feature*) sròn *f*

bluff *v*, **I was only ~ing** cha robh mi ach mas fhìor

blunt *adj* **1** maol; **2** (*person, character*) aithghearr

blush *n* rudhadh *m*, rudhadh-gruaidhe *m*

blush *v*, **she ~ed** ruadhaich *vi* a gruaidh *f*, thàinig rudhadh *m* na gruaidh

blushing *adj* ruiteach

boar *n* torc *m*, cullach *m*, **wild** ~ torc allaidh/fiadhaich

board[1] *n* **1** (*plank &c*) bòrd *m*, dèile *f*, clàr *m*; **2** (*notice* ~) bòrd *m*, **put a notice up on the** ~ cuir suas sanas *m* air a' bhòrd; **3** (*sign* ~) clàr *m*, **direction** ~ clàr seòlaidh *m*; **4** (*for playing games &c*) bòrd *m*, **chess** ~ bòrd tàileisg *m*, ~ **game** cluich-bùird *m*; **5** (*ship, plane*) *in expr* **on** ~ air bòrd

board² *n* (*governing &c body*) bòrd *m*

board *v* rach *vi* air bòrd *m* (bàta *m gen*, plèana *mf gen*)

boast *n* bòst *m*

boast *v* dèan bòst *m*

boastful *adj* 1 (*person*) bòstail; 2 ~ **talk, tales or chatter** rabhd *m*, ràbhart *m*

boasting *n* bòstadh *m*

boat *n* 1 bàta *m*, **steam-~** bàta-smùide, **ferry** ~ bàt'-aiseig; 2 (*esp a rowing boat*) eathar *or* eithear *mf*, geòla *f*

bobbin *n* iteachan *m*, piorna *mf*

bodily *adj* corporra

body *n* 1 (*of any living creature*) corp *m*, **parts of the** ~ buill *mpl* a' chuirp, ~ **and soul** corp is anam; 2 (*human* ~) bodhaig *f*, colann *f*; 3 (*dead* ~: *human*) corp *m*, (~ *usu not human*) closach *f*; 4 (*fam: a person*) creutair *m*, **a poor** ~ creutair bochd; 5 (*group of people*) buidheann *mf*, **research** ~ buidheann-sgrùdaidh *mf*; 6 (*collection, accumulation*) stòras *m*, cruinneachadh *m*, **a large** ~ **of historical material** stòras mòr de stuth *m* eachdraidheil

bog *n* boglach *f*, fèith(e) *f*; *in expr* **peat** ~ poll-mòna(ch) *&* poll-mònadh *m*

bog-cotton *n* canach *mf* (an t-sleibh)

boil *n* neasgaid *f*

boil *v* goil *vti*

boiler *n* goileadair *m*

boiling *adj* goileach

bold *adj* 1 (*intrepid*) cruadalach, dàna; 2 (*shameless, impudent*) ladarna, dàna; 3 (*of typog*) trom

boldness *n* dànadas *m*

bolt *n* crann *m*, **nut and** ~ cnò *f* is crann

bond *n* 1 (*abstr*) ceangal *m*, (*stronger*) dlùth-cheangal *m*, **there was a close/strong** ~ **between them** bha dlùth-cheangal eatarra; 2 (*phys: in imprisonment &c*) ceangal *m*, **he threw off his** ~**s** thilg e dheth a cheanglaichean; 3 (*fin &c agreement*) urras *m*

bond *v* tàth *vt*

bondage *n* 1 (*lit*) cuibhreachadh *m*, slaibhreas *m*; 2 (*more fig*) braighdeanas *m*, tràilleachd *f invar*

bonding *n* tàthadh *m*

bone *n* cnàimh *&* cnàmh *m*, *in expr* **the collar** ~ ugan *m*, cnàimh an ugain

bony *adj* cnàmhach

book *n* leabhar *m*

bookcase *n* preas-leabhraichean *m*

booklet *n* leabhran *m*, leabhrachan *m*

boot *n* 1 bròg-mhòr *f*, bròg *f* throm; 2 (*usu Wellington* ~) bòtann *mf*; 3 (*of car*) ciste(-càir) *f*; 4 *in expr* **to** ~ cuideachd *adv*, a bharrachd air sin, **they've a boat, and a caravan to** ~ tha bàta aca, agus carabhan *f* cuideachd

booty *n* cobhartach *mf*, (*more trad: in cattle raids &c*) creach *f*

booze *n* deoch *f*, deoch-làidir *f invar*, **he's fond of the** ~ tha e measail air an deoch

boozer *n* pòitear *m*, drungair *m*

boozing *n* pòitearachd *nf invar*

border *n* **1** (*of territory &c*) crìoch *f*, **The** ~**s** Na Crìochan, Crìochan Shasainn; **2** (*of material &c*) oir *f*

bore[1] *v* (*hole &c*) toll *vti*

bore[2] *v* (*cause tedium*) is *v irreg def* liosda (*with prep* le), **you** ~ **me** is liosda leam thu

bored *adj* bi *vi irreg* fadachd *f invar* (*with prep* air), **I was** ~ **all the time he was talking** bha fadachd orm fhad 's a bha e a' bruidhinn, **a** ~ **little girl** caileag bheag is fadachd oirre

boredom *n* fadachd *f invar*, fadal *m*

boring *adj* fadalach, liosda, màirnealach

born *past part*, *rendered by passive forms of irreg v* beir, **he was** ~ rugadh e, *also* chaidh a bhreith, **before you were** ~ mun do rugadh tusa

borrow *v* gabh/faigh *vt* air iasad *m* (**from** o/bho)

borrowed *adj & past part* air iasad *m*, **a** ~ **suit** deise *f* air iasad

borrowing *n* iasad *m*,

bosom *n* **1** (*general breast area*) uchd *m*, com *m*, broilleach *m*, **she clasped the boy to her** ~ theannaich i am balach ri a h-uchd; **2** (*woman's* ~) cìochan (*pl of* cìoch *f*)

boss[1] *n* (*in woodwork &c*) cnap *m*

boss[2] *n* (*of firm &c*) ceannard *m*

botanical *adj* luibheach

botanist *n* luibh-eòlaiche *m*

botany *n* luibh-eòlas *m*

botcher *n* uaipear *m*, cearbair(e) *m*

both *adv & adj* **1** (*of things, actions &c*) gach cuid *f*, an dà chuid, gach, **give me** ~ **sugar and salt** thoir dhomh gach cuid siùcar *m* is salann *m*, **meat or cheese? both!** feòil *f* no càise *mf*? an dà chuid!, **you/one can't** ~ **drink and drive** chan fhaod thu/chan fhaodar an dà chuid dràibheadh *m* agus òl *m*; **2** (*of people*) le chèile, nan dithis, **they** ~ **left** dh'fhalbh iad le chèile/nan dithis, *in expr* ~ **of you** an dithis agaibh; **3** (*before adjs*) eadar, **they came,** ~ **small and great** thàinig iad, eadar bheag agus mhòr (*note that both adjs are lenited*); **4** (*as adj*) gach, **on** ~ **sides** air gach taobh *m*

bother *n* dragh *m*, **I don't want to put you to any** ~ chan eil mi airson dragh (sam bith) a chur oirbh

bother *v* **1** (*annoy, upset, disturb*) cuir dragh (*with prep* air), (*more fam*) bodraig *vt*, cuir *vt* suas no sìos, **the noise is** ~**ing me** tha am fuaim a' cur dragh orm, **it's not** ~**ing me** chan eil e gam bhodraigeadh, **the news didn't** ~ **me in the least** cha do chuir an naidheachd *f* suas no sìos mi; **2** (*take the trouble to*) bodraig *vi*, **did you pay the bill? I didn't** ~ na phàigh thu a' bhileag? cha do bhodraig mi; **3** *in expr* **you needn't** ~

cha leig/ruig thu a leas *m invar*, **you needn't ~ grumbling all the time!** cha leig/ruig thu a leas a bhith a' gearan fad na h-ùine!

bottom *adj* **1** as ìsle (*superlative of* ìosal *adj*), **the ~ rung** an rong *f* as ìsle; **2** *in expr* **the ~ lip** am beul-ìochdair

bottom *n* **1** (*base of something*) bonn *m*, bun *m*, **the ~ of the hill** bonn/bun a' chnuic; **2** (*lowest part*) an ceann as ìsle, **hold the ~ of it** gabh grèim *m* air a' cheann *m* as ìsle dheth; **3** (*of river, well &c*) grinneal *m*; **4** *in expr* **~ of the sea** grunnd *m* na mara; **5** (*backside, bum*) (*fam*) màs *m*, tòn *f*

bough *n* meang(l)an *m*, geug *f*

boulder *n* ulbhag *f*, ulpag *f*

boundary *n* crìoch *f*, **this is the ~ of my land** is e seo crìoch an fhearainn agam, **the parish ~** crìoch na sgìre, **~ wall** gàrradh-crìche *m*

bourgeois *adj & n* bùirdeasach *m*

bourgeoisie *n* bùirdeasachd *f invar*

bow[1] *n* (*before royalty &c*) ùmhlachd *f invar*

bow[2] *n* **1** (*of boat*) toiseach *m*; **2** (*weapon*) bogha(-saighde) *m*; **3** (*for stringed instrument*) bogha *m*

bow *v* **1** crom *vt*, lùb *vt*, **she ~ed her head** chrom i a ceann *m*, **~ the knee** lùb a' ghlùin; **2** (*before royalty &c*) dèan ùmhlachd *f invar*

bowed *adj* **1** lùbte; **2** (*of head*) crom

bowels *n* innidh *f invar*

bowl *n* cuach *f*, (*fam*) bobhla *m*

bow-legged *adj* camachasach, gòbbhlach

bowstring *n* taifeid *f*

box *n* bogsa *m*, bucas *m*

boxer *n* bogsair *m*

boxing *n* bogsadh & bogsaigeadh *m*

boy *n* **1** gille *m*, balach *m*, **a wee ~** gille/balach beag, **do you have a family? we have three ~s** a bheil teaghlach *m* agaibh? tha triùir ghillean *gen* againn; **2** (*fam, of a male of any age*) balach *m*, gille *m*, **you're right ~!** tha thu ceart a ghille (*also* 'ille)/a bhalaich!

boyfriend *n* leannan *m*, (*fam*) car(a)bhaidh *f*

brace *n* (*ie pair*) càraid *f*, caigeann *f*

bracelet *n* bann-làimhe *m*

bracken *n* raineach *f*, roineach *f*

bracket *n* (*typog*) camag *f*, **square/round ~** camag cheàrnach/chruinn

braid *v* fill *vt*, dualaich *vt*

braided *adj & past part* fillte

brain, brains *n* eanchainn *f*, **she's got a good ~** tha eanchainn mhath innte

brain *v* (*fam*) cuir an eanchainn *mf* (*with prep* à), **he ~ed him** chuir e an eanchainn às

brainless *adj* faoin, baoth

brainy *adj* inntinneach

brainteaser *n* tòimhseachan *m*

brake *n* (*on wheel &c*) casgan *m*

bramble *n* 1 (*plant*) dris *f*; 2 (*fruit*) smeur *f*

bran *n* garbhan *m*

branch *n* 1 (*of tree, family, river, organisation &c*) meur *f*; 2 (*of tree*) geug *f*, meang(l)an *m*

branch *v* meuraich *vi*

brand *n* (*make, variety*) seòrsa *m*

brand-new *adj* ùr-nodha

brandish *v* crath *vt*, **he ~ed his fist/sword** chrath e a dhòrn *m*/a chlaidheamh *m*

brass *adj* 1 pràiseach; 2 *in exprs* **I don't have a ~ farthing** chan eil sgillinn *f* ruadh agam, **~ neck** aghaidh *f*, bathais *f*

brass *n* pràis *f*

brat *n* 1 (*fam*) droch isean *m*, ablach *m*, peasan *m*; 2 *in expr* **a spoilt ~** uilleagan *m*

brave *adj* 1 (*esp phys*) gaisgeil, treun, **~ heroes** gaisgich *mpl* threuna; 2 (*esp rashly ~*) dàna; 3 (*esp morally ~*) misneachail

bravery *n* 1 (*esp phys*) gaisge *f invar*, gaisgeachd *f invar*; 2 (*esp rash ~*) dànadas *m*; 3 (*esp moral ~*) misneach *f*, misneachd *f invar*

brawl *n* tuasaid *f*, (*more serious*) sabaid *f*

brawl *v* sabaid *vi*, dèan sabaid *f*, (**with** ri)

brawny *adj* (*of person's build*) tomadach, calma

brazen *adj* ladarna, gun nàire

breach *n* 1 (*gap*) beàrn *m*; 2 (*infraction, contravention*) briseadh *m* (**of** air), **~ of regulations** briseadh air riaghailtean *f*

breadth *n* farsaingeachd *f invar*, leud *m*

break *v* 1 bris(t) *vti*, **he broke the window** bhris e an uinneag, **when day broke** nuair a bhris an latha *m*, **the marriage broke up** bhris am posadh às a chèile; 2 (*~ promise &c*) rach *vi* air ais (*with prep* air), **he broke his promise** chaidh e air ais air a ghealladh *m*

break *n* 1 bris(t)eadh *m*; 2 (*short pause, rest*) stad (beag), *in expr* **take a ~** gabh/leig d' (*&c*) anail *f*

breast *n* 1 (*woman's ~*) cìoch *f*; 2 (*general breast area*) uchd *m*, com *m*, broilleach *m*, **she clasped the boy to her ~** theannaich i am balach ri a h-uchd, **his heart beating in his ~** a chridhe a' bualadh na chom; 3 *in exprs* **~ stroke** buille *m* uchd, **~ bone** cliathan *m*

breath *n* 1 anail *f*, **draw ~** tarraing anail, **under her ~** fo a h-anail, **get your ~ back** leig d' anail; 2 (*~ of life*) deò *f invar*, **as long as there's ~ in my body** fhad 's a bhios an deò annam; 3 *in expr* **a ~ of wind** deò gaoithe *f gen*, oiteag *f*, ospag *f*

breathalyser *n* poca *m* analach

breathe *v* analaich *vi*

breather *n* (*short rest*) stad (beag) *m*, **take a ~** dèan stad, (*more colloquial*) gabh/leig d' (*&c*) anail *f*

breed *v* **1** (*plants, animals*) tàrmaich *vt*; **2** (*humans & animals*) gin *vti*

breeding *n* **1** (*humans & animals*) gineadh *m*; **2** (*of cattle*) dàir *f*, ~ **cattle** crodh-dàra *m*; **3** (*of people: good* ~) modh *f*

breeze *n* oiteag *f*, ospag *f*, gaoth bheag, osnadh *m*

brewer *n* grùdair(e) *m*

brewery *n* taigh-grùide *m*

brewing *n* grùdaireachd *f invar*

bridge *n* **1** drochaid *f*, **the Skye** ~ Drochaid an Eilein Sgitheanaich; **2** *in expr* **the** ~ **of the nose** bràigh *m* na sròine

brief *adj* goirid, **a** ~ **tour** cuairt ghoirid

briefcase *n* màileid *f*

brier *n* dris *f*

bright *adj* **1** (*light &c*) soilleir; **2** (*mentally* ~) toinisgeil, eirmseach

brilliance *n* (*of light*) lainnir *f*

brilliant *adj* **1** (*of light*) lainnireach; **2** (*intellectually* ~) sàr-thoinisgeil, air leth toinisgeil

brimstone *n* pronnasg *m*

brindled *adj* riabhach

bring down *v* (*ie cause to fall*) leag *vt*

bring *v* thoir *vt* **1** (*phys & lit, also fig*) thoir *vt*, ~ **it to me** thoir thugam e, ~ **water from the well** thoir uisge *m* on tobair *mf*, ~ **to a conclusion** thoir gu buil *f*, ~ **to an end** thoir gu crìch (*dat of* crìoch *f*), ~ **into being/ existence** thoir gu/am bith *f invar*, ~ **into the open**, ~ **to light** thoir am follais *f invar*; **2** (*other phys & lit uses*) ~ **solace/comfort** furtaich *vi* (**to** air), **we will** ~ **you solace** furtaichidh sinn oirbh, ~ **together** cruinnich *vt*, ~ **up** (*food*) tilg *vt*, cuir *vt* a-mach, **she brought up her dinner** thilg i/chuir i a-mach a dìnnear *f*; **3** (*other fig uses*), ~ **a complaint** dèan casaid *f* (**against** air), ~ **out** (*books &c*) foillsich *vt*, cuir (leabhar *m &c*) an clò *m*, ~ **up** (*children, livestock &c*) tog *vt*, **I was brought up in Coll** thogadh mi ann an Colla

bristle *n* (*esp on body of animals*) frioghan *m*, calg *m*

broad *adj* farsaing, leathann

broadcast *n* craoladh *m*, craobh-sgaoileadh *m*

broadcast *v* craoil *vti*, craobh-sgaoil *vti*

broadcaster *m* craoladair *m*

broadcasting *n* craoladh *m*, craobh-sgaoileadh *m*

broaden *v* leudaich *vti*

broadened *adj* leudaichte

broadly *adv*, *in expr* ~ (**speaking**) san/anns an fharsaingeachd *f invar*

broadsword *n* claidheamh *m* leathann

brochure *n* leabhrachan *m*, leabhran *m*

broke *adj* gun sgillinn *f* ruadh, **I'm flat** ~ chan eil sgillinn ruadh (no geal) agam

broken *adj & past part* briste

bronze *n* umha *m invar*, **the** ~ **Age** Linn *mf* an Umha

broth *n* brot *m*, (*trad*) eanraich *f*
brow *n* mala *f*, bathais *f*, clàr *m* an aodainn, maoil *f*
brown *adj* donn, **dark** ~ dubh-dhonn
brown-haired *adj* donn
bubble *n* gucag *f*, builgean *m*
bucket *n* **1** bucaid *f*, peile *m*, (*more trad*) cuinneag *f*; **2** (*esp for milking*) cuman *m*
bucket *v*, *in expr* (*of weather*) **it was ~ing down** bha dìle bhàthte ann
bud *n* gucag *f*
budget *n* buidseat *m*
buffoon *n* bumalair *m*, baothair *m*
buffoonery *n* bumalaireachd *f invar*, baothaireachd *f invar*
bugger *n* **1** (*mild swear*) bugair *m*, **the ~s!** na bugairean!; **2** *in expr* (*fam*) **I don't give a ~ (for X)** cha toir mi ho-ro-gheallaidh *m invar* (air X)
bugle *n* dùdach *f*, dùdag *f*
build *n* (*physique*) dèanamh *m*
build *v* tog *vt*, **he built himself a house** thog e taigh *m* dha fhèin
builder *n* togalaiche *m*, fear-togail *m* (*pl* luchd-togail *m sing coll*)
building *n* **1** (*abstr*) togail *f*; **2** (*con*) togalach *m*, **the roof of the ~** mullach *m* an togalaich, ~ **society** comann *m* togalaich *gen*
built *adj & past part*, *in expr* **well ~ house** taigh *m* air a dheagh thogail
bulb *n* (*plant & light* ~) bolgan *m*
bulge *n* bogha *m*
bulky *adj* tomadach, tomaltach
bull *n* tarbh *m*
bullet *n* peilear *m*
bulling *adj* (*of cattle*) fo dhàir *f*, **a ~ cow** bò *f* fo dhàir, bò is an dàir oirre
bullock *n* damh *m*
bully *n* burraidh *m*, maoidhear *m*
bullying *n* burraidheachd *f invar*, maoidheadh *m*
bulwark *n* mùr *m*, dìdean *f*
bum *n* (*fam*) màs *m*
bundle *n* pasgadh *m*, pasgan *m*, ultach *m*
bundle *v* **1** ~ **up/together** tru(i)s *vt*; **2** (*push roughly*) brùth *vt*, sàth *vt*, **they ~d him into the car** bhrùth iad a-steach dhan chàr *m* e
bungler *n* cearbair *m*, uaipear *m*
buoy *n* put(a) *m*
buoyancy *n* fleòdradh *m*
burden *n* (*lit & fig*) eallach *m*, uallach *m*, **love is a heavy ~** (*trad*) is trom an t-eallach an gaol
burial *n* tiodhlacadh *m*
burial ground *n* cill *f*, cladh *m*
burly *adj* (*of person's build*) tomadach, dèanta, leathann
burn[1] *n* (*injury*) losgadh *m*

burn[2] *n* (*stream*) allt *m*, sruth(an) *m*

burn *v* loisg *vti*, (*less seriously, singe*) dàth *vt*

burnt *adj* loisgte

burst[1] *n* **1** (*sudden onset of noise &c*) brag *m*, (*esp of laughter*) lasgan *m*; **2** (*of energy &c*) sgairt *f*

burst[2] *n* (*in pipe &c*) sgàineadh *m*

burst *v* **1** (*pipes &c*) sgàin *vti*, spreadh *vi*; **2** (*people out of a building, shoots from the ground &c*) brùchd *vi* (**out of/from** à)

bury *v* (*the dead*) tiodhlaic *vt*, adhlaic *vt*

bus *n* bus *m*

bush *n* dos *m*, preas *m*

business *n* **1** (*commercial ~*) gnothach *m*, gnìomhachas *m*, **set up a new ~** cuir gnìomhachas ùr air chois (*dat of cas f*), **~ park** raon *m* gnìomhachais, **~ card** càirt-gnìomhachais *f*, **do/transact ~** dèan gnothach (**with** ri), **his ~ failed** dh'fhàillig an gnothach/gnìomhachas aige, **go to France on ~** rach don Fhraing *f* air cheann ghnothaich; **2** (*commercial, but usu more abstr*) malairt *f*, **do ~** dèan malairt; **3** (*more widely, affair, matter*) nì *m*, gnothach *m*, cùis *f*, **it was a bad ~** 's e droch nì a bh' ann, **their divorce was a bad ~** 's e droch ghnothach a bh' anns an sgaradh-pòsaidh *m* aca, **that's no ~ of yours!** chan e sin do ghnothach-sa!, **how did the ~ go/turn out?** ciamar a chaidh a' chùis?

businessman *n* fear-gnothaich *m*, fear-malairt *m*, fear-gniomhachais *m*

businesswoman *n* tè-ghnothaich *f*, tè-mhalairt *f*, tè-ghniomhachais *f*

bus-stop *n* àite-stad *m* bus *m gen*

bustle *n* drip *f*, sgairt *f*

busy *adj* **1** (*of people*) trang, **I'm ~** tha mi trang, **we're ~ at the fishing** tha sinn trang ris/aig an iasgach *m*; **2** (*of situations*) dripeil, **things are hell/ heck of a ~ just now** tha cùisean *f* garbh dripeil an-dràsta

butcher *n* bùidsear *m*, (*more trad*) feòladair *m*

butcher *v* casgair *vt*

butchering, butchery *n* spadadh *m*, casgairt *f invar*

butt 1 (*archery &c*) targaid *f*; **2** (*fig: target, recipient &c*) cùis *f*, culaidh *f*, (*followed by gen*) **they were a ~ of ridicule** bha iad nan cùis-mhagaidh/ nan culaidh-mhagaidh

butter *n* ìm *m*

butter *v* **1** cuir ìm *m* (*with prep* air), **~ bread** cuir ìm air aran *m*; **2** (*fig*) *in expr* **~ someone up** dèan miodal *m* do chuideigin/ri cuideigin

butterfly *n* dealan-dè *m*

buttock *n* màs *m*

button *n* putan *m*, **fasten/undo ~s** dùin/fuasgail putanan *mpl*

buy *v* ceannaich *vti*, **~ at a good price** ceannaich air deagh phrìs *f*

buyer *n* ceannaiche *m*

buying *n* ceannachd *nf invar*, ceannach *m*

buzzard *n* clamhan *m*

buzz *n* crònan *m*

buzz *v* dèan crònan *m*

buzzer *n* (*alarm &c*) srannan *m*

buzzing *n* crònan *m*

by *adv, in exprs* **put** ~ cuir mu seach, **pass** ~ rach seachad; ~ **and** ~ ri tìde *f*

by *prep* **1** (*introducing the means or the agent of an action &c*) le (*before the art* leis; *takes the dat*), *prep prons* ~ **me** leam(sa), ~ **you** (*sing*) leat(sa), ~ **him/it** (*m*) leis(-san), ~ **her/it** (*f*) leatha(se), ~ **you** (*pl*) leibh(se), ~ **us** leinn(e), ~ **them** leotha(san), **he was killed** ~ **a bullet** chaidh a mharbhadh le peilear *m*, **he came by (the) train** thàinig e leis an trèan *f*; **2** (*motion*) seachad air, **he passed** ~ **the house** chaidh e seachad air an taigh; **3** (*beside*) ri taobh *m* (*with gen*), **a tree** ~ **the road** craobh *f* ri taobh an rathaid; **4** (*misc exprs & idioms*) ~ **and large** san/anns an fharsaingeachd *f invar*, ~ **the way/in the ~-going** san dol seachad, ~ **day and** ~ **night** a latha *m* 's a dh'oidhche *f*, **little** ~ **little** beag is beag, beag air bheag, mean air mhean, (*of time*) ~ **and** ~ mu dheireadh thall, ri tìde *f*, **close** ~ faisg air làimh (*gen of làmh f*), faisg (*with prep* air), **the bank is close** ~ tha am banca faisg air làimh, **close** ~ **the station** faisg air an stèisean *m*

bye-law *n* frith-lagh *m*

by-election *n* fo-thaghadh *m*

by-name *n* far-ainm *m*, frith-ainm *m*

bypass *n* seach-rathad *m*

byre *n* bàthach *f*, bàthaich *f*

C

cab *n* (*ie taxi*) tagsaidh *m*

cabbage *n* càl *m*

caber *n* cabar *m*

cabin *n* **1** bothan *m*; **2** (*on ship &c*) cèabain *m*

cabinet *n* (*pol*) caibineat *m*

cabinetmaker *n* saor-àirneis *m*

cable *n* càball *m*

cache *n* stòr *m* (falaichte)

cack (*fam, vulg*) *n* cac *m*

cackle *v* gloc *vi*

cackle, cackling *n* gloc *m*, glocail *f invar*, gogail *f invar*

cadence *n* (*Lit, music*) dùnadh *m*

cadge *v* (*gifts of food &c*) dèan faoighe *f invar*

cadging *n* (*for gifts of food &c*) faoighe *f invar*

café *n* cafaidh *mf*, taigh-bìdh *m*

cage *n* cèidse *f*

cairn *n* càrn *m*

cake *n* cèic *f*

calamitous *adj* dosgainneach

calamity *n* dosgainn *f*

calculate *v* **1** (*distance, speed &c*) tomhais *vt*; **2** (*sums &c*) àireamhaich *vti*, obraich *vt* a-mach

calculation *n* tomhas *m*, àireamhachadh *m*

calculator *n* (*pocket &c*) àireamhair *m*

calendar *n* mìosachan *m*

calf *n* **1** (*the animal*) laogh *m*; **2** (*~ of leg*) calpa *m*

call *n* **1** (*cry*) gairm *f*, glaodh *m*, èigh *f*; **2** (*visit*) tadhal *m*, (*esp informal ~*) cèilidh *mf*

call *v* **1** (*cry, shout: lit & fig*) gairm *vti*, glaodh *vi*, èigh *vi*, **~ing to each other** a' gairm ri chèile, **they ~ed on her to do that** ghairm iad oirre sin a dhèanamh, **~ an election** gairm taghadh *m*; **2** (*visit*) tathaich *vti*, tadhail *vi*, (**on** air), **~ on friends** tadhail air caraidean *mpl*; **3** (*refer to as*) can *vi* (*with prep* ri), **Fair-haired Davie, as they ~ him** Dàibhidh Bàn, mar a chanas iad ris, **the song ~ed 'Càrlabhagh'** an t-òran ris an canar Càrlabhagh, (*when equivalent to* 'what's his (*&c*) name?') dè an t-ainm *with v irreg* bi *& prep* air, **what's the boy ~ed?** dè an t-ainm a th' air a' bhalach *m*?; **4** *misc uses with* cuir *vt*, **they ~ed off the strike** chuir iad stad *m* air an stailc *f*, chuir iad dheth an stailc, **~ into question** cuir teagamh *m* (*with prep* an), **he ~ed my competence into question** chuir e teagamh na mo chomas *m*, (*telephone*) **I'll ~ them tomorrow** cuiridh mi fòn *mf* thuca a-maireach, **~ to mind** cuir na (*&c*) c(h)uimhne *f*,

it ~ed to mind the days of my youth chuir e nam chuimhne làithean *mpl* m' òige *f gen*

calling *n* **1** (*shouting &c*) gairm *f*, èigheachd *f invar*; **2** (*visiting*) tadhal *m* (*with prep* air); **3** (*vocation*) gairm *f*

calm *adj* ciùin, **a ~ morning** madainn chiùin

calm *n* **1** (*esp of temperament, atmosphere*) ciùineas *m*; **2** (*esp of weather*) fèath *mf*

calm *v* ciùinich *vti*, tàlaidh *vti*, **~ down** ciùinich *vti*, socraich *vti*

calmness *n see* **calm** *n* **1**

calumny *n* **1** (*the action*) cùl-chàineadh *m*; **2** (*the words spoken*) cùl-chainnt *f*

camel *n* càmhal *m*

camera *n* **1** camara *m*; **2** (*meetings &c*) *in expr* **(hold) in ~** (cùm *vt*) ann an dìomhaireachd *f invar*

camouflage *n* breug-riochd *m*

camp *n* campa *m*, *in expr* **~ site** ionad *m* campachaidh *m*

camp *v* campaich *vi*

camping *n* campachadh *m*, **~ing ground** ionad *m* campachaidh *gen*

campaign *n* (*in aid of something, to achieve something, also military*) iomairt *f*, **election ~** iomairt-taghaidh *f*

campaign *v* (*for cause, pol &c*) dèan iomairt *f*

campaigner *n* neach-iomairt (*pl* luchd-iomairt *m sing coll*)

campaigning *n* iomairt *f*

Campbell *adj* Caimbeulach, **a ~ guy/fellow/man gave me it** thug fear Caimbeulach dhomh e

Campbell *n* Caimbeulach *m*

camping *n* campachadh *m*

can *n* **1** (*for drinks, food &c*) cana *m*, canastair *m*; **2** *in expr* **watering ~** peile-frasaidh *m*

can *v* **1** (*be permitted or allowed to*) faod *vi def*, **~ we go? yes** am faod sinn falbh? faodaidh; **2** (*may, might*) faod *vi def*, **it could be that there is life on Mars** dh'fhaodadh e a bhith gu bheil beatha *f* air Màrt *m*, **he could be ill** faodaidh gu bheil e tinn; **3** (*ability, capability*) urrainn *f invar* (*with v is & prep* do), bi *vi irreg, followed by n & prep* aig, **~ they do it? yes** an urrainn dhaibh a dhèanamh? is urrainn, **I ~'t swallow** chan urrainn dhomh slugadh, **I couldn't help being sad** cha b' urrainn dhomh gun a bhith brònach, **~ you read/write?** a bheil leughadh/sgrìobhadh *m* agad?, *note also exprs* **~ you swim?** an dèan thu snàmh *m*?, **~ you drive (&c)?** an tèid dràibheadh *m* (*&c*) agad?; **4** (*expr possibility, feasibility &c*) gabh *vi*, **~ that be done? no!** an gabh sin a dhèanamh? (*also an gabh sin dèanamh?*) cha ghabh!, **as hot as ~ be** cho teth 's a ghabhas; **5** (*other exprs*) **she did it as well as she could** rinn i e cho math agus a rachadh aice, **she did what she could** rinn i na bha na comas

Canadian *n & adj* Canèidianach *m*

cancel *v* **1** (*function &c*) cuir *vt* dheth; **2** (*entry in document &c*) dubh *vt* a-mach

cancellation *n* **1** (*function &c*) cur *m* dheth; **2** (*entry in document &c*) dubhadh *m* a-mach

cancer *n* aillse *f invar*

candid *adj* fosgailte, faoilidh, fosgarra

candidate *n* **1** (*in election &c*) tagraiche *m*, neach-tagraidh *m* (*pl* luchd-tagraidh *m sing coll*); **2** (*at job interview &c*) neach-iarraidh *m* (*pl* luchd-iarraidh *m sing coll*); **3** (*in exam*) deuchainniche *m*

candle *n* coinneal *f*, *in expr* ~ **holder** coinnlear *m*

Candlemas *n* an Fhèill Brìde *f*

candlestick *n* coinnlear *m*

candour *n* fosgailteachd *f invar*, fosgarrachd *f invar*

cane *n* **1** (*the material*) cuilc *f*; **2** (*~ walking-stick &c*) bata(-cuilce) *m*

canine *adj* conail, ~ **teeth** fiaclan *fpl* conail

canister *n* canastair *m*

cannabis *n* cainb *f*, (*the plant*) cainb-lus *m*

canoe *n* curach *f* Innseanach

canteen *n* biadhlann *f*

canvas *n* cainb *f*, canabhas *m*

canvass *v*, ~ **for support/votes** sìr taic *f*/bhòtaichean *fpl*

cap *n* (*headgear*) ceap *m*, bonaid *mf*

cap *v* **1** (*limit*) cuibhrich *vt*, ~ **a grant/expenditure** cuibhrich tabhartas *m*/caiteachas *m*; **2** (*beat*) thoir bàrr *m* (*with prep* air), **that ~s everything I ever saw** tha sin a' toirt bàrr air a h-uile càil *m invar* a chunna mi (a-)riamh

capability *n* comas *m*, **all that's beyond my** ~ tha sin uile thar mo chomais *gen*

capable *adj* **1** comasach (**of** air), **a** ~ **man** duine comasach, **I'm not** ~ **of (working) miracles** chan eil mi comasach air mìorbhailean *fpl* a dhèanamh; **2** *in expr* **she did what she was** ~ **of** rinn i na bha na comas *m*

capacious *adj* **1** (*premises &c*) farsaing; **2** (*of vessel &c: able to take a large load/cargo*) luchdmhor

capacity *n* **1** (*abstr*) tomhas-lìonaidh *m*; **2** *in expr* (*more con*) **a lorry with a** ~ **of two tons** làraidh *f* a ghabhas *vt* dà thunna *m*; **3** (*ability, skill*) comas *m*, ~ **of speech**, comas bruidhne *f gen*, **that's beyond my** ~ tha sin thar mo chomais *gen*; **4** (*role &c*) dreuchd *f*, **in my** ~ **as chairman** na mo dhreuchd mar chathraiche *m*

cape *n* **1** (*ie headland*) maol *m*, rubha *m*; **2** (*garment*) cleòc *m*, (*esp plaid*) tonnag *f*

caper *v* leum *vi*, ~**ing** a' leumadaich

capercaillie, capercailzie *n* capall-coille *m*

capering *n* leumadaich *f invar*

capillary *n* cuisle chaol

capital *n* **1** (*fin*) calpa *m*, ~ **expenditure** caiteachas *m* calpa, ~ **gain** buannachd *f* calpa; **2** (~ *city*) prìomh-bhaile *m*; **3** (*orthog*) litir mhòr

capital *adj* **1** (*fin*) calpach; **2** (*first rate*) anabarrach math, barraichte; **3** *in exprs* ~ **letter** litir mhòr, ~ **city** ceanna-bhaile *m*, prìomh bhaile *m*

capitalism *n* calpachas *m*

capitalist *n* calpaiche *m*

capitulate *v* strìochd *vi* (**to** do)

capitulation *n* strìochdadh *m* (**to** do)

capping *n* (*limiting*) cuibhreachadh *m*

caprice *n* baogaid *f*

capricious *adj* caochlaideach, baogaideach

capsize *v* **1** (*as vt*) cuir *vt* thairis, **they ~d her** chuir iad thairis i; **2** (*as vi*) rach *vi* thairis, **the boat ~d** chaidh am bàta thairis, *also* chaidh car *m* dhen bhàta *m*

captain *n* caiptean *m*, sgiobair *m*

captivated *adj* fo gheasaibh (*obs dat pl of* geas *f*) (**by** le *or* aig), **I was ~ by it** bha mi fo gheasaibh leis/aige

captivating *adj* meallach, tàlaidheach

captive *adj* an làimh (*dat of* làmh *f*), an sàs *m*, **I am ~** tha mi an làimh/an sàs

captive *n* prìosanach *m*, ciomach *m*, (neach &c) an làimh (*dat of* làmh *f*)/an sàs *m*, **I am a ~** tha mi nam phrìosanach, tha mi an làimh/an sàs

captivity *n* braighdeanas *m*, ciomachas *m*

capture *n* glacadh *m*, grèim *m*

capture *v* glac *vt*, cuir *vt* an làimh (*dat of* làmh *f*), **the police ~d him** ghlac am poileas e

captured *adj & past part* glacte, an làimh (*dat of* làmh *f*), an sàs *m*

car *n* càr *m*, (*trad*) carbad *m*, ~ **park** pàirc *f* chàraichean *pl gen*

carbon *n* gualan *m*

carbuncle *n* niosgaid *f*, guirean *m*

carcase *n* **1** corp (marbh) *m*; **2** (*usu not human: esp at butcher's &c*) closach *f*

card *n* cairt *f*, **Christmas ~** cairt Nollaig, **playing ~** cairt-chluiche, **a pack of ~s** paca *m* chairtean *pl gen*, **credit ~** cairt-iasaid, **business ~** càirt-ghnìomhachais

cardboard *n* cairt-bhòrd *m*

cardinal *adj* prìomh, (*of compass*) ~ **points** prìomh phuingean *fpl* (combaist *f gen*)

Cardinal *n* Càirdineal *m*

care *n* **1** (*carefulness, caution*) faiceall *f*, aire *f invar*, **a lack of ~** cion *m invar* faicill *gen*, **take ~** thoir an aire; **2** (*tending, charge, responsibility*) cùram *m*, ~ **of the elderly** cùram sheann daoine *mpl*, **in Donald's ~** air cùram Dhòmhnaill, ~ **of the sick** (*trad*) eiridinn *m invar*; **3** (*worry*) cùram *m*, iomagain *f*, **without (a) ~** gun chùram, **full of ~** làn iomagaine

care *v* **1** (*~ for, tend: esp the sick*) altraim *vt*, eiridnich *vt*, **~ for the sick/ill** eiridnich na h-euslaintich *mpl*; **2** (*expr affection*) bi *v irreg* measail (*with prep* air), **I ~ for you** tha mi measail ort; **3** (*expr disapproval, dislike*) is *v irreg def* beag orm &c, **she doesn't ~ for his house** is beag oirre an taigh aige, *note also* **I don't ~ much for him** chan eil mòran agam mu dheidhinn; **4** (*expr indifference*) *in exprs* **I don't ~** tha mi coma!, **I don't ~ in the least** tha mi coma co-dhiù, **I don't ~ if he comes or not** is coma leam an tig e no nach tig

career *n* dreuchd *f*

careful *adj* cùramach, faiceallach, **be ~** bi *v irreg* faiceallach, thoir an aire *f invar*

caress *v* cniadaich *vt*, brìodail *vt*

caressing *n* cniadachadh *m*

caretaker *n* neach-gleidhidh (*pl* luchd-gleidhidh *m sing coll*)

cargo *n* cargu & carago *m*, luchd *m*, eallach *m*

carnage *n* dòrtadh-fala *m*, bùidsearachd *f invar*, (*trad*) àr *m*

carnal *adj* feòlmhor, collaidh

carnation *n* càrnaid *f*

carnivore *n* feòil-itheadair *m*, ainmhidh feòil-itheach

carnivorous *adj* feòil-itheach

carousal, carousing *n* pòitearachd *f invar*

carouse *v* pòit *vi*

carpenter *n* saor *m*

carpentry *n* saorsainneachd *f invar*

carpet *n* brat-ùrlair *m*, brat-làir *m*

carrageen *n* carraigean *m*

carriage *n* **1** (*vehicle*) carbad *m*; **2** (*abstr: transportation*) giùlan *m*; **3** (*the charges levied for ~*) faradh *m*

carriageway *n* rathad *m*, slighe *f* (carbaid *m*)

carrier *n* **1** (*individual*) neach-giùlain (*pl* luchd-giùlain *m sing coll*); **2** (*firm*) companaidh *mf* ghiùlain *m gen*, companaidh iomchair *m gen*

carrion *n* **1** ablach *m*; **2** *in expr* **~ crow** feannag dhubh

carrot *n* curran *m*

carry *v* **1** giùlain *vt*, (*less usu*) iomchair *vt*; **2** *in expr* **~ out** (*a task, process &c*) coilean *vt*, cuir *vt* an gnìomh *m*, gnìomhaich *vt*; **3** *in expr* **~ on** (*continue, persevere*) cùm *vi*, lean *vi*, (*with prep* air), **we carried on in spite of the rain** chùm/lean sinn oirnn a dh'aindeoin an uisge; **4** *in expr* **~ on** (*ie behave*) giùlain f(h)èin/fhìn, **he was ~ing on as if there was no-one else in the room** bha e ga ghiùlan fhèin mar nach robh duine eile anns an rùm *m*, *note also* **I don't think much of the way they ~ on/their way of ~ing on** is beag orm an dol-a-mach *m invar* (a tha) aca

carry-on, carrying-on *n* (*ie behaviour, often questionable*) dol-a-mach *m invar*, **what a carry-on!** abair dol-a-mach!

cart *n* cairt *f*

cartoon *n* dealbh-èibhinn *mf*, cartùn *m*

carve *v* **1** (*wood &c*) snaigh *vt*; **2** (*meat*) geàrr *vt*

carving *n* **1** (*wood &c: the process*) snaigheadh *m*, (*the product*) obair-shnaighte *f*; **2** (*meat*) gearradh *m*

cascade *n* (*waterfall*) eas *m*, leum-uisge *m*, spùt *m*

case *n* **1** (*luggage*) màileid *f*, ceas *m*; **2** (*legal*) cùis *f*, cuis-lagha *f*, **the ~ went against her** chaidh a' chùis na h-aghaidh; **3** (*gram*) tuiseal *m*, **the genitive ~** an tuiseal ginideach; **4** (*fact, situation, eventuality &c*) *in exprs* **in that ~**, **if that is the ~** mas ann mar sin a tha a' chùis, **if it is the ~ that he is lazy** mas e (an rud e) 's gu bheil e leisg; **5** *in expr* **in ~** air eagal (*with conj* gu), mus *conj*, **he kept hold of her in ~ she should fall** chùm e grèim *m* oirre air eagal 's gun tuiteadh i, chùm e grèim oirre mus tuiteadh i; **6** *in expr* **in any ~** co-dhiù, **I'm leaving in any ~** tha mise a' falbh co-dhiù

cash *n* **1** (*as opposed to credit &c*) airgead *m*, **~ price** prìs *f* airgid (*gen, used adjectivally*); **2** (*ready money, ~ carried about one*) airgead *m* ullamh, airgead làimhe (*gen of* làmh *f, used adjectivally*)

cask *n* baraille *m*

cassette *n* cèiseag *f*

cassock *n* casag *f*

cast[1] *n* (*in play &c*) muinntir *f*, sgioba *mf*, **the ~ of the play** muinntir na dealbh-cluiche

cast[2] *n* (*throw*) tilgeadh *m*, tilgeil *f*, (*esp of thrown weapon*) urchair *f*

cast *v* **1** tilg *vt*, caith *vt*, (**at** air), **~ a stone** tilg clach *f*, **she ~ a foal** thilg i searrach *m*; **2** (*fig exprs*) **~ a glance** thoir sùil *f* (aithghearr) (**at** air), **~ doubt on something** cuir rudeigin an teagamh *m*, **~ a vote** cuir bhòt *f*

castigate *v* cronaich *vt*

castle *n* caisteal *m*, (*esp early fortified ~*) dùn *m*

castrate *v* spoth *vt*, **castrating lambs** a' spodh uan *m gen pl*

castration *n* geàrradh *m*, spothadh *m*

castrato *n* caillteanach *m*

casual *adj* **1** (*pej: of person, attitude*) coma co-dhiù, mì-dhìcheallach; **2** *in expr* **~ violence** droch-ionnsaigh(ean) *mf* gun adhbhar *m*, fòirneart *m* gun adhbhar; **3** *in expr* **a ~ stroll** cuairt shocrach

casualty *n* (*in accident, war &c*) leòinteach *m*

cat *n* **1** cat *m*, **wild ~** cat fiadhaich; **2** (*idioms*) **it was raining ~s and dogs** bha dìle bhàthte ann, **put/set the ~ among the pigeons** cuir an ceòl air feadh na fidhle

catastrophe *n* sgrios *m*, (*stronger*) leirsgrios *m*, mòr-sgrios *m*

catch *v* **1** glac *vt*, **the police caught him** ghlac am poileas e, **we didn't ~ the plane** cha do ghlac sinn am plèana *mf*; **2** *in expr* **~ (up with)** beir *vi irreg* (*with prep* air) **we caught (up with) him yesterday** rug sinn air an-dè; **3** (*~ illness &c*) gabh *vt*, **we caught the cold** ghabh sinn an cnatan; **4** *in expr* **~ sight** faigh sealladh *m* (**of** air), (*usu at a distance*) faigh faire *f* (**of** air)

catching *adj* (*ie infectious*) gabhaltach

catchment area *n* sgìre *f*, ~ **of a school** sgìre-sgoile, **the ~ of the school** sgìre na sgoile

catechise *v* (*relig*) ceasnaich *vt*

catechism *n* 1 (*relig: the book*) leabhar-cheist *m*, **the ~** leabhar nan ceist; 2 (*the act of asking the questions*) ceasnachadh *m*

catechist *n* (*relig*) ceistear *m*

categorical *adj* (*firm, clear, definite*) deimhinne, **a ~ answer** freagairt dheimhinne

categorically *adv* 1 (*firmly, definitely*) gu deimhinne, gun teagamh *m* (sam bith), **I can tell you ~ that the moon's a balloon** faodaidh mi innse dhuibh gu deimhinne/gun teagamh sam bith gur e bailiùn *m* a th' anns a' ghealaich *f*; 2 (*utterly*) gu buileach, uile-gu-lèir, **I deny that ~ly!** tha mi ag àicheadh sin gu buileach/uile-gu-lèir!

category *n* seòrsa *m*, gnè *f*

cater *v* 1 (*in restaurant, refectory &c*) ullaich biadh *m*; 2 (*supply by way of trade &c*) solair *vti*, solaraich *vti*, (**for** do), ~ **for tourists** solar/solaraich (seirbheisean *&c*) do luchd-turais *m sing coll*; 3 (*meet, satisfy*) coilean *vt*, leasaich *vt*, ~ **for every need** coilean gach feum *m*/gach easbhaidh *f*

catering *n* ullachadh *m* bìdh (*gen sing of* biadh *m*)

cathedral *n* cathair-eaglais *f*

Catholic *n & adj* Caitligeach *m*, (*not PC*) Pàpanach *m*

cattle *n* crodh *m*, **dairy ~** crodh-bainne, **~-grid** cliath *f* chruidh *gen*

caught *adj & past part* an sàs, an làimh, glacte, **the robber is/has been ~ now** tha am mèirleach an sàs a-nise

cauldron *n* coire *m*

cauliflower *n* càl-colaig *m*

cause *n* 1 adhbhar *m*, fàth *m*, cùis *f*, (*all followed by gen*) **prime ~** màthair-adhbhar *m*, **the ~ of my sadness** adhbhar/fàth mo mhulaid *m*, **a ~ of mockery** adhbhar/fàth magaidh *m*, ~ **for complaint** cùis-ghearain *f*; 2 (*principle, belief system &c*) adhbhar *m*, **she laboured in the ~ of women's rights** shaothraich i ann an adhbhar còraichean *fpl* nam ban (*gen pl of* bean *f*)

cause *v* 1 is *v irreg def* adhbhar *m* (*with prep* do), is *v irreg def* coireach (*with prep* ri), **A ~s B** 's e A as adhbhar do B, **you ~d the accident** is tu a bu choireach ris an tubaist *f*; 2 *in expr* ~ **to be** *v* cuir *vt followed by abstr n* (*with prep* air), fàg *vt followed by adj*, **you ~d me to be afraid** chuir sibh (an t-)eagal *m* orm, **you ~d me to be sad** dh'fhàg sibh muladach mi

causeway *n* cabhsair *m*

caustic *adj* (*remarks &c*) geur, guineach, searbh

caution *n* 1 (*prudence*) faiceall *f*; 2 (*warning*) earalachadh *m*, rabhadh *m*

caution *v* 1 (*esp legal*) earalaich *vt* (**about** air); 2 (*more general*) thoir rabhadh *m* (*with prep* do), **they ~ed me** dh'earalaich iad mi, thug iad rabhadh dhomh

cautious *adj* faiceallach

cavalry *n* eachraidh *m sing coll*

cave, cavern *n* uaimh *&* uamh *f*

cavity *n* toll *m*

caw *n* gràg *m*, ròcail *f*

caw *v* dèan gràgail *f invar*

cawing *n* gràgail *f invar*, ròcail *f*

cease *v* **1** (*come to an end*) thig *vi* gu crìch (*dat of* crìoch *f*), sguir *vi*, **the fighting ~d** thàinig an t-sabaid gu crìch, **the noise ~ed** sguir am fuaim; **2** (*desist from, give up*) leig *vt* seachad, sguir (*with or without prep* de), **she ~d smoking** leig i seachad smocadh *m*, sguir i (de) smocadh

ceaseless *adj*, **ceaselessly** *adv*, gun sgur, **ceaseless noise** fuaim *mf* gun sgur, **grumbling ceaselessly** a' gearan gun sgur

ceilidh *n* cèilidh *mf*, **ceilidh-dance** cèilidh agus dannsa *m*

ceiling *n* mullach-seòmair *m*, **the ~** mullach an t-seòmair

celebrate *v* **1** (*praise &c*) mol *vt*, luaidh *vt*; **2** (*observe festival &c*) cùm *vt*, glèidh *vt*, **~ New Year** cùm a' Bhliadhna Ùr

celebrated *adj* cliùiteach, iomraiteach

celebrity *n* **1** (*abstr*) ainmealachd *f invar*; **2** (*person*) neach *m* ainmeil

celery *n* soilire *m*

celestial *adj* **1** (*incl relig senses*) nèamhaidh; **2** (*esp of phys heavens*) speurach

celibacy *n* (*esp of males*) gilleadas *m*, (*of both sexes*) seachnadh *m* feise *f gen*

celibate *n* (neach *&c*) a sheachnas feise *f*

cell *n* **1** (*biol*) cealla *f*; **2** (*of saint &c*) cill *f*

Celt *n* Ceilteach *m*

Celtic *adj* Ceilteach, **the ~ languages** na cànanan *fpl* Ceilteach

cement *n* saimeant *m invar*, (*more trad*) tàth *m invar*

cement *v* tàth *vt* (**together** ri chèile)

cemetery *n* cladh *m*, clachan *m*, cill *f*

censorious *adj* cronachail, coireachail

censure *n* cronachadh *m*

censure *v* cronaich *vt*

census *n* cunntas *m* sluaigh *m gen*

centilitre *n* ceudailiotair *m*

centimetre *n* ceudameatair *m*, **cubic ~** ceudameatair ciùbach, **square ~** ceudameatair ceàrnagach

centipede *n* ceud-chasach *m*

central *adj* meadhanach

centralisation *n* meadhanachadh *m*

centralise *v* meadhanaich *vti*

centre *n* **1** meadhan *m*, **the town ~** meadhan a' bhaile, **right in the ~** anns a' cheart-mheadhan, **in the dead ~ of the field** ann an teis-meadhan an achaidh; **2** (*location for particular activities &c*) ionad *m*, **day ~** ionad latha, **job ~** ionad obrach, **health ~** ionad slàinte, **sports ~** ionad spòrsa, **management ~** ionad stiùiridh, **resource ~** ionad ghoireasan

centrifugal *adj* meadhan-sheachnach

century *n* linn *m*

cereal *n* arbhar *m*, gràn *m*

ceremony *n* **1** (*formal event*) deas-ghnàth *m*; **2** *in expr* (*at ceilidh &c*) **the master of ceremonies** fear *m* an taighe

certain *adj* **1** (*sure, definite*) cinnteach, (*more trad*) deimhinn(e), (**of** às), **I'm ~ of it** tha mi cinnteach às, **are you ~ she'll come?** a bheil thu cinnteach gun tig i?; **2** (*Bibl, trad stories &c*) àraidh, **a ~ widow, having three sons** banntrach *f* àraidh, agus triùir mhac aice; **3** (*specified, particular*) sònraichte, **we must buy it in a ~ place on a ~ day** feumaidh sinn a cheannach ann an àite sònraichte air là sònraichte

certainly *adv* gu dearbh, **are you well? I ~ am!** a bheil thu gu math? tha gu dearbh!

certainty *n* cinnt *f*, **I can say with ~ that I am right!** faodaidh mi a ràdh le cinnt gu bheil mi ceart!

certificate *n* teisteanas *m*, **birth ~** teisteanas-breith *m*

certify *v* thoir teisteanas *m*

cessation *n* stad *m*

chafe *v* (*skin of hand &c*) rùisg *vt*

chaff *n* càth *f*, moll *m*

chagrin *n* frionas *m*

chagrined *adj* frionasach

chain *n* cuibhreach *m*, slabhraidh *f*, *in expr* **put in ~s** cuibhrich *vt*

chain (up) *v* cuibhrich *vt*, cuir *vt* air slabhraidh *f*

chair *n* cathair *f*, (*less trad*) sèithear *m*

chairman *n* cathraiche *m*, fear-cathrach *m*

chairperson *n* cathraiche *m*, neach-cathrach *m* (*pl* luchd-cathrach *m sing coll*)

chalk *n* cailc *f*

challenge *n* dùbhlan *m*

challenge *v* **1** thoir dùbhlan (*with prep* do), **he ~d me to tell the truth** thug e dùbhlan dhomh an fhìrinn innse; **2** (*~ decision &c*) cuir *vi* an aghaidh (*with gen*)

chamber *n* seòmar *m*

champion *n* curaidh *m*

chance *adj* tuiteamach, **~ occurrences** tachartasan *mpl* tuiteamach

chance *n* **1** (*luck &c*) tuiteamas *m*, **it happened by ~** thachair e le tuiteamas; **2** (*opportunity*) cothrom *m* (**of** air), **a ~ of a better life** cothrom air beatha *f* as fheàrr; **3** (*idiom*) **we gave them a sporting ~** thug sinn cothrom *m* na Fèinne dhaibh

chance *v* **1** tuit *vi* (*with prep* do), **I ~d to see her on the street** thuit dhomh a faicinn air an t-sràid; **2** *in expr* **~ upon** tachair *vi* air, amais *vi* air

chancellor *n* seansalair *m*

change *n* **1** atharrachadh *m*, caochladh *m*, (*often for the worse*) mùthadh *m*, **a ~ in the weather** atharrachadh-sìde *f*, (*idiom*) **what a ~ has come upon**

us! (*trad*) nach (ann) oirnn a thàinig an dà là *m*!; 2 (*new situation, experience &c*) ùrachadh *m*, **that will be/make a ~ for you** bidh sin na ùrachadh dhut; 3 (*money*) iomlaid *f*, **~ for/of a pound** iomlaid nota *f gen*, **I didn't get any ~** cha d'fhuair mi iomlaid, *in expr* **small ~** airgead pronn

change *v* 1 atharraich *vti*, caochail *vi*, (*often for the worse*) mùth *vi*; 2 (*~ money*) **can you ~ a pound?** a bheil iomlaid *f* nota *f* agad?

changeable *adj* caochlaideach, **~ weather/personality** sìde/pearsantachd chaochlaideach

chanter *n* (*piping*) feadan *m*

chaos *n* 1 (*cosmology*) eu-cruth *m*; 2 (*fam: disorder, untidiness &c*) *in expr* **in ~** troimh-a-chèile, **the office was in ~** bha an oifis troimh-a-chèile

chapel *n* caibeal *m*

chaplain *n* seaiplin *m*

chapter *n* (*of book*) caibideil *mf*

character *n* 1 nàdar *m*, (*esp of humans*) mèinn *f*, (*esp hereditary*) dualchas *m*, **it's in his ~ to be proud** is e a dhualchas a bhith àrdanach, *also* tha e dualach a bhith àrdanach; 2 (*in play &c*) caractar *m*, (*less usu*) pearsa *m*

characteristic *n* (*esp inherent*) feart *m*, **we get many ~s from our forebears/ ancestors** gheibh sinn mòran fheartan *pl gen* bhor sinnsirean *mpl*

charcoal *n* gual-fiodha *m*

charge *n* 1 (*responsibility &c*) cùram *m*, **in Donald's ~** air cùram Dhòmhnaill, **in ~ of** an urra ri, **I was in ~ of the Post Office** bha mi an urra ri Oifis a' Phuist, (*idiom*) **she took ~ of the house** ghabh i an taigh os làimh (*gen of* làmh *f*); 2 (*cost, payment*) cosgais *f*, **bank(ing) ~s** cosgaisean banca(ireachd); 3 (*fee &c*) tuarastal *m*, **the lawyer didn't make a ~** cha do ghabh am fear-lagha tuarastal, *in expr* **free of ~** saor ('s an asgaidh), **there'll be no ~ for that** bidh sin saor 's an asgaidh, *in expr* **freight ~** faradh *m*; 4 (*legal: accusation*) casaid *f*; 5 (*military: attack*) ionnsaigh *f*

charge *v* 1 (*make responsible*) cuir uallach *m* (*with prep* air), **they ~d me with the respnsibility for the journey** chuir iad orm uallach an turais; 2 (*~ for goods &c*) iarr pàigheadh *m* (**for** airson); 3 (*banking &c*) **~ to an account** cuir *vt* ri cunntas *m*; 4 (*military: attack*) thoir ionnsaigh *f* (*with prep* air), (*trad*) rach *vi* sìos; 5 (*legal*) cuir casaid *f* (*with prep* air)

charitable *adj* 1 (*apt to give charitably*) tabhairteach; 2 (*involved in charity*) carthannach, **~ trust** urras carthannach; 3 (*of person: kindly disposed &c*) coibhneil

charity *n* 1 (*abstr*) carthannas *m*, carthannachd *f invar*; 2 (*organisation: a ~*) buidheann-carthannais, buidheann-carthannach; 3 (*con: alms, charitable gifts*) dèirc *f*; 4 (*Bibl: Christian ~*) carthannachd *f invar*, gràdh *m*

charm *n* 1 (*magical*) geas *f*, seun *m*, ortha *f*; 2 (*personal ~*) taitneas *m*, ciatachd *f invar*

charming *adj* 1 (*person*) taitneach, ciatach, tlachdmhor; 2 (*person & place*) grinn

chart *n* **1** (*map &c*) cairt *f*, **navigation ~** cairt-iùil; **2** (*table &c*) clàr *m*, (*IT*) **flow ~** clàr-ruith *m*, sruth-chlàr *m*

charter *n* cairt *f*, cùmhnant *m* sgrìobhte

chase *n* **1** tòir *f*, ruaig *f*; **2** (*hunting*) ruaig *f*

chase *v* **1** rua(i)g *vt*, ruith *vi* às dèidh (*with gen*); **2** *in expr* **~ away** rua(i)g *vt*, fuadaich *vt*, **the dog ~d away the fox** ruaig/dh'fhuadaich an cù an sionnach, *also* chuir an cù teicheadh *m* air an t-sionnach

chaste *adj* geanmnaidh

chasten *v* ùmhlaich *vt*, nàraich *vt*

chastise *v* peanasaich *vt*

chastity *n* geanmnachd *f invar*

chat *n* **1** còmhradh (beag), **we had a wee ~** rinn sinn còmhradh beag; **2** (*words used, opinions expressed &c*) còmhradh *m*, (*fam*) craic *f*, **listening to their ~** ag èisdeachd ris an còmhradh

chat *v* dèan còmhradh (beag), (*idiom*) **~ting about this and that** a' còmhradh a-null 's a-nall

chattels *npl* **1** (*bits & pieces*) treal(l)aich *f sing coll*; **2** (*possessions*) **goods and ~** maoin *f*

chatter, chattering *n* cabadaich *f*, cabaireachd *f invar*, gobaireachd & gabaireachd *f invar*, goileam *m*

chatty *adj* còmhraideach, bruidhneach

cheap *adj* **1** (*in price*) saor, air bheag prìs *m*, air prìs ìseal; **2** (*derog: petty, unworthy &c*) suarach, **a ~ ploy** plòigh shuarach

cheat *n* cealgair(e) *m*, mealltair *m*, fear-foille *m*

cheat *v* **1** meall *vt*, thoir an car (*with prep* à), dèan foill *f* (*with prep* air), **they ~ed her** mheall iad i, thug iad an car aiste, rinn iad foill oirre; **2** (*as vi: in games &c*) bi *vi irreg* ri foill *f*, **they're ~ing!** tha iad ri foill!

cheated *adj* air a (*&c*) m(h)ealladh

cheating *adj* meallta(ch)

cheating *n* foill *f*, mealladh *m*

check *v* **1** (*examine for errors &c*) sgrùd *vt*, dèan ath-sgrùdadh *m* (*with prep* air), thoir sùil *f* (*with prep* air); **2** (*stop, restrain*) cuir stad *m* (*with prep* air), bac *vt*, cuir bacadh *m* (*with prep* air)

check-out *n* àite-pàighidh *m*

check-up *n* àth-sgrùdadh *m*, **dental ~** àth-sgrùdadh-fhiacail, àth-sgrùdadh fhiaclan *fpl gen*

cheek *n* **1** gruaidh *f*, (*esp plump, rosy*) pluic *f*; **2** (*fam: nerve, insolence*) aghaidh *f*, bathais *f*, **what a ~!** abair aghaidh!, **what a ~ they've got!** nach ann orra a tha an aghaidh/a' bhathais!

cheep, cheeping *n* bìd *m*, bìogail *f*

cheep *v* bìog *vi*

cheer *n* **1** (*sign of approval*) iolach *f*, **raise a ~** dèan/tog iolach; **2** (*mood, spirits &c*) misneachail, **they were of good ~** bha iad misneachail, *also* bha deagh shunnd *m invar* orra

cheer *v* 1 dèan/tog iolach *f* (*with prep* do), **the people ~ed (him)** rinn/thog an sluagh iolach (dha); 2 *in expr* ~ **up** tog a (*&c*) c(h)ridhe *m*, **that ~ed me up** thog sin mo chridhe, (*as vi: idiom*) ~ **up!** tog ort!

cheerful *adj* greannmhor, aighearach, cridheil, sunndach

cheerfulness *n* aighear *m*, sunnd *m invar*

cheerio! *excl* tìoraidh!

cheery *adj* (*esp person*) aighearach, (*person, atmosphere &c*) cridheil

cheese *n* càise *mf*

chef *n* còcaire *m*, (*female* ~) ban-chòcaire *f*

chemical *adj* ceimigeach, *in expr* ~ **substance** ceimig *f*

chemical *n* ceimig *f*

chemist *n* 1 ceimigear *m*; 2 (*pharmacist*) neach *m* chungaidhean, *in expr* ~**'s shop** bùth-chungaidh *f*

chemistry *n* ceimigeachd *f invar*

chess *n* tàileasg *m*

chest *n* 1 (*thorax*) cliabh *m*, broilleach *m*; 2 (*furniture &c*) ciste *f*, **linen** ~ ciste anairt *m gen*, **treasure** ~ ciste ionmhais *m gen*

chew *v* 1 cnàmh *vti*, cagainn *vti*, cnuas & cnuasaich *vti*; 2 *in expr* ~ **over** (*ideas, events &c*) cnuas & cnuasaich (*with prep* air), ~ **over the news** cnuasaich air an naidheachd *f*; 3 *in exprs* (*of animals*) ~**ing the cud**, (*also, fam, of humans*) ~**ing the fat**, a' cnàmh na cìre

chick *n* isean *m*

chicken *n* (*young*) isean *m*, eireag *f*, (*mature*) cearc *f*, **roast** ~ cearc ròsta

chide *v* cronaich *vt*, càin *vt*

chief *adj* prìomh, àrd, (*precede the noun, which is lenited where possible*) ~ **clerk** prìomh-chlèireach *m*, ~ **justice** àrd-bhreitheamh *m*

chief *n* 1 (*leader &c*) ceannard *m*; 2 (*of clan*) ceann-cinnidh *m*, ceann-feadhna *m*, ~ **of the MacDonalds** ceann-cinnidh nan Dòmhnallach

chilblain *n* cusp *f*

child *n* (*see also* **children** *below*) 1 (*abstr & general*) duine cloinne *m*, **how many ~ren do you have? one** ~ cia mheud duine cloinne a th' agaibh? tha aon duine cloinne; 2 (*particular* ~, *generally young/infants*) leanabh *m*, pàisde & pàiste *m*, leanaban *m*, naoidhean *m*, (*boy* ~, *esp a little older*) balach *m* (beag), (*girl* ~, *esp a little older*) caileag *f* (bheag), **she had a** ~ bha pàiste aice; 3 (*misc exprs*) **unruly/badly-behaved** ~ (*fam*) droch isean *m*, ~ **minder** freiceadan *m* cloinne, ~ **care** cùram-cloinne *m*

childhood *n* leanabas *m*

childish *adj* leanabail

childless *adj* gun chlann *f sing coll*, ~ **couple** càraid *f* gun chlann

children *n* (*see also* **child** *above*) clann *f sing coll*, **little** ~ clann bheaga, **two** ~ dìthis chloinne, **girl** ~ clann-nighean, **how many** ~ **do you have?** cia mheud duine cloinne a th' agaibh?

chill *adj* (*lit & fig*) fuaraidh, fionnar

chill *n* 1 (*abstr*) fionnarachd *f invar*, (*colder*) fuachd *f invar*; 2 *in expr* **catch a** ~ gabh fuachd *f invar*

chill *v* fuaraich *vti*, meilich *vti*

chilly *adj* **1** (*lit & fig*) fuaraidh, fionnar; **2** (*of welcome, reception*) fuar, fionnar

chimney *n* **1** similear *m*; **2** (*marine, industrial &c*) luidhear *m*

chip *n* (*IT*) sgealb *f*

chips *npl* sliseagan-buntàta *fpl*

chirp, chirping *n* bìd *m*, bìogail *f*

chirp *v* bìog *vi*

chisel *n* gilb *f*

chocolate *n & adj* teòclaid *&* seòclaid *f*

choice *adj* taghta

choice *n* **1** (*the thing &c chosen*) roghainn *mf*, **my own ~ of music** mo roghainn fhìn de cheòl *m*; **2** (*alternative*) roghainn *mf*, **we've no ~** chan eil roghainn (eile) againn; **3** (*abstr*) taghadh *m*

choir *n* còisir *f*, còisir-chiùil *f*

choke mùch *vt*, tachd *vt*

choose *v* **1** (*select*) tagh *vt*, roghnaich *vti*, **he chose the team** thagh e an sgioba; **2** (*single out*) sònraich *vt*

chop *v* **1** (*wood &c*) sgud *vti*; **2** *in expr* **~ off** sgath *vt* dheth; **3** *in expr* (*food &c*) **~ up** (*esp finely*) mion-gheàrr *vt*

chopper *n* làmhthuagh *f*

chosen *adj & past part* **1** (*selected*) taghta; **2** (*singled out*) sònraichte

Christendom *n, used with art,* a' Chrìosdachd *f invar*

Christian *adj* Crìosdail, **the ~ Church** an Eaglais Chrìosdail

Christian *n* Crìosdaidh *m*

Christianity *n* **1** (*the faith*) Crìosdaidheachd *f invar*; **2** (*conduct, way of life*) Crìosdalachd *f invar*

Christmas *n* Nollaig *f*, **Merry ~!** Nollaig Chridheil!, **~ Day/Eve** Là *m*/ Oidhche (na) Nollaig, **at ~ time** aig àm *m* na Nollaig(e)

chuffed *adj* toilichte, (*more fam: idiom*) **he's ~** tha e air a dheagh dhòigh *m*

chunk *n* cnap *m*, geinn *m*

church *n* eaglais *f*, **the ~ of Scotland** Eaglais na h-Alba, **~ officer** maor-eaglais *m*

churchyard *n* cladh *m*, clachan *m*, cill *f*

churlish *adj* iargalt(a), droch-nàdarrach

churn *n* crannag *f*, muidhe *m*, crannachan *m*

cigarette *n* toitean *m*

cinder *n* èibhleag *f*

cinema *n* taigh-dhealbh *m*

cinnamon *n* caineal *m*

circle *n* cearcall *m*, **dancing in a ~** a' dannsadh ann an cearcall

circle *v* iadh *&* iath *vt*, *in expr* **~ around** cuartaich *&* cuairtich *vt*

circuit *n* **1** (*route &c*) cuairt *f*; **2** (*elec*) cuairt *f* dealain *m gen*

circular *adj* cruinn, cearclach

circular *n* (*corres*) cuairt-litir *f*

circulate *v* **1** (*as vi*) rach *vi* timcheall, rach *vi* mun cuairt, **a rumour about them was circulating** bha fathann *m* mun deidhinn a' dol timcheall/ mun cuairt; **2** (*as vt*) cuir *vt* timcheall, cuir *vt* mun cuairt, **we ~d a rumour about them** chuir sinn timcheall/mun cuairt fathann mun deidhinn

circulation *n* cuairteachadh *m*, **~ of blood** cuairteachadh fala (*gen of* fuil *f*)

circumspect *adj* aireach, faiceallach

circumspection *n* aire *f*, faiceall *f*

circumstance *n* **1** cùis *f*, suidheachadh *m*, **if ~s allow me** ma cheadaicheas cùisean dhomh, **in unfortunate ~s** ann an suidheachadh mì-fhortanach; **2** (*eventuality*) cor *m*, **don't sign it under any ~s** na cuir d' ainm *m* ris air chor sam bith

citizen *n* **1** (*general*) neach-àiteachaidh (*pl* luchd-àiteachaidh *m sing coll*); **2** (*of a country*) saoranach *m*, neach-dùthcha (*pl* luchd-dùthcha *m sing coll*), **a French ~** saoranach Frangach; **3 ~s** poball *m sing*, sluagh *m sing*, **consult the ~s** cuir comhairle *f* ris a' phoball

citizenship *n* **1** (*the status*) saoranachd *f invar*, inbhe *f* neach-dùthcha *m*; **2** (*the associated rights &c*) còir *m* dùthcha (*gen of* duthaich *f*), **seek/ apply for ~** sir/iarr còir dùthcha

city *n* baile mòr, (*esp cathedral ~*) cathair *f*

civic *adj* catharra, **~ responsibility** dleastanas catharra

civil *adj* **1** (*polite*) modhail, cùirteil; **2** (*relating to the citizens of a state*) sìobhalta, catharra, **~ servant** seirbheiseach catharra, seirbheiseach sìobhalta, seirbheiseach stàite, **~ war** cogadh catharra, **~ court/liberty** cùirt/saorsa chatharra; **3** *in expr* **~ engineer** innleadair-thogalach *m*

civilian *n* sìobhaltair *m*

civility n modh *f*

civilisation *n* sìobhaltachd *f invar*

cladding *n* còmhdach *m*

claim *n* (*law, insurance &c*) tagairt *f*, tagradh *m*

claim *v* **1** (*~ rights, possessions &c: law, insurance &c*) tagair *vt*, **~ing his prize/reward** a' tagairt a dhuais; **2** (*assert*) cùm a-mach, **he ~ed that the world wasn't round** chùm e a-mach nach robh an cruinne cruinn

claimant neach-tagraidh (*pl* luchd-tagraidh *m sing coll*), tagraiche *m*

clamour *n* gleadhraich *f*

clamp *n* teanchair & teannachair *m*, glamradh *m*

clan *n* cinneadh *m*, clann *f*, (*more trad*) fine *f*, **~ Donald** C(h)lann Dhòmhnaill, **~ MacLeod** C(h)lann Leòid, **~ chief** ceann-cinnidh *m*, *also* ceann-feadhna *m*

clang *n* gliongadaich *f*

clang *v* dèan gliongadaich *f*

clanging *n* gliongadaich *f*

clannish *adj* cinneadail

clansman *n* fear-cinnidh *m*

clanswoman *n* bean-chinnidh *f*

clap *v* buail basan/(*more fam*) boisean *fpl*, **the audience ~ped** bhuail an luchd-èisteachd *m sing coll* am basan/boisean

clapping *n* bas-bhualadh *m*, bois-bhualadh *m*

clarification *n* soilleireachadh *m*

clarify *v* soilleirich *vt*

clarity *n* siolleireachd *f invar*

clarsach *n* clàrsach *f*

clash *n* **1** (*noise*) gliongadaich *f*; **2** (*confrontation*) connsachadh *m*, connspaid *f*

clash *v* **1** (*make noise*) dèan gliongadaich *f*; **2** (*disagree &c*) connsaich *vi* (**with** le)

clasp *n* cromag *f*

class *n* **1** (*school*) clas *m*; **2** (*social ~*) seòrsa *m*; **3** (*idiom: of quality, competence &c*) **he's not in the same ~ as her** cha tig e an uisge *m* na stiùrach dhi

classical *adj* clasaigeach

classification *n* seòrsachadh *m*

classified *adj & past part* **1** seòrsaichte; **2** (*of document &c, confidential*) dìomhair

classify *v* seòrsaich *vt*

clattering *n* glagadaich *f*

claw *n* ìne *f*

clay *n* crèadh *f*

claymore *n* claimheadh-mòr *m*, claidheamh leathann *m*, (*less correctly*) claidheamh dà-làimh *m*

clean *adj* glan

clean *v* **1** glan *vt*; **2** ~ **out** (*byre &c*) cairt *vt*

cleanse *v* glan *vt*

cleanliness *n* glaine *f invar*

clear *adj* **1** (*of light, day &c*) soilleir; **2** (*esp of sounds, sights, audible, visible*) taisbeanach; **3** (*of area of ground &c*) rèidh; **4** (*evident &c*) follaiseach, (*more trad*) lèir (*with v irreg & def* is *& prep* do), **it's ~ that he's not guilty** tha e follaiseach nach eil e ciontach, **it was ~ to him that he was lost** bu lèir dha gun robh e air chall; **5** (*of argument, explanation &c*) soilleir

clear *v* **1** (*population*) fàsaich *vt*, fuadaich *vt*; **2** (~ *obstacles, problems &c*) rèitich *vt*, ~ **the road/way** rèitich an rathad; **3** ~ **up** (*untidiness &c*) rèitich *vt*, sgioblaich *vt*, ~ **up that mess!** rèitich/sgioblaich am bùrach sin!; **4** ~ **up** (*situations, relationships &c*) rèitich *vt*; **5** *in expr* ~ **up** (*intellectual difficulties & misunderstandings*) soilleirich *vt*; **6** (*idiom, fam*) ~ **off/out!** thoir do chasan leat!

clearance *n* (*of population*) fàsachadh *m*, fuadach *m*, fuadachadh *m*, (*hist*) **the (Highland) ~s** Na Fuadaichean

cleared *adj & past part* (*area of ground &c*) rèidh

cleg *n* creithleag *f*

clemency *n* iochd *f invar*, tròcair *f*

clement *adj* **1** (*esp of weather*) ciùin, sèimh; **2** (*of judge, ruler &c*) iochdmhor, tròcaireach

clergy *n* clèir *f*, (*usu used with art*) a' chlèir

clergyman *n* ministear *m*, clèireach *m*, pears-eaglais *m*

clerical *adj* **1** (*relig*) clèireachail; **2** (*secretarial &c*) clèireachail, clèireachd (clèireachd *f invar*, *used adjectivally*), **~ staff** luchd-obrach *m sing coll* clèireachail, luchd-clèireachd *m sing coll*

clerk *n* **1** (*in office &c*) clèireach *m*, (*of higher status*) clàrc *m*, **~ of the Parliament** Clàrc na Parlamaid; **2** *in expr* (*crofting*) **the township/ grazings ~** clàrc *m* a' bhaile

clever *adj* **1** (*esp mentally*) glic, eirmseach; **2** (*esp practically*) tapaidh, gleusta & gleusda, deas; **3** (*resourceful*) innleachdach

cleverness *n* **1** (*esp mental*) gliocas *m*; **2** (*esp practical*) tapachd *f invar*; **3** (*resourcefulness*) innleachd *f*

cliff *n* creag *f*, bearradh *m*, stalla *m*

climate *n* clìomaid *f*

climb *v* **1** (*hill &c*) dìrich *vt*, s(t)reap *vti*; **2** *in expr* **~ down** crom *vi*, teirinn & teàrn *vi*, **he ~ed down from the donkey's back** chrom e bhon asail *f*, **he ~ed down the rock** chrom e leis a' chreig *f*, **she ~ed down from the wall** theirinn i bhàrr a' ghàrraidh *m*

clinking *n* gliong *m*, gliongartaich *m invar*, clagarsaich *f invar*

clip *n* (*ie for fastening*) cromag *f*, ceangal *m*

clip *v* **1** (*cut*) geàrr *vt*; **2** (*~ sheep*) lom *vt*, rùisg *vt*

cloak *n* cleòc *m*

clock *n* gleoc *m*, cloc & cleoc *m*

clockwise *adv* deiseil & deiseal

clod *n* (*of earth*) ploc *m*, fòid & fòd *f*

clog *v* stop *vt*

cloister *n* clabhstair *m*

close *adj* **1** (*ie near*) faisg, (*less usu*) dlùth, (**to** air), **~ together/to each other** faisg air a chèile, **~ to the village/township** faisg air a' bhaile; **2** *in exprs* **a ~ connection/link/bond** dlùth-cheangal *m* (**with** ri, **between** eadar), **~ on a month ago** teann air mìos *mf* air ais; **3** (*of weather*) bruicheil, bruthainneach

close *n* (*in tenement &c*) clobhsa *m*

close *n* crìoch *f*, **bring to a ~** thoir *vt* gu crìch (*dat*)

close *v* **1** (*as vt*) dùin *vt*, thoir *vt* gu crìch (*dat of* crìoch *f*), crìochnaich *vt*, **~ the door** dùin an doras, **the chairman will ~ the meeting** dùinidh am fear-cathrach a' choinneamh, bheir am fear-cathrach a' choinneamh gu crìch; **2** (*as vi*) dùin *vi*, **the shop was closing** bha a' bhùth a' dùnadh, **the window ~d with a bang** dhùin an uinneag *f* le brag *m*

closed *adj* & *past part* (*buildings, objects &c*) dùinte

closeness *n* faisge *f invar*, dlùths *m*

closet *n* clòsaid *f*

closure *n* dùnadh *m*

cloth *n* 1 (*material*) clò *m*, aodach *m*; 2 (*for dishes, dusting &c*) clùd *m*, clobhd *m*, brèid *m*

clothes, clothing *n* 1 (~ *in general*) aodach *m*, (*less usu*) trusgan *m*, *in expr* **a piece/an item of clothing** ball-aodaich *m*; 2 (*esp one's clothing at a given time*) cuid *f* aodaich *m gen*, **she put on her** ~ chuir i oirre a cuid aodaich; 3 (*misc exprs*) **clothes peg** cnag-aodaich *f*, **clothes-line** ròp-aodaich *m*, **suit of clothes** deise *f*, culaidh & culaidh-aodaich *f*, **bedclothes** aodach-leapa *m*, **nightclothes** aodach-oidhche *m*

cloud *n* neul *m*, sgòth *f*

cloud (over) *v* neulaich *vti*

cloudy *adj* neulach, sgòthach

clove *n* clòbha *f*

clover *n* clòbhar *m*, seamrag *f*

clown *n* 1 (*in circus &c*) cleasaiche *m*, tuaistear *m*; 2 (*ridiculous, incompetent &c person*) amadan *m*, bumailear *m*, **he's a** ~ 's e amadan/bumailear a th' ann (dheth)

club[1] *n* 1 (*weapon*) cuaille *m*; 2 (*for sport*) caman *m*, **golf** ~ (*ie driver, wedge &c*) caman *m* goilf *m gen*

club[2] *n* (*association &c*) comann *m*, club *m*, **youth** ~ comann òigridh *f*, **golf** ~ club goilf *m gen*

cluck *v* dèan gogail *f invar*

clucking *n* gogail *f invar*

clump *n* bad *m*

clumsy *adj* (*person, action*) cearbach, *in expr* **a** ~ **person** cearbair *m*

cluster *n* 1 (*of nuts, fruits &c*) bagaid *f*; 2 (*of people*) grunnan *m* (dhaoine)

co- *prefix* co-, *eg* **co-education** *n* co-fhoghlam *m*, **co-operate** *v* co-obraich *vi*

coach[1] *n* (*transport*) coidse *f invar*

coach[2] *n* (*instructor &c*) neach-teagaisg *m*, (*esp sport*) neach-trèanaidh *m* (*pl* luchd-teagaisg/trèanaidh *m sing coll*)

coach *v* 1 teagaisg *vt*; 2 (*sport &c*) trèan *vt*

coal *n* gual *m*

coalition *n* co-bhanntachd *f*

coalmine *n* mèinn(e)-ghuail *f*

coarse *adj* 1 (*to the touch*) garbh, ~ **material** stuth *m* garbh; 2 (*uncouth*) garbh, borb; 3 (*crude, lewd &c*) drabasta, draosta

coarseness *n* 1 (*to the touch*) gairbhe *f invar*, gairbhead *m*; 2 (*crudeness, lewdness*) drabastachd *f invar*, draostachd *f invar*

coast *n* oirthir *f*, costa *m*

coastguard *n* 1 (*the organisation*) maoras-cladaich *m*; 2 (*individual* ~) maor-cladaich *m*

coat *n* 1 (*garment*) còta *m*, *in expr* ~ **hanger** crochadair-còta *m*; 2 (*layer, covering*) còta *m*, **a** ~ **of paint** còta peanta *m*, còta de pheant

coat *v* còmhdaich *vt*, cuir brat *m* (*with prep* air)

cobbler *n* greusaiche *m*

cobweb *n* lìon *m* damhain-allaidh *m*

cock *n* **1** (*male domestic fowl or game bird*) coileach *m*; **2** (*vulg: penis*) slat *f* (*vulg/fam*)

cock *v* (*gun*) cuir *vt* air lagh *f*

cock-crow *n* gairm *f* coilich (*gen of* coileach *m*)

cocked *adj & past part* (*of gun*) air lagh *f*

cockle *n* coilleag *f*, srùban *m*

cockroach *n* càrnan *m*

cocoa *n* còco *m invar*

coconut *n* cnò-bhainne *f*, cnò-còco *f*

cod *n* trosg *m*, bodach-ruadh *m*

coddle *v* (*treat over gently, spoil*) mùirnich *vt*, maothaich *vt*

code *n* **1** (*cypher &c*) còd *m*, (*IT*) **binary** ~ còd dà-fhillte, **machine** ~ còd inneil *m gen*; **2** (*rules, guidelines &c*) còd *m*, ~ **of practice** còd obrachaidh *m gen*

co-education *n* co-fhoghlam *m*

coffee *n* cofaidh *mf*

coffin *n* ciste-laighe *f*

cognate *adj* dàimheil

coin *n* bonn *m* airgid *m gen*, *in expr* **toss a** ~ cuir crainn (*pl of* crann *m*)

coincide *v* co-thuit *vi*

coincidence *n* co-thuiteamas *m*

coincidental *adj* **1** co-thuiteamach; **2** (*irrelevant, unconnected*) **that's** ~ chan eil sin a' buntainn ris a' chùis *f*

coke *n* (*fuel*) còc *m invar*

cold *adj* **1** (*phys: weather, objects &c*) fuar, **a** ~ **day** là fuar, **the porridge is getting** ~ tha am brochan a' fàs fuar; **2** (*emotionally* ~) fuar, fad' às, **a** ~ **person** duine/neach fuar, duine/neach fad' às; **3** (*welcome, atmosphere &c*) fionnar

cold *n* **1** (*phys*) fuachd *mf*, **I can't stand/bear the** ~ **of winter** chan fhuiling mi fuachd a' gheamhraidh; **2** (*the ailment: used with art*) an cnatan *m*, (*less usu*) am fuachd *m*, **I'm getting a/the** ~ tha an cnatan a' tighinn orm, **we caught a/the** ~ ghabh sinn an cnatan

coldly *adv* (*of emotions, behaviour &c*) gu fionnar, **she answered** ~ fhreagair i gu fionnar

coldness *n* (*esp phys*) fuachd *mf*, (*phys & emotional*) fionnarachd *f invar*

Coll *n* Col(l)a *m*, *in expr* **a** ~ **man/person** Col(l)ach *m* (*also adj*)

collaborate *v* **1** (*work together*) co-obraich *vi*; **2** *in expr* ~ **with the enemy** thoir taic *f* don nàmhaid *m*

collaboration *n* co-obrachadh *m*

collar *n* coilear *m*

collarbone, the *n* cnà(i)mh *m* an uga(in), cnà(i)mh a' choileir

colleague *n* co-obraiche *m*, companach *m*

collect *v* **1** (*esp people*) cruinnich *vi*, tionail *vi*, **a crowd ~d in front of the house** chruinnich/thionail sluagh (mòr) air beulaibh an taighe; **2** (*things*) cruinnich *vt*, co-chruinnich *vt*, **he ~s furniture** bidh e a' cruinneachadh àirneis *f invar*

collection *n* **1** (*abstr & con*) cruinneachadh *m*; **2** (*anthology*) co-chruinneachadh *m*

collective *adj* coitcheann, **~ responsibility** uallach coitcheann

college *n* colaiste & colaisde *f*, **private ~** colaiste phrìobhaideach

collide *v* co-bhuail *vi*

collision *n* co-bhualadh *m*

colon *n* **1** (*typog*) dà-phuing *f*, còilean *m*; **2** (*part of intestine*) snathainn *f*

colony *n* colonaidh *m*

colour *n* **1** dath *m*, **what ~'s the coat?** dè an dath a th' air a' chòta?; **2** (*of person's features, at a particular moment*) tuar *m*, snuadh *m*

colour *v* dath *vt*, cuir dath *m* (*with prep* air)

colour-blind *adj* dath-dhall

coloured *adj & past part* dathte

column *n* (*architecture, newspaper*) colbh *m*

comb *n* **1** cìr *f*; **2** (*of game bird &c*) cìrean *m*

comb *v* cìr *vt*, **~ your hair** cìr d' fhalt *m*

combat *n* còmhrag *f*

combat *v* sabaid *vi*, strì *vi*, (*with prep* ri), **~ crime** sabaid/strì ri eucoir *f*

combine *v* measgaich *vt*, co-mheasgaich *vti*

combination *n* measgachadh *m*

come *v* **1** *exprs with* thig *vi irreg*, **~ in!** thig a-steach! **she didn't ~ with me** cha tàinig i còmhla rium, **coming this way** a' tighinn an taobh seo, **before winter ~s** mus tig an geamhradh, **~ to an agreement/ understanding** thig gu còrdadh *m*/gu aonta *m*, **~ to a decision/ conclusion** thig gu co-dhùnadh *m*, **~ together** thig còmhla, **the bus hasn't ~** tha am bus gun tighinn, **~ out of retirement** thig air ais bho chluaineas *m*, **~ to my arms!** thig nam chom *m*/nam achlais *f*!, **~ to be** thig gu bith, **~ upon** thig air, tachair *vi* air, buail *vi* air, tuit *vi* air, **we came upon an abandoned boat** thachair sinn air bàta trèigte, **she came round/came to** (*ie recovered consciousness*) thainig i thuice fhèin; **2** (*other misc idioms & exprs*), (*book &c*) **~ out** nochd *vi* (an clò *m*), **in the weeks to ~** anns na seachdainnean *fpl* (a tha) ri teachd, **~ along/~ on** (**with me** *understood*), *also* **~ here**, tiugainn, trobhad (*pl* trobhadaibh) *imper*, (*expr mild protest*) **~**, **~!** *or* **~ on now!** *excl* ud, ud!, **~ back** till *vi*, **coming (back) home** a' tilleadh dhachaigh, **~ close** dlùthaich *vi* (**to** ri), **we were ~ing close to the sea** bha sinn a' dlùthachadh ris a' mhuir *mf*, **~ down** teirinn & teàrn *vti*, **he came down from the pulpit** theirinn e às a' chùbaid *f*, **coming down the hillside** teàrnadh a' bhruthaich *mf*, **~ in useful/handy** dèan feum *m*, **scissors would ~ in useful/handy just now** dhèanadh siosar *mf* feum an-dràsta, **~ about** thachair *vi*,

that's how it came about 's ann mar sin a thachair, **the tide came in** lìon am muir, thàinig an làn *m* (a-steach)

comedian *n* cleasaiche *m*

comedy *n* **1** (*abstr*) àbhachd *f invar*; **2** (*film, play &c*) cleas-chluich *f*

comely *adj* ceanalta

comfort *n* **1** (*spiritual, emotional & phys*) cofhurtachd *f invar*; **2** (*~ for pain, worry &c*) furtachd *f invar* (**for** air), **~ for his anguish** furtachd air a dhòrainn *f*

comfort *v* furtaich *vi* (*with prep* air), cofhurtaich *vt*, **we will ~ you** furtaichidh sinn oirbh

comfortable *adj* **1** (*phys*) cofhurtail, seasgair; **2** (*fin*) **~, comfortably off** airgeadach, math dheth

comforting *adj* (*spiritually, emotionally*) sòlasach

comic *n* (*ie a comedian*) cleasaiche *m*

comic, comical *adj* èibhinn, (*less usu*) àbhachdach

coming *n* teachd *m invar*, **the ~ of Spring** teachd an Earraich

comma *n* cromag *f*, **inverted ~s** cromagan turrach

command *n* **1** (*abstr*) ceannas (**of, over** air) *m*; **2** (*an instruction &c*) òrdugh *m*, reachd *m invar*

command *v* **1** (*order, tell*) thoir òrdugh *m* (*with prep* do), **they ~ed me to shut the gates** thug iad òrdugh dhomh na geataichean *mpl* a dhùnadh; **2** (*be in command of*) bi *vi irreg* an ceann (*with gen*), **the officer ~ing the regiment** an t-oifigeach (a tha/bha &c) an ceann na rèiseamaid(e)

commander *n* ceannard *m*, **~-in-chief** àrd-cheannard *m*

commanding *adj* (*personality &c*) ceannsalach

commemorate *v* cuimhnich *vt*

commemoration *n* **1** (*abstr*) cuimhne *f invar*, **service of ~** seirbheis *f* chuimhne, seirbheis cuimhneachaidh *m gen*; **2** (*phys monument &c*) cuimhneachan *m*

commemorative *adj* cuimhneachaidh *gen of* cuimhneachadh *m used adjectivally, in expr* **~ medal** bonn-cuimhneachaidh *m*

commence *v* tòisich *vti* (*with preps* air & ri), **~ work** tòisich air an obair *f*, **~ ploughing** tòisich a' treabhadh, tòisich ri treabhadh, tòisich air/ris an treabhadh *m*, **the battle ~d** thòisich am blàr

commencement *n* toiseachadh *m*

comment *v* thoir (seachad) beachd *m* (**on** air)

commerce *n* ceannachd *f invar*, ceannach *m*, malairt *f*

commercial *adj* **1** malairteach, **~ sponsorship** goistidheachd *f invar* mhalairteach; **2** *in expr* **~ traveller** fear-reic *m* siubhail, reiceadair-siubhail *m*

commercial *n* (*on TV &c*) sanas-reic *m*

commission *n* **1** (*official task &c*) teachdaireachd *f invar*; **2** (*body of officials &c*) coimisean *m*, **the European Commission** An Coimisean Eòrpach, Coimisean na Roinn Eòrpa; **3** (*payment*) tuarastal *m*; **4** (*in armed services*) barantas *m* (oifigich *m gen*); **5** (*for work of art &c*) òrdugh *m*

commission *v* (*work of art &c*) òrdaich *vt*

commit *v* **1** (*carry out*) dèan *vt*, gnìomhaich *vt*, ~ **a crime** dèan eucoir *f*; **2** *in exprs* ~ **suicide** cuir às dha (*&c*) fhèin/fhìn, cuir làmh *f* na (*&c*) b(h)eatha *f*, **we will ~ suicide** cuiridh sinn às dhuinn fhìn, cuiridh sinn làmh nar beatha, ~ **to prison** cuir *vt* an làimh (*dat of* làmh *f*), cuir *vt* don phrìosan *m*, ~ **to memory** meòmhraich & meamhraich *vt*, cùm *vt* air mheomhair *f*

commitment *n* dealas *m* (**to** airson)

committee *n* comataidh *f*, **the Housing** ~ Comataidh an Taigheadais

common *adj* **1** coitcheann, ~ **stair** staidhre *f* choitcheann, **the ~ Market** am Margadh Coitcheann, a' Mhargaidh Choitcheann; **2** (*crofting*) **the ~ grazing** am monadh *m*; **3** *in expr* ~ **sense** toinisg *f*, ciall *f*; **4** (*frequently met with*) cumanta, **a ~ occurence** tachartas cumanta; **5** (*uncouth &c*) mì-mhodhail, garbh, (*stronger*) borb

common *n* **1** (*common land*) coitcheann *m invar*, (*in crofting context: common grazings*) am monadh; **2** *in expr* **the House of Commons** Taigh *m* nan Cumantan; **3** *in expr* **they haven't much in ~** chan eil mòran aca an cumantas *m*

commonly *adv* gu tric, an cumantas *m*, am bitheantas *m*

commonwealth *n*, **the (British) Commonwealth** An Co-fhlaitheas *m*

commotion *n* ùpraid *f*

communal *adj* coitcheann, ~ **facilities** goireasan *mpl* coitcheann

commune *n* co-chomann *m*

communicant *n* (*relig*) comanaiche *m*

communicate *v* **1** com-pàirtich *vt*, ~ **information** com-pàirtich fios *m*, cuir fios (**to** gu); **2** (*be in touch*) *in expr* **we still ~ with them** bidh sinn a' cur ar cuid naidheachdan *fpl* thuca fhathast, tha muinntireachd *f invar* eadarainn fhathast; **3** (*express, cause to understand*) cuir *vt* an cèill (*dat of* ciall *f*), **I cannot ~ my feelings to you** chan urrainn dhomh m' fhaireachdainnean *fpl* a chur an cèill dhut; **4** (*relig: receive communion*) comanaich *vi*

communication *n* **1** (*abstr*) conaltradh *m*, eadar-theachdaireachd *f invar*, **means of ~**, *also* ~ **media** meadhanan *mpl* conaltraidh *gen*, ~ **skills** sgilean *mpl* conaltraidh *gen*, ~ **centre** ionad *m* eadar-theachdaireachd; **2** (*con: an individual message*) fios *m*, teachdaireachd *f*, **we received your ~** fhuair sinn ur teachdaireachd; **3** (*the act of communicating*) com-pàirteachadh *m*, (*in a social context*) muinntearachd *f invar*,

Communion *n* **1** (*relig*) comanachadh *m*; **2** (*Presbyterianism: the ~ season, the sequence of services including the sacrament of ~*) òrdaighean *mpl*

communism *n* co-mhaoineas *m*

communist *n* & *adj* co-mhaoineach *m*

community *n* **1** (*a district & its people*) coimhearsnachd *f*; **2** (*commune &c*) comann *m*, co-chomann *m*

compact *adj* **1** (*dense &c*) dlùth, dòmhail & dùmhail; **2** (*small, miniature*) mion, meanbh, (*IT*) ~ **disc** meanbh-chlàr *m*

compact *n* (*agreement*) co-chòrdadh *m*, cùmhnant *m*

compact *v* teannaich *vti*

companion *n* companach *m*

companionable *adj* cèilidheach, cuideachdail

companionship *n* companas *m*

company *n* 1 (*commerce &c*) companaidh *mf*, **international companies** companaidhean eadar-nàiseanta; 2 (*social*) cuideachd *f invar*, comann *m*, **in my ~** nam chuideachd, **I like the ~ of young people** is toigh leam cuideachd/comann na h-òigridh, *in expr* **fond of** ~ cuideachdail, cèilidheach; 3 (*of troops &c*) còmhlan *m*, **~ of soldiers** còmhlan shaighdearan *mpl gen*

comparable *adj* coimeasach

comparative *adj* (*gram*) coimeasach, **~ adjective** buadhair coimeasach

compare *v* dèan coimeas *m* (*with prep* eadar), coltaich *vt* (**to** ri), samhlaich *vt* (**to** ri), **~ X and Y** dèan coimeas eadar X is Y, **~ X to Y** coltaich/ samhlaich X ri Y

compared *adj & past part*, **~ to** an coimeas, an taca, (**with** ri), **she's clever ~ to her brother** tha i comasach an coimeas/an taca ri a bràthair *m*

comparison *n* 1 coimeas *f* (**between** eadar); 2 *in expr* **in ~ to** an coimeas ri, an taca ri, **she's clever in ~ to her brother** tha i comasach an coimeas/an taca ri a bràthair; 3 *in expr* (*gram*) **adjective of** ~ buadhair coimeasach

compass *n* combaist *f*

compassion *n* iochd *f invar*, truas *m*, truacantas *m*, **take ~** gabh truas (**on** de), **won't you take ~ on me?** nach gabh thu truas dhìom?

compassionate *adj* 1 (*merciful*) iochdmhor, truacanta; 2 (*sympathetic*) co-fhulangach, co-mhothachail

compatibility *n* co-fhreagarrachd *f invar*, (*esp of people*) co-chòrdalachd *f invar*

compatible *adj* co-fhreagarrach, freagarrach (**with** do *or* air), **the wheel and the axle were not ~** cha robh a' chuibhle agus an aiseal *f* co-fhreagarrach, **Iain and Mòrag were very ~** bha Iain agus Mòrag glè fhreagarrach dha chèile/air a chèile

compel *v* thoir *vi* air, co-èignich *vt*, **she ~led me to leave** thug i orm falbh, **he'll ~ me to do it eventually** bheir e orm a dhèanamh aig a' cheann thall

compensate *v* (*fin*) dìol *vt*, cuidhtich *vi*

compensation *n* (*fin*) dìoladh *m*, cuidhteachadh *m*

compère *n* (*at ceilidh &c*) fear *m* an taighe *m*

competence *n* comas *m*, **beyond his ~** thar a chomais (*gen*)

competent *adj* comasach

competition *n* 1 (*for prizes, awards &c*) co-fharpais *f*, farpais *f*, **the Mod ~s** co-fharpaisean a' Mhòid; 2 (*rivalry between individuals, firms, nations &c*) còmhstri *f*

competitive *adj* 1 (*in character*) farpaiseach, strìtheil; 2 (*in business &c*) farpaiseach, **a ~ tender** tairgse fharpaiseach, *also* tairgse air deagh phrìs *f*

competitor *n* **1** (*for prizes, awards &c*) co-fharpaiseach *m*, farpaiseach; **2** (*rival in business &c*) còmhstritheach *m*

compilation *n* co-chruinneachadh *m*

complain *v* **1** gearain *vi*, (*less usu*) talaich *v*, (**about** air, **to** ri), ~ **to the manager** gearain ris a' mhanaidsear *m*; **2** *in expr* **apt to** ~ gearanach

complaining *adj* gearanach

complaint *n* **1** (*grumble &c*) gearan *m*; **2** (*official, legal* ~) casaid *f*, **make/bring a** ~ dèan casaid (**against** air); **3** (*ailment*) gearan *m*, galar *m*, tinneas *m*

complete *adj* **1** (*entire, intact*) iomlan, slàn, gu lèir *adv*, **a** ~ **Pictish standing stone** tursa Cruithneach iomlan/slàn, **a** ~ **month** mìos *m* gu lèir; **2** (*finished*) deiseil, ullamh, **the project is** ~ tha am pròiseict ullamh; **3** (*utter*) dearg (*precedes the noun*), gu chùl *m*, **a** ~ **fool** dearg amadan *m*, amadan gu chùl

complete *v* cuir crìoch *f* (*with prep* air), thoir *vt* gu buil *f*, thoir *vt* gu crìch (*dat of* crìoch *f*), thoir *vt* gu ceann *m*, **she ~ed her novel** chuir i crìoch air an nobhail *f* aice, **we ~d the project** thug sinn am pròiseict gu buil/gu crìch/gu ceann

completed *adj & past part* crìochnaichte

completely *adv* **1** (gu) buileach, gu h-iomlan, gu tur, **I'm** ~ **certain** tha mi buileach cinnteach, *also* tha mi làn-chinnteach, **it was** ~ **destroyed** chaidh a sgrios gu h-iomlan/gu tur, **the two things are** ~ **different** tha an dà rud gu tur eadar-dhealaichte; **2** (*more fam*) dearg, **she's** ~ **spoilt** tha i air a dearg mhilleadh, ~ **naked** dearg rùisgte; **3** *in expr* ~ **opposed to,** ~ **against** calg-dhìreach an aghaidh (*with gen*), **I'm** ~ **against hunting** tha mi calg-dhìreach an aghaidh sealgaireachd *f invar*

complex *adj* **1** (*in structure &c*) iomadh-fhillte; **2** (*hard to understand*) deacair, amalach

complex *n* (*ie group of buildings & facilities*) ionad *m*, **sports** ~ ionad spòrs

complexion *n* **1** (*of person's features*) dreach *m*, tuar *m*; **2** (*appearance, significance, interpretation*) coltas *m*, cruth *m*, **that puts a different** ~ **on the matter** tha sin a' cur coltais/cruth eile air a' chùis *f*

complexity *n* **1** (*in structure &c*) iomadh-fhillteachd *f invar*; **2** (*difficulty of understanding*) deacaireachd *f invar*; **3** (*complication, problem*) duilgheadas *m*, **one of the complexities of this situation** fear de dhuilgheadasan an t-suidheachaidh *m* seo ·

compliance *n* gèilleadh *m*

compliant *adj* umha(i)l, macanta, strìochdach

complicated *adj* **1** (*in structure &c*) iomadh-fhillte; **2** (*hard to understand, solve*) deacair, amalach

compliment *n* **1** moladh *m*, **I paid him a** ~ rinn mi moladh air; **2** (*in corres*) **with ~s** le deagh dhùrachd *m*

compliment *v* dèan moladh *m* (*with prep* air), **she ~ed me on my Gaelic** rinn i moladh air (cho math 's a bha) mo chuid *f* Gàidhlig

complimentary *adj* **1** luaidheach, molaidh (*gen of* moladh *m*, *used* *adjectivally*), ~ **words** briathran *mpl* luaidheach/molaidh; **2** (*free*) an asgaidh, **a ~ ticket** ticead *f* an asgaidh

comply *v* **1** (*submit &c*) gèill *vi* (**with** do); **2** (*regulations, agreements &c*) cùm *vi* (**with** ri)

comportment *n* giùlan *m*, iomchar *m*, dol-a-mach *m*

compose *v* **1** (*write &c*) dèan *vt* (suas), cuir *vt* ri chèile, **I ~d some poetry** rinn mi bàrdachd *f invar*, **a song ~d by X** òran *m* air a chur ri chèile le X **2** (*regain composure*) socraich *vt*, **she had no time to ~ herself** cha robh ùine *f*/tìde *f* aice i fhèin a shocrachadh

composed *adj & past part* **1** (*written &c*) dèanta; **2** (*calmed &c*) socraichte

composer *n* ùghdar *m*, sgrìobhadair *m*, (*mus*) ceòl-sgrìobhaiche *m*

compound *adj* fillte, ~ **interest** riadh fillte

comprehend *v* **1** (*facts &c*) tuig *vti*; **2** (*esp people, behaviour: less usu*) fidir *vt*

comprehension *n* tuigse *f invar*

compress *v* teannaich *vt*

compressed *adj & past part* teannaichte

compression *n* teannachadh *m*

compromise *n* co-rèiteachadh *m*, còrdadh *m*

compulsion *n* co-èigneachadh *m*

compulsive *adj, in expr* **he was a ~ gambler** bha e na thràill *m* do cheàrrachas *m*, cha b' urrainn dha cèarrachas a sheachnadh

compulsory *adj* èigneachail, do-sheachainte

computation *n* tomhas *m*, àireamhachd *f invar*

compute *v* (*distance, speed &c*) tomhais *vt*

computer *n* coimpiutair *m*, *in expr* ~ **terminal** ceann-obrach *m*

computerisation *n* coimpiutaireachadh *m*

computing *n* coimpiutaireachd *f invar*

comrade *n* companach *m*

con *prefix* co-, *eg* **concord** co-chòrdadh *m*

conceal *v* cuir *vt* am falach *m*, falaich *vt*, ceil *vt* (**from** air), **they ~ed the ammunition** chuir iad an connadh-làmhaich am falach, ~ **it from her** ceil oirre e

concealed *adj & past part* am falach, falaichte

concealment *n* ceileadh *m*, ceiltinn *f invar*, falach *m*, cleith *f*

concede *v* **1** (*relinquish &c*) gèill *vi*; **2** (*agree, recognise*) aidich *vi*, **I ~ that I was wrong** tha mi ag aideachadh gun robh mi ceàrr

conceit *n* fèin-mholadh *m*, mòr-chùis *f*, leòm *f*

conceited *adj* mòrchuiseach, mòr às (*&c*) fhèin/fhìn

conceive *v* **1** (*become pregnant*) gin *vti*; **2** (*think up &c*) innlich *vt*, ~ **a trick/a stratagem** innlich cuilbheart *f*

concentric *adj* co-mheadhanach

concept *n* bun-bheachd *m*

conception *n* **1** (*gynaecology &c*) gineamhainn *m invar*; **2** (*of plan, invention &c*) innleachadh *m*; **3** (*understanding*) tuigse *f*, **you have no ~ of what I mean** chan eil tuigse sam bith agad dè a tha mi a' ciallachadh

concern *n* **1** (*interest, attention*) aire *m*, for *m* invar, (**for** air), **with ~ for nothing but his own affairs** gun aire/gun for aige ach air a ghnothaichean *mpl* fhèin; **2** (*worry*) iomagain *f*, dragh *m*, **a cause for ~** adhbhar *m* iomagain/dragha *gen*; **3** (*~ for others*) co-fhulangas *m*, co-mhothachadh *m*; **4** (*business, firm*) gnothach *m*; **5** *in expr* **that's no ~ of yours!** chan e sin do ghnothach-sa!

concern *v* **1** (*affect &c*) buin *vi* (*with preps* do *&* ri), **that doesn't ~ you** chan eil sin a' buntainn dhutsa/riutsa, *or* (*stronger: ie none of your business*) chan e sin do ghnothach-sa *m*; **2** *in expr* **~ oneself** (*ie worry*) gabh uallach *m* (**about** mu); **3** *in expr* **as far as . . . is ~ed**, a thaobh (*with gen*), **as far as the election is ~ed** a thaobh an taghaidh

concerned *adj & past part* **1** (*worried*) *in exprs* **she's ~ about the state of the world** tha uallach *m* oirre mu staid *f* an t-saoghail, **become ~** gabh uallach (**about** mu); **2** (*relevant, involved*) *in expr* **the people ~** na daoine *mpl* ris am buin a' chùis, na daoine a tha an sàs anns a' ghnothach *m*

concerning *prep* **1** (*to do with*) a thaobh (*with gen*), **he has problems ~ money** tha duilgheadasan *mpl* aige a thaobh airgid *m gen*; **2** (*about*) mu dheidhinn (*with gen*), **they're saying dreadful things ~ the minister** tha iad ag ràdh rudan *mpl* uabhasach mu dheidhinn a' mhinisteir, **a rumour ~ing him** fathann *m* mu dheidhinn

concert *n* cuirm-chiùil *f*

concierge *n* dorsair *m*

conciliate *v* (*opposing parties &c*) thoir *vt* gu rèite *f*

conciliation *n* rèiteachadh *m*

conciliator *n* neach-rèiteachaidh (*pl* luchd-rèiteachaidh *m sing coll*)

concise *adj* **1** (*speech &c: to the point*) pongail; **2** (*short*) goirid, **~ dictionary** faclair goirid

conclude *v* **1** (*come to a decision or conclusion*) co-dhùin *vi*; **2** (*as vt: bring to a close*) thoir *vt* gu crìch (*dat of* crìoch *f*), thoir *vt* gu ceann *m*, crìochnaich *vt*

conclusion *n* **1** (*of meeting, train of thought &c*) co-dhùnadh *m*, **come to a ~** thig *vi* gu co-dhùnadh, co-dhùin *vi*; **2** *in expr* **bring to a ~** (*project &c*) thoir *vt* gu buil *f*, (*meeting, event &c*) thoir *vt* gu co-dhùnadh *m*

conclusive *adj* deimhinnte, dearbhte, **~ evidence** fianais dheimhinnte/ dhearbhte

concord *n* co-chòrdadh *m*, **~ between the nations** co-chòrdadh eadar na nàiseanan *mpl*

concrete[1] *adj* saimeant (*gen of* saimeant *m invar*), **~ walls** ballaichean *mpl* saimeant

concrete[2] *adj* **1** (*actual, specific &c*) sònraichte, **a ~ example** eisimpleir shònraichte; **2** (*opposite of abstr*) nitheil

concubine *n* coimhleapach *mf*

condemn *v* **1** (*criticise severely*) cronaich *vt*, **they ~ed our conduct** chronaich iad (gu mòr) ar dol-a-mach *m invar*; **2** (*sentence &c*) dìt *vt*, **~ to death** dìt *vt* gu bàs *m*

condemnation *n* dìteadh *m*

condensation *n* (*vapour*) co-dhlùthachadh *m*

condense *v* **1** (*abridge: book &c*) giorraich *vt*; **2** (*vapour*) co-dhlùthaich *vti*

condition *n* **1** (*state*) cor *m*, staid *f*, **the pitiful ~ of the refugees** cor truagh nam fògarrach; **2** (*stipulation*) cor *m*, cumha *m*, cùmhnant *m*, **on ~ that you marry me** air chor/air chumha 's gum pòs thu mi, **on this ~** air a' chùmhnant seo

conditional *adj* **1** (*gram*) cumhach, **the ~ tense** an tràth cumhach *m*; **2** (*dependent*) an crochadh (**on** air), a rèir (*with gen*), **the price is ~ on the colour** tha a' phrìs an crochadh air an dath *m* (a th' air &c), tha a' phrìs a rèir an datha

condom *n* casgan *m*

conduct *n* giùlan *m*, dol-a-mach *m invar*, **I don't think much of your ~ is** beag orm an dhol-a-mach agad

conduct *v* **1** (*~ a legal case, an argument*) tagair *vt*; **2** (*~ tourists &c*) treòraich; **3** (*~ orchestra*) stiùir *vti*; **4** (*behave*) *in expr* **~ oneself** giùlain *vt* e/i (*&c*) fhèin/fhìn, **I'm ~ing myself very well indeed!** tha mi gam ghiùlan fhìn uabhasach math!; **5** (*carry out*) cuir *vt* an gnìomh *m*, **~ an investigation** cuir sgrùdadh *m* an gnìomh; **6** (*~ elec current*) giùlain *vt*

conductor *n* **1** (*of orchestra*) stiùireadair *m*; **2** (*of elec current &c*) stuth-giùlain *m*

cone *n* **1** (*geometry &c*) còn *m*; **2 pine/fir ~** durcan *m*

confederation *n* (*of countries*) co-fhlaitheas *m*

conference *n* co-labhairt *f invar*, còmhdhail *f*

confess *v* **1** (*to misdeed &c*) aidich *vti*; **2** (*relig*) dèan faoisid *f*, faoisidich *vti*

confession *n* **1** (*relig*) faoisid *f*, **make ~** dèan faoisid; **2** (*legal &c*) aideachadh *m*

confessor *n* (*relig*) sagart-faoisid *m*

confidant(e) *n* fear-rùin *m*, (*pl* luchd-rùin *m sing coll*), bean-rùin *f*

confide *v* leig a (*&c*) rùn *m* (**in ri**), **don't ~ in them** na leig do rùn riutha

confidence *n* **1** (*trust &c*) earbsa *f invar* (**in** ann, às), **they have no ~ in you** chan eil earbsa aca annaibh/asaibh; **2** (*~ in oneself*) misneachd *f invar*, fèin-mhisneachd *f invar*, (*excessive*) fèin-spèis *f*, fèin-mholadh *m*; **3** (*secret &c*) rùn *m*, **let me into your ~** leig do rùn rium.

confident *adj* **1** (*assured*) misneachail, **self-~** fèin-mhisneachail; **2** (*hopeful*) dòchasach, làn dòchais *m gen*, **I'm ~ about the future** tha mi dòchasach mun àm a tha ri teachd; **3** (*certain*) cinnteach, **are you ~ she'll come?** a bheil thu cinnteach gun tig i?

confidential *adj* dìomhair

confidentiality *n* dìomhaireachd *f invar*

confirm *v* **1** (*prove: truths, principles, theories &c*) dearbh *vt*; **2** (*assert, strengthen: faith &c*) daingnich *vt*, **she ~ed her faith by becoming a nun** dhaingnich i a creideamh *m* le a bhith a' dol na caillich-dhuibh

conflict *n* còmhrag *f*, còmhstri *f*, strì *f*

confluence *n* comar *m*, inbhir *m*

confront *v* (*oppose, face up to*) seas *vi* (*with prep* ri), (*esp phys*) seas *vi* mu choinneimh (*with gen*), **we ~ed the committee** sheas sinn ris a' chomataidh *f*, **she ~ed the thief** sheas i mu choinneimh a' mheirlich

confuse *v* **1** (*mix up*) measgaich *vt* suas, **~ different things** measgaich suas rudan *mpl* eadar-dhealaichte; **2** (*puzzle, disorentiate*) breislich *vt*, cuir *vt* am breisleach *m*, cuir *vt* troimh-a-chèile, **you're confusing me now** tha thu gam bhreisleachadh/gam chur troimh-a-chèile a-nis

confusion *n* **1** (*of different things, one for the other*) measgachadh *m* suas; **2** (*in crowds: disturbance &c*) ùpraid *f*; **3** (*of things, in situations, places &c: disorder, disarray*) in expr **in ~** troimh-a-chèile, thar a chèile, **the entire house was in ~** bha an taigh air fad troimh-a-chèile/thar a chèile; **4** (*mental ~*) breisleach *m*

congenial *adj* taitneach, **I find that ~** is taitneach leam sin, *also* tha sin a' còrdadh rium

congested *adj* (*places, buildings, gatherings &c*) dòmhail & dùmhail, loma-làn

congestion *n* dùmhlachd *f invar*

congratulate *v* cuir meal-a-naidheachd (*with prep* air), **I ~d them after the wedding** chuir mi meal-a-naidheachd orra an dèidh na bainnse

congratulations *excl* meal do naidheachd! *f* (*lit 'enjoy your news!'*)

congregate *v* (*esp of people*) tionail *vi*, thig *vi* còmhla, cruinnich *vi*

congregation *n* coitheanal *m*

congress *n* **1** (*an organisation & its meetings*) còmhdhail *f*, **Trades Union Congress** Còmhdhail nan Aonaidhean *mpl* Ciùird (*gen of* cèard *or* ceàrd *m*); **2** (*sexual ~*) co-ghineadh *m*, cuplachadh *m*

conical *adj* cònach, air chumadh *m* còn *m*

coniferous *adj* cònach

conjectural *adj* tuaireamach, baralach

conjecture *n* tuaiream *f*, tuairmeas *m*

conjecture *v* thoir tuairmeas, beachdaich *vi*, (**about** air)

conjunction *n* (*gram*) naisgear *m*

conjurer *n* cleasaiche *m*, caisreabhaiche *m*

conjuring *n* cleasachd *f invar*, caisreabhachd *f invar*

connect *v* ceangail *vt* (**to** ri), (**~ together**) co-cheangail *vt*

connected *adj & past part* **1** (*abstr & con*) ceangailte, co-cheangailte, **global warming and the climate are ~ (to one another)** tha blàthachadh *m* na cruinne is a' chlìomaid co-cheangailte (ri chèile); **2** (*associated*) **~ with** an lùib (*dat of* lùb *f*), an cois (*dat of* cas), (*both with gen*), **theft and the loss ~ with it** goid *f* agus an call a tha na lùib/na cois

connection *n* **1** (*abstr & con*) ceangal *m*, co-cheangal *m*; **2** (*association, link*) ceangal *m*, gnothach *m* (**with** ri), **I have no ~ with that firm** chan eil ceangal sam bith/gnothach sam bith agam ris a' chompanaidh *mf* sin; **3** (*esp family ~*) buinteanas *m*, **I have ~s with Skye** tha buinteanas agam ris an Eilean *m* Sgitheanach; **4** *in expr* **in ~ with** a thaobh (*with* *gen*), **he has problems in ~ with money** tha duilgheadasan *mpl* aige a thaobh airgid *m*

conquer *v* ceannsaich *vt*, thoir buaidh *f* (*with prep* air)

conqueror *n* ceannsaiche *m*

conquest *n* ceannsachadh *m*

conscience *n* cogais *f*, **my ~ was tormenting me** bha mo chogais gam shàrachadh

conscientious *adj* dìcheallach

conscientiousness *n* dìcheall *m*, dìcheallachd *f invar*

conscious *adj* **1** (*not unconscious, in possession of one's faculties*) fiosrach; **2** (*aware, cognisant*) fiosrach, mothachail, (**of** air), **~ of the danger** fiosrach/mothachail air a' chunnart *m*, *in expr* **be ~ of** (*ie perceive*) mothaich *vt* (*with prep* do), **we were ~ of the movement of the boat** mhothaich sinn do ghluasad *m* a' bhàta

consciousness *n* **1** (*possession of one's faculties*) fiosrachd *f invar*; **2** (*awareness*) mothachadh *m* (**of** air)

consecrate *v* coisrig *vt* (**to** do *or* gu)

consecrated *adj & past part* coisrigte (**to** do *or* gu), **~ (communion) wafer** abhlan coisrigte

consecration *n* coisrigeadh *m* (**to** do *or* gu)

consecutive *adj* an ceann *m* a chèile, an sreath *mf* a chèile, co-leanailteach

consensus *m* co-aontachd *f*

consent *n* aonta(dh) *m*, cead *m*, **get your parents' ~** faigh aonta/cead do phàrantan *mpl gen*

consent *v* aontaich *vti*, co-aontaich *vti*, (**to** ri)

consequence *n* (*of action &c*) toradh *m*, buaidh *f*, buil *f*, **the ~(s) of your behaviour** toradh do dhol-a-mach *m invar*, **as a ~ of that** mar thoradh air sin

conservancy *n* glèidhteachas *m*, **nature ~** glèidhteachas nàdair *m gen*

conservation *n* glèidhteachas *m*

conservationist *n* neach-glèidhteachais (*pl* luchd-glèidhteachais *m sing coll*)

conservative *adj* glèidhteach

Conservative *adj* (*pol*) Tòraidheach

Conservative *n* (*pol*) Tòraidh *m*

conserve *v* glèidh *vt*, **they're being ~d in a museum** tha iad gan gleidheadh ann an taigh-tasgaidh *m*

conserved *adj & past part* glèidhte

consider *v* **1** (*think, be of the opinion*) saoil *vi*, creid *vi*, **I ~ him to be an idiot** saoilidh mi gur e bumailear *m* a th' ann (dheth); **2** (*think over*) beachdaich *vi*, gabh beachd *m*, smaoin(t)ich *vi*, (*more fam*) cnuasaich *vi*, (*all with prep* air), **will you ~ it?** an smaoin(t)ich thu air?, am beachdaich thu air?, **~ing the events of the day** a' smaoin(t)eachadh air tachartasan *mpl* an latha; **3** (*observe, contemplate*) beachdaich *vt* (*with prep* air), **~ the stars** beachdaich air na reultan *fpl*

consideration *n* **1** (*~ for others*) co-fhulangas *m*; **2** (*thinking over*) beachdachadh *m* (**of** air); **3** *in expr* **take into** ~ cuir *vt* san àireimh *f*, **we'll take the boy's age into** ~ cuiridh sinn san àireimh aois *f* a' ghille; **4** (*fee &c*) tuarastal *m*, duais *f*

consistent *adj* **1** (*unvarying*) seasmhach, neo-chaochlaideach; **2** (*tallying with*) co-chòrdail (**with** ri), **it's** ~ **with what he said** tha e co-chòrdail ris na thubhairt e

consolation *n* furtachd *f invar*, cofhurtachd *f invar*, ~ **for his anguish** furtachd air a dhòrainn *f*

console *v* (*after pain, worry &c*) furtaich *vi* (*with prep* air), cofhurtaich *vt*, **we will** ~ **you** furtaichidh sinn oirbh

consolidate *v* (*structure, building, situation &c*) co-dhaingnich *vt*

consonant *n* (*lang*) co-fhoghar *m*, consan *m*, cònnrag *f*

conspicuous *adj* faicsinneach, follaiseach, suaicheanta

conspicuousness *n* faicsinneachd *f invar*

conspiracy *n* (*plot &c*) co-fheall *f*, cuilbheart *f*

conspire *v* dèan co-fheall *f*, innlich cuilbheart *f*, (**against** an aghaidh *with gen*)

constable *n*, (*crofting, police*) constabal *m*

constancy *n* **1** (*durability &c*) maireannachd *f invar*, seasmhachd *f invar*; **2** (*loyalty*) dìlseachd *f invar*, seasmhachd *f invar*

constant *adj* **1** (*lasting*) buan, maireannach, seasmhach; **2** (*unchanging*) neo-atharrachail; **3** (*loyal*) dìleas, seasmhach, **a** ~ **friend** caraid *m* dìleas; **4** (*ceaseless*) gun sgur *adv*, ~ **bickering** connsachadh *m* gun sgur

constantly *adv* gun sgur, daonnan, **they're** ~ **on at me** tha iad an sàs annam gun sgur

constellation *n* reul-bhad *m*

constituency *n* (*pol*) roinn *f* taghaidh *m gen*, roinn-phàrlamaid *f*

constituent *n* **1** (*a part*) pàirt *mf*, earrann *f*; **2** (*pol*) neach-taghaidh (*pl* luchd-taghaidh *m sing coll*)

constitution *n* **1** (*phys, of person*) dèanamh *m*; **2** (*of country, organisation &c*) bun-reachd *m invar*, bonn-stèidh *f*

constitutional *adj* **1** (*to do with a country's &c constitution*) bun-reachdail, ~ **law** lagh bun-reachdail; **2** (*in accordance with the constitution*) co-chòrdail ris a' bhun-reachd *f invar*, **the act was not** ~ bha/chaidh an achd *f* an aghaidh a' bhun-reachd

constrict *v* teannaich *vt*, fàisg *vt*, tachd *vt*

constriction *n* teannachadh *m*

construct *v* **1** cum *vt*, dealbh *vt*, dèan *vt*; **2** (*building &c*) tog *vt*

consul *n* consal *m*

consular *adj* consalach

consult *v* sìr beachd *m* (*with gen*), gabh comhairle *f* (*with prep* o/bho), **he** ~**ed the committee** shìr e beachd na comataidh

consultation *n* co-chomhairle *f*, sìreadh *m* beachd *m* (*with prep* o/bho) gabhal *m* comhairle *f* (*with gen*)

consume *v* caith *vt*

consumer *n* (*esp of goods*) neach-caitheimh (*pl* luchd-caitheimh *m sing coll*), caitheadair *m*, (*esp of services, amenities &c*) neach-cleachdaidh *m* (*pl* luchd-cleachdaidh *m sing coll*)

consumption *n* **1** (*business, fin &c*) caitheamh *f*; **2** (*the illness: used with the art*) a' chaitheamh *f*

contact *n* **1** (*phys*) beantainn *m*, suathadh *m*, (**with** ri), ~ **lens** lionsa-suathaidh *f*; **2** *in expr* **in (physical)** ~ **with** an taice ri; **3** (*social relations, corres &c*) muinntearreachd *f invar*, conaltradh *m*, **we're still in** ~ **with them** tha muinntireachd eadarainn fhathast

contact *v* cuir fios *m* (*with prep* gu), ~ **the bank** cuir fios chun a' bhanca *m*

contain *v* **1** (*have capacity for*) gabh *vt*, **it can** ~ **a gallon** gabhaidh e galan *m*; **2** (*have inside*) **that cage** ~**s a lion** tha leòmhann *m* sa chèidse *f* sin

contaminate *v* (*environment &c*) truaill *vt*

contamination *n* truailleadh *m*

contemplate *v* **1** (*mentally*) meòmhraich & meamhraich *vi*, (*more fam*) cnuas & cnuasaich *vi*, (*all with prep* air); **2** (*mentally &/or visually*) beachdaich *vt* (*with prep* air), ~ **the stars** beachdaich air na reultan *fpl*

contemporary *adj* **1** (*occurring at the same period*) co-aimsireil; **2** (*modern &c*) an là *m* (*gen sing*) an-diugh, ~ **clothes/customs** aodach *m sing coll*/ dòighean *fpl* an là an-diugh

contemporary *n* co-aois *m*, co-aoiseach *m*, **A and B were contemporaries** bha A agus B nan co-aoisean/nan co-aoiseachan

contempt *n* tàir *f*, tarcais *f*, dìmeas *m*, (**of, towards** air)

contemptible *adj* tàireil, suarach

contemptuous *adj* tarcaiseach, tailceasach

content *n* (*of book, argument &c*) susbaint *f*, brìgh *f invar*

content *adj* toileach, sona, (*stronger*) riaraichte, toilichte

content, contentment *n* toileachas *m*, toil-inntinn *f*, toileachas-inntinn *m*

content *v* toilich *vt*, riaraich *vt*

contented *adj* toileach, sona

contention *n* connspaid *f*

contentious *adj* connspaideach

contentment *n see* **content** *n above*

contents *n*, **1** na tha/bha ann, na tha/bha am broinn (*with gen*), **the** ~ **of the chest** na tha/bha sa chiste *f*, na tha/bha am broinn *f* na ciste; **2** (*list of* ~, *of book &c*) clàr-innse *m*; **3** (*abstr, intellectual* ~: *matter, substance of book &c*) susbaint *f invar*, brìgh *f invar*

contest *n* **1** strì *f invar*, (*esp in games &c*) farpais *f*

contestant *n* farpaiseach *m*

continent *n* **1** (*general*) roinn *f*, mòr-roinn *f*, mòr-thìr *f*, **the** ~ **of Europe** (An) Roinn-Eòrpa; **2** (*usu from a more local point of view*) tìr-mòr *m*, **on the** ~ (*ie Europe from the perspective of the British Isles*) air tìr-mòr (na h-)Eòrpa *f invar*

continental *adj* **1** mòr-roinneach, mòr-thìreach; **2** (*European, from the perspective of the British Isles*) Eòrpach, na Roinn-Eòrpa, ~ **cheeses** càisean *mfpl* na Roinn-Eòrpa

contingency *n* tuiteamas *m*, ~ **plan** plana *m* tuiteamais *gen*

contingent *adj* tuiteamach

contingent *n* (*troops &c*) buidheann *f*, còmhlan *m*, cuideachd *f*

continual *see* **continuous**

continue *v* **1** lean *vi*, **the bad weather** ~**d** lean an droch aimsir *f*; **2** (*persevere, with task &c*) lean *vi* (*with prep* air), cùm *vi* a' dol, **she ~d, (even) though she was tired** lean i oirre/chùm i a' dol, ged a bha i sgìth, ~**!** lean ort!, cùm ort!

continuity *n* leantalachd *f invar*, leanailteachd *f invar*

continuous, continual *adj* leanailteach, leantainneach, gun sgur *m*, ~ **rain** uisge *m* leanailteach, ~ **stationery/assessment** pàipear *m*/measadh *m* leantainneach, ~ **complaining** gearan *m* gun sgur

contraception, contraceptive *n* casg-gineamhainn *m invar*

contraceptive *adj* casg-gineamhainneach

contract *n* (*legal, official, fin &c*) cunnradh *m*, cùmhnant *m*, ~ **of employment** cunnradh-obrach *m*

contract *v* (*ie shrink &c*) teannaich *vti*, lùghdaich *vti*, fàisg *vt*, rach *vi* a-steach

contradict *v* cuir *vi* an aghaidh (*with gen*), **she ~ed them** chuir i nan aghaidh

contraption *n* inneal *m*, innleachd *f*

contrast *v* cuir *vt* an aghaidh (*with gen*), dèan eadar-dhealachadh *m* (*with prep* eadar), ~ **A and B** cuir A an aghaidh B, dèan eadar-dhealachadh eadar A agus B

contribute *v* **1** (*to charity &c*) thoir *vt* seachad (airgead *&c*); **2** (*assist in project &c*) cuidich *vi* (**to** le), cuir *vti* (**to** ri)

contribution *n* **1** (*to charity &c*) dèirc *f*; **2** (*regular payment(s) for specific purpose*) tabhartas *m*, **pension/National Insurance ~s** tabhartasan peinnsein *m*/Àrachais *m* Nàiseanta; **3** (*non-fin:* ~ *to project &c*) cuideachadh *m* (**to** le); **4** (~ *to magazine &c*) cuid-sgrìobhaidh *f*, làmh-sgrìobhainn *mf*

contrive *v* **1** (*invent, improvise: idea or object*) innlich *vt*, (*object*) dealbh *vt*, ~ **an emergency plan** innlich plana-èiginn *m*; **2** (*manage, succeed*) rach *vi* impersonal (*with prep* aig) (**to** air), **he ~d to bring them together** chaidh aige air an toirt còmhla

contrived *adj & past part* (*attitudes, emotions &c: insincere*) fallsa, breugach

contrivance *n* **1** (*abstr*) innleachdadh *m*; **2** (*con: the object contrived*) inneal *m*, innleachd *f*

control *v* **1** (*people, emotions &c: gain/regain control*) ceannsaich *vt*, ~ **a disturbance** ceannsaich aimhreit *f*; **2** (*maintain control*) cùm smachd *m* (*with prep* air)

controversial *adj* connspaideach

controversy *n* connspaid *f*

conundrum *n* tòimhseachan *m*

convene *v* gairm *vt*, **~ a meeting** gairm coinneamh *f*

convenience *n* (*abstr & con*) goireas *m*, **(public) ~s** goireasan

convenient *adj* **1** goireasach, (*more fam*) deiseil, **that will be ~ for you** bidh sin deiseil dhuibh; **2** *in expr* **~ for** faisg air **~ for the shops** faisg air na bùithtean *mfpl*

convent *n* clochar *m*

convention *n* **1** (*gathering*) co-chruinneachadh *m*; **2** (*document, agreement*) cùmhnant *m*, **Human Rights ~** Cùmhnant air Còraichean *fpl* a' Chinne Daonna; **3** (*accepted practice*) gnàth *m*, cleachdadh *m*, **literary ~** gnàth litreachail

convential *adj* gnàthach

converge *v* co-aom *vi*

convergence *n* co-aomadh *m*

conversant *adj* eòlach (**with** air), **~ with computers** eòlach air coimpiutairean *mpl*

conversation *n* (*in more formal context*) agallamh *m*, (*more everyday*) còmhradh *m*, (*fam*) craic *f*, **we had a wee ~** rinn sinn còmhradh beag, bha beagan còmhraidh againn

converse *v* dèan còmhradh, bruidhinn *vi* (**with** ri)

conversion *n* **1** (*esp relig*) iompachadh *m*; **2** (*of dwelling &c*) leasachadh *m*, atharrachadh *m*

convert *n* (*relig*) iompachan *m*, (*Presbyterianism: usu derog, implying a degree of devoutness the speaker considers excessive*) neach *m* fo chùram *m*

convert *v* **1** (*relig*) iompaich *vt*, **she was ~ed** chaidh a h-iompachadh, (*Presbyterianism: usu derog, implying a degree of devoutness the speaker considers excessive*) ghabh i an cùram *m*; **2** (*dwelling &c*) leasaich *vt*, atharraich *vt*

converted *adj & past part* **1** (*relig*) iompaichte, (*Presbyterianism: usu derog, implying a degree of devoutness the speaker considers excessive*) fo chùram *m*; **2** (*dwelling &c*) leasaichte

convey *v* **1** (*transport*) giùlain *vt*, (*less usu*) iomchair *vt*; **2** (*legal*) thoir thairis còraichean *fpl* (taighe *&c*); **3** (*make understood*) cuir *vt* an cèill (*dat of* ciall *f*) (**to do**), **how will I ~ to you the extent of my grief?** ciamar a chuireas mi an cèill dhut meud *m* mo bhròin *m*?

conveyance *n* **1** (*transport*) carbad *m*, seòl-iomchair *m*; **2** (*legal:* (*the process*) toirt *f invar* thairis chòraichean *fpl gen* (taighe *&c*), (*the documents*) còir *f* sgrìobhte (taighe *&c*)

conveyancing *n* toirt *f invar* thairis chòraichean *fpl gen* (taighe *m &c*)

conviction *n* (*legal*) dìteadh *m*

convivial *adj* **1** (*person*) cuideachdail, cèilidheach; **2** (*gathering &c*) làn cridhealais *m*

conviviality *n* cridhealas *m*,

coo *v* (*of doves, pigeons*) dèan dùrdail *f*

cooing *n* dùrdail *f*

cook *n* còcaire *m*, (*female* ~) ban-chòcaire *f*

cooker *n* cucair *m*, **gas/electric** ~ cucair-gas/dealain

cookery, cooking *n* còcaireachd *f invar*, *in expr* **cooking pot** prais *f*

cool *adj* (*lit & fig*) fionnar, fuaraidh, (*esp fig*) leth-fhuar, **she answered ~ly** fhreagair i gu fionnar, **a ~ welcome/reception** fàilte fhionnar/leth-fhuar, *also* fàilte gu math fuar

cool, cool down *v* fionnraich *vti*, fuaraich *vti*

co-operate *v* co-obraich *& co*-oibrich *vi*

co-operation *n* co-obrachadh *m*

co-operative *adj*, co-obrachail

co-operative *n* co-chomann *m*, **crofters'** ~ co-chomann chroitearan *mpl gen*

co-ordinate *v* co-òrdanaich *vt*

copious *adj* lìonmhor, pailt

copper *n* copar *m*

coppersmith *n* ceàrd-copair *m*

copulate *v* co-ghin *vi*, cuplaich *vi*, (*of male*) ~ **with** rach air muin *f invar* (*with gen*), **the bull ~d with the cow** chaidh an tarbh air muin na bà

copulation *n* co-ghineadh *m*, cuplachadh *m*

copy *n* **1** (*exact reproduction*) mac-samhail *m*, lethbhreac *m*; **2** (*one of a number of identical books, newspapers &c*) lethbhreac *m*, **he signed copies of his novel** chuir e ainm *m* ri lethbhreacan den nobhail *f* aige

coquette *n* guanag *f*

coquettish *adj* guanach, *in expr* ~ **girl** guanag *f*

coracle *n* curach *f*

cord *n* còrd *m*

core *n* eitean *m*, buillsgean *m*, **an apple** ~ eitean ubhail *m gen*, **the earth's** ~ eitean na talmhainn

core *adj in expr* (*ed*) **a ~ subject** prìomh chuspair *m*, bun-chuspair *m*

cork *n* àrc *m*, (*esp for bottle*) corcais *f*, **draw/pull a cork** tarraing corcais

corn[1] *n* (*agric*) arbhar *m*

corn[2] *n* (*on foot*) còrn *m*

corner *n* **1** (*esp internal*) cùil *f*, còrnair *m*, **he was sitting in the** ~ bha e na shuidhe sa chùil/sa chòrnair; **2** (*external & internal*) oisean *m & *oisinn *f*, **at the** ~ **of the house** aig oisean an taighe; **3** (*usu external*) uileann *& *uilinn *f*; **4** (*fig: predicament &c*) *in expr* **a tight** ~ cùil-chumhang *f*

Cornish *adj* Còrnach

Cornishman *n* Còrnach *m*

corn-yard *n* iodhlann *f*

coronation *n* crùnadh *m*

corporal *adj* corporra, ~ **punishment** peanas corporra

corporal *n* corpailear *m*

corporate *adj* corporra, **a ~ body** buidheann chorporra

corpse *n* corp (marbh) *m*, (*less usu*) marbhan *m*

corpulent *adj* sultmhor

correct *adj* **1** ceart, **the answers are** ~ tha na freagairtean *fpl* ceart; **2** (*calculations &c*) cruinn; **3** (*idiom*) **if I remember ~ly** mas math mo chuimhne *f*

correct *v* ceartaich *vt*, cuir *vt* ceart

correction *n* ceartachadh *m*

correspond *v* **1** bi *vi irreg* co-fhreagarrach (**to do**), **X ~s to Y** tha X co-fhreagarrach do Y; **2** (*by letter &c*) co-fhreagair *vi*, sgrìobh *vi* gu chèile

correspondence *n* **1** (*abstr*) co-fhreagairt *f*; **2** (*letters &c*) co-fhreagairt *f*, co-sgrìobhadh *m*

correspondent *n* **1** (*by letter &c*) co-sgrìobhadair *m*, co-sgrìobhaiche; **2** (*journalism*) neach-naidheachd (*pl* luchd-naidheachd *m sing coll*), naidheachdair *m*

corresponding *adj* co-fhreagarrach (**to** ri)

corridor *n* trannsa *f*

corrie *n* coire *m*

corroborate *v* co-dhearbh *vt*

corrosion *n* **1** (*abstr*) meirgeadh *m*; **2** (*con*) meirg *f*

corrugate *v* preas

corrugated *adj* preasach

corrupt *adj* **1** (*esp financially, politically &c*) coirbte, ~ **businessman/ politician** fear-gnothaich/fear-poileataics coirbte; **2** (*esp morally, sexually*) truaillte, (*esp sexually*) draosta, drabasda

corrupt *v* coirb *vt*, (*esp morally, sexually*) truaill *vt*

corrupted *adj & past part* coirbte, (*esp morally, sexually*) truaillte

corruption *n* **1** (*abstr*) coirbteachd *f invar*, (*esp moral, sexual*) truaillidheachd *f invar*; **2** (*action of corrupting*) coirbeadh *m*, (*esp morally, sexually*) truailleadh *m*

cosmonaut *n* speuradair *m*, speurair *m*

cost *n* cosgais *f*, cosg *m invar*, **the ~ of living** cosgais bith-beò *m*, **travel ~s** cosgaisean siubhail *m gen*

cost *v* cosg *vt*, **how much does it ~?** dè a chosgas e/i?, dè a tha e/i a' cosg?, *also* (*more fam*) dè na tha e/i?

costly *adj* cosgail, daor

costume *n* (*stage, party &c*) culaidh *f*, **fancy dress** ~ culaidh-choimheach

cosy *adj* seasgair, cofhurtail

cotton *n* cotan *m*, (*more trad*) canach *mf*

couch *n* langasaid *f*

cough *n* casadaich *f invar*, casad *m*

cough *v* dèan casad *m*, casadaich *vi*

coughing *n* casadaich *f invar*

council *n* comhairle *f*, **The Scottish Arts Council** Comhairle Ealain na h-Alba, **regional** ~ comhairle-roinneil, ~ **house** taigh-comhairle, ~ **tax** cìs chomhairle

councillor *n* (*local authority &c*) comhairliche *m*

counsel *n* **1** (*advice*) comhairle *f*, **take/get** ~ gabh comhairle (**from** o/bho); **2** (*legal representative, advocate &c*) neach-tagraidh (*pl* luchd-tagraidh *m sing coll*)

counsellor *n* neach-comhairle (*pl* luchd-comhairle *m sing coll*)

count *v* **1** cunnt *vti*, cunntais *vti*, **~ing sheep** a' cunntadh/a' cunntas chaorach *fpl gen*; **2** (*matter*) cunnt *vi*, **he** (*emph*) **doesn't** ~ chan eil esan a' cunntadh

counter *n* (*shop &c*) cuntair *m*

counter *v* rach *vi* an aghaidh (*with gen*)

country *n* **1** dùthaich *f*, tìr *mf*, (*esp as political entity*) rìoghachd *f*, **foreign countries** dùthchannan/tìrean cèin; **2** (*territory of a given group &c*) dùthaich *f*, **the Mackay** ~ Dùthaich MhicAoidh; **3** (*rural area*) dùthaich *f*, **we lived/were living in the** ~ bha sinn a' fuireach air an dùthaich

county *n* siorrachd *f*, siorramachd *f invar*

couple *n* **1** (*man & wife*) càraid *f*, **childless** ~ càraid gun chlann *f sing coll*, **married** ~ càraid phòsta; **2** (*pair, twosome*) dithis *f* (*usu used of people only*), **they came in ~s** thàinig iad nan dithisean; **3** (*fam: a few, one or two*) *the appropriate n sing followed by* no dhà, **in a** ~ **of days** an ceann là *m* no dhà, **give me a** ~ **of apples** thoir dhomh ubhal *m* no dhà

couple *v* **1** (*connect carriages &c*) co-cheangail *vt*; **2** (*sexually*) cuplaich *vi*

coupling *n* **1** (*carriages &c*) co-cheangal *m*; **2** (*sexually*) cuplachadh *m*, (*of cattle*) dàir *f*

coupon *n* cùpon *m*

courage *n* **1** (*phys*) gaisge *f invar*, gaisgeachd *f invar*, (*sometimes rash* ~) dànadas *m*, braisead *f*; **2** (*esp inner & moral* ~) misneach *f*, misneachd *f invar*, smior *m*

courageous *adj* **1** (*phys*) gaisgeil, (*sometimes rashly*) dàna, bras; **2** (*esp morally*) misneachail

courier *n* teachdaire *m*

course *n* **1** (*academic &c*) cùrsa *m*, **Gaelic ~s** cùrsaichean Gàidhlig, **immersion** ~ cùrsa-bogaidh *m*; **2** (*seafaring &c*) cùrsa *m*, gabhail *mf*, (*less usu*) seòl *m*, **keeping her on** ~ ga cumail air chùrsa, (*fig, fam*) **you knocked me off** ~ chuir thu às mo ghabhail mi; **3** *in expr* (*of time*) **in due** ~ ri tìde; **4** *in expr* **golf** ~ raon *m* goilf *m gen*

court *n* (*royal &c*) cùirt *f*, **law** ~ cùirt-lagha

court *v* **1** (*amorously*) dèan suirghe *f invar* (*with prep* ri), **he ~ed a girl** rinn e suirghe ri nighean; **2** (*through ambition &c*) dèan miodal *m* (*with prep* do), dèan sodal *m* (*with prep* ri), **he ~ed the important people** rinn e miodal do/rinn e sodal ris na daoine (*pl of* duine *m*) mòra

courtesan *n* siùrsach *f*, strìopach *f*

courteous *adj* cùirteil, sìobhalta, modhail, suairc(e)

courtesy *n* modhalachd *f invar*, sìobhaltachd *f invar*, modh *f*

courting *n* suirghe *f invar*, leannanachd *f invar*

courtly *adj* cùirteil

courtship *n* suirghe *f invar*, leannanachd *f invar*

cousin *n* co-ogha *mf*

cove *n* geòdha *mf*, camas *m*, bàgh *m*, òb *m*

covenant *n* (*legal, official, fin &c*) cùmhnant *m*, cunnradh *m*

Covenanter *n* (*hist*) Cùmhnantach *m*

cover *n* còmhdach *m*, (*of book*) **hard/soft** ~ còmhdach cruaidh/bog

cover *v* còmhdaich *vt*

covered *adj & past part* **1** còmhdaichte; **2** ~ **in** (*esp natural phenomena*) fo *prep* (*lenites the following cons where possible & takes the dat*), **mountains** ~ **in mist/cloud/snow** beanntan (*pl of* beinn *f*) fo cheò *m*/fo sgòth *f*/fo shneachd *m*

covering *n* còmhdach *m*, **floor** ~ còmhdach ùrlair *m*

coverlet *n* cuibhrig *f*

covert *adj* falaichte, dìomhair

covertly *adv* os ìosal

covet *v* sanntaich *vt*, miannaich *vt*, (*less usu*) togair *vt*

covetous *adj* sanntach

covetousness *n* sannt *m*

cow *n* bò *f*, for *pl* crodh (*m sing coll*) can also be used, **dairy** ~**s** crodh-bainne

cow *v* cuir *vt* fo eagal *m*

cowed *adj & past part* fo eagal *m*

coward *n* gealtaire *m*, cladhaire *m*

cowardice *n* gealtachd *f invar*, cladhaireachd *f invar*

cowardly *adj* gealtach, cladhaireach

coy *adj* màlda

crab *n* partan *m*, (*larger*) crùbag *f*

crabbit *adj* greannach, cròst(a), diombach

crack *n* **1** (*noise*) brag *m*, pleasg *m*; **2** (*split &c*) sgoltadh *m*; **3** (*fam: conversation*) craic *f*

crack *v* **1** (*noise*) dèan pleasg *m*, dèan brag *m*; **2** (*split &c*) sgàin *vti*, sgoilt & sgolt *vti*

cracking *n* (*splitting &c*) sgoltadh *m*

cradle *n* creathail *f*

craft *n* ceàird *f*

craftsman *n* fear-ceàirde & fear-ciùird (*pl* luchd-ceàirde/ciùird *m sing coll*)

crafty *adj* carach, seòlta, fiar

crag *n* creag *f*, carraig *f*

craggy *adj* creagach

cramp *n* (*used with art*) an t-orc, **I've got** ~ tha an t-orc orm

crane *n* **1** (*for lifting*) crann *m*; **2** (*bird*) corra-mhonaidh *f*

crannog *n* crannag *f*

crap 1 (*fam, vulg: excrement*) *n* cac *m*; **2** (*fig: useless &c*) *in expr* **it's a load of** ~ 's e tòrr *m* caca a th' ann

crash *n* **1** (*impact*) bualadh *m*; **2** (*noise*) stàirn *f*; **3** (*accident*) tubaist *f* rathaid *m gen*; **4** *in expr* ~ **helmet** cloga(i)d-dìona *f*

crawl *v* snàig *vi*, crùb *vi*

creak, creaking *n* dìosgan *m*, dìosgail *f invar*

creak *v* dèan dìosgan *m*

cream *n* **1** (*of milk*) uachdar *m*, bàrr (a' bhainne) *m*; **2** (*cosmetic* ~) cè *m*, **hand** ~ cè làimhe *f gen*

creamy *adj* uachdarach

crease *n* preasag *f*, filleadh *m*

crease *v* preas *vt*, fill *vt*

create *v* cruthaich *vt*, innlich *vt*

creation *n* **1** (*artistic &c*) cruthachadh *m*; **2** (*of plans, devices &c*) innleachadh *m*; **3** (*relig*) cruitheachd *f*, *used with art*, **Creation** A' Chruitheachd; **4** *in expr* (*relig*) **the King/Lord of** ~ Rìgh *m* nan Dùl (*gen pl of* dùil *f*)

creative *adj* **1** (*in arts &c*) cruthachail, ~ **writing** sgrìobhadh cruthachail; **2** (*innovative, inventive*) innleachdach, tionnsgalach

creativity *n* (*innovation, inventiveness*) tionnsgal *m*, tionnsgalachd *f invar*, innleachd *f*,

creator *n* **1** (*esp relig*) cruithear *m*, **the** ~ An Cruithear; **2** (*arts &c*) ùghdar *m*; **3** (~ *of more technical things*) tionnsgalair *m*

creature *n* creutair *m*, (*also fam, of humans*) **the poor** ~! an creutair bochd!

credibility *n* creideas *m*

credible *adj* so-chreidsinn

credit *n* **1** (*fin*) dàil *f*, **buy/sell on** ~ ceannaich/reic *vti* air dàil; **2** *in expr* ~ **card** cairt-iasaid *f*; **3** (*idiom*) **he took the** ~ **for what I did!** chuir e na rinn mise às a leth fhèin!

creed *n* (*relig &c*) creud *f*, creideamh *m*

creel *n* cliabh *m*, **lobster** ~ cliabh ghiomach *mpl gen*

creep *v* èalaidh, snàig, ~ **off home** èalaidh dhachaigh *adv*

crescent *n* corran *m*

crest *n* **1** (*of cock; also clan &c emblem*) cìrean *m*, (*of other birds*) topan *m*; **2** (*of hill*) mala *f* (cnuic *&c*)

crestfallen *adj* gun mhisneachd *f invar*

crevice *n* còs *m*, sgoltadh *m*

crime *n* eucoir *f*, **commit a** ~ dèan eucoir

criminal *adj* eucorach, ~ **law** lagh *m* na h-eucorach (*gen of* eucoir *f*)

criminal *n* eucorach *m*

crimson *adj* crò-dhearg

cringe *v* crùb *vi*, strìochd *vi*

cripple *n* crioplach *&* cripleach *m*

crisis *n* èiginn *f*, cruaidh-chàs *m*, gàbhadh *m*

criterion *n* slat-thomhais *f*

critic *n* **1** (*one who finds fault*) cronadair *m*; **2** (*arts &c*) neach-sgrùdaidh (*pl* luchd-sgrùdaidh *m sing coll*), sgrùdair *m*, breithniche *m*

critical *adj* 1 (*finding fault*) càineach; 2 (*crucial*) deatamach, riatanach

criticise *v* 1 (~ *adversely*) càin *vti*, faigh cron *m* (*with prep* do); 2 (*review arts &c*) sgrùd *vt*, breithnich *vt*

criticism *n* 1 (*adverse*) càineadh *m*, cronachadh *m*; 2 (*review of arts &c*) sgrùdadh *m*, breithneachadh *m*, *in expr* **piece of** ~ lèirmheas *m*

critique *n* sgrùdadh *m*, breithneachadh *m*, (*esp of arts*) lèirmheas *m*

croak *n* ròcail *f*, gràg *m*

croak *v* dèan gràgail *f*

croaking *n* ròcail *f*, gràgail *f invar*

croft *n* croit & cruit *f*, (*in the Gaelic of some districts*) lot *f*

crofter *n* croitear & cruitear *m*, **The Crofters Commission** Coimisean *m* nan Croitearan, **a ~s' co-operative** co-chomann *m* chroitearan *mpl gen*

crofting *n* croitearachd *f invar*

cromag *n* cromag *f*

crony *n* seana-charaid *m*

crook *n* 1 (*person*) eucorach *m*; 2 (*bend in object, river &c*) lùb *m*, caime *f*; 3 (*shepherd's* ~) cromag *f*

crooked *adj* crom, fiar, **a ~ stick** bata crom

crop[1] *n* (*agric* ~ & ~s) bàrr *m*, pòr *m*

crop[2] *n* (*of bird*) sgròban *m*

cross *adj* crost(a) & crosda, (*stronger*) feargach

cross *n* 1 crois *f*, **(make) the sign of the** ~ (dèan) comharradh *m* na croise; 2 (*for crucifixion*) crann-ceusaidh *m*; 3 (*heraldry &c*) **St Andrew's Cross** An Crann

cross *v* 1 rach *vi* tarsainn (*with gen*), **they ~ed (over)** chaidh iad tarsainn, **they ~ed (over) the bridge/the mountains** chaidh iad tarsainn na drochaid *f*/nam beanntan *fpl*; 2 (*thwart &c*) rach *vi* an aghaidh (*with gen*), **don't ~ me!** na rach nam aghaidh!; 3 (*relig*) *in expr* ~ **oneself** dèan comharradh *m* na croise

crossbar *n* crann-tarsainn *m*

cross-border *adj* tar-chrìochail

cross-examine *v* cruaidh-cheasnaich *vt*, mion-cheasnaich *vt*

cross-fertilise *v* tar-thoraich *vt*

crossing *n* (*of water*) aiseag *mf*

cross-reference *n* tar-iomradh *m*

crosspiece *n* rong *f*, rongas *m*

cross-roads *n* crois *f* rathaid *m gen*

crossword *n* tòimhseachan-tarsainn *m*

crotchet *n* (*mus*) dubh-nota *m*

crouch *n* crùban *m*, crùbagan *m*

crouch *v* dèan crùban *m*, dèan crùbagan *m*, rach *vi* na (*&c*) c(h)rùban/c(h)rùbagan, crùb *vi*, **they ~ed down** rinn iad crùban, chaidh iad nan crùban/nan crùbagan, chrùb iad

crouched, crouching *adj & adv* na (*&c*) c(h)rùban *m*, na (*&c*) c(h)rùbagan *m*, **he was ~ed down/crouching** bha e na chrùban/na chrùbagan

crow[1] *n* feannag *f*, **carrion** ~ feannag dhubh, **hooded** ~ feannag ghlas

crow[2] *n* (*of cock*) gairm *f*

crow *v* (*cock &c*) gairm *vi*

crowd *n* **1** grunn *m*, (*bigger*) sluagh (mòr) *m*, (*derog*) gràisg *f*, prabar *m*, **there was a good ~ there** bha grunn math (dhaoine) ann; **2** (*fam:* "*gang*" *&c*) treud *m*, **Ian and Alan and all that ~** Iain is Ailean agus an treud sin uile

crowd *v* **1** (*as vt*) **they ~ed the hall** lìon iad an talla; **2** (*as vi*) **they ~ed into the hall** chaidh/thàinig iad a-steach dhan talla nan ceudan *mpl*

crowded *adj* (*places, buildings, gatherings &c*) dòmhail *&* dùmhail, loma-làn

crowdie *n* gruth *m*, slaman *m*

crown *n* **1** (*for royalty &c*) crùn *m*; **2** (*~ of head*) mullach *m* (a' chinn)

crown *v* crùn *vt*

crowning *n* crùnadh *m*

crucial *adj* deatamach

crucifix *n* crann-ceusaidh *m*, crois *f*

crucifixion *n* ceusadh *m*

crucify *v* ceus *vt*

crude *adj* (*in unprocessed state*) amh, ~ **oil** ola *f* amh

cruel *adj* cruaidh, an-iochdmhor

cruelty *n* an-iochd *f invar*

cruisie *n* (*trad*) crùisgean *m*

crumb *n* (*of bread &c*) criomag *f*, sprùilleag *f*, ~**s** sprùilleach *m sing coll*

crumble *v* **1** (*as vt*) criomagaich, **she ~d the bread** chriomagaich i an t-aran; **2** (*as vi*) rach *vi* na (*&c*) c(h)riomagan *fpl*, **the bread ~d in the bag** chaidh an t-aran na chriomagan sa phoca *m*

crunch, crunching *n* cnagadh *m*

crunch *v* cnag *vi*, **the shingle was ~ing beneath his feet** bha am mol a' cnagadh fo chasan *fpl*

crusade *n* cogadh-croise *m*

crush *v* preas *vt*, pronn *vt*

crust *n* plaosg *m*, rùsg *m*, **the Earth's ~** rùsg na Talmhainn

crutch *n* **1** (*of body, trousers*) gobhal *&* gabhal *m*; **2** (*walking aid*) crasg *f*, croitse *f*

crux *n*, *in expr* **the ~ of the matter** cnag *f* na cùise

cry *n* **1** (*call, shout*) gairm *f*, èigh *f*, glaodh *m*; **2** (*~ of pain, anguish &c*) gaoir *f*

cry *v* **1** (*call, shout*) gairm *vi*, èigh *&* èibh *vi*, glaodh *vi*; **2** (*weep*) guil *vi*, gail *vi*, caoin *vi*, (*vigorously*) ràn *vi*

crying *n* **1** (*calling, shouting*) gairm *f*, èigheachd *f invar*; **2** (*weeping*) gul *m*, caoineadh *m*, (*usu vigorous*) rànail *m invar*, rànaich *m invar*

crystal *n* criostal *m*

cub *n* cuilean *m*

cube *n* ciùb *m*

cubic *adj* ciùbach

cuckold *n* cèile *m* meallta

cuckold *v*, **she ~ed her husband** mheall i a cèile *m* (le fear *m* eile)

cuckoo *n* cuthag *f*

cucumber *n* cularan *m*

cud *n* cìr *f*, **chewing the ~** a' cnàmh na cìre

cudgel *n* cuaille *m*

Culdee *n* (*relig hist*) Cèile-Dè *m*

cull *v* tanaich *vt*

cull, **culling** *n* tanachadh *m*

culpability *n* coireachd *f invar*

culpable *adj* coireach, ciontach

cultivate *v* (*land*) àitich *vt*, obraich *vt*

cultivated *adj* **1** (*land*) àitichte; **2** (*person*) culturail

cultural *adj* culturach

culture *n* cultar *m*, **Gaelic ~** cultar na Gàidhlig(e)

cumin n lus-MhicCuimein *m*

cumulative *adj* tionalach

cunning *adj* carach, seòlta, fiar, innleachdach

cunning *n* seòltachd *f invar*, innleachd *f*

cup *n* **1** cupa *m*, cùp *m*, (*dimin*) cupan *m*, copan *m*, **a ~ of tea** cupa teatha; **2** (*as trophy &c*) cuach *f*, **the World ~** Cuach na Cruinne

cupboard *n* preas(a) *m*, **clothes ~** preas-aodaich *m*

curb *n* bacadh *m*

curb *v* bac *vt*, cuir bacadh *m* (*with prep* air)

curd(s) *n* gruth *m*, slaman *m*

cure *n* leigheas *m*, ìocshlaint *f*, (**for** air), **a ~ for asthma** leigheas air a' chuing

cure *v* **1** (*~ the malady & the patient*) leighis *vt*, slànaich *vi*, (*~ the patient*) cuir *vt* am feabhas *m*; **2** (*bacon, fish &c*) ciùraig *vt*

curious *adj* **1** (*strange*) neònach; **2** (*desiring knowledge, information*) ceasnachail, faighneach, faighneachail

curl *n* bachlag *f*, camag *f*, dual *m*

curl *v* (*hair*) bachlaich *vt*, dualaich *vt*

curled, **curly** *adj* (*of hair*) bachlach, camagach, dualach

curlew *n* guilbneach *m*

curling *n* (*sport*) crolaidh *m invar*, (*less trad*) curladh *m*

currency *n* **1** (*con*) airgead *m*, **weak/strong ~** airgead lag/làidir; **2** (*more abstr: ~ rates*) ruith-airgid *f*, **~ fund** ciste *f* ruith-airgid, **speculate on currencies** dèan tuairmeas *m* air ruith-airgid

current *adj* **1** (*in effect or existence at present*) làithreach, an latha (*gen*) an-diugh, **~ legislation** reachdas *m* làithreach, **the ~ situation** suidheachadh an latha an-diugh, *also* an suidheachadh a th' ann a-nis; **2** *in expr* (*banking*) **~ account** cunntas *m* làithreil, cunntas ruith (*gen of* ruith *f*, used adjectivally*)

current *n* **1** (*water*) sruth *m*, **against the** ~ ris an t-sruth, **with the** ~ leis an t-sruth; **2** (*elec*) sruth(-dealain) *m*

curriculum *n* clàr-oideachais *m*

curriculum vitae *n* cunntas-beatha *m*

curse *n* **1** (*malediction*) mallachd & mollachd *f*; **2** (*swear*) mionn *mf*, mionnan *m*

curse *v* **1** (*as vt:* ~ *someone*) mallaich; **2** (*as vi: swear*) mionnaich

cursed *adj* mallaichte & mollaichte

cursing *n* **1** (*malediction*) mallachadh *m*; **2** (*swearing*) mionnachadh *m*, speuradh *m*

cursor *n* (*IT &c*) cùrsair *m*

cursory *adj* aithghearr, cabhagach, **a** ~ **look at the accounts** sùil *f* aithghearr air na cunntasan *mpl*

curtail *v* **1** (*shorten, make shorter*) giorraich *vt*; **2** (*cut short*) cuir stad *m* (*with prep* air), **the meeting was** ~**ed** chaidh stad a chur air a' choinneimh *f* (ron àm *m*/ron mhithich *f invar*)

curtailed *adj & past part* giorraichte

curtailment *n* giorrachadh *m*

curtain *n* cùirtean *m*, cùirtear *m*

curvature *n* caime *f*, lùbadh *m*

curve *n* **1** caime *f*, lùb *f*; **2** (*in a river*) camas *m*

curve *v* crom *vti*, lùb *vti*

curved *adj* cam, lùbte, crom, **a** ~ **stick** bata crom

cushion *n* pillean *m*, cuisean *m*

custard *n* ughagan *m*

custody *n* **1** (*care, responsibility*) cùram *m*, **she had** ~ **of the child, the child was in her** ~ bha am pàiste air a cùram-sa; **2** (*museum &c*) **have** ~ **of** (*an object*) glèidh *vt*; **3** (*prison &c*) **in** *expr* **in** ~ an greim *m*, an làimh (*dat of* làmh *f*), **remand in** ~ cuir *vt* an greim/an làimh

custom *n* **1** (*esp of an individual*) àbhaist *m*, cleachdadh *m*, **it was a** ~ **of mine to take a glass of brandy** b' àbhaist dhomh/bu chleachdadh dhomh glainne *f* branndaidh *f* a ghabhail; **2** (*more general*) cleachdadh *m*, dòigh *m*, **the** ~**s of the country** dòighean/cleachdaidhean na dùthcha; **3** (*esp trad* ~*s*) gnàth *m*, gnàths *m*, nòs *m*

customary *adj* àbhaisteach, gnàthach, (*looser*) cumanta

customer *n* **1** (*esp for goods*) neach-ceannach(d) (*pl* luchd-ceannach(d) *m sing coll*); **2** (*esp for professional services*) neach-dèilige (*pl* luchd-dèilige *m sing coll*)

customs *n* cusbainn *f invar*, ~ **officer** oifigear *m* na cusbainn, ~ **duty** cìs-chusbainn *f*

cut *n* **1** gearradh *m*; **2** (*fig: fin &c* ~*s*) gearraidhean *mpl*, **he lost his job on account of the** ~**s** chaill e obair *f* air sgàth nan gearraidhean

cut *v* **1** geàrr *vt*, ~ **down** geàrr sìos; **2** ~ **up** (*esp finely*) mion-gheàrr *vt*; **3** (*crops*) buain *vt*, ~ **the corn** buain an t-arbhar; **4** (*misc exprs*) **I** ~ **out**

smoking leig mi seachad smocadh *m*, **~ out the middleman** dùin a-mach am fear meadhanach, **I ~ him dead** chuir mi mo chùl ris, chaidh mi seachad air mar nach robh e ann

cutting *adj* **1** (*of remarks &c*) geur, guineach; **2** (*made for ~*) gearraidh (*gen of* gearradh *m, used adjectivally*), **a ~ edge** faobhar *m* gearraidh

CV *n* cùnntas-beatha *m*

cycle *n* **1** (*pedal ~*) baidhsagal *m*, (*more trad*) rothar *m*; **2** (*economics, science &c*) cuairt *f*

cyclic, cyclical *adj* cuairteach

cycling *n* baidhsagalachd *f invar*, (*more trad*) rothaireachd *f invar*

cyclist *n* baidhsagalair *m*

cymbal *n* tiompan *m*

D

dab *v* suath *vt*

dabble *v*, **he ~s in/with carpentry** tha làmh *f* aige ann an saorsainneachd *f invar*

Daddy *n* (*fam*) dadaidh *m*

daddy-longlegs *n* breabadair *m*

daffodil *n* lus-a'-chrom-chinn *m*

daft *adj* gòrach, amaideach, **don't be ~!** na bi gòrach!

dagger *n* biodag *f*

daily *adj* làitheil

daily *adv* gach là *m*, a h-uile là, **we see him ~** bidh sinn ga fhaicinn gach là/a h-uile là

dainty *adj* mìn

dairy *n* taigh-bainne *m*, *in expr* **~ cows/cattle** crodh-bainne *m*

daisy *n* neòinean *m*

dale *n* gleann *m*, (*smaller*) gleannan *m*

dam *n* dàm *&* dam *m*

damage *v* mill *vt*, dochainn *vt*

damage *n* milleadh *m*, cron *m*, damaiste *m invar*

damaged *adj* millte

damn *n*, (*idioms*) **I don't give a ~ for X** (*fam*) cha toir mi ho-ro-gheallaidh *m invar* air X, chan eil diù *m invar* a' choin agam mu X

damn *v* **1** (*lit*) dìt *vt*; **2** (*in excls*) **~ it!** mac an donais!, **~ them!** taigh *m* na galla dhaibh!

damnation *n* dìteadh *m*

damned *adj* **1** mallaichte; **2** (*as excl, swear*) **the ~ hammer!** òrd *m* na croiche!, **~ car!** càr *f* na galla!

damp *adj* tais

damp *n* taiseachd *f invar*

dampen *v* taisich *vt*

dampness *n* taise *f invar*, taiseachd *f invar*, dampachd *f invar*

damp-proof *adj* taise-dhìonte, taise-dhìonach

dance *n* dannsa *m*, *in expr* **~ floor** ùrlar *m*

dance *v* danns *vti*

dancer *n* dannsair *m*

dancing *n* dannsadh *m*

dandelion *n* beàrnan-Brìde *m*

dandruff *n* càrr *&* càir *f*

danger *n* cunnart *m*, (*usu stronger*) gàbhadh *m*, **in ~** ann an cunnart, ann an gàbhadh, **mortal ~** cunnart-bàis *m*

dangerous *adj* cunnartach, (*usu stronger*) gàbhaidh, (*esp of situation*) cruadalach, *in expr* **a ~ situation** cruaidh-chàs *m*

dangle *v* **1** (*as vi*) bi *vi irreg* air bhodagan *m*, bi a' bogadan, **it ~d/was dangling at the end of a rope** bha e air bhodagan/a' bogadan aig ceann *m* ròpa *m*; **2** (*as vt*) cuir air bhodagan, **I ~d it above him** chuir mi air bhodagan e os a chionn

dank *adj* tais agus fuar

dare *v* **1** dùraig *vi*, **we didn't ~ (to) leave the house** cha do dhùraig sinn an taigh *m* fhàgail; **2** (*challenge, defy to do something*) thoir dù(bh)lan *m* (*with prep* do & *infin of verb*), **I ~d him to steal the apple** thug mi dùlan dha an t-ubhal a ghoid; **3** (*idiom*) **don't (you) ~ move!** na gabh (thusa) ort gluasad *m*

daring *adj* dàna, (*esp rashly ~*) bras

daring *n* dànadas *m*, (*esp rash ~*) braisead *f*

dark *adj* **1** dorch(a), ciar, (*esp ~ & gloomy*) doilleir, **~ cloud** neul dorcha, **the Dark Ages** Na Linntean *fpl* Dorcha, *in expr* **the evening grew ~** chiar *vi* am feasgar; **2** (*qualifying a colour*) dubh-, **~ blue** dubh-ghorm, **~ brown** dubh-dhonn; **3** (*of person's complexion*) ciar

darken *v* **1** ciar *vi*, doilleirich *vti*; **2** (*drawing &c: shade, make darker*) duibhrich *vt*

dark-haired *adj* dubh, dorcha, **a ~ woman** boireannach dubh

darkness *n* **1** dorchadas *m*, duibhre *f*; **2** *in expr* **shroud/cover in ~** duibhrich *vt*, sgàil *vt*

darling *adj* gaolach, **my ~ girl** mo chaileag ghaolach

darling *n* **1** luaidh *m*; **2** (*as affectionate voc expr*) **(my) ~!** a ghaoil!, a luaidh!, **my ~!** m' eudail!, m' ulaidh!

darn *v* càirich *vt*

dart *n* gath *m*, guin *m*

dash *n* **1** ruith *f*, (*usu stronger*) dian-ruith & deann-ruith *f*; **2** (*typog*) sgrìob *f*

dash *v* **1** ruith *vi*; **2** *in expr* **they ~ed off/away** ~ dh'fhalbh iad nan ruith *f*

data *n* dàta *m invar*, fiosrachadh *m*, (*IT*) **~ processing** obrachadh-dàta *m*, gnìomhachadh-dàta *m*, **~ security** tèarainteachd *f invar* dàta, **~ protection** dìon *m* dàta

database *n* (*IT*) stòr-dàta *m*

date[1] *n* **1** (*calendar*) ceann-là & ceann-latha *m*; **2** *in expr* **bring up to ~** ùraich *vt*

date[2] *n* (*fruit*) deit *f*

date *v* **1** (*~ document &c*) cuir ceann-là *m* (*with prep* air), **~ a letter** cuir ceann-là air litir *f*; **2** (*become outdated*) rach *vi irreg* às an fhasan *m*

dated *adj* sean(n)-fhasanta, às an fhasan *m*

dative *adj* (*gram*) tabhartach, **the ~ case** an tuiseal tabhartach

daub *v* smeur & smiùr *vt*

daughter *n* nighean *f*

daughter-in law *n* bana-chliamhainn *f*, bean-mhic *f*

daunt *v* cuir *vt* fo eagal *m*, cuir eagal *m* (*with prep* air), geiltich *vt*

dawn *n* **1** camhana(i)ch *f* an latha *m*, bris(t)eadh *m* an latha; **2** (*idiom*) **from ~ to dusk** o mhoch gu dubh

day *n* **1** là & latha *n*, **the ~s of the week** làithean na seachdainn, **what ~ is it?** dè an là a th' ann?, **by night and by ~** a dh'oidhche *f* 's a là, **the other ~** an là roimhe, **one of these ~s** latha no latheigin, **a ~ off** là dheth, **~ unit** ionad-latha *m*, *in expr* **the next/following ~** làirne-mhàireach & làrna-mhàireach *m invar*; **2** (*lifetime*) là & latha *m*, rè *f invar*, linn *mf*, **at the end of my ~s** aig deireadh *m*/crìoch *f* mo là, **in my grandfather's ~** an rè mo sheanar *m*, ri linn mo sheanar

daybreak *n* bris(t)eadh *m* an latha

daylight *n* solas *m* an latha

dead *adj* **1** marbh, **the king is ~** tha an rìgh marbh, *in exprs* **~ body** corp *m*, corp marbh *m*, (*less usu*) marbhan *m*, **~ and buried** san uaigh *f*; **2** (*exact*) *in expr* **in the ~ centre of the field** ann an teis-meadhan *m*/ann an ceart-mheadhan *m* an achaidh; **3** (*completely*) *in expr* **~ against** calg-dhìreach an aghaidh (*with gen*)

deadline *n* ceann-ama *m*

deadly *adj* marbhtach, bàsmhor

deaf *adj* **1** bodhar; **2** (*idiom*) **he's as ~ as a post** cha chluinn e bìd *m*

deafen *v* bodhair *vt*

deafness *n* buidhre *f*

deal *n* **1** (*business ~*) cunnradh *m*; **2** (*arrangement, agreement*) cùmhnant *m*; **3** (*degree, extent*) *in exprs* **a good ~**, **a great ~** fada (*with comp adj*), **this one is a great ~ better/bigger/stronger** tha am fear seo fada nas fheàrr/nas motha/nas trèine

deal *v* **1** (*playing cards*) riaraich *vti*, roinn *vti*; **2** **~ with** dèilig *vi* (*with prep* ri), **I'll ~ with it tomorrow** dèiligidh mi ris a-màireach, **~ with customers** dèilig ri luchd-ceannaich *m sing coll*; **3** (*buy & sell*) dèilig *vi*, **~ in shares** dèilig ann an sèaraichan *mpl*

dealer *n* (*commerce &c*) neach-dèiligidh (*pl* luchd-dèiligidh *m sing coll*)

dear *excl*, **~ oh ~** dhuine! dhuine!, obh! obh!, **~ me!** O mo chreach *f*!

dear *adj* **1** (*expensive*) daor, cosgail; **2** (*person*) ionmhainn, gaolach, caomh, **her ~ friend** a caraid *m* ionmhainn; **3** (*affectionate address*) **my ~** a ghràidh, m' eudail; **4** (*in corres*) **~ Sir** A Charaid, **~ Sirs** A Chàirdean, **~ Madam** A Bhanacharaid, **~ Mr Fraser** A Mhaighstir Fhriseil, **~ Morag** A Mhòrag a bhanacharaid, **~ Donald** A Dhòmhnaill a charaid, (*more personal or affectionate*) A Dhòmhnaill chòir,

dearth *n* cion *m invar*, gainne *f*, dìth *m*

death *n* **1** bàs *m*, caochladh *m*, (*trad*) eug *m*, **~ certificate** urras *m* bàis, **~ throes** grèim-bàis *m*; **2** *in expr* **I was scared to ~** bha eagal *m* mo bheatha *m* orm

death-bed *n* leabaidh *f* bhàis *f gen*

death-dealing *adj* marbhtach, bàsmhor

debar *v* bac *vt*

debase *v* **1** (*person: humiliate*) ìslich *vt*, maslaich *vt*, dèan *vi irreg* dìmeas *m* invar (*with prep* air), cuir *vt* (ann) an suarachas *m*; **2** (*person: corrupt*) truaill *vt*; **3** (~ *currency*) dì-luachaich *vt*

debate *n* deasbad *mf*, connsachadh *m*, (**about** air, mu, mu dheidhinn)

debate *v* deasbad *vti*, deasbair *vi*, connsaich *vi*, (**about** air, mu, mu dheidhinn)

debauch *v* claon *vt*, coirb *vt*, truaill *vt*

debauchery *n* **1** (*sexual*) mì-gheanmnachd *f invar*, strìopachas *m*; **2** (*drinking*) pòitearachd *f invar*

debilitate *v* lagaich *vti*, fannaich *vti*

debility *n* laigse *f*

debris *n* sprùilleach *m*

debt *n* **1** fiach *m*, **repay a** ~ dìoghail fiach; **2** (*moral &c, not fin*) comain *f*, **I'm greatly in your** ~ tha mi fada nad chomain

debtor *n* fèichear *m*

decade *n* deichead *m*

decadence *n* claonadh *m*

decadent *adj* air claonadh

decapitate *v* dì-cheannaich *vt*

decapitation *n* dì-cheanna(cha)dh *m*

decay *n* lobhadh *m*, seargadh *m*

decay *v* lobh *vi*, caith *vi*, crìon *vi*

deceit *n* mealladh *m*, cealg *f*, foill *f*

deceitful *adj* mealltach, cealgach, fallsa, foilleil

deceive *v* meall *vt*, cealg *vt*, dèan foill *f* (*with prep* air)

deceived *adj* meallta

deceiver *n* mealltair *m*, cealgair(e) *m*

December *n* Dùbhlachd *f invar*, *used with art*, an Dùbhlachd, **the first of** ~ a' chiad là *m* den Dùbhlachd

decency *n* beusachd *f invar*

decent *adj* **1** (*persons: moral, honest &c*) còir, beusach; **2** (*persons: fair, reasonable*) cothromach; **3** (*actions, arrangements &c: reasonable, appropriate*) cothromach, iomchaidh, **a** ~ **salary** tuarastal cothromach/iomchaidh

deception *n* mealladh *m*, cealg *f*, foill *f*

deceptive *adj* mealltach

decide *v* **1** (*make a decision*) co-dhùin *vi*, thig *vi* gu co-dhùnadh *m*; **2** *in expr* ~ **on/upon** (*ie choose, appoint*) sònraich *vt*, ~ **on a day for the meeting** sònraich latha *m* airson na coinneimh; **3** (*form a plan or intention*) cuir *vt* romham, romhad (*&c*) (*with infinitive of verb*), **I ~d to close the shop** chuir mi romham a' bhùth a dhùnadh (*also* rinn mi suas m' inntinn *f* a' bhùth a dhùnadh)

deciduous *adj* seargach

decimal *adj* deicheach, ~ **place** ionad deicheach

decimal *n* deicheamh *m*

decipher *v* fuasgail *vt*

decision *n* co-dhùnadh *m*, **come to/reach a ~** co-dhùin *vi*, thig *vi* gu co-dhùnadh

decision-making *n* co-dhùnadh *m*

decisive *adj* **1** (*persons: ~ in character, actions*) duineil; **2** (*leading to a decision*) co-dhùnaidh (*gen of* co-dhùnadh *m*), **it was he who made the ~ speech** is esan a rinn an òraid cho-dhùnaidh; **3** (*main, crucial*) prìomh, **the ~ element in this situation** a' phrìomh ealamaid anns an t-suidheachadh seo

decisiveness *n* (*in character, actions*) duinealas *m*

declare *v* **1** abair *vti irreg*, can *vti def*, cuir *vt* an cèill (*dat of* ciall *f*); **2** *in expr* **~ war** gairm cogadh *m*

decline *n* lughdachadh *m*, crìonadh *m*

decline *v* **1** (*deteriorate &c*) lughdaich *vi*, crìon *vi*, rach *vi* nas miosa; **2** (*turn down &c*) diùlt *vt*

decompose *v* lobh *vi*, bris *vi* sìos

decomposition *n* lobhadh *m*, bris(t)eadh *m* sìos

decorate *v* maisich *vt*, sgeadaich *vt*

decoration *n* maiseachadh *m*, sgeadachadh *m*

decorative *adj* sgeadachail

decorous *adj* **1** (*well-behaved*) beusach, modhail; **2** (*proper, acceptable*) cubhaidh, iomchaidh

decorum *n* stuaim *f*, deagh bheus *f*, modh *mf*

decrease *n* lùghdachadh *m*

decrease *v* lùghdaich *vti*

decree *n* òrdugh *m*

decree *v* òrdaich *vi*

decrepit *adj* (*people*) breòite, anfhann

decriminalise *v* dì-eucoirich *vt*

decriminalisation *n* dì-eucoireachadh *m*

dedicate *v* coisrig *vt* (**to** gu)

dedication *n* coisrigeadh *m* (**to** gu)

deduce *v* dèan *vt irreg* a-mach, obraich *vt* a-mach, dèan *vt irreg* dheth

deduct *v* (*subtract*) thoir *vt* air falbh (**from** bho & o)

deduction *n* **1** (*subtraction*) toirt *f invar* air falbh (**from** bho & o); **2** (*intellectual process*) dèanamh *m* a-mach, obrachadh *m* a-mach, dèanamh dheth

deed *n* **1** (*action*) gnìomh *m*, **bad ~** droch ghnìomh; **2** (*feat*) euchd *m*

deep *adj* **1** (*lit: phys*) domhainn; **2** (*fig: of personality, character*) domhainn, dìomhair

deep freeze *n* reothadair *m*

deep *n* dubh-aigeann *m invar*, doimhne *f invar*, *used with art*, **the ~** an dubh-aigean, an doimhne

deepen *v* doimhnich *vti*

deer *n* **1** (*general term*) fiadh *m*; **2** (*particular* ~) **red** ~ (*stag*) damh *m*, (*hind*)
  eilid *f*, **roe** ~ (*buck*) boc(-earba) *m*, (*female*) earb *f*; **3** *in expr* ~ **forest** frìth *f*

deface *v* mill *vt*

defamation *n* tuaileas *m*, mì-chliù *m*

defamatory *adj* tuaileasach

defame *v* cùl-chàin *vt*, mì-chliùitich *vt*

defeat *n* call *m*, (*esp military, involving rout*) ruaig *f*

defeat *v* **1** faigh buaidh *f*, (*more fam*) dèan an gnothach *m*/a' chùis,
  buadhaich *vi*, (*all with prep* air), **we ~ed them** fhuair sinn buaidh orra,
  rinn sinn an gnothach orra; **2** (*esp of things one fails to achieve*) fairtlich
  vi, failich *vi*, (*with prep* air), **I wanted to climb the mountain but it ~ed
  me** bha mi airson a' bheinn a dhìreadh ach dh'fhairtlich/dh'fhailich
  i orm

defecate *v* cac *vi*

defecation *m* cacadh *m*

defect *n* (*moral or phys*) fàillinn *f*, meang *f*

defect *v* trèig *vi* (**to** gu)

defective *adj* **1** (*having a defect*) meangail; **2** (*incomplete*) neo-iomlan, **a** ~
  verb gnìomhair *m* neo-iomlan

defence *n* dìon *m*, **Centre for** ~ **Studies** Ionad *m* airson Eòlas-dìona *m*

defenceless *adj* gun dìon *m*

defend *v* dìon *vt*

defendant *n* (*law*) neach-dìona *m* (*pl* luchd-dìona *m sing coll*)

defender *n* dìonadair *m*

defensible *adj* so-dhìonta

defer *v* **1** cuir *vt* air (an) ath là *m*, cuir *vt* air dàil *f*, cuir dàil (*with preps* ann
  an *or* air), ~ **the meeting** cuir a' choinneamh air ath là, ~ **construction
  of the bridge** cuir dàil ann an/air togail *f* na drochaid(e); **2** (*give way*)
  gèill *vi* (**to** do), **he ~red to the manager** ghèill e don mhanadsair *m*

deference *n* urram *m*, ùmhlachd *nf invar*

deferential *adj* umha(i)l

defiance *n* dùbhlan & dùlan *m*

deficiency *n* **1** (*lack*) easbhaidh *f*, dìth *m*; **2** (*fault, failing*) fàilligeadh *m*

deficient *adj* **1** (*missing, in short supply*) easbhaidheach, a dhìth; **2** (*faulty*)
  easbhaidheach

deficit *n* **1** easbhaidh *f*, dìth *m*; **2** (*in balance sheet &c*) call *m*

defile *v* (*places, objects, relig, morals &c*) truaill *vt*, salaich *vt*

defilement *n* truailleadh *m*

define *v* mìnich *vt*, soilleirich *vt*, ~ **your terms** mìnich na briathran *mpl* a
  tha thu a' cleachdadh

definite *adj* cinnteach, deimhinne/deimhinnte

definitely *adv* gu dearbh, gun teagamh, **are you tired? I** ~ **am!** a bheil thu
  sgìth? tha gu dearbh!, **will she come tomorrow?** ~! an tig i a-màireach?
  thig gun teagamh!

definition *n* mìneachadh *m*

deflation *n* (*economics*) seargadh *m*

deforestation *n* dì-choilleachadh *m*

deform *v* cuir *vt* à cumadh *m*

deformity *n* **1** (*abstr*) mì-chumadh *m*; **2** (*specific: phys*) meang *f*

defraud *v* feallaich *vt*, dèan foill *f* (*with prep* air)

defrost *v* dì-reoth *vti*

deft *adj* deas, ealamh

defunct *adj* **1** (*of persons*) marbh, nach maireann; **2** (*of systems, ideas &c*) a chaidh à cleachdadh *m*

defy *v* thoir dù(bh)lan *m* (*with prep* do *& infinitive of verb*), **we defied them** thug sinn dùlan dhaibh, **he defied me to tell the truth** thug e dùlan dhomh an fhìrinn innse

degeneracy *n* (*moral*) coirbteachd *f invar*

degenerate *adj* (*morally*) coirbte

degenerate *v* (*phys, morally &c*) rach *vi* sìos, rach *vi irreg* am miosad *f*

degradation *n* ìsleachadh *m*

degrade *v* ìslich *vt*

degree *n* **1** (*of heat, angles*) puing *f*; **2** (*of progress, development, ability &c*) ìre *f invar*; **3** (*university* ~) ceum *m*

dehydrate *v* sgreubh *vt*, crìon *vti*, searg *vti*

dehydration *n* sgreubhadh *m*, crìonadh *m*, seargadh *m*

deity *n* **1** (*abstr*) diadhachd *f invar*; **2** (*a god*) dia *m*, **a Roman** ~ dia Ròmanach, dia nan Ròmanach *mpl*

dejected *adj* fo bhròn, dubhach, smalanach, fo smalan *m*, (*more fam*) sìos na (*&c*) inntinn *f*, **we were** ~ bha sinn sìos nar n-inntinn

dejection *n* bròn *m*, smalan *m*, smuairean *m*

delay *n* dàil *f*, maille *f invar*, **without** ~ gun dàil

delay *v* **1** (*hinder*) cuir maille *f invar*, cuir dàil *f*, (*with prep* air *or* ann), cùm *vt* air ais, **that ~ed the project** chuir sin maille/dàil air a' phròiseact *mf*/ anns a' phròiseact, **I don't want to** ~ **you** chan eil mi airson ur cumail air ais, (*idiom*) **if they're ~ed** ma thèid maille *f invar* orra; **2** (*drag one's heels*) màirnealaich *vi*, bi *vi irreg* màirnealach

delectable *adj* blasmhor

delegate *n* riochdaire *m*

delegate *v* tiomain *vt* (**to** do), ~ **authority** tiomain ùghdarras *m*

delegation *n* **1** (*abstr:* ~ *of authority, responsibility &c*) tiomnadh *m* (**to** do); **2** (*con: a* ~) buidheann *mf* riochdachaidh *m*

delete *v* dubh *vt* às, dubh *vt* a-mach

deliberate *adj* a dh'aon ghnothach *m*, a dh'aon rùn *m*

deliberate *v* (*reflect upon inwardly; also of committee &c, discuss*) beachdaich *vi* (**upon, about** air)

deliberately *adv* a dh'aon ghnothach *m*, a dh'aon rùn *m*

deliberation *n* beachdachadh *m* (**upon, about** air)

delicacy *n* **1** (*abstr: refinement*) finealtas *m*; **2** (*abstr: phys or emotional vulnerability*) maothachd *f invar*

delicate *adj* **1** (*refined &c*) finealta; **2** (*phys or emotionally vulnerable*) maoth

delicious *adj* ana-bhlasta

delight *n* aighear *m*, aoibhneas *m*, sòlas *m*

delight *v* toilich *vt*, riaraich *vt*

delighted *adj & past part* **1** làn-thoilichte, riaraichte, sòlasach; **2** (*idiom*) **he's ~** tha e air a dheagh dhòigh

delightful *adj* taitneach, ciatach

delinquency *n* coire *f*, ciontachd *f invar*

delinquent *n* coireach *m*, ciontach *m*

delirious *adj* breisleachail

delirium *n* breisleach *m*

deliver *v* **1** (*~ goods &c*) lìbhrig *vt*, liubhair *vt*; **2** (*set free*) saor *vt*, fuasgail *vt*; **3** (*~ baby*) asaidich *vt*; **4** (*~ speech &c*) gabh *vt*, thoir *vt* seachad, **he ~ed a speech** ghabh e òraid *f*, thug e seachad òraid, *also* rinn e òraid

deliverance *n* saorsa *f*, fuasgladh *m*

delivery *n* **1** (*of goods &c*) lìbhrigeadh *m*, liubhairt *m*; **2** (*of baby*) asaid *f*

delude *v* meall *vt*, **she was deluding herself** bha i ga mealladh fhèin

deluge *n* tuil *f*, dìle *f*, (*stronger*) dìle bhàthte,

delusion *n* mealladh *m*

delusory *adj* mealltach

delve *v* rannsaich *vt*, cladhaich *vt*, **delving into his family history** a' rannsachadh eachdraidh *f* a theaghlaich (fhèin)

demand *n* **1** iarrtas *m*; **2** (*economics, business*) fèill *f*, margadh *m*, **will there be a ~ for it?** am bi fèill/margadh air?

demand *v* iarr *vt*, **they ~ed a pay rise** dh'iarr iad àrdachadh *m* pàighidh (*gen of* pàigheadh *m*)

demean *v* dìblich *vt*, ìslich *vt*

demented *adj* **1** air bhoile *f invar*, air chuthach *m*, (*more fam*) às a (*&c*) rian *m*, às a (*&c*) c(h)iall *f*; **2** (*idiom*) **it was nearly driving me ~** bha e gus mo chur dhìom fhìn, *also* bha e gus mo chur às mo rian

demi- *prefix* leth-, *eg* **demigod** leth-dhia *m*

democracy *n* deamocrasaidh *m*, (*more trad*) sluagh-fhlaitheas *m*

democrat *n* deamocratach *m*

democratic *adj* deamocratach

demolish *v* leag *vt*, sgrios *vt*

demolition *n* leagail *f*, sgrios *m*

demon *n* deamhan *m*

demonstrate *v* **1** (*prove*) dearbh *vt*; **2** (*~ products, techniques &c*) taisbean *vt*; **3** (*pol &c: take part in march, rally &c*) tog *vt* fianais *f*

demonstration *n* **1** (*proof*) dearbhadh *m*; **2** (*~ of products, techniques &c*) taisbeanadh *m*; **3** (*pol &c: march, rally*) fianais-dhùbhlain *f*, (*esp march*) caismeachd *f*

demoralize *v* mì-mhisnich *vt*

demote *v* ìslich *vt*

demure *adj* stuama

den *n* **1** (*topog*) lag *mf*; **2** (*of animal &c*) garaidh *m*

denial *n* àicheadh *m*

denigrate *v* dèan dìmeas *m invar* (*with prep* air), **he ~d the First Minister** rinn e dìmeas air a' Phrìomh Mhinistear

denounce *v* **1** (*betray*) brath *vt*; **2** (*oppose, speak out against*) cuir *vi* an aghaidh, rach *vi irreg* an aghaidh, (*with gen*), **they ~d the war** chuir iad an aghaidh a' chogaidh

dense *adj* **1** (*of trees, hair, vegetation &c*) dòmhail & dùmhail, dlùth, tiugh; **2** (*mentally ~*) maol, maol-aigneach, (*fam*) tiugh

density *n* dlùths *m invar*, tiughad *m*, tighead *m*

dent *n* beàrn *f*, tulg *m*

dental *adj* deudach, fiaclach, *in expr* **~ surgery** (*ie the place*) ionad *m* fiaclaire *m*

dentist *n* fiaclair(e) *m*

dentistry *n* fiaclaireachd *f invar*

dentures *n* fiaclan-fuadain *fpl*

denunciation *n* **1** (*betrayal*) brathadh *m*; **2** (*opposition, speaking out against*) cur *m* an aghaidh (*with gen*)

deny *v* **1** (*~ accusation &c*) àicheidh *vt*, **~ing his guilt** ag àicheadh a chionta *m*; **2** (*reject, disown*) diùlt *vti*, àicheidh *vt*, **she won't ~ her own daughter** cha diùlt i a nighean *f* fhèin, **~ing his faith** ag àicheadh a chreideimh *m*; **3** (*deprive of*) cùm *vt* air ais (*with prep* o, bho), **the soldiers denied them food** chùm na sàighdearan *mpl* biadh *m* air ais bhuapa

depart *v* falbh *vi*, (*less usu*) imich *vi*, **they ~ed yesterday** dh'fhalbh iad an-dè

department *n* roinn *f*, (*ed*) **the French ~** Roinn na Fraingis

departmental *adj* roinneil

departure *n* falbh *m*

depend *v* **1** (*accept support or help from*) cuir taic *f* (*with preps* air *or* ri), **~ on me** cuir do thaic orm/rium; **2** (*trust*) cuir creideas *m*, cuir earbsa *f invar*, (*with prep* ann), **can we ~ on him?** an urrainn dhuinn creideas/earbsa a chur ann?; **3** (*vary according to*) bi *vi irreg* an crochadh (**on** air), **that will ~ on the price** bidh sin an crochadh air a' phrìs *f*

dependable *adj* (*person, business &c*) urrasach

dependence *n* eisimeileachd *f invar*, eisimeil *f*

dependent *adj* **1** an eisimeil *f* (*with gen*), eisimeil (**on** air), **the company was ~ on its shareholders** bha a' chompanaidh an eisimeil an luchd-earrann *m sing coll* aice, **~ on her brother** an eisimeil a bràthar; **2** (*addicted*) an urra (**on** ri), na *&c* t(h)ràill *m* (**on** do), **they were ~ on drugs** bha iad an urra ri drogaichean *fpl*, bha iad nan tràillean do dhrogaichean

dependent *n* neach-eisimeil *m* (*pl* luchd-eisimeil *m sing coll*)

depict *v* dealbh

deplorable *adj* maslach, tàmailteach

deplore *v* is *v irreg & def* beag (*with prep* air), is olc (*with prep* le), **I ~ the opinions you expressed** is beag orm na beachdan *mpl* a chuir sibh an cèill (*dat of* ciall *f*)

deploy *v* (*measures, strategies &c*) cuir *vt* an gnìomh *m*

depopulate *v* fàsaich *vt*

depopulation *n* fàsachadh *m*

deport *v* fuadaich *vt*

deportment *n* giùlan *m*

deposit *n* **1** (*fin: advance payment on purchases &c*) eàrlas *m*; **2** (*fin: payment into account*) tasgadh *m*

deposit *v* taisg *vt*

depot *n* **1** (*store &c*) batharnach *m*; **2** (*base, centre, for business &c operations*) ionad *m*

deprecate *v* coirich *vt*

depress *v* **1** (*lit, phys*) brùth *vt* sìos; **2** (*sadden &c*) cuir *vt* sìos, fàg *vt* dubhach, fàg *vt* fo smalan *m*, **the news ~ed me** chuir an naidheachd *f* sìos mi, dh'fhàg an naidheachd dubhach mi

depressed *adj* fo bhròn *m*, dubhach, smalanach, fo smalan *m*, (*more fam*) sìos na (*&c*) inntinn *f*, ìosal/ìseal, **we were a bit ~** bha sinn rud beag sìos nar n-inntinn, bha sinn car ìosal

depression *n* **1** (*of mood*) bròn *m*, smalan *m*, smuairean *m*, leann-dubh *m*; **2** (*of mood or weather*) ìsleachadh *m*

deprivation *n* **1** (*the action*) cumail *f* air ais; **2** (*the state of poverty, homelessness &c*) easbhaidh *f*

deprive *v* cùm *vt* air ais (*with prep* o, bho), **the soldiers ~d them of food** chùm na sàighdearan *mpl* biadh *m* air ais bhuapa

depth *n* doimhneachd *f invar*

deputation *n* buidheann-tagraidh *mf*

depute, deputy *adj* iar-, leas-, *suffixes, eg* ~ **director** iar-stiùiriche *m*, leas-stiùiriche *m*

deputy *n* neach-ionaid *m* (*pl* luchd-ionaid *m sing coll*), **she appointed her ~** dh'ainmich i an neach-ionaid aice

derelict *adj* trèigte

deride *v* mag *vi*, dèan fanaid *f*, (*with prep* air)

derision *n* magadh *m*, fanaid *f*, (**of** air)

derisive *adj* **1** (*deriding, apt to deride*) magail; **2** (*~ly inadequate*) suarach

derivation *n* **1** (*abstr: the activity of etymologising &c*) freumh-fhaclachd *f invar*, freumhachadh *m*; **2** (*con: esp ~ of words*) freumh *m*, bun *m*, tùs *m*, (an fhacail &c)

derivative *adj* iasadach

derive *v* **1** (*as vi*) thig *vi irreg* (**from** bho, o), **A ~s from B** thàinig A bho B; **2** (*to translate vt*) **X ~s this word from French** a rèir X, thig am facal seo on Fhrangais *f*

derogatory *adj* cur-sìos, ~ **statements** briathran *mpl* cur-sìos

derrick *n* crann(-togail) *m*

descend *v* **1** (*phys*) teirinn & teàrn *vti* (*with prep* à, *or direct object*), crom *vi* (*with preps* o/bho & le), thig *vi* sìos/a-nuas, **he ~ed from the pulpit** theirinn e às a' chùbaid *f*, **~ing the hillside** a' teàrnadh a' bhruthaich *mf*, **he ~ed from the donkey's back** chrom e bhon asail (*dat of* asal *f*), **he ~ed the rock** chrom e leis a' chreig (*dat of* creag *f*); **2** (*be a descendant of*) *see* **descendant** & **descended** *below*

descendant *n* fear *m*/tè *f* de shìol *m coll*, fear/tè de shliochd *m coll* (*with gen of ancestor*), **she's a ~ of Diarmad** is e/i tè de shìol Diarmaid a tha innte, **~s** sìol/sliochd (*with gen of ancestor*), **(the) ~s of Diarmad** sìol/ sliochd Diarmaid

descended *past part* de shliochd *m coll*, de shìol *m coll*, **he's ~ from the Lord of the Isles** is ann de shìol Tighearna *m* nan Eilean *mpl* a tha e

descent *n* **1** (*phys*) teàrnadh *m*, cromadh *m*; **2** (*one's ancestry, genealogy*) sinnsearachd *f invar*

describe *v* thoir tuairisgeul *m* (*with prep* air)

description *n* **1** (*of person or thing*) tuairisgeul *m*, **the police already have the thief's ~** tha tuairisgeul a' mhèirlich aig a' phoileas *m* mu thràth; **2** (*of events &c*) cunntas *m*

descriptive *adj* dealbhach, tuairisgeulach

desert *n* fàsach *mf*, (*less usu*) dìthreabh *f*, **the ~s of Africa** fàsaichean Afraga *m gen*

desert *v* **1** trèig *vt*, dìobair *vt*, **he ~ed his family** thrèig/dhìobair e a theaghlach *m*, **the people ~ed the island** thrèig na daoine *mpl* an t-eilean; **2** (*soldiers &c*) teich *vi*

deserted *adj* & *past part* **1** (*empty, lonely*) uaigneach, fàsaichte, fàs, *in expr* **a ~ place** fàsach *mf*; **2** (*of a person, of an abandoned house &c*) trèigte

deserter *n* fear-teichidh *m* (*pl* luchd-teichidh *m sing coll*)

desertification *n* fàsachadh *m*

desertion *n* **1** (*from army &c*) teicheadh *m*; **2** (*~ of people*) trèigsinn *m invar*

deserve *v* **1** bi *vi irreg* airidh (*with prep* air), **they ~ praise/to be praised** tha iad airidh air moladh *m*, (*also: idiom*) tha iad rim moladh; **2** (*idiom*) **we thoroughly ~d it** bu mhath an airidh sinn

deserving *adj* airidh, (*less usu*) toillteanach, (**of** air)

desiccate *v* tiormaich *vti*

design *n* dealbh & deilbh *mf*

design *v* (*technical & artistic objects*) dealbh & deilbh *vt*, dealbhaich *vt*, **~ machines** dealbh/deilbh innealan *mpl*

designate *v* (*specify person or thing*) sònraich *vt*, (*esp person*) ainmich *vt*

designer *n* dealbhaiche & deilbhiche *m*, neach-deilbh *m* (*pl* luchd-deilbh *m sing coll*)

designing *n* dealbhadh & deilbheadh *m*, dealbhachadh *m*

desire *n* **1** (*abstr & con*) miann *mf*, rùn *m*, (*con*) togradh *m*, (*less usu*) dèidh *f*; **2** (*sexual ~*) miann *mf*, **a small flame of ~** lasair bheag miann

desire *v* **1** (*wish for*) miannaich *vt*; **2** (~ *to do something*) rùnaich *vt*, togair *vti*, (*the latter is often used as vi in relative future tense*), **just as you** ~ dìreach mar a thogras sibh

desist *v* leig *vi*, sguir *vi*, (**from** de)

desk *n* deasg *m*

desolate *adj* **1** fàsail, **a ~ land** tìr *mf* fhàsail; **2** (*of person*) trèigte, truagh

despair *n* eu-dòchas *m*

despicable *adj* suarach, tàireil

despise *v* dèan tàir *f*, dèan tarcais *f*, (*with prep* air), cuir *vt* suarach, **we ~ them** tha sinn gan cur suarach

despite *prep* a dh'aindeoin (*with gen*), ~ **the rain** a dh'aindeoin an uisge

despised *adj & past part* fo dhìmeas

despondency *n* mì-mhisneachd *f invar*

despondent *adj* gun mhisneach *f*, dubhach, smalanach

despot *n* aintighearna *m*, deachdaire *m*

despotism *n* aintighearnas *m*, deachdaireachd *f invar*

dessert *n* mìlsean *m*

dessert-spoon *n* spàin-mìlsein *f*

destabilise *v* dì-dhaingnich *vt*

destination *n* ceann-uidhe *m*

destined *adj & past part* an dàn (**for** do), **what was ~ for him** na bha an dàn dha

destiny *n* dàn *m*, crannchur *m*, **oppose/go against** ~ cuir *vi* an aghaidh dàin, **if that is my ~** mas e sin mo chrannchur, *also* mas e sin a tha an *prep* dàn dhomh

destitute *adj* airceach, ainniseach

destitution *n* airc *f*, ainnis *f*

destroy *v* mill *vt*, sgrios *vt*, cuir *vi* às (*with prep* do)

destruction *n* milleadh *m*, sgrios *m*

destructive *adj* millteach, sgriosail

detach *v* dealaich *vt*

detached *adj & past part* **1** dealaichte, ~ **house** taigh dealaichte; **2** (*of person-ality*) fad' às, dùinte

detachment *n* **1** (*abstr*) dealachadh *m*; **2** (~ *of troops &c*) buidheann *mf*, còmhlan *m*, cuideachd *f*

detail *n* **1** mion-phuing *f*; **2** *in exprs* **attentive to** ~ mion-chùiseach, **question in** ~ mion-cheasnaich *vt*

detailed *adj* mionaideach, mion- (*prefix*), **a ~ enquiry/study** sgrùdadh mionaideach, ~ **knowledge/acquaintance** mion-eòlas *m* (**of/with** air)

detain *v* **1** (*delay, keep back*) cùm *vt* air ais; **2** (~ *in custody*) cùm *vt* an làimh (*dat of* làmh *f*), cùm *vt* an grèim *m*/an sàs *m*

detect *v* lorg *vt*, faigh lorg *f* (*with prep* air)

detection *n* lorg *f*

detector *n* lorgair *m*

detention *n* **1** (*abstr*) làmh *f*, grèim *m*, sàs *m*, **in ~** an làimh, an grèim, an sàs (*all dat*); **2** (*the act of detaining*) cumail *f* an làimh/an grèim/an sàs

deter *v* bac *vt*, caisg *vt*

deteriorate *v* **1** mùth *vi*, rach *vi* am miosad *m*; **2** (*of person*) rach *vi* bhuaithe (*&c*), tuit *vi* bhuaithe (*&c*), **she ~d** chaidh i bhuaipe

deterioration *n* **1** mùthadh *m*, dol *m invar* am miosad *m*, fàillinn *f*; **2** (*of person*) dol *m invar* bhuaithe (*&c*), tuiteam *m* bhuaithe (*&c*)

determination *n* daingneachd *f invar*, rùn suidhichte

determine *v* **1** (*form a plan &c*) cuir roimhe (*&c*), **they ~ed to build a house** chuir iad romhpa taigh *m* a thogail; **2** (*discover, elucidate &c*) dearbh *vt*

determined *adj & past part* **1** (*persistent, forceful*) daingeann, suidhichte, **a ~ effort** ionnsaigh dhaingeann; **2** (*firmly resolved*) mionnaichte, suidhichte, **she was ~ it wouldn't get the better of her** bha i mionnaichte nach fairtlicheadh e oirre

deterrent *n* bacadh *m*, seòl *m* bacaidh *gen*, casg *m*

detest *v* fuathaich *vt*, bi *vi irreg* gràin *f* aig (*with prep* air), **I ~ them** tha gràin agam orra

detestable *adj* gràineil, fuathach

detour *n* bealach *m*, **take/make a ~** gabh bealach

detrimental *adj* millteach (**to** air)

devalue *v* dì-luachaich *vti*

devaluation *n* dì-luachadh *m*

devastate *v* lèir-sgrios *vt*

devastation *n* lèir-sgrios *m*

develop *v* **1** (*as vt: improve, modernise &c*) leasaich *vt*, **~ the town centre** leasaich meadhan *m* a' bhaile; **2** (*as vi: make progress &c*) thig *vi* air adhart, **he/it's ~ing nicely** tha e a' tighinn air adhart gu dòigheil

developing *adj*, *in expr* **~ country** tìr *mf* fo leasachadh *m*

development *n* **1** (*improvement, modernisation &c*) leasachadh *m*, **a ~ board** bòrd *m* leasachaidh *gen*, **~ plan** plana *f* leasachaidh *gen*; **2** (*esp of persons: progress in skill, knowledge &c*) adhartas *m*, piseach *m*

deviate *v* saobh *vi* (**from** o/bho)

deviation *n* saobhadh *m* (**from** o/bho)

device *n* **1** (*mechanical*) inneal *m*, innleachd *f*; **2** (*idiom*) **leave them to their own ~s** leig *vi* leotha

devil *n* diabhal *m*, **the ~** an Diabhal, an Donas *m*

devilish *adj* diabhlaidh

devious *adj* **1** (*person, behaviour*) fiar, carach; **2** (*route &c*) cuairteach

devise *v* innlich *vt*, dealbh *vt*, (*less usu*) tionnsgail *&* tionnsgain *vt*, **~ a stratagem/a machine** innlich cuilbheart *f*/inneal *m*

devoid (of) *adj* às aonais, às eugmhais, (*with gen*)

devolution *n* tiomnadh *m* chumhachdan *fpl gen*, sgaoileadh-cumhachd *m*

devolve *v* tiomnaich *vt* (**to** do), **~ power** tiomnaich cumhachd *f*

devolved *adj & past part* tiomnaichte

devote *v* coisrig *vt* (**to gu**)

devotion *n* **1** (*relig: abstr*) cràbhadh *m*, diadhachd *f invar*; **2** *in expr* ~**s** (*ie relig observances*) adhradh *m*, ùrnaigh *f*; **3** (*intense love for a person*) teas-ghràdh *m*

devour *v* glam & glamh (*also* glàm & glàmh) *vt*, sluig *vt*, ith *vt* gu glàmach

devout *adj* **1** cràbhach, diadhaidh; **2** (*idioms*) **she is very** ~ tha i làn den Fhìrinn *f*, **become very** ~ (*usu derog, implying a degree of devoutness the speaker considers excessive*) gabh an cùram

devoutness *n* cràbhadh *m*, diadhachd *f invar*

dew *n* dealt *mf*, dr(i)ùchd *m*

dewy *adj* dealtach

dexterity *n* deas-làmhachd *f invar*

dexterous *adj* làmhach, deas-làmhach

diabetes *n* tinneas *m* an t-siùcair

diabolical *adj* diabhlaidh

diagonal *adj* trastanach

diagonal *n* trastan *m*

diagram *n* diagram *m*, (*more trad*) dealbh-chumadh *mf*

dial *n* (*of clock, instruments &c*) aodann *m*, aghaidh *f*

dial *v* dèan àireamh *f* (fòn *mf gen*)

dialect *n* dualchainnt *f*

dialogue *n* co-chòmhradh *m*, còmhradh-dithis *m*

diametrically *adj*, *in expr* ~ **opposed to** calg-dhìreach an aghaidh (*with gen*)

diamond *n* daoimean *m*

diaphragm *n* sgairt *f*

diarrhoeia *n* buinneach *f*, sgàird *f*, spùt *m*, *all used with art*, a' bhuinneadh, an sgàird, an spùt

diary *n* leabhar-latha *m*

dice *n see* **die** *n*

dictate *v* **1** (~ *letter &c*) deachd *vt*; **2** (*command &c*) òrdaich *vi*

dictation *n* (*of letter &c*) deachdadh *m*

dictator *n* **1** (*pol &c*) deachdaire *m*; **2** (*of letter &c*) neach-deachdaidh *m* (*pl* luchd-deachdaidh *m sing coll*)

dictatorial *adj* deachdaireach, ceannsalach

dictatorship *n* deachdaireachd *f invar*

diction *n* labhradh *m*

dictionary *n* faclair *m*

dicy *adj* **1** (*dodgy, shaky*) cugallach; **2** (*risky*) cunnartach, *in expr* **a** ~ **situation** cruaidh-chàs *m*

didactic *adj* oideachail

die *v* **1** (*esp of persons*) caochail *vi*, siubhail *vi*, (*trad*) eug *vi*; **2** (*of other creatures*) bàsaich *vi* (*though this is also used by some speakers to refer to humans*), *note also* **the dog** ~**d** chailleadh an cù

die, *pl* **dice**, *n* (*sing*) dìsinn *m* & dìsne *mf*, (*pl*) dìsnean *m*

diesel *n* dìosail *m invar*

diet *n* riaghailt *f* bìdh (*gen of* biadh *m*)

difference *n* **1** diofar *m* (*also* difir *m invar* & deifir *f*), eadar-dhealachadh *m*, **what's the ~ between A and B?** dè an diofar/an t-eadar-dhealachadh (a th') eadar A agus B?; **2** (*idiom*) **it makes no ~** chan eil e gu diofar, chan eil diofar ann

different *adj* **1** diof(a)rach, diofraichte & deifrichte, (*stronger*) eadar-dhealaichte; **2** (*idiom*) **you and I are ~** chan ionann thusa is mise

differentiate *v* eadar-dhealaich, dèan eadar-dhealachadh *m*, dèan sgaradh *m*, (**between** eadar)

differentiation *n* eadar-dhealachadh *m*

difficult *adj* **1** (*~ to do, solve &c*) doirbh, duilich, **a ~ question/problem** ceist dhoirbh/dhuilich, **that's ~ to say** tha sin doirbh a ràdh, **trigonometry isn't ~** chan eil triantanachd *f invar* doirbh; **2** (*~ to understand*) deacair, **a ~ book** leabhar deacair; **3** (*of circumstances &c: ~ to bear, deal with*) cruaidh, duilich; **4** *in expr* **a ~ situation** (*ie predicament, emergency &c*) cruaidh-chàs *m*, èiginn *f invar*

difficulty *n* **1** (*problem*) duilgheadas *m*, **we've got difficulties where money is concerned** tha duilgheadasan againn a thaobh airgid *m gen*; **2** (*predicament, danger*) càs *m*, (*more serious*) cruaidh-chàs *m*, èiginn *f invar*, **an aeroplane in ~ above the airport** itealan *m* ann an èiginn/na h-èiginn os cionn a' phuirt-adhair; **3** (*effort*) *in expr* **with ~** air èiginn *f*, **it was with ~ that he opened his eye** 's ann air èiginn a dh'fhosgail e a shùil *f*

diffident *adj* diùid, nàrach

diffuse *adj* sgaoilte, sgaipte *or* sgapta

diffuse *v* craobh-sgaoil *vti*

diffusion *n* craobh-sgaoileadh *m*

dig *v* cladhaich *vti*, ruamhair *vi*

digest *v* **1** (*lit*) cnàmh *vti*; **2** (*fig: mentally ~ information &c*) cnuasaich *vt*

digestion *n* cnàmh *m*, *used with art*, an cnàmh

digging *n* cladhach *m*

digit *n* (*arith &c*) figear *m*

digital *adj* (*IT &c*) figearail, **~ clock** gleoc figearail

dignified *adj* stàiteil, stòlda, stuama

dignify *v* àrdaich *vt*, urramaich *vt*

dignity *n* **1** (*abstr: rank, status*) urram *m*, inbhe *f*, mòralachd *f invar*; **2** (*~ of manner or appearance*) stàitealachd *f invar*, stòldachd *f invar*; **3** (*idiom*) **it is beneath my ~ to speak to him** cha diù leam bruidhinn *f* ris

digs *n* lòistinn *m*, taigh-loidsidh *m*

dilatory *adj* màirnealach, slaodach

dilemma *n* imcheist *f*, **in a ~** an/fo imcheist *dat*

diligence *n* dìcheall *m*

diligent *adj* dìcheallach

dilute *v* tanaich *vt*, lagaich *vt*

dilute *adj*, **diluted** *adj & past part*, tanaichte

dim *adj* **1** (*of light &c*) doilleir; **2** (*unintelligent*) maol-aigneach, (*fam*) tiugh; **3** *in expr* **I take a ~ view of X** is ciar leam X, is beag orm X

dim *v* doilleirich *vti*

dimension *n* **1** (*size*) meud *m invar*, meudachd *f invar*; **2** (*measurement*) tomhas *m*, **take ~s** gabh tomhasan

diminish *v* lùghdaich *vti*, beagaich *vti*

diminution *n* lùghdachadh *m*, beagachadh *m*

diminutive *adj* meanbh, bìodach, crìon

dimple *n* tibhre *m*

din ùpraid *f*, gleadhar *m*, othail *f*, iorghail *f*

dine *v* gabh dìnnear *f*, **we ~ at eight** gabhaidh sinn ar dìnnear *f* aig a h-ochd

dingy *adj* **1** (*dark*) doilleir; **2** (*grubby*) mosach, luideach

dining-room *n* seòmar-bìdh *m*, rùm-bìdh *m*

dinner *n* dìnnear *f*, (*more trad*) diathad *f*, *used with art*, an diathad, **what have we got/what are we getting/having for our ~?** dè a th' againn air ar dìnnear?, **she brought up her ~** chuir i a-mach a dìnnear

dinner-time *n* àm dìnnearach, (*more trad*) tràth dìnnearach

diocese *n* sgìre-easbaig *f*, sgìreachd-easbaig *f*

dip *n* **1** (*the action: in liquid*) tumadh *m*, bogadh *m*; **2** (*for sheep: the liquid*) dup *m*

dip *v* **1** (*~ in liquid*) tum *vt*, bog *vt*; **2** (*~ sheep*) dup *vti*

diploma *n* teisteanas *m*

diplomacy *n* dioplòmasaidh *mf*

diplomat *n* rìochdaire dioplòmasach

diplomatic *adj* dioplòmasach

dipping *n* **1** (*in liquid*) tumadh *m*, bogadh *m*; **2** (*~ sheep*) dupadh *m*

dipsomania *n* tinneas *m* na dighe

direct *adj* dìreach

direct *v* **1** (*conduct, show way &c*) treòraich *vt*, stiùir *vt*; **2** (*run, manage*) stiùir *vt*

direction *n* **1** taobh *m*, rathad *m*, **they're coming in this ~** tha iad a' tighinn an taobh/an rathad seo; **2** (*compass ~*) àird *f*; **3** *in pl* **~s** (*instructions, guidelines &c; also for route-finding &c*) seòlaidhean *mpl*, **I followed your ~s** lean mi na seòlaidhean agaibh; **4** *in expr* (*at roadside &c*) **~ board** clàr *m* seòlaidh

directly *adv* **1** (*straight*) calg-d(h)ìreach, **go ~ to the office** rach calg-d(h)ìreach don oifis *f*; **2** (*immediately*) gun dàil *f*, air ball, anns a' bhad *m*; **3** (*shortly*) a dh'aithghearr, an ceart(u)air, **I'll be with you ~** bidh mi agaibh an ceartair; **4** (*idiom*) **~ opposed to** calg-d(h)ìreach an aghaidh (*with gen*)

director *n* neach-stiùiridh *m* (*pl* luchd-stiùiridh *m sing coll*), stiùiriche *m*, *in expr* ~ **General** Àrd-stiùiriche *m*

directory *n* (*for phone &c*) leabhar-seòlaidh *m*

dirge *n* tuireadh *m*

dirk *n* biodag *f*

dirt *n* salchar *m*

dirty *adj* salach, rapach

dis- *prefix* **1** ana- *prefix, eg* **disadvantage** *n* anacothrom *m*; **2** eas- *prefix, eg* **disobedient** eas-umhail; **3** mì- *prefix, eg* **disadvantage** *v* mì-leasaich *vt*

disability *n* ciorram *m, in expr* ~ **allowance** cuibhreann-ciorraim *m*

disabled *adj* ciorramach, *in exprs* **a** ~ **person** ciorramach *m*, neach *m* ciorramach (*pl* luchd-ciorramach *m sing coll*), **the** ~ na ciorramaich *mpl*

disadvantage *n* anacothrom *m*, mì-leas *m*

disadvantage *v* mì-leasaich *vt*

disadvantaged *adj & past part* **1** (*esp person*) fo anacothrom *m*; **2** (*region &c*) mì-leasaichte

disagree *v* rach *vi* an aghaidh (*with gen*), easaontaich *vi*, (*less confrontational*) **I** ~ chan eil mi(se) den aon bheachd *m*, chan eil mi a' dol leis a sin, cha tèid mi le sin

disagreeable *adj* neo-thaitneach

disagreement *n* **1** (*the act of disagreeing*) dol *m invar* an aghaidh (*with gen*); **2** (*abstr & con*) easaonta *f*, mì-chòrdadh *m*, **(a)** ~ **arose between us** dh'èirich *vi* easaonta eadarainn; **3** (*idiom*) **we were in total** ~ bha sinn calg-d(h)ìreach an aghaidh a chèile

disallow *v* mì-cheadaich *vt*

disappear *v* rach *vi* à sealladh *m*

disappoint *v* meall *vt*, leig *vt* sìos

disappointment *n* bris(t)eadh-dùil *m*, mealleadh-dùil *m*

disapproval *n* coireachadh *m*, dol *m invar* an aghaidh (*with gen*)

disapprove *v* **1** coirich *vt*, rach *vi* an aghaidh (*with gen*); **2** (*idioms*) **we** ~ **of that** chan eil sinn a' dol le sin, **I** ~ **of your conduct** is beag orm do dhol-a-mach *m invar*

disarm *v* dì-armaich *vti*

disarmament *n* dì-armachadh *m*

disarray *n* mì-riaghailt *f*

disaster *n* tubaist *f*, mòr-thubaist *f*, calldachd *f*

disbelief *n* às-creideamh *m*

disc, disk *n* **1** clàr *m*, (*IT*) **compact** ~ meanbh-chlàr, **hard/floppy** ~ clàr cruaidh/sùbailte, ~ **drive** clàr-inneal *m*; **2** (*in spine*) clàr *m*, **(a) slipped** ~ (*con*) clàr sgiorrte, (*the medical condition*) leum-droma *m*

discard *v* tilg *vt* air falbh

discernible *adj* follaiseach, so-fhaicinn

discerning *adj* tuigseach

discernment *n* tuigse *f*

discharge *v* **1** (*duties, obligations &c*) coilean *vt*; **2** (*debt*) ìoc *vt*, pàigh *vt*; **3** (*person from army &c*) saor *vt*; **4** (*gun*) loisg *vt*, tilg *vt*; **5** (*cargo &c*) di-luchdaich *vti*

disciple *n* deisciobal *m*

disciplinary *adj* smachdachaidh (*gen of* smachdachadh *m, used adjectivally*), ~ **tribunal** tribiunal smachdachaidh

discipline *n* **1** smachd *m invar*; **2** (*ed: field of study*) cuspair *m*

discipline *v* **1** (*assert authority over*) smachdaich *vt*, cuir smachd *f* (*with prep* air); **2** (*punish*) peanasaich *vt*

disclose *v* foillsich *vt*, leig *vt* ris

disclosure *n* (*abstr*) foillseachadh *m*, leigeil *m* ris

disco *n* diosgo *m invar*

discomfort *n* anshocair *f*

disconcert *v* buair *vt*

disconnect *v* neo-cheangail *vt*, sgaoil *vt*

disconsolate *adj* brònach, dubhach

discontent *n* mì-thoileachadh *m*, diomb & diumb *m invar*

discontented *adj* mì-thoilichte, diombach & diumbach

discontinue *v* (*an activity &c*) cuir stad *m* (*with prep* air), leig *vt* seachad, sguir *vi* (*with prep* de), **she ~d the correspondence** chuir i stad air a' cho-sgrìobhadh *m*, **I'm discontinuing the music lessons** tha mi a' leigeil seachad nan leasanan *m* ciùil *m*

discord *n* **1** (*abstr & con*) easaonta *f*, mì-chòrdadh *m*, ~ **arose between us** dh'èirich easaonta/mì-chòrdadh eadarainn; **2** (*music*) dì-chòrda *m*

discount *n* (*trade &c*) lùghdachadh *m* prìse/phrìsean *f gen*, ìsleachadh *m* prìse/phrìsean, **buy at a** ~ ceannaich *vti* air prìs(ean) ìsleachaidh *gen*

discount *v* **1** (*trade &c*) leag/lùghdaich/ìslich prìs(ean) *f*, reic *vti* air prìs(ean) ìsleachaidh *m gen*; **2** (*ignore, not take into account*) **I am ~ing everything he said** chan eil mi a' cur sùim *f* ann an càil *m invar* sam bith a thuirt e

discourage *v* **1** mì-mhisnich *vt*; **2** (*dissuade from*) thoir comhairle *f* (*with prep* air *followed by* gun & *infinitive of verb*), **I ~d him from joining the army** thug mi comhairle *f* air gun a dhol dhan arm *m*

discouragement *n* **1** (*the action*) mì-mhisneachadh *m*; **2** (*the state of mind*) mì-mhisneachd *f invar*

discourteous *adj* mì-mhodhail

discourtesy *n* mì-mhodh *m*

discover *v* **1** (*facts &c*) faigh *vt* a-mach; **2** (*objects &c*) lorg *vt*

discredit *n* **1** (*loss of trust, credibility*) mì-chreideas *m*; **2** (*loss of reputation*) mì-chliù *m*

discreet *adj* **1** (*keeping confidentiality*) rùnach; **2** (*tactful &c*) tuigseach

discrepancy *n* eadar-dhealachadh *m*, diofar *m*, (**between** eadar)

discretion *n* **1** (*tact, good judgement*) tuigse *f*, breithneachadh *m*; **2** *in exprs* **at**

your ~ mar as roghnach leibh, **we left it to their own** ~ dh'fhàg sinn aca fhèin e

discriminate *v* 1 (*unjustly*) dèan lethbhreith *f* (**against** an aghaidh, *with gen*); 2 (*neutral: differentiate &c*) eadar-dhealaich *vi*, dèan eadar-dhealachadh *m*, (**between** eadar)

discrimination *n* 1 (*unjust bias &c*) lethbhreith *f*; 2 (*capacity to judge, assess*) breithneachadh *m*; 3 (*abstr: making of distinctions*) eadar-dhealachadh *m* (**between** eadar)

discriminatory *adj* (*showing unjust bias &c*) lethbhreitheach

discuss *v* deasbair *vi* (*with prep* mu), deasbad *vi*, beachdaich *vi*, (*both with prep* air)

discussion *n* 1 (*abstr*) deasbaireachd *f invar*; 2 (*con*) **a** ~ deasbad *mf*

disdain *n* tarcais *f*, tailceas *m*, tàir *f*, dìmeas *m*

disdain *v* dèan tarcais *f*, dèan tàir *f*, dèan dìmeas *m*, (*all with prep* air)

disdainful *adj* tarcaiseach, tailceasach, tàireil

disease *n* tinneas *m*, galar *m*, euslaint *f*, **heart** ~ tinneas cridhe *m*, **infectious** ~**s** tinneasan gabhaltach

disembark *v* rach *vi* air tìr *mf*

disentangle *v* (*objects, situations &c*) rèitich *vt*, (*objects*) fuasgail *vt*, ~ **this wool for me** rèitich/fuasgail a' chlòimh seo dhomh

disentangled *adj & past part* (*wool &c*) rèidh

disgrace *n* 1 (*abstr*) masladh *m*, tàmailt *f*; 2 (*source of* ~) cùis-mhaslaidh *f*, **it's a** ~! 's e cùis-mhaslaidh a th' ann!

disgrace *v* nàraich *vt*, maslaich *vt*

disgraceful *adj* maslach, tàmailteach, nàr, **that's** ~! is nàr sin!

disgruntled *adj* diombach *&* diumbach, gruamach, mì-riaraichte

disguise *n* breug-riochd *m*

disgust *n* gràin *f*, sgreamh *m*

disgust *v* sgreamhaich *vt*, cuir sgreamh *m* (*with prep* air)

disgusting *adj* gràineil, sgreamhail

dish *n* soitheach *m*, **do/wash the** ~**es** dèan na soitheachan

dish-cloth *n* brèid-shoithichean *m*

dishonest *adj* eas-onarach, mì-onarach

dishonesty *n* mì-onair *m*

dishonour *n* eas-onair *f*, eas-urram *m*

dishonourable *adj* eas-urramach

dishwasher *n* nigheadair-shoithichean *m*

disillusion *v* bris misneachd *f*, **I don't want to** ~ **you** chan eil mi airson do mhisneachd a bhris(t)eadh

disillusionment *n* call *m* misneachd *f*

disinclined *adj* aindeònach, leisg, **I was** ~ **to follow them** bha mi aindeònach an leantainn, (*more trad*) bu leisg leam an leantainn, *also* bha leisg *f* orm an leantainn

disingenuous *adj* cealgach, fallsa

disinherit *v* thoir/cùm oighreachd *f* (*with prep* bho/o), **his father ~ed him** thug/chùm athair oighreachd bhuaithe

disinterested *adj* neo-thaobhach

disjointed *adj* **1** (*lit*) às an alt *m*; **2** (*discourse &c*) briste

disk *n see* **disc**

dislike *n* mì-thaitneamh *m*

dislike *v*, **I ~ him** is beag orm e, cha toigh leam e

dislocate *v* (*joint*) cuir *vt* às an alt *m*

disloyal *adj* mì-dhìleas, neo-dhìleas

disloyalty *n* mì-dhìlseachd *f invar*, neo-dhìlseachd *f invar*

dismal *adj* **1** (*of weather, light*) doilleir; **2** (*of persons: depressed &c*) dubhach, sìos na (*&c*) inntinn *f*; **3** (*of condition, outlook, performance &c*) bochd, truagh, **a ~ excuse** leisgeul bochd

dismantle *v* thoir *vt* às a chèile

dismay *n* mì-mhisneach *f*

dismay *v* **1** (*discourage*) mì-mhisnich *vt*; **2** (*alarm*) cuir eagal *m* (*with prep* air)

dismiss *v* **1** cuir *vt* air falbh; **2** (*employee &c*) cuir *vt* à dreuchd *f*

dismissal *n* (*of employee &c*) cur *m* à dreuchd *f*

dismount *v* teirinn *&* teàrn *vi* (**from** bho/o)

disobedience *n* eas-ùmhlachd *f invar*

disobedient *adj* eas-umhail

disobey *v* rach *vi* an aghaidh (*with gen*)

disorder *n* **1** (*lack of orderliness*) mì-rian *m*, mì-riaghailt *f*, *in expr* **in ~** troimh-a-chèile, **after the accident everything was in ~** an dèidh na tubaist bha a h-uile cail *m invar* troimh-a-chèile; **2** (*emotional, moral ~*) buaireas *m*; **3** (*mental ~*) mì-rian *m*; **4** (*civil ~*) aimhreit *f*, buaireas *m*

disorderly *adj* mì-rianail, mì-riaghailteach, buaireasach, aimhreiteach

disown *v* diùlt *vt*, àicheidh *vt*, **she won't ~ her own daughter** cha diùlt i a nighean fhèin

disparage *v* dèan tàir *f* (*with prep* air), cuir *vt* an suarachas *m*

disparagement *n* **1** (*abstr*) tàir *f*; **2** (*the action*) cur *m* an suarachas *m*

disparaging *adj* tàireil

disparate *adj* (gu tur) eadar-dhealaichte

disparity *n* neo-ionannachd *f invar*

dispense *v* **1** (*supply*) solair *vt*, riaraich *vt*; **2** *in expr* **~ with** dèan *vi irreg* às aonais (*with gen*)

dispersal *n* sgaoileadh *m*, sgapadh *m*

disperse *v* sgaoil *vti*, sgap *vti*

display *n* (*of art, goods, techniques &c*) taisbeanadh *m*

display *v* **1** (*esp art, goods, techniques &c*) taisbean *&* taisbein *vt*; **2** (*IT, electronics &c*) sealladh *m*, clàr *m* taisbeanaidh *m*, **digital ~** sealladh figearail

displease *v* mì-thoilich *vt*

displeasure *n* **1** mì-thoileachas *m*; **2** (*esp towards another person*) diomb *&* diumb *m invar*

disposal *n* **1** (*getting rid of*) faighinn *f invar* cuidhteas *m*; **2** (~ *by sale*) reic *m invar*; **3** (*idiom*) **I won't manage with the means at my** ~ cha dèan mi a' chùis leis na tha ri mo làimh (*dat of* làmh *f*)

dispose *v* **1** (*place, arrange &c*) suidhich *vt*, socraich *vt*; **2** *in expr* ~ **of something** faigh cuidhteas *m* rudeigin

disposition *n* (*temperament*) nàdar *m*, mèinn *f*, aigne *f*

dispossess *v* cuir *vt* à seilbh *f*

disprove *v* breugnaich *vt*

disputatious *adj* connsachail, connspaideach

dispute *n* connsachadh *m*, connspaid *f*

dispute *v* **1** (*as vi: argue*) connsaich *vi*; **2** (*as vt:* ~ *the truth &c of*) ceasnaich *vt*, cuir *vt* an ceist *f*

disqualification *n* dì-cheadachadh *m*

disqualify *v* dì-cheadaich *vt*

disquiet *n* iomagain *f*, imcheist *f*

disregard *n* **1** (*lack of concern*) neo-chùram *m* (**for** air), ~ **for safety** neo-chùram air tèarainteachd *f invar*; **2** (*lack of respect*) dìmeas *m* (**for** air)

disregard *v, in expr* **they ~ed my instructions** cha robh sùim *f* aca de na h-òrduighean *mpl* agam

disreputable *adj* **1** (*in appearance*) cearbach, luideach, grodach; **2** (*in character, behaviour*) neo-mheasail, (*fam*) fiadhaich, (*more disapproving*) tàmailteach, maslach

disrepute *n* mì-chliù *m*, **bring X into** ~ tarraing mì-chliù air X

disrespect *n* dìmeas *m invar*, eas-urram *m*

disrupt *v* (*event, meeting &c*) buair *vt*, cuir *vt* troimh-a-chèile, cuir *vt* thar a chèile

disruption *n* **1** (*the action*) buaireadh; **2** (*the state of affairs*) aimhreit *f*; **3** (*relig hist*) **The Disruption** Bris(t)eadh *m* na h-Eaglaise

dissatisfaction *n* mì-thoileachadh *m*

dissatisfy *v* mì-thoilich *vt*

dissembler *n* cealgair(e) *m*

dissembling *adj* cealgach

disseminate *v* sgaoil *vt*, craobh-sgaoil *vt*

dissemination *n* sgaoileadh *m*, craobh-sgaoileadh *m*

dissent *n* (*abstr & con*) easaonta *f*, ~ **arose between us** dh'èirich easaonta eadarainn

dissent *v* easaontaich *vi* (**from** ri)

dissenting *adj* easaontach

dissertation *n* tràchdas *m*

disservice *n* mì-sheirbheis *f*

dissident *adj* easaontach

dissident *n* easaontaiche *m*

dissimilar *adj* eu-coltach (**to** ri)

dissimilarity *n* eu-coltas *m*

dissimulation *n* cealgaireachd *f invar*

dissipate *v* (*wealth*) struidh *vt*, caith *vt*, ana-caith *vt*

dissipation *n* struidheadh *m*, ana-caitheamh *f*

dissolve *v* **1** leagh *vti*; **2** *in expr* ~ **parliament** sgaoil pàrlamaid *f*

dissuade *v* thoir comhairle *f* (*with prep* air *or* do), thoir *vt* (*with prep* air), (*both followed by* gun *and infinitive of verb*), **I ~d him from joining the army** thug mi comhairle *f* dha gun a dhol dhan arm *m*, thug mi air gun a dhol dhan arm

distance *n* astar *m*

distant *adj* **1** fad air falbh, cèin, iomallach; **2** (*of person*) fad' às

distaste *n* gràin *f* (**for** air)

distasteful *adj* gràineil, mì-chàilear

distend *v* at *vi*, sèid *vi*

distil *v* (*spirits*) tarraing *vti*

distillation *n* (*of spirits*) tarraing *f*, grùdadh *m*

distiller *n* grùdair(e) *m*

distillery *n* **1** taigh-staile *m*; **2** (*illicit* ~) taigh dubh, poit dhubh

distinct *adj* **1** (*esp sounds, sights: clear*) taisbeanach; **2** (*different, separate*) eadar-dhealaichte, air leth, (*more trad*) fa leth, (*less strong*) diof(a)rach, **a ~ species** seòrsa *m* eadar-dhealaichte/air leth

distinction *n* **1** (*difference*) eadar-dhealachadh *m* (**between** eadar); **2** (*pre-eminence*) àrd-urram *m*, òirdheirceas *m*

distinctive *adj* air leth, àraidh

distinctly *adv* gu taisbeanach, gu soilleir, **he saw/heard them** ~ chunnaic/chuala e gu taisbeanach/gu soilleir iad

distinguish *v* eadar-dhealaich, dèan eadar-dhealachadh *m*, (**between** eadar)

distinguished *adj* (*ie pre-eminent*) barraichte, òirdheirc

distort *v* **1** (*lit: phys*) cuir *vt* à cumadh *m*; **2** (*misquote, misrepresent*) dèan mì-aithris *m*, thoir claon-iomradh *m*, (*with prep* air), **you have ~ed what I said** tha sibh air mì-aithris a dhèanamh/claon-iomradh a thoirt air na thuirt mi

distortion *n* **1** (*lit: phys*) ath-chumadh *m*; **2** (*misquotation, misrepresentation &c*) mì-aithris *m*, claon-iomradh *m*

distract *v* tarraing aire *f invar* (**from** bho/o)

distracted *adj & past part* **1** (*preoccupied*) fad' às; **2** (*in intense mental state*) às a (*&c*) rian *m*

distraction *n* **1** (*pastime*) caitheamh-aimsir *m*, cur-seachad *m*; **2** (*intense mental state*) boile *f invar*

distress *n* (*mental state, also danger*) èiginn *f invar*, **a boat in** ~ bàta *m* ann an èiginn, bàta na èiginn

distress *v* (*mentally, emotionally*) sàraich *vt*, cràidh *vt*, pian *vt*, tàmailtich *vt*

distressed *adj* na (*&c*) èiginn *f invar*, cràidhte, air a (*&c*) s(h)àrachadh, air a (*&c*) t(h)àmailteachadh

distribute *v* roinn *vt*, riaraich *vt*, sgaoil *vt*

distribution *n* roinn *f*, riarachadh *m*, sgaoileadh *m*

district *n* ceàrn *m*, sgìre *f*, tìr *mf*, **remote** ~ ceàrn iomallach, ~ **council** comhairle *f* sgìre *gen*

distrust *n* mì-earbsa *m*, amharas *m*

distrustful *adj* mì-earbsach, amharasach

disturb *v* **1** (*bother, intrude upon &c*) cuir dragh *m* (*with prep* air); **2** (*disrupt situation &c; also* ~ *emotionally*) buair *vt*

disturbance *n* **1** (*the action*) buaireadh *m*; **2** (*the result*) aimhreit *f*, buaireas *m*, an-fhois *m*

disunity *n* eas-aonachd *f invar*

disuse *n* mì-chleachdadh *m*, *in expr* **fall into** ~ rach *vi irreg* à cleachdadh *m*

ditch *n* clais *f*, dìg *f*

ditty *n* duanag *f*, luinneag *f*

dive *v* dàibh *vi*, dàibhig *vi*

diver *n* dàibhear *m*

diverge *v* dealaich *vi* ri chèile, **their paths** ~**d** dhealaich na slighean *fpl* aca ri chèile

diverse *adj* caochladh *n* (*followed by gen pl of noun*), de dh'iomadach seòrsa *m* (*follows noun*), ~ **methods** caochladh dhòighean, ~ **excuses** leusgeulan *mpl* de dh'iomadach seòrsa

diversion *n* **1** (*fun, entertainment*) dibhearsan *m*, spòrs *f*, (*more trad*) fearas-chuideachd *f*; **2** (~ *of traffic*) tionndadh *m* slighe *f*

diversity *n* iomadachd *f invar*

divert *v* **1** (*phys, also* ~ *funds &c*) tionndaidh *vt* a leth-taobh *m*; **2** (*amuse &c*) thoir dibhearsan *m* (*with prep* do)

diving *n* dàibheadh *m*, dàibhigeadh *m*

divide *v* **1** pàirtich *vt*, riaraich *vt*, roinn *vt*; **2** (*by force, through disunity &c*) sgar *vt*

divided *adj & past part* **1** (*lit*) roinnte; **2** (*of persons:* ~ *by force, disagreements &c*) air a (*&c*) sgaradh; **3** (*arith*) air a roinn (**by** le), **72** ~ **by 3** 72 air a roinn le 3

dividend *n* **1** (*gain*) buannachd *f*, **the peace** ~ buannachd na sìthe; **2** (*from shares*) duais-shèaraichean *f*

divine *adj* **1** diadhaidh; **2** (*coming from God*) Dhè (*gen of* Dè *m, used adjectivally*), ~ **grace** gràs *m* Dhè

divinity *n* **1** (*abstr: the attribute of a god*) diadhachd *f invar*; **2** (*the subject of study &c*) diadhaireachd *f invar*

division *n* **1** (*abstr: the process*) pàirteacheadh *m*; **2** (*through disagreement, by force &c*) sgaradh *m*; **3** (*arith &c*) roinn *f*; **4** (*con: eg in football*) roinn *f*, **the second** ~ an dàrna roinn

divorce *n* sgaradh-pòsaidh *m*

divorce *v* dealaich *vi* (*with prep* ri), **he ~d his wife** dhealaich e ris a' mhnaoi (*dat of* bean *f*) aige

divot *n* fàl *m*, ploc *m*, sgrath & sgroth *f*

divulge *v* foillsich *vt*, innis *vt*

dizziness *n* tuainealaich *f*, (*less usu*) luasgan *m*

dizzy *adj* tuainealach

do *v* **1** dèan *vt irreg*, **~ your duty** dèan do dhleastanas *m*, **don't ~ that!** na dèan sin!, **I did my best** rinn mi mo dhìcheall *m* (**to** air), **didn't you ~ well!**, *also* **well done!** nach math a rinn thu!, **well done!** math fhèin, math thu fhèin!, **that will ~**, **that will ~ the job/trick!** nì sin an gnothach, nì sin a' chùis!, **~ business** dèan gnothach *m* (**with** ri), **it will ~ you good** nì e feum *m* dhut, **that won't be done** cha tèid sin a dhèanamh, **that can't be done** cha ghabh sin a dhèanamh, cha ghabh sin dèanamh; **2 don't** *neg imperative, expr by neg particle* na, *followed by imperative of the relevant verb*, **don't leave it on the floor!** na fàg air an làr *m* e!, **don't have anything to ~ with him/it!** na gabh gnothach *m* ris!; **3** (*be sufficient*) foghain *vi*, **will that ~?** am foghain sin?, (*to children &c*) **that will ~!** fòghnaidh sin!; **4** (*other idioms & exprs*) (*fam*) **how are you ~ing?** dè an dòigh (a th' ort)?, dè do chor?, **a wee stroll would ~ you good** b' fheàirrde thu cuairt bheag, **what's ~ing?** (*fam*) dè (a) tha (a') dol?, **~ away with** cuir *vi* às do, **~ up** (*ie renovate &c*) leasaich *vt*, nuadhaich *vt*, càraich *vt*, cuir *vt* air dòigh *f*

docile *adj* **1** sèimh, ciùin, sàmhach; **2** (*biddable*) macanta, umha(i)l

docility *n* **1** sèimhe *f invar*, ciùineas *m*; **2** (*obedience*) macantas *m*, ùmhlachd *f invar*

dock[1] *n* (*bot*) copag *f*

dock[2] *n* (*in seaport &c*) doca *m*

dock[1] *v* **1** (*cut, shorten*) giorraich *vt*, cut & cutaich *vt*; **2** (*fam: reduce*) **they ~ed my pay** lùghdaich iad am pàigheadh *m invar* agam

dock[2] (*ship &c: as vt*) cuir *vt* san doca *m*, (*as vi*) rach *vi* a-steach dhan doca

docken *n* (*bot*) copag *f*

docker *n* docair *m*

doctor *n* **1** (*medical*) do(c)tair *m*, (*more trad*) lighiche *m*; **2** (*non-medical, PhD &c*) ollamh *m*, **~ Campbell** An t-Ollamh Caimbeul

doctorate *n* ollamhachd *f invar*

doctrine *n* teagasg *m*

document *n* sgrìobhainn *f*, pàipear *m*

documentary *adj* **1** sgrìobhte, **~ evidence** fianais *f* sgrìobhte; **2** (*media &c*) aithriseach, **a ~ film** film *m* aithriseach

documentary *n* (*media &c*) film *m*/prògram *m* (*&c*) aithriseach

dodge *n* (*stratagem &c*) innleachd *f*, (*more fam*) plòigh *f*

dodgy *adj* **1** (*dubious*) cugallach; **2** (*risky*) cunnartach

doff *v* cuir *vt* (*with prep* de), **we ~ed our caps** chuir sinn dhinn ar ceapannan *mpl*

dog *n* **1** cù *m*; **2** (*more trad: of any canine species*) madadh *m*

dogged *adj* **1** (*as term of praise: persistent &c*) leanailteach, dìorrasach; **2** (*as adverse criticism: stubborn, intractable*) dùr, rag, rag-mhuinealach

dogmatic *adj* (*intractable in one's opinions*) rag-bharaileach

dole *n* dòil *m invar*

dole out *v* riaraich *vt*

doleful *adj* brònach, smalanach

doll *n* liùdhag *f*, doileag *f*

dollar *n* dolair *m*

dolt *n* bumailear *m*, ùmaidh *m*, stalcaire *m*

domestic *adj* taigheil

domesticate *v* callaich *vt*

domesticated *adj* **1** (*of animals*) calla & callda; **2** (*of home-loving person*) dachaigheil

domestication *n* callachadh *m*

domicile *n* àite-fuirich *m*, àite-còmhnaidh *m*, dachaigh *f*

dominance *n* smachd *m*, làmh *f* an uachdair, (**over** air), **he achieved ~ over them** fhuair e smachd/làmh an uachdair orra

dominant *adj* **1** (*exerting power, authority*) ceannsalach, smachdail; **2** (*principal, main &c*) prìomh (*precedes the noun, which it lenites where possible*), **the ~ group of the party** prìomh bhuidheann *mf* a' phàrtaidh

dominate *v* **1** (*achieve dominance over*) ceannsaich *vt*, smachdaich *vt*, cuir *vt* fo smachd *m*, faigh smachd (*with prep* air); **2** (*be in a position of dominance over*) cùm *vt* fo smachd, **the Romans ~d them for many years** chùm na Ròmanaich *mpl* fo smachd iad fad iomadach bliadhna *f*

domineering *adj* ceannsalach

donate *v* tiodhlaic *vt*, thoir *vt* (seachad), (**to** do)

donation *n* tabhartas *m*, tiodhlac *m*, (**to** do)

done *adj* & *past part* **1** dèanta & dèante; **2** (*fam: finished*) deiseil, ullamh, **are you nearly ~?** a bheil thu gu bhith deiseil?, **have you ~ with the phone?** a bheil thu deiseil den fòn *mf*?; **3** *in expr* **well ~!** math fhèin!, math thu-fhèin!, nach math a rinn thu!

donor *n* tabhartaiche *m*, tabhairteach *m*

don't *neg imperative, see* **do 2**

doomsday *n* Là-luain *m*

door *n* **1** doras *m*, **the main/front ~** an doras mòr, **the ~ handle** làmh *f* an dorais, **bar the ~** cuir an crann air an doras, **living next ~** a' fuireachd an ath-dhoras, **out of ~s** a-mach air doras; **2** (*idiom*) **at death's ~** ri uchd *m* a' bhàis; *Note: traditionally* doras *was used for the door opening while the door leaf was* còmhla *mf, but* doras *is now often used for both*

doorman *n* dorsair *m*, portair *m*

doorpost *n* ursainn *f*

doorstep *n* leac *f* (an) dorais

doorway n doras m (see Note under **door**)

dormant adj na (&c) c(h)adal m, na (&c) t(h)àmh m

dormitory n seòmar-cadail m

dose n tomhas m (ìocshlaint f)

double adj dùbailte

double v (numbers, quantities &c) dùblaich vti

double-barrelled adj, **a ~ shotgun** gunna dùbailte

doubt n 1 teagamh m, **without (a) ~** gun teagamh, **there's no ~ about it** chan eil teagamh ann, **cast ~ (up)on** cuir vt an (prep) teagamh m, **they cast ~ on his veracity** chuir iad an teagamh an fhìreantachd aige; 2 (perplexity, puzzlement) imcheist f, iomadh-chomhairle f, **in ~ as to what I would do** an/fo imcheist dè a dhèanainn, ann an iomadh-chomhairle dè a dhèanainn

doubt v 1 (cast ~ (up)on) cuir vt an teagamh m, cuir vt an amharas m, cuir teagamh (with prep ann an), **they ~ed his innocence** chuir iad an teagamh/an amharas an neo-chiontachd f invar aige, chuir iad teagamh san neo-chiontachd aige; 2 (fail to believe) **will he go back? I ~ it** an tèid e air ais? cha chreid mi gun tèid

doubtful adj teagmhach

doubting adj teagmhach, amharasach

doubtless adv gun teagamh

dough n taois f

dour adj dùr, gruamach

dove n calman m

dowdy adj cearbach, luideach, robach

down adv 1 (movement) sìos, **my shares have gone ~** tha mo shèaraichean mpl air a dhol sìos; 2 (movement: from point of view of person(s) making the movement) sìos, **go ~** rach vi sìos, **he went ~ (towards them)** chaidh e sìos (dhan ionnsaigh); 3 (movement: from point of view of person(s) towards whom the movement is made) a-nuas, **come ~** thig a-nuas, **he came ~ (towards me)** thàinig e a-nuas dham ionnsaigh; 4 (position) shìos, **they're all ~ there** tha iad uile shìos an sud; 5 (misc idioms & exprs) **sit ~** dèan suidhe m, (more fam) suidh vi sìos, (less usu) suidh a-bhàn, **go ~** (of sun) laigh vi, **knock ~, throw ~, let ~,** leag vt, **he let ~ the window** leag e an uinneag, **she's lying ~** tha i na laighe, **she was a bit ~** bha i rud beag sìos na h-inntinn, also bha i rud beag ìseal/ìosal, **she walked ~ the slope** choisich i leis a' bhruthaich mf, **slow ~** (as vt) cuir maille f invar (with preps air or ann), **slow ~ the improvements** cuir maille air na leasachaidhean mpl

downcast adj smalanach, fo smalan m, dubhach, (more fam) sìos na (&c) inntinn f, ìseal & ìosal

downhill adv 1 leis a' bhruthaich mf; 2 (idiom: fig) **she went ~** chaidh vi i bhuaipe

downpour n dìle f, (heavier) dìle bhàthte

downstairs *adj* **1** (*position*) shìos an staidhre *f*, **they are** ~ tha iad shìos an staidhre; **2** (*movement*) sìos an staidhre, **they went** ~ chaidh iad sìos an staidhre

downstream *adv* (*movement*) leis an t-sruth

downwards *adv* sìos

dowry *n* tochradh *m*

doze *n* clò-chadal *m*, leth-chadal *m*, dùsal *m*, norrag *f*

doze *v* **1** dèan dùsal *m*, dèan norrag (bheag); **2** (*idioms*) **I** ~**d off** chaidh *vi* mi nam chlò-chadal *m*, thàinig *vi* clò-chadal orm

dozen *n* dusan *m*

dozy *adj* **1** (*with sleep*) cadalach; **2** (*mentally slow*) maol-aigneach

drab *adj* (*in colour*) lachdann, odhar, doilleir

draft *n* (*of document*) dreachd *f*, dreachdadh *m*

drag *v* **1** tarraing *vti*, slaod *vti*, (**at/on** air), dragh *vt*; **2** (*fig*) *in expr* ~ **one's heels** màirnealaich *vi*

dragonfly *n* tarbh-nathrach *m*

drain *n* **1** (*agric, plumbing &c*) clais *f*, drèana *f*; **2** (*source of fin waste or loss*) traoghadh *m* (**on** de), **a** ~ **on resources** traoghadh den mhaoin *f*

drain *v* **1** (*empty a container &c*) tràigh *vt*; **2** (*drain liquids from container &c*) taom *vt*; **3** (*cookery*) taom *vt*, ~ **the carrots** taom na currain *mpl*; **4** *in expr* ~ **away** sìol *vi* às, **the waters** ~**ed away** shìol na h-uisgeachan *mpl* às

drainage *n* drèanadh *m*

drainpipe *n* pìob *f* drèanaidh *m gen*

drake *n* ràc *m*, dràc *m*

dram *n* drama *m*, dràm *m*, **will you take a** ~? an gabh thu drama?

drama dràma *m*

dramatic *adj* dràmadach & dràmatach

dramatist *n* sgrìobhaiche *m* dràma *m gen*, dràmaire *m*

draught *n* (*of liquid*) tarraing *f*, (*fam*) balgam *m*, sgailc *f*, steallag *f*

draughtboard *n* bòrd-dàmais *m*

draughts *n* (*game*) dàmais *f invar*

draw *n* (*football match &c*) geama *m* ionannach

draw *v* **1** (*pull, drag*) tarraing *vti*, slaod *vti*, (**on** air), dragh *vt* ~ **on the rope** tarraing air an ròpa *m*, ~ **breath/blood** tarraing anail *f*/fuil *f*, ~ **a pint/a cork** tarraing pinnt *m*/corcais *f*; **2** (*less lit uses*) tarraing *vt*, ~ **a picture** tarraing dealbh *m*, ~ **to a close** tarraing *vi* gu crìch (*dat of* crìoch *f*); **3** *in exprs* ~ **lots** cuir croinn (*pl of* crann *m*), tilg croinn, ~**ing lots** (*ie the action*) crannchur *m*; **4** *in expr* ~ **near** dlùthaich *vi*, teann *vi*, (**to** ri), **we were** ~**ing near to the sea** bha sinn a' dlùthachadh/a' teannadh ris a' mhuir *mf*; **5** (~ *weapon, sword*) rùisg *vt*

drawer *n* drabhair *m*

drawing *n* dealbh *mf*

drawing-pin *n* tacaid *f*, tacaid-bhalla *f*

dread *n* uamhann & uabhann *m*, oillt *f*, uabhas *m*

dreadful *adj* **1** oillteil; **2** (*often with attenuated meaning*) eagalach, uabhasach, sgriosail, **the music was just ~!** bha an ceòl dìreach eagalach/uabhasach/sgriosail!

dreadfully *adv*, uabhasach, eagalach, garbh, **~ poor** uabhasach/eagalach bochd, **things are ~ busy just now** tha cùisean *fpl* garbh dripeil an-dràsta

dream *n* bruadar *m*, aisling *f*

dream *v* **1** bruadair *vi* (**about/of** air), **I was ~ing about you** bha mi a' bruadar ort; **2** *in expr* **you're ~ing!** tha thu ri bruadar!, tha thu ag aisling!

dreamer *n* aislingiche *m*

dreary *adj* **1** (*mournful*) tiamhaidh; **2** (*dull, tedious*) slaodach

dregs *n* (*in liquids*) grùid *f*

drench *v* drùidh *vi* (*with prep* air), **the rain ~ed me** dhrùidh an t-uisge orm

drenched *adj & past part* drùidhte, bog fliuch

dress *n* **1** (*woman's garment*) dreasa *f*; **2** (*mode of ~*) èideadh *m*, **Highland ~** an t-èideadh Gàidhealach

dress *v* **1** (*~ oneself*) cuir *vti* (*with prep* mu), **I ~ed** chuir mi umam, chuir mi umam m' aodach *m*; **2** (*~ someone else*) cuir aodach (*with prep* air), **I ~ed him** chuir mi aodach air; **3** *in expr* **~ up** sgeadaich *vt*

dressed *adj & past part, in exprs* **I got ~** chuir mi umam (m' aodach *m*), **well ~** spruiseil

dresser *n* (*furniture*) dreasair *m*

dressing-gown *n* còta-leapa *m*

dried *adj & past part* **1** tiormaichte; **2** *in expr* **~ up** crìon, seac

drift *n*, (*idiom*) **you made me lose my ~** chuir thu às mo ghabhail *mf* mi

drift *v* (*snow &c*) cath *vi*

drifter *n* (*fishing*) drioftair *m*

drill[1] *n* (*tool*) drile *f*, (*more trad*) snìomhaire *m*, tolladair *m*

drill[2] *n* (*army &c*) drile *f*

drill[1] *v* toll *vt*, *in expr* (*oil industry*) **~ing platform** clàr *m* tollaidh *m gen*

drill[2] *v* (*army &c*) drilich *vi*, dèan drile *f*

drink *n* **1** (*of all kinds*) deoch *f*, **a ~ of milk/of water** deoch bhainne *m*/uisge *m*; **2** (*alcoholic ~*) deoch *f*, deoch-làidir *f invar*, **he's fond of the ~** tha e measail air an deoch

drink *v* **1** òl *vti*, gabh *vt*, **~ a cup of tea** òl/gabh cupan *m* teatha *f invar*; **2** (*alcoholic drinks*) òl *vti*, **I don't ~ at all** cha bhi mi ag òl idir

drinker *n* (*usu excessive*) pòitear *m*, misgear *m*

drinking *n* **1** (*general & of alcoholic drinks*) òl *m*; **2** (*of alcohol: usu excessive*) pòitearachd *f invar*; **3** *in exprs* **~ companion** co-phòitear *m*, **~ spree** (*now rather trad*) daorach *f*

drip, dripping *n* **1** (*abstr & con*) sileadh *m*, snighe *m*; **2** (*the sound*) gliog *m*

drive *v* **1** (*~ a vehicle*) dràibh *vti*, dràibhig *vti*; **2** (*propel machinery &c*) iomain *vt*,

~ **a machine by steam** iomain inneal *m* le smùid *f*; **3** (*sport: propel*) iomain *vt*, ~ **a ball** iomain bàla *m*; **4** (*other exprs & idioms*) ~ **(on)** (*esp livestock*) iomain *vt*, ~ **on** (*people, animals*) greas *vt*, ~ **away** fuadaich *vt*, **the dog drove away the fox** dh'fhuadaich an cù an sionnach, *also* chuir an cù teicheadh *m* air an t-sionnach, ~ **out** *or* **away** *v* rua(i)g *vt*, fògair *vt*, fuadaich *vt*, **the people were ~n from/out of the glen** dh'fhògradh an sluagh *m* às a' ghleann *m*, **it was nearly driving me mad/demented/ out of my mind** bha e gus mo chur dhìom fhìn/far mo chinn (*gen of* ceann *m*)/às mo rian *m*

drivel *n* **1** seile *m invar*, ronn *m*; **2** (*fig: foolish talk, nonsense &c*) amaideas *m*, (*fam*) sgudal *m*

driver *n*, (*of a vehicle*) dràibhear *m*

driving *n* (*a vehicle*) dràibheadh *m*

drizzle *n* ciùbhran & ciùthran *m*

drizzle *v* braon *vi*

droll *adj* èibhinn, ait

drone[1] *n* (*of bagpipe*) dos *m*

drone[2] *n* **1** (*bee*) seillean *m* dìomhain; **2** (*sound of bee*) torman *m*

droning *n* torman *m*

droop *v* searg *vi*

drop *n* **1** boinne *f*, braon *m*, drùdhag *f*, **a ~ of milk** boinne bhainne *m*, **won't you take a ~ of tea?** nach gabh thu drùdhag tì?; **2** (*on end of nose*) boinneag *f*, **a ~ on his nose** boinneag ri shròin (*dat of* sròn *f*)

drop *v* **1** (*as vi*) tuit *vi*, **the glasses ~ped** thuit na gloinneachan *fpl*; **2** (*as vt: let fall accidentally*) leig *vt* às, **I ~ped the glasses** leig mi às na gloinneachan *fpl*; **3** (*as vt: release deliberately*) leag *vt*, ~ **bombs** leag bomaichean *mpl*; **4** (*other exprs & idioms*) ~ **to bits** rach *vi* na (*&c*) c(h)riomagan *fpl*, **the toys were ~ping to bits** bha na dèideagan *fpl* a' dol nan criomagan, **I ~ped off** (*ie dozed*) chaidh mi nam chlò-chadal *m*, thàinig clò-chadal orm

drought *n* tiormachd *f invar*, tart *f*

drove *n* **1** (*of cattle*) dròbh *m*; **2** (*fig: in pl*) ~**s** mìltean *mpl*, dròbhan *mpl*, **they came in ~s** thàinig iad nam mìltean/nan dròbhan

drover *n* (*of cattle*) dròbhair *m*

drown *v* **1** bàth *vt*, **he was ~ed** chaidh a bhàthadh *m*; **2** (*sounds*) ~ **(out)** bàth *vt*

drowsy *adj* cadalach

drudge *n* tràill *mf*, sgalag *f*

drudgery *n* tràilleachd *f invar*, obair *f* sgalaig *f*

drug *n* **1** (*medical*) cungaidh *f*, cungaidh-leighis *f*; **2** (*medical & illicit*) droga *f*

druid *n* draoidh *m*

drum *n* (*mus*) druma *f*

drunk *adj* **1** air mhisg *f*, air an daoraich (*dat of* daorach *f*), leis an daoraich, **I'm ~** tha mi air mhisg, tha mi air an daoraich, tha an daorach orm, tha mi leis an daoraich, (*stronger: fam*) tha smùid *f* orm, tha mi air mo phronnadh; **2** *in exprs* **make** ~ cuir misg *f*, cuir an daorach *f*, (*with prep* air), **they made me** ~ chuir iad misg/an daorach orm, **half** ~ air leth-mhisg

drunkard *n* pòitear *m*, misgear *m*

drunkenness *n* daorach *f*, misg *f*, (*fam*) smùid *f*

dry *adj* **1** tioram, **here's a dry towel for you** seo agad tubhailte thioram, **the loch was** ~ bha an loch *m* tioram; **2** (~ *from thirst*) pàiteach, tartmhor, ìotmhor; **3** *in exprs* ~ **spell**, ~ **weather, spell of** ~ **weather** (*esp following a rainy period*) turadh *m*

dry *v* **1** tiormaich *vti*, **the dishes haven't been dried** chan eil na soithichean *mfpl* air an tiormachadh; **2** *in expr* ~ **up** (*ie wither*) crìon *vti*

dryer *n* tiormadair *m*

dryness *n* **1** tiormachd *f invar*; **2** (*from thirst*) pathadh *m*, tart *m*, ìota *m*

dual *adj* dùbailte

dubious *adj* **1** (*having doubts*) teagmhach, amharasach; **2** (*arousing doubts, unreliable*) neo-earbsach, cugallach

duchess *n* ban-diùc *f*

duck *n* tunnag *f*, (*wild* ~) lach *f*

duck *v* (*in liquid*) tum *vt*

ducking *n* (*in liquid*) tumadh *m*

due *adj* **1** (*fitting*) dligheach, cubhaidh, iomchaidh, ~ **respect** meas dligheach; **2** (*expr that a time limit &c has expired*) bi *vi irreg followed by prep* ri *and a verbal noun*, **this book is** ~ **back/**~ **to be returned** tha an leabhar *m* seo ri thoirt air ais, **this bill is** ~ **(to be paid)** tha an cunntas seo ri phàigheadh; **3** (*owed*) **you're** ~ **ten pounds from me** tha ceithir notaichean *fpl* agad orm; **4** *in expr* **in** ~ **course** ri tìde *f*, **we'll get it in** ~ **course** gheibh sinn ri tìde e

due *n* (*what one is entitled to*) dlighe *f invar*, dleas *m*

duel *n* còmhrag-dithis *f*

duet *n* òran-dithis *m*

duke *n* diùc *m*

dull *adj* **1** (*of light, colours &c*) doilleir, ciar; **2** (*tedious*) liosda, slaodach

dull *v* **1** (*esp light*) doilleirich *vti*; **2** (~ *pain &c*) faothaich *vti*, lasaich *vt*

dulse *n* (*bot*) duileasg *m*

duly *adv* gu dligheach

dumb *adj* (*permanently or temporarily*) balbh

dumbness *n* balbhachd *f invar*

dump *n* **1** (*rubbish heap &c*) òtrach *m*; **2** (*place: shabby &c*) àite grodach, (*not worth frequenting*) àite *m* gun fheum

dun *adj* odhar, ciar, lachdann, (*less usu*) riabhach

dunce *n* bumailear *m*, ùmaidh *m*, stalcaire *m*

dung *n* (*used as manure*) innear & inneir *f*, todhar *m*, **cow** ~ buachar *m*, ~ **heap** dùnan *m*, òtrach *m*, siteag *f*

dunghill *n* dùnan *m*, siteag & sitig *f*, òtrach *m*

duodenum *n* beul *m* a' chaolain

dupe *v* thoir an car (*with prep* à), dèan foill *f* (*with prep* air), cealg *vt*, **he ~d me** thug e an car asam, rinn e foill orm

duplicate *n* **1** mac-samhail *m*, lethbhreac *m*, (**of** de); **2 document** (*&c*) **in ~** sgrìobhainn *f* (*&c*) le lethbhreac

duplicate *v* dèan mac-samhail *m*/lethbhreac *m* (*with prep* de)

duplicity *n* cealg *f*, foill *f*

durable *adj* buan, maireannach,

duration *n*, *in expr* **for the ~ of the meeting** fad na coinneimh, fhad 's a bha a' choinneamh a' dol

during *prep* **1** ann an, fad, (*occas*) ri, **it was snowing ~ the night** bha e a' cur an t-sneachda *m* san oidhche *f* (*also* air an oidhche), **it was snowing ~ the (whole) night** bha e a' cur sneachda fad na h-oidhche; **2** *in expr* **he fell asleep ~ her talk** chaidh/thuit e na chadal *m* is i a' toirt seachad na h-òraid aice

dusk *n* **1** duibhre *f invar*, eadar-sholas *m*, camhanaich *f* na h-oidhche, beul *m* na h-oidhche; **2** (*idiom*) **from dawn to ~** o mhoch gu dubh

dusky *adj* (*of persons*) ciar

dust *n* duslach *m*, dust *m invar*, stùr *m*

dustbin *n* bucaid *f*

duster *n* dustair *m*

dusty *adj* dustach, stùrach

Dutch *adj* Duitseach

Dutchman *n* Duitseach *m*

dutiful *adj* dleastanach

duty *n* **1** dleastanas *m*, (*less usu*) dleas *m*, **they did their ~** rinn iad an dleastanas; **2** (*tax*) cìs *f*, **customs ~** cìs-chusbainn *f invar*, **~ free** saor o chìsean

dwang *n* rong *m*, rongas *f*

dwarf *n* luchraban *m*, troich *mf*

dwell *v* **1** (*live*) fuirich *vi*, (*less usu*) tàmh *vi*; **2** (*settle in, inhabit*) tuinich *vi*, àitich *vt*, gabh còmhnaidh *f*, **the first race that dwelt in America** a' chiad chinneadh *m* a thuinich ann an Ameireagaidh *f*

dweller *n* **1** (*esp in house, town &c*) neach-còmhnaidh *m* (*pl* luchd-còmhnaidh *m sing coll*); **2** (*esp in a country, continent*) neach-àiteachaidh *m* (*pl* luchd-àiteachaidh *m sing coll*), tuiniche *m*

dwelling *n* **1** (*abstr*) còmhnaidh *f*; **2** (*con: ~ place*) àite-còmhnaidh *m*, àite-fuirich *m*; **3** (*~ house*) taigh *m*, taigh-còmhnaidh *m*, (*more trad*) fàrdach *f*

dye *n* dath *m*

dye *v* dath *vt*, cuir dath *m* (*with prep* air)

dyed *adj* dathte

dyke *n* gàr(r)adh *m*

dynamic *adj* innsgineach

dynasty *n* gineal *mf*, cineal *m*, sliochd *m coll*

E

each *adj* **1** gach, ~ **house** gach taigh *m*, **I went there ~ day** chaidh mi ann gach là *m*, ~ **and every** gach aon, gach uile, ~ **and every house** gach aon taigh, **she's on at me about ~ and every thing** bidh i an sàs annam mu gach uile nì *m*; **2** *as pron in expr* ~ **other** a chèile, (*less usu*) cach a chèile, **they kissed ~ other** phòg iad a chèile, **talking to ~ other** a' bruidhinn ri chèile, **seeing ~ other** a' faicinn càch a chèile; **3** (*per capita*) an urra *f*, **they received a thousand pounds ~** fhuair iad mìle not(a) *f* an urra

eager *adj* **1** (*pursuit, endeavour &c*) dian; **2** (*person*) dealasach, (*esp to work, oblige &c*) èasgaidh

eagerness *n* dealas *m*, èasgaidheachd *f invar*, dealasachd *f invar*

eagle *n* iolair(e) *f*, **golden ~** iolair(e) bhuidhe

ear *n* **1** cluas *f*, ~ **drum** druma *mf* (na) cluaise, faillean *m*, ~ **piercing** tolladh-chluasan *m*; **2** (*idiom*) **give an ~** dèan èisteachd *f invar* (**to** do); **3** (~ *of corn*) dias *f*

earache *n* greim-cluaise *m*

eardrum *n* faillean *m*

earl *n* iarla *m*

earldom *n* iarlachd *f invar*

early *adj* moch, tràth (*advs*), (*usu Lit/poet*) òg (*adj*), **in the ~ morning** moch/ tràth sa mhadainn *f*, san òg-mhadainn

early *adv* **1** moch, tràth, ~ **in the morning** moch/tràth sa mhadainn *f*; **2** (*before set or expected time*) tràth *adv*, ron mhithich *f invar*, ron àm *m*, ~ **for the meeting** tràth airson na coinneimh, **it's too ~ for ripe apples** tha e ro thràth airson ùbhlan *mpl* abaich, **she retired ~** leig i seachad/ leig i dhith an obair *f* ron mhithich/ron àm, ~ **departure** falbh *m* ron mhithich/ron àm, **we arrived ~** ràinig *vi* sinn ron àm

earmark *n* (*on livestock*) comharradh-cluaise *m*

earmark *v* **1** (*livestock*) cuir comharradh-cluaise *m* (*with prep* air); **2** (*fig: general*) comharraich *vt*

earn *v* coisinn *vt*, buainnich *vt*, **~ing big money** a' cosnadh airgid *m gen* mhòir

earnest *adj* **1** (*in character, personality*) dùrachdach, stòlda; **2** (*more temporary*) *in exprs* **in~** ann an da-rìribh *adv*, **they weren't in ~** cha robh iad ann an da-rìribh, **half in ~** eadar fealla-dhà *f invar* is da-rìribh

earnings *n* cosnadh *m*, tuarastal *f*

ear-ring *n* cluas-fhail *f*

earth *n* **1** (*the planet*) *used with art*, **the ~** an cruinne *mf*, an cruinne-cè *mf*, an talamh *m* (*f in gen sing*), **the surface of the ~** uachdar *m* na cruinne, **on the face of the ~** air aghaidh na talmhainn; **2** (*soil, ground*) talamh *m* (*f in gen sing*), (*less usu*) ùir *f*, **they put him into the ~** chuir iad san talamh/san ùir e; **3** (*idioms*) **where on ~ did he go?** càit' idir an deach e?, **where on ~ is he?** càite fon ghrèin (*dat of* grian f) a bheil e?, **why on ~ did you do it?** carson, a chiall a rinn thu e?

earthly *adj* **1** talmhaidh *adj*, **an ~ creature** creutair talmhaidh; **2** (*temporal, opposite of spiritual, heavenly*) saoghalta, talmhaidh

earthquake *n* crith-thalmhainn *f*

earthworm *n* cnuimh-thalmhainn *f*, boiteag *f*

ear-wax cèir-chluaise *f*

earwig *n* gobhlag *f*, fiolan *m*, fiolan-gobhlach *m*

ease *n* **1** fois *f*, socair *f*, *in expr* **take your ~** gabh fois, gabh *vi* air do shocair; **2** (*in personality, character, mood*) **at (his** &c**) ~** socair, socrach (*adjs*); **3** (*financial ~*) seasgaireachd *f invar*

ease *v* **1** (*suffering* &c) faothaich *vti*, lasaich *vt*; **2** (*bonds* &c) fuasgail *vt*

easel *n* sorchan-dealbha *m*

easier *comp adj* nas fhasa, **that will be ~** bidh sin nas fhasa

easiest *sup adj*, as fhasa (*in past & conditional tenses* a b' fhasa), **the ~ thing was to come back** b' e an rud *m* a b' fhasa tilleadh *m*

easing *n* **1** (*of pain, suffering*) faothachadh *m*, furtachd *f invar*; **2** (*of bonds* &c) fuasgladh *m*

east *adj* sear *adj*, an ear *f invar*, **the ~ side** an taobh sear, an taobh an ear, **an ~ wind** gaoth *f* on ear

east *adv* an ear *f invar*, sear *adv*, **going ~** a' dol an ear, **~ of Eden** an ear air Eden, sear air Eden

east *n* ear *f invar*, **the ~** (*ie compass direction*) an àird an ear, **in the ~** san ear, **from the ~** on ear, **a wind from/out of the ~** gaoth *f* às an ear, **the ~** (*ie location, part of a country* &c) an taobh *m* an ear *or* an taobh sear

Easter *n* (*used with the art*) a' Chàisg, **~ Monday** Diluain *m invar* na Càisge

easterly *adj* an ear *f invar*, **an ~ wind** gaoth *f* an ear

eastern *adj* an ear *f invar*, sear *adj*, **the ~ towns** na bailtean *mpl* an ear, na bailtean sear

eastwards *adv* an ear, chun an ear, chun na h-àirde an ear, **sailing ~** a' seòladh (chun) an ear

easy *adj* **1** furasta, soirbh, simplidh, **an ~ job** obair fhurasta, **an ~ question** ceist shoirbh; **2** (*financially ~*) seasgair; **3** (*idioms*) **take things ~** gabh *vi* air do (&c) s(h)ocair *f*, (*excl*) **take it ~!, go ~!** socair! *or* air do shocair!

easy-going *adj* **1** (*patient, apt to put up with annoyances* &c) foighidneach; **2** (*not disciplinarian*) ceadach; **3** (*nonchalant; can also be pej, implying 'couldn't care less' attitude*) coma-co-dhiù

eat *v* **1** ith *vti*; **2** (*idiom*) **he came home to ~** thàinig e dhachaigh gu bhiadh *m*

eatable *adj* ion-ithe

eating *n* ithe & itheadh *m*

eaves *n* anainn *f*

eavesdrop *v* dèan farchluais *f*

eavesdropping *n* farchluais *f*

ebb *n* (*of tide*) tràghadh *m*, traoghadh *m*

ebb *v* (*of tide*) tràigh *vi*, traogh *vi*

eccentric *adj* (*of person, behaviour*) neònach, às a' chumantas, rudanach

ecclesiastic, ecclesiastical *adj* eaglaiseil

ecclesiastic *n* eaglaiseach *m*, pears-eaglais *m*

echo *n* mac-talla *m*, sgailc-creige *f*

echo *v* ath-ghairm *vi*

eclectic *adj* ioma-sheòrsach, **an ~ collection** cruinneachadh *m* ioma-sheòrsach

eclipse *n* dubhadh *m*, **~ of the sun/of the moon** dubhadh na grèine/na gealaich

eclipse *v* duibhrich *vti*

economic *adj* (*related to economics, the economy*) eaconamach

economical *adj* **1** (*thrifty*) cunntach, caomhantach, cùramach (a-thaobh airgid); **2** (*cheap, not excessive*) **an ~ price** deagh phrìs *f*, prìs chothromach/dhòigheil; **3** *in expr* **~ with the truth** cunntach leis an fhìrinn *f*

economics *n* eaconamachd *f invar*, eaconamas *m*

economise *v* caomhain *vti*, glèidh *vt*, sàbhail *vt*

economist *n* eaconamair *m*

economy *n* **1** eaconamaidh *m*, **the national ~** eaconamaidh na dùthcha, **free market ~** econamaidh saor-mhargaidh; **2** *in exprs* **domestic ~** taigheadas *m*, banas-taighe *m invar*, **make economies** geàrr *vi* sìos, geàrr *vi* air ais, (**in air**), **make economies in our expenditure** geàrr sìos air an teachd-a-mach *m invar* againn

ecstasy *n* mire *f*, meadhail *f invar*, meadhradh *m*, **in ~** air mhire

ecstatic *adj* air mhire *f*, **make someone ~** cuir cuideigin air mhire

eddy *n* cuairteag *f*

edge *n* **1** iomall *m*, oir *f*, **the ~ of the wood** iomall na coille, **the ~ of the roof** oir a' mhullaich; **2** (*of blade, tool &c*) faobhar *m*, **cutting ~** faobhar gearraidh *m gen*, *in expr* **put an ~ on** (*blade, tool &c*) faobharaich *vt*; **3** *in expr* (*of person*) **on ~** clisgeach

edgy *adj* clisgeach

edible *adj* ion-ithe

edict *n* riaghailt *f*, reachd *m invar*

edit *v* deasaich *vt*

editing *n* deasachadh *m*

edition *n* **1** (*abstr*) deasachadh *m*; **2** (*con*) clò-bhualadh *m*, **a new ~ of his novel** clò-bhualadh ùr den nobhail *f* aige

editor *n* deasaiche *m*, neach-deasachaidh *m* (*pl* luchd-deasachaidh *m sing coll*)

educate *v* foghlaim *vt*, teagaisg *vt*, thoir sgoil *f* (*with prep* do), **~ the new generation** teagaisg an ginealach ùr

educated *adj* foghlaimte, foghlamaichte, ionnsaichte

education *n* foghlam *m*, ionnsachadh *m*, oideachas *m*, sgoil *f*, **pre-school/ nursery** ~ foghlam fo-sgoile, **adult** ~ foghlam-inbhidh, **Gaelic-medium** ~ foghlam tro meadhan *m* na Gàidhlig, **the Education Department** Roinn *f* an Fhoghlaim, **we got our** ~ **in Lewis** fhuair sinn ar sgoil ann an Leòdhas

educational *adj* **1** (*providing education or information*) oideachail; **2** (*to do with education*) foghlaim (*gen of* foghlam *m*, *used adjectivally*) ~ **facilities** goireasan *mpl* foghlaim

eel *n* easgann *f*

eery *adj* iargalta, uaigealta

effect *n* **1** (*of action &c*) toradh *m*, buil *f*, buaidh *f*, èifeachd *f invar*, **the** ~**(s) of your behaviour** toradh do dhol-a-mach *m invar*, **the greenhouse** ~ buaidh an taigh-ghlainne; **2** (*impression &c made on someone*) drùidheadh *m*, *in expr* **have an** ~ **on someone** drùidh *vi* air cuideigin; **3** *in expr* **put into** ~ (*plan, ideas &c*) cuir *vt* an gnìomh *m*

effective *adj* èifeachdach

effectiveness *n* èifeachdachd *f invar*, èifeachdas *m*

effects *npl* **1** (*one's belongings in general*) sealbh & seilbh *f sing coll*; **2** *in expr* **household** ~ àirneis (taighe) *f sing coll invar*

effeminacy *n* boireanntachd *f invar*

effeminate *adj* boireannta

effervescence *n* (*of person*) beòthalas *m*

effervescent *adj* **1** (*of liquid*) builgeanach; **2** (*of person*) beòthail

efficiency *n* èifeachdachd *f invar*, èifeachdas *m*

efficient *adj* èifeachdach

effigy *n* ìomhaigh *f*

effluent *n* às-shruthadh *m*

effort *n* **1** (*abstr*) saothair *f*, **it's not worth the** ~ **(to you)** chan fhiach dhut do shaothair; **2** (*con; an* ~) oidhirp *f*, (*esp a strenuous* ~) spàirn *f*, **make an** ~ thoir oidhirp (**at** air); **3** (*results of* ~) oidhirpean *fpl*, **the editor didn't like my** ~**s** cha bu toigh leis an fhear-deasachaidh *m* na h-oidhirpean agam

effrontery *n* ladarnas *m*, (*more fam*) aghaidh *f*, bathais *f*, **what** ~**!** abair ladarnas!, abair aghaidh!

egalitarian *adj* co-ionannachail

egg *n* ugh *m*

egg-cup *n* gucag-uighe *f*

egg-shaped *adj* ughach

egg-white *n* gealagan *m*

ego *n*, *used with art*, **the** ~ am fèin *m invar*

egoist, egotist *n* fèinear *m*

egoism, egotism *n* fèineachd *f invar*

egotistical *adj* fèineil

Egypt *n, used with art*, An Eipheit *f invar*

Egyptian *n & adj* Eipheiteach

eiderdown *n* clòimhteachan *m*

eight *numeral & adj* ochd, (*of people*) ochdnar *mf*

eighteen *numeral & adj* ochd-deug

eighth *adj* ochdamh

eighth *n* ochdamh *m*

eightsome *n* ochdnar *mf*, **an ~ reel** ruidhle-ochdnar *m*

eighty *num & adj* ceithir fichead, (*in alternative numbering system*) ochdad *m*

either *adv* **1** nas motha, **I won't go home! I won't ~!** cha tèid mi dhachaigh! cha tèid mise nas motha! (*also* cha tèid no mise!), **no-one else saw me ~** cha mhotha (a) chunnaic duine eile mi; **2** *in expr* **~ ... or** an dara/dàrna cuid ... no, (*in neg sentences*) an aon chuid ... no, **give me ~ meat or fish** thoir dhomh an dara cuid feòil *f* no iasg *m*, (*in neg sentences*) **I won't go ~ to Glasgow or to Edinburgh** cha tèid mi an aon chuid a Ghlaschu no a Dhun Eideann

eject *v* tilg *vt* a-mach, cuir *vt* a-mach, (**from** à)

elaborate *adj* **1** (*involving much work*) saothrach; **2** (*detailed*) mionaideach; **3** (*multi-faceted*) iomadh-fhillte

elaborate *v* **1** (*create, develop*) innlich *vt*, tionnsgail *vt*, obraich *vt* a-mach; **2** (*give more detail*) leudaich *vi* (**on** air), **he ~d on his plans** leudaich e air na planaichean *mpl* aige

elastic *adj* sùbailte, **~ band** bann sùbailte

elastic *n* lastaic & lastaig *f invar*

elasticity *n* sùbailteachd *f invar*

elated *adj & past part* aoibhneach, (*fam*) air a (*&c*) d(h)eagh dhòigh *f*, **they were ~** bha iad air an deagh dhòigh

elbow *n* uileann & uilinn *f*

elbow *v* uillnich *vti*, thoir ùpag(an) *f* (*with prep* do)

elder[1] *n* **1** (*church ~*) èildear *m*, (*more trad*) foirfeach *m*; **2** (*older of two*) am fear/an tè (*&c*) as sine, **John is the ~** is e Iain am fear *m* as sine

elder[2] *n* (*the tree*) ruis *f*, droman *m*

elect *v* (*esp pol*) tagh *vt*, **they weren't ~ed** cha deach an taghadh *m*

elected *adj & past part* taghte

election *n* taghadh *m*, **~ campaign** iomairt *f* taghaidh *gen*, **~ expenses** cosgaisean *fpl* taghaidh

elector *n* neach-taghaidh *m* (*pl* luchd-taghaidh *m sing coll*)

electoral *adj* taghaidh (*gen of* taghadh *m, used adjectivally*), **~ district** sgìre *f* taghaidh

electorate *n* luchd-bhòtaidh *m sing coll*

electric *adj* dealain (*gen of* dealan *m, used adjectivally*), **~ light/fire** solas *m*/teine *m* dealain, **~ current** sruth *m* dealain, **~ cooker** cucair *m* dealain

electrical *adj* **1** dealain (*gen of* dealan *m, used adjectivally*); **2** *in expr* **~ engineer** innleadair-dealain *m*

electrician *n* dealanair *m*

electricity *n* dealan *m*, **the Electricity Board** Bòrd *m* an Dealain

electrify *v* **1** (*lit*) dealanaich *vt*; **2** (*fig*) cuir gaoir *f* (*with prep* air), **she electrified the audience** chuir i gaoir air an luchd-èisteachd *m sing coll*

electronic *adj* **1** eileagtronaigeach, dealanach, ~ **keyboard** meur-chlàr dealanach; **2** *in exprs* ~ **mail, e-mail** post *m* dealain *m gen*

elegance *n* grinneas *m*, snas *m*

elegant *adj* grinn, fìnealta, eireachdail

elegiac *adj* tuireach

elegy *n* cumha *m*, marbhrann *m*, tuireadh *m*

element *n* (*general, also science &c*) eileamaid *f*

elementary *adj* **1** bunaiteach; **2** (*not profound*) sìmplidh; **3** *in expr* ~ **knowledge** bun-eòlas *m* (**of, about** air)

elevate *v* àrdaich *vt*

elevator *n* àrdaichear *m*

eligibility *n* ion-roghnachd *f invar*, freagarrachd *f invar*

eligible *adj* **1** ion-roghnach, freagarrach; **2** (*qualified*) uidheamaichte

eliminate *v* **1** (*expel, remove, cut out &c*) thoir *vt* (**from** à), cuir *vt* a-mach (**from** à), geàrr *vt* às, **he was ~d from the competition** chaidh a thoirt às an fharpais *m*, **the council is eliminating** (*financial*) **waste** tha a' chomhairle a' geàrradh às ana-caitheimh *m*; **2** (*destroy, kill*) cuir *vi* às (*with prep* do), **they ~d their enemies** chuir iad às do na nàimhdean *mpl* aca

elimination *n* **1** (*removal &c*) toirt *f* (**from** à), cur *m* a-mach (**from** à), geàrradh *m* às; **2** (*destruction, killing*) cur *m* às (*with prep* do); **3** (*expulsion from body &c*) tilgeadh *m*, tilgeil *f*, toirt *f invar* air falbh

elision *n* (*gram*) bàthadh *m*

elm *n* leamhan *m*

elongate *v* sìn *vti*, fadaich *vti*

elope *v* teich *vi* (**with** còmhla ri)

elopement *n* teicheadh *m* (**with** còmhla ri)

eloquence *n* fileantachd *f invar*, deas-bhriathrachd *f invar*

eloquent *adj* fileanta, deas-bhriathrach

else *adj* **1** eile, **something** ~ rud *m* eile, **somewhere** ~ (ann an) àiteigin *m invar* eile, **who** ~ **was there?** cò eile a bh' ann?, **I don't want anything** ~ chan eil mi ag iarraidh càil *m invar* eile; **2** *in exprs* **anything** ~, **nothing** ~ an còrr *m invar*, **she didn't say anything** ~ cha tuirt i an còrr, **there was nothing** ~ **to it (than that)** cha robh an còrr ann (ach sin)

elucidate *v* mìnich *vt*, soilleirich *vt*

elucidation *n* mìneachadh *m*, soilleireachadh *m*

elude *v* siolp *vi* air falbh, èalaidh *vi* às, èalaidh *vi* air falbh, (*all with prep* air), seachain *vt*, **he managed to** ~ **me** chaidh aige air èalaidh/siolpadh air falbh orm, chaidh aige air mo sheachnadh

elusive *adj* doirbh a ghlacadh, doirbh a lorg

emaciated *adj* seang, seargte

e-mail *n* post *m* dealain *m gen*

emanate *v* thig (**from** a-mach à), **news emanating from Poland** naidheachdan *fpl* (a tha) a' tighinn a-mach às a' Phòlainn *f invar*

emancipate *v* saor *vt*, fuasgail *vt*, (**from** bho/o)

emancipation *n* **1** (*the action*) saoradh *m*, fuasgladh *m*, (**from** bho/o); **2** (*the state*) saorsa *f* (**from** bho/o)

emasculate *v* (*castrate*) spoth *vt*, geàrr *vt*

embargo *n* bacadh *m*, **trade ~** bacadh-malairt *m*

embark *v* **1** (*as vi*) rach *vi* air bòrd (*with gen*), **we ~ed** chaidh sinn air bòrd (a' bhàta/na luinge *&c*); **2** (*as vt*) cuir *vt* air bòrd (*with gen*); **3** *in expr* **~ on** (*begin, undertake*), tòisich *vi* (**on/upon** air), rach *vi* an sàs *m* (**on/upon** ann an), gabh *vt* os làimh (*dat of* làmh *f*), **we ~ed on a new project** thòisich sinn air pròiseact *mf* ùr, chaidh sinn an sàs ann am pròiseact ùr,

embarrass *v* **1** (*cause to feel shame*) nàraich *vt*, tàmailtich *vt*, maslaich *vt*; **2** (*make uneasy*) cuir *vt* troimh-a-chèile, buair *vt*

embarrassed *adj & past part* **1** (*through shame*) nàrach; **2** (*through uneasiness*) troimh-a-chèile, air (a *&c*) b(h)uaireadh; **3** (*through shyness*) diùid, nàrach, air a (*&c*) nàrachadh

embarrassment *n* **1** (*through shame*) nàire *f invar*, tàmailt *f*, masladh *m*; **2** (*through uneasiness*) buaireas *m*; **3** (*through shyness*) diùide *f invar*, nàire *f invar*

embassy *n* **1** (*abstr*) tosgaireachd *f*; **2** (*the premises & institution*) ambasaid *f*

embellish *v* maisich *vt*, sgeadaich *vt*, snuadhaich *vt*

embellishment *n* maiseachadh *m*, sgeadachadh *m*, snuadhachadh *m*

ember *n* èibhleag *f*

embitter *v* searbhaich *vt*

embittered *adj & past part* searbhta

emblem *n* suaicheantas *m*

embrace *v* **1** teannaich *vt*, **embracing each other** a' teannachadh a chèile, *also* an gàirdeanan a chèile, **she ~d him** theannaich i (ri a broilleach *m*/ri a h-uchd *m*) e; **2** (*include*) gabh *vt* a-steach, **his work ~s that of X and Y** tha/bidh an obair aige a gabhail a-steach obair X agus Y; **3** (*adopt enthusiastically &c*) gabh *vi* (*with prep* ri) **we ~d communism** ghabh sinn ri co-mhaoineas *m*

embroidery *n* **1** (*the activity*) grèis *f*; **2** (*the product*) obair-ghrèis(e) *f*

embryo *n* tùs-ghinean *mf*

emerald *n* smàrag *f*

emerge *v* **1** (*from building &c*) thig *vi* a-mach (**from** à); **2** (*of facts &c: become known, apparent*) thig *vi* am follais *f invar*, **it ~d this week that she was married** thàinig e am follais air an t-seachdain-sa *f* gun robh i pòsta; **3** (*come to the fore*) thig *vi irreg* an uachdar *m*, **he ~d as leader of the party** thàinig e an uachdar mar cheannard *m* a' phàrtaidh

emergency *n* **1** (*situation*) cruaidh-chàs *m*; **2** (*more abstr*) èiginn *f invar*, (*often used adjectivally*) **an ~ exit** doras-èiginn *m*

emigrant *n* eilthireach *m*

emigrate *v* fàg a (*&c*) d(h)ùthaich *f* fhèin, rach *vi irreg* a null thairis, **he ~d** dh'fhàg e a dhùthaich fhèin

emigration *n* às-imrich *f*

émigré *n* eilthireach *m*

eminence *n* 1 (*rank, honour &c*) mòr-inbhe *f*; 2 (*topog*) àird *f*

eminent *adj* 1 (*most important &c*) prìomh (*precedes the noun, which it lenites where possible*), **the ~ people of the town** prìomh dhaoine *mpl* a' bhaile; 2 (*distinguished &c*) inbheil, **an ~ surgeon** làmh-lèigh *m* inbheil

emit *v* cuir *vt* (a-mach), leig *vt* a-mach, **~ fumes** cuir a-mach deatach *f*

emotion *n* faireachdainn *f*, (*more extreme or troubled*) buaireas *m*

emotional *adj* 1 (*person: affected by ~*) gluaiste, (*more extreme or troubled*) buairte; 2 (*event &c: involving or arousing emotion*) gluasadach, drùidhteach, (*more extreme or troubling*) buaireasach; 3 *in expr* **~ arousal** gluasad *m*

emotive *adj* gluasadach, drùidhteach, (*more extreme or troubling*) buaireasach

empathy *n* co-fhaireachdainn *f*

emperor *n* ìompaire *m*

emphasis *n* cudthrom *m*, **put/lay great ~ on X** cuir/leig cudthrom mòr air X

emphasise *v* cuir/leig cudthrom *m* (*with prep* air), **~ how good her qualifications are** leig cudthrom air cho math agus a tha an t-uidheamachadh *m* aice

emphatic *adj* deimhinn(e), deimhinnte, cinnteach, làidir, **an ~ denial** àicheadh *m* deimhinn/deimhinnte

empire *n* ìompaireachd *f*

employ *v* 1 (*use*) cleachd *vt*, (*less usu: esp ~ tools, weapons*) iomair *vt*; 2 (*~ workers &c*) fastaich, *also* fasdaich *&* fastaidh, *vt*, thoir obair *f* (*with prep* do)

employee *n* neach-obrach *m* (*pl* luchd-obrach *m sing coll*), obraiche *&* oibriche *m*, cosnaiche *m*

employer *n* fastaidhear *m*, fastaiche *m*

employment *n* 1 (*abstr*) cosnadh *m*, obair *f*, **the ~ Minister** Ministear *m* a' Chosnaidh; 2 (*the act of employing people*) fastadh *m*

empower *v* thoir ùghdarras *m*, thoir cumhachd *mf*, (*with prep* do)

empowered *adj & past part* ùghdarraichte

empress *n* ban-ìompaire *f*

emptiness *n* fal(a)mhachd *f invar*

empty *adj* 1 falamh; 2 (*of place: deserted*) falamh, (*stronger*) fàs, **the glens are ~** tha na gleanntan falamh/fàs; 3 (*without substance*) dìomhain, **~ words** faclan dìomhain

empty *v* 1 falmhaich *vt*; 2 (*esp liquids from container &c*) tràigh *&* traogh *vt*, taom *vt*; 3 (*~ of population*) fàsaich *vt*

empty-headed *adj* faoin

enable *v* cuir *vt* na (*&c*) c(h)omas *m*, thoir comas/cothrom *m* (*with prep* do), **that ~d us to pay the bill** chuir sin nar comas/thug sin cothrom dhuinn an cunntas a phàigheadh

enamel *n* cruan *m*

enchant *v* cuir *vt* fo gheasaibh (*obs dat pl of* geas *f*)

enchanted *adj & past part* **1** (*lit*) seunta; **2** (*lit & fig*) fo gheasaibh (*obs dat pl of* geas *f*) (**by** aig), **he was ~ by the girl** bha e fo gheasaibh aig an nighean

enchantment *n* **1** (*abstr*) geasachd *f invar*; **2** (*con: a spell &c*) geas *f*

encircle *v* cuartaich *vt*

enclose *v* **1** cuartaich *vt*, iadh & iath *vt*; **2** (*esp in corres, packets &c*) cuir *vt* an cois (*dat of* cas *f*) (*with gen*), cuir *vt* an lùib (*dat of* lùb *f*) (*with gen*), **~ something in a letter** cuir rudeigin an cois litreach *f gen*

enclosed *adj & past part* **1** cuairtichte; **2** (*corres &c*) an cois (*dat of* cas *f*) (*with gen*), an lùib (*dat of* lùb *f*) (*with gen*), **~ with this letter** an cois na litreach seo

enclosure *n* **1** (*the action*) cuairteachadh *m*, iathadh *m*; **2** (*con: an enclosed piece of ground &c*) lann *f*, (*esp for livestock*) crò *m*; **3** *in expr* (*corres*) **~s with this letter** (pàipearan *&c*) an cois (*dat of* cas *f*) na litreach seo

encompass *v* **1** (*encircle*) cuairtich *vt*; **2** (*embrace, contain*) gabh *vt* a-steach

encourage *v* **1** (*raise spirits &c*) misnich *vt*; **2** (*urge*) cuir impidh *m* (*with prep* air), brosnaich *vt*, coitich *vt*, **they ~d me to give away all my money** chuir iad impidh orm mo chuid *f* airgid *m gen* air fad a thoirt seachad

encouragement *n* **1** (*raising of spirits &c*) misneachadh *m*; **2** (*urging*) brosnachadh *m*, coiteachadh *m*

encouraging *adj* misneachail, brosnachail

encumber *v* uallaich *vt*

encumbrance *n* uallach *m*, eallach *m*

end *n* **1** (*the phys ~ of something*) ceann *m*, **the ~ of the bridge** ceann na drochaid(e), **the ~ of my tether** ceann mo theadhrach (*gen of* teadhair *f*); **2** (*more abstr, & esp of time*) deireadh *m*, crìoch *f*, **the ~ of the world** crìoch na cruinne, **come to an ~** thig *vi* gu crìch (*dat*), **at the ~ of my days/life** aig deireadh/crìch mo là, **the ~ of the month** deireadh a' mhìosa, **at the ~ of the day** (*also* **in the ~**) aig deireadh an là, *also* aig a' cheann thall; **3** *in expr* **on ~** (*ie in succession*), an ceann a chèile, an sreath *mf* a chèile, **three days on ~** trì làithean *mpl* an ceann a chèile

end *v* **1** (*complete, bring to an ~*) cuir crìoch *f* (*with prep* air), thoir *vt* gu crìch (*dat of* crìoch *f*), crìochnaich *vt*; **2** (*esp meeting*) co-dhùin *vti*

endanger *v* cuir *vt* an cunnart *m*

endangered *adj & past part* an cunnart *m*, **an ~ species** gnè *f invar*/seòrsa *m* an cunnart

endearments *npl* faclan *m*/briathran *m* gaoil (*gen of* gaol *m*)

endeavour *n* iomairt *f*, oidhirp *f*

endeavour *v* feuch *vi* (**to** ri), dèan iomairt *f*/oidhirp *f* (**to** gus *or* air)

ending *n* (*of meeting, work of art &c*) co-dhùnadh *m*, crìoch *f*, deireadh *m*

endless *adj* 1 (*continual*) gun sgur *m*, ~ **criticism** càineadh *m* gun sgur; 2 (*eternal*) sìorraidh, bith-bhuan

endorse *v* 1 (*cheque &c*) cuir ainm *m* (*with prep* ri); 2 (*support*) cuir aonta *m* (*with prep* ri)

endurance *n* cruas *m*, cruadal *m*, fulang *m*, fulangas *m*

endure *v* 1 fuiling & fulaing *vti*, **they had to ~ cold and hunger** b' fheudar dhaibh fuachd *mf* is acras *m* fhulang; 2 (*continue, last, persist*) lean *vi*

enduring *adj* 1 (*persisting*) leantainneach; 2 (*eternal*) maireannach, buan, bith-bhuan

enemy *n* nàmhaid *m*

energetic *adj* lùthmhor, brìghmhor, sgairteil

energy *n* 1 lùth *m*, ~ **conservation** caomhnadh *m* lùtha *gen*, ~ **source** bun-lùtha *m*; 2 (*of individuals*) lùth(s) *m*, brìgh *f invar*, spionnadh *m*, sgairt *f*

enfeeble *v* lagaich *vti*, fannaich *vti*

enforce *v* cuir *vt* an gnìomh *m*, ~ **the law** cuir an lagh *m* an gnìomh

engage *v* dèan *vt*, bi *vi irreg* an sàs *m* (*with prep* ann an), ~ **in trade/commerce** dèan malairt *f*, *also* malairtich *vi*, ~ **in politics** bi an sàs ann am poileataics *f invar*

engaged *adj & past part*, 1 (*betrothed*) **they got ~ yesterday** thug iad gealladh-pòsaidh *m* (dha chèile) an-dè; 2 (*phone, salesperson &c*) trang, **he's ~ just now** tha e trang an-dràsta, *also* chan eil e saor an-dràsta

engagement *n* 1 (*betrothal*) gealladh-pòsaidh *m*, ~ **ring** fàinne-gealladh-pòsaidh *mf*; 2 (*appointment &c*) coinneamh *f*, **I have a prior ~** tha coinneamh agam mu thràth

engine *n* einnsean *m*, **a car ~** einnsean-càir, *in expr* **a fire ~** carbad-smàlaidh *m*

engineer *n* einnseanair *m*, innleadair *m*, **electrical ~** innleadair-dealain *m*, **civil ~** innleadair-thogalach *m*

engineer *v* innlich *vt*

engineering *n* einnseanaireachd *f invar*, innleadaireachd *f invar*

English *adj* Sasannach

English *n* 1 (*lang*) Beurla *f*, *often used with art*, a' Bheurla; 2 (*people*) **the ~** na Sasannaich *mpl*

engrave *v* gràbhail *vt*

engraver gràbhalaiche *m*

engraving *n* gràbhaladh *m*, gràbhalachd *f invar*

enhance *v* 1 (*increase, augment*) meudaich *vt*; 2 (*improve*) leasaich *vt*; 3 (~ *appearance*) sgeadaich *vt*

enhancement *n* 1 (*increase*) meudachadh *m*, *in expr* ~ **of salary** àrdachadh *m* pàighidh (*gen of* pàigheadh *m used adjectivally*), àrdachadh tuarastail *m gen*; 2 (*improvement*) leasachadh *m*; 3 (~ *of appearance*) sgeadachadh *m*

enigma *n* tòimhseachan *m*, snaidhm *m*

enjoy *v* **1** gabh tlachd *f invar* (*with prep* ann an), (*less usu*) meal *vt*; **2** (*most frequently expressed using the vi* còrd, *with prep* ri) **how are you ~ing that?** ciamar a tha sin a' còrdadh ribh?, **I didn't ~ the music at all** cha do chòrd an ceòl rium idir

enjoyable *adj* **1** tlachdmhor; **2** a chòrdas (*with prep* ri), **~ music, music I find ~** ceòl *m* a chòrdas rium

enjoyment *n* tlachd *f invar*, toil-inntinn *f*, toileachas *m*

enlarge *v* **1** (*as vt*) meudaich *vt*, leudaich *vt*; **2** (*as vi*) rach *vi irreg* am meud *m invar*, leudaich *vi*

enlarged *adj* meudaichte, leudaichte

enlargement *n* meudachadh *m*, leudachadh *m*

enlighten *v* soilleirich *vt*

enlightened *adj & past part* (*aware, broad-minded &c*) tuigseach, toinisgeil, saor-inntinneach

enlightenment *n* soilleireachadh *m*, soillseachadh *m*, (*hist*) the Enlightnment An Soilleireachadh, An Soillseachadh *m*, **the age of ~** linn *mf* an t-soilleireachaidh/an t-soillseachaidh

enlist *v* (*esp in armed forces*) liostaig *vi*, gabh *vi* san arm *m* (*&c*)

enliven *v* beothaich *vt*, brosnaich *vt*, brod *vt*

enmity *n* nàimhdeas *m*

ennoble *v* uaislich *vt*

enormous *adj* ro-mhòr, (*more fam*) uabhasach/eagalach mòr

enough *n* **1** gu leòr *adv*, leòr *f invar*, **we've ~ food** tha biadh gu leòr againn, tha gu leòr de bhiadh againn, tha gu leòr bìdh (*gen of* biadh *m*) againn, (*more trad*) tha ar leòr de bhiadh againn, **have you got ~?** a bheil gu leòr agad?, **I got (more than) ~ of it** fhuair mi mo leòr dheth, **right ~!** ceart gu leòr!; **2** *using* foghain *vi*, **will that be ~?** am foghain sin?, (*to noisy children &c*) **that's ~!** fòghnaidh (siud)!, (*saying/idiom*) **~ is ~, ~ is as good as a feast** fòghnaidh na dh'fhòghnas; **3** (*idiom*) **I've got more than ~** tha tuilleadh 's a chòir agam

enquire *v* faighnich *vi* (**of** de *or* do)

enquiry *n* **1** ceist *f*; **2** (*investigation*) rannsachadh *m*, faighneachd *f*

enrage *v* cuir an fhearg (*with prep* air), feargaich *vt*, **he ~d his father** chuir e an fhearg air athair

enraged *adj & past part* air bhoile *f invar*, air bhàinidh *f invar*, air chuthach *m*

enrich *v* **1** beartaich *& beairtich *vi*, saoibhrich *vt*; **2** (**~ soil**) mathaich *vt*

enrol (*at college &c*) clàraich *vti*

enrolment *n* clàrachadh *m*

enslave *v* tràillich *vt*

enslavement *n* **1** (*abstr*) tràilleachd *f invar*; **2** (*act of enslaving*) tràilleachadh *m*

ensnare *v* rib *vt*, glac *vt* (ann an ribe *f*)

entangle *v* amail *vt*, aimhreitich *vt*, *in expr* **~ oneself, get ~d** rach an sàs *m* (**in** ann)

enter *v* **1** rach/thig a-steach (*with prep* do), inntrig *vi*; **2** (*on keyboard, calculator &c*) put *vt* ann, cuir *vti* a-steach

enterprise *n* iomairt *f*, **Highlands and Islands Enterprise** Iomairt na Gaidhealtachd, ~ **zone** ceàrn *f* iomairt *gen*

enterprising *adj* iomairteach, ionnsaigheach, gnìomhach

entertainment *n* **1** dibhearsan *&* dibheirsean *m*; **2** (*hospitality*) fèisteas *m*

enthusiasm *n* **1** (*in general*) dealas *m*; **2** (*about a particular thing &c*) dèidhealachd *f invar* (**about** air)

enthusiastic *adj* **1** (*in general*) dealasach; **2** (*about a particular thing &c*) dèidheil (**about** air)

entice *v* meall *vt*, tàlaidh *vt*, breug *vt*

enticement *n* mealladh *m*, tàladh *m*

enticing *adj* meallach, tàlaidheach

entire *adj* **1** (*not divided, fragmented &c*) iomlan, slàn, **one was broken but the other was** ~ bha an dàrna fear *m* briste ach bha am fear eile iomlan/slàn; **2** (*in its entirety*) gu lèir, air fad, **the** ~ **army** an t-arm gu lèir, **an** ~ **month** mìos *mf* gu lèir, mìos air fad

entirely *adv* gu tur, gu buileach, gu h-iomlan, uile-gu-lèir, **the two things are** ~ **different** tha an dà rud *m* gu tur/gu buileach eadar-dhealaichte, ~ **useless** gun fheum *m* uile-gu-lèir

entitled *adj & past part* airidh (**to** air), **she is** ~ **to it** tha i airidh air, *also* tha còir *f* aice air

entitlement *n* **1** (*abstr*) dlighe *f invar*, dleas *m*, còir *f*, airidheachd *f invar*; **2** (*con: amount, allowance &c one is entitled to*) cuibhreann *mf*

entrails *n* **1** mionach *m*, innidh *f invar*; **2** (*usu of animals*) greallach *f*

entrance *n* **1** (*abstr*) teachd-a-steach *m invar*, inntrigeadh *m*; **2** (*con: way in*) rathad *m* inntrigidh (*gen of* inntreagadh *m used adjectivally*), slighe *f* inntrigidh, (*by a door*) doras *m* inntrigidh; **3** (*admission to ed establishment &c*) inntrigeadh *m*, ~ **exam/test** deuchainn *f* inntrigidh *gen*

entrant *n* **1** (*in competition*) farpaiseach *m*; **2** (*in exam*) deuchainniche *m*

entreat *v* guidh *vi*, iarr *vi* gu dian, cuir impidh *m*, (*all with prep* air), **I'm ~ing you to stay!** tha mi a' guidhe ort fuireach!

entreaty *n* guidhe *mf*, impidh *f*

entrepreneur *n* neach-iomairt *m* (*pl* luchd-iomairt *m sing coll*)

entrust *v* earb *vt* (**to** ri), cuir cùram *m* (*with gen*) (**to** air), leig *vt* (**to** le), **don't ~ yourself to them** na h-earb thu-fhèin riutha, **he ~ed his family to me** 's ann ormsa a chuir e cùram a theaghlaich *m*, ~ **the child's upbringing to her** leig leathase togail *f* a' phàiste, leig leathase am pàiste a thogail

entry *n* **1** (*mainly abstr*) inntrigeadh *m*, teachd-a-steach *m invar*, **right of** ~ còir-inntrigidh *f*; **2** (*con*) doras *m*/rathad *m* (*&c*) inntrigidh *gen* (*cf* **entrance** *n* 2 above); **3** (*tenement close*) clobhsa *m*

entwine *v* suain *vt*

entwined *adj & past part* **1** air suaineadh, fillte; **2** (*unintentionally, inconveniently*) air amaladh

enunciate *v* cuir *vt* an cèill (*dat of* ciall *f*)

envelop *v* paisg *vt*, suain *vt*

envelope *n* cèis *f*, cèis litreach (*gen of* litir *f*)

envious *adj* **1** farmadach, **an ~ woman** boireannach farmadach; **2** *in exprs* **she became/grew/felt ~ of her sister** (*esp at a given moment*) gabh i farmad *m* ri piuthar, **she was ~ of her sister** (*ie a more permanent feeling*) bha farmad aice ri piuthar

environment *n* àrainneachd *f invar*

envoy *n* tosgaire *m*

envy *n* farmad *m*, (*less usu*) tnù(th) *m*

envy *v* gabh farmad *m* (*with prep* ri), (*more permanent feeling*) **he envied his sister** bha farmad aige ri phiuthar *f*

ephemeral *adj* diombuan, siùbhlach

epilogue *n* dùnadh *m*, faclan-dùnaidh *mpl*

epicentre *n* teis-meadhan *m*

episcopal *adj* easbaigeach

Episcopalian *n & adj* Easbaigeach

episode *n* (*of drama series &c*) earrann *f*

epitaph *n* marbhrann *m*

equal *adj* co-ionann *&* co-ionnan (**to, with** ri), **~ pay** pàigheadh *m* co-ionann, **the scores were ~** bha na sgòraichean *mpl* co-ionann

equal *n* **1** coimeas *m*, mac-samhail *m*, seis(e) *m*, **I never saw his ~** chan fhaca mi a choimeas/a mhac-samhail a-riamh, **she met her ~** fhuair i a seis; **2** *in expr* **she's not the ~ of her mother** chan fhiù i a màthair

equal *v* ionann (*with v* is), co-ionann (*with v* bi), **X ~s Y** is ionann X agus Y, **2 times 2 ~s 4** tha 2 uiread 2 co-ionann ri 4, *also* tha 2 uiread 2 a' dèanamh 4

equality *n* co-ionannachd *f invar*, **~ of opportunity** co-ionannachd cothruim *m gen*

equanimity *n* socair *f* (inntinn *f gen*), rèidheachd *f invar* (inntinn)

equation *n* (*maths*) co-aontar *m*

equator *n*, *used with art*, **the ~** am meadhan-chearcall *m*

equidistant *adj* co-astarail (**from** bho/o)

equilibrium *n* **1** meidh *f*, cothrom *m*, **in ~** air mheidh, **put into ~** cuir *vt* air meidh; **2** (*~ of two objects*) co-chothrom *m*

equip *v* uidheamaich *vt*

equipment uidheam *f*, acainn *f*

equipped *adj* uidheamaichte, acainneach

equitable *adj* cothromach, dìreach, gun chlaonadh *m*

equivalence *n* co-ionannachd *f invar*

equivalent *adj* co-ionann

equivocal *adj* dà-sheaghach

era *n* linn *f*

eradicate *v* cuir às (*with prep* do), spìon *vt* (às a *&c* b(h)un *m*)

erase *v* dubh *vt* às, **~ it** dubh às e

erect *adj* dìreach, **stand ~** seas *vi* dìreach

erect *v* tog *vt*

erode *v* criom *vt*, cnàmh *vt*, bleith *vt*

erosion *n* criomadh *m*, cnàmhadh *m*, bleith *f*

err *v* **1** rach *vi* air iomrall *m*, rach *vi* air seachran *m*, deàn mearachd *f*; **2** (*esp from spiritual point of view*) peacaich *vi*

errand *n* teachdaireachd *f invar*, **going on an ~** a' dol air theachdaireachd, *also* a' dol air gnothach *m*

erratic *adj* neo-chunbhalach, caochlaideach, carach, luasganach

erring *adj* seachranach, **an ~ spouse** cèile seachranach

erroneous *adj* mearachdach, iomrallach, **an ~ rumour** fathann mearachdach

error *n* **1** (*abstr*) iomrall *m*; **2** (*con*) mearachd *f*, **make an ~** deàn mearachd, rach *vi* air iomrall

erudite *adj* foghlaimte, foghlamaichte, **an ~ man** duine foghlaimte, *also* sgoilear *m*, eòlaiche *m*

erudition *n* sgoilearachd *f invar*

erupt *v* **1** brùchd *vt* (**from, out of** à, a-mach à), **the shoots ~ed out of the ground** bhrùchd na h-òganan *npl* a-mach às an talamh *m*; **2** (*volcano*) spreadh *vi*

eruption *n* **1** brùchdadh *m* (**from, out of** à, a-mach à); **2** (*of volcano*) spreadhadh *m*

escape *n* **1** (*abstr, & act of escaping*) teicheadh *m*, tàrradh *&* tàireadh *m* às; **2** (*means of ~*) dol-às *m invar*, **there was no ~ for us now** cha robh dol-às againn a-nis, **~ route** slighe *f* dol-às *gen*, rathad *m* dol-às

escape *v* teich *vi*, tàrr *&* tàir *vi* às, **the soldiers ~d** theich na saighdearan *mpl*, thàir na saighdearan às

escort *n* (*guard &c*) coimheadach *m*, freiceadan *m sing & coll*, faire *f coll*

escort *v* **1** (*accompany*) rach *vi* còmhla (*with prep* ri), **he ~ed her back** chaidh e air ais còmhla rithe; **2** (**~ under supervision**) thoir *vt irreg* (**to** gu), **the police ~ed him to the frontier** thug am polas chun na crìche e

Eskimo *adj & n* Easgiomach *m*

especially *adv* **1** (*as qualifying adj or adv*) air leth, **~ good/well** air leth math; **2** (*in particular*) gu h-àraidh, gu sònraichte, **I like sport, ~ football** is toigh leam spòrs *f*, gu h-àraidh ball-coise *m*

espouse *v* (*fig*) taobh *vi* (*with prep* ri), **~ a policy** taobh ri poileasaidh *m*

essay *n* aiste *f*

essayist *n* aistear *m*

essence *n* (*lit & fig*) brìgh *f invar*, sùgh *m*, **the ~ of his philosophy** brìgh na feallsanachd aige

essential *adj* **1** (*indispensable*) riatanach, deatamach, do-sheachainte; **2** (*basic, fundamental*) bunaiteach

establish *v* **1** (*inaugurate, set up*) stèidhich *vt*, cuir *vt* air b(h)onn *m*, cuir *vt* air chois (*dat of* cas *f*); **2** (*of facts &c: find out, demonstrate*) dearbh *vt*

establishment *n* **1** (*abstr*) stèidheachadh *m*, cur *m* air b(h)onn *m*, cur air chois (*dat of* cas *f*); **2** (*con*) ionad *m*, **the proprietor of this** ~ sealbhadair *m* an ionaid seo

estate *n* **1** (*landed* ~) oighreachd *f*; **2** (*housing* ~) ionad-thaighean *m*, sgeama-thaighean *m*, *in expr* (*council &c*) ~**s office** oifig *f* fearann-thogalach; **3** (*misc exprs*) ~ **agent** ceannaiche-seilbhe *m*, **industrial** ~ raon *m* gnìomhachais *m*

esteem *n* meas *m*, urram *m*, onair *f*

esteem *v* meas *vt*

esteemed, estimable *adj* measail, urramach, miadhail

estimate *n* meas *m invar*, tuaiream *f*, tuairmeas *m*, tuairmse *f*

estimate *v* **1** meas *vt*, thoir tuaiream *f* (*with prep* air); **2** (~ *value*) cuir luach *m invar* (*with prep* air)

estuary *n* beul *m* aibhne (*gen of* abhainn *f*), inbhir *m*

eternal *adj* maireannach, sìorraidh, bith-bhuan, sìor-mhaireannach, ~ **life** beatha mhaireannach

eternity *n* sìorraidheachd *f invar*

ethereal *adj* adharail, spioradail, neo-chorporra

ethical *adj* beusail, (*less trad*) eiticeil

ethics *n* beus-eòlas *m*, beusalachd *f invar*, (*less trad*) eitic *f*

ethnic *adj* (*relating to ethnicity*) cinealach

ethnicity *n* cinealachd *f invar*

ethos *n* **1** (*essential feature(s) of something*) brìgh *f*, susbaint *f*; **2** (*rationale behind something*) feallsanachd *f invar*, **the** ~ **of the course** feallsanachd a' chùrsa

etymology *n* **1** (*the discipline*) freumh-fhaclachd *f invar*; **2** (*of a particular word, name &c*) freumh *m*, bun *m*, tùs *m* (an fhacail, an ainm *&c*)

eulogy *n* **1** (*abstr*) moladh *m*; **2** (*con: poem*) dàn-molaidh *m*, (*prose* ~) aiste-mholaidh *f*, (*spoken* ~) òraid-mholaidh *f*

euro *n* euro *mf* (*pl* eurothan), **the** ~ **zone** ceàrn *m* an euro

Europe *n* An Roinn *f* Eòrpa *f invar*, (*less usu*) Eòrpa *f invar*

European *adj & n* Eòrpach, Na Roinn *m* Eòrpa *f invar*, **the European Commission** An Coimisean Eòrpach, *also* Coimisean na Roinn Eòrpa

evacuate *v* falmhaich *vt*, (*esp of people*) fàsaich *vt*

evacuation *n* falmhachadh *m*, (*esp of people*) fàsachadh *m*

evacuee *n* fògrach *m*, neach-fuadain *m* (*pl* luchd-fuadain *m sing coll*)

evade *v* èalaidh *vi* air falbh, siolp *vi* air falbh, (*both with prep* air), seachain *vt*, **he managed to** ~ **me** chaidh aige air èalaidh/siolpadh air falbh orm, chaidh aige air mo sheachnadh *m*

evaluate *v* **1** (*monetary value*) luachaich *vt*, cuir luach *m invar* (*with prep* air); **2** (*more generally*) meas *vt*

evaluation *n* **1** (*of monetary value*) luachachadh *&* luachadh *m*; **2** (*more generally*) measadh *m*

evaporate *v* deataich *vi*

evaporation *n* deatachadh *m*

evasive *adj* (*persons, answers to questions &c*) mì-fhosgarra, fiar

eve *n* (*of specific days*) oidhche *f*, **New Year's Eve** Oidhche Challainn *f gen*

even *adj* **1** (*ground, surface &c*) còmhnard, rèidh; **2** (*numbers: not odd*) cothrom, **~ number** àireamh chothrom; **3** (*steady, regular*) cunbhalach, cothromach, **at an ~ pace** air ceum cunbhalach; **4** (*equal*) co-ionann, **the scores were ~** bha na sgòraichean *mpl* co-ionann

even *adv* **1** eadhon, fiù is/agus, uiread is/agus **I didn't ~ have two pounds** cha robh eadhon dà nota *f* agam, cha robh fiù is/uiread is dà nota agam, **without ~ so much as a piece of bread** gun uiread agus pìos *m* arain *m gen*, **they didn't ~ look at us** cha do rinn iad fiù agus sùil *f* a thoirt oirnn; **2** (*idiom*) **~ Calum grew afraid** thàinig an t-eagal air Calum fhèin

even-handed *adj* cothromach, **he is ~** tha e cothromach, *also* chan eil e taobhach

evening *n* feasgar *m*, **good ~!** feasgar math!, **we'll be in in the ~** bidh sinn ann feasgar, **in/during/in the course of the ~** air an fheasgar, **the ~ star** reul *f* an fheasgair

event *n* **1** (*occurrence*) tachartas *m*, tuiteamas *m*; **2** (*case, circumstance*) *in exprs* **in the ~ of his being guilty** mas e an rud e 's gu bheil e ciontach, **I'm not going in any ~** chan eil mise a' dol ann co-dhiù; **3** (*at sports meeting &c*) co-fharpais *f*

eventful *adj* tachartach

eventuality *n* (*circumstance*) cor *m*, **don't touch it in any ~** na buin ris air chor sam bith, *also* na buin ris ge b' e dè a thachras

eventually *adv* aig a' cheann *m* thall, mu dheireadh thall, luath no mall, **we built the house ~** thog sinn an taigh aig a' cheann thall/mu dheireadh thall, **we'll manage it ~** thèid againn air luath no mall/aig a' cheann thall

ever *adv* **1** (*with neg v*) gu bràth tuilleadh, **he won't ~ come back** cha till e gu bràth tuilleadh; **2** *in expr* **for ~** gu bràth, gu sìorraidh, a-chaoidh, **Ben Nevis will be there for ~** bidh Beinn Nibheis ann gu bràth/gu sìorraidh, **I'll love you for ~** bidh gaol *m* agam ort a-chaoidh, **for ~ and ~** gu sìorraidh bràth; **3** *in expr* **you'll hardly ~ see the likes of him** is gann a chì thu a leithid *f*

evergreen *adj* sìor-uaine, (*of trees*) neo-sheargach

everlasting *adj* maireannach, **~ life** beatha mhaireannach

every *adj* a h-uile, gach, **~ day** a h-uile là *m*, **~ single day** gach aon là, **each and ~ day** gach uile là, **~ one of them** a h-uile fear *m* aca, (*corres &c*) **with ~ good wish** leis gach deagh dhùrachd *m*

everybody, everyone *pron* a h-uile duine *m*, (*esp ~ concerned*) na h-uile *pron*, **~ will die in the end** gheibh a h-uile duine bàs *m* aig a' cheann *m* thall, **~ lost their money** chaill a h-uile duine/na h-uile an cuid *f* airgid *m gen*

everyday *adj* làitheil

everyone *pron, see* **everybody**, *above*

everything *n* a h-uile càil *m invar*, a h-uile sìon *m*, gach (aon) rud *m*, gach (aon) nì *m*

evict *v* cuir *vt* a-mach (**from** à)

evidence *n* 1 (*testimony given*) fianais *f*, teisteanas *m*, **give** ~ thoir fianais; 2 (*proof*) dearbhadh *m* (**of** air), ~ **of his guilt** dearbhadh air a chionta *m*

evident *adj* follaiseach, soilleir, **it's** ~ **that he's not guilty** tha e follaiseach nach eil e ciontach

evidentness *n* follais *f invar*

evil *adj* 1 olc; 2 *in exprs* **the** ~ **one** an Donas *m*, **the** ~ **eye** an droch-shùil *f*

evil *n* donas *m*, (*stronger*) olc *m*, **good and** ~ am math is an t-olc

evil-natured, evil-tempered *adj* droch-nàdarrach

evolution *n* (*of life forms &c*) meanbh-chinneas *m*, mùthadh *m*

evolve *v* 1 (*life forms &c*) mùth *vi*; 2 (*develop*) atharraich *vi* (mean air mhean), **his philosophy** ~**d over the years** dh'atharraich an fheallsanachd aige mean air mhean rè nam bliadhnachan *mpl*

ewe *n* caora *f*, **in lamb** ~ caora-uain, ~ **with a lamb at foot** caora is uan *m* na cois (*dat of* cas *f*), ~ **with twin lambs** caora-chàraid

exact *adj* 1 (*accurate*) ceart, (*sums, figures &c*) cruinn, grinn; 2 (*person, work &c*) pongail, mionaideach; 3 *in exprs* **in the** ~ **centre of the field** ann an ceart-mheadhan *m* an achaidh, **the** ~ **thing I needed** an dearbh rud *m* a bha dhìth orm

exactly *adv* dìreach, ~ **as I would wish** dìreach mar a thograinn, (*expr agreement*) ~! dìreach (sin)!

exalt *v* àrdaich *vt*, cuir *vt* an àirde *f invar*

examination *n* 1 (*in school &c*) deuchainn *f*, **entrance** ~ deuchainn inntrigidh (*gen of* inntrigeadh *m*); 2 (*medical &c*) sgrùdadh *m*, **dental** ~ sgrùdadh fhiaclan *fpl gen*

examine *v* 1 (*in school &c*) ceasnaich *vt*, thoir deuchainnean *fpl* (*with prep* do); 2 (*medical &c*) sgrùd *vt*, dèan sgrùdadh *m* (*with prep* air)

examinee *n* deuchainniche *m*

examiner *n* 1 sgrùdaiche *m*; 2 (*school &c* ~) neach-ceasnachaidh *m* (*pl* luchd-ceasnachaidh *m sing coll*)

example *n* eisimpleir *m*, **for** ~ mar eisimpleir (*abbrev* m.e.)

exasperate *v* leamhaich *vt*

exasperated *adj & past part* frionasach, diombach, sàraichte

exasperating *adj* frionasach, leamh

exceed *v* rach *vi irreg* thairis, rach seachad, (*with prep* air), **you** ~**ed my instructions** chaidh sibh thairis/seachad air na h-òrduighean *mpl* a thug mi dhuibh

exceedingly *adv* anabarrach, ro- *prefix*, uabhasach (fhèin), cianail fhèin, ~ **good** anabarrach math, (*more trad*) ro-mhath, (*more fam*) uabhasach (fhèin) math, ~ **slow** cianail fhèin slaodach

excellence *n* feabhas *m*, (*more trad or formal*) òirdheirceas *m*

excellent *adj* air leth, air leth math, math dha-rìribh, (*more trad or formal*) òirdheirc, **an ~ bottle of wine** botal air leth de dh'fhìon, **that was ~** bha sin air leth math/math dha-rìribh

exception *n, in expr* **with the ~ of** ach a-mhàin, **everyone returned home, with the ~ of Iain** thill a h-uile duine *m* dhachaigh, ach a-mhàin Iain

exceptional *adj* air leth, às a' chumantas *m*, **an ~ man** duine *m* air leth

excess *n*, cus *m*, tuilleadh 's a' chòir, **an ~ of food/noise** cus bìdh *m gen*/ fuaim *m gen*, **drink to ~** òl cus, **there was an ~ of it** bha tuilleadh 's a' chòir dheth ann

excessive *adj* **1** cus *m*, **~ noise/rain** cus *m* fuaim/uisge *gen*; **2** (*occas: esp with abstr nouns of feeling, psychological states &c*) ro- *prefix* (*lenites following cons where possible*), *eg* **~ anxiety** ro-chùram *m*

excessively *adv* ro (*lenites following cons where possible*), **~ permissive** ro cheadachail

exchange *n* **1** malairt *f*, (*more trad*) iomlaid *f*; **2** (*currency*) iomlaid *f*, **the ~ rate** luach *m* na h-iomlaid, *also* co-luach *m* an airgid

exchequer *n* Roinn *f* an Ionmhais

excite 1 (*esp emotions*) tog *vt*; **2** (*people*) brod *vt*, gluais *vt*, spreòd *vt*, cuir *vt* air bhioran *m*; **3** (*sexually*) brod *vt*

excited *adj & past part* air bhioran *m*, togarrach, meanmnach, (*more extreme*) am boile *f*, air bhoile

excitement *n* togarrachd *f invar*, meanmnachd *f invar*, (*more extreme*) boile *f invar*

exclamation *n* **1** clisgeadh *m*; **2** (*gram*) clisgear *m, in expr* **~ mark** clisg-phuing *f*

exclude *v* cùm *vt* (**from** bho/o), dùn *vt* a-mach (**from** à), **~ him from the room** cùm bhon rùm *m* e, dùn a-mach às an rùm e

exclusion *n* às-dùnadh *m*

excrement *n* cac *m*

excursion *n* cuairt *f*, sgrìob *f*, (**to do**), **an ~ to the islands** cuairt/sgrìob do na h-eileanan *mpl*

excuse *n* leisgeul *m*

excuse *v* **1** thoir leisgeul *m* (*with prep* do), math *vt*, **we ~d her** ghabh sinn a leisgeul; **2** (*excl*) **~ me!** gabh(aibh) mo leisgeul!; **3** (*allow to leave*) thoir cead *m invar* falbh (*with prep* do), (*allow to be absent*) thoir cead *followed by* gun *& infin of the verb*, **the chairman ~d him from the meeting** thug an caithriche cead dha gun a bhith aig a' choinneimh *f*

execute *v* **1** (*a task, process &c*) thoir *vt* gu buil *f*, gnìomhaich *vt*; **2** (*kill*) cuir *vt* gu bàs *m*

executive *adj* gnìomhach

executive *n* **1** gnìomhaiche *m*; **2** (*coll*) **the ~** an roinn-gnìomha *f*; **3** *in expr* (*pol*) **The Scottish Executive** Riaghaltas *m* na h-Alba

exempt *adj* saor (**from** bho/o), neo-bhuailteach (*with prep* do), **~ from taxes** saor o chìsean *fpl*, neo-bhuailteach do chìsean

exempt *v* saor *vt* (**from** bho/o)

exemption *n* saoradh *m* (**from** bho/o)

exercise *n* (*phys, ed &c*) eacarsaich *f*

exercise *v* **1** (*make use of*) cleachd *vt*, ~ **power** cleachd cumhachd *mf* invar; **2** (*put into effect*) cuir *vt* an gnìomh *m*, ~ **rights** cuir an gnìomh còraichean *fpl*; **3** (*take exercise*) bi *vi irreg* ag eacarsaich

exhaust *n* (*of engine*) tràghadh & traoghadh *m*, ~ **pipe** pìob-thràghaidh *f*

exhaust *v* **1** (*person*) claoidh *vt*; **2** (*use up resources &c*) caith *vt*

exhausted *adj* & *past part* **1** (*person*) claoidhte; **2** (*resources &c*) caithte, cosgte

exhaustion *n* **1** (*of people*) claoidheachd *f* invar; **2** (*of resources &c*) (*abstr*) caithteachd *f* invar, (*the action*) caitheamh *m*

exhibit *v* **1** seall *vt*, **~ing signs of weariness** a' sealltainn chomharraidhean *mpl* sgìths *f* invar; **2** (*art &c*) taisbean & taisbein *vt*

exhibition *n* **1** (*of art, goods, techniques &c*) taisbeanadh *m*, ~ **hall** taisbean-lann *f*, talla-taisbeanaidh *f*; **2** (*bad behaviour*) in *expr* **what an ~!** abair dol-a-mach!

exhilarate *v* cuir aoibhneas *m*/sunnd *m* (*with prep* air), sunndaich *vt*

exhort *v* brosnaich *vt*, earalaich *vt*, (**to** gu)

exhortation *n* brosnachadh *m*, earail *f*, earalachadh *m*, (**to** gu)

exile *n* **1** (*the state*) fuadan *m*, fògradh *m*, fògairt *f* invar; **2** (*the person*) neach-fuadain *m* (*pl* luchd-fuadain *m sing coll*), fòg(ar)rach *m*, eilthireach *m*

exile *v* fuadaich *vt*, fògair *vt*, **they were ~d** chaidh am fuadach(adh), chaidh am fògradh

exist *v* **1** bi *vi irreg* ann, **fairies don't ~** chan eil sìthichean *mpl* ann; **2** (*live*) mair *vi* beò, bi *vi irreg* beò, **I couldn't ~ without music** cha mhairinn beò/cha b' urrainn dhomh a bhith beò gun cheòl *m*

existence *n* **1** bith *f*, **bring into ~** thoir *vt* am bith, **pass out of ~** rach *vi* à bith; **2** (*con: life*) beatha *f*, **a wretched ~** beatha thruagh

exit *n* **1** doras *m* dol *m* a-mach, slighe *f* dol a-mach; **2** in *expr* (*pol*) ~ **poll** cunntas *m* sgaoilidh *m gen*

exonerate *v* saor *vt* o choire *f*

exotic *adj* allmharach, coigreach

expand *v* **1** leudaich *vti*, meudaich *vti*; **2** (*swell*) sèid *vi*, at *vi*

expanded *adj* **1** leudaichte, meudaichte; **2** (*swollen*) sèidte, air sèid(eadh)

expansion *n* **1** leudachadh *m*, meudachadh *m*; **2** (*by swelling*) sèideadh *m*

expect *v* **1** (*anticipate*) coimhead *vi* (*with prep* ri), **we're ~ing storms** tha sinn a' coimhead ri stoirmean *fpl*; **2** (~ *a visit*) **I ~/am ~ing her** tha dùil/sùil/fiughair (*all f*) agam rithe; **3** (*suppose*) bi *vi irreg* an dùil *f* (*with prep* aig & *conj* gu), bi *vi irreg* an dùil (*with conj* gu), **I ~ he'll come** tha dùil agam gun tig e, **I don't ~ he'll manage it** chan eil mi an dùil gun tèid aige air; **4** (*with double neg constr*) *eg*, **I'll be drunk tonight! I ~ you will!** bidh mi air an daoraich *dat* a-nochd! cha chreid mi nach bi!

expectation *n* dùil *f*, fiughair *f*

expedient *adj* iomchaidh, freagarrach

expedient *n* innleachd *f*, seòl *m*

expedition *n* turas *m*

expel *v* fògair *vt*, cuir *vt* a-mach, (*with prep* à), **the people were ~led from the glen** dh'fhògradh an sluagh às a' ghleann *m*

expenditure *n* teachd-a-mach *m invar*, caiteachas *m*

expense *n* cosgais *f*, **travelling ~s** cosgaisean-siubhail *fpl*

expensive *adj* cosgail, daor

experience *v* **1** (*~ sensations, emotions*) mothaich *vt*; **2** (*know, live through*) aithnich *vt*, (*esp emotions*) bi *vi irreg* fo (*prep*), **we didn't ~ poverty** cha do dh'aithnich sinn bochdainn *f*, **like a person experiencing fear/a nightmare** mar neach *m* a bhiodh fo eagal *m*/fo throm-laighe *mf*

experience *n* eòlas *m* (**of** air), **~ of the world** eòlas air an t-saoghal

experienced *adj* eòlach, fiosrach, (**in** air), cleachdte (**in** ri)

experiment *n* deuchainn *f*, dearbhadh *m*

expert *adj* **1** (*knowledgeable*) eòlach (**in, on, about** air); **2** (*~ at performing tasks &c*) teòma (**in, at** ann an)

expert *n* **1** (*knowledgeable person*) eòlaiche *m*; **2** (*~ at performing tasks &c*) ealantach *m*

expertise *n* **1** (*knowledge*) eòlas *m*; **2** (*~ in performing tasks &c*) ealantachd *f invar*, teòmachd *f invar*

expiation *n* rèite *f*

explain *v* mìnich *vt*, soilleirich *vt*

explanation *n* **1** mìneachadh *m*, soilleireachadh *m*; **2** (*reason: idiom*) **what's the ~ for that?** dè as coireach ri sin?

explanatory *adj* mìneachail

explode *v* spreadh *vti*

exploit *n* euchd *m*, cleas *m*, (*fam*) plòigh *f*

exploit *v* **1** dèan feum *m* (*with prep* de), thoir brìgh *f invar* (*with prep* à); **2** (*~ more unfairly*) gabh brath *m*, gabh fàth *m invar*, (*with prep* air)

explore *v* rannsaich *vt*

explorer *n* rannsachair *m* (dhùthchannan *fpl gen*)

explosion *n* spreadhadh *m*

explosives *npl* stuth-spreadhaidh *m*

export *n* **1** (*abstr*) às-mhalairt *f*, **~ market** margadh *mf* às-mhalairt *gen*; **2** (*con: products &c ~ed*) às-bhathar *m sing coll*

export *v* às-mhalairtich *vti*, reic *vt* an cèin

exporter *n* às-mhalairtear *m*

expose *v* **1** leig *vt* (*with prep pron* ris), thoir *vt* am follais *f invar*; **2** (*~ body*) rùisg *vt*

exposed *adj* ris, rùisgte, nochdte, **his back was ~** bha a dhruim *m* ris, **~ to the sun** ris a' ghrèin (*dat of* grian *f*)

exposition *n* cunntas *m*, mìneachadh *m*

exposure *n* **1** leigeil *m* ris, toirt *f invar* am follais *f invar*; **2** rùsgadh *m*

express *adj* **1** (*rapid*) luath, *often as prefix in this sense, eg* **~ train** luath-thrèana *f*, ~ **service** luath-sheirbheis *f*; **2** (*precise, deliberate*) **I did it with the ~ purpose/intention of annoying you** rinn mi e a dh'aon ghnothach *m*/a dh'aon rùn *m* gus dragh *m* a chur ort.

express *n* (*train*) luath-thrèana *f*

express *v* cuir *vt* an cèill (*dat sing of* ciall *f*), ~ **your feelings** cuir ur faireachdainnean *fpl* an cèill

expression *n* **1** (*transient facial ~*) fiamh *m*, mèinn *f*, coltas *m*; **2** (*more permanent facial ~*) gnùis *f*; **3** (*lang: idiom, phrase &c*) abairt *f*, dòigh-labhairt *f*; **4** (*abstr: act of expressing feelings &c*) cur *m* an cèill (*dat sing of* ciall *f*)

expressly *adv* a dh'aon ghnothach *m*, a dh'aon rùn *m*, **I wrote the letter ~ to bring the matter to an end** sgrìobh mi an litir a dh'aon ghnothach/a dh'aon rùn airson/gus a' chùis *f* a thoirt gu ceann *m*

extend *v* **1** (*increase size*) leudaich *vti*; **2** (*hold or stretch out*) sìn (a-mach) *vti*, ~ **the hand of friendship to them** sìn làmh a' chàirdeis dhaibh/thuca

extended *adj* **1** (*increased in size*) leudaichte; **2** (*held or stretched out*) sìnte (a-mach)

extension *n* **1** (*increase in size*) leudachadh *m*; **2** (*holding or stretching out*) sìneadh *m*

extensive *adj* **1** (*sizeable &c*) farsaing, leathann, mòr; **2** (*opposite of intensive*) sgaoilte

extent *n* **1** (*phys*) farsaingeachd *f invar*; **2** (*more abstr: degree, intensity &c*) meud *m invar*, **the ~ of her anxiety** meud a h-iomagain

exterior *n* (an) taobh a-muigh, **the ~ of the building** taobh a-muigh an togalaich

external *adj* (*phys*) an taoibh (*gen of* taobh *m*) a-muigh, (*also more fig*) **an ~ student** oileanach *m* an taoibh a-muigh

extinct *adj* (*volcano, species &c*) marbh, à bith *f invar*

extinguish smà(i)l *vt* (às), cuir *vt* às, mùch *vt*, tùch *vt*, ~ **the fire** cuir às/ smàil às an teine *m*

extinguisher *n* smàladair *m*, mùchadair *m*

extract *n* earrann *f* (**from** de *or* à)

extract *v* (*pull or take out*) thoir *vt* às, tarraing *vt* às, **he ~ed the tooth** thug e às an fhiacail

extraordinary *adj* às a' chumantas, air leth

extravagant *adj* caith(t)each

extreme *adj* **1** anabarrach, (*occas: esp with abstr nouns of feeling, psychological states &c*) ro- *prefix* (*lenites following cons where possible*), ~ **anxiety** ro-chùram *m*; **2** (*exceptional*) **an ~ example** eisimpleir *m* air leth

extreme *n* (*eg of climate*) anabarr *m*

extremely *adv* anabarrach, air leth, (*occas: esp with abstr nouns of feeling, psychological states &c*) ro- *prefix* (*lenites following cons where possible*), ~ **good** air leth math, anabarrach math, math dha-rìribh, gu dearbh fhèin math, ~ **willing** ro-thoileach, ~ **white** ro-gheal

extremity *n* **1** (*of extended area*) iomall *m*, crìoch *f*; **2** (*of a line*) ceann *m*; **3** (*a crisis &c*) èiginn *f invar*

exuberance *n* suilbhireachd *f invar*

exuberant *adj* suilbhir

eye *n* **1** sùil *f*, ~ **contact** glacadh *m* sùla, **the evil** ~ an droch-shùil *f*; **2** *in exprs* ~ **socket** gluc *f*, ~ **of a needle** crò *m* snàthaid *f gen*

eyeball *n* clach *f* na sùla

eyebrow *n* mala *f*

eyelash *n* fabhra *m*, rosg *m*

eyelid *n* fabhra *m*

eyesight *n* fradharc *&* radharc *m*, lèirsinn *f invar*

eyewitness *n* sùil-fhianaise *f*

F

fable *n* uirsgeul *m*, fionnsgeul *m*

facade *n* **1** (*of building &c*) aghaidh *f*; **2** (*outward pretence &c*) sgàil *f*

face *n* **1** (*of person*) aodann *m*, aghaidh *f*, ~ **to** ~ aghaidh ri aghaidh, **she struck me full in the** ~ bhuail i mi an clàr m' aodainn, **I told her the truth to her** ~ dh' innis mi an fhìrinn dhi an clàr a h-aodainn; **2** (*topog: ~ of hill &c*) aghaidh *f*, **the** ~ **of the mountain** aghaidh na beinne, **on the** ~ **of the earth** air aghaidh na talmhainn

face *v* **1** (*turn towards*) cuir a (*&c*) aghaidh *f* (*with prep* ri), **I ~d the wall** chuir mi m' aghaidh ris a' bhalla; **2** (*be orientated towards*) bi *vi irreg* mu choinneimh (*with gen*), (*less usu*) bi *vi irreg* fa chomhair (*with gen*), **I was facing her** bha mi mu coinneimh, **I was facing the window** bha mi mu choinneimh na h-uinneig(e); **3** *in expr* ~ **up to** seas *vi* (*with prep* ri), ~ **up to problems/enemies** seas *vi* ri duilgheadasan *mpl*/ri nàimhdean *mpl*

facility *n* **1** goireas *m*, **the club has lots of facilities** tha goireasan gu leòr/gu leòr de ghoireasan aig a' chlub *m*; **2** (*natural bent, flair*) alt *m* (**for** air)

facing *adv* mu choinneimh, (*less usu*) fa chomhair, (*with gen*), **I sat down** ~ **the window** shuidh mi sìos mu choinneimh na h-uinneige

facsimile *n* mac-samhail *m*, lethbhreac *m*

fact *n* fìrinn *f*, rud *m*, **it's a ~!** 's e an fhìrinn a th' ann!, **the** ~ **is, I was tired** 's e an rud a th' ann gun robh mi sgìth, *or* is ann gun robh mi sgìth, **if it is a** ~ **that he is lazy** mas e (an rud e) 's gu bheil e leisg

factor[1] *n* (*of estate &c*) bàillidh *m*, maor *m*

factor[2] *n* (*aspect, element*) adhbhar *m*, eileamaid *f*, **one of the ~s in his decision** fear de dh'adhbharan a cho-dhùnaidh *m gen*, **the main** ~ **in this situation** a' phrìomh eileamaid san t-suidheachadh *m* seo

faculty *n* **1** comas *m*, ~ **of speech**, comas-bruidhne *f*, comas-cainnte *f*, comas-labhairt *f*; **2** *in expr* **the** ~ **of movement/motion** lùth *m*

fade *v* crìon *vti*

fail *v* **1** (*as vi: person, business &c*) fàillig *vi*, (*esp business*) rach *vi* fodha, **he ~ed** dh'fhàillig e, **his business ~ed** dh'fhàillig an gnìomhachas aige, chaidh an gnìomhachas aige fodha; **2** (*as vt*) fàillig *vt*, **he ~ed his exams** dh'fhàillig e na deuchainnean *fpl* aige; **3** (~ *in health*) rach *vi* bhuaithe, **she is ~ing** tha i a' dol bhuaithe

failing *n* fàilligeadh *m*, fàillinn *f*

failure *n* fàilligeadh *m*

faint *adj* **1** fann, lag, **a** ~ **voice** guth fann, ~ **from/with hunger** lag leis an acras *m*; **2** (*idiom*) **I haven't the ~est idea** chan eil càil *m invar* a dh'fhios *m* agam

faint *n* neul *m*, laigse *f*

faint *v* fannaich *vi*, fanntaig *vi*, rach *vi irreg* an laigse *f*, rach *vi irreg* an neul *m*

faint-hearted *adj* meata

fair *adj* **1** (*attractive*) bòidheach, maiseach; **2** (*of hair, complexion*) bàn; **3** (*just &c*) cothromach, reusanta, **a ~ man** duine cothromach, **a ~ decision** breith chothromach; **4** (*idiom*) **we gave them ~ odds** thug sinn cothrom *m* na Fèinne dhaibh

fair *n* (*market; also rides, amusements &c*) fèill *f*, faidhir *f*, **The Mull Fair** An Fhaidhir Mhuileach

fair-haired *adj* bàn

fairly *adv* **1** (*quite, pretty*) an ìre mhath, car *m*, caran *m*, **we were ~ tired** bha sinn an ìre mhath sgìth/car sgìth; **2** (*in a fair manner*) gu cothromach

fairy *n* sìthiche *m*, bean-sìth(e) *f*, **the ~ folk, the fairies** na daoine-sìth *mpl*, na sìthichean *mpl*

faith *n* creideamh *m*, **the Islamic ~** an creideamh Ioslamach

faithful *adj* dìleas

faithfulness *n* dìlseachd *f invar*

faithless *adj* mì-dhìleas

fake *adj* fuadain, brèige (*gen of* fuadan *m*/breug *f used adjectivally*), **~ diamonds** daoimeanan *mpl* brèige

fake *n* **1** (*person: dissembler &c*) mealltair *m*, cealgair(e) *m*; **2** (fake object) rud *m* (*&c*) brèige (*gen of* breug *used adjectivally*)

fall[1] *n* tuiteam *m*

fall[2] *n* (*autumn*) foghar *m*

fall *v* **1** tuit *vi*, **stumbling and ~ing** a' tuisleadh 's a' tuiteam, **shares fell today** thuit sèaraichean *mpl* an-diugh, **it fell to him to be a soldier** thuit dha a bhith na shaighdear *m*, (*idiom*) **~ing to bits** a' dol na (*&c*) c(h)riomagan *fpl*; **2** (*come to rest*) laigh *vi* (**on** air), **her shadow fell on me** laigh a faileas *m* orm; **3** *in expr* **~ out** (*ie quarrel*) rach *vi irreg* thar a chèile, rach *vi irreg* a-mach air a chèile, **I caused them to ~ out** chuir mi thar a chèile iad, **they have ~en out** tha iad troimh-a-chèile

fallow *adj* bàn, **~ land/ground** talamh bàn

falls *n* (*waterfall*) eas *m*, leum-uisge *m*, linne *f*, spùt *m*

false *adj* **1** (*deceitful &c*) meallta, mealltach, fallsa; **2** (*artificial*) fuadain, brèige (*gen of* breug *f used adjectivally*), **~ teeth** fiaclan-fuadain *mpl*, **~ moustache** stais bhrèige; **3** (*wrong*) ceàrr, **a ~ conclusion** co-dhùnadh ceàrr

fame *n* cliù *m invar*, (*stronger*) glòir *f invar*, **win ~** coisinn cliù

familiar *adj* **1** (*knowledgeable*) eòlach (**with** air), **~ with computers** eòlach air coimpiutairean *mpl*; **2** (*accustomed*) cleachdte (**with** ri), **~ with her ways** cleachdte ri a dòigh(ean) *f*; **3** (*frequently met with*) cumanta, (*less usu*) gnàthach, **~ complaints** gearanan *mpl* cumanta

familiarity *n* eòlas *m* (**with** air), **~ with computers** eòlas air coimpiutairean *mpl*

family *n* **1** (*esp immediate ~*) teaghlach *m*; **2** (*extended ~*) càirdean (*pl of* caraid *m*), daoine (*pl of* duine *m*), cuideachd *f*, **all my ~ are in Stornoway** tha mo chàirdean/mo dhaoine air fad ann an Steòrnabhagh

famine *n* gort(a) *f*

famous *adj* ainmeil, cliùiteach, iomraiteach

famously *adv*, (*idiom*) **we get on** ~ tha sinn gu math mòr aig a chèile

fan *m* (*for ventilation &c*) gaotharan *m*

fank *n* (*the structure, also the activity of dipping &c at the* ~) faing *f*, fang *m*, **there'll be a** ~ **tomorrow** bidh faing ann a-màireach

far *adj & adv* **1** (*phys distance*) fad(a), **how** ~ **is it?** dè cho fada 's a tha e?, ~ **away/off** fad(a) air falbh, ~ **and wide** fad is farsaing, *in expr* **as** ~ **as** (*ie up to*) gu ruige *prep* (*with nom*), **we'll go as** ~ **as the ridge** thèid sinn gu ruige an druim; **2** (*time*) *in expr* **so** ~ (*ie up to the present*) gu ruige seo, chun a seo, **we haven't made any mistakes so** ~ cha do rinn sinn mearachdan *fpl* gu ruige seo/chun a seo; **3** (*intensifying adv: much*) fada, ~ **better** fada nas fheàrr, ~ **older** fada nas sine, (*idiom*) **we had** ~ **too much** bha tuilleadh 's a' chòir againn

faraway *adj* fad air falbh, cèin

fare[1] *n* (*on bus &c*) faradh *m*

fare[2] *n* (*provisions*) biadh *m*, lòn *m*

farewell *n* **1** cead *m*, **we bade them** ~ ghabh sinn ar cead dhiubh; **2** (*as excl*) ~! soraidh *f* leat/leibh!, beannachd *f* leat/leibh!, slàn leat/leibh!

far-fetched *adj* (a thèid) thar na fìrinn, *in expr* ~ **talk/stories/tales** rabhd *m*, ràbhart *m*,

farm *n* tuathanas *m*, *in expr* **home** ~ mànas *m*

farmer *n* tuathanach *m*

farming *n* **1** (*the activity*) tuathanachas *m*; **2** (*the subject, the theory of* ~) àiteachas *m*

fascinated *adj* fo gheasaibh (*obs dat pl of* geas *f*), **I was** ~ **by it** bha mi fo gheasaibh leis, **she had me** ~ bha mi fo gheasaibh aice

fashion *n* fasan *m*, **a new** ~ fasan ùr, **in** ~ san fhasan, **out of** ~ às an fhasan

fashion *v* cum *vt*, dealbh *vt*

fashionable *adj* fasanta, san fhasan *m*

fast *adj* luath, **a** ~ **train** luath-thrèana *f*

fast *n* trasg *f*, trasgadh *m*, ~ **day** là-traisg *m*, là-trasgaidh *m*

fast *v* bi *vi irreg* na (*&c*) t(h)rasg *f*, traisg *vi*, **they are** ~**ing** tha iad nan trasg, tha iad a' trasgadh

fasten *v* ceangail *vt*

fastening *n* ceangal *m*

fast-flowing *adj* cas, bras

fastidious *adj* òrraiseach

fat *adj* reamhar, sultmhor

fat *n* **1** crèis *f*, geir *f*, saill *f*; **2** (*body* ~) sult *m*

fatal *adj* marbhtach

fate *n* dàn *m*, (*more trad*) crannchur *m*, **oppose/go against** ~ cuir *vi* an aghaidh dàin, **he accepted his** ~ ghabh e ris na bha an dàn dha, **if that is my** ~ mas e sin mo chrannchur

fated *adj* an dàn (**for** do), **that was ~ for him** bha sin an dàn dha

fatten *v* reamhraich *vti*

fatty *adv* crèiseach

faucet *n* goc *m*

fault *n* **1** (*defect in person or object*) fàillinn *f*, gaoid *f*; **2** (*defect in object*) easbhaidh *f*, cearb *f*; **3** (*moral defect in person*) meang *f*; **4** (*geological ~, ~ in metal &c*) sgàineadh *m*; **5** (*guilty action*) ciont(a) *m*; **6** *in exprs* **at ~** coireach, ciontach, **it wasn't my ~** cha mhis' a bu choireach (ris), **find ~** faigh coire *f* (**with** do)

favour *n* fàbhar *m*, seirbheis *f*, bàidh *f*, **he did you a ~** rinn e fàbhar/ seirbheis/bàidh dhut

favour *v* **1** (*side with*) cùm taobh (*with prep* ri); **2** (*prefer*) is *v irreg & def* fheàrr (*with prep* le), **I ~ the other applicant** 's e an neach-tagraidh *m* eile as fheàrr leam

favourable *adj* fàbharach

fawn *adj* odhar

fawn *n* mang *f*

fawn *v* dèan miodal *m* (**on** do), dèan sodal *m* (**on** ri)

fawning *n* miodal *m* (**on** do), sodal *m* (**on** ri)

fax *n* (*IT*) facs *m*, **~ machine** inneal *m* facsa *gen*, **send a ~** cuir facs (**to** gu)

fax *v* cuir (litir *&c*) na facs *m* (*with prep* gu), **I'll ~ you it/I'll fax it to you** cuiridh mi thugad e na facs

fear *n* **1** eagal (*occas* feagal) *m*, (*less usu*) fiamh *m*; **2** *in expr* **for ~ that** air eagal 's/is (*with conj* gun), mus (*also* mun *& mum*) *conj*, **for ~ that I miss the train** air eagal 's gun caill mi an trèana *f*, **he held the ladder for ~ she should fall** chùm e grèim *m* air an fhàradh *m* mus tuiteadh i

fearful *adj* eagalach

feasibility *n* ion-dhèantachd *f invar*

feasible *adj* ion-dhèanta

feast *n* **1** (*banquet*) cuirm *f*, fèis (*also* fèisd *& fèist*) *f*, fleadh *m*; **2** (*idiom/ saying*) **enough is as good as a ~** fòghnaidh na dh'fhòghnas; **3** (*relig ~*) fèill *f*, **the ~ of St Bride/Bridget** An Fhèill Brìde *f gen*

feast-day *n* latha-fèille *m*

feat *n* euchd *m*, cleas *m*

feather *n* ite *f*, (*small*) iteag *f*

feathered *adj* iteach, iteagach

feature *n* (*characteristic &c*) feart *m*

February *n* Gearran *m*, *used with art*, an Gearran, *also* a' mhìos mharbh

fecund *adj* torach *& torrach*

fee *n* (*charged by lawyer &c*) tuarastal *f*

feeble *adj* fann, lag, lapach, meata, **a ~ voice** guth fann

feeble-minded *adj* lag na (*&c*) inntinn *f*

feel *v* **1** fairich *vti*, **~ cold and heat** fairich fuachd *mf* is teas *m invar*, **how are you ~ing/how do you ~ today?** ciamar a tha thu a' faireachdainn an-diugh?, **~ing disgruntled** a' faireachdainn diombach; **2** (*be conscious of*) mothaich *vt*, **we felt the motion of the boat** mhothaich sinn gluasad *m* a' bhàta; **3** (*touch, handle &c*) làimhsich *vt*; **4** *in expr* **~ the absence/lack of** ionndrainn *vt*

feeling *adj* mothachail

feeling *n* **1** (*phys, emotional*) faireachdainn *f*; **2** (*abstr: the sense or faculty of ~*) mothachadh *m*; **3** (*the act of ~*) faireachdainn, mothachadh *m*

fell *v* leag *vt* (gu làr *m*)

fellow *n* **1** (*man, guy &c*) fear *m*, **that ~ over yonder** am fear ud thall, **a ~ by the name of Campbell told me** dh'innis fear Caimbeulach dhomh (e); **2** (*misc usages*) (*compliment*) **aren't you the (clever &c) ~!** nach tusa an gille/am balach!, **the old ~** am bodach, (*excl*) **the poor ~!** an duine/an creutair bochd!, an truaghan!, *also used in voc case* a dhuine bhochd!, a chreutair bhochd!

fellow- *prefix, expressed by prefix* co-, *eg* **fellow-worker** co-oibriche *m*, **fellow-feeling** co-fhulangas *m*, co-bhàidh *m*

fellowship *n* **1** (*company, friendship*) comann *m*, cuideachd *f*, caidreabh *m*, conaltradh *m*; **2** (*body, association &c*) comann *m*, caidreabh *m*

female *n* (*of humans*) boireannach *m*, tè *f invar*, **a male and a ~** fireannach *m* agus boireannach

female *adj* boireann

feminine *adj* **1** boireannta; **2** *in expr* (*gram*) **the ~ gender** a' ghnè bhoireann

fence *n* feansa *f*, (*more trad*) callaid *f*

fern(s) *n* raineach *f*

ferocious *adj* garg

ferocity *n* gairge *f invar*

ferret *n* feòcallan *m*

fertile *adj* **1** (*land, plants &c*) to(r)rach; **2** *in expr* **make ~** toraich *vt*

fertilisation *n* torachadh *m*, sìolachadh *m*

fertilise *v* **1** (*ground*) leasaich *vt*, mathaich *vt*; **2** (*egg, embryo*) toraich *vt*

fertilised *adj* to(r)rach, **~ egg** ugh to(r)rach

fertiliser *n* leasachadh *m*, mathachadh *m*

fertility *n* torachas *m*

fervent *adj* (*person*) dùrachdach, (*persons, emotions, deeds*) dian

fervour *n* dèine *f invar*

festival *n* **1** fèis (*also* fèisd & fèist) *f*, **literature/music ~** fèis litreachais *m* gen/chiùil (*gen of* ceòl *m*); **2** (*esp relig ~*) fèill *f*

festive *adj* cuirmeach

fetch *v* **1** faigh *vt*, **~ bread from the kitchen** faigh aran *m* às a' chidsin *m*; **2** *in expr* **go to/and ~ something** falbh *vi*/rach *vi irreg* a dh'iarraidh rudeigin, **go** (*imperative*) **and ~ my book** thalla a dh'iarraidh an leabhar agam

fetter *n* geimheal *m*

fetter *v* geimhlich *vt*

fettle *n, in expr* **he's in fine** ~ tha e ann an deagh thriom *m*/air a (dheagh) dhòigh *f*

feud *n* falachd *f invar*, connsachadh *m*

fever *n* fiabhras *m*, teasach *m*, **scarlet/yellow** ~ am fiabhras dearg/buidhe

few *adj, in exprs* **he has very** ~ **friends** tha glè bheag de charaidean *mpl* aige, **his friends were** ~ (*trad*) bu thearc a charaidean, **as** ~ **as three** cho beag ri a trì

few *n* (*persons or things*) beagan *m*, (*more positive*) grunnan *m*, (*with gen*), **he has a** ~ **friends** tha beagan/grunnan charaidean *mpl gen* aige, **has he any friends? only a** ~ a bheil caraidean aige? chan eil ach beagan, **did you see your friends? I saw a** ~ (**of them**) am faca tu na caraidean agad? chunna mi beagan/grunnan dhiubh

fickle *adj* caochlaideach, carach

fiction *n* uirsgeul *m*

fictional, fictitious *adjs* uirsgeulach

fiddle *n* fidheall *f*, **a tune on the** ~ port *m* air an fhidhill *dat*

fiddler *n* fìdhlear *m*

fidelity *n* dìlseachd *nf invar*

fidgety *adj* luasganach

field *n* **1** (*mainly agric*) achadh *m*, pàirc(e) *f*; **2** (*for a variety of uses*) raon *m*, **playing** ~ raon-cluiche *m*, **air**~ raon-adhair *m*, **oil** ~ raon-ola *m*; **3** (*area of knowledge, expertise &c*) raon *m*, **that's not my** ~ chan e sin mo raon-sa; **4** (*IT*) raon *m*

field glasses prosbaig *f sing*

fiendish *adj* diabhlaidh

fierce *adj* **1** (*pursuit, fighting, contest &c*) dian; **2** (*person*) garg, fiadhaich

fierceness *n* gairge *f invar*

fifteen *n & adj* còig-deug, ~ **minutes** còig mionaidean *fpl* deug

fifteenth *adj* còigeamh-deug, **the** ~ **day** an còigeamh là *m* deug

fifth *adj* còigeamh

fifty *n* **1** leth-cheud *m*, ~ **women** leth-cheud boireannach (*sing*), **the fifties** na leth-cheudan, **a man in his fifties** duine (is e) na leth-cheudan; **2** (*in alt numbering system*) caogad *m*

fig *n* **1** fìogais *f*, fìge *f*; **2** (*idiom*) **I don't give a** ~ **for X** (*fam*) cha toir mi ho-ro-gheallaidh air X, chan eil diu a' choin (*gen of* cù *m*) agam do X

fight *n* **1** (*esp phys*) sabaid *f*, còmhrag *f*, (**with, against** ri), (*less serious*) tuasaid *f*; **2** (*usu verbal*) trod *m*; **3** (*more abstr*) strì *f invar*, **the** ~ **for women's rights** an strì airson chòraichean (*gen pl of* còir *f*) nam ban (*gen pl of* bean *f*)

fight *v* **1** sabaid *vi*, gleac *vi*, (**with, against** ri); **2** (*usu verbally*) troid *vi* (**with** ri)

fighting *n* sabaid *f*, còmhrag *f*, (**with, against** ri)

fig-tree *n* crann *m* fìogais *m gen*, crann-fìge *m*

figurative *adj* figearach

figure *n* **1** (*shape*) cruth *m*, dealbh *mf*, **I made out the ~ of a man** rinn mi a-mach cruth duine *m gen*; **2** (*person's physique*) dèanamh *m*, *in expr* **a fine ~ of a man** duine air a dheagh thogail; **3** (*arith &c*) àireamh *f*, figear *m*

file[1] *n* (*metalwork &c*) eighe *f*

file[2] *n* (*paperwork, IT &c*) faidhle *m*

fill *n* làn *m*, leòr *f invar*, **I got my ~ of it** fhuair mi mo làn/mo leòr dheth

fill *v* lìon *vti*

filled *adj* lìonta

filler *n* lìonadair *m*

filly *n* loth *f*

film *n* **1** (*thin covering*) sgàil(e) *f*; **2** (*cinema, photography*) film *m*

filter *n* sìol(t)achan *m*

filter *v* sìolaidh *vti*

filtering, filtration *n* sìoladh *m*

filth *n* salchar *m*

filthy *adj* salach

fin *n* ite *f*

final *adj* deireannach, **on the ~ day** air an là *dat* dheireannach

finally *adv* **1** (*eventually*) aig deireadh an là, aig a' cheann thall, **he managed it ~** chaidh aige air (a dhèanamh) aig a' cheann thall; **2** (*at long last*) mu dheireadh thall, **he ~ managed it** chaidh aige air mu dheireadh thall

finance *n* (*admin &c*) ionmhas *m*

financial *adj* ionmhasail

find *v* **1** faigh *vt irreg*, lorg *vt*, (*implying more difficulty*) faigh lorg *f* (*with prep* air), **she found a penny on the pavement** fhuair/lorg i sgillinn *f* air a' chabhsair *m*, **you'll ~ him in the pub** gheibh sibh san taigh-seinns' *m* e; **2** **~ out** (*discover, learn*) faigh *vt* a-mach, **they found out that he was broke/bankrupt** fhuair iad a-mach gun robh e briste; **3** (*consider &c*) *in exprs* **I ~ it good** is math leam e, **I ~ that pleasing** is toigh leam sin

fine *adj* **1** (*in texture or dimensions*) mìn; **2** (*in appearance, quality*) gasda & gasta, àlainn, brèagha, grinn, **the soldiers looked ~** bha na saighdearan *mpl* a' coimhead gasta, **a ~ house** taigh *m* àlainn, **a ~ day** là brèagha; **3** (*of weather*) math, brèagha, **~ weather** sìde mhath, sìde bhrèagha; **4** (*fam: as excl*) **~!** taghta!, **your dinner's in the oven, ~!** tha do dhìnnear san àmhainn, taghta!; **5** (*fam: excellent, "great"*) glan, gasta, **that's just ~** tha sin dìreach glan/gasta; **6** (*of person: ~ in health or spirits*) air a (*&c*) d(h)òigh *f*, gu dòigheil, **Murdo was in ~ fettle** bha Murchadh air a (dheagh) dhòigh *f*, **how are you? I'm ~** ciamar a tha thu? tha (mi) gu dòigheil

fine *n* ùnnlagh *m*, càin *f*

finger *n* corrag *f*, meur *f*, **little/pinkie ~** lùdag *f*, **ring ~** mac-an-aba *m*

finger *v* làimhsich *vt*

fingerprint *n* meur-lorg *f*

finish *v* **1** (*as vt*) cuir crìoch *f* (*with prep* air), crìochnaich *vt*, **she ~ed her**

novel chuir i crìoch air an nobhail *f* aice; **2** *as vi, corres to Eng perfect tense* **have you ~ed** *&c, see* **finished 2** *below*

finished *adj & past part* **1** (*task &c*) coileanta, crìochnaichte; **2** (*of person: having completed a task &c*) deiseil, ullamh, **have/are you ~ yet?** a bheil thu deiseil/ullamh fhathast?, **have you ~ with the phone?** a bheil thu deiseil/ullamh den fòn *mf*?, **the police had ~ questioning him** bha am poileas ullamh de cheasnachadh *m*

finite *adj* crìoch(n)ach

fir *n* giuthas *m*, *in expr* **~ cone** durcan *m*

fire *n* **1** teine *m*, **light/put out the ~** cuir air/cuir às an teine, **go on ~** rach *vi* na (*&c*) t(h)eine, **set ~** cuir teine (**to** ri), **las** *vt*, **electric ~** teine-dealain, **~ grate** cliath-theine *f*; **2** *in expr* **~ engine** carbad-smàlaidh *m*

fire *v* **1** (*a firearm*) tilg *vt*, loisg *vti*; **2** *in expr* **~ an arrow** leig saighead *f*; **3** (*sack, dismiss*) cuir *vt* à dreuchd *f*

fire-extinguisher *n* inneal-smàlaidh *m*

fireplace *n* teallach *m*, teinntean *m*

fireside *n* cagailt *f*, taobh *m* an teine, teallach *m*, **by the ~** ris a' chagailt

firm *adj* **1** (*constant, steady*) cunbhalach; **2** (*solid*) teann, daingeann; **3** (*in actions, character*) duineil

firm *n* companaidh *mf*

firmament *n*, *used with art*, **the ~** an iarmailt *f*

first *adj* **1** ciad, *usu with art*, **the ~ lesson** a' chiad leasan *m*, **in the ~ place** anns a' chiad àite *m*, **in the ~ instance** anns a' chiad dol-a-mach *m invar*, **~ thing in the morning** a' chiad char *m* sa' mhadainn *f*, **~ aid** ciad-fhuasgladh *m*; **2** *in expr* (**he fell** *&c*) **head ~** (thuit e *&c*) an comhair a chinn (*gen of* ceann *m*)

first *adv* **1** (*~ of a series*) an toiseach *m*, **Flora came ~** thàinig Flòraidh an toiseach; **2** (*~ in time*) **at ~** an toiseach, **I didn't like him at ~** cha bu toigh leam e an toiseach, **~ of all, at the very ~** an toiseach tòiseachaidh *m gen*

firstly *adv* sa chiad àite *m*, **~, I must welcome you all** sa chiad àite, feumaidh mi fàilte *f* a chur oirbh uile

firth *n* linne *f*

fish *n* iasg *m sing & coll*

fish *v* iasgaich *vi*

fisher, fisherman *n* iasgair *m*

fishing *n* iasgach *m*, **they're at the ~** tha iad aig/ris an iasgach, **~ net** lìon-iasgaich *m*, **fishing-boat** *n* bàta-iasgaich *m*, **~ rod** slat-iasgaich *f*, *in expr* **~ line** driamlach *mf*

fishmeal *n* min-èisg *f*

fissure *n* sgoltadh *m*, sgàineadh *m*

fist *n* dòrn *m*, (*derog*) cròg *f*

fistful *n* làn *m* dùirn (*gen of* dòrn *m*), dòrlach *m*, **I had a ~ of coins** bha làn mo dhùirn de bhuinn (*pl of* bonn *m*) airgid *m gen* agam

fit *adj* **1** (*well*) slàn, fallain, (*fam*) ann an deagh thriom *m*; **2** (*fam: ready to tackle task &c*) deiseil, ullamh, **are you** ~? a bheil sibh deiseil?; **3** (*phys able*) air chothrom (*with infin of verb*), ~ **to go out** air chothrom a dhol a-mach; **4** (*suitable*) freagarrach, cubhaidh, **a land** ~ **for heroes** tìr *mf* a tha freagarrach do ghaisgich *mpl*, **a pool** ~ **for swimming** linne fhreagarrach airson snàimh (*gen of* snàmh *m*)

fit *n* **1** (*outburst &c*) lasgan *m*, **a** ~ **of anger** lasgan feirge (*gen of* fearg *f*); **2** *in expr* **a fainting** ~ neul *m*, laigse *f*

fit *v* **1** (*clothing*) thig *vi* (*with prep* do), **will it** ~ **me?** an tig e dhomh?; **2** (*go into available space*) teachd *vi*, **will it** ~ **in the back of your car?** an teachd e an cùl *m* do chàir *m gen*?; **3** (*premises, boat &c*) ~ **out** uidheamaich *vt*

fitted out *adj & past part* uidheamaichte, acainneach

fitting *adj* **1** freagarrach, cubhaidh, iomchaidh, **a** ~ **conclusion** co-dhùnadh freagarrach/cubhaidh; **2** *in exprs* **as was** ~ **for you/on your part** (*trad*) mar bu chubhaidh dhut, **as was (only)** ~ mar bu chòir, **he repaid it, as was (only)** ~ dh'ath-dhìol e e, mar bu chòir (dha)

fittings *npl* (*in finished boat &c*) uidheam *f*, acainn *f*

five *n & num adj* (a) còig, (*of people*) còignear *mf invar* (*takes gen pl*), ~ **minutes** còig mionaidean *fpl*, **how many?** ~ cia mheud? a còig, ~ **ministers** còignear mhinistearan *mpl gen*

fivesome *n* còignear *mf invar* (*takes gen pl*)

fix *n* (*difficult situation*) èiginn *f invar*, staing *f*, cruaidh-chas *m*, **I'm in a** ~ tha mi ann an èiginn/ann an (droch) staing, tha mi nam èiginn

fix *v* **1** (*repair objects, machines &c*) càraich *vt*, cuir *vt* ceart, cuir *vt* air dòigh *f*; **2** (*sort out situations &c*) rèitich *vt*, socraich *vt*; **3** ~ **together** tàth *vt*, ceangail *vt* ri chèile

fixed *adj & past part* **1** (*firmly in place*) teann, suidhichte; **2** (*of situations &c: put right*) rèidh, socraichte; **3** (*repaired*) càraichte; **4** (*settled, consistent*) seasmhach, suidhichte, **of no** ~ **abode** gun àite-còmhnaidh seasmhach

fjord *n* loch-mara *m*

flabby *adj* (*lit: of body*) sultach, (*lit & fig*) bog

flair *n* liut *f* (**for** air)

flame *n* lasair *f*, **going up in** ~**s** a' dol na (*&c*) lasair, a' dol na (*&c*) lasraichean *fpl*

flame *v* las *vi*

flaming *adj* lasrach

flammable *adj* lasanta

flannel *n* flanainn *f*

flare *v*, ~ **up** *v* las *vi*

flash *n* **1** lasair *f*, drithleann *m*; **2** (*fam: instant of time*) plathadh *m*, **it went past in a** ~ chaidh e seachad ann am plathadh

flash *v* deàlraich *vi*

flashing *adj* lasrach, ~ **eyes** sùilean *fpl* lasrach

flashy *adj* (*esp in dress*) spaideil

flask *n* searrag *f*

flat *adj* còmhnard, rèidh

flat *n* (*ie dwelling*) lobht(a) *m*

flattened *adj* leudaichte, **his nose was ~ against the window pane** bha a shròn *f* leudaichte ris an lòsan *m*

flatter *v* dèan miodal *m*, dèan brìodal *m*, (*with prep* do)

flattery *n* miodal *m*, brìodal *m*

flatulence *n*, *used with art*, a' ghaoth

flatulent *adj* gaothach

flaw *n* **1** (*moral*) meang *f*; **2** (*in object*) fàillinn *f*, easbhaidh *f*, gaoid *f*

flawless *adj* **1** (*of person*) gun mheang *f*; **2** (*of object*) gun fàillinn *f*

flax *n* lìon *m*

flea *n* deargad *f*, deargann *f*

flee *v* tàrr *vi* às (*also* tàir *vi* às), teich *vi*

fleece *n* rùsg *m*

fleece *v* **1** (*sheep*) ruisg *vti*; **2** (*fam: rob, cheat*) spùill *vt* gu buileach

fleet *n* (*of vehicles, ships*) cabhlach *m*, (*of ships*) loingeas & luingeas *m*

fleeting *adj* **1** (*transient*) diombuan; **2** *in expr* **~ glimpse** boillsgeadh *m*, plathadh *m*, (**of** de), **I got a ~ glimpse of her** fhuair mi boillsgeadh/plathadh dhith

flesh *n* feòil *f*

fleshly, fleshy *adj* feòlmhor

flex *n* (*elec*) fleisg *f*

flexibility *n* sùbailteachd *f invar*

flexible *adj* lùbach, sùbailte

flight *n* **1** (*of bird &c*) iteag *f*, **in ~** air iteig (*dat*); **2** (*in battle &c*) ruaig *f*, ruith *f*, teicheadh *m*, *in expr* **put to ~** cuir an teicheadh, cuir an ruaig, (*with prep* air), rua(i)g *vt*, **we put them to ~** chuir sinn an teicheadh/an ruaig orra

flimsy *adj* **1** (*material &c*) tana; **2** (*easily broken*) brisg

fling *v* tilg *vt* (**at** air)

flipper *n* (*of divers*) clabar-snàimh *m*

flit *v* imrich *vi*, dèan *vt irreg* imrich *f*

flitting *n* imrich *f*

float *v* **1** (*as vt: set afloat*) cuir *vt* air flod *m*; **2** (*as vi*) bi *vi irreg* air fleòdradh *m*, **the ball is ~ing** tha am ball air fleòdradh

flock *n* **1** (*of animals*) treud *m*, greigh *f*; **2** (*of birds*) ealt(a) *f*

flock *v* **1** (*birds*) cruinnich *vi* (nan eultan *fpl*); **2** (*fig: people*) *in expr* **they ~ed to the fair** chaidh/thàinig iad dhan fhèill *f* nan ceudan *mpl*

flood *n* dìle *f*, tuil *f*

floor *n* **1** ùrlar *m*, làr *m*, **a stone ~** ùrlar cloiche (*gen of* clach *f*), **~ covering** còmhdach *m* ùrlair *gen*; **2** (*storey*) lobht(a) *m*

floppy *adj* sùbailte, (*IT*) **~ disc** clàr sùbailte

flour *n* flùr *m*, min-flùir *f*

flow *v* dòirt *vi*, sruth *vi*, ruith *vi*, sil *vi*, (*esp liquids from container &c*) taom *vi*

flow *n* **1** (*of liquids*) sruth *m*; **2** (*of conversation &c*) sruth *m*; **3** *in expr* **the minister** (*&c*) **was in full** ~ bha am ministear (*&c*) a' cur dheth

flower *n* dìthean *m*, flùr *m*, sìthean *m*

flowery *adj* (*covered in flowers*) flùranach

fluctuating *adj* caochlaideach

fluent *adj* (*in a lang*) fileanta, ~ **in Gaelic** fileanta sa Ghàidhlig *f*, *in expr* **a** ~ **speaker** (*of a lang*) fileantach *m*

fluently *adv* gu fileanta, *in expr* **she speaks Gaelic** ~ tha i fileanta sa Ghàidhlig *f*, *also* tha a' Ghàighlig aice gu fileanta

flush *n* (*on face*) rudhadh *m*, rudhadh-gruaidhe *m*

flushed *adj* ruiteach

flute *n* cuisle-chiùil *f*

flutter *v* (*esp wings, heart*) plap *vi*, (*more severe*) plosg *vi*

fluttering *n* (*esp of heart, wings*) plap *m invar*, (*more severe*) plosg *m*, plosgartaich *f*

fly *n* **1** cuileag *f*; **2** (*for fishing*) maghar *m*

fly *v* itealaich *vi*, rach *vi irreg* air iteig (*dat of* iteag *f*), sgiathaich *vi*

flying *adj & pres part* air iteig (*dat of* iteag *f*)

flying *n* **1** (*abstr*) iteag *f*; **2** (*the action*) itealaich *f*

fly-over *n* (*in road system*) os-rathad *m*

foam cop *m*, cobhar *m*

foaming *adj* copach

fodder *n* connlach *f sing coll*, fodar *m*

foe *n* nàmhaid *m*, eascaraid *m*

fog *n* ceò *m*

foggy *adj* ceòthach, ceòthar

fold¹ *n* (*for livestock: esp sheep*) crò *m*, (*esp for cattle*) buaile *f*

fold² *n* (*in material &c*) filleadh *m*

fold *v* **1** fill *vt*, preas *vt*, *in expr* ~ **up** paisg *vt*; **2** (*fig: fail*) rach *vi* fodha, **the company** ~**ed** chaidh a' chompanaidh fodha

folded *adj & past part* fillte

folder *n* pasgan *m*

foliage *n* duilleach *m*

folk *n* **1** (*people*) daoine *mpl*, **many/lots of** ~ mòran dhaoine *gen*, **the fairy** ~ na daoine-sìth *mpl*; **2** (*inhabitants of a particular area &c*) muinntir *f*, **Uist** ~ muinntir Uibhist *gen*

folks *npl* (*relatives*) daoine *mpl*, cuideachd *f*, càirdean *mpl*, **my** ~**s** mo dhaoine, mo chuideachd *f*, mo chàirdean

follow *v* lean *vti*

follower *n* **1** neach-leanmhainn *m* (*pl* luchd-leanmhainn *m sing coll*); **2** ~**s** muinntir *f*, cuideachd *f*, **his** ~**s left him** dh'fhàg a mhuinntir e

following *adj & pres part* **1** a leanas (*rel fut of* lean *vi*), **read the ~ words** leugh na faclan *mpl* a leanas; **2** (*next*) ath (*precedes the noun, which it lenites where possible: usu used with the art*), **the ~ week** an ath sheachdain *f, also* an t-seachdain an dèidh sin

folly *n* gòraiche *f invar*

fond *adj* **1** dèidheil, measail, (**of** air), **she was ~ of me** bha i dèidheil/ measail orm; **2** (*misc exprs*) **~ of the opposite sex** leannanach, **~ of company** cèilidheach, **~ of talking** còmhraiteach

fondle *v* cnèadaich & cniadaich *vt*

fondness *n* dèidh *f*

food *n* biadh *m*, (*less usu*) lòn *m*, **frozen ~** biadh reòta

fool *n* amadan *m*, òinseach *f* (*trad of a female, but also used of males*), bumailear *m*, ùmaidh *m*, stalcaire *m*

foolish *adj* gòrach, amaideach, faoin, baoth

foolishness *n* gòraiche *f invar*, amaideas *m*, faoineas *m*

foot *n* **1** (*part of body*) cas *f*, **on ~** de chois (*dat*), **on one's feet** air chois; **2** (*bottom or base of something*) bun *m*, bonn *m*, **the ~ of the hill** bun/bonn a' chnuic; **3** (*measurement*) troigh *f*, **two feet long** dà throigh a dh'fhad

football *n* ball-coise *m*

footpath *n* frith-rathad *m*

footprint *n* lorg(-coise) *f*, **in my own ~s** air mo lorgan fhìn

footstep *n* ceum *m*

footwear *n* caisbheart *f*

for *prep* **1** do (*takes the dat, lenites following consonant where possible*), **~ me** dhomh(sa), **~ you** (*sing*) dhu(i)t(sa), **~ him/it** (*m*) dha(san), **~ her/it** (*f*) dhi(se), **~ us** dhuinn(e), **~ you** (*pl*) dhuibh(se), **~ them** dhaibh(san), **I'll do that ~ you** nì mi sin dhut, **it's hard ~ me** tha e doirbh dhomh, (*trad*) is duilich leam e, **how did it go/turn out ~ you?** ciamar a chaidh dhut?; **2** airson (*with gen*), **she went ~ some eggs** dh'fhalbh i airson uighean *mpl*, **don't be sorry ~ her** na bi duilich air a son, **she wrote an essay ~** (*ie to oblige*) **her brother** sgrìobh i aiste *f* airson a bràthar *m*, **he lost his life ~** (**the sake of**) **the Prince** chaill e a bheatha *f* airson a' Phrionnsa *m*, **are you ~ leaving/~ a pint?** a bheil thu airson falbh *m*/airson pinnt *m*?, **they voted ~ the government** bhòt iad airson an riaghaltais *m*; **3** (*of time: since*) o chionn & bho chionn (*with gen*), **I've been working here ~ a year** tha mi ag obair an seo bho chionn bliadhna *f*, (*idiom*) **I haven't seen you ~ a long time!** 's fhada o nach fhaca mi thu!; **4** (*of time: during*) fad (*with gen*), airson (*with gen*), car (*with dat*), **we were there ~ a fortnight** bha sinn ann fad cola-deug *m invar*, **we were in Glasgow ~ a while** bha sinn ann an Glaschu airson greis *f, also* bha sinn treis mhath/greis mhath an Glaschu

for *conj* (*rather formal: as, because*) oir, **he left, ~ the night was growing dark** dh'fhalbh e, oir bha an oidhche a' fàs dorch

forbid *v* toirmisg *vt*

forbidden *adj & past part* toirmisgte

force *n* **1** (*pol &c* ~) cumhachd *mf invar*; **2** (*phys* ~) neart *m*, spionnadh *m*; **3** (*excessive* ~, *violence*) fòirneart *m*, ainneart *m*, èiginn *f invar*, **take by** ~ thoir *vt* air èiginn; **4** (*body of people*) feachd *f*, **the Air Force** Feachd an Adhair, **a work**~ feachd obrach/oibre (*gen of* obair *f*)

force *v* thoir *vt* (*with prep* air), co-èignich *vt*, **she** ~**d me to leave** thug i orm falbh, **he'll** ~ **me to do it eventually** bheir e orm a dhèanamh aig a' cheann thall

fore- *prefix* ro- (*also* roi(mh)-) *prefix, eg* **foretaste** ro-bhlasad *m*, **foretell** *v* ro-innis *vt*

forearm *n* ruighe *mf*

forecast *n* (*esp weather*) ro-aithris *f*

forecaster *n* tuairmsear *m*

forehead *n* bathais *f*, maoil *f*, clàr *m* aodainn *m gen*

foreign *adj* cèin, coimheach, thall thairis, ~ **country** dùthaich chèin, ~ **language** cànan cèin

foreigner *n* coigreach *m*, eilthireach *m*, (*less usu*) coimheach *m*

foreleg *n* cas *f* toisich (*gen of* toiseach *m used adjectivally*)

foreman *n* maor *m*, maor-obrach *m*

foremost *adj* prìomh (*precedes the noun, which it lenites where possible*), **the** ~ **singer in Scotland** a' phrìomh sheannadair *m* ann an Alba

foresee *v* ro-aithnich *vt*

foresight *n* ro-shealladh *m*

foreskin *n* ro-chraiceann *m*

forest *n* coille (mhòr), *in exprs* **pine** ~ giùthsach *f*, **deer** ~ (*trad*) frith *f*

forester *n* forsair *m*

forestry *n* forsaireachd *f invar*, *in expr* ~ **worker** forsair *m*, coillear *m*

forewarn *v* cuir *vt* air earalas *m*

foreword *n* ro-ràdh *m*

forge *n* ceàrdach *f*, teallach *m* (ceàrdaich *gen*)

forget *v* **1** dìochuimhnich & di-chuimhnich *vt*; **2** (*idioms & exprs*) **when was that? I** ~ cuine a bha sin? chan eil cuimhne *f invar* agam, **I forgot/have forgotten it** chaidh e às mo chuimhne, **the old songs were forgotten** chaidh na sean òrain *mpl* air dìochuimhne *f invar*

forgetful *adj* dìochuimhneach

forgetfulness *n* dìochuimhne *f invar*

forgotten *adj & past part* air dìochuimhne *f invar*, **be** ~ rach *vi irreg* air dìochuimhne, bi *vi irreg* air a (*&c*) leigeil air dìochuimhn'

forgive *v* math & maith *vi*, thoir mathanas, (*with prep* do), ~ **me!** maith dhomh!

forgiveness *n* mathanas *m*

fork *n* **1** gobhal & gabhal *m*, ~ **in the road** gobhal san rathad, ~ **of a bicycle** gobhal-baidhsagail *m*; **2** (*table* ~) forc(a) *f*, greimire *m*; **3** (*farm or garden* ~) gobhlag *f*, gràpa *m*

forked *adj* gobhlach, ~ **tail/lightning** earball/dealanach gobhlach

form[1] *n* 1 (*shape*) cumadh *m*, cruth *m*, dealbh *mf*, **I made out the ~ of a man** rinn mi a-mach cumadh/cruth duine *m gen*; 2 (*artistic ~*) cruth *m*, (*Lit &c*) **matter and ~** cuspair *m* is cruth; 3 (*borrowed or copied ~*) riochd *m*, **a ghost in the ~ of a cat** taibhse *mf* an riochd cait *m gen*; 4 (*mood, spirits*) dòigh *f*, gleus *mf*, **Murdo was on good ~** bha Murchadh air a (dheagh) dhòigh/air (deagh) ghleus

form[2] *n* (*seat*) furm *m*

form[3] *n* (*to fill in*) foirm *mf*

form *v* cum *vt*, dealbh *vt*, **he ~ed an image out of the stone** chum e ìomhaigh *f* às a' chloich (*dat of* clach *f*)

formal *adj* foirmeil, ~ **language/speech** cainnt fhoirmeil

former *adj* sean(n), a bha ann (*&c*) roimhe, **a ~ policeman** sean phoileasman *m*

forsake *v* trèig *vt*, cuir a (*&c*) c(h)ùl (*with prep* ri), **he forsook his family** thrèig e a theaghlach *m*, ~ **the faith of your forefathers** trèig creideamh *m* ur sinnsirean *mpl gen*

fort *n* 1 daingneach *f*; 2 (*hist*) **hill ~** dùn *m*

fortify *v* (*structure, building &c*) daingnich *vt*

fortitude *n* misneach *f*, misneachd *f invar*, cruadal *m*

fortnight *n* cola-deug *m invar*, **we'll be back in/after a ~** bidh sinn air ais an ceann cola-deug *gen*

fortress *n* daingneach *f*

fortuitous *adj* tuiteamach, ~ **occurrences** tachartasan *mpl* tuiteamach

fortunate *adj* fortanach

fortune *n* 1 (*luck*) fortan *m*, sealbh *m*, **good ~** deagh fhortan, **the wheel of ~** cuibhle *f* an fhortain, *in expr* ~ **teller** fiosaiche *m*; 2 (*financial ~*) beartas *m*, ionmhas *m*, saidhbhreas *m*, stòras *m*, **the family ~** ionmhas an teaghlaich *m*, *in expr* **he made a ~** rinn e airgead mòr, mòr, rinn e fhortan

Fort William *n* An Gearastan *m*

forty *num* dà fhichead, (*in alt numbering system*) ceathrad *m*

forwards *adv* (*of vehicle, movement &c*) air adhart *f*, air aghaidh *f*, an comhair a (*&c*) t(h)oisich

foster brother/sister *n* co-alta *mf*

foul *n* (*sports & games*) fealladh *m*

found *v* cuir *vt* air chois (*dat of* cas *f*), cuir *vt* air bhonn *m*, ~ **a business** cuir gnothach *m* air chois/air bhonn

fountainhead *n* màthair-uisge *f*

four *n & num adj* 1 (*used of objects*) ceithir 2 (*used of people*) ceathrar *mf invar* (*with gen pl*), **there are ~ (people) there** tha ceathrar ann, ~ **sons** ceathrar mhac; 3 (*idiom*) **he's on all ~s** tha e air a mhàgan/a mhàg(a)ran *fpl*

four-legged *adj* ceithir-chasach

foursome *n* ceathrar *mf invar*

fourteen *n & num adj* ceithir-deug

fourth *n* ceathramh *m*

fourth *num adj* ceathramh

four-wheeled *adj* ceithir-chuibhleach

fox *n* sionnach *m*, madadh-ruadh *m*, balgair *m*

foyer *n* (*of public building*) for-thalla *m*

fraction *n* (*maths &c*) bloigh *f*

fragment *n* bìdeag *f*, criomag *f*, bloigh *f*

fragment *v* rach *vi* na (*&c*) b(h)ìdeagan *fpl*

fragmented *adj & past part* briste, na (*&c*) c(h)riomagan *fpl*, pronn

fragrant *adj* cùbhraidh

frame *n* **1** cèis *f*, frèam *m*, **picture** ~ cèis-dealbha, **climbing** ~ cèis-streap *m*, **bicycle** ~ cèis-bhaidhsagail; **2** *in expr* ~ **of mind** fonn *m*, gean *m*, gleus *mf* inntinn *f gen*, **what** ~ **of mind is he in today?** dè am fonn/an gean a th' air an-diugh?

framework *n* frèam *m*

frank *adj* fosgarra, fosgailte

fraud *n* foill *f*

fraudulent *adj* foilleil

fraudulently *adv* le foill *f*, **obtain goods** ~ faigh bathar *m sing coll* le foill

free *adj* **1** (*at liberty*) saor, mu sgaoil *m invar*, mu rèir, **the prisoner is** ~ tha am prìosanach saor/mu sgaoil, *in expr* **set** ~ cuir *vt*/leig *vt* mu sgaoil, fuasgail *vt*, saor *vt*; **2** (*at leisure*, ~ *from*) saor (**from** bho/o, is), an tàmh *m*, **are you** ~? a bheil sibh nur tàmh?, ~ **from anxiety** saor o chùram *m*, **I'm** ~ **of debts now** tha mi saor o fhiachan *mpl* a-nis; **3** (~ *of charge, gratis*) saor, (*stronger*) saor 's an asgaidh *f*, **I got my food (completely)** ~ fhuair mi mo bhiadh *m* saor 's an asgaidh; **4** *in expr* ~ **verse** saor-rannaigheachd *f invar*

free *v* **1** (*liberate*) fuasgail *vt*, cuir *vt* mu sgaoil *m invar*, leig *vt* mu sgaoil, cuir/leig *vt* mu rèir; **2** (~ *tangled, caught &c object*) fuasgail *vt*

freedom *n* saorsa *f invar*

free-standing *adj* neo-eisimeileach

freeze *v* reòdh & reòth *vti*

freezer *n* reothadair *m*

freight *n* luchd *m*, *in expr* ~ **charge** faradh *m*

French *adj* Frangach

French *n* (*lang*) Fraingis *f, used with art*, an Fhraingis

Frenchman *n* Frangach *m*

frequency *n* (*abstr, also elec*) tricead *m*

frequent *v* tathaich *vi* (*with prep* air)

frequently *adv* (gu) tric, gu bitheanta, (*less usu*) gu minig, **he falls** ~ bidh e a' tuiteam gu tric, **she doesn't come as** ~ **as she used to** cha tig i cho tric agus a chleachd (i)/agus a b' àbhaist dhi, **he's** ~ **late** is tric a bhios e air dheireadh, *in expr* ~ **met with** cumanta

fresh *adj* **1** ùr, **~ herring/butter** sgadan *m*/ìm *m* ùr, **a ~ start** tòiseachadh *m* ùr, **make a ~ start** tòisich *vi* as ùr; **2** (*of weather*) fionnar

fretful *adj* frionasach

friction *n* **1** suathadh *m*; **2** (*fig: between people*) mì-chòrdadh *m*

Friday *n* Dihaoine *m invar*, **~ afternoon/evening** feasgar *m* Dihaoine, Feasgar-haoine *m*

fridge *n* frids *m*, (*more trad*) fuaradair *m*

fried *adj & past part* ròsta, **~ potatoes** buntàta *m sing coll* ròsta

friend *n* **1** caraid *mpl* caraidean **a good ~ of mine** deagh charaid dhomh, **female/woman ~** banacharaid; **2** (*idiom*) **we are great ~s** tha sinn gu math mòr aig a chèile

friendly *adj* càirdeil

friendship *n* càirdeas *m*

fright *n* **1** (*abstr*) eagal *m*, (*occas*) feagal *m*, **take ~** gabh eagal; **2** (*con: a ~*) clisgeadh *m*, **he gave me a ~** chuir e clisgeadh orm

frighten *v* cuir eagal *m* (*with prep* air), **he ~ed me** chuir e eagal orm

frightful *adj* eagalach, uabhasach, oillteil

frightfully *adv* eagalach, **that was ~ good** bha sin eagalach math

frill *n* fraoidhneas *m*

fringe *n* **1** (*periphery*) iomall *m*, oir *f*, **on the ~(s)** (*ie remote*) air an iomall; **2** (*on material, hair &c*) fraoidhneas *m*

frivolity *n* aotramas *m*, (*more pej*) faoineas *m*

frivolous *adj* aotram, (*more pej*) faoin

frock *n* froca *m*

frog *n* losgann *m*

from *prep* **1** (*expr direction, point of origin &c*) bho & o (*takes the dat, lenites following consonant where possible*), **~ me** (bh)uam, **~ you** (*sing*) (bh)ua(i)t, **~ him** (bh)uaithe, **~ her** (bh)uaipe, **~ us** (bh)uainn, **~ you** (*pl*) (bh)uaibh, **~ them** (bh)uapa, **she went up ~ the beach** chaidh i suas bhon chladach *m*, **get some fish ~ the van** faigh iasg *m* on bhan *f*, **a letter from Murdo** litir *f* o Mhurchadh, (*much less common in this sense*) de & dhe (*takes the dat, lenites following consonant where possible*), **~ me** dhìom(sa), **~ you** (*sing*) dhìot(sa), **~ him/it** (*m*) dheth(san), **~ her/it** (*f*) dhith(se), **~ us** dhinn(e), **~ you** (*pl & formal sing*) dhibh(se), **~ them** dhiubh(san), **lift stones ~ the ground** tog clachan *fpl* den làr *m*; **2** (*expr point of origin*) à (*before the art* às), **food ~ Tesco's/~ the shop** biadh *m* à Tesco's/às a' bhùth *mf*, **a band ~ Scotland** còmhlan-ciùil à Alba, **where are you ~?** cò às a tha thu/sibh?, **where did he come/spring ~?** cò às a nochd esan?; **3** (*expr a sequence of time*) bho & o (*takes the dat, lenites following consonant where possible*), **~ morning till night** o mhoch gu dubh, **~ that time forward/on** bhon àm *m* sin air adhart, **~ Monday to Friday** bho Dhiluain *m invar* gu Dihaoine *m invar*

front *adj* **1** toisich (*gen of* toiseach *m*), **~ leg** cas-toisich *f*; **2** *in expr* **~ door** doras mòr, doras-aghaidh *m*

front *n* **1** (*the front part of anything*) toiseach *m*, **at the** ~ aig/anns an toiseach, *also* an toiseach, **in the** ~ (*ie in the cab*) **of the lorry** ann an toiseach na làiridh, ~ **end first** an comhair a thoisich; **2** (*the front surface of anything*) beulaibh *m invar*, aghaidh *f*, **the** ~ **of the building** beulaibh an togalaich, **back to** ~ cùlaibh *m invar* air beulaibh; **3** *in expr* **in** ~ (*ie ahead*) air thoiseach (**of** air), **Iain was in** ~ bha Iain air thoiseach, **a long way in** ~ **of us** fada air thoiseach òirnn; **4** *in expr* **in** ~ (*ie facing, opposite, a person, object &c*) mu choinneimh, fa chomhair, (*with gen*), ro (*before art* ron), **in** ~ **of me** mu mo choinneimh, fa mo chomhair, romham, **in** ~ **of the shop** ron bhùth *mf*; **5** (*a weather* ~) aghaidh *f*, **a warm/cold** ~ aghaidh bhlàth/fhuar

frontier *n* crìoch *f*

frontwards *adv* an comhair a thoisich *m*, an comhair a chinn (*gen of* ceann *m*)

frost *n* reothadh *m*, **hoar** ~ liath-reothadh *m*

froth cop *m*, cobhar *m*

frothy *adj* copach

frown *n* mùig *m*, gruaim *f*, sgraing *f*

frown *v* cuir mùig *m*, cuir gruaim *f*, (*with prep* air), **she** ~**ed** chuir i mùig/gruaim oirre

frowning *adj* gruamach

frozen *adj* reòdhta *&* reòthte, **my feet are** ~! tha mo chasan *fpl* reòthte!

fruit *n* **1** meas *m*, ~ **tree** meas-chraobh *f*, ~ **juice** sùgh-measa *m*; **2** (*crop, produce*) toradh *m*, **the** ~**(s) of the earth** toradh na talmhainn

fruitful *adj* tor(r)ach

fruitless *adj* **1** (*trees &c*) gun mheas *m*; **2** (*fig: vain*) dìomhain, gun tor(r)adh *m*

fruity *adj* measach

fry *v* frighig *vt*, ròist *&* ròst *vt*

fuck *v* (*vulg/taboo*) rach *vi* air muin *f invar*, **he** ~**ed her** chaidh e air a muin

fuel connadh *m sing coll*

fugitive *n* fògrach *&* fògarrach *m*

full *adj* **1** (*filled*) làn, lìonta, ~ **up**, ~ **to the brim** loma-làn, **half** ~ leth-làn; **2** (*complete*) làn, iomlan, **a** ~ **length film** film *m* làn fhada, **he fell** ~ **length** thuit e a làn-fhada, ~**-time job** obair *f* làn-thìde/làn-ùine, **a** ~ **orchestra** orcastra *f* iomlan; **3** *in expr* (*typog*) ~ **stop** stad-phuing *f*, puing-stad *f*; **4** *in exprs* **a** ~ **account** cunntas/iomradh mionaideach, ~ **of holes** tolltach, (*idioms*) **he left at** ~ **tilt/at** ~ **speed** dh'fhalbh e na dhian-ruith *f*, dh'fhalbh e aig peilear *m* a bheatha *f gen*

full *adv*, *in expr* **she struck him** ~ **in the face** bhuail i e an clàr *m* aodainn *m gen*

full *v* (*cloth*) luaidh *vt*

full-grown *adj* **1** (*of person*) inbheach; **2** *in exprs* ~ **man** duine foirfe, **become** ~ thig *vi* gu ìre *f invar*

fulling *n* (*of cloth*) luadhadh *m*

full-length *adj* làn-fhada

fully *adv* **1** gu h-iomlan, uile-gu-lèir, **we succeeded** ~ shoirbhich leinn gu h-iomlan/uile-gu-lèir; **2** (*misc exprs*) ~ **grown** inbheach, **I was** ~ **aware** bha làn-fhios *m* agam, **there are** ~ **two thousand of them there** tha dà mhìle *m* dhiubh ann aig a' char *m* as lugha

fulmar *n* fulmair *m*

fulness *n* lànachd *nf invar*

fumes *n* deatach *f*, **emit/give out** ~ cuir (a-mach) deatach

fun *n* **1** spòrs *f*, dibhearsan *&* dibheirsean *m*, **we had (some)** ~ **last night** bha spòrs againn a-raoir, **have** ~ **at someone's expense** faigh spòrs air cuideigin *mf invar*, *in expr* **full of** ~ spòrsail; **2** *in expr* **make** ~ dèan fanaid *f*, mag *vi*, (**of** air), **they were making** ~ **of him** bha iad a' fanaid air/a' magadh air, bha iad a' dèanamh fanaide *gen* air

function *n* **1** (*purpose, use*) gnìomh *m*, feum *m*; **2** (*post, occupation*) oifis *f*, dreuchd *f*, obair *f*; **3** (*task, action*) gnìomh *m*, **bodily** ~**s** gnìomhan-bodhaig *mpl*, (*IT*) ~ **key** iuchair-ghnìomha *f*; **4** (*formal meal &c*) cuirm *f*

function *v* obraich, *occas* oibrich, *vti*

fund *n* **1** (*fin*) maoin *f*, *in expr* **a trust** ~ ciste-urrais *f*; **2** (*large accumulation*) stòr *m*, **a** ~ **of knowledge** stòr-eòlais *m*

fund *v* maoinich *vt*

funeral *n* tiodhlacadh *m*, adhlacadh *m*, tòrradh *m*

funnel *n* **1** (~ *of ship, industrial chimney &c*) luidhear *m*, similear *m*; **2** (*for pouring*) lìonadair *m*

funny *adj* **1** (*amusing*) èibhinn, (*less usu*) àbhachdach; **2** (*peculiar &c*) neònach, àraid

furious *adj* air chuthach *m*, air bhoile *f invar*, air bhàinidh *f invar*, (*fam*) fiadhaich, **become** ~ rach *vi* air chuthach/air bhoile/air bhàinidh, **I was** ~ **after what he said to me** (*fam*) bha mi fiadhaich an dèidh na thuirt e rium

furlough *n* fòrladh *m*

furnace *n* fùirneis *f*

furnish *v* **1** (*fit out factory &c*) uidheamaich *vt*; **2** (~ *house*) cuir àirneis *f invar coll* (ann an taigh *m*); **3** (*purvey, supply*) solair *vt*

furnishings *npl* àirneis *f*, àirneis bhog

furrow *n* **1** (*in ground*) clais *f*, sgrìob *f*; **2** (*in brow*) preas *m*, preasan *m*

furrow *v* **1** (*ground*) sgrìob *vt*, claisich *vt*; **2** (*brow*) preas *vt*

furry *adj* molach

further *adj* **1** (*additional*) a bharrachd, tuilleadh, eile, **we don't need anything** ~ chan fheum sinn càil *m invar* a bharrachd, **send (us) a** ~ **two lorries** cuiribh dà làraidh *f* a bharrachd thugainn, **give me** ~ **information** thoir dhomh tuilleadh fiosrachaidh *m gen*, **she received a** ~ **letter** fhuair i litir *f* eile; **2** *in expr* ~ **education** foghlam *m* (aig) àrd-ìre *f invar*,

furthermore *adv* a bharrachd air sin, a thuilleadh air sin

fury *n* cuthach *m*, bàinidh *f invar*

fussy *adj* **1** ro-chùramach, ro-phongail; **2** *in expr* **I'm not ~** (*ie don't mind*) is coma leam, tha mi coma co-dhiù

futile *adj* faoin, dìomhain, **the ~ endeavours of mankind** oidhirpean *fpl* faoin mhic-an-duine *m sing coll* (*gen*)

futility *n* faoineas *m*

future *adj* **1** ri teachd, **~ years/generations** na bliadhnachan *fpl*/na ginealaich *mpl* (a tha) ri teachd; **2** (*gram*) teachdail, **the ~ tense** an tràth teachdail

future *n* **1** (*with art*), **the ~** an t-àm ri teachd; **2** *in expr* **in ~** bho seo a-mach, turas *m* eile, **in ~, make sure you're wearing a safety helmet!** bho seo a-mach/turas eile, dèan cinnteach gu bheil clogaid-dìona *m* ort!

G

Gael *n* Gaidheal & Gàidheal *m*

Gaelic *n* **1** Gàidhlig *f*, **I speak** ~ tha Gàidhlig/a' Gàidhlig agam, **translate English into** ~ cuir Gàidhlig air Beurla *f invar*, **where did you learn/ pick up your** ~? càit an do thog thu do chuid *f* Gàidhlig? *gen, also often used with art*, **speaking in** ~ bruidhinn sa Ghàidhlig; **2** (*used adjectivally*) **The Gaelic Society of Inverness** Comann Gàidhlig Inbhir Nis, **the Gaelic Association** Comann na Gàidhlig, ~ **people/speakers** luchd *m sing coll* na Gàidhlig

gaffer *n* maor *m*, maor-obrach *m*

gain *n* (*fin*) prothaid *f*, buannachd *f*

gain *v* coisinn *vt*, buannaich *vt*, ~ **a reputation** coisinn cliù *m invar*

gait *n* gluasad *m*, giùlan *m*

gale *n* gèile *m*

gallery *n* (*for exhibitions, art &c*) taisbean-lann *f*, gaileiridh *m*

galling *adj* leamh, frionasach

gallon *n* galan *m*

gallows *n* croich *f*

gambler *n* ceàrraiche & cèarraiche *m*

game *n* **1** cluich & cluiche *m*, geam(a) *m*, **board** ~ cluich-bùird; **2** (*esp football*) geam(a) *m*, **will you be going to the** ~? am bi thu a' dol dhan gheam(a)?; **3** (*hunted creatures*) sitheann *f*, (*as food*) geam(a) *m*

gamekeeper *n* geamair *m*

gang *n* **1** (*of labourers, criminals &c*) buidheann *mf*; **2** (*fam/pej: crowd, group*) treud *m*, **the** ~ **he goes to the pub with** an treud leis am bi e a' dol dhan taigh-sheinnse *m*

gannet *n* sùlaire *m*, (*young* ~) guga *m*

gap *n* beàrn *f*, fosgladh *m*, **a** ~ **in the wall** beàrn sa ghàr(r)adh *m*, **a** ~ **in the market** fosgladh sa mharcaid *f*

garage *n* garaids *f*

garb *n* èideadh *m*, **the** ~ **of the Gael** an t-èideadh Gàidhealach

garden *n* gàrradh & gàradh *m*, (*more trad*) lios *mf*, *in expr* ~ **centre** ionad-gàirnealaireachd *m*, margadh-gàrraidh *mf*

gardener *n* gàirnealair *m*

gardening *n* gàirnealaireachd *f invar*

garlic *n* creamh *m*

garrison *n* gearastan & gearasdan *m*

garron *m* gearran *m*

garrulous *adj* beulach, (*more fam*) cabach, gobach

garter *n* gartan *m*

gas *n* **1** deatach *f*, **emit/give out** ~ cuir (a-mach) deatach; **2** (*domestic* ~) gas *m*, ~ **cooker** cucair *m* gas

gasp, gasping *n* plosg *m*

gasp *v* (*for breath*) plosg *vi*

gate *n* geata *m*

gather *v* **1** (*people*) cruinnich *vti*, tionail *vi*, thig còmhla, **they ~ed/he ~ed them in the barn** chruinnich iad/chruinnich e iad san t-sabhal *m*; **2** (*livestock*) cruinnich *vt*, tionail *vt*, tru(i)s *vt*; **3 ~ together** (*people & things*) co-chruinnich *vti*; **4** (*esp of clothing: bundle up, tuck up &c*) tru(i)s *vt*, **her petticoats were ~ed up** bha na còtaichean-bàna *mpl* aice air an trusadh

gathered *adj* (*people*) cruinn, **the congregation was ~ in the church** bha an coitheanal cruinn san eaglais *f dat*

gathering *n* (*of people: abstr & con*) cruinneachadh *m*, co-chruinneachadh *m*, tional *m*

gauge *n* tomhas *m*, meadhadair *m*

gauge *v* tomhais *vt*

gear[1] *n* **1** (*assorted possessions &c: fam*) treal(l)aich *f*, **tidy up your ~** sgioblaich do threallaich; **2** (*one's tools, equipment &c*) uidheam *f*, acainn *f*

gear[2] *n* (*engin*) gèar *f invar*, giodhar *m*

gear up *v* uidheamaich *vt*

geared up *adj & past part* uidheamaichte, acainneach

gelding *m* gearran *m*

gender *n* **1** gin *f*, gnè *f invar*; **2** (*gram*) gnè *f invar*, **the feminine/masculine ~** a' ghnè bhoireann/fhireann

gene *n* gine *f*

general *adj* **1** coitcheann, **~ knowledge/education** foghlam/eòlas coitcheann, **~ election** taghadh-coitcheann, **~ strike** stailc choitcheann; **2** *in expr* **in ~** (*on the whole*) san fharsaingeachd *f invar*, **in ~ the majority are against him** san fharsaingeachd tha a' mhòr-chuid na aghaidh; **3** *in expr* **in ~** (*normally, usually*) an cumantas *m*, am bitheantas *m*, mar as trice

general *n* seanailear *m*

generally *adv* **1** (*on the whole, ~ speaking*) san fharsaingeachd *f invar*; **2** (*normally, usually*) an cumantas *m*, am bitheantas *m*, mar as trice

generation *n* **1** (*with emph on time*) linn *m*, **from ~ to ~** bho linn gu linn; **2** (*with emph on people*) ginealach *m*, **two ~s of my family** dà ghinealach den teaghlach *m* agam, **the sixties ~** ginealach nan trì-ficheadan *mpl*

generator *n* gineadair *m*

generosity *n* fialaidheachd *f invar*

generous *adj* fialaidh, fial, faoilidh, tabhartach

genitals *n* buill-ghineamhainn *mpl*, **female ~** pit *f*, ròmag *f*, **male ~** bod *m*, (*fam/vulg*) slat *f*

genitive *adj* (*gram*) ginideach, **the ~ case** an tuiseal ginideach, (*as noun*) **the ~** an ginideach

genteel *adj* (*in manners &c*) uasal

gentility *n* (*abstr quality*) uaisle *f invar*

gentle *adj* (*person, weather*) ciùin, sèimh

gentleman *n* duine uasal *m*, (*trad*) uasal *m*

genuine *adj* **1** (*authentic*) fìor (*precedes the n, lenites a following consonant where possible*), ~ **gold** fìor òr *m*, **a ~ expert** fìor eòlaiche *m*; **2** (*sincere, trustworthy &c*) neo-chealgach, dìreach

geography *n* cruinn-eòlas *m*, tìr-eòlas *m*

geology *n* geòlas *m*

germ *n* bitheag *f*

German *n & adj* **1** Gearmailteach *m*; **2** (*the language*) *used with art*, a' Ghearmailtis *f invar*

Germany *n, used with art*, A' Ghearmailt *f invar*

germinate *v* ginidich *vi*

germination *n* ginideachadh *m*

gesture *n* **1** gluasad *m*; **2** (*beckoning ~*) smèideadh *m*

gesture *v* (*esp to summon or greet someone*) smèid *vi* (**to** air)

get *v* **1** (*obtain*) faigh *vt irreg*, ~ **some fish from the van** faigh iasg *m* on bhan *f*, **I didn't ~ the job** cha d'fhuair mi an obair; **2** (*become, grow*) fàs *vi* (*with adj*), rach *vi* (*often with abstr n*), **they got tired** dh'fhàs iad sgìth, **she's ~ting old** tha i a' fàs sean, ~ **used** fàs *vi* cleachdte (**to** ri), ~ **better** (*heal & improve*) rach am feabhas *m*, *also* thig *vi* bhuaithe, **she got better** (*ie recovered*) chaidh i am feabhas, thàinig i bhuaithe, **the local services are ~ting better** tha na seirbheisean *fpl* ionadail a' dol am feabhas, ~ **bigger** rach am meud *m invar*; **3** (*misc exprs & idioms*) **go to ~ something** falbh *vi* a dh'iarraidh rudeigin, ~ **advice** gabh comhairle *f*, ~ **the upper hand** faigh/gabh làmh *f* an uachdair (**of** air), ~ **the better of** failich *also* fairtlich *vi* (*with prep* air), (*esp of a person: slightly fam*) dèan an gnothach *m*, dèan a' chùis *f* (*both with prep* air), **I wanted to climb the mountain but it got the better of me** bha mi airson a' bheinn a dhìreadh ach dh'fhailich i orm, **we got the better of the other team** rinn sinn an gnothach/a' chùis air an sgioba *mf* eile, **they got engaged** thug iad gealladh-pòsaidh *m* dha chèile, ~ **involved in politics** rach an sàs ann am poileataics *f invar*, ~ **acquainted with/~ to know someone** cuir aithne *f invar*/eòlas *m* air cuideigin, ~ **used to it!** cleachd thu fhèin ris!, *also* faigh eòlas *m* air!, ~ **up** (*from bed, sitting position &c*) èirich *vi*, **I got up late yesterday** dh'èirich mi anmoch an-dè, (*more idiomatic*) bha mi fada gun èirigh an-dè, ~ **down** (*ie descend*) teirinn & teàrn *vi*, **she got down from the wall** theirinn i bhàrr a' ghàrraidh *m*, ~ **down** (*ie into crouching position*) rach *vi* na (*&c*) c(h)rùbagan *m*, dèan crùban *m*, ~ **on someone's nerves** leamhaich cuideigin, ~ **a move on!** cuir car *m* dhiot!, tog ort!, **she got over it** thàinig i bhuaithe, ~ **over an operation** faigh *vi* seachad air opairèisean *mf*, ~ **on well/smoothly with someone** bi *vi irreg* rèidh ri cuideigin, **we ~ on well (with each other)** tha sinn gu math mòr aig a chèile, ~ **out!** thoir do chasan *fpl* leat!, ~ **rid/shut of**

something faigh cuidhteas *m* (de) rudeigin, ~ **stuck in** teann *vi* ris an obair *f*, crom *vi* air an obair, ~ **to** (*affect*) drùidh (*with prep* air), **the news didn't ~ to her** cha do dhrùidh an naidheachd *f* oirre, (*more fam*) cha do chuir an naidheachd suas no sìos i, **how did you ~ on?** ciamar a chaidh dhut/dhuibh?, ciamar a dh'èirich dhut/dhuibh?

ghost *n* taibhse *mf*, tannasg *m*

giant *n* famhair *m*, fuamhair(e) *m*

gibbet *n* croich *f*

giddiness *n* **1** tuainealaich *f*, luasgan *m*; **2** (*fig: of character*) guanalas *m*

giddy *adj* **1** (*lit & fig*) tuainealach, guanach; **2** *in expr* ~ **girl** guanag *f*

gift *n* **1** tiodhlac *m*, gibht *f*, tabhartas *m*; **2** (*natural ~, talent*) tàlann *m*

gift *v* tiodhlaic *vt*, thoir *vt* seachad

gill *n* (*of fish*) giùran *m*

ginger *adj* (*hair, animal's coat &c*) ruadh

girl *n* **1** caileag *f*, nighean *f*, **a little ~** caileag bheag, **~s** clann-nighean *f sing coll*; **2** (*mostly used in songs*) gruagach *f*, cailin *f*, nìghneag *f*

give *v* **1** thoir (**to do**) *vt irreg*, thoir *vt* seachad, tiodhlaic *vt*, **she gave us a present** thug i tiodhlac *m* dhuinn, ~ **advice** thoir comhairle *f*, ~ **evidence** thoir fianais *f*, ~ **me your hand** thoir dhomh do làmh *f*; **2** (*deliver, perform &c*) gabh *vt*, ~ **a talk** gabh òraid *f*, ~ **us a song!** gabh òran *m*!; **3** (*misc exprs & idioms*) ~ **up** leig *vt* de *&* leig *vt* seachad, **I've ~n up smoking** leig mi seachad smocadh *m*, **he gave up his job** leig e dheth obair *f*, **don't ~ up!** (*ie persevere*) cùm *vi* ris!, **we didn't ~ the game away** cha do leig *vi* sinn òirnn, ~ **a row to** càin *vt*, ~ **in**, ~ **way** gèill *vi* (**to do**), (*of traffic*) ~ **way** gèill slighe *f*, ~ **out** (*ie emit*) cuir *vt* (a-mach)

giver *n* (*to charity &c*) tabhartaiche *m*, tabhairteach *m*

glad *adj* **1** (*happy, pleased*) toilichte, **I got the job! I'm ~** fhuair mi an obair! tha mi toilichte; **2** (*willing*) toileach, **I'd be ~ to do that for you** bhithinn toileach sin a dhèanamh dhut

gladness *n* gàirdeachas *m*, toileachas *m*, toil-inntinn *f*, toileachas-inntinn *m*

glance *n* plathadh *m*, sùil *f* (aithghearr), (**at** air)

gland *n* fàireag *f*, **sweat ~** fàireag an fhallais

glass *n* glainne *&* gloinne *f*

glasses *npl* **1** (*ie spectacles*) glainneachan *mpl*, speuclairean *mpl*; **2** *in expr* **field ~es** prosbaig *f sing*,

glasshouse *n* taigh-glainne *m*

glen *n* gleann *m*

glimpse *n* aiteal *m*, plathadh *m*, (**of** de)

glint *n* lainnir *f*, deàlradh *m*

glitter *n* lainnir *f*, deàlradh *m*

glitter *v* deàlraich *vi*

global *adj* **1** cruinneil; **2** *in expr* ~ **warming** blàthachadh *m* na cruinne

globe *n* cruinne *mf* (*f in gen sing*)

gloom, gloominess *n* **1** (*of light*) doilleireachd *f invar*; **2** (*of mood &c*) gruaim *f*, smalan *m*

gloomy *adj* **1** (*of setting &c*) ciar; **2** (*of light*) doilleir; **3** (*of mood &c*) doilleir, gruamach, mùgach

glorify *v* glòirich *vt*

glorious *adj* glòrmhor, òirdheirc

glory *n* **1** (*fame*) cliù *m invar*, glòir *f*; **2** (*spiritual, heavenly ~*) glòir *f*

gloss *n* (*lustre*) lìomh *f*

glossy *adj* lìomharra

glove *n* làmhainn *f*, miotag *f*, meatag *f*, **a pair of ~s** paidhir *mf* mhiotagan *pl gen*

glue *n* glaodh *m*

glue *v* glaodh *vt*

glug *v* plubraich *vi*, plub *vt*

glutton *adj* geòcaire *m*, craosaire *m*

gluttonous *adj* geòcach, craosach

gluttony *n* geòcaireachd *f invar*, craos *m*

gnash *v* gìosg *vt*, **~ing his teeth** a' gìosgail fhiaclan *fpl gen*

gnaw *v* cagainn *vti*

go *v* **1** (*make one's way, proceed*) rach *vi irreg*, falbh *vi*, gabh *vti*, **~ to Glasgow** rach do Ghlaschu, **~ to bed** rach a chadal *m*, **~ to fetch/get something** rach/falbh a dh'iarraidh rudeigin, **~ on an errand** rach air gnothach *m*, **~ in** rach a-steach, *also* inntrig *vi*, **she went her way** ghabh i an rathad *m*, **they went to the hill** ghabh iad chun a' mhonadh *m*, thug iad am monadh orra, *note also* thalla (*for falbh*) *and* theirig (*for rach*) *used as imper, eg* (**off you**) **~ home/to the shop!** thalla dhachaigh/dhan bhùth *mf*!, **~ to bed!** theirig a chadal *m*!; **2** (*expr changed states*) rach *vi irreg*, **~ off/downhill** rach bhuaithe, **~ mad/insane** rach air chuthach *m*/air bhoile *f invar*/air bhàinidh *f invar*, **~ astray/wrong** (*lit or morally*) rach air iomrall *m*; **3** (*leave*) falbh *vi*, **they went (away) yesterday** dh'fhalbh iad an-dè, **right! I'm ~ing** ceart! tha mi a' falbh, **she's ~ne** tha i air falbh; **4** (*misc idioms & exprs*) **let us ~!** tiugainn! *imper of vi def*, **~ back** till *vi*, **~ing back home** a' tilleadh dhachaigh, **~ bad/rotten** lobh *vi*, **~ to see/visit someone** tadhail *vi* air cuideigin, **keep ~ing!** cùm *vi* ort!, **how did it ~?** ciamar a chaidh (dhut/dhaibh &c)?

goal *n* **1** (*aim, ambition*) miann *mf*, rùn *m*; **2** (*football &c*) tadhal *m*

goat *n* gobhar *mf*

gob *n* (*fam*) gob *m*, cab *m*, **shut your ~!** duin do ghob/chab!

gobble *v* glam & glamh *vt*

God, god *m* Dia, dia *m*, **~'s grace** gràs *m* Dhè *gen*, **the ~s of the Romans** diathan nan Ròmanach *mpl*

goddess *n* ban-dia *f*

godfather *n* goistidh *m*

godhead *n* diadhachd *f invar*

godliness *n* diadhachd *f invar*

gold *n* òr *m*

gold *adj* òir (*gen sing of* òr *m*), **a ~ coin/medal** bonn *m* òir

golden eagle *n* iolair(e)-bhuidhe

goldsmith *n* òr-cheàrd & òr-cheard *m*

golf *n* go(i)lf *m*, **~ club** (*the stick*) caman *m* (goilf), **~ course** raon *m* goilf *gen*

good *adj* **1** math, **~ at singing** math air seinn *f*, math air òrain *mpl*, **that's ~!** 's math sin!, **very ~** glè mhath, **~ morning/night!** madainn/oidhche mhath!, **~ for you!** math thu-fhèin!, **it's ~ to see you!** 's math d' fhaicinn!, **it's ~ that you're here** 's math gu bheil thu ann; **2** deagh (*precedes the noun, which it lenites where possible*), **he's a ~ singer** is e deagh sheinneadair *m* a th' ann (dheth), **that's a ~ sign!** is e deagh chomharradh *m* a tha sin!, **he's a ~ friend of mine/to me** tha e na dheagh charaid *m* dhomh; **3** (*expr good measure*) pailt, **a ~ three feet in length** trì troighean *f* pailt de dh'fhad *m*; **3** (*misc exprs*) **~ grief!** an dòlas!, O mo chreach *f*!, mo chreach-s' a thàinig!, **~ heavens!** a chiall *f*!, **full of ~ sense** làn cèille (*gen of* ciall *f*), (*idiom*) **a wee stroll** (*&c*) **would be ~ for you** b' fheàirrde thu cuairt bheag (*&c*)

good *n* feum *m*, (*occas*) math *m*, **~ and evil** am math is an t-olc; **this machine's no ~** chan eil feum anns an inneal *m* seo, **what's the ~ of talking?** dè am feum/am math a bhith a' bruidhinn?, **do ~** dèan feum (**to do**), **the holidays will do you ~** nì na saor-làithean feum dhuibh, (*idiom*) **a drink of water** (*&c*) **would do you ~** b' fheàirrde thu deoch *f* uisge *m gen* (*&c*)

good- *prefix* deagh-, *eg* **~hearted** deagh-chridheach

goodbye *excl* beannachd *f* leat/leibh!, slàn leat/leibh!, (*more fam*) mar sin leat/leibh!

goodness *n* **1** (*moral &c*) mathas *m*; **2** (**~ in food &c**) brìgh *f*, susbaint *f*; **3** (*as excl*) **~!** a chiall!, (**my**) **~ me!** obh! obh!

goods *n* **1** (*merchandise*) bathar *m sing coll*, **~ vehicle** carbad-bathair *m*; **2** (*possessions, worldly ~*) maoin *f*, *in expr* **my worldly ~** (*trad*) mo chuid *f* den t-saoghal *m*

goodwill *n* deagh-thoil *f*, deagh-ghean *m*

goose *n* gèadh *mf*, *in expr* **solan ~** sùlaire *m*

gooseberry *n* gròiseid *f*

gore *n* fuil *f*

gorgeous *adj* greadhnach

gorse *n* conasg *m*

gory *adj* fuil(t)each, **~ battle** cath fuilteach

gossip *n* **1** (*abstr & con*) seanchas *m*; **2** (*person who gossips*) goistidh *m*

gossip *v* bi *vi irreg* ri seanchas *m dat*

govern *v* (*a country &c*) riaghail *vti*, riaghlaich *vti*

government *n* **1** (*abstr*) riaghladh *m*; **2** (*con*) riaghaltas *m*, **a national/local ~** riaghaltas nàiseanta/ionadail

governor *n* riaghladair *m*

gown *n* gùn *m*

grab *v* gabh grèim *m* (*with prep* air), **he ~bed her bag** ghabh e grèim air a' mhàileid *f dat* aice

grace *n* gràs *m*, **God's/divine ~** gràs Dhè (*gen of* Dia *m*)

graceful *adj* eireachdail, gràsmhor

gracefulness *n* gràsmhorachd *f invar*

graceless *adj* gun ghràs *m*

gracious *adj* gràsmhor

graciousness *n* gràsmhorachd *f invar*

grade *n* ìre *f invar*

gradient *n* caisead *m*

gradually *adv* mean air mhean, uidh *f* air n-uidh, beag air bheag

graduate *v* gabh ceum *m*, ceumnaich *vi*

graduation *n* ceumnachadh *m*

grain *n* **1** gràinnean *m*, **a ~ of salt/sugar** gràinnean salainn *m gen*/siùcair *m gen*; **2** (*from cereal crops*) gràn *m sing coll*, (*a single ~*) gràinne *f*

graip *n* gràpa *m*

gram(me) *n* gram *m*, **a hundred ~s of sugar** ceud gram de shiùcar *m*

grammar *n* gràmar *m*

grammatical *adj* gràmarach

grand *adj* **1** (*important, self-important*) mòr, mòr aige (*&c*) fhèin, mòr às (*&c*) fhèin, (*ironic*) **the ~ folk** na daoine *mpl* mòra; **2** (*fam: expr approval*) glan, gasta, sgoinneil, (*esp as excl*) taghta, **that was just ~** bha sin dìreach glan/gasta/sgoinneil, **We'll see you tomorrow as usual. ~!** Chì sinn a-maireach thu, mar as àbhaist. Taghta!

grandchild *n* ogha *m*

granddaughter *n* ban-ogha *f*

grandeur *n* mòrachd *f invar*

grandfather *n* seanair *m*

grandmother *n* seanmhair *f*, (*fam*) granaidh *f*

grandson *n* ogha *m*

granite clach-ghràin *f*, eibhir *f*

granny *n* (*fam*) granaidh *f*

grant *n* (*fin*) tabhartas *m*

grant *v* builich *vt* (**to** air)

granular *adj* gràinneach

grape *n* fìon-dearc *f*

graph *n* graf *m*

grasp *n* grèim *m*, glacadh *m*

grasp *v* **1** glac *vt*, gabh grèim *m* (*with prep* air), greimich *vi* (*with prep* air *or* ri); **2** (*understand*) tuig *vt*

grass *n* feur *m*

grass park *n* faiche *f*, pàirc(e) *f*

grasshopper *n* fionnan-feòir *m*

grassy *adj* feurach

grate *n* grèata *m*, *in expr* **fire** ~ cliath-theine *f*

grateful *adj* taingeil, buidheach

gratification *n* toileachadh *m*

grating[1] *n* (*scraping &c*) sgrìobadh *m*

grating[2] *n* (*grid &c*) cliath *f*

gratitude *n* taing *f*, taingealachd *f invar*, buidheachas *m*

grave *adj* **1** (*of person's character*) stòlda; **2** (*of state of affairs &c*) fìor dhroch (*precedes the noun, which it lenites where possible*), ~ **news** fìor dhroch naidheachd *f*

grave *n* uaigh *f*

gravel *n* grinneal *m*, morghan *m*

gravestone *n* leac *f*, leac uaighe *f gen*, clach-chinn *f*

gravity *n* (*force*) iom-tharraing *f*

graze[1] *v* (*skin of hand &c*) ruisg *vt*

graze[2] *v* (*livestock &c*) feuraich *vt*, **ionaltair** *vi*

grazing *n* **1** (*abstr*) feurachadh *m*, ionaltradh *m*; **2** (*con: pasture*) feurach *m*, ionaltradh *m*, clua(i)n *f*; **3** *in exprs* (*in crofting context*) **common** ~ monadh *m*, **the ~s clerk** clàrc *m* a' bhaile

grease *n* crèis *f*

greasy *adv* crèiseach

great *adj* **1** mòr, **a** ~ **crowd** sluagh mòr *m*, **a** ~ **poet** bàrd mòr, **a** ~ **deal of money** (*fam*) airgead mòr, (*idiom*) **we are** ~ **friends** tha sinn gu math mòr aig a chèile; **2** (*expr approval &c: fam*) gasta, (*esp as excl*) taghta, **that was just** ~ bha sin dìreach gasta, **I'll do the dishes for you.** ~! Nì mi na soithichean *mpl* dhut. Taghta!

great- *prefix* (*for family relationships*) iar-, *eg* **great-grandchild** iar-ogha *mf*

greatcoat *n* còta-mòr *m*

greater *comp adj* **1** mò/motha, **the** ~ **nation** an nàisean *m* as motha/(*in past & conditional tenses*) a bu mhotha, **that nation is** ~ 's e an nàisean sin as motha; **2** *in expr* **the** ~ **part** a' mhòr-chuid *f*, **the** ~ **part of his life** a' mhòr-chuid de (a) bheatha *f*

great-grandchild *n* iar-ogha *m*

greatly *adv* gu mòr

greatness *n* **1** (*size, extent*) meudachd *f invar*, **the** ~ **of their debts** meudachd nam fiachan *mpl* aca; **2** (*in prestige, reputation &c*) mòrachd *f invar*

Greece *n* (*used with art*) A' Ghrèig

greed *n* (*for wealth, food*) gionaiche *m invar*, (*for food*) sannt *m*, geòcaireachd *f invar*

greedy *adj* (*for wealth, food*) gionach, (*for food*) sanntach, geòcach

Greek *adj* Greugach

Greek *n* **1** (*person*) Greugach *m*; **2** (*the language*) *used with art*, a' Ghreugais *f invar*

green *adj* uaine, gorm, (*less intense* ~) glas, ~ **grass** feur gorm/uaine, ~ **hillocks** tulaichean *mpl* glasa

green *n* **1** (*colour*) dath *m* uaine; **2** (*expanse of grass*) rèidhlean *m*

greenhouse *n* taigh-glainne *m*, **the ~ effect** buaidh *f* an taigh-ghlainne

greens *n* (*ie vegetables*) glasraich *f sing coll invar*

greet *v* fàiltich *vt*, cuir fàilte *f* (*with prep* air)

greeting *n* fàilte *f*, dùrachd *m*

gregarious *adj* greigheach, cèilidheach

grey *adj* **1** glas, ~ **trousers** briogais ghlas; **2** (*of landscape, hair*) liath, *in expr* **turn/become/go** ~ liath *vi*, fàs *vi* liath

grey *v* liath *vi*, **her hair is ~ing** tha a falt *m* a' liathadh

greyhound *n* mìolchu *m*

grid *n* cliath *f*, **cattle ~** cliath-chruidh (*gen of* crodh *m sing coll*), (*on maps*) ~ **line** loidhne-clèithe (*gen of* cliath) *f*, ~ **reference** comharradh-clèithe *m*, ~ **square** ceàrnag *f* clèithe

griddle, gridiron *n* (*baking*) greideal *f*

grief *n* **1** mulad *f*, (*stronger*) dòlas, (*excl*) **good ~!** an dòlas!, O mo chreach *f*!, mo chreach-s' a thàinig!

grievance *n* cùis-ghearain *f*

grieve *v* **1** caoidh *vti*, (*saying*) **what the eye doesn't see the heart doesn't ~ over** cha chaoidh duine *m* an rud *m* nach fhaic e; **2** (*mourn*) bi *vi irreg* ri bròn *m*, **they are grieving** tha iad ri bròn

grievous *adj* crài(dh)teach

grill *n* (*for cooking*) grìos *m*

grill *v* **1** (*cookery*) grìosaich *vt*; **2** (*interrogate*) mion-cheasnaich *vt*

grind *v* **1** (*general*) pronn *vt*; **2** (*esp corn*) meil *vt*, bleith *vt*

grip *n* grèim *m*, glacadh *m*, **keep a ~ on something** cùm grèim air rudeigin

grip *v* gabh grèim *m* (*with prep* air), ~ **the ladder** gabh grèim air an fhàradh *m*, (*idiom*) **she was ~ping his hand** bha grèim aice air làimh *f dat* air

grizzled *adj* riabhach

groan *n* (*of pain or grief*) cnead *m*, **she let out a ~** leig i cnead (aiste)

groan *v* dèan cnead *m*, leig cnead, **she ~ed** rinn i cnead, leig i cnead (aiste)

grocer *n* grosair *m*

groove *n* clais *f*

grope *v* **1** (*in search of something*) rùraich *vi*; **2** (*feel one's way blindly*) smeuraich *vi*

gross *adj* **1** (*in character*) garbh, borb; **2** (*of sums of money*) iomlan, slàn, ~ **interest** riadh *m* iomlan

grotty *adj* (*fam*) grod, mosach, dràbhail

grouchy *adj* crost(a) & crosda, gruamach, fo ghruaim *f dat*

ground *adj* & *past part* pronn

ground *n* **1** (*land*) talamh *m* (*f in gen sing*), fearann *m*, **arable/**

cultivated ~ talamh-àitich, **fallow** ~ talamh bàn, **cultivate/till the ~** àitich am fearann, **a piece of** ~ pìos *m* fearainn *gen*; **2** (*the surface of the ~*) làr *m*, **he knocked him/it to the ~** leag e gu làr e, **stretched out on the ~** sìnte air an làr; **3** (*of pibroch & other music*) ùrlar *m*; **4 ~s** (*ie reason(s), justification &c*) adhbhar *m*, **the ~s for his complaint** adhbhar a ghearain *m gen*

groundless (*without justification*) gun adhbhar *m*

grounds[1] *npl* (*cause, justification*) see **ground** *n* **4**

grounds[2] *npl* (*in liquids*) grùid *f*

group *n* **1** (*of people*) grunn *m*, (*smaller*) grunnan, **there was a ~ of people at the bus stop** bha grunn(an) dhaoine *mpl gen* aig àite-stad *m* nam busaichean *mpl*; **2** (*esp a ~ formed for a specific purpose*) còmhlan *m*, buidheann *mf*, **a pressure ~** buidheann-strì, **a research ~** buidheann-rannsachaidh, (*music*) **a ~** còmhlan-ciùil *m*

grouse[1] *n* (*the bird*) coileach-fraoich *m*, *in expr* **red ~** cearc *f* ruadh, cearc-fhraoich

grouse[2] *n* (*grumble &c*) gearan *m*

grouse *v* gearain *vi*

grove *n* doire *mf*

grow *v* **1** fàs *vi*, **it's barley that's ~ing here** 's e eòrna *m invar* a tha a' fàs ann a sheo, **the boy's ~ing pretty quickly** tha am balach a' fàs gu math luath; **2** (*become*) fàs *vi* (*with adj*), thig *vi* (*with n & prep* air), rach *vi* (*with prep* an/am & *abstr n*), **~ old** fàs sean, **they grew tired (of it)** dh'fhàs iad sgìth (dheth), **I grew afraid/sorrowful/hungry** thàinig eagal *m*/mulad *m*/acras *m* orm, **~ bigger** rach am meud *m invar*, **~ worse** rach am miosad *f*; **3 ~ up** (*pass through childhood*) tog *vt* (*in passive voice*), (*reach maturity*) thig *vi irreg* gu inbhe *f*, **I grew up in Coll** thogadh mi ann an Colla; **4** (*of sky &c*) **~ dark** ciar *vi*, fàs *vi* dorcha, **the evening grew dark** chiar am feasgar

growl, growling *n* dranndan *m*, dranndail *f invar*, grùnsgal *m*

growl *v* dèan dranndan *m*, *in expr* **apt to ~** dranndanach

grown *adj & past part*, **a ~ man** duine dèanta/foirfe, duine a th' air fàs suas, *in expr* **fully ~** inbheach

grown-up *adj & n* inbheach *m*

growth *n* (*con & abstr*) fàs *m*, cinneas *m*, **new/fresh ~** ùr-fhàs *m*, **economic ~** cinneas eaconamach

grub[1] *n* (*of insect*) cnuimh *f*

grub[2] *n* (*food*) biadh *m*

grumble *n* gearan *m*

grumble *v* **1** gearain *vi* (**about** air), (*less usu*) talaich *vi*, **you needn't bother grumbling all the time!** cha leig thu a leas a bhith a' gearan/ri gearan fad na h-ùine!; **2** *in expr* **apt to ~** gearanach

grumbling *adj* gearanach

grumbling *n* gearan *m*

grumpiness *n* gruaim *f*

grumpy *adj* gruamach, fo ghruaim *f dat*, crost(a) *&* crosda

grunt *n* 1 gnòsail *f*; 2 (*esp of pig*) rùchd *m*

grunt *v* 1 dèan gnòsail *f*; 2 (*esp of pig*) rùchd *vi*

guarantee *n* 1 (*general*) bar(r)antas *m*; 2 (*esp in fin matters*) urras *m*, **stand as ~ for someone** rach *vi* an urras air cuideigin

guarantee *v* rach *vi* an urras *m* (**that . . .** gu . . .)

guard *n* 1 (*abstr: soldier &c*) faire *f*, **be on ~** dèan/cùm faire; 2 (*coll; con*) faire *f*, freiceadan *m*, **put a ~ on it** cuir faire air; 3 (*a single ~, a member of the ~*) fear-faire *m*; 4 *in expr* **put someone on his/her ~** cuir cuideigin air earalas *m*

guess *n* tuaiream *f*, tuairmse *f*, tomhas *m*, **take a ~ at it** thoir tuaiream air

guess *v* tomhais *vt*, thoir tuaiream *f*, **~ how many there are** tomhais cia mheud a th' ann

guest *n* aoigh *m*

guidance *n* 1 treòrachadh *m*, iùl *m*, (*ed*) **~ teacher** tidsear-treòrachaidh *m*; 2 (*advice*) comhairle *f*

guide *n* 1 neach-iùil *m* (*pl* luchd-iùil *m sing coll*), (*esp tourist ~*) neach-treòrachaidh *m* (*pl* luchd-treòrachaidh *m sing coll*); 2 *in expr* **~ book** leabhar-iùil *m*

guide *v* treòraich *vt*, seòl *vt*, stiùir *vt*, **~ tourists** treòraich luchd-turais *m sing coll*

guideline(s) *n(pl)* stiùireadh *m*, seòladh *m*

guilt *n* ciont(a) *m*, (*less usu*) coill *f invar*

guiltless *adj* neo-chiontach

guilty *adj* ciontach, coireach, (**of** air), *in expr* **~ person** ciontach *m*, coireach *m*

gull *n* faoileag *f*, **great black-backed ~** farspag *&* arspag *f*, **lesser black-backed ~** (f)arspag bheag

gullet *n* slugan *m*

gulp, gulping *n* glug *m*, glugan *m*

gum *n* (*plant substance & adhesive*) bìth *f*, (*adhesive*) glaodh *m*

gum(s) *n* (*of mouth*) càireas *m*, càirean *m*

gumption *n* toinisg *f*, ciall *f*

gun *n* gunna *m*, (*artillery ~*) gunna mòr

gunner *n* gunnair *m*

gurgle, gurgling *n* 1 (*of persons*) glug *m*; 2 (*of liquids*) glugan *m*, plubraich *f*

gust *n* osag *f*, oiteag *f*

gut *n* 1 (*intestine*) caolan *m*, (*idiom: vulg*) **I spewed my ~s up** chuir mi a-mach rùchd *m* mo chaolanan; 2 (*~s of other creatures & fam for human stomach*) mionach *m*, **fish ~s** mionach-èisg (*gen of* iasg *m*)

gut *v* (*fish &c*) cut *vti*

gutter[1] *n* (*for drainage*) guitear *m*

gutter[2] *n* (*of fish &c*) cutair *m*

H

habit *n* cleachdadh *m*, àbhaist *m*, gnàth *m*

habitat *n* àrainn *f*

habitual *adj* àbhaisteach, (*less usu*) gnàthach

hag *n* **1** (*pej*) cailleach *f*; **2** *in expr* **peat ~** poll-mòna(ch) *m*, poll-mònadh *m*

haggis *n* taigeis *f*

hail, hailstone *n* clach-mheallain *f*

hair *n* **1** (*coll: on human head*) falt *m sing coll*, gruag *f sing coll*, (*a single ~*) fuiltean *m*, ròineag *f*; **2** (*~ of animal*) fionnadh *m sing coll*, gaoisid *f sing coll*; **3** (*idiom*) **~ of the dog** leigheas *m* na poit

hairdresser *n* gruagaire *m*

hairdryer *n* tiormaichear-gruaig *m*

hairy *adj* fionnach, molach, robach, ròmach

half *adv* **1** leth, leitheach, **~ dead** leth mharbh, **~ awake** na (*&c*) leth-dhùsgadh *m* (*also* na (*&c*) leth-dhùisg), **we were ~ awake** bha sinn nar leth-dhùsgadh/nar leth-dhùisg, **~ full** leitheach làn, **it's ~ past four** tha e leth uair *f* an dèidh a ceithir; **2** (*idiom*) **~ in jest/earnest** eadar fealla-dhà *f invar* is da-rìribh *adv*

half *n* **1** leth *f*, leth-chuid *f*, **the other ~** an leth eile, **a mile and a ~** mìle *mf* gu leth, **~ and ~** leth mar leth, **how much did you lose? ~ (of it)** dè a chaill thu dheth? an dàrna leth; **2** *in expr* **~ as much** (a) leth uiread *m invar*, **~ as much again** leth-uiread eile, **~ as much as Peter has** leth uiread agus a tha aig Peadar

halfhearted *adj* leth-fhuar, **a ~ welcome** fàilte *f* leth-fhuar

halfway *adv* leitheach-slighe, leitheach-rathaid, (**between** eadar), **~ between X and Y** leitheach-slighe eadar X is Y

hall *n* talla *m*, **the village/town ~** talla a' bhaile

Halloween *n* Oidhche *f* Shamhna (*gen of* Samhain *f*)

halo *n* fàinne-solais *f*

hamlet *n* clachan *m*

hammer *n* òrd *m*

hand *n* **1** làmh *f*, (*derog: of large, clumsy &c hand*) cròg *f*, **he didn't shake my ~** cha do rug e air làimh *dat* orm, **the back of the ~** cùl *m* na làimh(e), **hollow of the ~** glac *f*, **helping ~** làmh-chuideachaidh *f*, **he's on his ~s and knees** tha e air a mhàg(ar)an, **what couldn't he turn his ~ to?** cò ris nach cuireadh e a làmh?, **take a matter in ~** gabh gnothach *m* os làimh *dat*; **2** *in expr* **on the other ~** air mhodh *mf* eile, air an làimh eile

hand *v* **1** sìn *vt* (*with prep* gu), **she ~ed me the key** shìn i thugam an iuchair; **2** *in exprs* **~ over** thoir *vt* seachad, **~ around** thoir *vt* mun cuairt, cuir *vt* mun cuairt

handbag *n* màileid-làimh *f*

handball *n* ball-làimhe *m*

handcuff *n* glas-làimhe *f*, ~s glasan-làimhe

handful *n* làn *m* dùirn (*gen of* dòrn *m*), dòrlach *m*, **I had a ~ of seed** bha làn mo dhùirn agam de shìol *m*

handgun *n* daga & dag *m*

handicap *n* **1** (*general*) bacadh *m*, **poverty is a great ~** 's e bacadh mòr a th' anns a' bhochdainn *f*; **2** (*phys ~*) ciorram *m*

handicapped *adj* **1** (*by a disability*) ciorramach, **mentally ~** ciorramach na (*&c*) inntinn *f*, *in exprs* **a ~ person** ciorramach *n*, **the ~** na ciorramaich *mpl*; **2** (*~ socially, economically &c*) ana-cothromach

handkerchief *n* neapaigear *m*

handle *n* **1** (*of tool &c*) cas *f*, **knife ~** cas-sgeine (*gen of* sgian *f*); **2** (*of jug, mug, cup, casserole &c*) cluas *f*

handle *v* **1** (*phys*) làimhsich *vt*, (*esp tool, weapon*) iomair *vt*; **2** (*~ situations, people &c*) dèilig *vi* (*with prep* ri), làimhsich *vt*

handlebar *n* crann-làmh *m*

handshake *n* crathadh-làimhe *m*

handsome *adj* gasta, eireachdail, **a sturdy, ~ man** duine calma, gasta

handwriting *n* làmh-sgrìobhadh *m*

handy *adj* **1** deiseil, ullamh, goireasach, **that'll be ~ for you** bidh sin deiseil/ ullamh dhut; **2** *in expr* **be/come in ~** dèan feum *m*, bi *vi irreg* feumail, **(for** do**), scissors would be ~/would come in ~ (for us) just now** dhèanadh siosar *mf* feum (dhuinn) an-dràsta, bhiodh siosar feumail (dhuinn) an-dràsta; **3** (*good with one's hands*) gleusta, deas-làmhach

hang *v* (*person, picture &c*) croch *vt*

hanged *adj* & *past part* crochte

hanging *adj* & *pres part* an crochadh *m*, crochte, **~ing behind the door** an crochadh air cùl *m* an dorais

hangman *n* crochadair *m*

hangover *n* ceann *m* daoraich *f gen*

happen *v* **1** (*occur, befall*) tachair *vi* (**to** do), **what's ~ing? nothing** dè a tha a' tachairt? chan eil càil, **what ~ed to James?** dè a thachair do Sheumas?, **that's how it ~ed** (*often impersonal in Gaelic*) 's ann mar sin a thachair, sin mar a thachair (e); **2** (*become of*) èirich *vi* (*with prep* do), **what ~ed to James?** dè a dh'èirich do Sheumas?; **3** (*chance: with Gaelic impersonal constrs*) tachair *vi*, tuit *vi* (*with prep* do), **I ~ed to see him on the street** thachair gum faca mi air an t-sraid e, thuit dhomh fhaicinn air an t-sràid; **4** *in expr* **~ on/upon** (*ie come across, stumble upon*) tachair *vi*, amais *vi*, (*with prep* air)

happening *n* tachartas *m*, tuiteamas *m*

happy *adj* toilichte, (*less common*) sona, **I'm ~ to do that for you** tha mi toilichte sin a dhèanamh dhut, **I hope they were ~** tha mi an dòchas gun robh iad toilichte/sona

happy-go-lucky *adj* guanach, (*can be pej*) coma-co-dhiù

harass *v* claoidh *vt*, sàraich *vt*

harassment *n* sàrachadh *m*, **sexual ~** sàrachadh gnèitheasach, sàrachadh drùiseach

harbour *n* port *m*, cala *m*

hard *adj* **1** (*lit & fig*) cruaidh, **~ work** obair chruaidh, **a ~ land** tìr *mf* c(h)ruaidh, (*of book*) **~ cover/back** còmhdach cruaidh, (*IT*) **~ disc** clàr cruaidh; **2** (*difficult, painful*) duilich, **it is ~ for me to leave** is duilich leam falbh; **3** (*difficult, taxing*) doirbh, **a ~ question** cèist dhoirbh *f*, **that's ~ to say** tha sin doirbh a ràdh; **4** (*of argument, book &c: ~ to understand*) deacair; **5** (*idiom*) **the army was ~ on their heels** bha an t-arm teann orra

harden *v* cruadhaich *vti*, **don't ~ your heart!** na cruadhaich do chridhe *m*!

hard-hearted *adj* cruaidh-chridheach

hardihood *n* cruadal *m*, cruas *m*

hardiness *n* cruas *m*, fulang *m*

hardly *adv* **1** (*to a small extent, rarely, with difficulty*) is gann (*with conj* a), **we ~ saw him** is gann a chunnaic sinn e, **he ~ uttered two words** is gann a leig e às dà fhacal *m*, **we ~ made out what she was saying** is gann a rinn sinn a-mach dè a bha i ag ràdh; **2** (*barely, scarcely*) cha mhòr (*with conj* gun), **he ~ uttered two words** cha mhòr gun do leig e às dà fhacal; **3** (*esp expr difficulty*) is ann air èiginn *f invar* (*with conj* a), **we ~ made out what she was saying** is ann air èiginn a rinn sinn a-mach dè a bha i ag ràdh

hardness *n* cruas *m*

hardship *n* cruadal *m*

hardworking *adj* gnìomhach, dèanadach, dìcheallach, èasgaidh, (*fam*) cruaidh air an obair *f dat*

hardy *adj* fulangach, cruadalach, cruaidh

hare *n* maigheach *f*, geàrr *f*

harm *n* **1** lochd *m*, milleadh *m*, beud *m*; **2** (*not usu phys*) cron *m*; **3** (*idiom*) **a pint (*&c*) wouldn't do me any ~** cha bu mhiste mi pinnt *m* (*&c*)

harm *v* **1** goirtich *vt*, mill *vt*; **2** (*not usu phys*) dèan cron *m* (*with prep* air); **3** (*~ someone's feelings, situation &c*) ciùrr *vt*

harmful *adj* lochdach, cronail, millteach, cunnartach

harmonious *adj* ceòlmhor

harmony *n* **1** (*music*) co-sheirm *f*; **2** (*lack of dissension &c*) co-aontachadh *m*, co-chòrdadh *m*; **3** (*idiom*) **they lived in ~ with their neighbours** bha iad rèidh ris na nàbaidhean *mpl* aca

harness *n* uidheam *f*, acainn *f*

harp *n* clàrsach *f*, (*more trad*) cruit *f*

harper *n* clàrsair *m*, (*more trad*) cruitear *m*

harpsichord *n* cruit-chòrda *f*

Harris *n*, *used with art*, Na Hearadh *f invar*, **~ Tweed** An Clò Hearach, An Clò Mòr, *in expr* **a man from ~** Hearach *m*

harrow *n* cliath *f*

harrow *v* **1** (*agric*) cliath *vti*; **2** (~ *emotionally*) cràidh *vt*

harrowing *adj* crài(dh)teach, dòrainneach, **a ~ story** sgeulachd dhòrainneach

harsh *adj* **1** (*person, situation*) cruaidh, garbh, **a ~ land** tìr *mf* c(h)ruaidh/ g(h)arbh, **a ~ man** duine cruaidh/garbh, **a ~ voice** guth garbh; **2** (*phys sensations, words, temperament*) geur, searbh, **a ~ taste** blas geur/searbh, **~ words** briathran *mpl* geura/searbha, **a ~ wind** gaoth gheur

harshness *n* cruas *m*, gèire *f invar*, searbhachd *f invar*

harvest *n* foghar *m*, buain *f*, **the barley ~** foghar an eòrna

haste *n* **1** cabhag *f*, (*stronger*) deann *f*, **in ~** ann an cabhaig *dat*, **he left in (great) ~** dh'fhalbh e na dheann, **make ~** dèan cabhag, (*as imper*) **make ~!** greas ort/greasaibh oirbh!, dèan/dèanaibh cabhag!

hasten *v* **1** (*make haste*) dèan cabhag *f*; **2** (*hurry on others*) cuir cabhag (*with prep* air)

hasty *adj* (*action &c*) cabhagach

hatch *v* **1** (*eggs*) guir *vti*; **2** (~ *a plot &c*) innlich *vt*

hatchet *n* làmhthuagh *f*, làmhadh *m*, làmhag *f*

hate *n* gràin *f*, fuath *m*

hate *v* fuathaich *vt*, *more usu expr by* bi *vi irreg* gràin *f with preps* aig *&* air, *eg* **I ~ him** tha gràin *f* agam air, **they ~ her** tha gràin aca oirre

hateful *adj* gràineil, fuathach

hatred *n* gràin *f*, fuath *m*

haugh *n* innis *f*

haughtiness *n* àrdan *m*, uaibhreas *m*, uabhar *m*

haughty *adj* uaibhreach, àrdanach

haul *v* tarraing *vti* (**on** air), slaod *vti*

haulage *n* **1** giùlan *m*; **2** (*the charges levied for* ~) faradh *m*

haunt *v* (*visit frequently, hang around in/at*) tathaich *vi* (*with prep* air)

have *v* **1** (*expr possession &c*) bi *vi irreg* (*with prep* aig), **I ~ a house and a dog** tha taigh *m* agus cù *m* agam, **she had a headache** bha ceann goirt aice; **2** *exprs with* gabh *vt*, thoir *vt*, **will you ~ a cup of tea?** an gabh thu cupan *m* tì *f invar*?, **don't ~ anything to do with him/it!** na gabh gnothach *m* ris!, **~ pity on them** gabh truas *m* dhiubh, **~ a look at the newspaper** thoir sùil *f* air a' phàipear-naidheachd *m*; **3 ~ to** (*ie must*) feum *vi*, 's fheudar, *in past & conditional tenses* b' fheudar (*with prep* do), **I ~ to admit that . . .** feumaidh mi aideachadh gu . . . , **do you ~ to go?** am feum sibh falbh?, **she has to/had to stop** 's fheudar/b' fheudar dhi sgur, *Note also constructions such as* **I ~ a lot to do** tha mòran agam ri dhèanamh, **I ~ a letter to write** tha litir *f* agam ri sgrìobhadh; **4 ~ to** (*be or feel compelled*), thig *vi irreg* (*with prep* air *& verbal noun*), **I had to do it** thàinig orm a dhèanamh *m*, (*also, using double neg constr*) cha b' urrainn dhomh gun a dhèanamh

hay *n* tràthach *m*

hay-fork *n* gobhlag *f*

hazardous *adj* cunnartach

haze *n* ceò *m*

hazel *n* calltainn *m*

hazelnut *n* cnò *f* challtainn *m gen*

hazy *adj* ceòthach

head *adj* prìomh (*precedes the noun, which it lenites where possible*), **the ~ clerk** a' phrìomh-chlèireach *m*, **the ~ office of the company** prìomh-oifis *f* a' chompanaidh

head *n* **1** ceann *m*, **he shook his ~** chrath e a cheann, **she bent/bowed her ~** chrom i a ceann, **~ first** an comhair *f invar* a chinn *gen*, **side of the ~** lethcheann *m*; **2** *in expr* **~ of hair** gruag *f*; **3** *in expr* (*of collision &c*) **~ on** an comhair a thoisich; **4** *in expr* **a ~** (*ie each*) an urra *f*, **we spent 50p a ~** chosg sinn leth-cheud sgillinn *f sing* an urra

headache *n* ceann *m* goirt, **I have a ~** tha mo cheann goirt

headgear *n* ceannbheart *f*

heading *n* (*in text &c*) ceann *m*

headland *n* rubha *m*

headline *n* ceann-naidheachd *m*

headlong *adj* na (*&c*) d(h)ian-ruith *f*, na *&c* d(h)eann *f*, **they left in a ~ rush** dh'fhalbh iad nan deann-ruith/nan deann

headlong *adv* an comhair *f invar* a (*&c*) c(h)inn *m gen*, **she fell ~** thuit i an comhair a cinn

headstrong *adj* **1** (*wilful*) ceann-làidir; **2** (*obstinate*) rag-mhuinealach

head-teacher *n* (*usu secondary school*) maighistir-sgoile *m*

heal *v* slànaich *vti*, leighis *vt*, **it ~ed** shlàinich e

healing *n* slànachadh *m*, leigheas *m*

health *n* **1** slàinte *f*, **~ centre** ionad-slàinte *m*; **2** *in exprs* **in good ~** slàn, fallain, **in bad ~** tinn, euslainteach, (*toast*) **good ~!** slàinte!

health-giving *adj* (*food &c*) fallain

healthy *adj* (*in good health, also health-giving*) slàn, fallain

heap *n* tòrr *m*, cruach *f*, (*small ~*) cruachan *m*

heap *v* cruach *vt*, càrn *vt*

hear *v* cluinn *vt irreg*, **he can't ~ a thing** cha chluinn e bìd *m*/bìog *f*, **I ~d you were ill** chuala mi gun robh thu tinn, **it's good to be ~ing from you!** 's math a bhith a' cluinntinn bhuat!

hearing *n* claisneachd *& c* claisteachd *f invar*, **I'm losing my ~** tha mi a' call mo chlaisneachd

heart *n* **1** cridhe *m*, **~ disease** tinneas *m* cridhe *gen*, **~ attack** clisgeadh *m* cridhe, grèim-cridhe *m*; **2** *in exprs* **in good ~** misneachail, **the ~ of the matter** cnag *f* na cùise

heartbeat buille *f* cridhe *m gen*

heartbreak *n* bris(t)eadh *m* cridhe *m gen*

heartbroken *adj & past part*, **she's ~** tha a cridhe *m* briste, **you left me ~** dh'fhàg thu mi 's mo chridhe briste

heartburn *n* losgadh-bràghad *m*

hearth *n* cagailt *f*, teallach *m*, teinntean *m*, **at the ~** ris a' chagailt *dat*

hearthstone *n* leac *f* theallaich *m gen*

heartiness *n* cridhealas *m*

hearty *adj* (*person, atmosphere &c*) cridheil, **a ~ welcome** fàilte chridheil

heat *n* teas *m invar*, **~ wave** tonn *mf* teasa *gen*

heat, heat up, *v* teasaich *vti*

heater *n* (*domestic &c*) uidheam *f* teasachaidh *m gen*

heath *n* **1** monadh *m*, sliabh *m*, mòinteach *f*; **2** (*the plant*) fraoch *m*

heathen *n* cinneach *m*

heather *n* fraoch *m*

heather-cock *n* coileach-fraoich *m*

heating *n* (*domestic &c*) teasachadh *m*, **~ appliance** uidheam *f* teasachaidh *gen*

heave *v* **1** (*throw*) tilg *vt*, caith *vt*; **2** (*haul &c*) tarraing *vi*, slaod *vi*, (**on air**)

heaven *n* **1** nèamh *m*, flaitheas *m*, pàrras *m*; **2** *in expr* **the ~s** an iarmailt *f*; **3** (*excl*) **good ~s!** obh! obh!, O mo chreach!; **4** *in expr* **why, in ~'s name**, (**did you do it &c**)? carson, a chiall, (a rinn thu e &c)?

heavenly *adj* nèamhaidh

heaviness *n* truimead *m*, **the ~ of my heart** truimead mo chridhe *m*

heavy *adj* trom, (*less usu*) cudthromach, **~ parcels** parsailean *mpl* troma, **a ~ step** ceum trom, **~ on the booze** (*fam*) trom air an deoch *f*, **with a ~ heart** le cridhe trom

Hebrew *n* (*lang*) Eabhra *f*

Hebrides *n*, **the ~** Innse Gall *fpl*

hectare *n* heactair *m*

hectic *adj* (*at work &c*) dripeil, **things are pretty ~ just now** tha cùisean *fpl* gu math dripeil an-dràsta

hedge *n* callaid *f*, fàl *m*

hedgehog *n* gràineag *f*

heed *n* aire *f invar*, feart & feairt *f*, **without paying ~ to it** gun aire/feart a thoirt air

heel *n* **1** sàil *f*, (*less usu*) bonn-dubh *m*; **2** (*command to dog*) (**come to my**) **~!** cùl *m* mo chois'! (*gen of* cas *f*); **3** (*idioms & exprs*) **the army was hard on their ~s** bha an t-arm teann orra, **he took to his ~s** thug e na buinn *mpl* às, thug e a chasan *fpl* leis, (*fig*) **drag one's ~s** màirnealaich *vi*, bi *vi irreg* màirnealach, bi slaodach

height *n* **1** (*lit*) àirde *f*, **what ~ is it?** dè an àirde a tha ann?; **2** (*fig*) *in expr* **at the ~ of his/her powers/strength** an treun *f invar* a neirt (*gen of* neart *m*), *also* aig àird *f* a c(h)omais (*gen of* comas *m*)

heir *n* oighre *m*

heiress *n* ban-oighre *f*

held *adj & past part* **1** glèidhte; **2** (**~ in captivity**) an grèim *m*, an sàs *m*, an làimh (*dat of* làmh *f*)

helicopter *n* heileacopta(i)r *m*

hell *n* **1** (*lit*) ifrinn *f*, (*less usu*) iutharn(a) *f*; **2** (*misc fig exprs & idioms*) ~ **of a** ... garbh *adv*, **things are ~ of a busy just now** tha cùisean *fpl* garbh dripeil an-dràsta, **they set off ~ for leather** dh'fhalbh iad nan dian-ruith *f*, thog iad orra nan deann *f*, (*as excl*) ~! mac *m* an donais!, (*with attenuated meaning*) **it was sheer ~!** bha e dìreach sgriosail!

hellish *adj* **1** (*lit*) ifrinneach; **2** (*with attenuated fig meaning*) sgriosail, **a ~ day** latha *m* sgriosail

hello *excl* halò

helm *n* falmadair *m*, ailm *f*

helmet *n* cloga(i)d *m*

help *n* **1** (*relief, aid*) cobhair *f*, (*as excl*) ~! (dèan) cobhair orm!, cuidich mi!; **2** (*more general*) cuideachadh *m*, **thank you for your ~** mòran taing *f* airson ur cuideachaidh *gen*; **3** *in expr* **financial ~** taic *f* airgid (*gen of* airgead *m*); **4** (*person who helps*) cuidiche *mf*, **home ~** cuidiche-taighe

help *v* **1** cuidich *vti*, dèan cobhair *f* (*with prep* air), **~ them** cuidich iad, (*more trad*) cuidich leotha, dèan cobhair orra, **a ~ing hand** làmh *f* cuideachaidh *m gen*; **2** (*avoid, prevent oneself &c*) **I can't ~/couldn't ~** ... chan urrainn/cha b' urrainn dhomh, *with conj* gun, **I couldn't ~ being sad** cha b' urrainn dhomh gun a bhith brònach; **3** (*idiom*) **it can't be ~ed** chan eil cothrom *m* air

helper *n* cuidiche *m*

helpful *adj* cuideachail

hem *n* fàitheam *m*

hemisphere *n* leth-chruinne *mf*

hemp *n* cainb *f*

hen *n* cearc *f*

her *poss adj* **1** a (*does not lenite a following noun*), ~ **mother** a màthair; **2** aice (*follows the noun and art: tends to be used with objects &c less intimately connected with the individual concerned*) ~ **pen** am peann aice (*though note exceptions such as* ~ **house** an taigh aice, ~ **husband** an duine aice)

her *pron* i, (*emph form*) ise

herb *n* luibh *mf*, lus *m*

herd *n* treud *m*, (*esp of cattle*) buar *m*

herd *v* (*usu cattle*) buachaillich *vi*

heritage *n* **1** (*lit & fig*) dìleab *f*, **the ~ of history** dìleab na h-eachdraidh; **2** (*inherited property &c*) oighreachd *f*; **3** (*cultural ~*) dualchas *m*

hermaphrodite *adj* fireann-boireann

hermaphrodite *n* fireann-boireann *m*

hero *n* curaidh *m*, gaisgeach *m*, laoch *m*

heroic *adj* gaisgeil

heroism *n* gaisge *f invar*, gaisgeachd *f invar*

heron *n* corra-ghritheach *f*

herself *reflexive pron* i-fhèin, *for examples of use cf* **myself**

hesitate *v* **1** (*through indecision*) màirnealaich *vi*, bi *vi irreg* an imcheist *f*, bi eadar-dhà-lionn; **2** (*through unwillingness*) is *v irreg & def* leisg, *with prep* le *& verbal noun*, **I ~ to admit it** is leisg leam aideachadh

hesitating *adj* (*undecided*) an imcheist *f*, eadar-dhà-lionn

heterogeneous *adj* ioma-sheòrsach

hibernation *n* cadal-geamhraidh *m*

hiccups *n* an aileag *f sing*, **I've got (the) ~** tha an aileag orm

hidden *adj & past part* falaichte, am falach *m*, air falach

hide[1] *n* (*pelt*) seiche *f*, bian *m*

hide[2] *n* (*place of concealment*) àite-falaich *m*

hide *v* **1** (*as vt*) cuir *vt* am falach *m*, ceil *vt* (**from** air), **~ it** cuir am falach e, **~ it from her** ceil oirre e; **2** (*as vi*) rach *vi* am falach *m* (**from** air), **they hid (from me)** chaidh iad am falach (orm)

hide-and-seek *n* falach-fead *m*

hide-out *n* àite-falaich *m*

hiding *n* falach *m*, **in ~** am falach, **go into ~** rach *vi* am falach

hiding place *n* àite-falaich *m*

high *adj* àrd

higher *adj* nas àirde (*in past & conditional tenses* na b' àirde), as àirde (*in past & conditional tenses* a b' àirde), **that hill is (the) ~** 's e an cnoc *m* sin as àirde, **a ~ hill** cnoc as àirde

highland *adj* (*topog*) àrd-thìreach

highland *n* (*topog*) àrd-thìr *mf*

Highland *adj* Gaidhealach *&* Gàidhealach, **~ Games** Geamannan *mpl* Gaidhealach

Highlander *n* Gaidheal *&* Gàidheal *m*

Highlands *n* Gaidhealtachd *&* Gàidhealtachd *f invar, used with art*, **the ~** a' Ghàidhealtachd, **in the ~** air a' Ghàidhealtachd

highlight *v* **1** soillsich *vt*; **2** (*fig: emphasise &c*) cuir cudthrom *m* (*with prep* air)

high-ranking *adj* inbheil

highway *n* rathad-mòr

high-yielding *adj* torach

hilarity *n* cridhealas *m*,

hill *n* **1** (*large ~, mountain*) beinn *f*, (*usu small to medium-sized*) cnoc *m*, (*small, usu rounded*) tom *m*, (*esp conical or mound shaped*) tòrr *m*, (*usu rounded or conical*) dùn *m*, (*usu conical*) cruach *f* (*dimin*) cruachan *m*, (*stony*) càrn *m*, (*usu rocky*) creag *f*, (*usu lumpy*) meall *m*; **2** (*esp agric &c: rough grazing &c*) monadh *m*, (*moorland*) mòinteach *f*, sliabh *m*

hillock *n* cnoc *m*, cnocan *m*, toman *m*, tulach *m*

hillside, hillslope *n* leathad *m*, ruighe *mf*

hilly *adj* cnocach, monadail

him *pron* e, (*emph form*) esan, **he saw ~** chunnaic e e

himself *reflexive pron* e-fhèin, *for examples cf* **myself**

hind *n* (*female of red deer*) eilid *f*

hinge *n* lùdag *f*, banntach *f*

hip *n* (*anat*) cruachann *f*

hippopotamus *n* each-aibhne *m*

hire *v* (*workers*) fastaich, *also* fasdaich & fastaidh, *vt*

hirsute *adj* ròmach

historian *n* eachdraiche *m*

historical *adj* eachdraidheil

history *n* eachdraidh *f*, **local ~** eachdraidh ionadail, **she did ~ at university** rinn i eachdraidh anns an oilthigh *m*

hither *adv* **1** an seo, a-bhos, an taobh seo, an taobh a-bhos, a-nall; **2** *in expr* **~ and thither** thall 's a-bhos

hitherto *adv* gu ruige seo

hoar frost *n* liath-reothadh *m*

hoard *n* tasgaidh *f*

hoard *v* taisg *vt*

hoarse *adj* **1** tùchanach; **2** (*idiom*) **I am ~, I have become ~** tha an tùchadh air tighinn orm; **3** *in expr* **a ~ voice** guth garbh

hoarseness *n* tùchadh *m*

hobby *n* cur-seachad *m*

hobnail *n* tacaid *f*

hoe *n* todha *m*

hoe *v* todhaig *vt*

hoeing *n* obair-thodha *f*

hog(g) *n* (*1-2 yr old ewe lamb*) othaisg *f*

hoist *v* tog *vt*, **~ the sails** togaibh na siùil *mpl*

hold *n* grèim *m*, **take ~ of something** gabh grèim air rudeigin, **keep ~ of something** cùm grèim air rudeigin

hold *v* **1** (*take hold of*) gabh grèim *m* (*with prep* air), (*keep hold*) cùm grèim (*with prep* air); **2** (*contain*) cùm *vt*, gabh *vt*, **will it ~ all my clothes?** an cùm e/an gabh e mo chuid *f* aodaich *m* gen air fad?, **the hall will ~ 300 people** gabhaidh an talla trì cheud duine *m sing*; **3** *in expr* **~ back, ~ up** (*ie delay*) cùm *vt* air ais, cuir maille *f invar* (*with prep* air *or* ann), **I won't ~ you back/up** cha chùm mi air ais sibh, **~ up the proceedings** cuir maille air/anns a' ghnothach *m*, (*idiom*) **if they're held up** ma thèid maille orra; **4** *in expr* **~ on to** (*ie keep, save*) cùm *vt*, glèidh *vt*, **~ on to this for me till Friday** cùm seo dhomh gu Dihaoine *m invar*; **5** (*idiom*) **she was ~ing his hand** bha grèim aice air làimh *dat* air

holding *n* (*of land*) lot *f*, croit *f*

hole *n* toll *m*, *in expr* **full of ~s** tolltach

hole *v* toll *vt*, **the boat was ~d** chaidh am bàta a tholladh

holiday *n* **1** (*esp vacation, time off*) saor-latha *m*, **~s** làithean-saora & saor-làithean *mpl*; **2** (*esp public ~*) latha-fèille *m*

holiness *n* naomhachd *f invar*

hollow *adj* còsach, falamh

hollow *n* **1** toll *m*; **2** (*topog*) còs *m*, glac *f*, lag *mf*

holly *n* cuileann *m*

holy *adj* **1** naomh, **the Holy Ghost/Spirit** An Spiorad *m* Naomh; **2** *in expr*
    ~ **Communion** comanachadh *m*

homage (*before royalty &c*) ùmhlachd *f invar*

home *adv* dhachaigh, **going** ~ a' dol dhachaigh, **I'm away** ~! tha mi a' falbh
    dhachaigh!, **the way** ~ an rathad *m* dhachaigh

home *n* **1** dachaigh *f invar*, **that's my** ~ 's e sin mo dhachaigh(-sa), **old**
    folks' ~ dachaigh nan seann daoine *mpl*; **2** *in exprs* **at** ~ aig an taigh *m*,
    away from ~, **not at** ~ on taigh, ~ **help** cuidiche *mf* taighe *gen*, ~ **farm**
    mànas *m*, **Home Secretary/Office** Rùnaire *m*/Oifis *f* na Dùthcha,
    ~ **rule** fèin-riaghladh *m*

homeland *n* dùthaich *f*, **the Mackay** ~ Dùthaich MhicAoidh

homesick *adj* cianalach

homesickness *n* cianalas *m*

homewards *adv* dhachaigh

homogeneous *adj* aon-seòrsach

homonym *n* co-ainmear *m*

homosexuality *n* fearas-feise *f*

honest *adj* onarach, ionraic

honesty *n* onair *f*, ionracas *m*

honey *n* mil *f*, **tasting of** ~ air blas *m* na meala (*gen of* mil)

honeycomb *n* cìr-mheala *f*

honeymoon *n* mìos *mf* nam pòg *fpl gen*

honeysuckle *n* iadh-shlat & iath-shlat *f*, lus *m* na meala (*gen of* mil *f*)

honorary *adj* onarach, urramach, **an** ~ **member of the society** ball *m*
    onarach/urramach den chomann *m*

honour *n* **1** (*personal* ~) onair *f*, **on my** ~! air m' onair!; **2** (*respect, distinction*)
    urram *m*, **confer an** ~ **on someone** cuir/builich urram air cuideigin;
    3 (*fame, renown*) cliù *m invar*, glòir *f*

honour *v* **1** (*bestow an honour on*) onaraich *vt*, cuir/builich urram *m* (*with*
    prep air); **2** (*respect, revere*) onaraich *vt*; **3** (*keep, stand by, fulfil*) coilean *vt*,
    he ~ed his commitment choilean e a ghealladh *m*

honourable *adj* onarach, urramach

hood *n* (*headgear*) cochall *m*

hoodie *n* (*crow*) feannag ghlas

hoof *n* (*of horse, cattle &c*) ìne *f*, ladhar *m*

hook *n* (*for fastenings, hanging objects, fishing, &c*) cromag *f*, dubhan *m*

hoolie *n* (*fam*) ho-ro-gheallaidh *m invar*

hooligan *n* glagaire *m*

hooliganism *n* miastachd *f invar*, glagaireachd *f invar*

hoop *n* (wooden) rong *f*

hooter *n* dùdach *f*, dùdag *f*

hope *n* **1** dòchas *m*, **without ~** gun dòchas, **put one's ~ in something** cuir dòchas ann an rudeigin; **2** (*expectation*) dùil *f*, **without ~ of returning** gun dùil ri tilleadh *m*

hope *v* bi *vi irreg* an dòchas *m*, **I ~ she won't come** tha mi an dòchas nach tig i, **it'll be a good day, I ~** bidh là math ann, tha mi an dòchas

hopeless *adj* gun dòchas

hopelessness *n* eu-dòchas *m*

horizon *n* fàire *f*, **on the ~** air fàire

horizontal *adj* còmhnard

horn *n* **1** (*of animal*) adharc *f*, (*also the material*) **a ~ spoon** spàin *f* adhairc *gen*; **2** (*drinking ~, musical instrument*) còrn *m*

hornless *adj* maol

horrible *adj* **1** uabhasach, oillteil; **2** (*of behaviour*) suarach (**to** ri), **I was ~ to her last night** bha mi suarach rithe a-raoir

horrify *v* cuir oillt *f* (*with prep* air), oilltich *vt*

horror *n* uamhann *&* uabhann *m*, oillt *f*, uabhas *m*, **~s of war** uabhasan cogaidh *m gen*

horse *n* each *m*, *in expr* **work~** each-oibre *&* each-obrach

horseback *n* muin *f invar* eich (*gen of* each *m*), **on ~** air muin eich

horsefly *n* creithleag *f*

horsehair *n* gaoisid *f*

horseman *n* marcaiche *m*, **horsemen** marcaichean *mpl*, eachraidh *m sing coll*

horsemanship *n* marcachadh *m*, marcachd *f invar*

horseshoe *n* crudha *m*

horticulture *n* tuathanachas-gàrraidh *m*

hose *n* (*for water*) pìob-uisge *f*

hospitable *adj* fialaidh, fial, fàilteachail, fàilteach, faoilidh

hospital *n* ospadal *m*, (*more trad*) taigh-eiridinn *m*, **in ~** anns an ospadal

hospitality *n* aoigheachd *f invar*, furan *m*

host[1] *n* (*at hotel*) òsdair *&* òstair *m*, (*at hotel, private house*) fear *m* (an) taighe *m*

host[2] *n* **1** (*body of people*) mòr-shluagh *m*; **2** (*an army*) feachd *f*

hostage *n* bràigh *mf*

hostel *n* òstail *f*

hostile *adj* nàimhdeil

hostility *n* nàimhdeas *m*

hot *adj* **1** teth; **2** (*idiom*) **~ off the presses** ùr on chlò *m*

hot-blooded *adj* lasanta

hotel *n* taigh-òsta *m*

hotelier *n* òstair *m*

hot-water-bottle *n* botal *m* teth

hour *n* uair *f*, **a quarter of an ~** cairteal *m* na h-uarach, **after an ~** an dèidh uair a (*for* de) thìde *f*, an dèidh uair an uaireadair, **at this ~** aig an uair seo

house *n* taigh *m*, (*less usu*) fàrdach *f*, **dwelling** ~ taigh-còmhnaidh *m*, **the man of the** ~ fear an taighe *m*, **the House of Commons/of Lords** Taigh nan Cumantan/nam Morairean

house *v* 1 (*people*) thoir taigh *m*, thoir lòistinn *m*, (*with prep* do); 2 (~ *objects in museum &c*) glèidh *vt*

housecoat *n* còta-leapa *m*

house-fly *n* cuileag *f*

housewife *n* bean *f* (an) taighe *m*

housework *n* obair-taighe *f*

housing *n* 1 (*abstr*) taigheadas *m*, **the Housing Committee** Comataidh *f* an Taigheadais; 2 (*con*) taighean *mpl*, ~ **scheme** sgeama-thaighean *m*

how *inter adv* 1 ciamar, ~ **are you today?** ciamar a tha thu an-diugh?, ~ **did he do it?** ciamar a rinn e e?, ~ **did you get on** ciamar a chaidh dhuibh?; 2 (*in exprs of quantity*) ~ **many** cia mheud & co mheud, ~ **many people were there?** cia mheud duine *m sing* a bha ann?, ~ **much milk have we got?** dè a tha againn de bhainne? *m*; 3 (~ *followed by an adj*) dè cho *plus adj plus* agus/'s *plus rel pron* a *plus verb*, ~ **long will you be here?** dè cho fada 's a bhios tu ann?, ~ **useful is it?** dè cho feumail 's a tha e?; 4 (*misc idioms*) ~ **are you (doing)?** (*fam*) dè do chor *m*?, dè an dòigh *f* (a th' ort)?, dè am fonn *m*?, (*cost*) ~ **much is it?** dè na tha e?, **that's ~ it is!** is ann mar sin a tha (e)!

howe *n* (*topog*) lag *mf*

however *adv* 1 ge-tà, co-dhiù, a dh'aindeoin chùis, **he didn't die,** ~ cha do chaochail e, ge-tà/co-dhiù/a dh'aindeoin chùis (*gen of* cùis *f*); 2 (*in concessive clauses*) air cho *plus adj plus* agus/is *plus conj* gu *plus verb*, ~ **tired you may be** air cho sgìth 's gu bheil thu/'s a tha thu, ~ **poor he was** air cho bochd 's gun robh e/'s a bha e

howl *n* (*esp of dog*) ulfhart *m*, donnal *m*

howl *v* 1 (*usu of animals*) nuallaich, (*esp dogs*) dèan ulfhart *m*; 2 (*of humans: weep noisily*) ràn *vi*

howling *n* 1 (*usu of animals*) nuallaich *f*, (*esp of dogs*) donnalaich *f*; 2 (*of humans: noisy weeping*) rànail *m invar*, rànaich *f*

hubbub ùpraid *f*, gleadhar, othail *f*, iorghail, toirm *f*

hue *n* 1 (*colour*) dath *m*; 2 (*esp of person's complexion*) fiamh *m*, neul *m*; 3 (*of person's features: not nec permanent*) tuar *m*

hug *v* 1 fàisg *vt*; 2 (*idioms*) **come and let me ~ you!** thig nam chom *m*!, thig nam achlais *f*!

hum *n* crònan *m*, torman *m*

human *adj* 1 daonna, **the ~ race** an cinne-daonna, ~ **rights** còraichean *fpl* daonna; 2 *in expr* ~ **being** duine *m*

humane *adj* truacanta, iochdmhor

humanity *n* (*humaneness; also the quality of being human*) daonnachd *f invar*

humanity, humankind *n* mac an duine *m sing coll*, (*used with art*) an cinne-daonna *m*

humble *adj* **1** (*in status &c*) ìosal & ìseal, iriosal & iriseal; **2** (*self-effacing &c*) umha(i)l, iriosal & iriseal

humble *v* (*humiliate &c*) ùmhlaich *vt*, irioslaich & irislich *vt*, islich *vt*

humbleness ùmhlachd *f invar*, irioslachd & irisleachd *f invar*

humid *adj* tais

humidity *n* taise *f invar*, taisead *m*

humiliate *v* ùmhlaich *vt*, irioslaich & irislich *vt*, ìslich *vt*

humiliation *n* ùmhlachadh *m*, irioslachadh & irisleachadh *m*, ìsleachadh *m*

humility *n* irioslachd & irisleachd *f invar*

humming *n* crònan *m*, torman *m*

humorous *adj* èibhinn, àbhachdach

humour *n* **1** àbhachd *f invar*, àbhachdas *m*; **2** (*mood*) gleus *mf*, gean *m*, **in good ~** air (deagh) ghleus, *also* gleusta, **good/bad ~** deagh/droch ghean, **what sort of ~ is he in today?** dè an gean a th' air an-diugh?

hump *n* (*on the back*) croit & cruit *f*

hump-backed *adj* crotach

hundred *n* ceud *m*, **a/one ~ people** ceud duine *m sing*, **~s of them came** thàinig iad nan ceudan, **several ~ years** iomadh ceud bliadhna *f sing*

hundredth *num adj* ceudamh

hung *adj & past part* crochte

Hungarian *n & adj* Ungaireach *m*

Hungary *n* (*with art*) An Ungair *f*

hungry *adj* **1** acrach, acrasach, *in exprs* **I am ~** tha an t-acras orm, **I grew ~** thàinig an t-acras orm; **2** (*fig: ~ for success &c*) gionach

hunt *n* sealg *f*, ruaig *f*

hunt *v* sealg *vti*

hunter, huntsman *n* sealgair *m*

hunting *n* sealg *f*

hurricane *n* doineann *f*

hurried *adj* cabhagach

hurry *n* cabhag *f*, **in a ~** ann an cabhaig *dat*, **he ate his dinner in a ~** ghabh e a dhìnnear *f* ann an cabhaig, **we're in a ~!** tha cabhag òirnn!

hurry *v* **1** (*as vi*) greas *vi* (*with prep* air), dèan cabhag *f*, **~ (up)!** greas ort! (*pl* greasaibh oirbh!), dèan cabhag!, **they ought to ~** bu chòir dhaibh greasad (*verbal noun of* greas *vi*) orra; **2** (*as vt*) **~ up/on** cuir cabhag *f* (*with prep* air), luathaich *vt*, **~ someone (up)** cuir cabhag *f* air cuideigin, **the teacher was ~ing us on** bha an tìdsear gar luathachadh/gar putadh air adhart

hurt *adj & past part* (*phys or emotionally*) ciùrrte, leònta & leònte, air a (*&c*) g(h)oirteachadh

hurt *n* ciùrradh *m*, leòn *m*, goirteas *m*

hurt *v* **1** (*as vt: ~ phys*) goirtich *vt*, (*phys or emotionally*) ciùrr *vt*, leòn *vt*; **2** (*as vi*) bi *vi irreg* goirt, **my back ~s** tha mo dhruim goirt

hurtful *adj* **1** (*esp emotionally*) cronail; **2** (*of remarks &c*) guineach

husband *n* duine *m*, cèile *m*, (*trad: affectionate*) companach *m*, **my** ~ an duine agam

hush! *excl* ist!, *pl* istibh!, *also* eist!, *pl* eistibh!

hush *v* ciùinich *vt*, (*esp child*) tàlaidh *vt*

husk *n* cochall *m*, plaosg *m*

hydro-electricity *n* dealan-uisge *m*

hydrogen *n* hàidraidean *m*

hymn *n* laoidh *mf*, dàn *m* spioradail

hyphen *n* tàthan *m*

hypocrisy *n* cealg *f*

hypocrite *n* cealgair(e) *m*

hypocritical *adj* cealgach

hypothesis *n* beachd-bharail *f*

hypothetical *adj* baralach

I

I *pers pron* mi, (*emph*) mise, mi-fhìn, ~ **did it** rinn mi e, ~ (*emph*) **did it!** is mise a rinn e!, rinn mi-fhìn e!

ice *n* eigh *or* eighre *or* deigh *f*, ~ **age** linn *mf* deighe *gen*

iceberg *n* cnoc *m* eighre *f gen*, beinn-deighe *f*

ice cream *n* reòiteag *f*

Iceland *n* Innis *f* Tìle

Icelander *n* Tìleach *m*

Icelandic *adj* Tìleach

icicle *n* caisean-reòta *m*, stob *m* reòta

Id *n* (*psych*), *used with art*, **the ~** an t-Eadh *m*

idea *n* **1** beachd *m*, beachd-smuain *f*, smuain *f*, **abstract ~** cùis-bheachd *m*; **2** (*idiom*) **I haven't the faintest ~**, **I've no ~** chan eil càil *m invar* a dh'fhios *m* agam

identical *adj* co-ionann (**to** ri), ionann (**to** agus/is), ~ **to X** co-ionann ri X, (*used with v* is) **X and Y are ~** is ionann X agus Y

idiom *n* (*lang*) gnàthas-cainnte *m*

idiomatic *adj* (*lang*) gnàthasach

idiot *n* amadan *m*, bumailear *m*, òinseach *f* (*trad a female but also used of males*)

idle *adj* **1** (*unoccupied, unemployed, not nec pej*) na (*&c*) t(h)àmh *m*, dìomhain, **the workers are ~ because of the strike** tha an luchd-obrach *m sing coll* na thàmh air sgàth na stailc; **2** (*pej: lazy*) leisg, *in expr* ~ **man/person** leisgeadair *m*; **3** *in expr* ~ **talk/chatter** rabhd *m*, ràbhart *m*

idleness *n* **1** (*inactivity: not nec pej*) tàmh *m*; **2** (*pej: laziness*) leisg(e) *f*

idol *n* ìomhaigh *f*, iodhal *m*

if *conj* **1** ma, (*in neg*) mur(a), ~ **it rains** ma tha/bhios an t-uisge ann, **have a break ~ you're tired** leig d' anail *f* ma tha thu sgìth, **I won't go ~ you're not keen on it** cha tèid mise (ann) mura bheil (*fam* mur eil) thusa air a shon; **2** (*in more hypothetical statements, in past and conditional tenses*) nan, ~ **I was/were rich I'd build you a castle** nan robh mi beartach thogainn caisteal *m* dhut

ignite *v* **1** (*as vt*) cuir teine *m* (*with prep* ri), las *vt*, **they ~d the bale** chuir iad teine ris a' bhèile *f*; **2** (*as vi*) rach *vi* na t(h)eine, **the bale ~d** chaidh a' bhèile na teine

ignominy *n* nàire *f*

ill *adj* **1** (*sick &c*) tinn, euslainteach, (*fam*) bochd; **2** *in expr* ~ **at ease** anshocrach; **3** (*bad, unfavourable &c*) **a)** *can be expressed in compounds with* droch(-) *adj* (*precedes the noun & lenites following consonant where possible*), *followed by n, adj, &c, eg* ~**-natured**, ~**-tempered** *adj* droch-nàdarrach, ~**-treatment** *n* droch-làimhseachadh *m*, **b)** *can be expressed by prefixes* eu- *or* mì-, *followed by the appropriate noun, eg* ~**-health** *n* euslàinte *f*, ~**-will** *n* mì-rùn *m* (*see further examples below*)

ill-bred *adj* mì-mhodhail
illegal *adj* mì-laghail
illegitimate *adj* **1** (*by birth*) dìolain; **2** (*morally, legally &c*) neo-dhligheil
illegitimacy *n* (*by birth*) dìolanas *m*
ill-health *n* tinneas *m*, euslaint(e) *f*, anfhannachd *f*
ill-humour *n* gruaim *f*, **in an ~** fo ghruaim *dat*
ill-humoured *adj* gruamach
ill-mannered *adj* mì-mhodhail
illness *n* **1** (*abstr: ill-health*) tinneas *m*, euslaint(e) *f*, **mental ~** tinneas-inntinn *m*; **2** (*con: an ~*) tinneas *m*, galar *m*
ill-tempered *adj* **1** crost(a), diombach, gruamach, greannach; **2** (*usu more permanent characteristic*) droch-nàdarrach
ill-timed *adj* mì-thràthail
ill-treatment *n* droch-làimhseachadh *m*
illuminate *v* soilleirich *vt*
illumination *n* soilleireachadh *m*
illustrate *v* dealbhaich *vt*
illustrious *adj* ainmeil, cliùiteach, iomraiteach, òirdheirc
ill-will *n* gamhlas *m*, mì-rùn *m*
im- *neg prefix* do-, mì-, eu-, *eg* **impossible** *adj* do-dhèanta, **impatience** *n* mì-fhoighidinn *f*, **improbable** *adj* eu-coltach
image *n* **1** (*in art, sculpture &c, also in mirror &c, Lit, publicity*) ìomhaigh *f*; **2** (*likeness*) mac-samhail *m*, **he was the ~ of his brother** is e mac-samhail a bhràthar *m gen* a bha ann
imagery *n* ìomhaigheachd *f invar*
imaginary *adj* mac-meanmnach
imagination *n* mac-meanmna *m*
imaginative *adj* mac-meanmnach, tionnsgalach
imagine *v* dealbh *vt*, **an event you couldn't ~** tachartas *m* nach b' urrainn dhut a dhealbhadh
immature *adj* an-abaich
immeasurable *adj* gun tomhas *m*, **at an ~ speed** aig astar *m* gun tomhas
immerse *v* (*in liquid*) bog *vt*, tum *vt*
immersion *n* **1** (*in liquid*) bogadh *m*, tumadh *m*; **2** (*lang teaching &c*) bogadh *m*, **~ course** cùrsa-bogaidh
immigrant *n*, fear-imrich *m*, in-imriche *m*
immigration *n* imrich *f* a-steach, in-imrich *f*
imminent *adj* a tha (*&c*) a' tighinn, **they talked of the ~ conflict** bhruidhinn iad mun chogadh *m* a bha a' tighinn
immoral *adj* mì-bheusach
immorality *n* mì-bheus *f*
immune *adj* saor, dìonta, (**from** o/bho)
impact *n* **1** (*lit: phys*) co-bhualadh *m*; **2** (*fig: effect*) buaidh *f*; **3** (*fig: ~ made on someone*) drùidheadh *m*

impartial *adj* cothromach, gun lethbhreith *f*

impatience *n* **1** mì-fhoighidinn *f*; **2** (*esp for something to be over*) fadachd *f invar*, fadal *m*

impatient *adj* **1** mì-fhoighidneach; **2** (*esp for something to be over: idiom*) **I was ~ all the time he was talking** bha fadachd *f invar* orm fhad 's a bha e a' bruidhinn

impede *v* cuir bacadh *m* (*with prep* air), cuir maille *f invar* (*with prep* air/ ann)

imperative *adj* **1** (*essential*) riatanach, deatamach; **2** (*gram*) àithneach, **the ~ mood** a' mhodh àithneach

imperfect *adj* neo-choileanta

imperial *adj* ìmpireil

impermeable *adj* neo-dhrùidhteach

impersonal *adj* **1** neo-phearsanta; **2** (*of atmosphere, person &c*) fuar, (*of person*) fad' às, dùinte

impersonate *v* pearsanaich *vt*, riochdaich *vt*

impertinence *n* mì-mhodh *m*, beadaidheachd *f invar*, dànadas *m*

impertinent *adj* mì-mhodhail, beadaidh, dàna, bathaiseach

impetuous *adj* bras, cas

impetus *n* deann *f*, dèine *f invar*

implacable *adj* neo-thruacanta

implement *n* inneal *m*, acainn *f*

implement *v* cuir *vt* an gnìomh *m*, thoir *vt* gu buil *f*

implicated *adj & past part*, **~ (in)** an lùib (*with gen*), an sàs (*with prep* ann an), **~ in the plot** an lùib na cuilbheirt

impolite *adj* mì-mhodhail

import[1] *n* (*trade*) bathar *m* a-steach, in-mhalairt *f*

import[2] *n* (*meaning, significance*) seagh *m*, brìgh *f*

import *v* thoir bathar *m sing coll* (*&c*) a-steach

importance *n* **1** diofar *m*, deifir *f*, cudthrom *m*, **it's of no ~** chan eil e gu diofar; **2** (*emphasis*) cudthrom *m*, **lay/put great ~ on X** leig cudthrom mòr air X

important *adj* **1** cudthromach, trom, **~ matters** gnothaichean *mpl* cudthromach, cuspairean *mpl* troma, **a big ~ man** (*ironic*) duine mòr cudthromach *m*; **2** *in expr* **it's not ~** chan eil e gu diofar

impossible, impracticable, *adjs* do-dhèanta

impractical *adj* **1** (*not in keeping with common sense, unrealistic*) neo-phrataigeach; **2** (*cannot be done*) do-dhèanta

impression *n* **1** (*phys mark made on something*) comharradh *m*, lorg *f*; **2** (*~ made on someone*) drùidheadh *m*, **make an ~** drùidh *vi* (*with prep* air), **the news made no ~ on her** cha do dhrùidh an naidheachd *f* oirre (idir), (*fam: idiom*) cha do chuir an naidheachd suas no sìos i; **3** (*mental ~, surmise &c*) **my ~ is that he's a liar** saoilidh mi gur e breugair a th' ann; **4** (*printing*) clò-bhualadh *m*

impressive *adj* drùidhteach

imprint *n* **1** (*phys*) lorg *f*; **2** (*publishing*) clò *m*

imprisonment *n* braighdeanas *m*, daorsa *f invar*, ciomachas *m*

improbable *adj* eu-coltach

impromptu *adj* gun ullachadh *m*

improper *adj* mì-iomchaidh

improve *v* **1** (*as vt*) leasaich *vt*, ~ **the company's profile/image** leasaich ìomhaigh *f* na companaidh; **2** (*as vi*) rach *vi* am feabhas *m*, **the local services are improving** tha na seirbheisean *fpl* ionadail a' dol am feabhas; **3** (*~ in a skill, activity &c: idiom*) **we're improving** tha (am) piseach a' tighinn òirnn

improvement *n* **1** leasachadh *m*, **an ~ grant** tabhartas *m* leasachaidh *gen*; **2** (*in skill, activity &c*) piseach *m*

impudence *n* beadaidheachd *f invar*, dànadas *m*

impudent *adj* beadaidh, dàna, bathaiseach

impulsive *adj* bras

in *prep* **1** (*position, situation*) ann an, ann am, (*with art*) anns an, anns a', sa, san (*&c*), ~ **a mess** ann am bùrach *m*, ~ **a house** ann an taigh *m*, ~ **danger** ann an cunnart *m*, ~ **the house** anns an taigh, ~ **general** san fharsaingeachd *f invar*, ~ **autumn** as t-fhoghar; **2** (*into*) do, **put a bag ~ the car** cuir màileid *f* dhan chàr *m*, **throw a stone ~ the loch** tilg clach *f* dhan loch *m*; **3** (*during*) ri, air, ann an, anns an (*&c*), ~ **my grandfather's time/day** ri linn *mf* mo sheanar, ~ **the afternoon/evening** anns an fheasgar *m*; **4** (*after*) an ceann (*with gen*), ~ **a short time** an ceann *m* ghoirid; **5** (*with compass directions*) mu, **islands ~ the north** eileanan *mpl* mu thuath; **6** (*misc exprs & idioms*) ~ **front of** ro & roimh, *before art* ron (*with the dat*), **a car was ~ front of the door** bha càr *m* ron doras *m*, ~ **Donald's care/charge** air cùram *m* Dhòmhnaill, **he put a piece in his pocket ~ case he should grow hungry** chuir e pìos *m* na phòca *m* gun fhios nach tigeadh an t-acras air

in- *neg prefix* mì-, do-, an-, eu- (*occas* ao-), neo-, *eg* **injustice** *n* mì-cheartas *m*, **innumerable** *adj* do-àireamh, **infirmity** *n* anfhannachd *f invar*, euslainte *f*, **incapable** *adj* neo-chomasach

inaccurate *adj* mearachdach

inactivity *n* tàmh *m*

inadequacy *n* uireasbhaidh *f*

inadequate *adj* uireasbhach

inadvertent neo-aireach

inappropriate *adj* neo-iomchaidh

incalculable *adj* gun tomhas *m*, **at an ~ speed** aig astar *m* gun tomhas

incantation *n* ortha *f*

incapable *adj* neo-chomasach

incessant *adj* leanailteach

incest *n* col *m*

incestuous *adj* colach

inch *n* òirleach *mf*, **he's every ~ a man** (*trad*) is duine *m* gach òirleach dheth

incident *n* tachartas *m*, tuiteamas *m*

incidental *adj* tuiteamach

incisor *n* (*tooth*) clàr-fhiacail *f*

inclination *n* 1 (*desire, wish*) togradh *m*; 2 (*tendency*) aomadh *m*

incline *n* 1 claonadh *m*; 2 (*topog*) leathad *m*, bruthach *mf*

incline *v* 1 crom *vti*, claon *vti*, **she ~ed her head** chrom i a ceann *m*; 2 (*tend*) aom *vi*

inclined *adj* dual(t)ach, buailteach, **they are ~ to be stingy/mean** tha iad dualach/buailteach a bhith spìocach

include *v* gabh *vt* a-steach, **Highland Region ~s Inverness** tha Roinn *f* na Gàidhealtachd a' gabhail a-steach Inbhir Nis

income *n* teachd-a-steach *m invar*, **in expr ~ tax** cìs-c(h)osnaidh *f*

incomer *n* coigreach *m*, srainnsear *m*

incoming *adj* a thig *vi* a-steach, **in expr ~ mail** post *m* a-steach

incompetence *n* neo-chomasachd *f invar*

incompetent *adj* neo-chomasach

incomplete *adj* neo-iomlan

inconsistent *adj* 1 (*liable to vary*) caochlaideach, neo-sheasmhach; 2 (*contradictory &c*) neo-chòrdail (**with** ri)

inconvenience *n* dragh *m*, **I don't want to put you to/cause you any ~** chan eil mi airson dragh a chur oirbh

inconvenience *v* cuir dragh *m* (*with prep* air), (*more fam*) bodraig *vt*, **I don't want to ~ you** chan eil mi airson dragh a chur oirbh/airson ur bodraigeadh

incorrect *adj* mearachdach, ceàrr, **~ report** aithisg mhearachdach

increase *n* 1 meudachadh *m*; 2 (*~ in pay*) àrdachadh *m*

increase *v* meudaich *vti*, cinn *vi*, rach *vi* am meud *m invar*

incumbent *adj* mar fhiachaibh (*obs dat pl of* fiach *m*) (*with prep* air), **it is ~ upon me to say a few words** (*formal*) tha e mar fhiachaibh orm facal *m* no dhà a ràdh

indebted *adj & past part* (*financially & fig*) fo fhiachaibh (*obs dat pl of* fiach *m*) (*with prep* do), **I'm ~ to them**, tha mi fo fhiachaibh dhaibh

indecent *adj* mì-bheusach

indecency *n* mì-bheusachd *f invar*

indeed *adv* 1 gu dearbh, **are you tired? I am ~!** a bheil thu sgìth? tha gu dearbh!, **he's rich! is he ~?** tha e beartach! a bheil gu dearbh? (*also* a bheil, a bheil?); 2 (*as intensifier of an adj or adv*) gu dearbh fhèin, uabhasach fhèin, cianail (fhèin), **very good/very well ~** gu dearbh fhèin math, uabhasach fhèin math, cianail (fhèin) math, *also* math dha-rìribh

indefinite *adj* neo-chinnteach

indentation *n* eag *f*

independence *n* neo-eisimeileachd *f invar*

independent *adj* neo-eisimeileach

index *n* **1** (*to contents of book &c*) clàr-amais *m*; **2** (*scale, yardstick*) clàr-innse *m*,
    ~ **of industrial production** clàr-innse toradh *m* gnìomhachais *m gen*

India *n, used with art,* na h-Innseachan *mpl*

Indian *n & adj* Innseanach *m*

indicate *v* comharraich *vt*

indicative *adj* (*gram*) taisbeanach, **the ~ mood** a' mhodh thaisbeanach

indicator *n* taisbeanair *m*

indifference *n* **1** (*the attitude of mind*) neo-shuim *f*; **2** (*idiom*) **it's a matter of**
    ~ **to me** is coma leam e

indifferent *adj* **1** coma, (*stronger*) coma-co-dhiù, **it's ~ to me** is coma leam
    e, **in the face of her husband's anger she was (completely)** ~ roimh
    fheirg (*dat of* fearg *f*) an duine aice bha i coma-co-dhiù; **2** (*~ quality*) ach
    meadhanach (math), *with neg v,* **the meal was** ~ cha robh am biadh ach
    meadhanach (math)

indigence *n* uireasbhaidh *f*, ainniseachd *f invar*

indigenous *adj* dùthchasach, tùsanach

indigent *adj* uireasbhach, *in expr* **an ~ person** uireasbhach *m*

indignant *adj* diombach & diumbach

indignation *n* diomb & diumb *m invar*

indignity *n* tàmailt *f*

indirect *adj* neo-dhìreach

indispensable *adj* riatanach

indissoluble *adj* do-sgaoilte

individual *adj* **1** (*relating to the individual*) pearsanta, ~ **duty** dleastanas
    pearsanta; **2** (*separate*) fa leth, **he questioned each ~ witness** cheasnaich
    e gach fianais *f* fa leth

individual *n* neach *m invar*, duine *m*, (*more trad*) urra *m*

individually *adv* fa leth, **he questioned each witness** ~ cheasnaich e gach
    fianais *f* fa leth

Indo-European *adj & n* Indo-Eòrpach *m*

indolence *n* leisg(e) *f*

indolent *adj* leisg

industrial *adj* **1** gnìomhachail, tionnsgalach; **2** *in expr* ~ **estate** raon *m*
    gnìomhachais *m gen*

industrious *adj* dèanadach, gnìomhach, dìcheallach

industriousness *n* dèanadas *m*, gnìomhachas *m*

industry *n* **1** (*the abstr quality*) dèanadas *m*; **2** (*manufacturing, manufacturers*
    &c) gnìomhachas *m*, **the electricity/food** ~ gnìomhachas an dealain/a'
    bhidhe

inebriate *v* cuir *vt* air mhisg *f*

inebriated *v* misgeach, air mhisg *f*

inefficiency *n* neo-èifeachdas *m*

inefficient *adj* neo-èifeachdach

inequality *n* eas-aontarachd *f invar*, neo-ionannachd *f invar*

infant *n* leanabh *m*, leanaban *m*, pàiste *m*

infantile *adj* leanabail

infectious *adj* gabhaltach, ~ **diseases** tinneasan *mpl* gabhaltach

inferior *adj* **1** (*in rank, in phys position*) ìochd(a)rach, (n)as ìsle; **2** (~ *in quality*) (n)as miosa (**to** na), **that one is** ~ tha am fear ud nas miosa, *also* chan eil am fear ud cho math

inferior *n* ìochdaran *m*

inferiority *n* ìochdaranachd *f invar*

infernal *adj* ifrinneach

infertile *adj* neo-thor(r)ach

infertility *n* neo-thor(r)achas *m*

infestation *n* plàigh *f*

infinite *adj* neo-chrìochnach

infinitive *adj* (*gram*) neo-chrìochnach

infinity *n* neo-crìochnachd *f invar*

infirm *adj* euslainteach, anfhann

infirmary *n* taigh-eiridinn *m*

infirmity *n* **1** euslaint(e) *f*, anfhannachd *f invar*; **2** (*more transient*) laigse *f*

inflame *v* (*fig: situation &c*) cuir lasair *f* (*with prep* ri)

inflammable *adj* lasanta

inflate *v* sèid *vt* (suas)

inflation *n* **1** (*lit*) sèideadh *m*; **2** (*fin*) atmhorachd *f invar*

inflexible *adj* rag

influence *n* **1** (*personal, political &c*) cumhachd *mf invar*, buaidh *f*; **2** *in expr* **under the** ~ **of** an lùib *f*, fo bhuaidh *f*, (*with gen*), **under the** ~ **of his friends** an lùib/fo bhuaidh a charaidean *mpl*; **3** *in expr* **under the** ~ (*ie of drink*) air mhisg *f*

influence *v* thoir buaidh *f* (*with prep* air)

influential *adj* buadhach, cumhachdach

inform *v* **1** thoir fios *m*, cuir fios, cuir brath *m*, (*all with prep* gu), innis *vti* (*with prep* do), **he** ~**ed me (of it)** thug e fios thugam (mu dheidhinn)

informal *adj* neo-fhoirmeil

informality *n* neo-fhoirmealachd *f invar*

information *n* **1** fiosrachadh *m*, **I'd like to receive** ~ **about the company/ firm** bu toigh leam fiosrachadh fhaighinn air a' chompanaidh *mf*, (*IT*) ~ **technology** teicneolas *m* fiosrachaidh *gen*; **2** (*facts, news &c*) fios *m*, **is there any** ~ **of/about Mary?** a bheil fios air Màiri?

informed *adj* fiosrach, fiosraichte, (**about** air)

infra- *prefix*, fo-, bun-, *prefixes, eg* **infra-red** *adj* fo-dhearg, **infrastructure** *n* bun-structair *m*

ingenious *adj* innleachdach, teòma, tionnsgalach

ingenuity *n* innleachd *f invar*, (*less usu*) tionnsgal *m*

ingredients *n* (*rather trad*) cungaidh *f*

inhabit *v* còmhnaich *vi*, fuirich *vi*, (*with prep* ann an), àitich *vt*

inhabitant *n* neach-àiteachaidh *m*, neach-còmhnaidh *m*, **~s** luchd-àiteachaidh *m sing coll*, luchd-còmhnaidh *m sing coll*, muinntir *f*

inherent *adj* **1** (*in a person*) dual(t)ach, **it's ~ in him to be hospitable** tha e dualach dha a bhith fàilteach; **2** (*in an object, situation &c*) bunaiteach, bunasach, gnèitheach

inherit *v* sealbhaich *vt* (mar oighreachd *f*), faigh *vt* mar oighreachd

inheritance *n* **1** (*esp material ~*) oighreachd *f*, **~ tax** cìs *f* oighreachd *gen*; **2** (*esp cultural ~*) dualchas *m*

inheritor *n* oighre *m*

inimical *adj* nàimhdeil

initial *adj* ciad, *used with art,* a' chiad (*for both m & f nouns*), *precedes the noun, which it lenites where possible,* **the ~ response** a' chiad fhreagairt *f*

initially *adv* an toiseach *m*, an toiseach tòiseachaidh *m gen*, sa chiad dol-a-mach *m invar*, sa chiad àite *m*

injure *v* **1** (*usu phys*) goirtich *vt*, (*phys or emotionally*) leòn *vt*, ciùrr *vt*; **2** (*not usu phys*) dèan cron *m* (*with prep* air)

injured *adj* **1** (*phys or emotionally*) leònta & leònte, ciùrrte; **2** (*as n: in accident, war &c*) **the ~** na leòintich *mpl*

injurious *adj* cronail, lochdach, millteach

injury *n* **1** (*phys or emotional*) leòn *m*; **2** (*not usu phys*) cron *m*

injustice *n* mì-cheartas *m*

ink *n* inc *m invar*, (*more trad*) dubh *m*

inn *n* taigh-òsta *m*

innards *n* innidh *f invar*, mionach *m*, (*esp of animals*) greallach *f*

innate *adj* **1** (*in a person*) dual(t)ach; **2** (*in an object*) gnèitheach

innkeeper *n* òstair *m*, fear *m* (an) taighe *m gen*

innocence *n* neo-chiontachd *f invar*

innocent *adj* neo-chiontach, neochionta

innuendo *n* leth-fhacal *m*

innumerable *adj* do-àireamh

input *n* cur-a-steach *m*

input *v* **1** cuir *vt* ann; **2** (*esp at keyboard*) put *vt* ann

inquiry *n* rannsachadh *m*

inquisitive *adj* ceasnachail, faighneachail

insane *adj* air chuthach *m*, air bhàinidh *f invar*, air bhoile *f invar*, (*more fam*) às a (*&c*) c(h)iall *f*, às a (*&c*) rian *m*, **go ~** rach *vi* air chuthach/air bhàinidh/air bhoile/às a (*&c*) c(h)iall

insanity *n* cuthach *m*, bàinidh *f invar*, boile *f invar*

insect *n* frìde *f*, meanbh-fhrìde *f*

inseparable *adj* do-sgaradh

inside *adv* **1** (*expr position*) a-staigh, **they are ~** tha iad a-staigh; **2** (*expr movement*) a-steach, **come ~!** thig(ibh) a-steach!

inside *n* **1** taobh *m* a-staigh, (*esp of building*) broinn *f*; **2** (*in expr*) ~ **out** caoin *f* air ascaoin *f*

inside *prep* **1** (*expr position*) a-staigh, am broinn (*with gen*), **we were ~ the barn** bha sinn a-staigh san t-sabhal *m*, bha sinn am broinn an t-sabhail, **there's a swimming pool ~ the house** tha amar-snàimh *m* am broinn an taighe *m*; **2** (*expr movement*) a-steach (*with prep* do), **come ~!** thig(ibh) a-steach! (*though note that* thig(ibh) a-staigh *is also commonly used in this sense*), **they went ~ the church** chaidh iad a-steach dhan eaglais *f*

insight *n* **1** (*abstr: the mental faculty or capacity*) tuigse *f invar*, (*less usu*) lèirsinn *f invar*; **2** (*con: knowledge or understanding coming suddenly to one*) geur-bheachd *m*

insignificant *adj* crìon, suarach

insipid *adj* leamhach

inspect *v* sgrùd *vt*

inspection *n* sgrùdadh *m*

inspector *n* neach-sgrùdaidh *m* (*pl* luchd-sgrùdaidh *m sing coll*)

inspire *v* misnich *vt*

instalment *n* earrann *f*

instance *n* **1** (*example*) eisimpleir *m*, **for ~** mar eisimpleir; **2** *in expr* **in the first ~** an *prep* toiseach *m*, anns a' chiad dol-a-mach *m invar*

instant *adj* grad (*precedes the noun, which it lenites where possible*), ~ **coffee** grad-chofaidh *f*

instant *n* **1** mòmaid *f*, plathadh *m*, tiota *m*; **2** (*idiom*) **in an ~** ann am priobadh *m* (na sùla)

instruct *v* **1** (*educate &c*) teagaisg *vt*, oileanaich *vt*, ~ **the new generation** teagaisg an ginealach ùr; **2** (*command &c*) òrdaich *vt* (*with prep* do), **they ~ed me to set fire to the house** dh'òrdaich iad dhomh teine *m* a chur ris an taigh *m*

instruction *n* **1** (*ed*) foghlam *m*, teagasg *m*, oileanachadh *m*; **2** (*command &c*) òrdugh *m*; **3** ~**s** (*for use, assembly &c*) seòladh *m*

instrument *n* **1** (*tool, device &c*) inneal *m*, ball-acainn *m*; **2** (*musical ~*) ionns(t)ramaid *f*, inneal-ciùil *m*

insubordinate *adj* eas-umhail

insulate *v* (*elec &c*) dealaich *vt* (**from** ri)

insulating *adj* (*ie non-conductive*) do-ghiùlan

insult *n* tàmailt *f*, tàir *f*, (**to** air)

insult *v* dèan tàir *f* (*with prep* air), tàmailtich *vt*

insulting *adj* tàmailteach, tàireil

insurance *n* àrachas *m*, urras *m*, ~ **policy** poileasaidh-àrachais *m*

integrity *n* ionracas *m*

intellect *n* inntinn *f*

intellectual *adj* **1** (*of book, person &c: having ~ qualities*) inntinneach; **2** (*to do with the intellect*) inntinn (*gen of* inntinn *f*), ~ **ability/capacity** comas *m* inntinn

intelligence *n* inntinn *f*, tuigse *f invar*

intelligent *adj* toinisgeil, tuigseach, eirmseach

intend *v* bi *vi irreg* airson, (*stronger resolve*) cuir *vt* roimhe (*&c*), rùnaich *vi*, **they ~ed to build a house** bha iad airson/chuir iad romhpa taigh *m* a thogail

intense *adj* **1** (*of persons, emotions, deeds*) dian; **2** (*of heat &c*) anabarrach

intensity *n* dèine *f invar*

intensive *adj* dian, dlùth, **~ farming** tuathanachas dian, **~ care** dlùth-aire *m*

intent, intention *n* rùn *m*, **that was my ~** b' e sin mo rùn, *also* b' e sin a bha mi airson a dhèanamh, **with the sole/express ~ of deceiving us** a dh'aon rùn/a dh'aon ghnothach *m* gus ar mealladh *m*

intentionally *adv* a dh'aon rùn *m*, a dh'aon ghnothach *m*

inter- *prefix* eadar-, *eg* **interface** *n* (*IT &c*) eadar-aghaidh *f*

inter *v* tiodhlaic *vt*, adhlaic *vt*

interact *v* eadar-obraich *vi*

intercourse *n* **1** (*social ~*) conaltradh *m*, caidreabh *m*; **2** (*sexual ~*) cleamhnas *m*, feis(e) *f*, co-ghineadh *m*, cuplachadh *m*; **3** *in exprs* **have (sexual) ~** faigh muin *f invar*, co-ghin *vi*, cuplaich *vi*, **he had ~ with her** chaidh e air a muin

interest *n* **1** ùidh *f* (**in** ann), **I have no ~ in it** chan eil ùidh agam ann, **take an ~ in something** gabh ùidh ann an rudeigin; **2** (*fin*) riadh *m*

interested *adj*, *in exprs* **I'm not ~ (in it)** chan eil ùidh *f* agam ann, **be ~ in something** gabh ùidh ann an rudeigin

interesting *adj* inntinneach, ùidheil

interface *n* (*IT &c*) eadar-aghaidh *f*

interfere *v* gabh gnothach *m* (**in/with** ri), buin *vi* (**in/with** do *or* ri)

interim *adj* eadar-amail

interior *n* taobh *m* a-staigh, (*esp of building*) broinn *f*

interlude *n* eadar-ùine *f*

intermarriage *n* eadar-phòsadh *m*

intermediate *adj* eadar-mheadhanach

intermingle, intermix *v* co-mheasgaich, co-measgaich & coimeasgaich *vti*

international *adj* eadar-nàiseanta, **~ companies** companaidhean *mfpl* eadar-nàiseanta

internet *n* eadar-lìon *m*, **~ site** ionad *m* eadar-lìn *gen*

interpret *v* **1** (*explain &c*) mìnich *vt*; **2** (*lang*) eadar-theangaich *vti*

interpretation *n* **1** mìneachadh *m*; **2** (*lang*) eadar-theangachadh *m*

interpreter *n* (*lang*) eadar-theangaiche *m*

interrogate *v* ceasnaich *vt*

interrogation *n* ceasnachadh *m*

interrogative *adj* ceisteach

interrogator *n* neach-ceasnachaidh *m* (*pl* luchd-ceasnachaidh *m sing coll*)

interrupt *v* bris(t) *vi* a-steach (*with prep* air)

interruption *n* casgadh *m*

interval *n* **1** (*esp in space*) beàrn *f*; **2** (*esp in time*) eadar-ùine *f*

interview *n* agallamh *m*

intestine *n* **1** caolan *m*; **2** ~s innidh *f invar*, (*esp of animals*) greallach *f*

intimate *adj* **1** dlùth, dlùth-chàirdeil; **2** *in exprs* ~ **knowledge/acquaintance** mion-eòlas *m* (**of/with** air); **3** (*sexually* ~) **he was** ~ **with her** chaidh e air a muin *f invar*

into *prep* **1** do, a-steach do, (*with dat*), **throw a stone** ~ **the loch** tilg clach *f* dhan loch *m*, **put cattle** ~ **the byre** cuir sprèidh *f* a-steach don bhàthaich *f*; **2** (*fam: interested in, keen on*) **he's** ~ **computing** tha ùidh mhòr aige ann an coimpiutaireachd *f invar*

intoxicating *adj* daorachail

intoxication *n* daorach *f*, misg *f*

intrepid *adj* dàna, cruadalach

intrepidity *n* dànadas *m*, cruadal *m*

introduce *v* (*people*) cuir *vt* an aithne *f invar* (*with gen*), **I ~d them (to each other)** chuir mi an aithne a chèile *m* iad

introduction *n* **1** (*of people*) cur *m* an aithne *f invar*; **2** (*in book &c*) ro-ràdh *m*

introvert *adj* dùinte

intuition *n* imfhios *m*

intuitive *adj* imfhiosach

inured *adj* dèanta (**to** ri), ~ **to war/poverty** dèanta ri cogadh *m*/bochdainn *f*

invalid *n* euslainteach *m*

invent *v* innlich *vt*, tionnsgail & tionnsgain *vt*

invention *n* (*abstr & con*) innleachd *f*, tionnsgal *m*

inventive *adj* innleachdach, tionnsgalach

inventiveness *n* innleachd *f*, tionnsgal *m*

inventor *n* tionnsgalair *m*, innliche *m*

invert *v* **1** (*turn over*) cuir *vt* bun-os-cionn; **2** (*maths &c: reverse position &c of*) cuir *vt* an àite a chèile, ~ **X and Y** cuir X agus Y an àite a chèile

inverted *adj* & *past part* **1** (*turned over*) bun-os-cionn; **2** *in expr* (*typog*) ~ **commas** cromagan *fpl* turrach

invest *v* (*fin*) cuir *vt* an seilbh *m*, ~ **money/capital** cuir airgead *m*/calpa *m* an seilbh

investigate *v* rannsaich *vt*

investigation *n* rannsachadh *m*

investment *n* **1** (*abstr, also the activity*) cur *m* an seilbh *m*, tasgadh *m*; **2** (*con: the funds invested*) airgead *m* an seilbh, airgead-tasgaidh *m*

investor *n* neach-tasgaidh *m* (*pl* luchd-tasgaidh *m sing coll*)

invigorate *v* neartaich *vt*

invitation *n* cuireadh *m*, fiathachadh *m*, (**to** gu), ~ **to a party** cuireadh gu pàrtaidh *m*, (*idiom*) (**we got) an** ~ **to a wedding** (fhuair sinn) fios *m* na bainnse (*gen of* banais *f*)

invite *v* iarr *vt* (*sometimes with prep* air – *see examples*), thoir cuireadh *m* (*with prep* do), (**to** gu), **we won't** ~ **you to come in** chan iarr sinn oirbh a thighinn a-steach, **they ~d me to a party** dh'iarr iad mi/dh'fhiathaich iad mi/thug iad cuireadh dhomh gu pàrtaidh *m*

invoice *n* cùnntas *m*

involved *adj & past part* **1** an sàs (*with prep* ann an), **~ in politics** an sàs ann am poileataics *f invar*, **get ~ in the work** rach *vi irreg* an sàs anns an obair *f*; **2** *in expr* **get ~** (*ie have to do with*) gabh gnothach *m* (**with** ri), **don't get ~ with those people** na gabh gnothach ris na daoine ud; **3** (*connected with, attached to*) an lùib (*with gen*), **there's plenty of work ~ in my new job** tha obair *f* gu leòr an lùib mo dhreuchd *f gen* ùir

ir- *prefix* mi-, neo-, eas-, *prefixes, eg* **irregular** *adj* mì-riaghailteach, **irresponsible** *adj* neo-chùramach, **irreverent** *adj* eas-umhail, eas-urramach

Ireland *n* Èirinn *f*

Irish *adj* Èireannach, na h-Èireann, **~ Gaelic** Gàidhlig *f* na h-Èireann

Irishman *n* Èireannach

iron *n* (*the metal; also the household implement*) iarann *m*, **the Iron Age** Linn *mf* an Iarainn

iron *v* (*clothes &c*) iarnaich & iarnaig *vti*

iron filings min-iarainn *f*

ironic(al) *adj* ìoranta

ironing *n* iarnachadh & iarnaigeadh *m*

irony *n* ìoran(t)as *m*

irreconcilable *adj* do-rèiteachail

irregular *adj* **1** mì-riaghailteach, mì-òrdail; **2** (*gram*) neo-riaghailteach, **~ verbs** gnìomhairean *mpl* neo-riaghailteach

irrelevant *adj* nach buin (*&c*) ris a' chùis *f*/ris a' ghnothach *m*, gun bhuntainneas *m*, nach eil (*&c*) buntainneach, **this letter is ~** chan eil an litir *f* seo buntainneach, **that remark is ~** chan eil am facal sin a' buntainn ris a' chùis

irresponsible *adj* neo-chùramach

irreverent *adj* eas-umhail, eas-urramach

irrigate *v* uisgich *vti*

irrigation *n* uisgeachadh *m*

irritable *adj* crost(a) & crosda, dranndanach, frionasach, cas

irritate *v* cuir greann *m*, cuir an fhearg, (*with prep* air), **the music ~d me** chuir an ceòl greann orm

irritating *adj* (*situations &c*) frionasach, **they're constantly asking me ~ questions** bidh iad a' cur chèistean *fpl* frionasach orm fad na h-ùine

is *v see under* **be**

Islamic *adj* Ioslamach

island *n* eilean *m*, (*less usu*) innis *f*, **on the ~** anns an eilean, air an eilean

islander *n* eileanach *m*

Islay *n* Ìle *f invar, in exprs* **an ~ person** Ìleach *m*, **from/belonging to ~** Ìleach *adj*

isle *n* eilean *m*, **the Western Isles** Na h-Eileanan Siar, **the Western Isles Council** Comhairle *f* nan Eilean (Siar), **the Isle of Man** Eilean Mhanainn *m gen*

isolated *adj* iomallach, ~ **areas/districts** ceàrnaidhean *mpl* iomallach

Israel *n* Iosrael *&* Israel *f invar*

Israeli *n* Iosralach *&* Israeleach *m*

Israelite *n & adj* (*Bibl, hist*) Iosralach *&* Israeleach *m*

issue *n* (*matter, problem &c*) ceist *f*, cùis *f*, gnothach *m*

issue *v* cuir *vt* a-mach

it *pron* (*f*) i, (*m*) e, **here's a glass, take** ~ seo glainne *f*, gabh i, **he saw** ~ (*m*) chunnaic e e, **he** (*emph*) **did** ~ rinn esan e, **that's** ~ sin e!, **can they do ~?** an urrainn dhaibh a dhèanamh?, (*impersonal* ~) **~'s my sister who left** is i/is e mo phiuthar *f* a dh'fhalbh

Italian *adj & n* **1** Eadailteach *m*; **2** (*lang: used with art*) an Eadailtis *f invar*

italics *npl* clò *m* eadailteach

Italy *n* (*used with art*) An Eadailt *f*

itch *n* tachas *m*

itch *v* tachais *vi*

ivy *n* eidheann *f*

J

jab *n* (*with elbow &c*) ùpag *f*

jab *v* (*esp with elbow*) uillnich *vti*, thoir ùpag *f* (*with prep* do)

jackdaw *n* cathag *f*

jagged *adj* eagach

jam *n* silidh *m invar*

jamb *n* ursainn *f*

janitor *n* dorsair *m*

January *n* Faoilleach, *also* Faoilteach, *m*, *used with art*, am Faoilleach, am Faoilteach, **the 20th of** ~ am ficheadamh là *m* den Fhaoilteach

jaundice *n* (*used with art*) a' bhuidheach

jaw *n* giall *f*, peirceall *m*

jawbone *n* peirceall *m*

javelin *n* gath *m*, sleagh *f*

jealous *adj* **1** (*esp sexually*) eudach & iadach, eudmhor; **2** (*envious*) farmadach

jealousy *n* **1** (*esp sexual*) eud & iad *m invar*, eudach & iadach *m*; **2** (*envy, non-sexual* ~) farmad *m*

jeans *n* dìnichean *fpl*

jeer *v* mag *vi* (**at** air)

jeering *adj* magail

jeering *n* magadh *m* (**at** air)

jelly *m* silidh *m invar*

jersey *n* geansaidh *m*

jest *n* fealla-dhà *f invar*, **half in** ~ eadar fealla-dhà 's da-rìribh *adv*

Jesus *proper name* Ìosa

Jew *n* Iùdhach *m*

jewel *n* seud *m*, àilleag *f*, leug *f*, (*esp one worn as an ornament*) usgar *m*

jeweller *n* seudaire *m*

Jewish *adj* Iùdhach

jiffy *n* (*instant*) priobadh *m* (na sùla), tiota *m*, (*dimin*) tiotan *m*, tiotag *f*, **in a** ~ ann an tiotag, ann am priobadh na sùla

jingle *v* dèan gliong *m*

jingling *n* gliong *m*, gliongartaich *f invar*

job *n* **1** obair *f*, cosnadh *m*, (*usu non-manual*) dreuchd *f*, **out of a** ~ gun obair, gun chosnadh, ~ **centre** ionad *m* obrach *gen*, ionad cosnaidh *gen*; **2** *in expr* (*fam*) **that'll do the** ~/**that's just the** ~ nì sin an gnothach/a' chùis

Jock and Doris *n* (*ie 'one for the road'*) deoch-an-dorais *f invar*

jog *n* (*with elbow &c*) ùpag *f*

jog *v* (*with elbow &c*) put *vt*, thoir ùpag *f* (*with prep* do)

join *v* **1** (*fix, connect*) ceangail *vt* , tàth *vt*, (**to** ri); **2** (*enlist &c*) gabh *vi* (*with prep* ann an), **he** ~**ed the navy** ghabh e san nèibhidh *m*

joint *adj* co- *prefix, eg* ~ **secretary** co-rùnaire *m*, ~ **venture** co-iomairt *f*

joint *n* (*anat*) alt *m*, **the elbow** ~ alt na h-uilne, *in expr* **finger-**~ rùdan *m*

jointed *adj* altach

joke *n* **1** (*usu verbal*) fealla-dhà *f invar*, (*verbal or non-verbal*) abhcaid *f*; **2** (*humorous story*) naidheachd *f*; **3** (*practical* ~) cleas *m*, car *m*, **they played a** ~ **on me** rinn iad cleas orm, thug iad an car asam

joke *v* bi *vi irreg* ri fealla-dhà *f invar*, **I'm not joking!** chan ann ri fealla-dhà a tha mi!, *also* tha mi ann an da-rìribh, tha mi ga chiallachadh

joking *n* fealla-dhà *f invar*

jollity *n* cridhealas *m*,

jostle *n* (*in crowd, in squabble &c*) ùpag *f*

jostle *v* uillnich *vti*, put *vti*

journal *n* **1** (*diary*) leabhar-latha *m*; **2** (*periodical*) iris *f*, ràitheachan *m*

journalist *n* fear-naidheachd *m*, neach-naidheachd *m*, naidheachdair *m*, ~**s** luchd-naidheachd *m sing coll*

journey *n* turas *m*, *in expr* ~**'s end** ceann-uidhe *m*

journey *v* siubhail *vi*, (*less usu*) imich *vi*, triall *vi*

jovial *adj* (*person, atmosphere &c*) cridheil

joy *n* gàirdeachas *m*, àgh *m*

joyful *adj* aighearach, greannmhor, àghmhor

judge *v* **1** breithnich *vti*, thoir breith *f invar* (*with prep* air); **2** *in expr* **judging by** a rèir, **judging by appearances, he's a foreigner** a rèir c(h)oltais *m gen*, 's e coigreach *m* a th' ann (dheth)

judg(e)ment *n* **1** (*the mental faculty or capacity*) tuigse *f invar*, toinisg *f*; **2** (*legal* ~) breith *f invar*, binn *f*, breithneachadh *m*, **pass** ~ thoir breith, thoir a-mach binn, (**on/upon**) air)

juggler *n* cleasaiche *m*

juggling *n* cleasachd *f invar*

juice *n* sùgh *m*, **fruit** ~ sùgh-measa *m*

juicy *adj* sùghmhor

July *n, used with art*, An t-Iuchar *m*

jumble *n* **1** (*collection of misc objects*) treal(l)aich *f*, truileis *f invar*, (*more worthless*) sgudal *m*; **2** (*state of untidiness, disorder*) bùrach *m*, **in a** ~ ann am bùrach *m*, *also* bun-os-cionn, thar a chèile, troimh-a-chèile

jump *n* leum *m*, sùrdag *f*, **standing** ~ cruinn-leum *m*

jump *v* **1** leum *vti*; **2** (*through fear, surprise*) clisg *vi*, **he** ~**ed** chlisg e, **he made me** ~ chuir e clisgeadh *m* orm, chlisg e mi

jumper *n* geansaidh *m*

jumpy *adj* (*nervous &c*) clisgeach

June *n, used with art*, An t-Òg-mhìos, An t-Òg-mhios, An t-Ògmhios *m*

junk *n* **1** (*misc objects, usu untidy*) treal(l)aich *f*, truileis *f invar*, **put that** ~ **on the floor and sit down** cuir an trealaich *m* sin air an làr agus dèan suidhe; **2** (*rubbish*) sgudal *m*

Jura *n* Diùra, *in expr* **a man/someone from** ~ Diùrach *m* (*also adj*)

jury *n* diùraidh *m*

just *adj* (*upright, fair*) dìreach, ceart, cothromach, còir, **a ~ man** duine dìreach/ceart/cothromach/còir, **a ~ decision** breith chothromach

just *adv* **1** (*simply, altogether*) dìreach, **that would be ~ great!** bhiodh sin dìreach sgoinneil!; **2** (*a moment ago*) dìreach, **he's ~ left** tha e dìreach an dèidh falbh; **3** (*expressing agreement*) **~ so!** dìreach (sin)!; **4** *in expr* **~ about** (*ie practically*) cha mhòr, an ìre mhath, **we see her ~ about every day** bidh sinn ga faicinn a h-uile là, cha mhòr, **the winter's ~ about over** tha an geamhradh an ìre mhath seachad; **5** (*in comparisons*) a cheart, **A's ~ as good as B** tha A a cheart cho math ri B

justice *n* ceartas *m*, còir *f*, ionracas *m*, **the Justice Department** Roinn *f* a' Cheartais, **standing up for ~** a' seasamh na còrach (*gen of* còir)

juvenile *adj* leanabail

K

kail *n* càl *m*

keel *n* 1 (*of boat*) druim *m*; 2 (*fig*) *in expr* **put/set on an even ~** (*situations, relationships &c*) rèitich *vt*

keen *adj* 1 èasgaidh, dùrachdach, dian, **~ to do it** èasgaidh a dhèanamh, **~ to get up in the morning** èasgaidh gu èirigh sa mhadainn *f*; 2 *in expr* **~ on** (*ie fond of, person &c*) dèidheil air, **~ on drink/music** dèidheil air deoch-làidir *f*/air ceòl *m*; 3 (*~ for success, ambitious*) gionach

keenness *n* dèine *f invar*

keep *v* 1 cùm *vti*, **~ a grip on/~ hold of something** cùm grèim *m* air rudeigin, **~ back!** cùm/cumaibh air ais!, **I won't ~ you back** cha chùm mi air ais sibh, **how are you ~ing?** ciamar a tha thu/sibh a' cumail?, **we didn't ~ New Year** cha do chùm sinn a' Bhliadhna Ùr, **~ going!** cùm ort!, *also* lean ort!, **~ at it!** cùm ris!, **~ time with someone** cùm caismeachd *f* ri cuideigin, **~ up/pace with someone** cùm ruith *f* ri cuideigin, **~ watch, ~ a look out** cùm faire *f*, *also* dèan faire, **~ away** (*from a specified place*) cùm às an làthair *f*, **~ away** (*from particular people, bad influences &c*) seachain(n) *vt*; 2 (*store, preserve*) glèidh *vt*, **they're being kept in a museum** tha iad gan gleidheadh ann an taigh-tasgaidh *m*

keepsake *n* cuimhneachan *m*

kelp *n* ceilp *f*

kelpie *n* each-uisge *m*

kennel *n* taigh *m* chon (*gen pl of* cù *m*)

kept *adj & past part* glèidhte

kerb *n* (*part of pavement*) iomall *m* cabhsair *m gen*

kernel *n* eitean *m*

kestrel *n* clamhan-ruadh *m*

kettle *n* coire *m*, **put the ~ on** cuir air an coire

key *n* 1 (*for locking &c; also of piano, typewriter, computer &c*) iuchair *f*, (*of pocket calculator &c*) putan *m*, (*IT*) **function ~** iuchair-ghnìomha *f*; 2 (*music: tonality*) gleus *mf*

key in *v* (*data &c*) put *vt* ann

keyboard *n* meur-chlàr *m*

khaki *adj* lachdann

kid *n* 1 (*young goat*) meann *m*; 2 (*child*) pàiste *& pàisde *m*

kid *v* 1 tarraing *vi* (*with prep* à), **I was ~ding you** bha mi a' tarraing asad/asaibh; 2 (*idiom*) **I was only ~ding** cha robh mi ach mas fhìor

kidney *n* dubhag *f*, àra *f*, àirne *f*

kill *v* marbh *vt*

killer *n* marbhaiche *m*, murtair *m*

killing *n* marbhadh *m*

kiln *n* àth *f*

kilo, kilogram *n* cilo *m*, cileagram *m*, **a ~ in weight** cileagram de chudthrom *m*

kilometre *n* cilemeatair *m*

kilt *n* fèile beag *&* fèileadh beag, èile beag *&* èileadh beag

kilt *v* (*ie ~ a garment*) tru(i)s *vt*, **her petticoats were ~ed** bha a còtaichean-bàna air an trusadh

kin *adj* càirdeach (**to** do), **I'm ~ to you** tha mi càirdeach dhut

kind *adj* **1** coibhneil, laghach; **2** (*in corres &c*) **with ~est regards** leis gach deagh dhùrachd *m*

kind *n* seòrsa *m*, (*less usu*) gnè *f invar*, **things of many ~s/of every ~** rudan *mpl* de dh'iomadach seòrsa/de gach seòrsa, **what ~ of a day is it?** dè an seòrsa là *m* a th' ann?, **a book of that ~** leabhar *m* den t-seòrsa

kindle *v* **1** (*as vt*) las *vt*; **2** (*as vi*) gabh *vi*, **the fire ~d** ghabh an teine

kindliness *n* coibhneas *m*

kindly *adj* coibhneil, còir, bàidheil

kindness *n* **1** (*abstr*) coibhneas *m*; **2** (*con: an act of ~*) bàidh *f*

king *n* rìgh *m*

kingdom *n* rìoghachd *f*

kingly *adj* rìoghail

kinship *n* càirdeas *m*, (*~ by blood*) càirdeas-fala (*gen of* fuil *f*), (*~ by marriage*) càirdeas-pòsaidh *m*, *also* cleamhnas *m*

kirkton *n* clachan *m*

kirkyard *n* cladh *m*, clachan *m*, cill *f*

kiss *n* pòg *f*

kiss *v* pòg *vt*

kitchen *n* cidsin *m*

kite *n* **1** (*the flying structure*) iteileag *f*; **2** (*the bird*) clamhan-gobhlach *m*

kitten *n* piseag *f*, isean *m* cait *m gen*

knack *n* liut *f* (**of, for** air), **I haven't got the ~ for that** chan eil an liut agam air sin

knead *v* (*dough*) fuin *vt*

knee *n* glùn *f*

kneecap *n* failmean *&* falman *m*

knees-up *n* (*fam*) ho-ro-gheallaidh *m invar*

knickers *n* drathais *&* drathars *fpl invar*

knight *n* ridire *m*

knit *v* figh *vti*

knitted *adj & past part* fighte

knitter *n* figheadair *m*

knitting *n* fighe *f invar*, **~ needle** bior-fighe *m*

knob *n* cnap *m*, cnag *f*

knobby, knobbly *adj* cnapach

knock *n* **1** (*esp the sound*) cnag *f*; **2** (*deliberate ~, on door &c*) gnogadh *m*; **3** (*blow, impact*) buille *f*, bualadh *m*

knock *v* **1** (*as vi*) cnag *vi*; **2** (*as vt*) gnog *vt*, ~ **at the door** gnog an doras; **3** (*strike*) buail *vt*; **4** *in expr* ~ **down** *v* leag *vt*

knocking *n* (*noise, on door &c*) gnogadh *m*

knoll *n* tom *m*, cnoc *m*, tulach *m*, (*smaller*) tolman *m*

know *v* **1** (*esp people*) bi *vi irreg* eòlach (*with prep* air), is *vi irreg & def* aithne *f invar* (*with prep* do), **that's Hugh, do you ~ him?** 's e sin Ùisdean, a bheil thu eòlach air?/an aithne dhut e?, **get to ~ someone** cuir aithne/eòlas *m* air cuideigin; **2** (*of facts, information*) bi *vi irreg* fios *m* (*with prep* aig), **I ~** tha f(h)ios agam, **they didn't ~ he was ill** cha robh fios aca gun robh e tinn, **no-one ~s/it's not ~n where he is** chan eil fios càite a bheil e; **3** *in expr* **let ~** cuir fios, leig fios, (*with prep* gu), **will you let us ~?** an cuir sibh/an leig sibh fios thugainn?

knowe *n* tom *m*, cnoc *m*, tulach *m*, (*small ~*) tolman *m*

knowledge *n* **1** (*information*) fios *m*, **has anyone any ~ of his whereabouts?** a bheil fios aig duine *m* càit a bheil e?; **2** (*more structured or learned ~*) eòlas *m*, **~ of computers/history** eòlas air coimpiutairean *mpl*/eachdraidh *f*

knowledgeable *adj* eòlach, fiosrach (**about/on** air)

knuckle *n* rùdan *m*

kyle, kyles *n* caol *m*, caolas *m*

L

label *n* bileag *f*

label *v* cuir bileag *f* (*with prep* air), bileagaich *vt*

laboratory *n* obair-lann *f*, deuchainn-lann *f*

labour *n* 1 saothair *f*, obair *f*, ~ **costs** cosgaisean *fpl* saothrach *gen*, ~ **relations** dàimhean-obrach *mpl*; 2 (*pol*) **Labour** na Làbaraich *mpl*, am Pàrtaidh Làbarach

labour *v* saothraich *vi*

labourer *n* oibriche *m*

lace *n* (*of shoe*) barrall *m*, iall *f* bròige *f gen*

lacerate *v* reub *vt*

lack *n* dìth *m*, cion *m invar*, easbhaidh *f*, ~ **of practice** dìth cleachdaidh *m gen*, ~ **of common sense** dìth cèille (*gen of* ciall *f*)

lack *v* 1 bi *vi irreg* às aonais (*with gen*), bi gun, **they ~ a house** tha iad às aonais taighe *m gen*, (*more usu*) chan eil taigh aca, **~ing common sense** gun chiall *f*; 2 (*exprs where the thing lacked is the subject in the Gaelic sentence*) bi a (*for* de) dhìth *m*, bi a dh'easbhaidh *f*, (*with prep* air), **they ~ a house** tha taigh *m* a dhìth orra, **what do they ~?** dè a tha a dhìth orra?

lacking *adj* 1 a dhìth, a dh'easbhaidh, **food is ~** tha biadh *m* a dhìth; 2 gun, às aonais (*with gen*), **a family ~ a place to stay** teaghlach *m* gun àite-còmhnaidh *m*

lad *n* gille *m*, balach *m*

ladle *n* ladar *m*, liagh *f*

lady *n* 1 (*polite for* **woman**) bean-uasal *f*; 2 (*female equivalent of* **lord**) baintighearna *f*, leadaidh *f*

ladybird *n* daolag-bhreac-dhearg *f*

lag (behind) *v* bi *vi irreg* air dheireadh

lair *n* garaidh *m*

laird *n* uachdaran *m*, tighearna *m*

lake *n* loch *m*, (*smaller*) lochan *m*

lamb *n* 1 (*the animal*) uan *m*; 2 (*the meat*) uainfheòil *f*

lame *adj* crùbach, bacach, cuagach, *in expr* ~ **person** crùbach *m*, bacach *m*

lament *n* tuireadh *m*, (*trad, Lit*) cumha *m*

lament *v* caoidh *vti*, caoin *vi*, dèan tuireadh *m*, **a man doesn't ~ what he doesn't see** cha chaoidh duine *m* an rud *m* nach fhaic e

lamentation *n* caoidh *f*, tuireadh *m*

lamp *n* lampa *mf*, (*less usu*) lòchran *m*, *in expr* **oil ~** crùisgean *m*

land *n* 1 (*territory, country*) dùthaich *f*, tìr *mf*, **a foreign ~** dùthaich/tìr chèin, **the Mackay ~s** Dùthaich MhicAoidh; 2 (*earth, agricultural ~*) talamh *m* (*f in gen sing*), fearann *m*, **arable/cultivated ~** talamh-àitich, **cultivate/till the ~** àitich am fearann, **fallow ~** talamh bàn, **a piece of ~** pìos *m* fearainn *gen*; 3 (~ *as opposed to sea*) tìr *mf*, **on ~** air tìr

land *v* laigh *vi*, **the plane ~ed** laigh a' phlèana *mf*

landing-place *n* **1** (*for boats*) laimrig *f*, cidhe *m*; **2** (*for aircraft*) raon-laighe *m*

landlady *n* (*of hotel, pub, boarding house &c*) bean *f* taighe *m gen*, **the ~** bean an taighe

landlord *n* (*of pub &c*) fear-taighe *m*, òstair *m*, **the ~** fear an taighe *m*

landmark *n* (*for navigation*) comharradh-stiùiridh *m*, iùl *m*

landowner *n* **1** neach-fearainn *m* (*pl* luchd-fearainn *m sing coll*); **2** (*esp landed gentry*) tighearna *m*, uachdaran *m*

landscape *n* **1** (*phys*) cruth-tìre *m*; **2** (*in art &c*) dealbh-tìre *mf*, sealladh-tìre *m*

lane *n* caol-shràid *f*, lònaid *f*

language *n* **1** (*esp in general & abstr sense*) cainnt *f*, **the faculty of ~** comas *m* cainnte *gen*, **bad ~** droch chainnt, **~ laboratory** cainnt-lann *f*; **2** (*national &c ~*) cànan *m*, cànain *f*, **the ~ of the Gaels** cànan nan Gàidheal *mpl*, **a foreign ~** cànan cèin, **a lesser-used/minority ~** mion-chànan *m or* cànan beag; **3** (*IT*) **programming ~** cànan-prògramaidh *m*

lanky *adj* caol, seang

lantern *n* lanntair *m*, lainntear *m*, (*less usu*) lòchran *m*

lap *n* uchd *m*, **the boy was sitting on her ~** bha am balach na shuidhe air a h-uchd

lap *v* imlich *vt*

lapwing *n* curracag *f*

large *adj* **1** mòr, (*esp bulky, burly*) tomadach *&* tomaltach, **a ~ estate** oighreachd mhòr, **a ~ quantity** meud mòr, **a ~ man** duine mòr, **a ~ book** leabhar tomadach; **2** *in expr* **by and ~** san fharsaingeachd *f invar*, **by and ~, the majority are against him** san fharsaingeachd, tha a' mhòr-chuid na aghaidh

larger *comp adj* mò/motha

lark *n* **1** (*bird*) uiseag *f*, topag *f*; **2** (*spree, fun*) plòigh *f*, spòrs *f*; **3** (*trick &c*) car *m*, cleas *m*

laser *n* leusair *m*, **~ beam** gath *m* leusair *gen*

lass, lassie *n* caileag *f*, nighean *f*

last *adj* mu dheireadh, deireannach, **this is the ~ opportunity you'll get** 's e seo an cothrom mu dheireadh a gheibh thu, **on the ~ day** air an là deireannach, air an là mu dheireadh

last *adv* **1** (*in final position*) air deireadh, **she came ~** thàinig i air deireadh; **2** (*of time*) *in expr* **at (long) ~** mu dheireadh (thall), **the rain stopped at (long) ~** sguir an t-uisge mu dheireadh (thall)

last *v* **1** (*survive, ~ out &c*) mair *vi*, **it won't ~ two days** cha mhair e dà là *m sing*; **2** (*continue, persist*) lean *vi*, **will the fine weather ~?** an lean an deagh aimsir *f*?

lasting *adj* maireannach, leantainneach, **~ peace** sìth mhaireannach

latch *n* clàimhean *m*

late *adj & adv* **1** (*after appointed time &c*) air deireadh, fadalach, **she came ~**

thàinig i air deireadh, **five minutes** ~ còig mionaidean *fpl* air deireadh, **I was** ~ bha mi fadalach; 2 (*advanced hour*) anmoch, ~ **at night** anmoch san oidhche *f*, **it was getting** ~ bha e a' fàs anmoch; 3 (*deceased person*) nach maireann (*verbal noun of* mair *vi*), **the** ~ **Johnny Campbell** Seonaidh Caimbeul nach maireann

Latin *adj* Laidinneach

Latin *n* (*lang*) Laideann *f*

latter *adj*, *in exprs* **at the** ~ **end** aig a' cheann *m* thall, **at the** ~ **day** air an là *m dat* dheireannach

lattice cliath-uinneig *f*

laugh *n* gàire *mf invar*

laugh *v* dèan gàire *mf invar*, gàir *vi*

laughing *n* gàireachdainn *f invar*, gàireachdaich *f invar*

laughing-stock *n* cùis-mhagaidh *f*, adhbhar *m* gàire *mf invar*, **they were a** ~ bha iad nan cùis-mhagaidh/nan adhbhar gàire

laughter *n* gàire *mf invar*, gàireachdainn *f invar*

launch *v* 1 (*boat*) cuir *vt* air flod *m*, cuir *vt* air bhog *f*; 2 (~ *company &c*) cuir *vt* air chois (*dat of* cas *f*), cuir *vt* air bhonn *m*

laundry *n* taigh-nighe *m*

law *n* lagh *m*, **against the** ~ an aghaidh an lagha

lawful *adj* 1 (*not against the law*) laghail; 2 (*legitimate*) dligheach

lawn *n* faiche *f*, rèidhlean *m*

lawsuit *n* cùis *f*, cuis-lagha *f*

lawyer *n* neach-lagha *m* (*pl* luchd-lagha *m sing coll*)

lay *n* (*poem, song*) laoidh *mf*

lay *v* 1 (*floortiles &c*) leag *vt*; 2 (*egg*) beir *vt*; 3 (*misc exprs*) ~ **bare** lom *vt*, ~ **blame** cuir coire *f* (**on** air), ~ **great emphasis on X** leig cudthrom mòr air X

laziness *n* leisg(e) *f*

lazy *adj* leisg

lazy-bed *n* feannag *f*

lazybones *n* leisgeadair *m*

lead *adj* (*principal &c*) prìomh, ~ **singer** prìomh sheinneadair *m*

lead *n* 1 (*example to be followed*) stiùir *f*, **give a/the** ~ thoir stiùir (**to do**); 2 (*leading position*) *in expr* **he was in the** ~ bha e air thoiseach; 3 (*dog's* ~) iall *f*

lead *n* (*metal*) luaidhe *mf invar*, **a** ~ **soldier** saighdear *m* luaidhe *gen*

lead *v* 1 treòraich *vt*, stiùir *vt*, **he led his congregation to Canada** threòraich e a choitheanal *m* gu Canada; 2 (*as vi: be in the lead*) bi *vi irreg* air thoiseach, **they led/were ~ing after five minutes** bha iad air thoiseach an dèidh chòig mionaidean *fpl*; 3 *in expr* ~ **astray** (*morally*) claon *vt*, (*phys or morally*) cuir *vt* air seachran *m*, cuir *vt* air iomrall *m*

leader *n* ceannard *m*

leadership *n* ceannardas *m*

leaf *n* (*of tree, book*) duilleag *f*

leaflet *n* (*publicity &c*) duilleachan *m*, bileag *f*

leak *n* aodion *m*

leaking *adj* aodionach

leakproof *adj* (*house, boat &c*) dìonach, uisge-dìonach

leaky *adj* aodionach

lean *adj* **1** (*of person*) tana, seang; **2** (*of meat*) gun saill *f*, neo-shultmhor

lean *v* **1** (*ie not upright*) bi *vi irreg* air fhiaradh *m*, **the post ~ed/was ~ing** bha am post air fhiaradh; **2** (*~ for support*) cuir/leig a (*&c*) t(h)aic *f*, cuir/leig a (*&c*) c(h)udthrom *m*, (**on** air, **against** ri), **~ on me**, cuir/leig do thaic orm, **~ against a tree** cuir/leig do thaic ri craoibh (*dat of* craobh *f*)

leaning *adj* **1** (*not vertical*) claon, air fhiaradh *m*; **2** (*supported*) an taic *f*, an tacsa *m*, (**against** ri), **~ against a tree** an taic ri craoibh (*dat of* craobh *f*)

leap *n* leum m

leap *v* leum *vti*

leap year *n* bliadhna-leum *f*

learn *v* ionnsaich *vti*, (*~ less formally*) tog *vt*, **I ~t my Gaelic in Skye** thog mi mo chuid *f* Gàidhlig *f* san Eilean *m* Sgitheanach

learned *adj* foghlaimte, foghlamaichte

learner *n* neach-ionnsachaidh *m* (*pl* luchd-ionnsachaidh *m sing coll*)

learning *n* **1** (*knowledge, scholarship*) ionnsachadh *m*, foghlam *m*, oideachas *m*; **2** (*traditional ~*) beul-oideachas *m*

lease *n* gabhail *mf*, **the farmer took the ~ of a farm** ghabh an tuathanach *m* tuathanas *m* air gabhail

lease *v* **1** (*~ out*) thoir *vt* (seachad) air gabhail *mf*/air mhàl *m*, **the landlord ~d (out) a farm** thug an t-uachdaran seachad tuathanas *m* air gabhail; **2** (*rent, take on lease*) gabh *vt* air mhàl *m*, **the farmer ~ed a farm** ghabh an tuathanach *m* tuathanas air mhàl

leash *n* iall *f*

least 1 *comp adj* lugha; **2** *in expr* **at ~** co-dhiù, **there were 2000 there at ~** bha dà mhìle *m sing* ann co-dhiù, **at ~, that's what he said** 's e sin a thuirt e, co-dhiù; **3** *in expr* **at the very ~** aig a' char *m* as lugha, **at the very ~ we lost two thousand pounds** aig a' char as lugha chaill sinn dà mhìle nota *f sing*

leather *adj* leathair (*gen of* leathar *m*), **a ~ jacket** seacaid *f* leathair

leather *n* leathar *m*

leave *n* **1** (*permission*) cead *m invar*, **by your ~** le ur cead; **2** (*parting*) cead *m invar*, *in expr* **take ~** gabh cead (**of** de), dealaich *vi* (*with prep* ri), **we took our ~ of them** ghabh sinn ar cead dhiubh, dhealaich sinn riutha; **3** (*~ from army &c*) fòrladh *m*

leave *v* **1** (*depart*) falbh *vi*, **they left yesterday** dh'fhalbh iad an-dè, **she's left** tha i air falbh; **2** (*depart from*) fàg *vt*, **leaving Stornoway** a' fàgail Steòrnabhaigh; **3** (*put, leave behind*) fàg *vt*, **where did you ~ the car?** càite na dh'fhàg thu an càr?; **4** (*make, cause to be, with adj*) fàg *vt*, **the**

journey left them tired dh'fhàg an turas sgith iad; **5** (*desert, abandon*) trèig *vt*, **he left his family** thrèig e a theaghlach *m*; **6** (~ *in one's will*) tiomnaich *vt* (**to** do); **7** (*entrust with a task &c*) leig *vt* (*with preps* le *or* do), ~ **it to her to bring up the child** leig leathase am pàiste a thogail, ~ **it to me** (*ie* I'll handle it/see to it *&c*) leig dhomhsa e

leavings *n* fuidheall *&* fuigheall *m*, **he got his pick of it, I got the** ~ fhuair esan a roghainn *mf* dheth, fhuair mise am fuidheall

lecher *n* drùisear *m*

lecherous *adj* drùiseach

lechery *n* drùis *f*

lecture *n* òraid *f*, **give a** ~ thoir seachad òraid, dèan òraid

lecturer *n* òraidiche *m*

ledge *n* **1** (*topog*) leac *f*; **2** (*of window*) oir *f* na h-uinneig(e)

leek *n* creamh-gàrraidh *m*

lees *n* (*in liquids*) grùid *f*

left *adj* **1** clì, ceàrr, **my** ~ **foot** mo chas chlì; **2** *in expr* **on his/her** ~ air a làimh (*dat of* làmh *f*) chlì

left-handed *adj* ciotach

leg *n* cas *f*

legacy *n* (*lit or fig*) dìleab *f*, **the** ~ **of history** dìleab na h-eachdraidh

legal *adj* **1** (*not against the law, also, to do with the law*) laghail; **2** (*legitimate &c*) dligheach

legend *n* uirsgeul *m*, fionnsgeul *m*, faoinsgeul *m*

legendary *adj* uirsgeulach

legible *adj* so-leughte

legislate *v* reachdaich *vi*

legislation *n* **1** (*the action*) reachdachadh *m*; **2** (*the actual laws &c*) reachdas *m*

legislature *n* reachdaireachd *f*

legitimate *adj* dligheach

leisure *n* **1** saor-ùine *f*; **2** *in exprs* **I am at** ~ tha mi nam thàmh *m*, ~ **pursuits/ activities** cur-seachadan *mpl*

leisurely *adj* socrach, **a** ~ **pace** ceum socrach

lemon liomaid *f*

lend *v* thoir *vt* air iasad *m*, thoir iasad (*with prep* de), (**to** do), **I lent James a pound** thug mi nota *f* do Sheumas air iasad, thug mi iasad de nota do Sheumas

length *n* fad *m*, **a mile in** ~ mìle *mf* a (*for* de) dh'fhad, **it flew the** ~ **of the house** dh'itealaich e air fad an taighe, **increasing in** ~ a' dol am fad

lengthen *v* **1** (*as vt*) cuir *vt* am fad, **we ~ed it** chuir sinn am fad e; **2** (*as vi*) rach *vi* am fad, **it's ~ing** tha e a' dol am fad, *also* tha e a' fàs nas fhaide

lenite *v* (*lang*) sèimhich *vt*

lenition *n* (*lang*) sèimheachadh *m*

lens *n* lionsa *f*

leopard *n* liopard *m*

leper *n* lobhar *m*

leprosy *n* luibhre *f invar*

lesbian *adj & n* leasbach *f*

-less *suffix* mì-, eu- (*occas* ao-), *eg* **careless** mì-chùramach, **hopeless** eu-dòchasach

lessen *v* **1** lùghdaich *vti*, rach *vi* sìos, **the noise ~ed** lùghdaich am fuaim, chaidh am fuaim sìos; **2** *in expr* **his suffering/pain ~ed** thàinig faothachadh *m* air

lesser *adj* **1** as lugha, (*in past & conditional tenses*) a bu lugha, **the ~ number/ quantity** an àireamh/am meud as lugha; **2** mion- *prefix*, beag, **lesser-used language** mion-chànan *m*, cànan beag; **3** (*in names of birds, animals &c*) beag, **~ black-backed gull** farspag bheag

lesson *n* leasan *m*

lest *conj* air eagal is gu, gun fhios nach, mus, **he put a piece in his pocket ~ he should grow hungry** chuir e pìos *m* na phòca *m* gun fhios nach tigeadh an t-acras air, **he kept hold of her ~ she should fall** chùm e grèim *m* oirre mus tuiteadh i/air eagal 's gun tuiteadh i

let *v* **1** (*permit*) leig *vt* (*with prep* le), **he ~ me buy it** leig e leam a cheannach, **~ her be!/~ her get on with it!** leig leatha!, **will you ~ us know?** an leig sibh fios *m* dhuinn?, *also* an cuir sibh fios thugainn?; **2** *in expr* **~ go** (*ie release*) leig às *vt*, saor *vt*, fuasgail *vt*, (*esp from captivity*) leig *vt* mu sgaoil *m invar*, cuir *vt* mu sgaoil, **~ the dogs go** leig às na coin (*pl of* cù *m*), **they ~ the prisoners go** leig/chuir iad na prìosanaich *mpl* mu sgaoil; **3** *in expr* **~ off/out** (*ie emit &c*) leig *vt* (*with or without adv* às), **he ~ off a fart** leig e braim *m* (às), *also* rinn e braim, **they ~ out a yell** leig iad às sgreuch *m*; **4** *in expr* **~ on** (*ie give the game away &c*) leig *vi* (*with prep* air), **we didn't ~ on** cha do leig sinn òirnn; **5** *in expr* **~ down** (*ie lower*) leag *vt*, **he ~ down the window** leag e an uinneag *f*; **6** *in expr* **~ down** (*ie disappoint &c*) leig *vt* sìos; **7** (*idiom*) **~ me see** fuirich ort, fan ort, **that happened . . . , ~ me see now . . . , in Stornoway** thachair sin . . . , fuirich ort . . . , ann an Steòrnabhagh; **8** (**~ property &c**) thoir *vt* (seachad) air mhàl *m*, **he has ~ his house** tha e air an taigh *m* aige a thoirt seachad air mhàl; **9** (*imper: can be archaic*) *expressed by imper forms of verb*, *eg* **~ us see** faiceamaid, **~ them hear** chluinneadh iad, **~ me not go** na racham

letter *n* (*corres, orthography*) litir *f*, **thank you for your ~** tapadh leat airson do litreach *gen*, **~s of the alphabet** litrichean na h-aibidil(e)

lettuce *n* leiteis *f*

level *adj* rèidh, còmhnard

level *n* **1** (*of progress, development, ability &c*) ìre *f invar*; **2** (*of rank, attainment, ability*) inbhe *f*; **3** (*of height, volume*) àirde *f*

lever *n* luamhan *m*

lewd *adj* drabasta, draosta, collaidh

lewdness *n* drabastachd *f invar*, draostachd *f invar*

Lewis *n* Leòdhas *or* Eilean *m* Leòdhais, *(nickname, in songs &c)* Eilean Fraoich *(gen of* fraoch *m)*

Lewisman *n* Leòdhasach *m*, **Lewis woman** ban *f* Leòdhasach

lexicography *n* faclaireachd *f invar*

liable *adj* buailteach, ~ **to change** buailteach do chaochladh *m*, ~ **to spend money** buailteach airgead *m* a chosg

liar *n* breugaire *m*

libel *n* tuaileas *m*

libel *v* cuir tuaileas *(with prep* air*)*

liberal *adj* **1** *(generous)* fialaidh, fial, tabhartach; **2** *(permissive &c)* ceadach, ceadachail; **3** *(pol)* libearalach *(m & adj)*, ~ **democrat** libearalach deamocratach

liberate *v* saor *vt*, cuir/leig *vt* mu sgaoil, fuasgail *vt*

library *n* leabharlann *mf*

lice *npl* mialan *fpl*

licence *n* cead *m invar*, **driving** ~ cead-dràibhidh *m*, **television** ~ cead telebhisein *m gen*

license *v* ceadaich *vt*, ùghdarraich *vt*

licensee *n* *(of public house, hotel)* òstair *m*, fear *m* (an) taighe

licensing *n* ceadachadh *m*, ùghdarrachadh *m*, *in expr* ~ **board** bòrd *m* ceadachaidh *gen*, bòrd-ceadachd *m*

lichen *n* crotal *m*

licit *adj* ceadaichte, laghail

lick *n* imlich *f*

lick *v* imlich *vti*

lie *n* breug *f*, **tell a** ~ innis breug

lie[1] *v* laigh *vi*, ~ **down** laigh sìos, **I lay down** laigh mi sìos, *in expr* **lying (down)** na *(&c)* laighe *mf invar*, **she's lying down** tha i na laighe, **they were lying (down) on the ground** bha iad nan laighe air an làr *m*

lie[2] *v* *(tell untruths)* innis/dèan breug(an) *f(pl)*

life *n* **1** *(abstr & con)* beatha *f*, *(more trad: con)* saoghal *m*, **a hard** ~ beatha chruaidh, **all my** ~ fad mo bheatha *gen*, **way of** ~ dòigh-beatha *f*, ~ **cycle** cearcall *m* (na) beatha, ~ **member** ball beatha *gen*, *in expr* **long** ~ **to you!** saoghal fada dhuibh!; **2** *(the breath of ~)* deò *f invar*, *(a spark of ~)* rong *m*, **as long as there's** ~ **in me** fhad 's a bhios an deò annam, **there wasn't a spark of** ~ **in her** cha robh rong innte; **3** *(lifespan, lifetime)* maireann *m*, beò *m*, là *m*, **he never left the island in his** ~ cha do dh'fhàg e an t-eilean ri bheò/ri mhaireann, **at the end of my** ~ aig crìoch *f* mo là *gen*; **4** *in exprs* **he was running for dear** ~ bha e a' ruith mar a bheatha, bha e a' ruith aig peilear *m* a bheatha, ~ **expectancy** dùil *f* aois *f gen*

life-belt *n* crios-sàbhalaidh *m*, crios-teasairginn *m*

lifeboat *n* bata-teasairginn *m*, bàta-coibhre *m*

life-jacket *n* seacaid-teasairginn *f*

lifelong *adj* fad-beatha

lifestyle *n* dòigh-beatha *f*

lifetime *n* maireann *m*, beò *m*, là *m*, rè *f invar*, linn *mf*, (*trad*) saoghal *m*, **in/during my** ~ rim mhaireann, rim bheò, rim latha, rim shaoghal, **in my grandfather's** ~ an rè mo sheanar *m gen*, ri linn mo sheanar, **at the end of my** ~ aig deireadh *f* mo là *gen*

lift *v* tog *vt* (**from** de, far), ~ **stones from the ground** tog clachan *fpl* den làr *m*/far na talmhainn (*gen f of* talamh *m*), ~ (**up**) **your head** tog do cheann *m*, **that ~ed my spirits** thog sin mo chridhe *m*

light *adj* aotrom, ~ **stones/music** clachan *fpl*/ceòl *m* aotrom

light *n* **1** (*natural or artificial*) solas *m*, **ray/beam of** ~ gath *m* solais, **put the** ~ **on/off** cuir air/às an solas, **electric** ~ solas-dealain *m*; **2** (*misc idioms & exprs*) **the Northern Lights** Na Fir *mpl* Chlis, **bring to** ~ thoir *vt* am follais *f invar*, **come to** ~ thig *vi* am follais

light *v* **1** las *vti*, ~ **a cigarette** las toitean *m*, (*fig*) **his face would** ~ **up** bhiodh aodann *m* a' lasadh; **2** (~ *fire, lamp &c*) cuir *vt* air, ~ **the fire** cuir air an teine *m*; **3** *in expr* ~ **upon** (*ie come to rest upon*) laigh *vi* (*with prep* air), **each thing his eye would** ~ **upon** gach rud *m* air an laigheadh a shùil *f*; **4** *in expr* ~ **upon** (*ie come upon by chance*) amais *vi* air

light-heartedness *n* mire *f invar*, sunnd *m invar*, aighearachd *f invar*

lightning *n* dealanach *m*

like *adj* **1** (*similar*) coltach (*with prep* ri), **she's not** ~ **her brother** chan eil i coltach ri a bràthair, ~ **each other** coltach ri chèile; **2** (*stronger: just/exactly* ~) ionann agus, *takes the v is*, **A is (exactly)** ~ **B** is ionann A agus B; **3** (*idioms*) **you look** ~ **a soldier** tha coltas *m* saighdeir *m gen* ort, **I'm tired! you look** ~ **it!** tha mi sgìth! tha a choltas (sin) ort!; **4** mar (*a following noun without the art is in the dat, & lenited*), **singing** ~ **a girl** a' seinn mar chaileig, **he left, just** ~ **his brother** dh'fhalbh e, dìreach mar a bhràthair; *NB: Note the difference between* **he is** ~ (*ie resembles*) **his sister** tha e coltach ri phiuthar, *and* **he sings** ~ **his sister** (*ie sings as his sister sings*) bidh e a' seinn mar a phiuthar

like *n* leithid *f*, coimeas *m*, samhail *m*, **a man the** ~(**s**) **of him** a *poss adj* leithid de dhuine *m*, **his/her** ~ **never existed** cha robh a leithid ann a-riamh, **I never saw his** ~ chan fhaca mi a-riamh a leithid/a choimeas/a shamhail, **the** ~(**s**) **of that** a leithid sin

like *v* **1** is *vi irreg def* toigh (*with prep* le), (*can be stronger: be fond of*) bi *vi irreg* dèidheil (*with prep* air), **I** ~ **my school/the teacher** is toigh leam an sgoil *f* agam/an tidsear *m*, **I** ~ **Mary/chocolate** tha mi dèidheil air Màiri/air teoclaid *mf*; **2** (*wish, desire*) togair *vti* (*often used as vi in relative future tense*), **we'll go on holiday, if you** ~ thèid sinn air laithean-saora *mpl*, ma thogras tu, **just as you** ~ dìreach mar a thogras sibh; **3** *in expr* (*in shop, café &c*) **what would you** ~? dè (a) tha a dhìth oirbh?

likeable *adj* tlachdmhor, taitneach, ciatach

likelihood *n* coltas *m*

likely *adj* coltach, **it's** ~ **that she'll come** tha e coltach gun tig i

liken *v* coimeas *vt*, dèan coimeas *m* (*with prep* eadar), ~ **A and B** coimeas A agus B, dèan coimeas eadar A agus B

likeness *n* **1** (*abstr: resemblance*) coltas *m*; **2** (*con: representation in portrait, sculpture &c*) ìomhaigh *f*; **3** (*shape, disguise &c*) riochd *m*, **he appeared in the** ~ **of a cat** nochd e an riochd cait *m gen*

likewise *adv* cuideachd, mar an ceudna, **I was good at dancing, my sister** ~ bha mi math air dannsadh, (agus) mo phiuthar cuideachd/ mar an ceudna

liking *n* **1** (*affection*) tlachd *f invar*, spèis *f*, bàidh *f*; **2** *in expr* **he has a** ~ **for (chocolate &c)** tha e dèidheil air (teoclaid *mf &c*)

lily *n* lili(dh) *f*

limit *n* **1** (*maximum permitted*) crìoch *f*, **speed** ~ crìoch astair *m gen*, astar-chrìoch *f*; **2** (*edge, boundary*) crìoch *f*, iomall *m*, **the ~(s) of the country** crìoch/iomall na dùthcha

limit *v* cuingealaich *vt* (**to** ri), cuir crìoch *f* (*with prep* ri), **~ed to five minutes** air a chuingealachadh ri còig mionaidean *fpl*, **he ~ed our costs** chuir e crìoch ri ar cosgaisean *fpl*

limited *adj* **1** (*people, attitudes*) cumhang; **2** (*business*) earranta, **a** ~ **company** companaidh *mf* earranta, **Birlinn** ~ Birlinn Earranta

limping *adj* cuagach, bacach, crùbach

line *n* **1** (*pencil* ~, *phone* ~ *&c*) loidhne *f*, **parallel ~s** loidhnichean co-shìnte, (*IT*) **on** ~ air loidhne; **2** (~ *of verse or prose, of people, objects*) sreath *mf*

line *v* (*curtains &c*) lìnig *vt*

linen *n* (*the material & things made from it*) anart *m*, **a shirt of** ~ lèine *f* anairt *gen*, **bed** ~ anart-leapa *m*

ling[1] *n* (*the fish*) langa *f*

ling[2] *n* (*the plant*) fraoch *m*

linguist *n* cànanaiche *m*

linguistic *adj* cànanach

linguistics *n* cànanachas *m*

lining *n* (*material*) lìnigeadh *m*

link *n* **1** (*con: in chain &c*) tinne *f*, ceangal *m*; **2** (*abstr: logical* ~, ~ *of cause & effect &c*} ceangal *m* (**with** ri, **between** eadar), **there is no** ~ **between the meat and the illness** chan eil ceangal sam bith eadar an fheòil agus an tinneas *m*, **a close** ~ dlùth-cheangal *m*; **3** (*relationship, association*) dàimh *mf invar* (**with** ri), **I have no ~(s) with that firm** chan eil dàimh sam bith agam ris a' chompanaidh *mf* sin; **4** (*family &c* ~) buinteanas *m*, **I have ~s with Skye** tha buinteanas agam ris an Eilean Sgitheanach

link *v* ceangail *vt*, co-cheangail *vt*, (**to/with** ri)

linkage *n* ceangal *m*, (*esp abstr*) co-cheangal *m*

linked *adj & past part* co-cheangailte (**to** ri), **global warming and the climate are** ~ **(to one another)** tha blàthachadh *m* na cruinne is a' chlìomaid co-cheangailte (ri chèile)

linn *n* linne *f*

lint *n* lìon *m*

lion *n* leòghann *&* leòmhann *m*

lip *n* **1** (*of mouth*) bile *f*, (*less usu*) li(o)p *f*, *in exprs* **lower** ~ beul-ìochdair *m*, **upper** ~ beul-uachdar *m*; **2** (*of container, jug &c*) bile *f*, oir *f*, iomall *m*

lipstick *n* dath-lipean *m*

liquid *adj* sruthach

liquid *n* lionn *m*

liquidate *v* **1** (*company &c*) leagh *vt*; **2** (*kill, execute*) cuir *vi* às (*with prep* do)

liquidation *n* (*of company &c*) leaghadh *m*

Lismore *n* Lios Mòr

lisp, lisping *n* liotachas *m*, *in expr* **she has a** ~ tha i liotach

lisp *v* bi *vi irreg* liotach, **she** ~**s** tha i liotach

lisping *adj* liotach

list *n* **1** (*general*) liosta *f*; **2** (*in publication*) clàr *m*, ~ **of contents** clàr-innse *m*, ~ **of names/people** clàr-ainmean *m*, clàr-dhaoine *m*

list *v* dèan liosta *f* (*with prep* de)

listen *v* èist (**to** ri), ~**ing to the songs** ag èisteachd ris na h-òrain *mpl*

listener *n* neach-èisteachd *m*, ~**s** luchd-èisteachd *m sing coll*

literal *adj* litireil

literary *adj* litreachail

literate *adj* litireach

literature *n* litreachas *m*, **Gaelic** ~ litreachas na Gàidhlig

litigious *adj* connspaideach, agartach

litre *n* liotair *m*

litter[1] *n* (*rubbish, untidiness*) truileis *f invar*, (*stronger*) sgudal *m*

litter[2] *n* (*young of animals*) cuain *f*, (*more trad*) àl *m*

little *adj* **1** beag, (*smaller*) meanbh, ~ **by** ~ beag air bheag, beag is beag, mean air mhean, uidh *f* air n-uidh; **2** *in expr* **the Little Minch** An Cuan Sgìth

little *n* **1** (*a certain amount*) beagan *m* (*with gen*), **I have a** ~ **money** tha beagan airgid *m* agam; **2** (*a very small or limited amount*) a' bheag *f* (*with prep* de), **there was only a (very)** ~ **room in the boat** cha robh ach a' bheag de rùm *m* sa bhàta *m*

littoral *n* oirthir *f*, costa *m*

live *adj* beò

live *v* **1** (*be alive*) bi *vi irreg* beò, (*more trad*) is *vi irreg def* beò, mair *vi* beò, **as long as I** ~ cho fad 's a bhios mi beò, cho fad 's a mhaireas mi beò, rim mhaireann *m*, rim shaoghal *m*, (*more trad*) cho fad 's as beò mi; **2** (*dwell &c*) fuirich *vi*, còmhnaich *vi*, fan *vi*, **we were living in Islay at the time** bha sinn a' fuireach/a' còmhnaidh ann an Ìle aig an àm *m*, ~ **with someone** fan/fuirich aig cuideigin; **3** (*survive, make a living*) thig *vi* beò, **how will we** ~ **in this place?** ciamar a thig sinn beò san àite seo?, **I can't** ~ **on that!** cha tig mi beò (*or* cha tig mi suas) air sin!

livelihood *n* teachd-an-tìr *m invar*, beòshlaint *f*, bith-beò *f*

lively *adj* **1** beothail; **2** (*idioms*) **look ~!** tog *vi* ort!, crath dhìot an cadal *m*!

liver *n* àdha *m*, (*usu of animal*) grùthan *m*

livestock *n* stoc *m*, (*esp cattle*) crodh *m*, sprèidh *f*

living *adj* **1** beò, **I didn't see a ~ soul** chan fhaca mi duine beò; **2** *in expr* **I'm still in the land of the ~** tha mi a' cumail beò, tha mi beò fhathast

living *n* **1** (*abstr*) bith-beò *f*, **the cost of ~** cosgais *f* bith-beò *gen*; **2** (*a livelihood*) teachd-an-tìr *m invar*, beòshlaint *f*; **3** (*an income*) teachd-a-steach *m invar*

lizard *n* laghairt *mf*

load *n* **1** (*burden &c, esp as carried by humans/animals*) eallach *m*, uallach *m*, (*esp carried by a human*) ultach *m*; **2** (*cargo*) luchd *m*; **3** (*in pl*) **~s** (*fam: a lot, lots, many*) tòrr *m* (*with gen*), **~s of people are of that opinion** tha tòrr dhaoine *mpl* den bheachd *m* sin

load *v* (*boat, vehicle &c*) luchdaich *vt*

loading *n* luchdachadh *m*

loads *npl* (*ie lots, many &c*) *see* **load** *n* **3**

loaf *n* lof *mf*, (*more trad: homemade bread ~, ~ of sugar &c*) buileann *f*

loan *n* iasad *m*, **get something on ~** gabh/faigh rudeigin air iasad, **get a ~ of something** faigh iasad de rudeigin

loanword *n* (*lang*) facal *m* iasaid *m gen*

loathe *v* fuathaich *vt*, (*but usu expressed as follows*) **I ~ him/them** &c tha gràin *f* agam air/orra

loathing *n* gràin *f*, fuath *mf*

loathsome *adj* gràineil, fuathach

lobster *n* giomach *m*

lobsterpot *n* cliabh *m* ghiomach *mpl gen*

local *adj* ionadail, **~ authority/history** ùghdarras *m*/eachdraidh *f* ionadail

locate *v* (*find, trace*) faigh lorg *f* air, **the police ~ed him** fhuair am poileas lorg air

location *n* (*site, position &c*) suidheachadh *m*, àite *m*

loch *n* loch *m*, **sea ~** loch-mara *m*

lochan *n* lochan *m*

lock[1] *n* (*on door &c*) glas *f*

lock[2] (*of hair*) dual *m*

lock *v* glais & glas *vt*, **~ the door** glais/glas an doras

locked *adj & past part* glaiste

locum *n* (*med*) neach-ionaid *m*

locust *n* lòcast *m*

lodge *v* **1** (*as vi*) fan *vi*, fuirich *vi*, **~ with someone** fan/fuirich aig cuideigin; **2** (*as vt: house, accommodate*) thoir taigh *m*, thoir lòistinn *m*, (*with prep* do); **3** (*deposit, eg in museum, bank &c*) taisg *vt*

lodger *n* lòistear *m*

lodging(s) *n* **1** lòistinn *m*, (*less usu*) fàrdach *f*; **2** *in expr* **a night's ~** cuid *f* oidhche *f gen*

loft *n* lobht(a) *m*

loggerheads *n*, **at ~** thar a chèile, troimh-a-chèile, **they were at ~** bha iad thar a chèile/troimh-a-chèile, **I set them at ~** chuir mi thar a chèile/ troimh-a-chèile iad

lonely, lonesome *adj* (*person or place*) aonaranach, uaigneach

long *adj* **1** (*in time & dimension*) fad(a), **how ~ is it?** dè cho fada 's a tha e? (*also* dè an fhad a th' ann), **don't be ~** na bi fada!, **the days were/ seemed ~ for us** bha na làithean *mpl* fada dhuinn; **2** (*~ and weary*) cian, **a ~ (weary) road** rathad cian; **3** *in expr* **~ drawn out** fadalach, màirnealach; **4** (*idioms*) **~ time no see!** 's fhada o nach fhaca mi (*&c*) thu!, (*to impatient child &c*) **it won't be ~ now** chan fhad' thuige a-nis

long *adv* **1** (*dimension*) de dh'fhad (*also* a dh'fhad), **a mile ~** mìle *mf* a dh'fhad, **it's two feet ~** tha dà throigh *f* de dh'fhad ann; **2** (*time*) fada, **as ~ as I live** cho fad(a) 's is beò mi, *also* (*more trad*) rim mhaireann *m*; **3** (*misc exprs*) **the whole night ~** fad na h-oidhche, **at ~ last** mu dheireadh thall, (*in stories &c*) **~ ~ ago** o chionn fada nan cian, fada fada ron a seo

long- *prefix* fad-, *eg* **long-lived** fad-shaoghalach, **long-sighted** fad-fhradharcach, **long-suffering** fad-fhulangach

long *v* **1** *in expr* **~ for** (*ie desire*) miannaich *vt*; **2** *in expr* **~ for** (*ie nostalgically*) ionndrainn *vt*

longing *n* **1** (*desire*) miann *mf*; **2** (*with nostalgia*) cianalas *m*; **3** (*with impatience*) fadachd *f invar* (**for** ri)

look *n* sùil *f* (**at** air), **a quick ~ at the newspaper** sùil aithghearr air a' phàipear-naidheachd *m*, **take/have a ~** thoir sùil (**at** air); **2** (*physical appearance, aspect*) dreach *m*, **with a ghostly ~** air dhreach taibhse *mf gen*; **3** (*of person's features, not nec permanent*) tuar *m*; **4** (*transient, on face, in eye*) fiamh *m*; **5** (*resemblance, appearance*) coltas *m*, (*idioms*) **you have the ~ of a soldier** tha coltas saighdeir *m gen* ort, **by the ~ of it** a-rèir c(h)oltais *gen*

look *v* **1** coimhead *vi*, thoir sùil *f*, (**at** air), **~ at her** coimhead oirre, **that ~s/is ~ing good!** (*fam*) tha sin a' coimhead math!; **2** (*resemblance: idioms*) **~ing like a ghost** air dhreach *m* taibhse *mf gen*, **you ~ like a soldier** tha coltas *m* saighdeir *m gen* ort; **3** *in expr* **~ for** sir *vt*, lorg *vt*, bi *vi irreg* an tòir *f* (*with prep* air), **the company is ~ing for workers** tha a' chompanaidh *mf* a' sireadh luchd-obrach *m sing coll*, **he went to town ~ing for his brother** chaidh e don bhaile *m* an tòir air a bhràthair; **4** (*idiom*) (**I'm tired!** *&c*) **you ~ it!** (tha mi sgìth! *&c*) tha a choltas (sin) ort!

loom *n* (*weaving*) beart-fhighe *f*

loop *n* lùb *f*

loose *adj* **1** fuasgailte, sgaoilte, neo-cheangailte; **2** (*fig: of immoral person, behaviour*) mì-bheusach

loose *v* leig (às) *vt*, **~ an arrow** leig (às) saighead *f*

loosen *v* (*fastenings &c*) fuasgail *vt*, sgaoil *vt*, lasaich *vt*, **~ a knot/a shoelace** fuasgail snaidhm *m*/barrall *m*

lord *n* **1** (*ruler, landowner &c*) tighearna *m*, (*hist*) **The Lord of the Isles** Tighearna nan Eilean *mpl gen*, Triath *m* nan Eilean; **2** (*peer &c*) morair *m*, **the House of ~s** Taigh *m* nam Morairean; **3** (*relig*) **The Lord** An Tighearna; **4** (*excl*) **Good ~!** a Thighearna!

lorry *n* làraidh *f*

lose *v* caill *vti*

loss *n* call *m*

lost *adj & past part* air chall *m*, caillte, **I'm ~** tha mi air chall, **we got ~** chaidh sinn air chall

lot[1] *n* **1** (*one's fate*) crannchur *m*, **if that is my ~** mas e sin mo chrannchur; **2** (*one's ~ in life*) **it was his ~ to be a soldier** thuit dha a bhith na shaighdear *m*; **3** *in exprs* **draw ~s** cuir crainn (*pl of* crann *m*), thilg crainn, cuir crannchur, **drawing of ~s** crannchur *m*

lot[2] *n* **1** (*considerable quantity*) mòran *m*, (*fam*) grunn *m*, (*fam*) tòrr *m*, (*all with gen*), gu leòr *adv* (*follows the noun*), **a ~ of food** mòran bìdh (*gen of* biadh) *m*, **I spent a ~ of years there** chuir mi seachad mòran/grunn bhliadhnachan *fpl* an sin, **~s of people** mòran/tòrr dhaoine *mpl*, **a ~ of money** mòran/tòrr airgid *m*, *also* (*fam*) airgead mòr, **we've got a ~ of troubles** tha trioblaidean *fpl* gu leòr againn; **2** (*misc exprs*) **thanks a ~!** mòran taing!, ceud *m* taing!, **a ~ better** fada/mòran nas fheàrr, **such a ~** na h-uibhir, na h-uiread, (*with prep* de), **there were such a ~ of people there** bha na h-uibhir/na h-uiread de dhaoine *mpl* ann

loth *adj* leisg, aindeònach, **I am ~ to sell it** is leisg leam a reic

lottery *n* crannchur *m*, **the national ~** an crannchur nàiseanta

loud *adj* **1** (*at high volume*) àrd; **2** (*noisy*) faramach, fuaimneach; **3** (*of style, garments &c*) spaideil

loudspeaker *n* glaodhaire *m*

louse *n* mial *f*

lout *n* duine borb

loutish *adj* gràisgeil

loutishness *n* gràisgealachd *f invar*

love *n* **1** (*esp sexual & intimate ~*) gaol *m*, (*for less intimate affection*) gràdh *m*, **she's in ~** tha i ann an gaol, **I gave my ~ to her** thug mi mo ghaol dhi, **young ~** gaol na h-òige, **my first ~** mo chiad ghaol, **the land of my ~, the land (that) I love** tìr *mf* mo ghràidh *gen*; **2** (*the person loved*) leannan *m*, **my ~** mo leannan; **3** (*in voc exprs: affectionate address*) **(my) ~!** (*esp to lovers and close family*) a ghaoil!, a luaidh!, (*usu for more general, less intimate use*) a ghràidh!, m' eudail!

love *v* **1** (*esp sexually, intimately*) bi *vi irreg* gaol *m* (*with preps* aig & air), (*for less intimate affection*) bi *vi irreg* gràdh *m* (*with preps* aig & air), **I ~ you** tha gaol *m* agam ort, tha gràdh agam ort; **2** *in expr* **the land (&c) I ~** tìr *mf* (*&c*) mo ghràidh (*gen of* gràdh *m*); **3** (*like or enjoy greatly*) is *vi irreg & def* toigh (*with prep* le), **I ~ football** is toigh leam (gu mòr) ball-coise *m*

loveliness *n* (*woman, place &c*) bòidhchead *f invar*, (*esp of woman*) maise *f invar*

lovely *adj* (*place, weather, girl &c*) brèagha, (*woman, place &c*) bòidheach, (*esp of woman*) maiseach

lover *n* leannan *m*, *in expr* **live-in** ~ coileapach *mf*

loving *adj* gaolach, gràdhach, maoth

low *adj* **1** (*of phys position, status, sound*) ìosal & ìseal, **in a ~ voice** ann an guth ìosal; **2** (~ *in spirit*) smalanach, sìos na (*&c*) inntinn *f*; **3** (~ *in morale*) gun mhisneach(d) *f*

low *v* (*cattle*) geum *vi*, (*cattle & esp deer*) langanaich *vi*

lower *adj* **1** (*in phys position, status, quality*) ìochd(a)rach; **2** *in expr* ~ **lip** beul-ìochdair *m*; **3** (*comp adj*) (n)as ìsle, (*in past & conditional tenses*) (n)a b' ìsle

lower *v* (*phys & fig*) ìslich *vt*, (*phys*) leag *vt*, **he ~ed the window** leag e an uinneag

lowing *n* (*cattle*) geumnaich *f*, (*cattle & esp deer*) langanaich *f*

Lowland *adj* Gallta, (*lang*) ~ **Scots** (*usu with art*) A' Bheurla Ghallta

Lowlander *n* Gall *m*

Lowlands *n* **1** (*of Scotland*) **the** ~ A' Ghalltachd *f invar*, A' Mhachair(e) Ghallta, Machair na h-Alba, **in the** ~ air a' Ghalltachd, air a' Mhachair Ghallta; **2** (*as general geographical term*) còmhnardan *mpl*

lowliness *n* ùmhlachd *f invar*, irioslachd & irisleachd *f invar*

lowly *adj* umha(i)l, ìosal & ìseal, iriosal & iriseal

loyal *adj* dìleas

loyalty *n* dìlseachd *f invar*, dìlse *m invar*

lubricate *v* ùillich *vt*

lubrication *n* ùilleachadh *m*

luck *n* fortan *m*, (*usu good* ~) sealbh *m*, **good/bad** ~ deagh/droch fhortan, **good** ~! fortan leat!, sealbh ort!

lucky *adj* **1** fortanach, sealbhach; **2** (*idiom*) **he'll be** ~ (**if he isn't killed** *&c*) 's math a dh'èireas dha (mura tèid a mharbhadh *&c*)

luggage *n* treal(l)aichean *fpl*, bagaichean *mpl*

Luing *n* Luinn *m*, Eilean *m* Luinn *gen*, *in expr* **a man from** ~ Luinneach *m* (*also as adj*)

lukewarm *adj* (*lit & fig*) leth-fhuar, (*welcome, attitude &c*) fionnar, ~ **tea** teatha leth-fhuar, **a** ~ **welcome** fàilte *f* leth-fhuar, fàilte fhionnar

lullaby *n* tàladh *m*, òran *m* tàlaidh *gen*

lumber *n* treal(l)aich *f*

lump *n* ceap *m*, cnap *m*, meall *m*, ~ **of peat** ceap mòna (*gen of* mòine *f*)

lumpy *adj* cnapach

lunch *n* **1** biadh *m* meadhan-là, (*trad: used with art*) an ruisean *m*; **2** (*for worker, schoolchild &c*) (**packed**) ~ pìos *m*

lung *n* sgamhan *m*

lurch *v* (*seas, ship, trees &c*) tulg *vi*, luaisg *vi*

lurching *n* tulgadh *m*
lure *v* tàlaidh *vt*, meall *vt*
lust *n* drùis *f*, ana-miann *m*
lust *v* miannaich *vi*, *in expr* ~ **after** miannaich *vt*
lustful *adj* drùiseach, drùiseil
Luxemburger *n* Lucsamburgach *m* (*also as adj*)
luxurious *adj* sòghail
luxury *n* sògh *m*
lying *adj* breugach

M

machair, machair-land *n* (*grassy stretches of land, esp adjoining the Atlantic seaboard*) machair(e) *f in nom case, m in gen sing*

machine *n* inneal *m*, **washing ~** inneal-nigheadaireachd *m*, inneal-nighe *m* (*also* nigheadair *m*), **fax ~** inneal-facsa *m*

mackerel *n* rionnach *m sing & coll*

mad *adj* **1** (*with rage, insanity*) air chuthach *m*, air bhàinidh *f invar*, air bhoile *f invar*, **go ~** rach *vi* air chuthach/bhàinidh/bhoile; **2** (*idioms*) **go quite/ totally ~ (with rage)** gabh an cuthach dearg, **it was nearly driving me ~** bha e gus mo chur dhìom fhìn/gus mo chur às mo rian *m*

Madam *n* Bean-Uasal *f*, (*voc*) A bhean-uasal

made *adj & past part* dèanta & dèante; *in exprs* **~ up** (*story &c*) uirsgeulach; **~ up** (*assembled*) co-dhèanta

madness *n* boile *f invar*, cuthach *m*

magazine *n* iris *f*, (*esp a quarterly*) ràitheachan *m*

maggot *n* cnuimh *f*, cnuimheag *f*

magic *adj* draoidheil, seunta

magic *n* draoidheachd *f invar*

magical *adj* draoidheil

magician *n* draoidh *m*

magistrate *n* maigh(i)stir *m* lagha (*gen of* lagh *m*)

magnanimity *n* mòr-mheanmna *m*, àrd-aigne *m*

magnanimous *adj* mòr-mheanmnach

magnet *n* clach-iùil *f*, (*less trad*) magnait *f*

magnetic *adj* iùil-tharraingeach, (*less trad*) magnaiteach

magnetism *n* iùil-tharraing *f*

magnificent *adj* greadhnach, glòrmhor, (*less usu*) òirdheirc

magnify *v* meudaich *vt*, **~ing glass** glainne-mheudachaidh *f*

magnitude *n* meudachd *f invar*, **the ~ of their debts** meudachd nam fiachan *mpl* aca

maid *n* **1** (*servant*) searbhanta *f*; **2** (*young woman*) maighdeann *f*, **old ~** seana-mhaighdeann; **3** (*virgin*) maighdeann *f*, òigh *f*, ainnir *f*

maidenhead, maidenhood *n* maighdeannas *m*

mail *n* post *m*, **the Royal Mail** Am Post Rìoghail, **air ~** post-adhair *m*, **e-mail** post-dealain *m*

main *adj* **1** prìomh (*precedes the noun, which it lenites where possible*), **the ~ town** am prìomh bhaile, **the ~ reason for his conduct** prìomh adhbhar a ghiùlain *m*; **2** *in expr* **~ door** doras mòr, **~ road** rathad mòr

mainland *n* tìr-mòr & tìr mòr *m* (*not usu with art*), **on the ~** air tìr-mòr

mains *n* (*agric*) mànas *m*

maintain *v* **1** (*assert*) cùm *vt* a-mach, **he ~s that Stalin was right** bidh e a' cumail a-mach gun robh Stalin ceart; **2** (*support*) cùm *vt* suas, **I've**

a family to ~ tha teaghlach *m* agam ri chumail suas; **3** (*machinery &c*) gleus *vt*, càirich *vt*

maintenance *n* **1** (*abstr: financial &c support*) cumail *m* suas; **2** (*keep, feed, of livestock &c*) beathachadh *m*; **3** (*of machinery &c*) gleusadh *m*, càradh *m*

majestic *adj* **1** greadhnach, glòrmhor; **2** (*like a monarch*) rìoghail

majesty *n* **1** (*abstr: royalty*) rìoghalachd *f invar*; **2** (*splendour, grandeur*) mòrachd *f invar*, greadhnachas *m*

major *adj* **1** (*principal*) prìomh (*precedes the noun, which it lenites where possible*), **the** ~ **town** am prìomh bhaile, **the** ~ **reason for his conduct** prìomh adhbhar a ghiùlain; **2** (*of great importance, gravity &c*) mòr, glè chudthromach, **a** ~ **accident** tubaist mhòr, **a** ~ **exhibition** taisbeanadh mòr/glè chudthromach

major *n* (*military rank*) màidsear *m*

majority *n* (*of objects &c & people*) mòr-chùid *f*, **the** ~ **of his life** a' mhòr-chuid de a bheatha *f*, **the** ~ **are in favour** tha a' mhòr-chùid air a shon

make *v* **1** dèan *vt irreg*, **I'll** ~ **jam tomorrow** nì mi silidh *m invar* a-màireach, **they made progress** rinn iad adhartas *m*, ~ **a profit** dèan prothaid *f*, ~ **war** dèan cogadh *m*, ~ **fun** dèan fanaid *f*, *also* mag *vi*, (**of** air), **they were making fun of her** bha iad a' dèanamh fanaid oirre/a' magadh oirre; **2** *in expr* ~ **for** (*ie head for*) dèan *vi* (*with prep* air), **he made for the boat** rinn e air a' bhàta *m*; **3** (*create, fashion*) dealbh *vt*, ~ **a statue** dealbh ìomhaigh *f*; **4** (*cause, force to do something*) thoir *vt* (*with prep* air), **she made me leave** thug i orm falbh, **he'll** ~ **me do it eventually** bheir e orm a dhèanamh aig a' cheann *m* thall; **5** (*transmit/arouse an emotion &c*) cuir *vt* (*with prep* air), **she made him angry** chuir i an fhearg air, **he made me jump** (*ie startled me*) chuir e clisgeadh *mf* orm, *also* chlisg e mi; **6** (*cause to be*) fàg *vt*, **the journey made them tired** dh'fhàg an turas sgìth iad; **7** (*misc idioms & exprs*) ~ **a mistake** rach *vi* air iomrall *m*, *also* dèan mearachd *f*, ~ **a start** tòisich *vi* (**on/at** air), ~ **a fresh start** tòisich *vi* as ùr (**on/at** air), ~ **an impression on** drùidh *vi* (*with prep* air), **the play made an impression on me** dhrùidh an dealbh-chluich *f* orm, ~ **new** *v* nuadhaich *vt*, ùraich *vt*, ath-nuadhaich *vt*, ~ **haste** greas *vi* (*with prep* air), ~ **haste!** greas ort, *pl* greasaibh oirbh, **they made haste** ghreas iad orra, ~ **off** (*escape &c*) tàrr/tàir *vi* às, ~ **up** (*face*) maisich *vt*, ~ **up** (*anecdote, incident &c*) **they asked (me) if I was making it up** dh'fhaighnich iad (dhomh) am b' e uirsgeul *m* a bh' agam/an e an fhìrinn a bh' agam, ~ **out** (*dissemble, pretend*) leig *vi* (*with prep* air), **the soldiers made out they were civilians** leig na saighdearan *mpl* orra gun robh iad nan sìobhaltairean *mpl*, ~ **out** (*assert*) cùm *vt* a-mach, **they are making out that the world will end tomorrow** tha iad a' cumail a-mach gun tig an saoghal *m* gu crìch (*dat of* crìoch *f*) a-màireach

maladministration *n* mì-rianachd *f invar*

malady *n* tinneas *m*, galar *m*

male *adj* fireann, fireannta, ~ **cat** cat fireann

male *n* fireannach *m*, ~s on the right and females on the left, please! fireannaich air an làimh (*dat of* làmh *f*) dheis is boireannaich *mpl* air an làimh chlì, mas e ur toil *f* e!

malevolence *n* gamhlas *m*, mì-rùn *m*

malevolent *adj* gamhlasach

malice *n* gamhlas *m*, mì-rùn *m*, nimh & neimh *m*

malicious *adj* gamhlasach, nimheil

mallet *n* fairche *m*

malnutrition *n* dìth *m* beathachaidh *m gen*

malpractice *n* mì-chleachdadh *m*

Mammy *n* mamaidh *f*

man *n* **1** (*emphasising gender*) fear *m*, fireannach *m*, **a ~ and a woman** fear is bean *f*, fear/fireannach agus boireannach *m*, **the ~ of the house** fear an taighe, **men on the right and women on the left, please!** fireannaich air an làimh (*dat of* làmh *f*) dheis is boireannaich *mpl* air an làimh chlì, mas e ur toil *f* e!; **2** (*stressing male gender less*) duine *m*, **I met a ~ on the stair** thachair mi ri duine air an staidhre *f*, **when I'm a ~** an uair a bhios mi nam dhuine; **3** (*mankind, humanity*) mac-an-duine *m sing coll*, an cinne-daonna *m*, **~'s futile efforts** oidhirpean *fpl* dìomhain mhic-an-duine *gen*

Man *n*, **the Isle of ~**, Eilean *m* Mhanainn *m gen*

manage *v* **1** (*~ firm, organisation &c*) stiùir *vt*, riaghail *vt*; **2** (*handle situation &c*) dèilig *vi* (*with prep* ri), làimhsich *vt*, **she ~d the problem extremely well** dhèilig i ris an duilgheadas uabhasach math; **3** (*succeed in doing something, be up to a task &c*) faigh *vi* (*with prep* air), rach *vi* agam (*&c*) (*with prep* air), dèan a' chùis (*with prep* air), **I'll ~ to go back there some time or other** gheibh mi air tilleadh ann uair no uaireigin, **will you ~ to find a job?** an tèid agad air obair *f* fhaighinn?, **the box is heavy, will you ~ it?** tha am bogsa trom, an dèan thu a' chùis air?; **4** (*live, get by*) thig *vi irreg* beò, thig suas, **I can't ~ on that!** cha tig mi beò/cha tig mi suas air sin!

management **1** (*abstr: the process*) stiùireadh *m*, riaghladh *m*, **~ centre** ionad-stiùiridh *m*; **2** (*con: the managers &c*) luchd-stiùiridh *m sing coll*, luchd-riaghlaidh *m sing coll*

manager *n* manaidsear *m*, neach-stiùiridh *m invar*, neach-riaghlaidh *m invar* (*pl* luchd-stiùiridh & luchd-riaghlaidh *m sing coll*)

manageress *n* bana-mhanaidsear *f*

mane *n* (*of horse, lion &c*) muing *f*

mangle *v* (*lacerate &c*) reub *vt*

manifest *v* **1** (*show, display qualities &c*) taisbein *vt*, nochd *vt*; **2** *in expr* **~ itself** thig *vi* an uachdar *m*, thig *vi* am follais *f invar*, nochd *vt*, **their bravery ~ed itself in wartime** thàinig an cuid *f* gaisge *f invar* an uachdar/am follais an àm *m* cogaidh *m gen*, nochd an cuid gaisge an àm cogaidh

manifold *adj* iomadh-fhillte

mankind *n* mac-an-duine *m*, an cinne-daonna *m* (*used with art*)

manliness *n* duinealas *m*, fearalachd *f invar*

manly *adj* duineil, fearail, ~ **qualities** feartan *mpl* duineil/fearail

man-made *adj* **1** (*manufactured*) saothraichte; **2** (*as substitute for the natural object &c*) fuadain, brèige

manner *n* **1** (~ *of doing something*) dòigh *m*, modh, nòs, **in a particular** ~ air dhòigh/mhodh àraidh, **the traditional** ~ (*esp of singing*) an seann nòs; **2** (*manner of behaving*) dol-a-mach *m invar*, **I didn't like his** ~ bu bheag leam/orm an dol-a-mach (a bha) aige

manners *n* beus *f*, (*good* ~) modh *f*, **good/bad** ~ deagh/droch bheus

mannish *adj* (*esp of woman*) duineil, firean(n)ta

manpower *n* **1** luchd-obrach *m sing coll*, **take on extra** ~ fastaich luchd-obrach a bharrachd; **2** (*more abstr*) sgiobachd *f invar*, ~ **planning** planaigeadh *m* sgiobachd

manslaughter *n* duine-mharbhadh *m*, murt *m*

manual *n* leabhrachan *m*, leabhran *m*, (*esp instruction* ~) leabhar-mìneachaidh *m*

manufacture *n* saothrachadh *m*

manufacture *v* saothraich *vt*, dèan *vt*

manufacturing *n* saothrachadh *m*

manure *n* **1** mathachadh *m*, leasachadh *m*, innear & inneir *f*; **2** *in expr* ~ **heap** siteag *f*, òtrach *m*, dùnan *m*

manure *v* (*land*) mathaich *vt*, leasaich *vt*, (*with seaweed*) feamainn *vt*

manuscript *n* làmh-sgrìobhainn *mf*

Manx *adj* Manainneach

Manxman *n* Manainneach *m*

many *adj* **1** mòran *m* (*with gen pl n*), iomadach *adj*, iomadh *adj*, (*both with nom sing n*), (*fam*) tòrr *m*, (*fam: usu less numerous*) grunn *m*, (*both with gen pl n*), ~ **people** mòran dhaoine *mpl*, ~ **thanks!** mòran taing *f*!, ~ **times**, ~ **a time** iomadach/iomadh uair *f*, ~ **people are of that opinion** tha tòrr dhaoine den bheachd *m* sin, **I spent a good** ~ **years there** chuir mi seachad grunn bhliadhnachan *fpl* an sin; **2** *in expr* **so** ~ uimhir *f invar*, uiread *m invar*, na h-uimhir, na h-uiread, **there were so** ~ **people there** bha (na h-)uimhir/(na h-)uiread de dhaoine *mpl* ann; **3** *in expr* **how** ~ cia mheud & co mheud (*with nom sing n*), **how** ~ **years?** co mheud bliadhna *f*?

many *n* mòran *m*, ~ **of them** mòran dhiubh, **there weren't** ~ **there** cha robh mòran ann, **did you buy books? not** ~ an do cheannaich sibh leabhraichean? cha do cheannaich mòran

map *n* clàr-dùthcha *m*, mapa *m*

mar *v* mill *vt*

marble *n* màrmor *m*

March *n* (*used with art*) Am Màrt

march[1] *n* (*boundary, limit*) crìoch *f*, **this is the ~ of my land** is e seo crìoch an fhearainn agam

march[2] *n* **1** (*of soldiers &c*) màrsail *f*, mèarrsadh *m*; **2** (*music*) caismeachd *f*

marching *n* màrsail *f*, mèarrsadh *m*

mare *n* làir *f*

margarine *n* margarain *m invar*

margin *n* iomall *m*, oir *f*, **at/on the ~(s)** (*ie remote*) air an iomall, air an oir, *also* iomallach *adj*

marginal *adj* iomallach, air an iomall *m*

mariner *n* maraiche *m*, seòladair *m*

maritime *adj* na mara (*gen of* muir *f*)

mark *n* **1** comharra(dh) *m*, (*school &c*) **good/bad ~s** deagh/droch chomharraidhean, (*livestock*) **ear ~** comharradh cluaise *f gen*, **~ of respect** comharradh-urraim *m*, **question ~** comharradh-ceiste *m*; **2** (*~ left by person, animal, object*) lorg *f*, comharradh *m*; **3** (*typog*) puing *f*, **exclamation ~** clisg-phuing *f*

mark *v* **1** (*leave a mark*) fàg lorg *f*, fàg comharradh *m*, (*with prep* air); **2** (*stain*) fàg spot *m*, fàg smal *m*, (*with prep* air); **3** (*teacher &c*) ceartaich *vt*, comharraich *vt*; **4** (*~ occasions &c*) comharraich *vt*, **to ~ his birthday** gus an ceann-bliadhna *m* aige a chomharrachadh

market *n* **1** margadh *mf*, marcaid *f*, (*esp for livestock*) fèill *f*, **~ town** baile-margaidh *m*, **a common ~** margadh coitcheann; **2** (*abstr: demand, for product &c*) margadh *mf*, fèill *f*, (**for** air), **will there be a ~ for it?** am bi margadh/fèill air?, *in expr* **free ~ economy** eaconamaidh saor-mhargaidh

marketing *n* margaideachd *f invar*

market-place *n* ionad-margaidh *m*

marking *n* (*teacher &c*) ceartachadh *m*, comharrachadh *m*, **~ scheme** sgeama-comharrachaidh *m*

marquee *n* puball & pùball *m*

marred *adj & past part* millte

marriage *n* pòsadh *m*

married *adj & past part* pòsta (**to** aig *or* ri), **a ~ couple** càraid phòsta, **~ to Andrew** pòsta aig/ri Anndra, **newly ~** nuadh-phòsta, *in expr* **get ~** pòs *vi*

marry *v* pòs *vti*

Mars *n* Màrt *m*

marsh *n* fèith(e) *f*, boglach *f*

mart[1] *n* (*Sc: beef animal*) mart *m*

mart[2] *n* (*market*) margadh *mf*, fèill *f*

marvel *n* iongnadh *m*, mìorbhail *f*

marvellous *adj* iongantach, mìorbhaileach

masculine *adj* **1** fireann, firean(n)ta; **2** (*gram*) fireann, **~ word/noun** facal/ainmear fireann, **the ~ gender** a' ghnè fhireann

mash *v* pronn

mashed *adj & past part* pronn, ~ **potato** buntata pronn

mask *n* **1** masg *m*; **2** (*as disguise, fancy dress &c*) aghaidh-choimheach *f*, aodannan *m*

mason *n* clachair *m*

mass *adj* mòr- *prefix, eg* ~ **production** *n* mòr-bhuileachadh *m*, ~ **media** mòr-mheadheanan *mpl*

mass[1] *n* **1** (*abstr: bulk, magnitude*) tomad *m*; **2** (*large quantity or number: of objects*) meud mòr, uimhir *f invar*, uiread *m invar*, **a** ~ **of paper** meud mòr pàipeir *m gen*, uimhir de phàipear; **3** (*of people*) sluagh mòr, meud mòr dhaoine *mpl gen*

mass[2] *n* (*relig*) aifreann *m*

massacre *n* casgairt *f*, mort *m*, (*hist*) **the** ~ **of Glencoe** Mort Ghlinne-Comhainn *m gen*

massacre *v* casgair *vt*

massage *n* suathadh *m* (bodhaig *f gen*)

massage *v* suath *vt*

mast *n* (*of ship &c*) crann *m*, **radio/television** ~ crann-craolaidh *m*

master *n* **1** (*one in authority, or in position of superiority over others*) maigh(i)stir *m*, uachdaran *m*; **2** (*of boat &c*) caiptean *m*, sgiobair *m*; **3** *in expr* (*at ceilidh &c*) ~ **of ceremonies** fear *m* an taighe; **4** *in expr* **question** ~ ceistear *m*, fear-ceasnachaidh *m*

master *v* **1** (*people, emotions &c*) ceannsaich *vt*, faigh làmh *f* an uachdair (*with prep* air); **2** (*a topic or activity*) faigh eòlas *m* (*with prep* air)

masterful *adj* ceannsalach, smachdail

masterly *adj* (*at performing task, as artist &c*) ealanta, barraichte

masterwork *n* sàr-obair *f*

masticate cnàmh *vt*, cnuas *vti*, cagainn *vti*

masturbate *v* brod *vt*, fèin-bhrod *vi*

masturbation *n* brodadh *m*, fèin-bhrodadh *m*

match[1] *n* (*for lighting; also football &c* ~) maids(e) *m*, (*for lighting: trad*) lasadair *m*

match[2] *n* (*worthy or superior opponent*) seis(e) *m*, **she met her** ~ **that day!** fhuair i a seis an là *m* sin!

match *v* freagair *vi*, co-fhreagair *vi*, (*with prep* do), **the coat** ~**es the hat** tha an còta a' co-fhreagairt don aid (*dat of* ad *f*)

matching *adj* co-fhreagarrach

mate *n* **1** (*pal*) companach *m*, (*less informal*) caraid *m*; **2** (*on ship*) meite *m*

mate *v* co-ghin *vi*, cuplaich *vi*

material *adj* **1** (*ie not abstr or spiritual*) corporra, stuthail, nitheil, rudail; **2** (*ie significant, weighty, meaningful*) cudthromach & cudromach, seaghach; **3** (*ie real, substantial*) fìor, ~ **gain/advantage** fìor bhuannachd *f*

material *n* **1** (*fabric, cloth &c*) stuth *m*; **2** (*more generally:* ~ *for creating or constructing something*) stuth *m*, adhbhar *m*, **building** ~**s** stuthan-togalaich *mpl*,

collecting ~ **for a book** a' cruinneachadh stuth airson leabhair *m gen*,
shoe-making ~(s) stuth/adhbhar bhròg *fpl gen*

materialism *n* saoghaltachd *f invar*

materialist *n* duine saoghalta

materialistic *adj* saoghalta

materially *adv* **1** (*ie financially*) a thaobh airgid *m gen*, a thaobh beartais *m gen*, **I'm no worse off** ~ chan eil mi dad *f invar* nas miosa dheth a thaobh airgid; **2** (*ie significantly, considerably*) gu mòr, gu ìre *f* mhòir (*dat*), **the situation has changed** ~ tha an suidheachadh air atharrachadh gu mòr/gu ìre mhòir

maternal *adj* **1** (*pertaining to a mother, motherly*) màthaireil; **2** (*in family relationships*) ~ **uncle** bràthair-màthar *m*, ~ **aunt** piùthar-màthar *f*, ~ **grandfather** athair-màthar *f*

maternity *n* màthaireachd *f invar*

mathematics, maths *n* matamataig(s) *m invar*

mating *n* co-ghineadh *m*, cuplachadh *m*

matter *n* **1** (*chem &c: material substance*) stuth *m*; **2** (*affair &c*) cùis *f*, gnothach *m*, **how did the ~ go/turn out?** ciamar a chaidh *vi* a' chùis/an gnothach?, **the nub/crux of the ~** cnag *f* na cùise; **3** (*subject ~*) cuspair *m*, (*Lit &c*) ~ **and form** cuspair is cruth *m*; **4** (*something wrong*) **what's the ~?** dè a tha ceàrr?, **what's the ~ with you?** dè a tha a' cur ort?, (*to sick person*) dè a tha thu a' gearan?; **5** *in expr* **reading ~** stuth *m* leughaidh (*gen of* leughadh *m*, *used adjectivally*); **6** (*pus*) brachadh *m*, iongar *m*

matter *v* bi *vi irreg* gu diofar (*freq in neg exprs*), **that doesn't ~** chan eil sin gu diofar, *also* is *v irreg def* coma sin, **it doesn't ~ whether she comes or not** is coma an tig i no nach tig

mattock *n* caibe *m*

mature *adj* **1** (*person*) inbheach, abaich, ~ **student** oileanach *m* inbheach; **2** (*fruits &c*) abaich

mature *v* abaich *vi*, (*esp people*) thig *vi* gu inbhe *f*, thig *vi* gu ìre *f invar*

maturity *n* **1** (*adulthood*) inbhe *f*, ìre *f invar*, **come to/reach ~** thig *vi* gu inbhe/gu ìre; **2** (*of fruits &c*) abaichead *m*

maul *v* **1** (*with hands*) làimhsich *vt*; **2** (*fam: in fight &c*) pronn *vt*, dochainn *vt*

maw *n* **1** (*mouth, esp voracious*) craos *m*; **2** (*craw, gizzard*) sgròban *m*; **3** (*stomach, esp greedy*) maodal *f*, mionach *m*

maximum *adj* as motha (*sup of* mòr), ~ **speed** astar *m* as motha

May *n* (*used with art*) An Cèitean *m*, (*less trad*) a' Mhàigh, **a ~ morning** madainn Chèitein (*gen used adjectivally*)

may *v* **1** (*ie be permitted, allowed to*) faod *vi def*, ~ **we go? yes/no** am faod sinn falbh? faodaidh/chan fhaod; **2** (*expr possibility*) faod *vi def*, **it ~ be that there is life on the moon** dh'fhaodadh e a bhith gu bheil beatha *f* air a' ghealaich *f*, **he ~ be ill** faodaidh gu bheil e tinn, *in expr* **be that as it ~** biodh sin mar a bhitheas e; **3** (*trad: expr wishes &c*) gum(a) *conj*, ~ **you be in good health!** fallain gum bi thu!, **long ~ you live!** guma fada beò thu! (*also* saoghal fada dhut!)

maybe *adv & conj*, is dòcha, (is) ma(th) dh'fhaodte (*also* 's mathaid), **it'll be a fine day**, ~ bidh là brèagha ann, 's dòcha/ma dh'fhaodte, ~ **it won't snow** 's dòcha/ma dh'fhaodte nach cuir i, ~ **he's ill** 's dòcha gu bheil e tinn, *also* faodaidh gu bheil e tinn, ~ **he'll come tomorrow** 's dòcha gun tig e a-màireach

mayor *n* mèar *m*

MC *n* (*at ceilidh &c*) fear *m* an taighe

me *pers pron* mi, (*emph*) mise, mi-fhìn, **don't you know** ~? **It's** ~ (*emph*)! nach aithnich thu mi? 's mise/'s mi-fhìn a th' ann!

meadow, meadowland *n* clua(i)n *f*, dail *f*, faiche *f*, lèana *f*, (*esp beside watercourse, loch*) innis *f*

meal[1] *n* (*ground cereals &c*) min *f*

meal[2] *n* biadh *m*, (*trad*) diathad *f*, lòn *m*, **the midday** ~ biadh meadhan-là *m gen*, *also* (*trad: with art*) an ruisean *m*

mealtime *n* tràth *m* bìdh/bidhe (*gen of* biadh *m*)

mean *adj* 1 (*petty, insignificant*) crìon, suarach; 2 (*stingy*) spìocach, mosach

mean *n* meadhan *m*

mean *v* 1 ciallaich *vt*, (*more fam*) minig *vt*, **what do you** ~? dè a tha thu a' ciallachadh?, (*more fam*) dè a tha thu a' minigeadh?, **what does this word** ~? dè a tha am facal seo a' ciallachadh?; 2 (*idiom: be serious*) bi *v irreg* ann an da-rìribh, **they didn't** ~ **it** cha robh iad ann an da-rìribh; 3 (*intend*) bi *vi irreg* airson, **I didn't** ~ **to do it** cha robh mi airson a dhèanamh, *also* cha robh mi a' ciallachadh a dhèanamh, cha do rinn mi a dh'aon rùn *m*/a dh'aon ghnothach *m* e

meander *v* (*river &c*) lùb *vi*

meandering *adj* (*road, river, argument &c*) lùbach

meaning *n* ciall *f*, (*esp sense of words & exprs*) brìgh *f invar*, seagh *m*, **words without** ~ faclan *mpl* gun chiall, **the** ~ **of (the) words** brìgh nam facal, **the word isn't used with that** ~ cha chleachdar am facal san t-seagh sin

meaningful *adj* brìghmhor

meaningless *adj* gun chiall

means *n* 1 dòigh *f*, meadhan *m*, ~ **of transport** dòigh(ean)-siubhail/giùlain *m*; 2 *in expr* **by** ~ **of** tro mheadhan *m* (*with gen*), **by** ~ **of the hammer** tro mheadhan an ùird (*gen of* òrd *m*); 3 (*wealth &c*) beartas *m*, saidhbhreas *m*, *in expr* **a man of** ~ duine airgeadach

meantime *n* eadar-ama *m*, **in the** ~ anns an eadar-ama

meanwhile *adv* rè na h-ùine seo/sin

measles *n used with art*, a' ghriù(th)lach *f*, (*idiom*) **she has (the)** ~ tha i sa ghriùlach

measure *n* 1 (*abstr, also device, tool*) tomhas *m*, **tape** ~ ribean-tomhais *m*; 2 (*a certain or limited amount*) na h-uimhir *f invar*, na h-uiread *m invar*, **we had a** ~ **of security** bha na h-uimhir/na h-uiread de thèarainteachd *f invar* againn; 3 (*expedient, solution &c*) ceum *m*, **take/implement** ~s gabh ceumannan (**to** gus), **safety** ~s ceumannan-sàbhailteachd *mpl*

measure *v* (*dimensions, speed, weight &c*) tomhais *vt*

measurement *n* tomhas *m*, **take ~s** gabh tomhasan

measuring *adj* tomhais (*gen of* tomhas *m*), **~ tape** teip *f* tomhais

meat *n* feòil *f*

mechanic *n* meacanaig *m*, (*more trad*) innleadair *m*

mechanical *adj* innealach

mechanism *n* **1** inneal *m*; **2** (*means, not nec mechanical*) meadhan *m*, **a ~ for collecting taxes** meadhan airson/gus cìsean *fpl* a thoirt a-steach

meddle *v* gabh gnothach *m* (**in/with** ri), buin *vi* (**in/with** do, ri), **don't ~ with it** na gabh gnothach ris, na buin dha/ris

media *npl, used with art*, **the ~** na meadhanan *mpl*

medical *adj* lèigheil, (*less trad*) meidigeach

medicine *n* **1** (*abstr: the science*) eòlas-leighis *m*; **2** (*con: medication*) leigheas *m*, ìocshlaint *f*, cungaidh *f*, cungaidh-leighis *f*, **cough ~** leigheas-chasad *m*

medieval *adj* meadhan-aoiseil

meditate *v* meòmhraich & meamhraich *vi* (**on/about** air)

meditation *n* meòmhrachadh & meamhrachadh *m* (**on/about** air)

Mediterranean *adj* Meadhan-thìreach

Mediterranean *n*, **the ~** Am Muir *mf* Meadhan-thìreach

medium *adj* meadhanach

medium *n* meadhan *m*, **through the ~ of** tro mheadhan *m* (*with gen*), **education through the ~ of Gaelic** foghlam *m* tro mheadhan na Gàidhlig

meek *adj* umha(i)l, macanta

meekness ùmhlachd *f invar*

meet *v* **1** (*congregate*) cruinnich *vi*, coinnich *vi*, thig *vi* còmhla, tionail *vi*, **they ~ in the village hall** bidh iad a' cruinneachadh ann an talla *m* a' bhaile; **2** (*encounter, by chance or by arrangement*) coinnich *vi*, tachair *vi*, (*with prep* ri), **I met X in the town** choinnich mi/thachair mi ri X sa bhaile, **did you ever ~ him?** an do choinnich thu a-riamh ris?; **3** *in expr* **go to ~ them** (*ie towards them*) rach *vi* nan coinneimh *f*

meeting *n* **1** (*business ~, ~ of societies &c*) coinneamh *f*, **annual ~** coinneamh bhliadhnail; **2** (*an encounter, by chance or arrangement*) coinneachadh *m*

melancholy *adj* **1** (*person, mood &c*) gruamach, dubhach, fo ghruaim *f dat*; **2** (*atmosphere, music &c*) tiamhaidh

melancholy *n* gruaim *f*, mulad *m*

melodious *adj* ceòlmhor, fonnmhor, binn

melody *n* port *f*, fonn *m*

melon *n* meal-bhucan *m*

melt *v* leagh *vti*

member *n* ball *m*

membership *n* ballrachd *f invar*

memorandum *n* cuimhneachan *m*, meòrachan & meamhrachan *m*

memorial *adj* cuimhneachaidh (*gen of* cuimhneachadh *m, used adjectivally*)

memorial *n* **1** cuimhneachan *m*; **2** (*in the form of a stone or monument*) clach *f* chuimhne *f invar*, clach *f* chuimhneachain *gen*, clach chuimhneachaidh (*gen of* cuimhneachadh *m, used adjectivally*)

memorise *v* meòmhraich & meamhraich *vt*, cùm *vt* air mheòmhair *f*, cùm *vt* air chuimhne *f invar*

memory *n* **1** (*the faculty and site of ~*) meòmhair & meamhair *f*, cuimhne *f invar*, **commit to ~** meòmhraich & meamhraich *vt*, cùm *vt* air mheòmhair, (*idiom*) **if my ~ serves me rightly/doesn't deceive me** mas math mo chuimhne, (*IT*) **random access ~ (RAM)** cuimhne thuairmeach, **read only ~ (ROM)** cuimhne bhuan; **2** (*what is remembered*) cuimhne *f invar* (**of** air), **I've no ~ of him** chan eil cuimhne agam air

menace *v* maoidh *vi*, bagair *vi*, (*with prep* air), **he was menacing me** bha e a' maoidheadh orm

menace *n* maoidheadh *m*

mend *v* **1** càirich *vt*, càir *vt*; **2** (*remedy, improve*) leasaich *vt*

menstruation *n* fuil-m(h)ìosa *f*

mental *adj* inntinn (*gen of* inntinn *f, used adjectivally*), inntinneach, inntinneil, **~ ability/capacity** comas *m* inntinn, **~ illness** tinneas-inntinn *m*, euslaint *m* inntinn

mention *n* iomradh *m*, guth *m*, tarraing *f*, (**of** air),

mention *v* **1** thoir iomradh *m*, thoir guth *m*, (*with prep* air), **he didn't ~ it** cha tug e iomradh/guth air; **2** *in expr* **not to ~** gun guth (*with prep* air), **pears are dear, not to ~ apples** tha peuran *fpl* daor, gun ghuth air ùbhlan *mpl*

menu *n* **1** clàr *m* bìdh (*gen of* biadh *m*); **2** (*IT*) clàr *m* iùil (*gen of* iùl *m*)

merchant *n* ceannaiche *m*, marsanta *m*

merciful *adj* iochdmhor, tròcaireach

mercury *n* airgead beò

mercy *n* iochd *f invar*, tròcair *f*, truas *m*, **God's mercies** tròcairean Dhè (*gen of* Dia *m*), **have ~** gabh truas (**on** de)

merge *v* co-m(h)easgaich *vti*, co-aonaich *vti*

merit *n* **1** (*worth, value*) luach *m invar*, fiù *m invar*, **without ~** gun luach, gun fhiù; **2** (*honour, reputation*) cliù *m invar*

merit *v* toill *vt*

meritorious *adj* airidh

mermaid *n* maighdeann-mhara *f*

merriment *n* cridhealas *m*, mire *f invar*

merry *adj* **1** aighearach; **2** (*tipsy*) air leth-mhisg *f*

mess *n* **1** (*litter, untidiness*) truileis *f invar*; **2** (*messy state*) bùrach *m*, **in a ~** ann am bùrach, *also* troimh-a-chèile, thar a chèile, bun-os-cionn

message *n* fios *m*, teachdaireachd *f invar*, **give him this ~** thoir am fios seo dha, **going on a ~** a' dol air theachdaireachd

messenger *n* teachdaire *m*

metal *adj* meatailt, de mheatailt *f*, ~ **doors** dorsan *mpl* meatailt, dorsan de mheatailt

metal *n* meatailt *f*

metallic *adj* meatailteach

metamorphosis *n* cruth-atharrachadh *m*

meteor, meteorite *n* dreag *f*

meteorology *n* eòlas-sìde *m*

meter *n* meidheadair *m*

method *n* 1 (*abstr: organisation, orderliness &c*) òrdugh *m*, riaghailt *f*, rian *m*; 2 (*way of doing something*) dòigh *f*, seòl *m*, alt *m*

methodical *adj* òrdail, riaghailteach, rianail

methodicalness *n* òrdugh *m*, riaghailt *f*, rian *m*

methodology *n* dòigh-obrach *f*

meticulous *adj* (*person, work &c*) mionaideach, mion-chùiseach, pongail, **a ~ enquiry/study** sgrùdadh mionaideach

metre *n* 1 (*unit of length*) meatair *m*; 2 (*poetic rhythm*) meadrachd *f invar*, rannaigheachd *f invar*

metric *adj* meatrach

metrical *adj* meadrachail

mew *v* dèan mialaich/miamhail *f invar*

mewing, miaowing, *n* mialaich *f invar*, miamhail *f invar*

microwave *n* meanbh-thonn *f*

midday *n* meadhan-là *m*, **the ~ meal** biadh *m* meadhan-là *gen*, (*trad*) an ruisean *m*

midden siteag *f*, òtrach *m*, dùnan *m*

middle *n* meadhan *m*, **a belt around my ~** crios *m* mum mheadhan, **the very/exact ~** an ceart-mheadhan, an teis-meadhan, **right in the ~ of the town** ann an ceart-mheadhan/ann an teis-meadhan a' bhaile

middle-age *n* meadhan-aois *f*

middle-aged *adj* leth-shean

middling *adj & adv* meadhanach, **I'm only ~ well today** chan eil mi ach meadhanach an-diugh, **you only did ~ well** cha do rinn thu ach meadhanach math

midge *n* meanbh-chuileag *f*

midget *n* luchraban *m*

midnight *n* meadhan-oidhche *m*

midsummer *n* leth *m invar* an t-samhraidh

midwife *n* bean-ghlùin *f*

midwinter *n* leth *m invar* a' gheamhraidh

mien *n* mèinn *f*, dreach *m*, snuadh *m*

might *n* 1 (*mainly abstr: pol, military &c*) cumhachd *mf invar*, **the ~ of the Roman Empire** cumhachd Ìompaireachd *f* na Ròimhe; 2 (*abstr, also often phys*) neart *m*, **Samson's ~** neart Shamsoin, (*saying*) **~ before right** thèid neart thar ceart *m*

might *v* **1** (*expressing possibility*) faod *vi def*, **it ~ be that there is life on Mars** dh'fhaodadh e a bhith gu bheil beatha *m* air Màrt *m*, **he ~ be ill** faodaidh gu bheil e tinn, *also* 's dòcha gu bheil e tinn, dh'fhaodte gu bheil e tinn; **2** (*expressing permission*) ~ **I leave now? no!** am faod mi falbh a-nis? chan fhaod!

mighty *adj* **1** (*pol, militarily &c*) cumhachdach; **2** (*phys*) neartmhor

migrant *n* fear-imrich *m*, neach-imrich *m*, ~**s** luchd-imrich *m sing coll*

migration *n* imrich *f*

mild *adj* **1** (*of person, weather &c*) ciùin, sèimh, **a ~ morning/breeze** madainn/oiteag chiùin; **2** (*of illness &c*) beag, **a ~ fever** fiabhras beag

mile *n* mìle *mf*

militant *adj* mileanta

militant *n* mileantach *m*

military *adj* armailteach

milk *n* bainne *m*, *in expr* ~ **cows** crodh-eadraidh *m*

milking *n* bleoghann *f invar*

mill *n* muileann *mf*, muilinn *f*

mill *v* (*corn &c*) meil *vt*, bleith *vt*

miller *n* muillear *m*

million *n* millean *&* muillean *m*

millstone *n* clach-mhuilinn *f*

mimic *v* atharrais *vt*

mimicry *n* atharrais *f invar*

Minch *n, used with art,* **the ~** A' Mhaoil , **the Little ~** An Cuan Sgìth

mind *n* **1** inntinn *f*, **she's got a good ~** tha inntinn mhath innte, **frame/state of ~** gleus *mf* inntinn *gen, also* fonn *m*, gean *m*, dòigh *m*, **peace of ~** toil-inntinn *f*; **2** (*preoccupation &c*) cùram *m*, aire *f invar*, **she is on my ~** tha i air mo chùram/air m' aire, *also* tha i fa-near dhomh, tha i nam inntinn *f*; **3** (*decision, intention*) *in expr* **make up one's ~** cuir *vt* (*with prep* ro), **they made up their ~s to build a house** chuir iad romhpa taigh *m* a thogail, *note also the idiom* **she had a ~ to tidy the house** bha e fa-near dhi an taigh a sgioblachadh; **4** (*memory*) cuimhne *f*, **keep in ~** cùm *vt* air chuimhne, **it slipped my ~** chaidh e às mo chuimhne, **call to ~** cuir *vt* na (*&c*) c(h)uimhne, **it called to ~ my mother's house** chuir e nam chuimhne taigh *m* mo mhàthar; **5** (*sanity &c*) ciall *f*, rian *m*, reusan *m*, **he lost his ~** chaill e a chiall, **she's out of her ~** tha i às a ciall/às a rian, **it was nearly driving me out of my ~** bha e gus mo chur às mo rian, *also* bha e gus mo chur dhìom fhìn

mind *v* **1** (*care, be concerned*) *in exprs* **I don't ~!** tha mi coma!, **I don't ~ in the least!** tha mi coma-co-dhiù!, **never ~!** coma leat!, dad ort!; **2** (*misc exprs*) **she was ~ed to tidy the house** bha e fa-near dhi/bha i am beachd an taigh a sgioblachadh, **pears are dear, never ~ apples** tha peuran *fpl* daor, gun ghuth *m* air ùbhlan *mpl*

mine *poss pron* **1** leam(sa), **it's ~** 's ann leamsa a tha e; **2** *in exprs* **he's a good**

friend of ~ tha e na dheagh charaid *m* dhomh, **a cousin of** ~ co-ogha *m* dhomh

mine *n* (*for coal &c, also explosive device*) mèinn(e) *f*

miner *n* mèinnear *m*

mineral *adj* mèinneach & mèinneil

mineral *n* mèinnear *m*, mèinnearach m

mineralogy *n* mèinn-eòlas *m*, mèinnearachd *f invar*

mingle *v* measgaich *vt*, co-mheasgaich, co-measgaich & coimeasgaich *vti*, (**with** ri) **~ed together** air am measgachadh ri chèile, *also* am measg a chèile

minimum *adj* as lugha

mining *n* mèinnearachd *f invar*

minister *n* (*religion, politics*) ministear *m*, **the First Minister** Am Prìomh Mhinistear, *in expr* **prime** ~ prìomhaire *m*

ministry *n* (*religion, politics*) ministrealachd *f*

minor[1] *adj* **1** (*ie less important, lesser-used &c than others*) mion- *prefix*, beag, ~ **language** mion-chànan *m*, cànan beag, ~ **road** rathad beag; **2** (*slight, not grave*) beag, **a** ~ **problem** duilgheadas beag

minor[2] *adj* (*of person: under-age*) mion-aoiseach

minor *n* (*ie under-age person*) mion-aoiseach *m*

minority *n* **1** mion-chuid *f*, beag-chuid *f*; **2** *in expr* ~ **language** mion-chànan *m*, cànan beag

minute *adj* **1** (*very small*) crìon; **2** (*detailed, meticulous*) mion- *prefix*, mionaideach, ~ **questioning** mion-cheasnachadh *m*, ceasnachadh mionaideach

minute *n* mionaid *f*, **twenty** ~**s** fichead mionaid, **wait a** ~**!** fuirich mionaid!

miracle *n* mìorbhail *f*, **capable of** ~**s** comasach air mìorbhailean

miraculous *adj* mìorbhaileach

mire *n* eabar *m*, poll *m*, **sinking into the** ~ a' dol fodha san eabar

mirth *n* mire *f invar*

mis- *prefix* mì-, *eg* **misfortune** *n* mì-shealbh *m*, **misinterpret** *v* mì-mhìnich *vt*

miscellaneous *adj* measgaichte, de gach seòrsa *m*

miscellany *n* measgachadh *m*

mischance *n* **1** (*abstr*) mì-shealbh *m*; **2** (*con*) tubaist *f*

mischief *n* donas *m*

misconduct *n* mì-ghiùlan *m*

miserable *adj* truagh, brònach

misery *n* truaighe *f*

misfortune *n* (*abstr*) mì-shealbh *m*, (*abstr & con*) dosgainn *f*, driod-fhortan *m*

mishap *n* tubaist *f*, driod-fhortan *m*

misinterpret *v* mì-mhìnich *vt*

misjudge *v* (*situation &c: assess wrongly*) mì-thuig *vt*

mislead *v* meall *vt*

misleading *adj* meallta

misprint *n* clò-mhearachd *f*

Miss *n* A' Mhaighdeann(-uasal) *f*, ~ **Campbell** A' Mhaighdeann(-uasal) Chaimbeul, (*voc, for corres &c*) **Dear ~ Campbell** A Mhaighdeann(-uasal) Chaimbeul, (*abbrev*) A Mh(-uas) Chaimbeul

miss *v* **1** (*fail to catch &c*) caill *vt*, **I ~ed the train** chaill mi an trèana *f*, **Didn't you see the film? You didn't ~ much!** Nach fhaca sibh am film? Cha do chaill thu mòran!; **2** (*pine for &c*) ionndrainn *vt*, bi *vi irreg* fadachd *f invar* orm (*&c*) (*with prep* ri), **she's ~ing you** tha i gad ionndrainn, tha fadachd oirre riut

missile *n* urchair *f*

missing *adj* a dhìth, (*less usu*) a dh'easbhaidh, **the cover of the book was ~** bha còmhdach *m* an leabhair a dhìth

mission *n* teachdaireachd *f invar*, rùn *m*, **going on a ~** a' dol air theachdaireachd

missionary *n* teachdaire *m*, (*less trad*) misionairidh *m*

mist *n* ceò *m*, (*less usu*) ceathach *m*

mistake *n* mearachd *f*, iomrall *m*, **make a ~** dèan mearachd, rach *vi* air iomrall

mistaken *adj* mearachdach, iomrallach, **~ opinion** beachd mearachdach

Mister *n* Maighstir *m* (*abbrev* Mgr), **~ Fraser** Maighstir Friseal, (*voc, for corres &c*) **Dear ~ Fraser** A Mhaighstir Fhriseil, (*abbrev*) A Mhgr Fhriseil

mistress *n* **1** (*woman in authority, or in position of superiority over others*) bana-mhàighistear *f*; **2** *in expr* **school~** ban(a)-mhàighstir-sgoile *f*; **3** (*sexual partner*) coileapach *f*

mistrust *n* mì-earbsa *m*

misty *adj* fo cheò *m*, ceòthach, **the hills are ~** tha na beanntan (*pl of* beinn *f*) fo cheò

mitigate *v* maothaich *vt*

mitten *n* miotag *f*

mix *v* measgaich *vt*, co-mheasgaich, co-measgaich & coimeasgaich *vt*, **~ed together** air am measgachadh ri chèile, *also* am measg a chèile

mixed *adj & past part* measgaichte

mixer *n* (*for food, cement &c*) measgaichear *m*

mixing, mixture *n* measgachadh *m*, co-m(h)easgachadh *m*

moan *v* **1** (*through grief &c*) caoin *vi*; **2** (*complain, grumble*) gearain *vi* (**about** air), **you needn't bother ~ing all the time!** cha leig thu a leas a bhith a' gearan fad na h-ùine!

mob *n* gràisg *f*, prabar *m*

mock *v* mag *vi*, dèan fanaid, (*with prep* air)

mockery *n* fanaid *f*, magadh *m*, (**of** air)

mocking *adj* magail

mod *n* mòd *m*, **local ~** mòd ionadail, **the National Mod** Am Mòd Nàiseanta

mode *n* (*of doing something*) dòigh *f*, (*more abstr*) modh *f*, ~s **of transport** dòighean-siubhail *mpl*, ~ **of governing** modh-riaghlaidh *m*,

model *n* mac-samhail *m*

moderate *adj* **1** (*not outstanding*) meadhanach; **2** (*esp of persons, behaviour, temperament: not excessive or given to excess*) measarra, stuama

modern *adj* ùr, ùr-nodha, **these ~ times** na h-amannan *mpl* ùra seo

modernisation *n* ùrachadh *m*

modernise *v* ùraich

modest *adj* **1** (*shy, self-effacing &c*) diùid, màlda; **2** (*of woman, decorous in dress, behaviour &c*) banail; **3** (*not excessive*) measarra; **4** (*not outstanding*) meadhanach; **5** (*in more positive contexts*) beag, **my mother left me a ~ legacy** thiomnaich mo mhàthair dìleab bheag dhomh, **a ~ bet on a horse** geall beag air each *m*

modicum *n* na h-uimhir *f invar*, **we had a ~ of security** bha na h-uimhir de thèarainteachd *f invar* againn

modish *adj* fasanta

Mohammedan *n & adj* Mohamadanach *m*

moist *adj* tais

moisten *v* taisich *vt*

moistness, moisture *n* taise *f invar*, taiseachd *f invar*

molar *n* (*tooth*) fiacail chùil (*gen of* cùl *m*, *used adjectivally*)

mole *n* **1** (*the animal*) famh *f*; **2** (*on skin*) ball-dòrain *m*

moment *n* **1** mòmaid *f*, tiota *m*, (*dimin*) tiotan *m*, tiotag *f*; **2** *in expr* **the ~** *conj* (*ie as soon as*), cho luath agus/is, **we began the ~ he came in** thòisich sinn cho luath agus a thàinig e a-steach

monastery *n* manachainn *f*

Monday *n* Diluain *m invar*

money *n* airgead *m*, **pocket ~** airgead-pòcaid, **ready ~** airgead ullamh, **that's a lot of ~!** 's e airgead mòr a tha sin!, **a waste of ~** call *m* airgid *gen*

monitor *n* (*IT*) foillsear *m*

monitor *vt* cùm sùil (*with prep* air)

monk *n* manach *m*

monkey *n* muncaidh *m*

monolith *n* tursa *m*

monster *n* uilebheist *m*, **the Loch Ness ~** Uilebheist Loch Nis *m gen*

month *n* mìos *mf*

monthly *adj* mìosach, mìosail

monument *n* clach *f* chuimhne *f gen*

moo *v* geum *vi*

mood *n* **1** gean *m*, gleus *m*, fonn *m*, **what ~ is he in today?** dè an gean/ am fonn a th' air an-diugh?, **in a good ~** air deagh ghleus, **in a bad ~** diombach & diumbach, dubhach, greannach; **2** (*gram*) modh *f*, **the imperative ~** a' mhodh àithneach, **the indicative ~** a' mhodh thaisbeanach

moody *adj* **1** (*of changeable disposition*) caochlaideach; **2** (*more temporary*) dubhach, diombach & diumbach, **aren't you the ~ one today!** nach tusa (a) tha dubhach/diombach/greannach an-diugh!

mooing *n* geumnaich *f*

moon *n* gealach *f*, **the harvest ~** gealach (bhuidhe) an abachaidh, **full ~** làn-ghealach, gealach làn, **the rays of the ~** gathan *mpl* na gealaich

moonshine *n* (*whisky*) poitean *m*

moor, moorland *n* mòinteach *f*, monadh *m*, sliabh *m*, aonach *m*

moral *adj* beusach, moralta

morale *n* misneach *f*, misneachd *f invar*

morality *n* moraltachd *f invar*

morals *n* beusan *fpl*, **good ~** deagh-bheusan

more *adv, pron & n* **1** tuilleadh *m invar*, barrachd *f invar*, **do you want (any/ some) ~?** a bheil thu ag iarraidh tuilleadh/barrachd?, **~ information** tuilleadh/barrachd fiosrachaidh *m gen*, **don't do that any ~** na dèan sin tuilleadh, **why aren't ~ records being made?** carson nach eil an tuilleadh chlàran *mpl gen* gan dèanamh?; **2** *in expr* **~ than** barrachd air, còrr *m invar* is, **~ than twenty miles** barrachd air/còrr is fichead mìle *mf sing*, **~ than I was expecting to see** barrachd air na bha mi an dùil fhaicinn, (*idiom*) **I've got ~ than enough** tha tuilleadh 's a' chòir agam; **3** (*corres to* else) a bharrachd, **I don't want anything ~** chan eil mi ag iarraidh càil *m invar* a bharrachd; **4** (*corres to* additional) a bharrachd, **two ~ workers** dithis neach-obrach *m* a bharrachd; **5** *in expr* **~ or less** an ìre mhath, **the winter's ~ or less over** tha an geamhradh an ìre mhath seachad

morning *n* **1** madainn *f*, **in/in the course of/during the ~** anns a' mhadainn, **this ~** madainn an-diugh, **yesterday ~** madainn an dè, **tomorrow ~** madainn a-màireach, **three in the ~** trì uairean *fpl* sa mhadainn, **the ~ star** reul *f* na maidne; **2** *in expr* **from ~ till night** o mhoch gu dubh

morose *adj* gruamach, mùgach

morrow *n, in expr* **on the ~** làirne-mhàireach & làrna-mhàireach *adv*

morsel *n* (*ie to eat*) grèim *m* bìdh (*gen of* biadh *m*)

mortal *adj* **1** (*not immortal*) bàsmhor, **your ~ body and your immortal soul** do chorp bàsmhor is d' anam *m* neo-bhàsmhor; **2** (*deadly, fatal*) marbhtach, bàsmhor, **a ~ blow** buille mharbhtach; **3** *in expr* **in ~ danger** an cunnart *m* bàis (*gen of* bàs *m*)

mortgage *n* morgaidse *m*

mortification *n* **1** (*humiliation*) ìsleachadh *m*, ùmhlachadh *m*; **2** (*shaming*) nàrachadh *m*

mortify *v* **1** (*humiliate*) ìslich *vt*, ùmhlaich *vt*; **2** (*shame*) nàraich *vt*

mosque *n* mosg *m*

moss *n* (*bot*) còinneach *f*

most *n* **1** a' mhòr-chuid *f*, a' chuid-mhòr, a' chuid as mò/as motha, **~ of his life** a' mhòr-chuid de a bheatha *f*, **~ people** a' mhòr-chuid, **~ of the**

bread a' chuid as motha den aran *m*; **2** *in expr* **at ~** aig a' char *m* as mò, **at ~ we will only lose twenty pounds** aig a' char as mò cha chaill sinn ach fichead nota *f sing*

most *sup adj* **1** *expr by* as (*in the past & conditional tenses* a bu, *in the future* a bhitheas & a bhios) *followed by the sup form of the adj*, **she is the ~ beautiful woman** is ise am boireannach as bòidhche, **he will be the ~ famous man** is esan am fear as ainmeile a bhitheas (ann); **2** (*very, exceptionally*) anabarrach, glè, **his talk was ~ interesting** bha an òraid aige anabarrach inntinneach

mostly *adv* mar as trice, **we ~ eat porridge** mar as trice bidh sinn ag ithe lite *f invar*

moth *n* leòman *m*

mother *n* màthair *f*

motherhood *n* màthaireachd *f invar*

mother-in law *n* màthair-chèile *f*

motherly *adj* màthaireil, màithreil

motion *n* (*movement, also parliamentary &c ~*) gluasad *m*

motionless *adj* gun ghluasad *m*

motive *n* adhbhar *m*, **~less** gun adhbhar

motor *n* motair *m*

motor-bike *n* motair-baidhg *m*, (*more trad*) motair-rothar *m*

motorcar *n* càr *m*, (*trad*) carbad *m*

mould[1] *n* clòimh *f* liath, clòimhteach *f* liath

mould[2] *n* (*for forming, shaping*) molldair *m*

mound *n* **1** (*topog: rounded hill*) tom *m*, tolman *m*, tòrr *m*; **2** (*heap &c*) tòrr *m*, **a ~ of sand** tòrr gainmhich *f gen*

mount *n* (*horse for riding*) each *m* (dìollaid *f gen*)

mount *v* **1** leum *vi* air muin *f invar* (*with gen*), **he ~ed the horse** leum e air muin an eich; **2** (*of animals mating*) rach *vi* air muin *f invar* (*with gen*), **the bull ~ed the cow** chaidh an tarbh air muin na bà; **3** (*~ an exhibition &c*) cuir *vt* air chois (*dat of* cas *f*)

mountain *n* beinn *f*, (*also, in some ~ names*) sliabh *m*

mountain ash *n* caorann *f*

mountainous *adj* beanntach, sliabhach, monadail

mourn *v* **1** (*as vi*) bi *vi irreg* ri bròn *m*, caoidh *vi*, caoin *vi*, dèan tuireadh *m*, **they are ~ing** tha iad ri bròn; **2** (*as vt*) caoidh *vt*, **he is ~ing his parents** tha e a' caoidh a phàrantan *mpl gen*

mourning *n* bròn *m*, **they are in ~** tha iad ri bròn

mouse *n* luch *f*, lùchag *f*

mouth *n* beul *m*, (*fam/vulg*) cab *f*, gob *m*, (*pej when used of humans*) craos *m*, **shut your ~!** dùin do bheul!, (*fam/vulg*) dùin do chab!

mouth music *n* port-a-beul *m*

mouthful *n* làn *m* beòil *m gen*, **I took a ~ of haggis** ghabh mi làn mo bheòil de thaigeis *f*

move *n* **1** (*flitting*) imrich *f*; **2** *in expr* **get a ~ on** dèan cabhag *f*!, tog ort!

move *v* **1** (*phys*) gluais *vti*, caraich *vti*, cuir car *m* (*with prep* de), **the army ~d towards the town** ghluais an t-arm chun a' bhaile, **don't ~ the table** na gluais/na caraich am bòrd, **don't ~ from the table** na caraich bhon bhòrd, **don't ~ it!** na cuir car dheth!; **2** *in expr* **unable to ~** gun lùth/ lùths *m*; **3** (*~ emotionally*) gluais *vti*, drùidh *vi* (*with prep* air), **I was ~d** chaidh mo ghluasad *m*, **the film ~d me** dhrùidh am film orm; **4** (*flit, ~ house*) imrich *vi*, dèan imrich *f*

movement *n* **1** gluasad *m*, **we heard a ~** chuala sinn gluasad; **2** (*the faculty or power of ~*) lùth *m*, lùths *m*

moving *adj* **1** (*in motion*) gluasadach, siùbhlach; **2** (*emotionally ~*) gluasadach, drùidhteach

moving *n* (*flitting*) imrich *f*

mow *v* (*grass &c*) lom *vt*, geàrr *vt*

much *adj, adv, n,* **1** (*quantity*) mòran *m*, **~ food** mòran bìdh (*gen of* biadh *m*), **I haven't (very) ~ money** chan eil mòran airgid *m gen* agam, **we didn't get (very) ~** cha d'fhuair sinn mòran, **thank you/thanks very ~** mòran taing *f*, **what's doing/happening? not ~** (*fam*) dè (a) tha (a') dol? chan eil mòran; **2** *in expr* **too ~** cus *m*, **too ~ talking** cus bruidhne (*gen of* bruidhinn *f*), **I drank too ~!** dh'òl mi cus!, *note also idiom* **far too ~** tuilleadh 's a' chòir; **3** (*in various kinds of comparative exprs*) mòran, fada, fiù is/agus, uimhir *f invar*, uiread *m invar*, **~ better** mòran/fada nas fheàrr, **~ older** mòran/fada nas sine, **there wasn't as ~ as a piece of bread left** cha robh fiù is pìos *m* arain *m gen* air fhàgail, **they didn't so ~ as look at us** cha do rinn iad fiù agus sùil *f* a thoirt òirnn, **give me as ~ again** thoir dhomh uimhir eile (dheth), **don't give me as ~ as James (has)!** na toir dhomh uimhir ri Seumas!, **half as ~** a leth uiread, **without so ~ as fifty pence** gun uiread agus lethcheud sgillin *f sing*, **I had so ~ money** bha (na h-)uimhir de dh'airgead *m* agam; **4** (*in direct & indirect questions*) *in expr* **how ~** dè, **how ~ is there (of it)?** dè a th' ann dheth? *also* dè an uimhir a th' ann?, **I don't know how ~ there is** chan eil fhios *m* agam dè a th' ann dheth; **5** (*misc idioms*) **I don't think ~ of her hat** is beag orm an ad aice, (*cost*) **how ~ is it?** dè na tha e?

muck out *v* (*byre &c*) cairt *vt*

mucus *n* ronn *m*

mud *n* poll *m*, eabar *m*

mug *n* (*for drinking*) muga *f*

mugging *n* brath-ghoid *f*

muggy *adj* (*of weather*) bruthainneach

Mull *n* Muile, **(The) Isle of ~** Eilean *m* Muile, (*poetic, in songs*) an t-Eilean Muileach

multi- *prefix* ioma-, *eg* **multilingual** *adj* ioma-chànanach, **multimedia** *adj* ioma-mheadhan, **multinational** *adj* ioma-thìreach, **multilateral** *adj* ioma-thaobhach

multiplication *n* (*maths*) iomadachadh *m*

multiply *v* **1** (*as vi: become more numerous*) cinn *vi*, meudaich *vi*; **2** (*as vt: maths*) iomadaich *vt* (**by** le), **two multiplied by four** a dhà air iomadachadh le a ceithir, *also* a dhà uiread a ceithir

Mummy *n* mamaidh *f*

munitions *n* connadh-làmhaich *m sing coll*

murder *n* mort & murt *m*

murder *v* mort & murt *vt*

murderer *n* marbhaiche *m*, mortair & murtair *m*

murmur, murmuring *n* (*of voices, water*) crònan *m*, monmhar *m*, (*esp of water*) torman *m*

muscle *n* fèith *f*

muscular *adj* fèitheach

muse *v* meòmhraich & meamhraich *vi*, (*more fam*) cnuas & cnuasaich *vi*, (**on, about** air)

museum *n* taigh-tasgaidh *m*

music *n* ceòl *m*

musical *adj* **1** ceòlmhor, fonnmhor; **2** *in expr* ~ **instrument** inneal-ciùil *m*, ionns(t)ramaid *f*

musician *n* neach-ciùil *m*, ~**s** luchd-ciùil *m sing coll*

Muslim *n* & *adj* Muslamach *m*, Mohamadanach *m*

mussel *n* feusgan *m*

must *v* feum *vi*, (*more trad*) is/'s fheudar dhomh (*&c*), **we** ~ **go/leave** feumaidh sinn falbh, 's fheudar dhuinn falbh, **I** ~ **admit that . . .** feumaidh mi aideachadh gu . . . , ~ **you go?** am feum sibh falbh?, (*used impersonally*) **there** ~ **be a strike** feumaidh gu bheil stailc *f* ann

mutate *v* mùth *vi*

mutation *n* mùthadh *m*

mutton *n* muilt-fheoil *f*, feòil-caorach *f*

mutual *adj* **1** *can be conveyed by a prep phrase including* (a *&c*) chèile, *eg* **their** ~ **respect/loathing** (*&c*) am meas/a' ghràin (*&c*) a th' aca air a chèile, **our** ~ **friend** an caraid againn, an caraid a th' againn le chèile; **2** *can also be conveyed by a noun with the prefix* co-, *eg* ~ **agreement** co-chòrdadh *m*, co-aontachd *f*, co-rèiteachadh *m*, ~ **consent** co-aontachadh *m*, ~ **acquaintance** co-eòlas *m*, ~ **assistance** co-chuideachadh *m*

my *poss adj* mo, *also very commonly expr by art plus noun followed by* agam, ~ **mother** mo mhàthair *f*, ~ **home** mo dhachaigh *f invar*, ~ **back is sore** tha mo dhruim *m* goirt, ~ **car/watch** an càr/an t-uaireadair agam, ~ **insurance policy** am poileasaidh-urrais agam, *as a general rule, the more intimate the connection, the more likely is* mo *to be used, note however examples such as the following,* ~ **wife** a' bhean agam, ~ **husband** an duine agam & (*from some speakers*) mo dhuine *m*, ~ **house** an taigh agam & mo thaigh

myself *reflexive pron* mi-fhìn, **I saw** ~ **in the mirror** chunnaic mi mi-fhìn san sgàthan *m*, **I was drying** ~ bha mi gam thiormachadh fhìn, **by** ~ leam fhìn, **I made the cake** ~ rinn mi-fhìn a' chèic, **as for** ~ air mo shon fhìn.

mysterious *adj* dìomhair

mystery *n* dìomhaireachd *f invar*

myth *n* uirsgeul *m*, fionnsgeul *m*, faoinsgeul *m*, miotas *m*

N

nail[1] *n* (*of finger, toe*) ìne *f*
nail[2] *n* (*joinery*) tarrang *f*, tarrag *f*
naked *adj* lomnochd, rùisgte, lom
nakedness *n* luime *f invar*
name *n* **1** ainm *m*, **what's your ~?** dè an t-ainm a th' ort/oirbh?, **my ~ is Angus** 's e Aonghas an t-ainm a th' orm, **second/family ~** sloinneadh *m*, cinneadh *m*; **2** (*reputation &c*) cliù *m invar*, **he made a ~ for himself** choisinn e cliù
name *v* ainmich *vt*, thoir ainm *m* (*with prep* air)
namely *adv* is/'s e sin (*in past tense* b' e sin), **one man arrived late, ~ MacDonald** thàinig aon fhear *m* air dheireadh, b' e sin an Dòmhnallach *m*
nap *n* norrag *f*, norrag chadail *m gen*, dùsal *m*, norradaich *f*, **take a ~** gabh norrag, dèan dùsal
napkin *n* neapaigin *f*
nappy *n* badan *m*
narration *n* (*abstr & con*) aithris *f*, (*con*) cùnntas *m*
narrow *adj* **1** (*phys*) caol, (*less usu*) cumhang, **a ~ bed** leabaidh chaol; **2** (*fig: in attitudes, opinions &c*) cumhang
narrow, narrows *n* caol *m*, caolas *m*
narrow *v* **1** (*as vi*) fàs *vi* caol, **the road ~ed** dh'fhàs an rathad *m* caol; **2** (*as vt; ~ down, restrict, reduce*) cuingealaich *vt* (**to** ri)
narrow-minded *adj* cumhang
nasty *adj* **1** (*esp in appearance*) mosach; **2** (*of person: in behaviour*) suarach (**to** ri), **I was ~ to her** bha mi suarach rithe
nation *n* nàisean *m*
national *adj* nàiseanta, **the ~ lottery** an crannchur nàiseanta, **~ insurance** àrachas *m* nàiseanta
nationalism *n* nàiseantachas *m*
nationalist *n* & *adj* nàiseantach *m*
nationality *n* nàiseantachd *f invar*
nationhood *n* nàiseantachas *m*
native *adj* **1** dùthchasach; **2** *in expr* **~ speaker** (*of a lang*) fileantach *m*
native *n* dùthchasach *m*
natural *adj* **1** (*in keeping with, or a product of, Nature*) nàdarra(ch), **~ selection** taghadh *m* nàdarra, **~ gas** gas *m* nàdarra; **2** (*in keeping with a person's nature*) dual(t)ach (**for,to** do), **it's ~ for him to be proud** tha e dualtach dha a bhith àrdanach
naturally *adv* **1** (*in a natural manner*) gu nàdarra(ch); **2** (*of course*) tha f(h)ios *m*, **that will be free of charge, ~** bidh sin saor 's an asgaidh *f*, tha f(h)ios
nature *n* **1** (*the natural world*) nàdar *m*, **~ conservancy** glèidhteachas *m* nàdair *gen*, **~ reserve** tèarmann *m* nàdair *gen*; **2** (*a person's temperament,*

character) nàdar *m*, aigne *f*, mèinn *f*; 3 (*esp hereditary* ~) dualchas *m*, **it's in his ~ to be proud** tha e na dhualchas dha a bhith àrdanach, *also* tha e dualtach dha a bhith àrdanach

naughty *adj* crost(a), dona, mì-mhodhail, **he's ~ today** tha e crosta an-diugh, **a ~ boy** gille dona

navel *n* imleag *f*

navy *n* 1 (*esp the force & institution*) nèibhi(dh) *mf*; 2 (*the vessels*) cabhlach *m*, loingeas *m*

Nazi *adj & n* Nàsach *m*

neap-tide *n* con(n)traigh *f*

near *adj* 1 faisg, **Christmas time is ~ now** tha àm *m* na Nollaig(e) faisg (òirnn) a-nis

near *prep* faisg (*with prep* air), dlùth (*with prep* do *or* air), an còir (*with gen*), **~ the town** faisg air a' bhaile *m*, dlùth don bhaile, **they didn't come ~ me** cha tàinig iad nam chòir

near *v* dlùthaich *vi* (*with prep* ri), teann *vi* (*with prep* ri *or* air), **we were ~ing the sea** bha sinn a' dlùthachadh ris a' mhuir *mf*, **it was ~ing midnight** bha e a' teannadh air meadhan-oidhche *m*

nearly *adv* 1 faisg air, teann air, **~ a month ago** faisg/teann air mìos *mf* air ais; 2 cha mhòr *adv*, theab *v def*, **we see her ~ every day** bidh sinn ga faicinn a h-uile là *m* cha mhòr, **we ~ missed the bus** theab sinn am bus a chall, **I ~ fell** theab mi tuiteam, **they ~ ruined me** theab iad mo sgriosadh; 3 *note also conj* gu(s) *plus verbal expr, & double neg expr* cha mhòr nach (*conj*), **I'm ~ ready** tha mi gu bhith deiseil, **he was ~ dropping the parcel** bha e gus am parsail a leigeil às, **I ~ lost my purse** cha mhòr nach do chaill mi an sporan agam

nearness *n* faisge *f invar*

neat *adj* (*esp of person*) grinn, cuimir, (*of person, object*) sgiobalta, (*esp of objects*) snasail, snasmhor, **a ~ wee boat** eathar beag snasmhor

neatness *n* grinneas *m*, sgiobaltachd *f invar*

necessary *adj* deatamach, riatanach, (*less usu & weaker*) feumail

neck *n* 1 amha(i)ch *f*, muineal *m*, **the back of the ~** cùl *m* na h-amhaich

neckband, necklace *n* crios-muineil *m*

nectar *n* neactair *m*

need *n* 1 feum *m*, (*more trad*) easbhaidh *f*; 2 *in expr* **in ~** feumach, easbhaidheach, (**of** air), **in ~ of improvement** feumach air (a) leasachadh *m*; 3 (*indigence*) airc *f*, uireasbhaidh *f*

need *v* feum *vti def*, bi *vi irreg* feum *m* agam (*&c*) (*with prep* air), bi *vi irreg* a dhìth/a dh'easbhaidh (*with prep* air), bi *vi irreg* feumach (*with prep* air), **it ~s a bit of tidying up yet** feumaidh e beagan *m* sgioblachaidh *m gen* fhathast, **I ~ money** feumaidh mi airgead *m*, tha feum agam air airgead, tha airgead a dhìth orm, **what do they ~?** dè a tha a dhith orra/a dh'easbhaidh orra?, **I ~ some peace** tha mi feumach air fois *f*; 2 (*often with implication* 'don't bother') cha leig/ruig thu (*&c*) (a) leas *m* *invar*, **you don't ~ to come with us** cha leig thu (a) leas tighinn còmhla rinn; **3** (*with 'at least' implied*) chan fhuilear *adv*, *with prep* do, **he ~s a fortnight off** chan fhuilear dha cola-deug *m invar* dheth

needed *adj* (*lacking*) a dhìth, **some pepper is ~** tha piobar *m* a dhìth

needle *n* **1** snàthad *f*; **2** *in exprs* **eye of a ~** crò-snàthaid *m*, **knitting ~** bior-fighe *m*

needlework *n* **1** (*the activity*) grèis *f*; **2** (*the product*) obair-ghrèis *f*

needy *adj* feumach, easbhaidheach, uireasbhach, *in expr* **a ~ person** uireasbhach *m*

negative *adj* àicheil

neglect *n* dearmad *m*

neglect *v* **1** (*fail to perform an action &c*) dearmaid *vi*, cuir *vt* air dhearmad *m*, **I ~ed to inform you** dhearmaid mi fios *m* a chur thugaibh, **~ to do something** cuir rudeigin air dhearmad; **2** (*~ something/someone*) dearmaid *vt*, leig *vt* air dhearmad *m*

neglectful *adj* dearmadach

negligence *n* dearmad *m*, dearmadachd *f invar*

negligent *adj* dearmadach

neigh *n* sitir *f*

neigh *v* sitrich *vi*

neighing *n* sitir *f*

neighbour *n* nàbaidh *m*, coimhearsnach *m*

neighbhourhood *n* coimhearsnachd *f invar*, nàbaidheachd *f invar*

neighbourly *adj* nàbaidheil

neither *adv* **1** nas motha, **I won't go home! ~ will I!** cha tèid mi dhachaigh! cha tèid mise nas motha!, *also* (*more idiomatic*) cha tèid no mise!; **2** *in constr* **~ ... nor** (*followed by nouns or proper nouns*) aon chuid *f* ... no, **he'll marry ~ Morag nor Mary** cha phòs e aon chuid Mòrag no Màiri, (*followed by adjs*) eadar, **he is ~ small nor big** tha e eadar beag agus mòr; **3** (*idiom*) **it's ~ one thing nor another** tha e eadar-dhà-lionn

neither *conj* cha mhotha (a), **~ did anyone else see me** cha mhotha (a) chunnaic duine *m* eile mi

neither *pron* (*for m nouns*) fear *m* seach fear, (*for f nouns*) tè *f* seach tè, **I've two sons but ~ (of them) is married** tha dà mhac agam ach chan eil fear seach fear dhiubh pòsta

neologism *n* nuadh-fhacal *m*

neophyte *n* (*relig*) iompachan *m*

nephew *n* (*brother's son*) mac *m* bràthar *m gen*, (*sister's son*) mac peathar (*gen of* piuthar *f*), **my ~** mac mo bhràthar *or* mac mo pheathar

Neptune *n* Neiptiùn *m*

nerve *n* **1** (*anat*) lèith *f*, nearbh *f*; **2** (*brass neck, cheek*) bathais *f*, aghaidh *f*, (*idioms*) **what a ~!** abair bathais/aghaidh, **what a ~ he's got!** nach ann air(san)/aige(san) a tha a' bhathais/an aghaidh!; **3** *in expr* **get on someone's ~s** leamhaich cuideigin

nervous, nervy *adj* clisgeach, nearbhach, frionasach

nest *n* nead *m*

net *adj* lom, ~ **weight** cudthrom *m* lom

net *n* lìon *m*, **fishing** ~ lìon-iasgaich

nether *adj* ìochd(a)rach

netting *n* lìon *m*

nettle *n* feanntag *f*, deanntag *f*

network *n* lìonra *m*

neuk *n* cùil *f*

neuter *adj* (*lang*) neodrach

neuter *v* spoth *vt*, geàrr *vt*

neutral *adj* neo-phàirteach

neutrality *n* neo-phàirteachd *f invar*

never *adv* **1** (*for past time: with a v in the neg*) a-riamh, **have you been to Egypt?** ~! an robh thu san Èipheit? cha robh a-riamh!; **2** (*for future time, with a v in the neg*) a-chaoidh, gu bràth, gu sìorraidh (tuilleadh), **they will ~ return** cha till iad a-chaoidh/gu bràth/gu sìorraidh tuilleadh; **3** (*misc exprs & idioms*) **pears are dear, ~ mind apples** tha peuran *fpl* daor, gun ghuth air ùbhlan *mpl*, ~ **mind!** coma leat!, dad ort!, **the twelfth of ~** là-luain *m*

nevertheless *adv* a dh'aindeoin chùis *f gen*, a dh'aindeoin sin, an dèidh sin, **he came last, but was pleased with himself ~** thàinig e air deireadh, ach bha e air a dhòigh a dh'aindeoin chùis/a dh'aindeoin sin

new *adj* ùr, nuadh, ~ **friends** caraidean *mpl* ùra, **New Year** a' Bhliadhna Ùr, **what's ~?** (*fam*) dè as ùr?, **brand/split ~** ùr-nodha, **the New Testament** An Tiomnnadh *m* Nuadh

newly *adv* ùr, nuadh, ~ **arrived from Glasgow** air ùr-thighinn à Glaschu, ~ **published** ùr on chlò *m*, air ùr-fhoillseachadh, ~ **wed** nuadh-phòsta

news *n* naidheachd *f*, fios *m*, guth *m*, (*TV, Radio &c*) **the ~** na naidheachdan, **is there any ~ of Mary?** a bheil fios/guth air Màiri?, **I haven't heard any ~ of him/it** cha chuala mi guth mu dheidhinn, (*idiom*) **there was (absolutely) no ~ of Murdo** sgeul *m* no fathann *m* cha robh air Murchadh

newsman *n* fear-naidheachd *m*, neach-naidheachd *m* (*pl* luchd-naidheachd *m sing coll*), naidheachdair *m*

newspaper pàipear-naidheachd *m*

next *adj* **1** ath (*precedes the noun, which is lenited where possible: usu used with the art*), ~ **week** an ath sheachdain *f*, **the ~ man/one** an ath fhear *m*, **living ~ door** a' fuireach an ath-dhoras; **2** *in expr* ~ **to** (*phys*) ri taobh *f* (*with gen*), làmh ri (*with dat*)

next *adv* an dèidh sin, **and ~ they went to the cinema** agus an dèidh sin chaidh iad don taigh-dhealbh *m*

nibble *v* creim *vt*, pioc *vt*

nice *adj* (*people, objects, situations*) snog (*slightly fam*), (*esp people*) laghach, **a ~ man** duine *m* snog/laghach, **that was ~!** bha siud snog!, **a ~ place** àite *m* snog

nick *n* **1** (*indentation &c*) eag *f*; **2** (*fam in Eng: form, condition*) gleus *mf*, **in good ~** air (deagh) ghleus *mf dat*

nickname *n* far-ainm *m*, frith-ainm *m*

niece *n* (*brother's daughter*) nighean *f* bràthar *m gen*, (*sister's daughter*) nighean peathar (*gen of* piuthar *f*), **her ~** nighean a bràthar *or* nighean a peathar

niggardly *adj* spìocach, mosach

niggling *adj* (*situations &c*) frionasach, **they're constantly asking me ~ questions** bidh iad a' cur chèistean *fpl* frionasach orm fad na h-ùine

night *n* **1** oidhche *f*, **Tuesday ~** oidhche-Mhàirt, **good ~!** oidhche mhath (leat/leibh)!, **a ~'s lodging/accommodation** cuid *f* oidhche *gen*, **by ~ and by day** a dh'oidhche 's a là *m*; **2** *in expr* **from morning till ~** o mhoch gu dubh

nightgown *n* gùn-oidhche *m*

nightmare *n* trom-laighe *mf*, **like a person in the grip of/having a ~** mar neach a bhiodh fo throm-laighe

nil *n* (*in scores &c*) neoni *f invar*

nimble *adj* **1** (*in performing tasks &c*) clis, deas, ealamh; **2** (*athletic, agile*) lùthmhor

nimbleness *n* **1** (*in performing tasks &c*) cliseachd *f invar*; **2** (*phys agility*) lùth *&* lùths *m*

nine *num* **1** naoi *or* naodh; **2** (*of people*) naoinear *mf*, **~ sons** naoinear mhac (*mpl gen*)

nineteen *num* naoi-deug *or* naodh-deug

no *adj* **1** *expr by neg forms of the verb followed by the appropriate noun*, **we have ~ money** chan eil airgead *m* againn, **this machine's ~ good/use** chan eil feum *m* anns an inneal *m* seo, **there are ~ fairies** chan eil sìthichean *fpl* ann, **we eat ~ meat** cha bhi sinn ag ithe feòla (*gen of* feòil *f*), **we found ~ gold** cha do lorg sinn òr *m* (sam bith/idir); **2** (*expr prohibition*) chan fhaodar (*present passive of* faod *vi*) *followed by the appropriate verbal noun*, **~ smoking** chan fhaodar smocadh *m*

no *adv*, *the negating word is expressed in Gaelic by putting the v of the question into the neg*, **is he there? ~** a bheil e ann? chan eil, **did you do it? ~** an do rinn thu e? cha do rinn, **is it a cat you've got? ~** an e cat *m* a th' agad? chan e, **are you Alan? ~** an sibhse Ailean? cha mhì

nobbly *adj* cnapach

nobility *n* **1** (*abstr quality*) uaisle *f invar*; **2** (*con*) **the ~** na h-uaislean *mpl*

noble *adj* uasal, flathail

noble, nobleman *n* duine-uasal *m*, flath *m*, mòr-uasal *m*

nobody, no-one *n* duine *m* (*after neg v*), **I saw ~ (at all)** chan fhaca mi duine (sam bith), chan fhaca mi duine no duine, **there was ~ on the road** cha robh duine (beò) air an rathad *m*, **~ saw it** chan fhaca duine e

no-claims discount *n* lughdachadh *m* neo-thagraidh *m gen*

nod *n* gnogadh *m* cinn (*gen of* ceann *m*)

nod *v* **1** gnog an ceann; **2** *in expr* ~ **off** rach *vi* na (*&c*) c(h)lò-chadal *m*, norradaich *vi*, **she ~ded off** chaidh/thuit i na clò-chadal

noise *n* fuaim *mf*, (*esp louder* ~) toirm *f*, faram *m*

noisy *adj* fuaimneach, faramach

nomad *n* iniltear *m*

nominate *v* ainmich *vt*

nomination *n* ainmeachadh *m*

non- *prefix* neo- *eg* **non-renewable** *adj* neo-leantainneach, **non-resident** *n* neo-àitiche *m*, **non-political** neo-phoileataigeach

non-commital *adj* leam leat, neo-cheangaltach

none *pron* **1** (*of objects*) gin *pron* (*after neg v*), **he was wanting nails but I had** ~ bha e ag iarraidh thairngean (*gen pl of* tarraing *f*) ach cha robh gin agam; **2** (*of people*) aon duine *m*, aon fhear *m*, aon tè *f*, *after neg verb*, **I invited a lot of people but ~ came** thug mi cuireadh *m* do mhòran dhaoine ach cha tàinig aon duine; **3** *in expr* **that's ~ of your business!** chan e sin do ghnothach-sa! *m*

nonetheless *adv* a dh'aindeoin chùis *f gen*, a dh'aindeoin sin, an dèidh sin, **he came last, but was pleased with himself** ~ thàinig e air deireadh, ach bha e air a dhòigh a dh'aindeoin chùis/a dh'aindeoin sin

nook *n* cùil *f*

noon *n* meadhan-là *m*

no-one *n* duine *m* (*after neg v*), **I saw ~ (at all)** chan fhaca mi duine (sam bith), chan fhaca mi duine idir/duine no duine, **there was ~ on the road** cha robh duine (beò) air an rathad *m*, ~ **saw it** chan fhaca duine e

noose *n* lùb *f*

nor *adv* **1** nas motha, **I won't go home! ~ will I!** cha tèid mi dhachaigh! cha tèid mise nas motha!, *also* (*more idiomatic*) cha tèid no mise!; **2** *in constr* **neither . . . ~** (*followed by nouns or proper nouns*) aon chùid *f* . . . no, **he'll marry neither Morag ~ Mary** cha phòs e aon chuid Mòrag no Màiri, (*followed by adjs*) eadar, **he is neither small ~ big** tha e eadar beag agus mòr; **2** (*idiom*) **it's neither one thing ~ another** (*ie* six and half a dozen) tha e eadar-dhà-lionn

nor *conj* cha mhotha (a), ~ **did anyone else see me** cha mhotha (a) chunnaic duine *m* eile mi

normal *adj* cumanta, àbhaisteach

normality *n* cumantas *m*

normally *adv* an cumantas *m*, am bitheantas *m*

Norse *adj* Lochlannach

Norseman *n* Lochlannach *m*

north *adj* tuath, **Perth is ~ of Kinross** tha Peairt tuath air Ceann Rois, **North Uist** Uibhist a Tuath, **the ~ country** an taobh tuath

north *n* **1** tuath *f invar*, **living in/going to the ~** a' fuireach/a' dol mu thuath, **the islands in the** ~ na h-eileanan *mpl* mu thuath, **a breeze from the** ~ oiteag *f* on tuath, **the** ~ (*of an area*) an taobh tuath, **the** ~ **of the country** taobh tuath na dùthcha (*gen of* dùthaich *f*), ceann a tuath na dùthcha; **2** (*the compass point*) an àird(e) *f* tuath

northerly *adj* mu thuath, **the** ~ **islands** na h-eileanan *mpl* mu thuath

northern *adj* **1** tuath, **the** ~ **part of the country** taobh tuath na dùthcha (*gen of* dùthaich *f*), ceann a tuath na dùthcha; **2** (*astronomy*) **the Northern Lights** Na Fir *mpl* Chlis

Norway *n* **1** Nirribhidh *f*, (*more trad*) Lochlann *f*; **2** *in expr* ~ **spruce** giuthas *m* Lochlannach

Norwegian *n & adj* Lochlannach *m*

nose *n* sròn *f*, **my** ~ **is bleeding** tha mo shròn a' leum, ~ **bleed** leum-sròine *m*

nostalgia *n* cianalas *m*, fadachd *f invar*, fadal *m*, (**for** ri)

nostalgic *adj* cianalach

nostril *n* cuinnean *m*

not *adv*, **1** *expressed by pre-verbal particles* cha, chan, cha do, nach, nach do, mur(a), na *&c*, **I will** ~ **go** cha tèid mi, **I'm** ~ **tired** chan eil mi sgìth, **I'm** ~ **doing it** chan eil mi ga dhèanamh, **I did** ~ **do that** cha do rinn mi sin, **he did** ~ **know her** cha b' aithne dha i, **I was** ~ **born there** cha do rugadh mi an sin, **isn't it empty?** nach eil e falamh?, **won't you go (there)?** nach tèid sibh ann?, **didn't you do it?** nach do rinn thu e?, **she said (that) she was** ~ **tired** thuirt i nach robh i sgìth, **if they do** ~ **go (there)** mur(a) tèid iad ann, **do** ~ **sing!** na seinn!; **2** (*rendered by* gun *followed by an infinitive in exprs such as*) **he asked me** ~ **to be rude** dh'iarr e orm gun a bhith mì-mhodhail

notch *n* eag *f*

note *n* **1** nota *f*, **take** ~**s** gabh notaichean, **send me a** ~ cuir nota thugam; **2** (*music*) pong *m*

note *v* **1** (*acknowledge*) thoir fainear (*with prep* do); **2** (*take mental note*) meòmhraich & meamhraich *vt*

nothing *n* **1** (*zero*) neoni *f invar*, (*also in fig expr*) **come to** ~ rach *vi* gu neoni; **2** (*in neg exprs*) càil *m invar* (sam bith), rud *m* sam bith, **I've got** ~ **at all** chan eil càil/rud sam bith agam, **what did you buy?** ~ dè a cheannaich thu? cha do cheannaich càil, **we've** ~ **to do** chan eil càil againn ri dhèanamh, ~ **would make me do it** chan eil càil a bheireadh orm a dhèanamh; **3** (*idioms*) **have** ~ **to do with him/it!** na gabh gnothach *m* ris!, **he said** ~ cha duirt e guth *m*/bìd *m*/smid *f* (*fam*)

notice *n* **1** (*attention*) aire *f invar*, feart *f*, for *m invar*, sùim *f*, **without taking (any)** ~ **of it** gun aire a thoirt dha, gun for/feart a thoirt air, **I'm not taking any** ~ **of what they said** chan eil sùim sam bith agam de na thuirt iad; **2** (*information displayed*) sanas *m*, **she put up a** ~ **on the board** chuir i sanas an àird/chuir i suas sanas air a' bhòrd *m*; **3** (*advance notification*) brath *f*, **receive** ~ faigh brath (**of** air)

notice *v* thoir an aire, thoir fa-near, (*with prep* do), mothaich *vt*, **she didn't ~ the car** cha tug i an aire/cha tug i fa-near don chàr *m*, **I ~d it in passing** mhothaich mi e san dol *m invar* seachad

notorious *adj* (*esp persons*) iomraiteach

nought *n* (*scores, marks &c*) neoni *f invar*, (*also in fig expr*) **come to ~** rach *vi* gu neoni

noun *n* ainmear *m*, **plural ~** ainmear iolra

nourishment *n* lòn *m*, beathachadh *m*

novel *adj* 1 (*new*) ùr, nuadh; 2 (*esp unusual, odd*) annasach

novel *n* nobhail *f*

novelist *n* nobhailiche *mf*

novelty *n* 1 (*abstr*) ùrachd *f invar*; 2 (*novel object, idea &c*) annas *m*

now *adv* 1 a-nis(e), (*more immediate: just ~, right ~, at the moment*) an-dràsta, (*less usu*) an ceart(u)air, **he's getting old ~** tha e a' fàs sean a-nis, **we'll do it (right) ~** nì sinn an-dràsta (fhèin)/an-ceartair e; 2 (*excl: expr disapproval*) **~ ~!** ud ud!

nub *n*, *in expr* **the ~ of the matter** cnag *f* na cùise

nuclear *adj* niuclasach, **~ waste** sgudal *m* niuclasach

nude *adj* lomnochd

nude *n* lom-neach *m*

nudity *n* luime *f invar*

nuisance plàigh *f*, dragh *m*

numb *adj* lapach, meilichte

numb *v* (*esp with cold*) meilich *vt*

number *n* àireamh *f*, figear *m*, **~ four** àireamh a ceithir, **phone ~** àireamh-fòn *f*, **a great ~ of people** àireamh mhòr dhaoine *mpl gen*, **cardinal/ordinal ~** figear àrdail/òrdail

numeral *n* (*arith &c*) figear *m*

numerous *adj* lìonmhor

nun *n* cailleach dhubh

nurse *n* nurs *f*, (*more trad*) banaltram *f*, bean-eiridinn *f*

nurse *v* eiridnich *vt*, altraim *vt*

nursery *n* 1 (*in house*) seòmar-cloinne *m*; 2 (*ed: ~ school*) sgoil *f* àraich (*gen of* àrach *m used adjectivally*); 3 *in expr* **~ education** foghlam *m* fo-sgoile; 4 (*gardening*) lios-àraich *m*

nursing *n* eiridinn *m invar*, banaltramachd *f invar*

nut *n* (*bot & engin*) cnò *f*, **hazel~** cnò-challtainn *f*, **a ~ and bolt** cnò is crann *m*

nutrients *npl* beathachadh *m*

nuts, nutty *adj* (*fam: mad*) às a (*&c*) c(h)iall *f*

nutty *adj* (*taste*) cnòthach

nylon *n* nàidhlean *m*, (*as adj*) nàidhlein *gen*, **a ~ shirt** lèine *f* nàidhlein

O

oak *n* darach *m*

oar *n* ràmh *m*

oath *n* (*testimony &c, also swear, curse*) mionn *mf*, mionnan *m*, bòid *f*, **take/swear an ~** thoir mionnan/bòid

oatmeal *n* min-choirce *f*

oats *n* coirce *m sing coll*

obedience *n* ùmhlachd *f invar*

obedient *adj* umha(i)l

obeisance *n* (*before royalty &c*) ùmhlachd *f invar*

obey *v* bi *vi irreg* umhail (*with prep* do)

object *n* **1** rud *m*, nì *m*; **2** (*butt, recipient*) cùis *f*, culaidh *f*, (*less usu*) fàth *m invar*, (*trad*) cuspair *m*, **they were an ~ of ridicule** bha iad nan cùis-mhagaidh *f*/nan culaidh-mhagaidh *f*, **an ~ of envy** culaidh-fharmaid *f*, **the ~ of his love** (*trad*) cuspair a ghràidh *m gen*; **3** (*reason, purpose*) adhbhar *m*, **the ~ of his journey** adhbhar an turais aige; **4** (*gram*) cuspair *m*

object *v* cuir *vi* an aghaidh (*with gen*), **~ to the proposals** cuir an aghaidh nam molaidhean *mpl*

objective *adj* cothromach, neo-phàirteach

objective *n* rùn *m*, amas *m*

objectivity *n* cothromachd *f invar*, neo-phàirteachd *f invar*

obligation *n* comain *f* (**to** aig), **under an ~ to X** fo chomain aig X

oblige *v* **1** (*exert moral compulsion*) cuir *vi* mar fhiachaibh (*obs dat pl of* fiach *m*) (*with prep* air), **they ~d me to accept the post** chuir iad mar fhiachaibh orm an dreuchd *f* a ghabhail; **2** (*do a favour*) dèan fàbhar *m*, dèan bàidh *f*, dèan seirbheis *f*, (*with prep* do), **they ~d me** rinn iad fàbhar/bàidh/seirbheis dhomh

obliged *adj & past part* **1** (*morally compelled*) **they made me feel ~ to accept the post** chuir iad mar fhiachaibh (*obs dat pl of* fiach *m*) orm an dreuchd *f* a ghabhail, **I was ~ to repay the loan** chaidh a chur mar fhiachaibh orm an t-iasad a dhìoladh; **2** (*grateful, in moral debt*) an comain (*with gen*), fo fhiachaibh (*obs dat pl of* fiach *m*) (**to** do), **I'm (very much) ~ to you** tha mi (fada) nad chomain, **I'm ~ to them**, tha mi fo fhiachaibh dhaibh

obliging *adj* èasgaidh, deònach

oblique *adj* claon, fiar

obliqueness *n* claonadh *m*

oblivion *n* dìochuimhne *f invar*, **pass into ~** rach *vi* air dìochuimhne

obscene *adj* **1** drabasta, draosta; **2** (*in expr*) **~ talk** rabhd *& ràbhart *m*

obscenity *n* drabastachd *f invar*, draostachd *f invar*

obscure *adj* **1** (*poorly lit &c*) doilleir; **2** (*abstruse*) deacair; **3** (*little known*) neo-ainmeil, neo-aithnichte

obscure *v* 1 (*darken*) doilleirich *vt*, neulaich *vt*; 2 (*conceal*) ceil *vt*, falaich *vt*

obsequious *adj* umha(i)l

obsequiousness ùmhlachd *f invar*

observance *n* (*of rules, principles &c*) glèidheadh *m*

observant *adj* mothachail, furachail

observe *v* 1 (*notice*) mothaich *vt*; 2 (*follow rules &c*) glèidh *vt*; 3 (*celebrate*) cùm *vt*, **we didn't ~ New Year** cha do chùm sinn a' Bhliadhna Ùr

obsession *n* beò-ghlacadh *m*

obsolete *adj* à cleachdadh *m*

obstacle *n* (*lit & fig*) bacadh *m*, cnap-starra *m*

obstinacy *n* raige *f invar*

obstinate *adj* rag, dùr, (*stronger*) rag-mhuinealach

obstruct *v* bac *vt*

obstruction *n* bacadh *m*, cnap-starra *m*

obtain *v* faigh *vt irreg*, **~ employment** faigh obair *f*/cosnadh *m*, **~ fraudulently** faigh *vt* le foill *f*

obvious *adj* follaiseach, soilleir, am follais, **it's ~ he's not guilty** tha e follaiseach/soilleir nach eil e ciontach, **become ~** thig *vi* am follais *f*

obviously *adv* 1 tha f(h)ios, **that will be free of charge, ~** bidh sin saor 's an asgaidh, tha fios; 2 *also rendered by* tha e follaiseach/soilleir, **he's ~ not guilty** tha e follaiseach/soilleir nach eil e ciontach

obviousness *n* follais *f invar*

occasion *n* 1 uair *f*, turas *m*, **I was there on one ~** bha mi ann uair, bha mi ann aon turas, *in expr* **some ~ or other** uair no uaireigin; 2 (*cause, reason*) adhbhar *m*, **we had ~ to complain** bha adhbhar-gearain *m* againn, bha adhbhar againn a bhith a' gearan; 3 (*event, function &c*) tachartas *m*, **a civic ~** tachartas catharra

occasional *adj* 1 corra (*precedes the noun, which it lenites where possible*), *also expr by adv phrase* bho àm gu àm, **I have the ~ pint with him** gabhaidh mi corra phinnt *m* còmhla ris, *also* gabhaidh mi pinnt còmhla ris bho àm gu àm

occasionally *adv* bho àm gu àm, an-dràsta 's a-rithist, uaireannan, air uairean (*trad* air uairibh)

occupant *n* (*of building &c*) neach-còmhnaidh *m* (*pl* luchd-còmhnaidh *m sing coll*)

occupation *n* obair *f*, (*usu non-manual*) dreuchd *f*

occur *v* 1 (*take place*) tachair *vi*, **it ~red two years ago** thachair e o chionn dà bhliadhna/dà bhliadhna *f sing* air ais; 2 (*come to mind &c*) thig *vi* a-steach (*with prep* air), **it ~red to me that they weren't listening** thàinig e a-steach orm nach robh iad ag èisteachd

occurrence *n* tachartas *m*, tuiteamas *m*

ocean *n* cuan *m*, fairge *f*, **the Atlantic Ocean** An Cuan Siar

o'clock *adv* uair *f*, uairean *fpl*, **at two ~** aig dà uair, **it's three ~** tha e trì uairean, **twelve ~** dà uair dheug

octave *n* (*music*) gàmag *f*

October *n* (*used with art*) An Dàmhair *f*

odd *adj* **1** (*not even*) còrr, ~ **number** àireamh chòrr; **2** (*occasional, rare*) corra (*precedes the noun, which it lenites where possible*), **the ~ person came in from time to time** thigeadh corra dhuine *m* a-steach bho àm *m* gu àm; **3** (*strange, unusual*) neònach, annasach

odds *npl in expr* **fair ~** cothrom *m* na Fèinne

odds and ends criomagan *fpl*, treal(l)aich *f*

odour *n* boladh *m*

oesophagus *n* slugan *m*

of *prep* de *&* dhe, (*takes the dat, lenites following consonant where possible*), ~ **me** dhìom(sa), ~ **you** (*sing*) dhìot(sa), ~ **him/it** (*m*) dheth(san), ~ **her/it** (*f*) dhith(se), ~ **us** dhinn(e), ~ **you** (*pl*) dhibh(se), ~ **them** dhiubh(san), **most ~ it** a' chuid *f* as mò dheth, **at this time ~ the year** aig an àm seo den bhliadhna *f*, **the twentieth ~ the month** am ficheadamh là *m* den mhìos *mf*, **full ~ milk** làn de bhainne *m*, **one ~ those who were there** fear *m* de na bha ann, **a fool ~ a man** amadan *m* de dhuine *m*, **a brooch ~ silver** bràiste *f* de dh'airgead *m*, *Note*: de / dhe *can occur as* a, *usu in set exprs, eg* ~ **one mind** (*ie unanimous*) a dh'aon rùn *m*

of course *adv* tha f(h)ios *m*, **that will be free of charge,** ~ bidh sin saor 's an asgaidh, tha fios, **are you pleased? ~ I am!** a bheil thu toilichte? tha fios gu bheil!, *also* 's mi a tha!

off *adv* **1** dheth, **the electricity's ~** tha an dealan dheth, **turn the radio ~** cuir dheth an rèidio *m*, **the cream's going ~** tha an t-uachdar a' dol dheth; **2** (*in phrases & idioms expr movement, departure*) **be ~!** tog ort!, ~ **you go home!** thalla(ibh) (*imper, for* falbh) dhachaigh! *adv*, ~ **you go to the shop for me!** thalla don bhùth *mf* dhomh!, **right! I'm ~** ceart! tha mi a' falbh, **she took herself ~/~ she went to America** thug i Ameireagaidh *f* oirre; **3** (*misc exprs*) **far ~, a long way ~** fad' air falbh, **I dropped/dozed ~** chaidh mi nam chlò-chadal *m*, **make ~** tàrr *vi* às, *also* tàir *vi* às, **put something ~ (till another day)** cuir rudeigin air ath là *m*, **go ~** (*ie detoriate*) rach *vi* bhuaithe, **she went ~** chaidh i bhuaithe, (*clothing &c*) **take ~** cuir *vt* dheth (*&c*), **take your coat ~** cuir dhìot do chòta *m*

off *prep* bhàrr (*for* de bhàrr *m*, *lit* from the top or surface (of)), *also* far, (*with gen*), **he took a book ~ the table** thug e leabhar bhàrr a' bhùird, **a stone fell ~ the wall** thuit clach *f* far a' ghàrraidh

offence *n* **1** oilbheum *m*, **give ~ to someone** dèan oilbheum do chuideigin; **2** (*illegal action*) coire *f*, eucoir *f*, **commit an ~** dèan coire, *also* ciontaich *vi*

offend *v* **1** (*give offence to*) dèan oilbheum *m* (*with prep* do), **she ~ed me** rinn i oilbheum dhomh; **2** (*law: commit an illegal action*) dèan coire *f*, ciontaich *vi*

offender *n* (*law*) ciontach *m*, coireach *m*

offensive *adj* **1** (*action &c*) oilbheumach, tàmailteach; **2** (*smell &c*) sgreamhail, sgreataidh

offer *n* tairgse *f*, **make an** ~ thoir tairgse (**for** air, **to** do)

offer *v* **1** tairg *vt*, tabhainn *vt*, **he ~ed his help** thairg e a chuideachadh *m*, **he ~ed to do it** thairg e a dhèanamh; **2** (*relig:* ~ *up as a sacrifice*) ìobair *vt*

offering *n* **1** tabhartas *m*; **2** (*relig: sacrificial* ~) ìobairt *f*

off-hand *adj* **1** (*welcome, reception &c*) fionnar; **2** (*attitude &c: uninterested*) coma-co-dhiù, (*not giving full attention*) fad' às

office *n* oifig *f*, oifis *f*, **the post** ~ oifis a' phuist, **the Scottish Office** Oifis na h-Alba

officer *n* **1** (*in forces &c*) oifigear *m*, oifigeach *m*; **2** *in expr* **church** ~ maor-eaglais *m*

official *adj* oifigeil, **let them know ~ly** cuir fios *m* thuca gu h-oifigeil

official *n* oifigeach *m*, **he's a council** ~ tha e na oifigeach aig a' chomhairle *f*

offspring *n* clann *f sing coll*, (*more remote generations*) gineal *mf sing coll*, sìol *m sing coll*, sliochd *m sing coll*

often *adv* (gu) tric, iomadach uair *f*, iomadh uair, (*more trad*) gu minig, **that ~ happens** bidh sin a' tachairt gu tric, **she doesn't come as ~ as she used to** cha tig i cho tric agus a chleachd (i)/agus a b' àbhaist, **we ~ used to go there** is tric a rachadh sinn ann, **I did it ~** rinn mi iomadach/iomadh uair e

oil *n* **1** ola *f*, ùillidh *m*, **vegetable** ~ ola-luis, **mineral** ~ ola-thalmhainn; **2** *in exprs* ~ **lamp** crùisgean *m*, ~ **rig** crann-ola *m*, ~ **tanker** tancair *m* ola *f gen*

oily *adj* ùilleach

ointment *n* ungadh *m*

OK, okay *adj, adv & excl* ceart gu leòr, **that's** ~ tha sin ceart gu leòr, **I got on** ~ chaidh dhomh ceart gu leòr, **do it tomorrow!** ~**!** dèan a-màireach e! ceart gu leòr!

old *adj* **1** (*of considerable age, also former*) sean (seann *before* d, s, t, l, n *or* r) *lenites following cons exc for* d, s & t, ~ **people** seann daoine *mpl*, **in the** ~ **days** sna seann làithean *mpl*; **2** (*as prefix*) sean(n)-, *eg* ~**-fashioned** sean-fhasanta; *note also the form* seana-, *eg* ~ **maid** seana-mhaighdeann *f*, ~ **bachelor** seana-ghille *m*

omen *n* manadh *m*

omission *n* dearmad *m*, **sins of** ~ peacaidhean *mpl* dearmaid *gen*

omit *v* **1** (*fail to include*) fàg às; **2** (*through negligence, fail to perform an action &c*) dearmaid *vi*, cuir *vt* air dhearmad *m*, **I ~ted to inform you** dhearmaid mi fios *m* a chur thugaibh, ~ **to do something** cuir rudeigin air dhearmad

omni- *prefix* uile-, *eg* ~**potent** uile-chumhachdach

on *prep* **1** air, ~ **me** orm(sa), ~ **you** (*sing*) ort(sa), ~ **him/it** *m* air(san), ~ **her/it** *f* oirre(se), ~ **us** òirnn(e), ~ **you** (*pl*) oirbh(se), ~ **them** orra(san), *prep prons*, ~ **the table** air a' bhòrd *m*, **a tune** ~ **the fiddle** port *m* air an

fhidhill (*dat of* fidheall *f*), **a book ~ history** leabhar *m* air eachdraidh
f, **~ a journey** air turas *m*, **~ my mind** air m' aire *f invar*, air m' aigne
f invar, air mo chùram *m*, **he was ~ good form** (*ie in fine fettle*) bha
e air a dheagh dhòigh *f*, **~ the spot** (*ie immediately*) anns a' bhad *m*,
an làrach *f* nam bonn *mpl*, **the television broke down ~ me** bhris an
telebhisean *m* sìos orm; **2** (*misc exprs*) **~ purpose** a dh'aon ghnothach,
~ my own nam aonar, leam fhìn, **~ drugs** a' gabhail dhrogaichean *fpl*,
air na drogaichean, **dependent ~ drugs** an urra ri drogaichean, na (*&c*)
t(h)ràill *mf* do dhrogaichean

on *adv* **1** (*expr progression, continuity*) air adhart, **from that time ~** bhon àm
m sin air adhart, **how are you getting ~?** ciamar a tha thu a' faighinn
air adhart, **her pupils are coming ~ well** tha na sgoilearan *mpl* aice
a' tighinn air adhart gu math, **and so ~** 's mar sin air adhart; **2** (*misc
exprs*) **they get ~ well (together)** tha iad gu math mòr aig a chèile, **the
light was ~** bha an solas air, **put your coat ~** cuir umad do chòta *m*,
we walked ~ choisich sinn romhainn, **she's always ~ at me!** tha i an
sàs annam an-còmhnaidh!, **he's got nothing ~** (*ie unclothed*) tha e dearg
rùisgte, **I've got nothing ~ at the moment** (*ie no commitments &c*) tha
mi saor an-dràsta, chan eil càil *m invar* agam ri dhèanamh an-dràsta,
what's ~ tomorrow? dè a tha a' dol a-màireach?

once *adv* **1** (*at some time in the past*) uair, uaireigin, **we were there ~** bha sinn
ann uair; **2** (*on a single occasion*) aon uair, aon turas *m*, **I went there ~**
chaidh mi ann aon uair/aon turas, **~ or twice** uair no dhà; **3** *in exprs*
~ upon a time fada fada ro seo, uaireigin den t-saoghal, **at ~** anns a'
bhad, air ball, gun dàil *f*

once *conj* (*ie as soon as*) aon uair is/'s/agus, **~ he got started everything
would be fine** aon uair 's gun tòisicheadh e bhiodh a h-uile càil *m
invar* air dòigh *f*

one *adj* **1** (*num*) aon (*lenites following cons exc for d, t & s*), (*emph*) aonan,
~ woman aon bhoireannach *m*, **it's ~** (*emph*) **pound he owes me, not
two** 's e aonan nota *f* a th' agam air, chan e na dhà; **2** (*often in contrast to
eile* **other**) an dara & an dàrna, **~ son is industrious but the other ~ is
lazy** tha an dara mac èasgaidh ach tha am fear eile leisg, **put to ~ side**
cuir an dara taobh *m*; **3** (*~ of a pair*) leth-, **on ~ leg** air leth-chois (*gen of
cas f*), **on ~ elbow** air mo/a &c leth-uilinn *f dat*

one *n* **1** (*representing a m sing noun*) fear *m*, **here are some books, take ~
or two of them** seo agad leabhraichean *mpl*, gabh fear no dhà dhiubh,
which ~ do you prefer? cò am fear as fheàrr leat?, (*idiom*) **I'm** (*&c*) **~ of
them** tha mise (*&c*) air fear dhiubh, **many people are tired of it, and
he's ~ of them** tha mòran dhaoine *mpl gen* sgìth dheth, agus tha esan
air fear dhiubh; **2** (*representing a f sing n*) tè *f invar*, **this ~ is smaller
than that ~** tha an tè seo nas lugha na an tè sin; **3** **~s** (*pl, of people &
objects*) feadhainn *f sing coll*, *used with art*, an fheadhainn, **these ~s are
going home** tha an fheadhainn seo a' dol dhachaigh, **the ~s that are**

on the shelf are broken but the other ~s are OK tha an fheadhainn a
th' air an sgeilp *f* briste ach tha an fheadhainn eile ceart gu leòr; **4** (*in
succession*) **~ after another/the other** an ceann *m* a chèile *m gen,* **aon an
dèidh aoin** *mf gen,* **three accidents ~ after the other** trì tubaistean *fpl*
an ceann a chèile/an dèidh a chèile; **5** (*in turn*) **~ after the other/~ by ~**
fear *m*/tè *f* mu seach, fear seach fear, tè seach tè, **~ after the other/~ by
~ they went through the door** fear mu seach/fear seach fear, chaidh
iad tron doras *m*; **6** (*idioms*) **it's all ~** (*ie indifferent*) chan eil e gu diofar,
that's all ~ to me is coma leam sin
one *pron* duine *m,* neach *m,* **it would amaze ~** chuireadh e iongnadh *m* air
duine, **a love ~ couldn't express** gaol *m* nach cuireadh neach an cèill
(*dat of* ciall *f*)
onerous *adj* trom
one-way *adj* aon-sligheach
onion *n* uinnean *m*
on-line *adj* air-loidhne
onlooker *n* neach-coimhid *m* (*pl* luchd-coimhid *m sing coll*)
onslaught *n* ionnsaigh *mf*
onus *n* uallach *m,* **the ~ is on you** (*emph*) 's ann oirbhse a tha an t-uallach
open *adj* **1** fosgailte, **an ~ window** uinneag fhosgailte, **the shop is ~** tha
a' bhùth *mf* fosgailte, **an ~** (*ie public*) **meeting** coinneamh fhosgailte;
2 (*of persons: frank, approachable &c*) fosgailte, fosgarra, faoilidh; **3** *in
exprs* **bring into the ~** thoir *vt* am follais *f,* **come into the ~** thig *vi* am
follais
open *v* fosgail *vti,* **~ the door!** fosgail an doras!, **the door ~ed** dh'fhosgail
an doras, **the shop's ~ing** tha a' bhùth *mf* a' fosgladh
opened *adj & past part* fosgailte,
open-handed *adj* fialaidh, fial
opener *n* fosglair *m*
opening *n* **1** (*aperture*) fosgladh *m,* beàrn *f;* **2** (*opportunity*) fosgladh *m,*
cothrom *m,* **an ~ in the market** fosgladh sa mhargadh *mf*
openness *n* (*of information, character*) fosgailteachd *f invar,* fosgarrachd *f
invar*
operate *v* obraich *vt,* **~ a machine** obraich inneal *m*
operation *n* **1** (*abstr*) gnìomh *m,* **put into ~** cuir *vt* an gnìomh; **2** (*con: project
&c*) gnothach *m,* **he'll be taking charge of the ~** bidh esan a' gabhail a'
ghnothaich os làimh (*dat of* làmh *f*); **3** (*medical ~*) opairèisean *m,* **she's
recovering from an ~** tha i a' faighinn seachad air opairèisean
opponent *n* **1** (*sport, competition &c*) farpaiseach *m;* **2** (*politics*) neach-
dùbhlain *m* (*pl* luchd-dùbhlain *m sing coll*)
opportune *adj* **1** (*timeous*) mithich, tràthail, na (*&c*) t(h)ràth *m,* **a word
(spoken) at an ~ moment** facal *m* na thràth; **2** (*appropriate, propitious*)
fàbharach, freagarrach
opportunity *n* cothrom *m,* fosgladh *m,* (*less usu*) fàth *m invar,* **opportunities**

for higher education cothroman air foghlam *m* àrd-ìre, **he saw an ~ in the clothing market** chunnaic e fosgladh ann am margadh *mf* an aodaich, **an ~ for some fun** fàth airson spòrsa *f gen*

oppose *v* cuir *vi* an aghaidh *(with gen)*

opposed *adj* an aghaidh *(with gen)*, **I'm (completely/totally) ~ to that** tha mi (calg-d(h)ìreach) an aghaidh sin, **they were (completely/totally) ~ to each other** bha iad (calg-d(h)ìreach) an aghaidh a chèile *m gen*

opposite *adv & prep*, mu choinneimh, fa chomhair, *(with gen)*, **the man ~ (me)** an duine a bha (na sheasamh &c) mum choinneimh, **I was ~ her** bha mi mu coinneimh, **he stopped ~ me** stad e fa mo chomhair

opposite *n* ceart-aghaidh *f*

opposition *n* **1** *(abstr)* cur *m* an aghaidh, dùbhlan *m*; **2** *(con: esp pol)* dùbhlanaich *mpl*, **the ~** na dùbhlanaich, *(as adj)* **~ parties** pàrtaidhean *mpl* dùbhlanach; **3** *(rivals in business, sport &c)* **the ~** na còmhstrithich *mpl*, na co-fharpaisich *mpl* (againn &c)

oppression *n* fòirneart *m*

oppressor *n* fear-fòirneirt *m* *(pl* luchd-fòirneirt *m sing coll)*

optic, optical *adj* fradharcach

option roghainn *mf*, **we've no ~** chan eil roghainn (eile) againn

or *conj* **1** no, **war ~ peace** cogadh *m* no sìth *f*; **2** *in expr* **~ else** air neo, **eat your dinner, ~ else you'll be hungry** gabh do dhìnnear *f*, air neo bidh an t-acras ort

oral *adj* **1** beòil *(gen of* beul *m, used adjectivally)*, **~ evidence** fianais-bheòil *f*; **2** *in expr* **~ tradition** beul-aithris *f*

orange *adj* orainds, dearg-bhuidhe, **what colour is it? (it's) ~** dè an dath a th' air? tha orainds

orange *n* **1** *(fruit)* orain(d)sear *m*; **2** *(colour)* orainds *f*, dearg-bhuidhe *m*

oration *n* òraid *f*

orbit *n* cuairt *f*, reul-chuairt *f*, **the sun's ~** cuairt na grèine

orchard *n* ubhalghort *m*

ordain *v* òrdaich *vt*

ordained *adj & past part* **1** òrdaichte; **2** *(fated)* an dàn *m* **(for** do), **what was ~ for him** na bha an dàn dha

ordeal *n* deuchainn *f*, *(stronger)* cruaidh-dheuchainn *f*

order *n* **1** *(command, also ~ in café &c)* òrdugh *m*, **he gave me an ~** thug e dhomh òrdugh; **2** *(correct sequence)* òrdugh *m*, **put in ~** cuir *vt* an òrdugh, òrdaich *vt*, **alphabetical ~** òrdugh aibidealach, **out of ~** a-mach à òrdugh; **3** *(orderliness, tidiness, organisation, as things should be)* òrdugh *m*, rian *m*, **in ~** ann an òrdugh; **4** *(working ~, condition)* dòigh *f*, gleus *mf*, òrdugh *m*, **in good ~** air dòigh, air (deagh) ghleus, *also* gleusta & gleusda *adj*, **put in good ~** cuir *vt* air dòigh, cuir *vt* air (deagh) ghleus, **out of ~** a-mach à òrdugh, *also* briste *adj*; **5** *in expr* **in ~ to** *conj* gus, **in ~ to clean the house** gus an taigh a ghlanadh

order *v* **1** *(instruct)* òrdaich *vi (with prep* do), **they ~ed me to shut the gates**

dh'òrdaich iad dhomh na geataichean *mpl* a dhùnadh; 2 (*in café &c*)
òrdaich *vti*

ordered *adj* òrdail, riaghailteach, rianail

orderliness *n* òrdugh *m*, riaghailteachd *f invar*, rian *m*

orderly *adj* òrdail, riaghailteach, rianail

ordinal *adj* òrdail, **an ~ number** cunntair *m* òrdail

ordinance *n* riaghailt *f*, reachd *m invar*

ordinary *adj* 1 àbhaisteach, cumanta, gnàthach; 2 (*as n*) *in expr* **out of the
~** às a' chumantas *m*

ore *n* mèinn(e) *f*

organ[1] *n* (*bodily ~*) ball(-bodhaig) *m*, **reproductive ~s** buill-ghineamhainn
mpl

organ[2] *n* (*mus*) òrgan *m*

organisation *n* 1 (*abstr*) òrdugh *m*, riaghailt *f*, rian *m invar*; 2 (*the act
of organising*) òrdachadh *m*, cur *m* an òrdugh *m*; 3 (*con: body &c*)
buidheann *mf*, **a charitable ~** buidheann-charthannachd

organise *v* 1 (*put in order*) cuir *vt* an òrdugh *m*, òrdaich *vt*, cuir rian *m* (*with
prep* air); 2 (*set up &c*) cuir *vt* air chois (*dat of* cas *f*), cuir *vt* air b(h)onn
m, **~ an investigation/a playgroup** cuir sgrùdadh *m*/croileagan *f* air
chois/air b(h)onn

origin *n* tùs *m*, (*prov*) **the fear of God is the ~ of wisdom** 's e tùs a' ghliocais
eagal *m* Dhè *gen, also* is e eagal an Tighearna tùs an eòlais

original *adj* 1 (*innovative &c*) ùr; 2 (*first, initial*) tùsail

originally *adv* o/bho thùs *m*, an toiseach *m* (tòiseachaidh *m gen*), sa chiad
àite *m*, **they were living here ~** bha iad a' fuireach an seo o thùs/an
toiseach

originate *v* tàrmaich *vt*

ornament *n* ball-maise *m*

ornithology *n* eun-eòlas *m*

oscillate *v* luaisg *vi*

oscillation *n* 1 (*abstr*) luasgadh *m*; 2 (*more con: an ~*) luasgan *m*

other *adj* 1 eile, **the ~ half** an leth *m invar* eile, **on the ~ hand** air an làimh
(*dat of* làmh *f*) eile, **give me the ~ one** thoir dhomh am fear *m*/an tè
f eile; 2 (*often in contrast to* an dara *&* an dàrna, **one**) eile, *eg* **one son
is industrious but the ~ (one) is lazy** tha an dara mac èasgaidh ach
tha am fear eile leisg; 3 (*in pl*) **the ~s** (*of persons*) càch *pron*, (*of persons
& things*) an fheadhainn *f sing coll* eile, **she did better than the ~s**
rinn i na b' fheàrr na càch, **I went, along with the ~s** chaidh mi
ann, còmhla ri càch/còmhla ris an fheadhainn eile; 4 *in expr* **each ~**
a chèile *m*, **they kissed each ~** phòg iad a chèile, **talking to each ~** a'
bruidhinn ri chèile; 5 *in expr* **or ~**, *expr by the appropriate noun followed
by* air choreigin, *eg* **something or ~** rud *m* air choreigin, **somebody or
~** duine *m* air choreigin; 6 (*misc exprs*) **the ~ day** an là *m* roimhe, **one
after the ~** (*in time or space*) an ceann a chèile, an dèidh a chèile, **three**

accidents one after the ~ trì tubaistean *fpl* an ceann a chèile/an dèidh a chèile

otherwise *adv* air neo, **eat your dinner, ~ you'll be hungry** gabh do dhìnnear *f*, air neo bidh an t-acras ort

otter *n* dòbhran *m*, (*informal*) biast-dhubh & beist-dhubh *f*

ought *v* bu chòir *f* (*impersonal, with prep* do), **I ~ to go/leave** bu chòir dhomh falbh *m*, **you ~ not to smoke** cha bu chòir dhut smocadh *m*, **it's not as good as it ~ to be** chan eil e cho math agus bu chòir (dha a bhith)

ounce *n* ùnnsa *m*

ourselves *reflexive pron* sinn fhìn, *for examples of use cf* **myself**

out *adv* & *prep* **1** (*esp of motion: lit* & *fig*) a-mach (of à), **he went ~** chaidh e a-mach, **~ of here!/get ~!** a-mach à seo (leat/leibh)!, **the way ~** an t-slighe (dol) a-mach, (*by a door*) an doras *m* (dol) a-mach, **a page ~ of a newspaper** duilleag *f* a-mach à pàipear-naidheachd *m*, **~ of work/a job** a-mach à obair *f*, *also* gun chosnadh *m*, **~ of order** a-mach à òrdugh *m*, **my book's (come) ~** thàinig an leabhar *m* agam a-mach, **~ of danger** a-mach à cunnart *m*, **make ~** (*ie assert*) cùm *vi* a-mach, **she was making ~ that Einstein was a fool** bha i a' cumail a-mach gum b' e amadan *m* a bh' ann an Einstein; **2** *expr by* à, às, **put the fire/the light ~** cuir às an teine/an solas *m*, **let ~** leig *vi* (*with prep* à), **I let ~ a shreik** leig mi sgreuch *m* asam, **~ of sight** à sealladh *m or* às an t-sealladh, **~ of his mind** às a chiall *f*, às a rian *m*, **~ of the ordinary** às a' chumantas *m*, **they got the hell ~ of it** thug iad na buinn (*pl of* bonn *m*) asta, thug iad an casan (*pl of* cas *f*) leotha, **way ~** (*ie solution, means of escape*) dol *m* *invar* às, **there was no way ~ for them** cha robh dol às aca; **3** (*outside*) a-muigh, **he's ~ in the garden** tha e a-muigh anns a' ghàrradh *m*; **4** (*misc exprs*) **~** (*ie not at home*) on taigh *m*, **my wife's ~** tha a' bhean agam on taigh, **~ in America** ann an Ameireagaidh thall, **~ of sorts** (*ie crotchety* &*c*) diombach & diumbach, (*usu of child*) crost(a) & crosda, **~ of sorts** (*ie not in best of health*) ach meadhanach (*after a verb in the neg*), **he's ~ of sorts today** chan eil e ach meadhanach an-diugh

outburst *n* (*of noise, emotion* &*c*) lasgan *m*

outcome *n* toradh *f*, buil *f*

outgoing *adj* **1** (*person*) faoilidh, cuideachdail, fàilteach; **2** *in expr* **~ mail** post *m* a-mach

outlaw *n* neach-cùirn *m* (*pl* luchd-cùirn *m sing coll*)

outlaw *v* cuir *vt* fon choill (*dat of* coille *f*)

outlawed *adj* & *past part* **1** (*person*) fon choill (*dat of* coille *f*); **2** (*substances, practices* &*c*) mì-laghail, toirmisgte, fo thoirmeasg *m*, neo-cheadaichte

output *n* (*of industry* &*c*) toradh *m*

outrageous *adj* uabhasach

outside *adv* **1** (*movement*) a-mach, **go ~** rach *vi* a-mach, thalla *imper* a-mach, **~ with you!** a-mach leat!; **2** (*position*) a-muigh, **where's Iain? he's ~** càit a bheil Iain? tha (e) a-muigh

outside *n* taobh *m* a-muigh (*with gen*), **on the** ~ air an taobh a-muigh, **the** ~ **of the building** taobh a-muigh an togalaich

outside *prep* air (an) taobh *m* a-muigh (*with gen*), ~ **the building** air taobh a-muigh an togalaich

outskirts *n* iomall *m sing*, **on the** ~ **of the town** air iomall a' bhaile

outstanding *adj* **1** (*of high quality*) air leth, air leth math, **an** ~ **man** duine *m* air leth, **that was** ~ bha sin air leth math; **2** (*bills, debts*) gun phàigheadh *m*

outwith *prep* **1** (*beyond*) thar (*with gen*), ~ **my competence** thar mo chomais *m gen*/mo chomasan *mpl gen*; **2** (*outside, furth of*) air taobh *m* a-muigh (*with gen*), ~ **the community/the country** air taobh a-muigh na coimhearsnachd *f invar*/na dùthcha (*gen of* dùthaich *f*)

oval *adj* ughach

oval *n* ughach *m*

ovary *n* ughlann *f*

over *adv* **1** (*usu expr movement*) thairis, **they went** ~ chaidh iad thairis, **turn** ~ cuir *vti* thairis, *also* cuir *vt* a (*&c*) c(h)eann *m* fodha, cuir *vt* bun-os-cionn; **2** (*misc exprs*) ~ **and** ~ **again** (*expr repetition*) uair *f* is uair, (*expr motion*) **rolling** ~ **and** ~ a' dol car *m* mu char, **all** ~ (*ie finished*) seachad, **that's (all)** ~ **now** tha sin seachad a-nis, **all** ~ (*ie everywhere*) anns a h-uile h-àite *m*, anns gach àite *m*, **it will be wet all** ~ bidh i fliuch anns a h-uile h-àite

over *prep* **1** (*expr position or movement*) thar (*with gen*), ~ **me** tharam(sa), ~ **you** (*sing*) tharad(sa), ~ **him/it** (*m*) thairis(-san), ~ **her/it** (*f*) thairte(se), ~ **us** tharainn(e), ~ **you** tharaibh(se), ~ **them** tharta(san), **he had a rifle** ~ **his shoulder** bha raidhfil *f* aige thar a ghuailne *f*, **they went** ~ **the ocean** chaidh iad thar a' chuain; **2** (*expr movement*) tarsainn air, thairis air, (*with dat*), **they went** ~ **the bridge/the mountains** chaidh iad tarsainn/thairis air an drochaid *f*/air na beanntan (*pl of* beinn *f*), **the plane passed** ~ **the town** chaidh am plèana thairis air a' bhaile *m*; **3** (*above*) os cionn (*obs dat of* ceann *m*) (*with gen*), **clouds** ~ **the ocean** neòil (*pl of* neul *m*) os cionn a' chuain, ~ **me** os mo chionn; **4** (*time: in the course of*) rè (*with gen*) ~ **the years** rè nam bliadhnachan *fpl*; **5** *in expr* **all** ~ (*in every part of*) air feadh (*with gen*), **all** ~ **the country** air feadh na dùthcha (*gen of* dùthaich *f*), **there were empty glasses all** ~ **the place** bha glainneachan *fpl* falamh air feadh an àite *m*

over- *prefix* ro-, *eg* **over-expose** *v* ro-nochd *vt*, **over-weight** *adj* ro-throm

overcoat *n* còta mòr *m*

overcome *v* **1** (*quell: people, emotions &c*) ceannsaich *vt*; **2** (*people, problems &c: vanquish, succeed over*) thoir buaidh *f* (*with prep* air), (*more colloquial*) dèan a' chùis *f*, dèan an gnothach *m*, (*both with prep* air), **we will** ~ **the enemy** bheir sinn buaidh air an nàmhaid *m*, nì sinn a' chùis/an gnothach air an nàmhaid

over-expose *v* ro-nochd *vt*

overflow *v* (*lit & fig*) cuir *vi* thairis, **the water ~ed** chuir an t-uisge thairis, **a land ~ing with creatures of every kind** tìr *mf* a' cur thairis le creutairean *mpl* de gach seòrsa *m*

overhead *adj* os-cinn, **~ cable** càball *m* os-cinn

overhead *adv* os a (*&c*) c(h)ionn (*obs dat of* ceann *m*), **I saw a plane ~** chunnaic mi plèana *mf* os mo chionn

overload *v* an-luchdaich *vt*

overlord *n* àrd-uachdaran *m*

overseas *adv* **1** (*expr movement*) a-null thairis, **they went ~** chaidh iad a-null thairis; **2** (*expr position*) thall thairis, **they are ~** tha iad thall thairis, **~ market** margadh *mf* thall thairis

oversight *n* (*careless omission*) dearmad *m*

overt *adj* follaiseach

overtime *n* còrr-ùine *f*, seach-thìm *f*

overturn *v* cuir a (*&c*) c(h)eann *m* fodha, cuir *vt* bun-os-cionn, (*esp boat*) cuir *vti* thairis

over-weight *adj* ro-throm

owe *v* **1** (*fin & moral debts*) bi *vi irreg* fo fhiachaibh (*obs dat pl of* fiach *m*) (*with prep* do), **we ~ them (money)** tha sinn fo fhiachaibh dhaibh; **2** (*fin debts: note that it is the person owed money who is said to* 'have' *the money* 'on' *the debtor*) **we ~ them fifty pounds** tha leth-cheud *m* not *f sing* aca òirnn, **they ~ us fifty pounds** tha leth-cheud not againn orra

owl *n* cailleach-oidhche *f*, (*esp a barn ~*) comhachag *f*

own *adj* **1** (*using the poss formed with* aig) aige (*&c*) f(h)èin/fhìn, **my ~ house** an taigh agam fhìn, **a house of his ~** taigh *m* aige dha fhèin; **2** (*using poss pron*) **he broke his ~ leg** bhris e a chas *f* fhèin

owner *n* **1** sealbhadair *m*, **share ~** sealbhadair-shèaraichean (*gen pl of* sèar *m*); **2** *in expr* **who's the ~ (of this lorry** *&c*)? cò leis a tha (an làraidh *f* seo *&c*)?

ox *n* damh *m*

ox-tail *n* earball *m* daimh *m gen*

oxygen *n* ocsaidean *m*

oyster-catcher *n* gille-brì(gh)de *m*, trìlleachan *f*

P

pace *n* **1** (*stride, step*) ceum *m*, **we quickened our** ~ luathaich sinn ar ceum, **take a** ~ **forward/back** gabh ceum air adhart/air ais; **2** (*speed*) astar *m*, **run at a good** ~ ruith *vi* aig deagh astar, **they were going at/making a good** ~ bha astar math aca; **3** *in expr* **keep** ~ cùm ruith *f* (**with** ri), **keep** ~ **with the others** cùm ruith ri càch *pron*

pace *v* ceumnaich *vi*

Pacific, *n* **the** An Cuan Sèimh

pacify *v* **1** (*calm &c*) ciùinich *vt*, sìthich *vt*, sèimhich *vt*, socraich *vt*; **2** (*subdue by force*) ceannsaich *vt*

pack[1] *n* paca *m*, **a** ~ **of cards** paca chairtean *fpl gen*

pack[2] *n* (*derog: mob, crowd of people*) gràisg *f*

pack *v* **1** (*parcel &c*) paisg *vt*; **2** *in fam exprs* ~ **up/in** (*break down*) bris *vi*, **my radio's** ~**ed up** tha an rèidio *m* agam briste/air briseadh/air a bhriseadh, ~ **in** (*give up*) leig *vt* dheth (*&c*), **she's** ~**ing in her job** tha i a' leigeil dhith a h-obrach

package parsail *m*, pasgadh *m*, pasgan *m*

packed *adj & past part* **1** (*places, buildings, gatherings &c*) loma-làn, dòmhail & dùmhail, **the hall was** ~ bha an talla loma-làn; **2** (*objects, woodland, people*) **closely** ~ dlùth

packed lunch *n* pìos *m*

packet *n* pacaid *f*

packing *n* pasgadh *m*

pact *n* còrdadh *m*

paddle *n* pleadhag *f*

paddle *v* (~ *canoe; also* ~ *with feet*) pleadhagaich *vti*

pagan *n & adj* pàganach *m*

page *n* (*of a book &c*) duilleag *f*, taobh-duilleig(e) *m*, (*abbrev* d *or* td, *pl* dd *or* tdd), **the Yellow Pages** Na Duilleagan Buidhe

pail *n* peile *m*, bucaid *f*, (*esp for milking*) cuman *m*, cuinneag *f*

pain *n* (*usu phys*) pian *f*, (*mental/emotional or phys*) cràdh *m*

pain *v* (*usu phys*) pian *vt*, (*mentally or emotionally*) cràidh *vt*, ciùrr *vt*

pained *adj* (*emotionally or mentally*) dòrainneach

painful *adj* (*phys*) goirt, (*emotionally/mentally*) dòrainneach, (*mentally/ emotionally or phys*) pianail, crài(dh)teach, **my back's** ~ tha mo dhruim *m* goirt, **a** ~ **reminder** cuimhneachan *m sing* cràiteach, **a** ~ **conversation/interview** agallamh dòrainneach

painstaking *adj* (*person, work &c*) mion-chùiseach, ro-phongail, ro-mhionaideach

paint *n* peant(a) *m*

paint *v* peant *vti*

painter *n* (*artist or tradesman*) peantair *m*

pair *n* **1** (*usu used of people*) dithis *f*, **they came in ~s** thàinig iad nan dithisean, **the ~ of you** an dithis agaibh; **2** *in expr* **~ of twins** càraid *f sing*; **3** (*of objects, creatures*) paidhir *mf*, **a ~ of gloves** paidhir mhiotagan *fpl gen*, **a ~ of oystercatchers** paidhir thrìlleachan *mpl gen*

pal *n* companach *m*, (*less informal*) caraid *m*

palace *n* pàileis *f*, (*more trad*) lùchairt *f*

pale-faced *adj* glas-neulach

palm[1] *n* (*of hand*) bas *f*, bois *f*, (*less usu*) glac *f*

palm[2] *n* (*the tree*) pailm *f*, craobh-phailm *f*

palpitate *v* (*esp heart*) plosg *vi*, (*less severe*) plap *vi*

palpitation *n* (*esp of heart*) plosg *m*, plosgadh *m*, plosgartaich *f*

pamphlet *n* leabhrachan *m*, leabhran *m*

pan *n* pana *m*

pancake *n* foileag *f*

pane *n* lòsan *m*

panel *n* pannal *m*, **a wooden ~** pannal-fiodha, **the Children's Panel** Pannal na Cloinne

pang *n* guin *m*

pannier *n* cliabh *m*

pant *n* plosg *m*

pant *v* plosg *vi*

panting *n* plosg *m*, plosgadh *m*, plosgartaich *f*

pants *n* **1** (*underwear*) drathais & drathars *fpl invar*; **2** (*trousers*) briogais *f*, triubhas *m*

paper *n* pàipear *m*, **wall~** pàipear-balla *m*, **news~** pàipear-naidheachd *m*

paper-mill *n* muileann-pàipeir *mf*

papist *adj* (*not PC*) pàpanach

Papist *n* (*not PC*) Pàpanach *m*

parable *n* cosamhlachd *f*

Paradise *n* Pàrras *m*, flaitheas *m*

paraffin *n* paireafain *m invar*

parallel *adj* co-shìnte, **~ lines** loidhnichean *fpl* co-shìnte

parcel *n* parsail *m*, pasgan *m*

parched *adj* **1** (*person*) ìotmhor; **2** (*ground &c*) tioram

pardon *n* mathanas *m*

pardon *v* **1** ma(i)th *vt*, thoir mathanas *m* (*with prep* do); **2** *in exprs* (*as apology*) **~ me!** gabh(aibh) mo leisgeul *m!*, (*on not catching what someone has said*) **~?** b' àill leibh?

parent *n* pàrant *m*

parenthesis *n* eadar-ràdh *m*

parish *n* sgìre *f*, sgìreachd *f*, paraiste *f*

parity *n* ionannachd *f invar*, co-ionannachd *f invar*

park *n* **1** (*recreation, agric &c*) pàirc(e) *f*, **car ~** pàirc-chàraichean *f*; **2** (*site for various activities*) raon *m*, **business ~** raon gnìomhachais *m gen*

parliament *n* pàrlamaid *f*

parliamentary *adj* pàrlamaideach

parrot *n* pearraid *f*

part *n* 1 (*a proportion of a whole*) cuid *f*, pàirt *m*, **give me ~ of it** thoir dhomh cuid dheth, **the greater ~ of his life** a' mhòr-chuid de (a) bheatha *f*, **~ of the book was good** bha pàirt den leabhar *m* math; 2 (*section, division*) earrann *f*, **the first ~ of her novel came out** thàinig a' chiad earrann den nobhail *f* aice a-mach; 3 (*portion, share*) cuid *f*, roinn *f*, **my ~ of the world's goods** mo chuid den t-saoghal; 4 (*in dispute &c*) taobh *m*, **she took our ~** ghabh i ar taobh, *also* chaidh i às ar leth; 5 (*misc exprs*) **spare ~s** pàirtean-càraidh *mpl*, **take ~** (*participate*) gabh pàirt, com-pàirtich *vt*, **~s of the body** buill *mpl* a' chuirp, **for my (own) ~ . . .** air mo shon fhìn . . .

part *v* dealaich *vti* (**from** ri), **death ~ed them** dhealaich am bàs iad, **they ~ed** dhealaich iad ri chèile, **you won't ~ him from his money!** cha dhealaich thu ri a chuid *f* airgid *m gen* e!

participant *n* com-pàirtiche *m*, (*esp in a competition*) farpaiseach *m*

participate *v* gabh pàirt *m*, gabh com-pàirt *f*, com-pàirtich *vi*

participation *n* com-pàirt *f*

particle *n* 1 mìr *m*, mìrean *m*; 2 (*gram*) mion-fhacal *m*

particular *adj* 1 àraidh, sònraichte, **it's a ~ house/one house in ~ that I want to buy** 's e taigh *m* àraidh a tha mi airson a cheannach, **a ~ sort** seòrsa *m* àraidh/sònraichte; 2 (*of person: precise, attentive to detail*) mion-chùiseach, pongail; 3 *in neg expr* **he's not ~** (*ie doesn't mind*) is coma leis, tha e coma co-dhiù

parting *n* dealachadh *m*

partition *n* pàirteacheadh *m*

partition *v* pàirtich *vt*, roinn *vt*

partner *n* 1 pàirtiche *m*, com-pàirtiche *m*; 2 (*sexual ~*) coileapach *mf*, companach *mf*

party *n* 1 pàrtaidh *m*, **a political ~** pàrtaidh poileataigeach, **The Labour/ Liberal Democrat/Tory Party** Am Pàrtaidh Làbarach/Libearalach Deamocratach/Tòraidheach, **The Scottish National Party** Pàrtaidh Nàiseanta na h-Alba; 2 (*social gathering*) pàrtaidh *m*, (*more boisterous; fam*) ho-ro-gheallaidh *m invar*

pass *n* 1 (*topog*) bealach *m*; 2 (*games*) pas *m*; 3 (*document*) cead *m* inntrigidh *m gen*, pas *m*

pass *v* 1 rach *vi* seachad (*with prep* air), **the train ~ed (me)** chaidh an trèana *f* seachad (orm), **the time ~ed quickly** chaidh an ùine seachad gu luath; 2 (*spend*) cuir *vt* seachad, caith *vt*, **~ time** cuir seachad ùine *f*; 3 (*misc exprs*) **~ away** (*ie die*) caochail *vi*, siubhail *vi*, **~ me the salt** sìn thugam an salann, **~ the biscuits round** cuir timcheall na briosgaidean *fpl*, **~ into oblivion** rach *vi* air dìochuimhne *f*, **the pain ~ed off** dh'fhalbh am pian *m*, **~ water** dèan mùn *m*, mùin *vi*, **I noticed it in ~ing** mhothaich mi dha san dol *m invar* seachad

passage *n* **1** (*in building*) trannsa *f*; **2** (*in book*) earrann *f*; **3** (*through hills*) bealach *m*; **4** (*across river, strait &c*) aiseag *mf*, (*longer, maritime*) turas-mara *m*, **a rough ~** turas(-mara) garbh

passenger *n* neach-siubhail *m* (*pl* luchd-siubhail *m sing coll*)

passionate *adj* (*person*) lasanta

passive *adj* fulangach, (*gram*) **the ~ voice** an guth fulangach

passport *n* cead-siubhail *m*, cead *m* dol *m invar* thairis

past *adj & adv* **1** seachad, **all that's ~ now** tha sin uile seachad a-nis, **~ time** an t-àm a chaidh seachad, *also* an t-àm a dh'fhalbh; **2** *in expr* **he's ~ his best** tha e air a dhol dheth, tha e air a dhol bhuaithe; **3** (*gram*) caithte, **the ~ tense** an tràth caithte

past, the *n* an t-àm a chaidh seachad, an t-àm a dh'fhalbh

paste *n* (*flour & water*) glaodhan *m*

pastime *n* cur-seachad *m*, **my favourite ~** an cur-seachad as fheàrr leam

pastry *n* pastra *f invar*

pasture *n* clua(i)n *f*, ionaltradh *m*, (*beside water*) dail *f*, innis *f*

pasture *v* feuraich *vt*

patch *n* **1** (*of material &c*) tuthag *f*, brèid *m*; **2** *in exprs* **~ of ground** pìos (beag) fearainn *m gen*, **~ of fog/mist** bad *m* ceò *m gen*

Paternoster *n* paidir *f*

path *n* frith-rathad *m*, slighe *f*, **the ~ of righteousness** slighe na fìreantachd *f invar*

patience *n* foighidinn *f*

patient *adj* foighidneach

patient *n* euslainteach *m*

patron *n* fear-taice *m*, goistidh *m*

patronage *n* taic(e) *f*, goistidheachd *f invar*

patronymic *n* sloinneadh *m*

pattern *n* pàtran *m*

paunch *n* maodal *f*, mionach *m*

pavement *n* cabhsair *m*

pavilion *n* pàillean *m*

paving stone (*for floor*) leac-ùrlair *f*, (*for pavement*) leac-chabhsair *f*

paw *n* cròg *f*, spòg *f*, màg *f*

paw *v* (*of persons: handle improperly, roughly*) (droch-)làimhsich *vt*

pay *n* pàigh *m invar*, pàigheadh *m*, tuarastal *m*, **a ~ rise** àrdachadh *m* pàighidh *gen*

pay *v* **1** pàigh *vti*, **~ a bill** pàigh cunntas *m*/bileag *f*, **he left without ~ing** dh'fhalbh e gun phàigheadh, **you'll ~ for your sins** pàighidh tu (airson) do pheacaidhean *mpl*; **2** (*misc exprs*) **~ attention** thoir an aire (**to** do), thoir fea(i)rt *f* (**to** air), **~ a compliment** dèan moladh *m* (*with prep* air), **~ X a visit** rach *vi* air chèilidh *mf* air X, cuir cèilidh air X, tadhail *vi* air X, **~ back** (*fin or in revenge*) dìoghail & dìol *vt*

payment *n* **1** pàigheadh *m*, dìo(gh)ladh *m*; **2** (*in reparation or in return for something: esp a ransom*) èirig *f*

pea *n* peasair *f*

peace *n* **1** (*opposite of war*) sìth *f*, **war or** ~ cogadh *m* no sìth; **2** (*tranquility*) fois *f*, sìth *f*, (*esp of the dead*) **they are at** ~ tha iad aig fois, *also* tha iad nan tàmh; **3** *in expr* ~ **of mind** toil-inntinn *f*

peaceful *adj* **1** (*opposite of warlike &c*) sìtheil; **2** (*calm, tranquil*) sàmhach, **a** ~ **sleep/evening** cadal/feasgar sàmhach

peach *n* pèitseag *f*

peak *n* **1** (*pointed mountaintop*) stùc *f*, binnean *m*; **2** *in expr* **he's at his** ~ tha e ann an treun *f invar* a neirt (*gen of* neart *m*), tha e aig àird *f* a neirt, tha e aig (a) àird

peal *n* **1** (*of bells*) seirm *f*, bualadh *m*; **2** *in expr* **a** ~ **of laughter** lasgan *m* gàire *mf invar*

peanut *n* cnò-thalmhainn *f*

pear *n* peur *f*

peasantry *n* tuath *f*

peat *n* **1** (*coll*) mòine *f sing coll*, ~ **bog**, ~ **hag**, ~ **bank** poll-mòna(ch) *or* poll-mònadh *m*, ~ **smoke**, ~ **reek** ceò *m* na mòna(ch)/na mònadh, **they're (working) at the** ~**(s)** tha iad aig a' mhòine, **win/cut/gather** ~ dèan/buain mòine; **2** (*a single* ~) fòid *f*, fàd *m* (mònach); **3** ~ **iron/spade** tairsgeir *f*

pebble *n* dèideag *f*, molag *f*

peck *v* (*birds &c*) pioc *vti*

pedal *n* troighean *m*

pedestrian *n* coisiche *m*

pee *n* mùn *m*, **have a** ~ dèan mùn, dèan dileag *f*

pee *v* dèan mùn *m*, mùin *vi*

peel *n* (*of fruit, vegetables &c*) rùsg *m*, plaosg *m*

peel *v* (*fruit, vegetables &c*) rùisg *vt*, plaoisg *vt*

peeled *adj & past part* rùisgte, ~ **potatoes** buntàta *m invar coll* rùisgte

peer *n* **1** (~ *of the realm*) morair *m*; **2** (*one's equal*) seise *m*

peevish *adj* frithearra, (*usu of child*) crost(a)

peewit *n* currcag *f*

peg *n* cnag *f*, **clothes** ~ cnag-aodaich *f*

pellet *n* (*ie as projectile*) peileir *m*

pelt *v* **1** tilg *vt*, caith *vt*, (*with prep* air), **they were** ~**ing me with eggs** bha iad a' tilgeil uighean *mpl gen* orm; **2** *in expr* ~ **with stones** clach *vt*

pen[1] *n* (*for writing*) peann *m*

pen[2] *n* (*for livestock*) buaile *f*, (*esp sheep*) crò *m*

penal *adj* peanasach

penalise *v* peanasaich

penalty *n* (*punishment*) peanas *m*

pencil *n* peansail *m*

penetrate *v* **1** (*make one's way into*) rach *vi* a-steach, (*more violently*) bris *vi* a-steach, (*with prep* do); **2** (*break or pierce hole(s) in*) toll *vt*; **3** (*pass or break through defences &c*) thig *vi*, rach *vi*, (*more violently*) bris *vi*, (*all with prep* troimh, *with dat*); 4 (*esp of water*) drùidh *vi*, **the rain ~ed to my skin** dhrùidh an t-uisge orm

penny *n* 1 sgillinn *f*, (*idiom*) **I haven't a ~ to my name** chan eil sgillinn ruadh (*no* geal) agam; 2 (*hist*) **Scots ~** peighinn *f*

pension *n* pein(n)sean *m*, **retirement ~** pein(n)sean-cluaineis *m*

pensioner *n* neach *m* pei(n)nsein *m gen* (*pl* luchd-pein(n)sein *m sing coll*)

Pentland Firth, the *n* An Caol Arcach

people *n* 1 (*human beings in general*) daoine (*pl of* duine *m*), **many/lots of ~** mòran dhaoine *mpl gen*; 2 (*populace*) sluagh *m*, (*esp rural: more trad*) tuath *f*, **unrest among the ~** aimhreit *f* am measg an t-sluaigh; 3 (*the ~ of a particular place*) muinntir *f*, poball *m*, **the ~ of this town(ship)** muinntir a' bhaile seo, **the ~ of Uist, Uist ~** muinntir Uibhist, **the ~ of Ireland, the Irish ~** poball na h-Èireann; 4 (*one's relatives, folks*) càirdean (*pl of* caraid *m*), daoine *mpl*, **my ~ are in Stornoway** tha mo chàirdean/ mo dhaoine ann an Steòrnabhagh; 5 (*associates, followers, companions*) muinntir *f*, cuideachd *f*, **he left the country but his ~ didn't go with him** dh'fhàg e an dùthaich *f* ach cha deach a mhuinntir/a chuideachd còmhla ris; 6 (*a race, tribe, &c*) cinneadh *m*, **the Eskimo ~** cinneadh nan Easciomach *mpl*

pep up *v* (*cooking; also fig*) piobraich *vt*

pepper *n* piobar *m*

pepper *v* piobraich *vt*

per capita *adv* an urra *f*, (*do &c*) gach pearsa *m*, **a thousand pounds ~** mìle not(a) *f sing* an urra

perceive *v* (*visually*) faic *vt*, (*visually, mentally*) mothaich *vt*

per cent *adv* sa cheud *m*, **four ~** ceithir sa cheud

perception *n* 1 (*the mental faculty or capacity*) tuigse *f invar*, lèirsinn *f invar*; 2 (*sight*) fradharc *&* radharc *m*, lèirsinn *f invar*; 3 (*idea, view*) beachd *m*, **his ~ of himself** am beachd a bh' aige air fhèin

perceptive *adj* geur-chùiseach, tuigseach, mothachail

perch *v* (*come to rest*) laigh *vi* (**on** air)

perfect *adj* 1 (*not usu in moral sense*) coileanta, (*gram*) **the ~ tense** an tràth coileanta; 2 (*esp morally*) foirfe; 3 (*fam: expr approval &c*) taghta!, **that's ~** tha sin taghta

perforate *v* toll *vt*

perform *v* 1 (*carry out, fulfil*) coilean *vt*, thoir *vt* gu buil *f*, **~ a task** coilean gnìomh *m*, coilean pìos *m* obrach (*gen of* obair *f*); 2 (*theatre, cinema*) cluich *vi*, cleasaich *vi*, **~ in a play** cluich ann an dealbh-chluich *mf*, (*in orchestra, band &c*) cluich *vi*; 3 (*~ song, music &c*) gabh *vt*, **~ a song** gabh òran *m*; 4 (*acquit oneself*) **he ~ed well** 's math a rinn e

performance *n* (*fulfilment of task &c*) coileanadh *m*, toirt *f invar* gu buil

perfume *n* cùbhrachd *f invar*

perhaps *adv & conj* 1 is/'s dòcha, (is) ma(th) dh'fhaodte (*also* is mathaid), theagamh, **it'll be a fine day, ~** bidh là brèagha ann, 's dòcha/ma dh'fhaodte; **2** (*as conj*) is/'s dòcha, (is) ma(th) dh'fhaodte, theagamh, faodaidh, (*all followed by conjs* gun/gum, nach *&c*), ~ **he'll come tomorrow** 's dòcha gun tig e a-màireach, ~ **it won't snow** ma dh'fhaodte nach cuir i, ~ **he's ill** faodaidh gu bheil e tinn, ~ **she won't come** theagamh nach tig i

peril *n* gàbhadh *m*, (*usu less strong*) cunnart *m*, **in** ~ ann an gàbhadh

perilous *adj* gàbhaidh, (*usu less strong*) cunnartach

period *n* **1** (*of time*) greis *f*, treis *f*, **he spent a** ~ **of time in Australia** chuir e seachad greis/treis ann an Astràilia *f invar*; **2** (*school lesson*) tràth(-teagaisg) *m*; **3** (*menstrual* ~) fuil-mìos *f*

periodical *n* iris *f*, (*esp a quarterly*) ràitheachan *m*

peripheral *adj* iomallach, ~ **areas/districts** ceàrnaidhean *mpl* iomallach

periphery *n* iomall *m*

permanent *adj* maireannach, buan

permeable *adj* so-dhrùidhteach

permissible *adj* ceadaichte

permission *n* cead *m invar*, **with your** ~ le ur cead, **I gave them** ~ **to leave** thug mi cead dhaibh falbh, **planning** ~ cead-dealbhaidh *m*

permissive *adj* ceadachail

permit *n* cead *m invar*

permit *v* leig *vi* (*with prep* le *or* do), ceadaich *vt*, **he ~ted me to buy it** leig e leam a cheannach, ~ **new development in the town centre** ceadaich leasachadh *m* ùr ann am meadhan *m* a' bhaile

permitted *adj & past part* ceadaichte

perplex *v* cuir *vt* an imcheist *f*

perplexed *adj* an/fo imcheist *f*, imcheisteach

perplexing *adj* imcheisteach

perplexity *n* imcheist *f*

persevere *v* cùm *vi* (*with prep* ri), lean *vi* (*with prep* air), ~! cùm ris!, **she ~d** lean i oirre

persevering *adj* leantainneach

persistent *adj* **1** (*of persons: tenacious &c*) gramail *&* greimeil; **2** (*of situations &c: long-lasting*) leanailteach

person *n* (*regardless of gender*) duine *m*, neach *m invar*, (*less usu*) pearsa *m*

personal *adj* pearsanta

personality *n* pearsantachd *f invar*

personnel *n* sgiobachd *f invar*, luchd-obrach *m sing coll*

perspiration *n* fallas *m*

perspire *v* bi *vi irreg* fallas *m* (*with prep* air), cuir fallas (*with prep* de), bi *vi irreg* na (*&c*) f(h)allas, **I'm perspiring** tha fallas orm, tha mi a' cur fallas dhìom, tha mi nam fhallas

persuade *v* cuir ìmpidh *f* (*with prep* air), iompaich *vt*, **they ~d me to give up my job/to retire** chuir iad ìmpidh orm mo dhreuchd *f* a leigeil dhìom

persuasion *n* ìmpidh *f*

persuasive *adj* impidheach

perverse *adj* (*obstinate*) rag, dùr, (*stronger*) rag-mhuinealach

perversion *n* claonadh *m*

perversity *n* (*obstinacy*) raige *f invar*

pervert *v* **1** (~ *persons*) truaill *vt*, claon *vt*; **2** (~ *justice &c*) claon *vt*

pest *n* (*rodent &c, also inconvenience*) plàigh *f*

pestiferous *adj* plàigheil

pestilence *n* plàigh *f*

pestilential *adj* plàigheil

pet *n* peata *m*

peter out *v* sìolaidh *vi* às

petition *n* tagradh *m*

petrol *n* peatro(i)l *&* peatrail *m*

petticoat *n* còta-bàn *m*

petty *adj* **1** (*on small scale*) mion- *prefix*, ~ **theft/pilfering** mion-bhraide *f*; **2** (*small-minded &c*) crìon, suarach

pharmacist *n* neach *m* chungaidhean *fpl gen*

pharmacy *n* **1** (*the premises*) bùth-chungaidh(ean) *f*; **2** (*knowledge, profession of* ~) eòlas *m* leigheasan *mpl gen*, eòlas-chungaidhean *m*

pheasant *n* easag *f*

phenomenal *adj* iongantach

phenomenon *n* **1** (*science & philo*) sìon *m*; **2** (*amazing thing*) iongantas *m*, mìorbhail *f*, (*less usu*) suaicheantas *m*

philosopher *n* feallsanach *m*

philosophy *n* feallsanachd *f*

phlegm *n* ronn *m*

phone *n* fòn *mf*, **I was talking to him on the** ~ bha mi a' bruidhinn ris air a fòn, **what's your** ~ **number?** dè an àireamh-fòn *f* a th' agad?

phone *v* cuir fòn *mf*, fòn *vi*, fònaig *vi*, (*all with prep* gu), **he ~d her** chuir e fòn thuice, dh'fhòn(aig) e thuice

photograph *n* dealbh *mf*, **take a** ~ tog dealbh

physical *adj* corporra

physique *n* dèanamh *m*

piano *n* piàna *&* piàno *m*

pibroch *n* ceòl mòr *m*, (*loosely*) pìobaireachd *f invar*

pick[1] *n* (*tool*) pic *m*, piocaid *f*

pick[2] *n* (*choice*) roghainn *f*, **you'll get your** ~ **of it** gheibh thu do roghainn dheth

pick *v* **1** (*select*) tagh *vt*, roghnaich *vt*; **2** (~ *flowers &c*) cruinnich *vt*; **3** (~ *at food*) pioc *vi*, creim *vi*; **4** ~ **up** tog *vt*, (*also fig*) **I ~ed up my Gaelic in Skye** (*emph*) 's ann san Eilean *m* Sgitheanach a thog mi mo chuid *f* Gàidhlig *f gen*

pickaxe *n* pic *m*, piocaid *f*

pickle *n* picil *f*

picnic *n* cuirm-chnuic *f*

Pict *n* Cruithneach *m*

picture *n* dealbh *mf*

picture *v* dealbh *vt*

piece *n* **1** (*bit, particle*) criomag *f*, bloigh *f*, (*smaller*) mìr *m*, **falling to ~s** a' dol/a' tuiteam na (*&c*) c(h)riomagan; **2** (*component part*) pìos *m*, earrann *f*; **3** (*sandwich*) pìos *m*; **4** (*misc exprs*) **they arrived in one ~** ràinig iad slàn is fallain, **bits and ~s** treal(l)aich *f sing*

pierce *v* toll *vt*

piercing *n* tolladh *m*, **ear ~** tolladh-chluasan *m*

piety *n* cràbhadh *m*, diadhachd *f invar*

pig *n* muc *f*

pigeon *n* **1** calman *m*; **2** (*idiom*) **put the cat among the ~s** cuir an ceòl air feadh na fidhle

piggy-back *n* (*a ~ ride*) gioma-goc *m*

pig-headed *adj* rag-mhuinealach

piglet *n* uircean *&* oircean *m*

pigsty *n* fail-mhuc *f*

pigtail *n* figheachan *m*

pile *n* cruach *f*, tòrr *m*, dùn *m*, (*smaller*) cruachan *m*

pile, pile up *v* càrn *vt*, cruach *vt*

pilfer *v* dèan mion-bhraide *f*

pilfering mion-bhraide *f*

pilgrim *n* eilthireach *m*

pilgrimage *n* eilthireachd *f*

pill *n* pile *f*

pillar *n* **1** (*architecture &c*) colbh *m*; **2** (*of rock*) carragh *f*

pillion *n* pillean *m*

pillow *n* cluasag *f*

pilot *n* pìleat *&* paidhleat *m*

pimple *n* plucan *m*, guirean *m*

pin *n* prìne *m*, (*less usu*) dealg *f*, **safety ~** prìne-banaltraim *m*

pincers *n* (*pair of ~*) teanchair *&* teannachair *m sing*

pinch *n* (*with fingers, nails*) gòmag *f*, pioc *m*

pinch *v* **1** (*with fingernails &c*) pioc *vti*; **2** (*steal*) goid *vti*, dèan braid *f*

pinching *n* **1** (*with fingernails &c*) piocadh *m*; **2** (*stealing*) goid *f*, braid *f*

pine *n* giuthas *m*, in exprs **~ wood/forest** giùthsach *f*, **~ cone** durcan *m*

pinhead *n* ploc-prìne *m*

pink *adj* pinc

pink *n* pinc *m*

pinkie *n* lùdag *f*

pinnacle *n* binnean *m*

pins and needles an cadal deilgneach

pint *n* pinnt *m*, **I fancy a** ~ tha mi airson pinnt

pipe *n* **1** pìob *f*, feadan *m*, **water** ~**s** pìoban-uisge, **exhaust** ~ pìob-thraoghaidh *f*; **2** (*for smoking*) pìob(-thombaca); **3** (*musical instrument*) cuisle *f*, cuislean *m*; **4** (*bag*~) pìob *f*, (*Highland bag*~) pìob mhòr, (*usu with art*) a' phìob mhòr, ~ **music** ceòl *m* na pìoba

piper *n* pìobaire *m*

piping *n* (*music & performance*) pìobaireachd *f invar*

piss *n* mùn *m*

piss *v* dèan mùn *m*, mùin *vi*, (*involuntarily*) caill mùn, **I almost** ~**ed myself** theab mi mo mhùn a chall

pistol *n* daga & dag *m*

pit *n* **1** (*topog &c, a hollow*) lag *mf*, glac *f*, sloc *m*; **2** (*for potatoes &c*) sloc *m*; **3** (*mining*) mèinn(e) *f*

pitch[1] *n* (*tar*) bìth *f*, tèarr & teàrr *f*

pitch[2] *n* (*for football &c*) raon-cluiche *m*

pitch[3] *n* (*musical* ~) àirde *f*

pitch *v* **1** (*throw*) tilg, (*esp carelessly*) sad *vt*; **2** (*seas, ship, trees &c*) tulg *vi*

pitch-fork *n* gobhlag *f*

piteous *adj* truagh, (*more pej*) suarach

pith *n* glaodhan *m*

pitiable, pitiful *adj* truagh, (*more pej*) suarach, *in expr* ~ **person/creature** truaghan *m*

pitiless *adj* neo-thruacanta, an-iochdmhor

pity *n* **1** iochd *f invar*, truas *m*, truacantas *m*, **won't you take** ~ **on me?** nach gabh thu truas dhìom/rium?; **2** *in expr* **that's a** ~! tha sin duilich!, (*more trad*) is duilich sin!, is truagh sin!, *also* (*idiom*) b' olc an airidh (e)!

pitying *adj* truasail

place *n* **1** (*general*) àite *m*, **a bonny** ~ àite brèagha, **in its proper** ~ na (h-)àite fhèin, **in** ~ **of strife** an àite strì *f invar*, **take** ~ gabh àite, *also* tachair *vi*; **2** (*esp* ~ *where a particular activity &c is carried out*) ionad *m*, ~ **of work** ionad oibre/obrach (*gen of* obair *f*), ~ **of worship** ionad-adhraidh *m*

place *v* cuir *vt*, (*more carefully or elaborately*) socraich *vt*, suidhich *vt*, **she** ~**d the book on the table** chuir i an leabhar *m* air a' bhòrd *m*, ~ **a bet** cuir geall *m* (**on** air), ~ **a statue on a column** socraich/suidhich ìomhaigh *f* air colbh *m*

place-name *n* ainm *n* àite *m gen*

plague *n* plàigh *f*, **a** ~ **of mice** plàigh de luchan *fpl*

plague *v* (*exasperate*) leamhaich *vt*, sàraich *vt*

plaid *n* **1** (*esp the material & pattern*) breacan *m*; **2** (~ *blanket*) plaide *f*

plain *adj* **1** (*evident*) soilleir, follaiseach, (*more trad*) lèir, **it was** ~ **to him that he was lost** bha e soilleir/follaiseach dha gun robh e air chall, (*more trad*) bu lèir dha gun robh e air chall; **2** (*of things, situations: uncomplicated*) sìmplidh, aon-fhillte; **3** (*unpretentious*) sìmplidh, lom

plain *n* (*topog*) còmhnard *m*, machair *mf*

plaintive *adj* tiamhaidh

plait *n* dual *m*, filleadh *m*

plait *v* (*hair, rope &c*) dualaich *vt*, fill *vt*

plaited *adj & past part* fillte

plan *n* **1** (*intention, also map, diagram &c*) plana *m*; **2** (*strategy, stratagem*) innleachd *f*; **3** (*technical drawing*) dealbh-chumadh *mf*

plan *v* **1** (*general*) planaig *vti*; **2** (*~ technical & artistic objects*) dealbh *&* deilbh *vt*; **3** (*~ a strategy, stratagem*) innlich *vt*

plane[1] *n* (*carpentry*) locair *f*, locar *m*

plane[2] *n* (*aircraft*) plèana *f*, itealan *m*

plane[3] *n* (*geometry &c*) raon *m*

planet *n* planaid *f*

plank *n* dèile *f*, clàr *m*

planner *n* neach-dealbhaidh *m* (*pl* luchd-dealbhaidh *m sing coll*)

planning *n* dealbhadh *m*, planaigeadh *m*, **~ permission** cead *m* dealbhaidh *gen*

plant[1] *n* (*botanical*) luibh *mf*, lus *m*

plant[2] *n* (*manufacturing &c*) **1** (*equipment &c*) uidheam *f*; **2** (*the premises*) factaraidh *f*

plant *v* cuir *vt*, **~ potatoes** cuir buntàta *m invar coll*

plaster *n* **1** (*for building &c*) sglàib *f invar*; **2** (*sticking ~*) plàsd *&* plàst *m*

plastic *n & adj* plastaig *f*

plate *n* **1** (*tableware*) truinnsear *m*; **2** (*metal &c ~*) lann *f*

platform *n* **1** (*in concert hall &c*) àrd-ùrlar *m*; **2** (*railway &c*) àrd-chabhsair *m*, còmhnard *m*; **3** (*oil industry*) clàr *m*, **drilling ~** clàr-tollaidh *m*

platter *n* mias *f*

play *n* **1** (*the activity*) cluich *&* cluiche *m*, (*esp children: less usu*) cleas *m*; **2** (*more con: stage ~*) dealbh-chluich *mf*; **3** *in expr* (*sport*) **foul ~** fealladh *m*

play *v* **1** cluich *vti*, **~ football/rugby** cluich ball-coise *m*/rugbaidh *m*, **~ Rangers** cluich (an aghaidh) Rangers, **~ Hamlet on the stage** cluich Hamlet air an àrd-ùrlar *m*, **~ the accordeon** cluich (air) a' bhogsa *m*, **~ a tune on the accordeon** gabh port *m* air a' bhogsa; **2** *in expr* **~ shinty** iomain *vi*, **they were ~ing shinty** bha iad ag iomain

player *n* (*stage, games, music*) cluicheadair *m*

playground *n* raon-cluiche *m*

playgroup *n* cròileagan *m*

playing *n* cluich *&* cluiche *m*, (*esp children: less usu*) cleas *m*

plea *n* **1** (*request*) guidhe *mf*; **2** (*law*) tagradh *m*, tagairt *f*

plead *v* **1** guidh *vi* (**with** air), **I'm ~ing with you to stay!** tha mi a' guidhe ort fuireach!, **he ~ed with us to let him go/set him free** ghuidh e òirnn a leigeil mu sgaoil; **2** (*in court of law*) tagair *vti*

pleasant *adj* (*of people, also things, situations*) tlachdmhor, taitneach (**to, for** ri), (*esp of people*) ciatach

pleasantness *n* taitneas *m*

please *v* **1** *(content, give pleasure)* còrd *vi (with prep* ri*)*, toilich *vt*, riaraich *vt*, taitinn *vi (with prep* ri*)*, **it ~d me** chòrd e rium; **2** *(wish, prefer)* togair *vi*, *usu in expr* mar a thogras *(rel fut)* tu/sibh, **black or white, (just) as you ~** dubh no geal, (dìreach) mar a thogras sibh; **3** *(polite request)* **~** mas e do thoil *f*/ur toil e, **~ close the door** dùin an doras *m*, mas e do thoil e

pleased *adj & past part* **1** *(satisfied, content)* toilichte, riaraichte, air a *(&c)* d(h)òigh *f*, air a d(h)eagh dhòigh, **I'm ~ to be here**, tha mi toilichte a bhith ann, **Murdo was very ~ (with himself)** bha Murchadh air a dheagh dhòigh; **2** *(proud, approving)* moiteil **(with** à**)**, **we're ~ with you** tha sinn moiteil asad

pleasing *adj* **1** *(persons, also things, situations)* tlachdmhor, taitneach, **(to** ri**)**; **2** *in expr* **I find that ~** is toigh leam sin, tha sin a' còrdadh rium

pleasurable *adj* tlachdmhor

pleasure *n* **1** tlachd *f invar*, taitneas *m*, toileachadh *m*; **2** *(esp mental ~)* toil-inntinn *f*, toileachas-inntinn *m*

pleat *n* filleadh *m*

pleat *v* fill *vt*

pleated *adj & past part* fillte

pledge *n* gealladh *m*, *(less usu in this sense)* geall *m*

pledge *v* geall *vti*, thoir gealladh *m*, rach *vi* an geall *m*

Pleiades, the *n* An Grioglachan *m sing*

plentiful *adj* pailt, lìonmhor

plenty *n* **1** *(ample sufficiency, superfluity)* pailteas *m*, **the land of ~** tìr *mf* a' phailteis; **2** *in expr* **~ of** gu leòr, **we've got ~ of time** tha ùine *f* gu leòr againn, **there are ~ of people around who think that (way)** tha gu leòr ann/tha daoine *mpl* gu leòr ann a tha den bheachd *m* sin

pliable *adj* sùbailte, so-lùibte, so-lùbadh

pliant *adj* lùbach

pliers *npl* greimire *m*

plop *n* plub *m*

plop *v* plubraich, plub

plot[1] *n* **1** *(conspiracy, stratagem)* cuilbheart *f*, innleachd *f*; **2** *(Lit)* sgeul *m*, **the ~ of her novel** sgeul na nobhail aice

plot[2] *n* **1** *(~ of ground)* pìos *m* fearainn *m gen*, pìos-talmhainn *m*; **2** *(flower &c bed)* ceapach *m*

plot *v* innlich *vt*, dèan co-fheall *m* **(against** an aghaidh *with gen)*, **~ an uprising** innlich ar-a-mach *m invar*, **~ against the government** dèan co-fheall an aghaidh an riaghaltais

plough *n* **1** *(agric)* crann *m*; **2** *(astronomy)* **The Plough** An Crann-arain

plough *v* treabh *vti*

ploughing *n* treabhadh *m*

plover *n* feadag *f*, **green ~** currcag *f*

ploy *n* **1** *(activity, escapade)* plòigh *f*; **2** *(stratagem, tactic)* innleachd *f*

pluck *n* (*courage &c*) smior *m*, misneach(d) *f*

pluck *v* (*flower, harpstring &c*) spìon *vt*

plug *n* (*for sink, container &c*) cnag *f*, (*for sink, container, powerpoint &c*) plucan *m*, (*electric ~*) cnag-dealain *f*

plumage *n* iteach *m*

plumber *n* plumair *m*

plunder *n* cobhartach *mf*, (*trad: esp cattle*) creach *f*

plunder *v* creach *vti*, spùill *&* spùinn *vti*

plunge *n* (*into liquid*) tumadh *m*

plunge *v* (*into liquid*) tum *vt*

plural *adj* (*gram*) iolra, ~ **noun** ainmear *m* iolra

plural *n* (*gram*) iolra *m*

Pluto *n* (*planet*) Pluta *m invar*

pm *adv* feasgar, **seven** ~ seachd uairean *fpl* feasgar

poacher *n* poitsear *m*

pocket *n* pòcaid *f*, ~ **money** airgead *m* pòcaid *gen*

pod *n* (*of peas & beans &c*) plaosg *m*

pod *v* (*vegetables &c*) plaoisg *&* plaosg *vt*

poem *n* dàn *m*, duan *m*, laoidh *mf*, pìos *m* bàrdachd *f invar*

poet *n* bàrd *m*, filidh *m*

poetic *adj* bàrdail

poetry *n* bàrdachd *f invar*, rann *m*, (*less usu*) dànachd *f invar*

poignant *adj* tiamhaidh

point *n* **1** (*of pencil, pin &c*) bior *m*, gob *m*, rinn *m*; **2** (*topog: promontory*) àird *f*, rubha *m*, sròn *f*, rinn *m*; **3** (*in a scale, series &c, in an argument &c*) puing *f*, ~ **of balance** puing-chothromachaidh *m*; **4** (*the ~ at issue*) ceist *f*, cùis *f*, **that's not the ~!** chan e sin a' cheist/a' chùis!, *also* chan e sin an rud *m*!, (*note also idiom*) **you made me wander from the** ~ chuir thu às mo ghabhail *mf* mi; **5** (*misc exprs*) **at/on the ~ of death** ri uchd *m* a' bhàis, **on the ~ of** gu(s), **we're on the ~ of leaving** tha sinn gu falbh, **on the ~ of losing my mind** gus mo chiall *f* a chall, ~ **of view** (*ie opinion*) barail *f*, beachd *m*, ~ **of view** (*ie perspective: lit & fig*) sealladh *m*, **from the ~ of view of the old folks** bho shealladh nan seann daoine, **~s of the compass** àirdean *fpl*, (*usu with art*) na h-àirdean

point *v* **1** (*with finger &c*) tomh *vi* (**at** ri); **2** *in expr* ~ **out** sònraich *vt*

pointed *adj* **1** (*sharp*) biorach; **2** (*speech &c: to the point*) pongail

pointless *adj* dìomhain, faoin, gun fheum *m*, ~ **pastimes** cur-seachadan *mpl* dìomhain

poison *n* puinnsean *m*, nimh *&* neimh *m*

poison *v* puinnseanaich *vt*

poisonous *adj* (*lit*) puinnseanach, (*lit & fig*) nimheil

poke *v* brodaich *vt*

poker *n* pòcair *m*

Poland *n*, *used with art*, A' Phòlainn *f invar*

polar bear *n* mathan bàn

pole *n* 1 cabar *m*, pòla *m*, **ridge** ~ cabar-droma *m*, maide-droma *m*; 2 (*geog*) pòla *m*, **the north/south** ~ Am Pòla a Tuath/a Deas; 3 *in expr* **the** ~ **star** an reul-iùil *f*

Pole *n* Pòlach *m*

police *n* poileas *m*, **a** ~ **car** càr-poileis *m*

policeman *n* poileasman *m*, poileas *m*

policewoman *n* ban-phoileas *f*

policing *n* obair *f* phoileis *m gen*

policy *n* (*government, insurance &c*) poileasaidh *m*

Polish *adj* Pòlach

polish *n* lìomh *f*

polish *v* lìomh *vt*

polished *adj* lìomharra

polite *adj* modhail, cùirteil

politeness *n* modhalachd *f invar*

political *adj* poileataigeach, ~ **asylum** tèarmann *m* poileataigeach

politician *n* neach-poileataics *m* (*pl* luchd-poileataics *m sing coll*)

politics *n* poileataics *f invar*

poll *n* 1 (*election, vote*) taghadh *m*; 2 (*head*) ceann *m*, (*hist*) ~ **tax** cìs-chinn *f*

pollutant *n* stuth-truaillidh *m*

pollute *v* (*environment &c*) truaill *vt*, salaich *vt*

polluted *adj & past part* truaillte

pollution *n* truailleadh *m*

poly- *prefix* ioma-, *eg* **polygamy** *n* ioma-phòsadh *m*, **polyglot** *adj* ioma-chànanach, **polygon** *n* ioma-cheàrnag *f*

pompous *adj* mòrchùiseach

pond *n* lochan *m*, lòn *m*, glumag *f*

ponder *v* cnuas & cnuasaich, meòmhraich & meamhraich *vi*, (*more rigorously*) beachd-smaoin(t)ich *vi*, (**about, upon** air)

ponderous *adj* 1 (*heavy*) trom; 2 (*lumbering &c*) slaodach

pony *n* pònaidh *m*

pony-tail *n* (*on head*) figheachan *m*

pool *n* lòn *m*, glumag *f*, (*esp below a waterfall*) linne *f*

poor *adj* 1 (*indigent*) bochd; 2 (*unfortunate*) truagh, bochd, (*excl*) ~ **man/fellow/creature!** a thruaghain!, a dhuine bhochd!; 3 (*of* ~ *quality, inadequate*) droch (*precedes the noun, which it lenites where possible*), suarach, ~ **weather** droch aimsir *f*, droch shìde *f*, **in a** ~ **state** ann an droch staid *f*, **it was pretty** ~ cha robh e ach suarach

poor *n* (*indigent*), **the** ~ am bochd *m sing coll*, na daoine *mpl* bochda, na daoine uireasbhach

poorly *adv* 1 gu dona, **they did** ~ 's ann gu dona a rinn iad, *also* cha do rinn iad ro mhath idir, **they fared** ~ 's ann gu dona a chaidh dhaibh, *also* cha deach dhaibh ro mhath idir; 2 (*unwell*) **he's** ~ tha e (gu math) bochd

Pope *n* Pàpa *m*, *usu with art*, Am Pàpa

popish *adj* (*not PC*) pàpanach

populace *n* sluagh *m*, muinntir *f*, poball *m*

popular *adj* **1** mòr-chòrdte; **2** (*pertaining to the people*) poibleach

population *n* **1** (*con: the people themselves*) sluagh *m*, muinntir *f*, poball *m*; **2** (*more abstr: the people as a statistic*) àireamh-shluaigh *f*

pork *n* feòil-muice *f*, muic-fheòil *f*

porpoise *n* pèileag *f*

porridge *n* lite *f invar*, brochan *m*

port[1] *m* **1** (*harbour &c*) port *m*; **2** (*a conurbation with a ~*) baile-puirt *m*, **Glasgow is a ~** 's e baile-puirt a th' ann an Glaschu

port[2] *n* (*wine*) fion-poirt *m*

portable *adj* so-ghiùlan

porter *n* **1** portair *m*; **2** (*doorkeeper*) dorsair *m*

portion *n* cuid *f*, cuibhreann *m*, roinn *f*, **a half ~** leth-chuid *f*

portray *v* **1** (*on stage &c*) riochdaich *vt*; **2** (*in painting, drawing &c*) dealbh *vt*, tarraing *vt*

portrayal *n* **1** (*on stage, screen*) riochdachadh *m*; **2** (*in painting, drawing &c*) dealbhadh *m*, tarraing *f*

Portugal *n*, *used with art*, A' Phortagail

Portuguese *n & adj* Portagaileach *m*

position *n* **1** (*job*) oifis *f*, dreuchd *f*; **2** (*phys, economic &c*) suidheachadh *m*, **the family was in a difficult ~** bha an teaghlach ann an suidheachadh doirbh; **3** *in expr* **a crouching ~** gurraban *m*

possession(s) *n* **1** seilbh *f*, maoin *f*; **2** (*idiom*) **my worldly ~s** mo chuid *f* den t-saoghal *m*

possessive *adj* seilbheach

possessor *n* seilbheadair & sealbhadair *m*

possible *adj* **1** ion-dhèanta; **2** *commonly expr by* gabh *vi*, **is that ~? no!** an gabh sin a dhèanamh? cha ghabh!, **as hot as ~** cho teth 's a ghabhas

post[1] *n* (*mail*) post *m*, **the Post Office** Oifis *f* a' Phuist

post[2] **1** (*wooden ~*) post *m*, (*fence ~*) stob *m*; **2** (*idiom*) **he's as deaf as a ~** cha chluinn e bid *m*/bìog *f*

post- *prefix* iar-, *eg* **post-graduate** iar-cheumaiche *m*

postal *adj* tron phost *m*, **~ vote** bhòt *f* tron phost

postcard *n* cairt-phuist *f*

postcode *n* còd *m* puist (*gen of* post *m*)

postie, postman *n* post(a) *m*, **Alec the ~** Ailig Post

postpone *v* cuir *vt* dheth, cuir *vt* air an ath là *m*, cuir *vt* air ais

postscript *n* fo-sgrìobhadh *m*

posture *n* giùlan *m*

pot *n* poit *f*, **flower~** poit-fhlùran, **tea-pot** poit-tì *f invar*

potato, potatoes *n & npl* buntàta *m invar sing & coll*, **plant potatoes** cuir buntàta, **potato blight** cnàmh *m*, gaiseadh *m* a' bhuntàta

poteen *n* poitean *m*

potent *adj* **1** (*ruler &c*) cumhachdach; **2** (*drink &c*) làidir; **3** (*remedy, course of action*) èifeachdach, buadhmhor

potential *n* comas *m* (*with gen*), **~ for growth** comas-fàis *m*

potter *n* crèadhadair *m*

pottery *n* crèadhadaireachd *f invar*

pound[1] *n* **1** (*Scots & Eng money*) not(a) *f*, **Irish ~** punnd *m* Èireannach; **2** (*weight*) punnd *m*

pound[2] *n* (*for holding animals &c*) punnd *m*

pound *v* pronn

pounded *adj* pronn

pounding *n* pronnadh *m*

pour *v* **1** dòirt *vti*, sil *vti*, ruith *vti*, **~ me a pint** dòirt pinnt *m* dhomh, **water ~ing through the roof** uisge *m* a' dòrtadh/a' sileadh tron mhullach *m*; **2** (*~ with rain*) sil *vi*, **it's ~ing** tha e a' sileadh

powder *n* pùdar & fùdar *m*, *in expr* **reduce to ~** pùdaraich *vt*

powder *v* pùdaraich & fùdaraich *vt*, cuir pùdar/fùdar *m* (*with prep* air)

power *n* **1** (*might: military &c*) cumhachd *mf invar*, neart *m*, **the ~ of the Roman Empire** cumhachd/neart Ìompaireachd *f* na Ròimhe; **2** (*pol & social ~*) cumhachd *mf invar*, ùghdarras *m*, smachd *m invar*, reachd *m invar*; **3** (*individual's vigour &c*) neart *m*, **he was at the height of his ~s** bha e ann an treun *f invar* a neirt *gen*, *also* bha e aig àird *f* a neirt; **4** (*electric ~*) cumhachd *mf invar*, dealan *m*, **the ~'s off** tha an cumhachd/an dealan dheth; **5** (*capacity, capability*) comas *m*, **~ of speech**, comas-bruidhne (*gen of* bruidhinn *f*), **intellectual ~s** comas-inntinn *f*, **that's beyond my ~s** tha sin thar mo chomais/mo chomasan *gen*; **6** *in expr* **the ~ of movement/motion** lùth *m*

powerful *adj* **1** (*phys*) làidir, neartmhor, lùthmhor; **2** (*pol, militarily*) cumhachdach

practicable *adj* ion-dhèanta, a ghabhas dèanamh

practically *adv* an ìre mhath, **the winter's ~ over** tha an geamhradh an ìre mhath seachad

practice *n* **1** (*music &c*) cleachdadh *m*, **~ makes perfect** is e an cleachdadh a nì teòma; **2** (*habit, custom*) cleachdadh *m*, àbhaist *f*, **it was my ~ to swim every day** bha e na chleachdadh agam a bhith a' snàmh a h-uile là *m*

praise *n* moladh *m*, luaidh *m invar*

praise *v* mol *vt*, luaidh *vt*, dèan moladh *m*, dèan luaidh *f*, (*both with prep* air)

praiseworthy *adj* ionmholta

prattle *n* goileam *m*, gobaireachd & gabaireachd *f invar*

prattling *adj* gobach

pray *v* **1** (*beseech &c*) guidh *vi* (*with prep* air); **2** (*relig*) dèan ùrnaigh *f* (**to** ri)

prayer *n* **1** (*entreaty*) guidhe *mf*; **2** (*relig*) ùrnaigh *f*, (*less usu*) guidhe *mf*, **the Lord's ~** Ùrnaigh an Tighearna, **a ~ meeting** coinneamh *f* ùrnaigh *gen*

pre- *prefix* ro- *also* roi(mh)-, *eg* **prefix** (*gram*) *n* ro-leasachan *m*, **pre-payment** *n* ro-phàigheadh *m*

preamble *n* ro-ràdh *m*

precarious *adj* **1** (*unreliable, shaky, 'dodgy'*) cugallach, **the world is (a) ~ (place)** (*trad*) is cugallach an saoghal; **2** (*risky*) cunnartach

precious *adj* **1** luachmhor, prìseil; **2** *in expr* ~ **stone** clach *f* uasal; **3** *excl* **(my)** ~**!** m' ulaidh!, m' eudail!

precipitate *adj* **1** (*actions &c*) cabhagach, bras; **2** (*stream, hillslope*) cas, (*stream*) bras

precipitation *n* (*of liquids*) sileadh *m*

précis *n* geàrr-chunntas *m*

precise *adj* **1** (*of person, description &c*) pongail, mionaideach; **2** (*of figures &c: accurate*) grinn, pongail

precision *n* (*accuracy*) pongalachd *f invar*

precocious *adj* luathaireach

predator *n* sealgair *m*

predestination *n* ro-òrdachadh *m*

predicament *n* **1** (*difficult situation*) càs *m*, cùil-chumhang *f*, **grave/extreme ~** cruaidh-chàs *m*; **2** (*state of indecision*) ioma(dh)-chomhairle *f*, imcheist *f*, **in a ~** ann an ioma-chomhairle, an/fo imcheist

predict *v* ro-innis *vt*

predictable *adj* ro-innseach

preface *n* ro-ràdh *m*

prefer *v* is *v irreg def* (*in past & conditional tenses* b'), *followed by* fheàrr *lenited comp adj of* math, *with prep* le, **I ~ meat** 's fheàrr leam feòil *f*, **they would ~ cheese** b' fheàrr leotha càise *m*

preference *n* roghainn *mf*, **my own ~ in music** mo roghainn *mf* fhìn de cheòl *m*

prefix (*gram*) *n* ro-leasachan *m*

pregnancy *n* leatrom *m*

pregnant *adj* torach & torrach, trom

prejudice *n* claon-bhàigh *f*, claon-bhreith *f*

premature *adj* **1** ron àm *m*, ron mhithich *f invar*; **2** (*esp birth*) an-abaich

prematurely *adv* ron àm *m*, ron mhithich *f invar*

premier *adj* prìomh (*precedes the noun, which it lenites where possible*), **the ~ league** a' phrìomh roinn *f*, **the ~ town of the district** prìomh bhaile *m* na sgìre *f*

premier *n* (*pol*) prìomhaire *m*

preoccupation *n* cùram *m*

preoccupied *adj* **1** (*through anxiety*) fo chùram *m*; **2** (*with one's thoughts or attention elsewhere*) fad' às

preparation *n* deasachadh *m*, uidheamachadh *m*, ullachadh *m*

prepare *v* **1** deasaich *vt*, ullaich *vt*, **~ food/a meal** deasaich biadh *m*, **they were preparing themselves for war** bha iad gan deasachadh fhèin airson cogaidh *m gen*; **2** (*by adjusting, tuning &c*) gleus *vt*; **3** (*by equipping, fitting out &c*) uidheamaich *vt*

prepared *adj & past part* **1** deiseil, ullamh, deas, **is the dinner ~?** a bheil am biadh deiseil/ullamh?; **2** (*engine, equipment &c*) air ghleus *mf*; **3** (*equipped, fitted out &c*) uidheamaichte; **4** (*willing*) deònach, **they're not ~ to do it** chan eil iad deònach (air) a dhèanamh

pre-payment *n* ro-phàigheadh *m*

preponderance *n* tromalach *f*

preposition *n* (*gram*) roimhear *m*

Presbyterian *n & adj* Clèireach *m*

Presbyterianism *n* Clèireachd *f invar*

Presbytery *n* Clèir *f*

pre-school *adj* fo-sgoile, **~ education** foghlam *m* fo-sgoile

prescribe *v* òrdaich *vt*

prescription *n* (*med*) òrdugh *m* cungaidh *f gen*

pre-selection *n* ro-thaghadh *m*

presence *n* **1** làthair *f*, **(get) out of my ~!** a-mach às mo làthair!; **2** (*abstr, the fact of being present*) làthaireachd *f invar*

present *adj* **1** an làthair *f*, ann, **I knew those who were ~** bha mi eòlach air na bha an làthair/ann; **2** (*current, contemporary &c*) *in exprs* **(at) the ~ time** (aig) an àm *m* seo, (*more immediate*) **I can't help you at the ~ time** chan urrainn dhomh ur cuideachadh an-dràsta, **the ~ situation** an suidheachadh sa tha sinn a-nis/aig an àm seo, **the ~ government** riaghaltas *m* an latha *m gen* (an-diugh)

present[1] *n* tiodhlac *m*, gibht *f*

present[2] *n* (*time*) *in exprs* **the ~** an t-àm a tha làthair, **at ~** aig an àm seo, a-nis, (*more immediate*) an-dràsta, (*more general: these days &c*) san latha *m* an-diugh

present *v* **1** (*products, techniques &c*) taisbean & taisbein *vt*; **2** (*as gift*) thoir (seachad) *vt*, tiodhlaic *vt*, **(to do)**

presentation *n* **1** (*~ of products, techniques &c*) taisbeanadh *m*; **2** (*formal ~ to official, retiree &c*) tabhartas *m*

preserve *v* glèidh *vt*, **God will ~ us** glèidhidh Dia sinn

preserved *adj & past part* glèidhte

president *n* (*of firm, company, country*) ceann-suidhe *m*

press *n* **1** (*printing ~, also publishing house*) clò *m*, **hot off the ~es** ùr on chlò, **the Ostaig ~** Clò Ostaig; **2** *in expr* **the ~** (*published media in general*) na pàipearan(-naidheachd) *mpl*

press *v* **1** (*phys: squeeze, compress*) fàisg *vt*, teannaich *vt*; **2** (*urge*) coitich *vt*, brosnaich *vt*; **3** (*cause to hurry*) cuir cabhag *f* (*with prep* air), greas *vt*

pressing *adj* (*ie urgent*) cabhagach, èiginneach, cudthromach

pressure *n* **1** cudthrom, cudrom & cuideam *m*, **atmospheric ~** cudthrom an àile; **2** (*psych: stress &c*) uallach *m*, **under ~** fo uallach

pretend *v* **1** leig *vi* (*with prep* air), **the soldiers ~ed that they were civilians**

leig na saighdearan *mpl* orra gun robh iad nan sìobhaltairean *mpl*; **2** (*esp kidding, joking*) *in expr* **I was only ~ing** cha robh mi ach mas fhìor

pretext *n* leisgeul *m*

pretty *adj* grinn, bòidheach, ceanalta

pretty *adv* gu math, an ìre mhath, **~ old** gu math aosta, **we were ~ tired** bha sinn gu math sgìth/an ìre mhath sgìth, **the winter's ~ well over** tha an geamhradh an ìre mhath seachad

prevent *v* bac *vt*, cuir bacadh *m* (*with prep* air), caisg *vt*, cuir casg *m* (*with prep* air)

prevention *n* casg *m*, casgadh *m*

preventive *adj* casgach

prey *n* cobhartach *mf*, creach *f*

price *n* prìs *f*, **high ~s** prìsean àrda, **buy at a good ~** ceannaich *vti* air deagh phrìs

prickle *n* bior *m*, calg *m*, dealg *f*

pride *n* **1** (*esp legitimate ~*) pròis *f*, moit *f*; **2** (*usu more excessive ~*) àrdan, mòrchuis *f*, uabhar *m*, uaibhreas *m*

prime *adj* **1** prìomh (*precedes the noun, which it lenites where possible*), **~ number** prìomh-àireamh *f*, **his ~ objective** am prìomh amas *m* a bha aige; **2** *in expr* (*philo*) **~ cause** màthair-adhbhar *m*

prime *n* treun *f invar* a (*&c*) neirt (*gen of* neart *m*), **in my ~** (ann) an treun mo neirt, *also* aig àird *f* mo neirt

prime minister *n* prìomhaire *m*

prince *n* prionnsa *m*

princely *adj* flathail

princess *n* bana-phrionnsa *f*

principal *adj* prìomh (*precedes the noun, which it lenites where possible*), **the ~ town** am prìomh bhaile *m*

principle *n* prionnsabal *m*, **in ~** ann am prionnsabal

print *n* **1** (*abstr & con: books &c*) clò & clòdh *m*, **appear in ~** nochd *vi* an clò; **2** (*trace, imprint of something*) lorg *f*, làrach *f*

print *v* (*books &c*) clò-bhuail *vt*, cuir *vt* an clò *m*

printed *adj & past part* clò-bhuailte, **~ by X** clò-bhuailte le X, *also* air a c(h)lò-bhualadh le X

printer *n* clò-bhualadair *m*

printing *n* **1** clò-bhualadh *m*; **2** *in expr* **~ error** clò-mhearachd *m*

prison *n* prìosan *m*

prisoner *n* prìosanach *m*, ciomach *m*

private *adj* **1** (*secret*) uaigneach, dìomhair; **2** (*confidential*) dìomhair, pearsanta; **3** (*place &c, not open to all*) prìobhaiteach; **4** (*not state-owned*) prìobhaiteach, **~ college** colaisde phrìobhaiteach, **the ~ sector** an roinn phrìobhaiteach

privately *adv* (*ie in secret, in confidence &c*) os ìosal & os ìseal, gu dìomhair

prize *n* duais *f*, **she won a ~ at the Mod** choisinn i duais aig a' Mhòd *m*

probability *n* coltachd *f invar*

probable *adj* coltach, **it's ~ that she'll come** tha e coltach gun tig i

probably *adv* tha (*&c*) e coltach *followed by conj* gu, **he'll ~ come tomorrow** tha e coltach gun tig e a-màireach

probity *n* ionracas *m*

problem *n* **1** (*point at issue*) ceist *f*, cùis *f*, **is it too costly? that's the ~** a bheil e ro chosgail? 's e sin a' cheist/a' chùis, *also* 's e sin an rud *m*; **2** (*difficulty*) duilgheadas *m*, trioblaid *f*, **we've got ~s where money is concerned** tha duilgheadasan againn a thaobh airgid *m gen*, **that won't be a ~ for him** cha bhi sin na dhuilgheadas dha, **social ~s** duilgheadasan sòisealta, **the loss of my job was the start of our ~s** b' e call *m* m' obrach (*gen of* obair *f*) toiseach *m* ar trioblaidean *gen*

proceed *v* rach *vi* air adhart (**with** le)

process *n* **1** (*industrial ~, IT function or procedure*) gnìomh *m*; **2** *in expr* **the ~ of law** modh *m* an lagha

process *v* **1** (*industry &c: deal with, prepare, treat materials &c, appropriately*) giùllaich *vt*, gnìomhaich *vt*, saothraich *vt*; **2** (*~ information*) làimhsich *vt*, cuir *vt* an eagar *m*; **3** (*IT*) gnìomhaich *vt*, obraich *vt*, **~ data** gnìomhaich/obraich dàta *m invar*

processing *n* **1** (*industry &c*) giùllachadh *m*, gnìomhachadh *m*, saothrachadh *m*; **2** (*IT*) *in exprs* **word ~** facladaireachd *f invar*, **data ~** gnìomhachadh-dàta *m*, obrachadh-dàta *m*

processor *n* (*IT*) gnìomh-inneal *m*, *in expr* (*IT*) **word ~** facladair *m*

proclamation *n* gairm *f*

procrastinate *v* màirnealaich *vi*, maillich *vi*

prodigal *adj* stròdhail *&* struidheil, **the ~ son** am mac stròdhail/struidheil

produce *n* (*of land, plants, industry &c*) toradh *m*

produce *v* (*industry &c*) saothraich *vt*, dèan *vt*, tàrmaich *vt*

producer *n* (*of film, play &c*) riochdaire *m*

product *n* **1** toradh *m*; **2** **~s** (*ie items, goods*) bathar *m sing coll*

productive *adj* (*land, plants &c*) torach

profane *v* (*places, objects, relig, morals &c*) truaill *vt*

profession *n* (*ie occupation*) dreuchd *f*

professional *adj* **1** (*relating to a job or profession*) dreuchdail, **~ terminology** briathrachas *m* dreuchdail; **2** (*working for payment, also having high ~ standards*) proifeiseanta, **a ~ singer** seinneadair proifeiseanta

professor *n* proifeasair *m*

proficiency *n* comas *m*

proficient *adj* comasach

profile *n* **1** (*phys*) leth-aghaidh *f*; **2** (*journalism &c: descriptive account*) cunntas *m*; **3** (*publicity &c*) ìomhaigh *f*, **improve the company's ~** leasaich ìomhaigh na companaidh *mf*

profit *n* **1** (*esp fin*) prothaid *f*, buannachd *f*, **make a ~** dèan prothaid; **2** (*more general*) buannachd *f*, tairbhe *f invar*

profit *v* tairbhich & tarbhaich *vi*

profitable *adj* tairbheach & tarbhach, buannachdail

profound *adj* domhainn, **a ~ book/thought** leabhar domhainn/smuain dhomhainn

progeny *n* **1** (*of humans*) gineal *mf*, sìol *m sing coll*, sliochd *m sing coll*; **2** (*of birds, animals*) àl *m*

program, programme *n* (*broadcasting, IT*) prògram *m*, (*IT*) **applications ~** prògram-chleachdaidhean *m*

programming *n* (*IT*) prògramadh *m*, **~ language** cànan *m* prògramaidh *gen*

progress *n* **1** (*the abstr concept*) adhartas *m*; **2** (*in skill, activity &c*) piseach *m*, adhartas *m*, **we're making ~** tha (am) piseach a' tighinn òirnn, tha sinn a' dèanamh adhartais *gen, also* (*more fam*) tha sinn a' tighinn air adhart

progressive *adj* adhartach

prohibit *v* toirmisg *vt*

prohibited *adj & past part* toirmisgte, fo thoirmeasg *m*

prohibition *n* toirmeasg *m*

prohibitive *adj* toirmeasgach

project *n* pròiseact *mf*, plana *m*

prologue *n* ro-ràdh *m*

prolong *v* sìn *vt* a-mach

promise *n* gealladh *m*, geall *m*

promise *v* geall *vti*, thoir gealladh *m* (*with prep* do), **he ~d me he wouldn't do it again** gheall e dhomh nach dèanadh e a-rithist e, **~ me you'll write to me** thoir gealladh dhomh gun sgrìobh thu thugam

promised *adj & past part* **1** geallta; **2** *in expr* **the ~ land** tìr *mf* a' gheallaidh *m*

promising *adj* gealltanach, **~ player/student** cluicheadair *m*/oileanach *m* gealltanach

promontory *n* àird *f*, sròn *f*, (*rounded*) maol *m*, (*usu coastal*) rubha *m*

promote *v* àrdaich *vt*

prompt *adj* **1** (*on time*) an deagh àm *m*, mithich; **2** (*person: in performing tasks*) deas, èasgaidh, ealamh

promptly *adv*, **he did it ~** (*quickly*) rinn e gu deas e, (*by the appointed time*) rinn e an deagh àm *m* e

prone *adj* **1** (*phys position*) air a (&c) b(h)eul *m* fodha, air a (&c) b(h)eul sìos, (*loosely*) sìnte, **they were ~** bha iad air am beul fodha/sìos; **2** (*having a tendency to*) buailteach (*with noun, & prep* do), **~ to laughter/change** buailteach do ghàireachdainn *f invar*/do chaochladh *m*, *also in exprs* **~ to fear** eagalach, **~ to anxiety/worry** *adj* cùramach, iomagaineach; **3** (*with verbal exprs*) dual(t)ach, buailteach, **~ to spend money** dual(t)ach/buailteach airgead *m* a chosg, **~ to tell lies** dual(t)ach/buailteach a bhith ag innse bhreugan *fpl gen*

pronoun *n* (*gram*) riochdair *m*

pronounce v (*lang*) fuaimnich vt

pronunciation n (*lang*) fuaimneachadh m

proof n dearbhadh m (**of** air), **~ of his guilt** dearbhadh air a chionta m

prop n taic(e) f

propagate v (*plants, animals*) tàrmaich vt

propel v (*~ machinery &c*) iomain vt, **~ a machine by steam** iomain inneal m le smùid f, (*sport*) **~ a ball** iomain bàla m

propellant n stuth-iomain m

proper adj 1 (*suitable, fitting*) dòigheil, iomchaidh & iomchuidh, cothromach, cubhaidh; 2 (*moral, decent*) beusach; 3 (*real, complete*) fìor, dearg (*both precede the noun, which is lenited where possible*), **a ~ fool** fìor amadan m, dearg amadan

properly adv gu dòigheil, **do it ~!** dèan gu dòigheil e!

property n 1 (*possessions*) sealbh m, seilbh f; 2 (*characteristic &c*) buadh f, feart m

prophecy n fàidheadaireachd f, fàisneachd f

prophesy v fàisnich vti

prophet n fàidh m, fiosaiche m

propitious adj fàbharach

proposal n moladh m, **the government's ~s for a new bridge** molaidhean an riaghaltais airson drochaid f gen ùire

propose v 1 (*intend to do something*) cuir vi roimhe (*&c*), rùnaich vi, **they ~ed to build a house** chuir iad romhpa taigh m a thogail; 2 (*offer, suggest*) tairg vi, **he ~d to do it** thairg e a dhèanamh; 3 (*put forward idea, recommend*) mol vti

propped adj & past part an taic f, an tacsa m, (**against** ri), **~ (up) against a tree** an taic/an tacsa ri craoibh (*dat of* craobh f)

proprietor n seilbheadair & sealbhadair m

prose n rosg m

prospective adj san t-sealladh m, san amharc m

prosper v soirbhich vi (*usu impersonal: followed by prep le, with dat*), **the business ~ed** shoirbhich leis a' gnìomhachas, **we ~ed** shoirbhich leinn

prosperity n soirbheachas m, soirbheachadh m

protection n 1 (*abstr & con*) tèarmann m, dìon m, **under the court's ~** fo thèarmann/fo dhìon na cùirte; 2 (*more con*) fasgadh m, **seek ~ from the downpour** sir fasgadh on dìle f; 3 in expr (*IT*) **data ~** dìon-dàta m, tèarainteachd f invar dàta m invar

protest n 1 (*general*) gearan m; 2 (*pol &c: demonstration, rally, march*) fianais-dhùbhlain f (**against** an aghaidh *followed by gen*)

protest v 1 (*general*) gearain vi; 2 (*pol &c: demonstrate, march &c*) tog fianais f (**against** an aghaidh *followed by gen*)

protester n (*pol &c: at demonstration, march &c*) neach-togail-fianais m (*pl* luchd-togail-fianais m sing coll), (**against** an aghaidh *followed by gen*)

Protestant *n & adj* Pròstanach *m*

proud *adj* **1** (*usu legitimately*) pròiseil, moiteil, (**of** à), **we're ~ of you** tha sinn pròiseil/moiteil asad; **2** (*usu excessively*) uaibhreach, àrdanach, mòrchuiseach

prove *v* dearbh *vt*

proved, proven *adj & past part* dearbhte

proverb *n* seanfhacal *m*, ràdh *m invar*

provide *v* **1** (*general*) thoir *vt* seachad; **2** (*esp traders &c*) solair *vt*, **~ accom-modation for the tourists** solair lòistinn *m* don luchd-turais *m sing coll*; **3** (*esp admin, fin &c*) ullaich *vt*, **~ finance for a new hospital** ullaich ionmhas *m* airson ospatail *m gen* ùir

provided *conj* air chumha is (*with conj* gu), cho fad is (*with conj* a), **~ (that) the salary is high** air chumha is gu bheil an turastal àrd, cho fad 's a tha an turastal àrd

providence *n* sealbh *m*, freasdal *m*

provision *n* ullachadh *m*, **~ of finance** ullachadh ionmhais *m gen*

provisional *adj* sealach

provisions *n* lòn *m*

provost *n* pròbhaist *m*

prow *n* toiseach *m*

proximity *n* faisge *f invar*

prudence *n* faiceall *f*, earalas *m*

prudent *adj* faiceallach

PS *abbrev see* **postscript**

psychiatrist *n* lighiche-inntinn *m*

psychiatry *n* leigheas-inntinn *m*

psychologist *n* inntinn-eòlaiche *m*

psychology *n* eòlas-inntinn *m*

puberty *n* inbhidheachd *f invar*

pubes *n*, **pubic hair** *n* ròm *mf invar*, gaoisid *& gaosaid f*

public *adj* **1** (*communal*) coitcheann, poblach, **~ swimming pool** amar-snàimh *m* coitcheann/poblach; **2** (*opposite of* private) follaiseach, poblach, **a ~ enquiry** rannsachadh follaiseach, **a ~ meeting** coinneamh fhollaiseach/phoblach, **a ~ company** companaidh *mf* p(h)oblach, **the ~ sector** an roinn phoblach, an earrann phoblach; **3** *in exprs* **~ address system** *n* glaodhaire *m*, **~ house** taigh-seinnse *m*

publication *n* **1** (*abstr*) foillseachadh *m*; **2** (*abstr & con*) clò-bhualadh *m*, **Gairm ~s** Clò-bhualaidhean Gairm; **3** (*con: periodical*) iris *f*, ràitheachan *m*

publicise *v* cuir *vt* am follais *f invar*, thoir *vt* am follais, foillsich *vt*

publicity *n* **1** (*abstr*) follaiseachd *f invar*, sanasachd *f invar*,; **2** (*con: public notices &c*) sanas(an) *m(pl)*, (*commercial*) sanas(an)-reic *m(pl)*,

publish *v* **1** foillsich *vt*, cuir *vt* an clò *m*; **2** *in exprs* **be ~ed** nochd *vi* an clò, **newly ~ed** ùr on chlò, air ùr-fhoillseachadh

publisher *n* foillsichear *m*

publishing *n* foillseachadh *m*

pudding *n* **1** mìlsean *m*; **2** (*savoury* ~) marag *f*, **black/white** ~ marag dhubh/gheal

puddle *n* glumag *f*, lòn *m*

pull *n* tarraing *f*, slaodadh *m*

pull *v* **1** tarraing *vti*, (*more heavily*) slaod *vti*, ~ **a cork** tarraing corcais *f*; **2** (*idiom*) **they were ~ing my leg** bha iad a' tarraing asam

pullet *n* eireag *f*

pulley *n* ulag *f*

pullover *n* geansaidh *m*

pulp *n* glaodhan *m*, pronnadh *m*, **wood** ~ glaodhan-fiodha *m*

pulpit *n* cùbaid *f*, (*less usu*) crannag *f*

pulverise *v* pronn *vt*

pulverised *adj & past part* pronn, air a (*&c*) p(h)ronnadh

pump *n* pumpa *m*

punctilious *adj* (*person, work &c*) mion-chùiseach, pongail, mionaideach

punctual *adj* pongail

puncture *n* toll *m*

puncture *v* toll *vt*

punish *v* peanasaich *vt*, smachdaich *vt*

punishment *n* peanas *m*, **corporal** ~ peanas corporra

punitive *adj* peanasach

pup *n* cuilean *m*

pupil *n* **1** (*school*) sgoilear *m*; **2** (*of eye*) dubh *m* (na sùla)

puppet *n* fear-brèige *m*, pupaid *f*

puppy *n* cuilean *m*

purchaser *n* neach-ceannach *m* (*pl* luchd-ceannach *m sing coll*)

purchasing *n* ceannach *m*

purgatory *n* purgadair *m*

purling *n* (*of stream*) crònan *m*, torman *m*

purple *adj* corcair, purpaidh

purple *n* purpar *m*, purpaidh *f*

purpose *n* rùn *m*; **2** *in expr* **on** ~ a dh'aon rùn, a dh'aon ghnothach *m*

purring *n* crònan *m*

pursue *v* rua(i)g *vt*, lean *vt* (gu dian)

pursuit *n* **1** tòir *f*, ruaig *f*, **in** ~ an tòir (*of* air); **2** (*military*) ruith *f*; **3** (*hobby &c*) cur-seachad *m*, **my favourite** ~ an cur-seachad as fheàrr leam

pus *n* brachadh *m*, iongar *m*

push *v* put *vt*, (*more roughly*) brùth *vt*, sàth *vt*

pustule *n* guirean *m*

put *v* **1** (*exprs with* cuir *vt*) ~ **coal on the fire** cuir gual *m* air an teine *m*, ~ **your clothes on** cuir ort/umad do chuid *f* aodaich *m gen*, ~ **money on a horse** cuir airgead *m* air each *m*, ~ **the light on/off** cuir air/às an solas *m*, ~ **the fire out** cuir às an teine *m*, **I had to** ~ **on weight**

b' fheudar dhomh cudthrom *m* a chur orm, ~ **one's hope in someone/ something** cuir dòchas *m* ann an cuideigin/rudeigin, ~ **into words** cuir *vt* an cèill (*dat of* ciall *f*), ~ **an end to** (*esp person*) cuir *vi* às (*with prep* do), ~ **an end to** (*process &c*) cuir stad *m*, cuir crìoch *f*, (*with prep* air), ~ **something off (till another day)** cuir rudeigin air ath là *m*, *also* (*less trad*) cuir rudeigin dheth (gu là *m* eile), ~ **by/aside** cuir *vt* mu seach, cuir *vt* an dara taobh *m*, ~ **into action** (*plan &c*) cuir *vt* an gnìomh *m*, ~ **at risk/in danger** cuir *vt* an cunnart *m*, ~ **to the test** cuir *vt* gu deuchainn *f*, *also* dearbh *vt*, ~ **down** (*belittle, humiliate someone*) cuir *vt* an suarachas *m*, ~ **out** (*publish*) cuir *vt* a-mach, ~ **right** (*wrongs &c*) cuir *vt* ceart, ~ **right,** ~ **in order** (*machinery &c*) cuir *vt* air ghleus *mf*, *also* gleus *vt*, **I don't want to** ~ **you to any trouble** chan eil mi airson dragh *m* sam bith a chur oirbh, ~ **Gaelic into French** cuir Frangais *f* air Gàidhlig *f*, (*idiom*) ~ **the cat among the pigeons** cuir an ceòl air feadh na fìdhle; **2** (*other misc exprs*) ~ **down** (*rebellion &c*) ceannsaich *vt*, mùch *vt*, ~ **(great) emphasis on X** leig cudthrom (mòr) air X, ~ **right,** ~ **in order** (*situations, relationships &c*) rèitich *vt*, leasaich *vt*, ~ **to shame** maslaich *vt*, ~ **up with** fuiling & fulaing *vt*, (*less trad*) cuir *vi* suas ri, **they had to** ~ **up with cold and hunger** b' fheudar dhaibh fuachd *mf* is acras *m* fhulang, b' fheudar dhaibh cur suas ris an fhuachd is ris an acras, ~ **up (for the night)** faigh cuid-oidhche *f*/cuid *f* na h-oidhche, **we** ~ **up for the night at the hotel** fhuair sinn (ar) cuid-oidhche/fhuair sinn cuid na h-oidhche aig an taigh-òsta *m*
putrefaction *n* grodadh *m*, lobhadh *m*, brèine *f*
putrefy *v* grod *vi*, lobh *vi*
putrid *adj* grod, lobhte
puzzle *n* tòimhseachan *m*, **crossword** ~ tòimhseachan-tarsainn *m*
puzzle *v* cuir *vt* an imcheist *f*
puzzled *adj & past part* an/fo imcheist *f*
puzzling *adj* imcheisteach

Q

quadrangle *n* ceithir-cheàrnag *f*

quadrilateral *adj* ceithir-cheàrnach

quadruped *adj & n* ceithir-chasach

quagmire *n* sùil-chritheach *f*, bog *m*, boglach *f*, fèith(e) *f*

quaich *n* cuach *f*

quaint *adj* neònach, annasach, sean-fhasanta

quake *n* **1** crith *f*; **2** (*earthquake*) crith-thalmhainn *f*

quake *v* bi *vi irreg* air chrith *f*, crith *vi*, **he was quaking with fear** bha e air chrith leis an eagal *m*, *in expr* **start to** ~ rach *vi* air chrith

qualification *n* **1** (*for employment, study &c*) uidheamachadh *m*; **2** (*esp in written form*) ~(s) teisteanas *m*, barrantas *m*

qualified *adj & past part* (*for employment, study &c*) uidheamaichte, barrantaichte, (*of the standard required*) aig ìre *f invar* (na h-obrach &c)

qualify *v* **1** (*be up to a particular job*) bi *vi* aig ìre *f invar* (na h-obrach); **2** (*esp by formal qualifications*: ~ *for employment, study &c*) bi *vi* uidheamaichte (airson na h-obrach/a' chùrsa &c)

quality *n* **1** (*attribute &c*) buadh *f*, feart *m*, beus *f*, **natural qualities** buadhan nàdarra(ch), **intellectual qualities** buadhan inntinn *f gen*; **2** (*degree of excellence &c*) mathas *m*

quandary *n* ioma(dh)-chomhairle *f*, imcheist *f*, **in a** ~ **as to what I would do** ann an ioma(dh)-chomhairle dè a dhèanainn

quantity *n* uimhir *f invar*, uiread *m invar*, meud *m invar*, **we had a (certain)** ~ **of food** bha na h-uimhir/na h-uiread de bhiadh *m* againn, **give me the same** ~ **as Seumas (has)** thoir dhomh uimhir ri Seumas, thoir dhomh uiread 's a tha aig Seumas, *in expr* **what** ~ **do you require?** dè a dh'fheumas sibh dheth?

quarrel *n* **1** (*usu verbal*) trod *m*, argamaid *f*, **a** ~ **arose between them** dh'èirich trod eatarra; **2** (*verbal or phys*) tuasaid *f*; **3** (*phys*) sabaid *f*

quarrel *v* **1** (*squabble &c, usu verbally*) troid *vi*, connsaich *vi*; **2** (*phys*) sabaid *vi* (**with** ri); **3** (*fall out*) rach *vi* thar a chèile, **they ~led/have ~led** chaidh iad thar a chèile, tha iad troimh-a-chèile

quarrelling *n* trod *m*, **I can't sleep on account of their** ~ chan urrainn dhomh cadal air sgàth an troid *gen*

quarrelsome *adj* connspaideach, connsachail, aimhreiteach

quarry[1] *n* (*for stone &c*) cuaraidh *m*

quarry[2] *n* (*of hunters &c*) creach *f*

quart *n* cairteal *m*

quarter *n* **1** ceathramh *m*; **2** (*clock time*) cairteal *m*, (*less usu*) ceathramh *m*, **a ~/three ~s of an hour** cairteal/trì chairteil na h-uarach (*gen of* uair *f*), **a** ~ **to four** cairteal gu ceithir; **3** (~ *of year*) ràith *f*

quarterly *n* (*periodical*) ràitheachan *m*

quarters *n* **1** (*military*) taigh-feachd *m*, gearastan *m*, cairtealan *mpl*; **2** (*non-military*) àite-fuirich *m*, lòistinn *m*

quaver *v* crith *vi*

quay *n* cidhe *m*, laimrig *f*

queen *n* banrigh *f*, bànrighinn *f*

queer *adj* neònach

quell *v* (*people, emotions &c*) ceannsaich *vt*, mùch *vt*, ~ **unrest** ceannsaich aimhreit *f*

quelling *n* ceannsachadh *m*

quench *v* **1** (*thirst*) bàth *vt*; **2** (*fire, spirit &c*) mùch *vt*

querulous *adj* gearanach

query *n* ceist *f*

question *n* **1** ceist *f*, *in exprs* **ask X a** ~ cuir ceist air X, ~ **master** ceistear *m*, ~ **mark** comharradh-ceiste *m*; **2** (*point at issue*) ceist *f*, cùis *f*, **is it too costly, that's the** ~ a bheil e ro chosgail, 's e sin a' cheist/a' chùis; **3** (*doubt*) **call into** ~ cuir *vt* an teagamh *m*

question *v* **1** (*put questions*) ceasnaich *vt*, cuir ceist(ean) *f* (*with prep* air); **2** (*doubt, contest*) cuir *vt* an teagamh *m*, cuir teagamh (*with prep* ann an), **they ~ed my integrity** chuir iad an teagamh an t-ionracas *m* agam, chuir iad teagamh san ionracas agam

questionable *adj* amharasach

questioner *n* ceistear *m*

questioning *n* ceasnachadh *m*

questionnaire *n* ceisteachan *m*

queue *n* ciudha *mf*

quick *adj* **1** (*in moving from place to place*) luath, astarach; **2** (*of person, in performing tasks &c*) clis, deas, tapaidh, ealamh; **3** (*mentally* ~) luath na (*&c*) inntinn *f*, geur-chùiseach, geur na (*&c*) inntinn; **4** (*brief, hurried*) aithghearr, **a** ~ **look at the clock** sùil *f* aithghearr air a' chleoc *m*

quicken *v* luathaich *vti*, **our pace ~ed** luathaich ar ceum *m*, **we ~ed our pace** luathaich sinn ar ceum

quickly *adv* gu luath, **the time passed** ~ chaidh an ùine seachad gu luath

quickness *n* **1** (*of person, in performing tasks &c*) luas *m*, cliseachd *f invar*; **2** (*mental or phys* ~) graide *f invar*

quick-tempered *adj* aithghearr, cas

quiet *adj* **1** (*person, atmosphere, weather &c*) ciùin, sàmhach, sèimh; **2** (*of persons: silent, not speaking*) tosdach; **3** *in expr* **be** ~! tosd!, ist! (*pl* istibh!) & eist! (*pl* eistibh!), bi/bithibh sàmhach

quiet *n* **1** (*silence*) tosd *m invar*; **2** (*calm*) ciùineas *m*, sàmhchair *f*

quieten *v* **1** (*silence*) tosdaich *vt*; **2** (*calm*) ciùinich *vti*, sìthich *vti*, socraich *vti*, tàlaidh *vt*

quietly *adv* os ìosal & os ìseal

quietness *n* **1** (*silence*) tosd *m invar*; **2** (*calm*) ciùineas *m*, sàmhchair *f*

quilt *n* cuibhrig *mf*

quit *adj* saor *adj* is, cuidhteas *m* (*with or without prep* de), **we're ~ of the bad lodgers** tha sinn saor is na droch lòisdearan *mpl*, fhuair sinn cuidhteas (de) na droch lòisdearan

quit *v* fàg *vt*, (*can be more drastic*) trèig *vt*, **she ~ her post/job** thrèig i a dreuchd *f*, **the people ~ the island** thrèig na daoine *mpl* an t-eilean

quite *adv* **1** (*completely*) (gu) buileach, gu tur, gu h-iomlan, gu leòr, **she's not ~ ready** chan eil i buileach deiseil, **~ different** gu tur eadar-dhealaichte, *in exprs* **I'm ~ certain** tha mi làn-chinnteach, **that's ~ right** tha sin ceart gu leòr, *also* (*stronger*) tha sin cho ceart ri ceart; **2** (*fairly, somewhat*) gu math, **we were ~ tired** bha sinn gu math sgìth, **~ old** gu math aosta; **3** (*expr agreement*) dìreach (sin)!, **I was wrong! ~!** bha mi ceàrr! dìreach!

quiver *v* bi *vi irreg* air chrith *f*, crith *vi*

quiz *n* ceasnachadh *m*

quota *n* cuid *f*, cuibhreann *mf*, (*less trad*) cuota *m*

R

rabbit *n* rabaid *f*, (*more trad*) coineanach *m*

rabble *n* prabar *m*, gràisg *f*

race[1] *n* **1** (*ethnicity*) cineal *m*, ~ **relations** dàimh-chinealan *f*; **2** (*more loosely: tribe, people, esp supposedly of common descent*) sìol *m sing coll*, cinneadh *m*, gineal *mf*, **the ~ of Diarmaid** (*the Campbells*) sìol Diarmaid *gen*; **3** *in expr* **the human ~** an cinne-daonna *m*

race[2] *n* (*sports &c*) rèis *f*

racial *adj* cinneadail, cinealtais (*gen of* cinealtas *m, used adjectivally*), ~ **discrimination** lethbhreith chinneadail, claonadh cinealtais

racialism, racism *n* gràin-chinnidh *f*, cinealtas *m*

racialist, racist *adj* cinealtach

racist *n* neach cinealtach

racket[1] *n* (*noise*) gleadhraich *f*, (*louder*) ùpraid *f*, othail *f*

racket[2] (*for sport*) racaid *f*

racket[3] (*dishonest business &c*) foill *f*, gnìomhachas foilleil, companaidh *mf* fhoilleil

radiance *n* deàlradh *m*, lainnir *f*

radiant *adj* deàlrach, lainnireach, boillsgeach

radiate *v* **1** (*shine*) deàlraich *vi*; **2** (*emit*) sgaoil *vt*

radio *n* rèidio *m*, **what's on the ~?** dè a th' air an rèidio?

radioactive *adj* rèidio-beò

raffle *n* crannchur-gill *m*

rafter *n* cabar *m*

rag *n* luideag *f*, clùd & clobhd *m*

rage *n* cuthach *m*, bàinidh *f invar*, boile *f invar*, **in a ~** air chuthach, air bhàinidh, air bhoile, **fly into a ~/go mad with ~** rach *vi* air chuthach, gabh an cuthach (dearg)

ragged *adj* cearbach, luideach

raging *adj* **1** (*of persons: with madness or anger*) air chuthach *m*, air bhàinidh *f invar*, air bhoile *f invar*; **2** (*of seas*) doineannach

raid *n* creach *f*

rail *n* rèile *f*

railings *n* rèilichean *fpl*

rain *n* uisge *m*, (*heavy*) dìle *f*, (*torrential*) dìle bhàthte, **the ~ stopped at long last** sguir an t-uisge mu dheireadh thall, *in expr* **acid ~** uisge-searbhaig *m*

rain *v* **1** bi *vi irreg* an t-uisge ann, sil *vi*, (*lightly*) fras *vi*, **it's ~ing** tha an t-uisge ann, (*usu more heavily*) tha e a' sileadh, **it always ~ed** bha/bhiodh an t-uisge ann an-còmhnaidh; **2** (*idiom*) **it was ~ing cats and dogs** bha dìle bhàthte ann

rainbow *n* bogha-frois *m*

raincoat *n* còta-froise *m*

rainfall *n* sileadh *m*

rainforest *n* coille-uisge *f*

rainproof *adj* uisge-dìonach

raise *v* 1 tog *vt*, ~ **your head** tog do cheann *m*, **that ~d my spirits** thog sin mo chridhe *m*, ~ **an issue** tog cuspair *m*, **I was ~d in Coll** thogadh mi ann an Colla; 2 *in expr* ~ **oneself** èirich *vi*, **she ~d herself (up) onto one elbow** dh'èirich i air a leth-uilinn *f*

rake *n* (*tool*) ràcan *m*, ràc *m*

rally *n* tional *m*, cruinneachadh *m*

rally *v* (*raise spirits, encourage*) misnich *vt*, ath-mhisnich *vt*

RAM *n* (*IT*) *abbrev* **random access memory** cuimhne thuaireameach

ram *n* (*tup*) rùda *m*, reithe *m*

rampart *n* mùr *m*

random *adj* 1 tuaireamach; 2 *in expr* **at** ~ air thuaiream *f*; 3 (*IT*) ~ **access memory** cuimhne thuaireameach

randy *adj* drùiseach, drùiseil

range *n* 1 (*scale, series*) raon *m*, sreath *mf*, ~ **of temperature** raon teothachd *f invar*, ~ **of responsibilities** sreath de dhleastanasan *mpl*; 2 (*for artillery &c practice*) raon-bualaidh *m*; 3 (*of hills, mountains*) sreath *mf*

ranger *n* maor *m*, **countryside** ~ maor-dùthcha *m*, **park** ~ maor-pàirce *m*

rank *n* (*in hierarchy, progression, armed services &c*) inbhe *f*

ransack *v* rannsaich *vt*

ransom *n* èirig *f*

ransom *v* fuasgail *vt* le èirig *f*, saor/saoraich *vt* le èirig

rape *n* èigneachadh *m*

rape *v* èignich *vt*

rapid *adj* 1 (*general*) luath; 2 (*of watercourse*) bras, cas; 3 (*of person's movements*) grad, aithghearr

rapier *n* claidheamh caol

rapist *n* èigneachair *m*

rare *adj* 1 (*in short supply, seldom met with*) gann, tearc, ainneamh; 2 (*unusual*) annasach; 3 (*fam: expr approval*) taghta, **that was ~!** bha sin taghta!

rarely *adv* gu tearc, *commonly rendered by* is *v irreg def* gann, (*less usu*) is ainneamh, (*both with conj* a), **you'll ~ see the likes of him** is gann a chì thu a leithid *f*

rarity *n* 1 (*abstr*) gainne *f invar*, gainnead *m invar*, teirce *f invar*; 2 (*con*) **a ~** annas *m*, (*less usu*) suaicheantas *m*

rat *n* radan *&* rodan *m*

rate *n* 1 (*of speed*) astar *m*, luas *m*, **they were going along at a good ~** bha astar math aca; 2 (~ *of progress &c*) ruith *f*, **at this ~** air an ruith seo; 3 (*fin: level*) luach *m invar*, ìre *f*, **the ~ of exchange** luach na h-iomlaid, co-luach an airgid, **the interest ~** ìre/luach an rèidh; 4 (*local taxes*) ~**s** reataichean *mpl*

rate *v* **1** (*evaluate*) meas *vt*, cuir luach *m* (*with prep* air), luachaich *vt*; **2** (*more fam*) *in expr* **how do you ~ (him/it** *&c*) dè do/ur b(h)eachd (air *&c*), **how do you ~ them as players?** dè do bheachd orra mar chluicheadairean? *mpl*

rather *adv* **1** (*fairly, somewhat*) car, caran, beagan, rudeigin, rud beag, **~ tired** car/caran/beagan/rudeigin/rud beag sgìth; **2** (*expr preference*) b' fheàrr leam (*&c*), **they would ~ have cheese** b' fheàrr leotha càise *mf*; **3** *in expr* **~ than** seach *prep*, **give us money ~ than promises** thoir dhuinn airgead *m* seach geallaidhean *mpl*

ratify *v* daingnich *vt*

ration *n* cuibhreann *m*

rational *adj* reusanta

rationale *n* feallsanachd *f*, **the ~ of/behind the proposals** feallsanachd nam molaidhean *mpl*

rattle *n* (*ie toy &c*) clach-bhalg *f*

rattling *n* (*of lighter objects*) clagarsaich *f invar*, (*louder*) glagadaich *f*, gleadhraich *f*

raven *n* fitheach *m*

ravish *v* (*ie rape*) èignich *vt*

ravisher *n* èigneachair *m*

raw *adj* (*uncooked, unprocessed*) amh, **~ meat** feòil *f* amh, **~ material(s)** stuth(an) *m(pl)* amh

ray *n* gath *m*, (*less usu*) leus *m*, **~ of light** gath solais *m gen*, **the ~s of the sun** gathan na grèine

raze *v* leag *vt*, **~ to the ground** leag *vt* gu làr *m*

razor *n* ealtainn *f*, (*less trad*) ràsair *m*

re(-) *reiterative prefix* ath- (*lenites following consonant where possible*) *eg* **reassess** *v* ath-mheas *vt* also (*more informal*) meas *vt* a-rithist, **re-count** *n* ath-chunntadh *m*

reach *v* **1** (*arrive at, win to*) ruig *vti*, **we ~ed Perth** ràinig sinn Peairt; **2** (*fig, abstr: arrive at, achieve*) thig *vi* (*with prep* gu), **~ an agreement/ understanding** thig gu còrdadh *m*/rèite *f*, **~ a decision/conclusion** thig *vi* gu co-dhùnadh *m*, also co-dhùin *vi*; **3** (*attain with hand &c*) ruig *vi* (*with prep* air), **can you ~ the top shelf?** an ruig thu air an sgeilp *f* as àirde?, **~ for my hand** ruig air mo làimh *f*; **4** (*pass*) sìn *vt* (*with prep* gu), **~ me the sugar** sìn thugam an siùcar

read *v* leugh *vti*

reader *n* leughadair *m*

reading *n* leughadh *m*

ready *adj* **1** (*prepared, finished &c*) deiseil, ullamh, (*less usu*) deas, **the food's/meal's ~** tha am biadh *m* deiseil/ullamh, **are you ~?** a bheil thu deiseil/ullamh?; **2** (*keen, willing*) èasgaidh (**to** gu), deònach, **~ to help you** èasgaidh gur cuideachadh, **~ to do it** deònach a dhèanamh, (*more trad*) deònach air a dhèanamh; **3** (*expr convenience, handiness*) ullamh, ~ **to hand** ullamh, ~ **money** airgead *m* ullamh; **4** *in expr* **get ~** deasaich *vt*, ullaich *vt*, **get the food** ~ deasaich am biadh, (*esp machines, equipment &c*) gleus *vt*, cuir *vt* air ghleus, uidheamaich *vt*

real *adj* **1** (*actual*) nitheil, fìor, rudail; **2** (*genuine*) fìor (*precedes the noun, which it lenites where possible*), ~ **gold** fìor òr *m*; **3** (*out & out*) fìor, dearg, (*precede the noun, which is lenited where possible*), gu c(h)ùl *m* (*follows the noun*), **they're ~ musicians** 's e fìor luchd-ciùil *m sing coll* a th' annta, **a ~ idiot** dearg amadan *m*, **a ~ Highlander** fìor Ghàidheal, Gàidheal gu chùl

realise *v* **1** (*comprehend, appreciate*) tuig *vti*, (*trad or formal*) fidir *vti*, **I ~ that!** tha mi a' tuigsinn sin!; **2** (*be/become aware*) thig *vi* a-steach (*with prep* air), **I ~d that they weren't listening** thàinig e a-steach orm nach robh iad ag èisteachd

realism *n* fìorachas *m*

reality *n* fìorachd *f invar*

really *adv* fìor (*precedes the adj, which it lenites where possible*), uabhasach fhèin (*precedes the adj*), gu dearbh, **the food was ~ good/~ excellent** bha am biadh fìor mhath/uabhasach fhèin math, **are you tired? I ~ am!** a bheil thu sgìth? tha gu dearbh!, **he's rich!, is he ~?** tha e beartach! a bheil gu dearbh?

reanimate *v* ath-bheothaich *vt*

reappraisal *n* ath-bheachdachadh *m* (**of** air)

reappraise *v* ath-bheachdaich *vi* (*with prep* air)

rear *n* **1** (*of group &c*) deireadh *m*, **she was in the ~** bha i air dheireadh, **she brought up the ~** thàinig i air deireadh; **2** (*of building &c*), (*outside*) cùl *m*, cùlaibh *m invar*, (*inside*) tòn *f*, **there were trees at the ~ of the church** bha craobhan *fpl* (ann) air cùl/air cùlaibh na h-eaglaise, **the ~ (part) of the hall** tòn an talla; **3** (*fam: backside, bum*) tòn *f*, màs *m*

rear *v* **1** (*children, livestock &c*) tog *vt*, **I was ~ed in Coll** thogadh mi ann an Colla; **2** *in expr* **~ up** (*surge upwards &c*) èirich *vi* (suas)

reason[1] *n* **1** (*the faculty of ~*) reusan *m*; **2** (*sanity*) ciall *f*, rian *m*, reusan *m*, **I nearly lost my ~** cha mhòr nach deach mi às mo chiall/mo rian, theab mi a dhol às mo chiall/mo rian

reason[2] *n* (*cause, explanation*) adhbhar *m*, cùis *f*, (*less usu*) fàth *m invar*, **the ~ for my sadness** adhbhar/fàth mo bhròin *m gen*; **2** *in expr* **what's the ~?** dè as coireach? (**for** air), **the electricity's off, what's the ~ for that?** tha an dealan *m* dheth, dè as coireach air sin?

reason *v* reusanaich *vi*

reasoning *n* reusanachadh *m*

reasonable *adj* **1** (*statements, situations &c: logical, consistent with reason or sense*) reusanta, ciallach; **2** (*situations &c: fair, appropriate*) cothromach, reusanta, **a ~ salary** tuarastal cothromach; **3** (*persons: amenable to, displaying, reason or common sense*) toinisgeil, ciallach

reassess *v* ath-mheas *vt*

reassessment *n* ath-mheasadh *m*

rebel *n* reubalach *m*

rebel *v* dèan ar-a-mach *m invar*, èirich *vi* (suas), (**against** an aghaidh *with gen*)

rebellion *n* ar-a-mach *m invar*

rebuke *n* achmhasan *m*

rebuke *v* cronaich *vt*, thoir achmhasan *m* (*with prep* do)

recall *v* **1** (*remember*) cuimhnich *vi* (*with prep* air), meòmhraich & meamhraich *vti*; **2** (*call back, summon again*) gairm *vt* air ais

receipt *n* (*for money &c*) cuidhteas *m*

recent *adj* ùr, **a ~ book** leabhar *m* ùr

recently *adv* (bh)o chionn ghoirid

reception *n* **1** (*welcome*) fàilte *f*, **what sort of a ~ did you get?** dè seòrsa *m* fàilte a fhuair sibh?; **2** (*desk in hotel &c*) ionad *m* fàilte *gen*; **3** (*function*) cuirm *m*, **(the) wedding ~** cuirm *f* na bainnse (*gen of* banais *f*)

receptionist *n* (*hotel &c*) fàiltiche *m*

recession *n* (*fin*) seacadh *m*

recitation *n* aithris *m*

recite *v* aithris *vt*

reckon *v* **1** (*arithmetic &c*) cunnt *vti*; **2** (*consider, think*) saoil *vi*, meas *vi*, (*slightly fam*) **I ~ it will rain soon** saoilidh mi gum bi uisge *m* ann a dh'aithghearr, **what do you ~?** dè do bheachd (air)?

reckoning *n* **1** (*arithmetic &c*) cunntas *m*, cunntadh *m*; **2** (*sum due*) cunntas *m*, bileag *f* (cunntais *gen*)

recline *v* **1** (*referring to the movement*) laigh *vi* (sìos); **2** (*referring to the position*) bi *v irreg* na (*&c*) laighe *mf invar*

recognised *adj* & *past part* aithnichte

recollect *v* cuimhnich *vi* (*with prep* air)

recollection *n* cuimhne *f invar* (**of** air), **I've no ~ of him** chan eil cuimhne agam air idir

recommend *v* mol *vt*

recommendation *n* moladh *m*, **the government's ~s for a new tax** molaidhean an riaghaltais airson cìse *f gen* ùire

reconcile *v* (*opposing parties &c*) rèitich *vt*

reconciliation *n* rèite *f*

record *n* **1** (*of events &c*) cunntas *m*, clàr *m*; **2** (*sound recording*) clàr *m*

record *v* **1** (*events &c*) clàraich *vt*, sgrìobh cunntas (**of** air, de); **2** (*sound*) clàraich *vt*

recording *n* **1** (*abstr*) clàrachadh *m*; **2** (*con*) clàr *m*; **3** *in expr* **~ tape** teip *f* chlàraidh (*gen of* clàradh *m*)

recount *v* **1** (*relate*) thoir cunntas *m* (*with prep* de or air), innis *vt*

re-count *n* ath-chunntadh *m*

re-count *v* ath-cunnt *vti*, (*more informal*) cunnt *vt* a-rithist

recover *v* **1** (*from illness & other ordeals &c*) rach *vi* am feabhas *m*, thig *vi* bhuaithe, **the invalid ~ed** chaidh an t-euslainteach am feabhas, thàinig an t-euslainteach bhuaithe, (*less trad*) dh'fhàs an t-euslainteach na b' fheàrr; **2** (*retrieve*) faigh *vt* air ais

recreate *v* ath-chruthaich *vt*

recreation *n* **1** (*creating anew*) ath-chruthachadh *m*; **2** (*pastime &c*) cur-seachad *m*

recruit *v* **1** (*workers, staff*) fastaich *vt*; **2** (*armed forces*) tog *vt*

rectangle *n* ceart-cheàrnach *m*, ceart-cheàrnag *f*

rectangular *adj* ceart-cheàrnach

rectify *v* ceartaich *vt*, cuir *vt* ceart, leasaich *vt*

rectum *n* tòn *f*

recycle *v* ath-chuairtich *vt*

red *adj* **1** (*of human hair, animal's coat*) ruadh, **a ~-haired man** fear ruadh, **~ grouse** cearc *f* ruadh; **2** (*usu brighter ~*) dearg, **~ corpuscle** frìde dhearg, **~ wine** fìon dearg

red *n* dearg *m*

redcoat *n* (*hist*) saighdear dearg

redcurrant *n* dearc dhearg

redden *v* **1** (*as vt: make red*) deargaich *vt*; **2** (*as vi: turn/become ~*) fàs *vi* dearg

reddish- *adj prefix* dearg-, *eg* **~brown** dearg-dhonn

reduce *v* lùghdaich *vti*, ìslich *vt*

reduction *n* lùghdachadh *m*, **rent ~** lùghdachadh màil (*gen of màl m*)

reed *n* **1** cuilc *f*; **2** (*of musical instrument*) ribheid *f*

reel *n* **1** (*for thread &c*) iteachan *m*, piorna *f*; **2** (*dance*) ruidhle *m*, ridhil *m*, **eightsome ~** ruidhle-ochdnar *m*

redundant *adj* anbharra

re-election *n* ath-thaghadh *m*

refectory *n* biadh-lann *f*

refer *v* **1** (*admin &c*) cuir *vt* (**to** gu), **~ the matter to the manager** cuir a' chùis chun a' mhanaidseir *m*, **~ back** cuir *vt* air ais (**to** gu); **2** (*mention, allude*) thoir iomradh *m*, thoir tarraing *f*, thoir guth *m*, (**to** air), (*esp persons*) ainmich *vt*, **~ to something** thoir iomradh/tarraing/guth air rudeigin

referee *n* (*sport*) rèitear *m*

reference *n* **1** (*as to character, qualifications &c*) teisteanas *m*; **2** (*mention*) iomradh *m*, tarraing *f*, guth *m*, (**to** air), **he made no ~ to it** cha tug e iomradh/tarraing/guth (sam bith) air

reflect *v* **1** (*think*) cnuas *vi*, cnuasaich *vi*, meòmhraich & meamhraich *vi*, (*more rigorously*) beachd-smaoin(t)ich *vi*, (**on/upon** air); **2** (*mirror*) tilg *vt* air ais, ath-thilg *vt*

reflection *n* **1** (*contemplation &c*) cnuasachadh *m*, meòmhrachadh & meamhrachadh *m*, (*more rigorous*) beachd-smaoin(t)eachadh *m*, (**on/upon** air); **2** (*reflected image*) faileas *m*, ath-ìomhaigh *f*, **the ~ of the moon on the surface of the loch** faileas na gealaich air uachdar *m* an locha

reformation *n* ath-leasachadh *m*, (*hist, relig*) **the Reformation** an t-Ath-leasachadh

reform *v* **1** (*reshape*) ath-chruthaich *vt*; **2** (*change for better &c*) leasaich *vt*, ath-leasaich *vt*

refrain *n* (*music, poetry*) sèist *mf*

refrain *v* cùm *vi* (**from** bho/o), seachain *vt*, ~ **from strong drink** cùm on deoch *f* làidir, seachain (an) deoch làidir

refresh *v* ùraich *vt*

refreshment *n* **1** (*abstr*) ùrachadh *m*; **2** (*con: meal &c*) biadh *m* (is deoch *f*), lòn *m*, beathachadh *m*

refrigerate *v* fionnaraich *vt*

refrigeration *n* fionnarachadh *m*

refrigerator *n* frids *m*, (*less usu*) fuaradair *m*

refuge *n* (*abstr & con*) tèarmann *m*, comraich *f*, dìon *m*, fasgadh *m*

refugee *n* fògrach & fògarrach *m*

refusal *n* diùltadh *m*

refuse *n* sgudal *m*, (*less usu*) fuighleach *m*

refuse *v* diùlt *vti*, **we ~d food** dhiùlt sinn biadh *m*, **their father ~d to let them leave** dhiùlt an athair *m* leigeil leatha falbh, **refusing to get up** a' diùltadh èirigh

refute *v* breugnaich *vt*

regal *adj* rìoghail

regard *n* **1** (*respect*) meas *m*, urram *m*, (**for** air), **I have a great deal of ~ for her** tha meas mòr agam oirre; **2** (*more affectionate ~*) spèis *f*; **3** (*attention, care, concern*) for *m invar* (**for** air), suim *f* (**for** de), **he continued, with no ~ for me** lean e air, gun for a thoirt ormsa, lean e air, gun suim aige dhìomsa; **4** (*corres &c*) **with kindest ~s** leis gach deagh dhùrachd *m*; **5** *in expr* **with ~ to** thaobh *or* a-thaobh (*with gen*), **with ~ to the war** (a-)thaobh a' chogaidh

regarding *prep* thaobh *or* a-thaobh (*with gen*), **he has problems ~ money** tha duilgheadasan aige (a-)thaobh airgid *m*

regiment *n* rèiseamaid *f*

region *n* **1** ceàrn *m*, sgìre *f*, tìr *mf*; **2** (*local government admin*) roinn *f*, (*formerly*) **Highland Region** Roinn *f* na Gaidhealtachd

register *v* clàraich *vti*

register *n* clàr *m*, ~ **of electors** clàr (an) luchd-taghaidh *m sing coll*

registration *n* clàrachadh *m*

regret *n* aithreachas *m*

regret *v* bi *vi irreg* duilich, (*more formal*) bi *vi irreg* an t-aithreachas *m* (*with prep* air & *conj* gu), **I ~ having done that** tha mi duilich gun do rinn mi sin, tha an t-aithreachas orm gun do rinn mi sin

regular *adj* **1** (*orderly, in accordance with rules &c*) riaghailteach, òrdail; **2** (*as regards time: consistent, evenly spaced &c*) cunbhalach; **3** (*gram*) riaghailteach, ~ **verbs** gnìomhairean *mpl* riaghailteach

regularise *v* riaghailtich *vt*

regularity *n* riaghailteachd *f invar*

regulate *v* riaghlaich *vt*, riaghailtich *vt*, riaghail *vt*

regulation *n* **1** (*abstr*) riaghladh *m*; **2** (*more con: a* ~) riaghailt *f*

rehearsal *n* aithris *f*

rehearse *v* aithris *vti*

reign *n* rìoghachadh *m*

reign *v* rìoghaich *vi*

reject *v* diùlt *vt*, **she won't** ~ **her own daughter** cha dhiùlt i a nighean *f* fhèin

rejection *n* diùltadh *m*

rejoice *v* dèan gàirdeachas *m* (**at** ri)

rejoicing *n* gàirdeachas *m*

relate *v* **1** (*recount*) innis *vt*, aithris *vt*, (**to do**), **I'll** ~ **what I know** innsidh mi na tha a (*for* de) dh'fhios agam (air); **2** (*be pertinent, connected*) bi *vi irreg* co-cheangailte (**to** ri), **this** ~**s to what I said yesterday** tha seo co-cheangailte ris na thubhairt mi an-dè

related *adj* **1** (~ *by kinship*) càirdeach (**to do**), **I'm** ~ **to you** tha mi càirdeach dhut; **2** (*linked*) co-cheangailte (**to** ri), **the two things are** ~ tha an dà rud *m sing* co-cheangailte (ri chèile)

relation *n* **1** (*kin*) caraid *m*, **my** ~**s** mo chàirdean (*pl of* caraid *m*), mo dhaoine (*pl of* duine *m*), **a** ~ **of mine** caraid dhomh (*note also* **he's a** ~ **of mine** tha e càirdeach *adj* dhomh), **all my** ~**s are in Stornoway** tha mo chàirdean/mo dhaoine air fad ann an Steòrnabhagh; **2** (*relevance*) buinteanas *m*, *in expr* **bear** ~ **to** buin *vi* ri, **that bears no** ~ **to the matter** chan eil sin a' buntainn ris a' chùis *f* (idir); **3** *in expr* **sexual** ~**s** cleamhnas *m*

relationship *n* **1** (*of kinship*) càirdeas *m*, **blood** ~ càirdeas-fola (*gen of* fuil *f*); **2** (*not necessarily of kinship*) càirdeas *m*, dàimh *mf invar*, **the** ~ **between the two families** an càirdeas/an dàimh eadar an dà theaghlach *m sing*; **3** (~ *between things, ideas &c*) ceangal *m*, co-cheangal *m*, (**to** ri, **between** eadar)

relative *adj* (*gram*) dàimheach, ~ **particle** mion-fhacal *m* dàimheach

relative *n* (*kin*) caraid *m*, **my** ~**s** mo chàirdean (*pl of* caraid *m*), mo dhaoine (*pl of* duine *m*), **a** ~ **of mine** caraid dhomh (*note also* **he's a** ~ **of mine** tha e càirdeach *adj* dhomh), **all my** ~**s are in Stornoway** tha mo chàirdean/mo dhaoine air fad ann an Steòrnabhagh

relax *v* **1** (*rest, take one's ease*) gabh fois *f*, bi *vi irreg* na (*&c*) t(h)àmh *m*; **2** (*take things easily*) gabh *vi* air a (*&c*) s(h)ocair *f*; **3** (*calm down, be less streseed &c*) socraich *vti*, *as excl* ~! socair!, air do shocair!; **4** (~ *grip, tension on object &c*) fuasgail *vt*

relaxation *n* fois *f*, socair *f*

relaxed *adj* (*esp people*) socair, (*people, atmosphere &c*) socrach, **a** ~ **pace** ceum socrach

release *v* **1** (*set free*) fuasgail *vt*, cuir/leig *vt* mu sgaoil *m invar*, saor *vt*; **2** (*fire*) leig *vt*, ~ **an arrow** leig saighead *f*; **3** (*let out, let go/slip*) leig *vt* às, ~ **the dogs** leig às na coin (*pl of* cù *m*); **4** (*bring out film, recording &c*) cuir *vt* a-mach

relevance *n* buinteannas *m* (**to** do, ri)

relevant *adj* **1** a bhuineas (*&c*) (*rel fut of* buin *vi*; **to** do, ri), buntainneach, (*law*) **evidence ~ to the case** fianais *f* a bhuineas don chùis *f dat*, **this letter is ~** tha an litir *f* seo a' buntainn ris a' ghnothach *m dat*; **2** *in expr* **be ~** buin *vi* (**to** do, ri), **that is ~ to the question** tha sin a' buntainn don chùis/ris a' chùis *f dat*

reliable *adj* **1** (*esp morally*) earbsach, urrasach; **2** (*esp practically*) seasmhach, cunbhalach

reliance *n* earbsa *f invar*, creideas *m*, **place ~ in someone** cuir earbsa ann an cuideigin *mf invar*, thoir creideas do chuideigin

relic *n* **1** (*residue &c*) fuidheall & fuigheall *m*, (*less usu*) iarmad *m*; **2** (*keepsake &c*) cuimhneachan *m*

relief *n* **1** (*from pain, worry &c*) furtachd *f invar* (**for/from** air), ~ **for/from his anguish** furtachd air a dhòrainn *f*; **2** (*from pain, suffering*) faothachadh & faochadh *m*, **he experienced some ~** thàinig faothachadh air

relieve *v* **1** (*pain, suffering*) faothaich *vti*; **2** (*pain, worry &c*) furtaich *vi*, (*with prep* air), **she ~d his anguish** dh'fhurtaich i air a dhòrainn *f*

religion *n* creideamh *m*, **the Islamic ~** an creideamh Ioslamach

religious *n* **1** diadhaidh, cràbhach; **2** (*idiom: not PC*) **they** (*&c*) **became very ~** ghabh iad (*&c*) an cùram

relinquish *v* leig *vt* (*with prep* de), leig *vt* seachad, trèig *vt*, **she ~ed her post** leig i dhith/leig i seachad a dreuchd *f*

relinquishment *n* leigeil *f* seachad, trèigsinn *m invar*

reluctance *n* leisg(e) *f*

reluctant *adj* leisg, aindeònach, *in expr* **be ~** is *v irreg & def* leisg (*with prep* le), bi *vi irreg* leisg(e) *f* (*with prep* air), **I am ~ to sell it** is leisg leam a reic, **I was ~ to leave** bha leisg(e) orm falbh

rely *v* cuir earbsa *f invar* (**on** ann), earb thu-fhèin (*&c*) (**on** ri), **don't ~ on them** na cuir earbsa annta, na h-earb thu-fhèin riutha

remain *v* **1** (*stay*) fuirich *vi*, fan *vi*, **you ~ where you are!** fuirich/fan thusa far a bheil thu!; **2** (*continue to be*) **it ~s a good hotel** 's e taigh-òsta math a th' ann fhathast

remainder *n* **1** (*residue*) fuidheall & fuigheall *m*, (*less usu*) iarmad *m*; **2** (*arithmetic*) fuidheall & fuigheall *m*

remark *n* facal *m*, **cutting ~s** faclan geura, *also* briathran *mpl* geura

remarkable *adj* air leth, sònraichte

remedial *adj* leasachaidh (*gen of* leasachadh *m used adjectivally*), ~ **education/unit** foghlam *m*/ionad *m* leasachaidh

remedy *n* **1** (*health*) leigheas *m*, ìocshlaint *f*, (**for** air), **a ~ for asthma** leigheas air a' chuing *f*; **2** (*for problem &c*) leasachadh *m*, fuasgladh *m*, **there**

was no ~ for the matter cha robh leasachadh air a' chùis, **a problem without a** ~ ceist *f*/duilgheadas *m* gun fhuasgladh

remedy *v* (*situation &c*) leasaich *vt*, cuir *vt* am feabhas *m*, cuir *vt* ceart

remember *v* **1** cuimhnich *vti*, meòmhraich & meamhraich *vi*, (*with prep* air); **2** (*idioms*) **I don't** ~ **(him/it** *&c*) chan eil cuimhne *f* agam (air *&c*), **if I** ~ **rightly** mas math mo chuimhne *f*

remembrance *n* cuimhne *f*

remind *v* **1** (*recall &c*) cuir *vt* na (*&c*) c(h)uimhne *f*, ~**ing me of my young days** a' cur nam chuimhne làithean *mpl* m' òige *f gen*; **2** (*jog memory*) cuimhnich *vi* (*with prep* do), cuir *vt* na (*&c*) c(h)uimhne, **he ~ed me to give him the key** chuimhnich e dhomh/chuir e nam chuimhne an iuchair a thoirt dha

remnant, remnants *n* fuidheall & fuigheall *m*, (*less usu*) iarmad *m*, **he got his pick of it, I got the ~s** fhuair esan a roghainn *mf* dheth, fhuair mise am fuidheall

remote *adj* **1** (*phys distant from centre &c*) iomallach, cèin, ~ **area/district** ceàrn *m* iomallach; **2** (~ *in time or space*) cian; **3** (*of place: isolated, lonely*) uaigneach; **4** (*of person: withdrawn &c*) fad' às, dùinte

remoteness *n* (*in time or space*) cian *m*

removal *n* **1** toirt *f invar* air falbh; **2** (*from within something*) toirt às; **3** (*flitting*) imrich *f*

remove *v* **1** thoir *vt* air falbh; **2** (*from within something*) thoir *vt* às

remuneration *n* (*from employment*) pàigh *m invar*, pàigheadh *m*, tuarastal *m*, (*less usu*) cosnadh *m*

rend *v* reub *vt*, srac *vt*

renew *v* **1** (*renovate, refresh*) ùraich *vt*, ath-nuadhaich *vt*; **2** (*replace*) ath-nuadhaich *vt*; **3** (*reaffirm &c*) ath-nuadhaich *vt*, **they ~ed their vows** dh'ath-nuadhaich iad an geallaidhean *mpl*

renewal *n* ùrachadh *m*, ath-nuadhachadh *m*

renovate *v* ùraich *vt*, nuadhaich *vt*, ath-nuadhaich *vt*, (*more colloquial*) cuir *vt* air dòigh *f*

renovation *n* ùrachadh *m*, nuadhachadh *m*, ath-nuadhachadh *m*, (*more colloquial*) cur *m* air dòigh *f*

renown *n* cliù *m invar*, glòir *f*

renowned *adj* (*persons or things*) ainmeil, (*esp persons*) iomraiteach, cliùiteach

rent[1] *n* (*for property &c*) màl *m*

rent[2] *n* (*rip*) reubadh *m*, sracadh *m*

rent *v* **1** (*as tenant*) gabh *vt* air mhàl *m dat*; **2** (*as landlord*) thoir *vt* seachad air mhàl *dat*

rented *adj & past part* air mhàl *m dat*, **a ~ house** taigh *m* air mhàl

repair *n* càradh *m*

repair *v* càraich *vt*

repairer *n* neach-càraidh *m* (*pl* luchd-càraidh *m sing coll*)

repay *v* dìoghail *&* dìol *vt*, **~ a debt** dìo(ghai)l fiach *m*

repayment *n* dìo(gh)ladh *m*

repeat *v* **1** (*verbally*) can *vt def* a-rithist; **2** (*actions &c*) dèan *vt* (*&c*) a-rithist, **she ~ed the song** ghabh i an t-òran a-rithist/turas *m* eile

replace *v* **1** (*return to its place*) cuir *vt* air ais (na (*&c*) àite *m*); **2** (*exchange, substitute*) cuir *vt* an àite *m* (*with gen*), **~ X by Y** cuir Y an àite X; **3** (**~** *broken, worn out object &c*) **we ~d the fridge** fhuair sinn/cheannaich sinn frids *m* ùr/eile

replacement *n* **1** (*stand-in &c*) neach-ionaid *m*; **2** (*for car &c*) **~ part**, pàirt-càraidh *mf*

replica *n* mac-samhail *m*, (*more trad*) lethbhreac *m*

reply *n* freagairt *f*, **I didn't get a ~** cha d'fhuair mi freagairt

reply *v* freagair *vi*, thoir freagairt *f* (**to do**), **he hasn't replied yet** cha do fhreagair e fhathast, **we'll ~ to you soon** bheir sinn freagairt dhuibh a dh'aithghearr

report[1] *n* **1** (*in newspaper &c*) iomradh *m*, aithisg *f*, cunntas *m*, **a ~ of the strike** iomradh air an stailc *f*; **2** (*pol, business &c: formal ~*) aithisg *f*

report[2] *n* (*of gunfire*) urchair *f*

repository *n* ionad-tasgaidh *m*

represent *v* (*lawyer, spokesman, actor, artist, sportsman, politician*) riochdaich *vt*

representation *n* riochdachadh *m*

representative *n* riochdaire *m*, **(trade) union ~** riochdaire-aonaidh *m*

repress *v* (*people, emotions &c*) ceannsaich *vt*, mùch *vt*

repression *n* (*of people, emotions &c*) ceannsachadh *m*, mùchadh *m*

repressive *adj* ceannsachail

reproach *n* tarcais *f*, tailceas *m*

reproach *v* cronaich *vt*, càin *vt*, **don't ~ her** na cronaich i; **2** (*with following complement*) tilg *vt* (*with prep air followed by conj gu, nach*), **they ~ed me with not being conscientious** thilg iad orm nach robh mi dìcheallach

reproachful *adj* tarcaiseach, tailceasach

reproduce *v* **1** (*breed*) gin *vti*, tàrmaich *vti*; **2** (*copy &c*) dèan lethbhreac *m*/mac-samhail *m* (*with prep de*), **~ this book** dèan lethbhreac den leabhar *m* seo

reproduction *n* **1** (*breeding*) gineadh *m*, gineamhainn *m invar*; **2** (*facsimile of book, picture &c*) lethbhreac *m*

reproductive *adj* gineamhainn *m invar gen used adjectivally*, **~ organs** buill-ghineamhainn *mpl*

reptile *n* pèist *f*

republic *n* poblachd *f*, **the Irish Republic** Poblachd na h-Èireann

republican *adj & n* poblachdach *m*

republicanism *n* poblachdas *m*

reputation *n* ainm *m*, cliù *m invar*

request *n* iarrtas *m*, (*less usu*) iarraidh *m*

request *v* iarr *vt*, **they ~ed a pay rise** dh'iarr iad àrdachadh *m* pàighidh (*gen of* pàigheadh *m*)

rescue *n* sàbhaladh *m*, **a ~ boat** bàta-sàbhalaidh *m*, *also* bàta-teasairginn *m*

rescue *v* teasairg *&* teasraig *vt*, sàbhail *vt*

research *n* rannsachadh *m*, sgrùdadh *m*

research *v* rannsaich, dèan rannsachadh *m* (*with prep* air), sgrùd *vi*, **she's ~ing the history of the country** tha i a' rannsachadh eachdraidh *f* na dùthcha (*gen of* dùthaich *f*), tha i a' dèanamh rannsachadh air eachdraidh na dùthcha

resemblance *n* samhladh *m*, coltas *m*, coimeas *f*

resemble *v* bi *vi irreg* coltach (*with prep* ri), bi *vi irreg* coltas *m* (*with gen and prep* air), **she doesn't ~ her brother** chan eil i coltach ri a bràthair, chan eil coltas a bràthar oirre

resembling *adj* coltach (*with prep* ri)

reservation *n* **1** (*booking*) gleidheadh *m*; **2** (*place set aside for particular group, species &c*) tèarmann *m*; **3** (*mental ~*) teagamh *m*, amharas *m*

reserve *n* **1** (*of money, goods &c*) stòr *m*, stòras *m*; **2** (*place set aside for particular group, wildlife &c*) tèarmann *m*, **nature ~** tèarmann-nàdair *m*; **3** (*in personality: reticence &c*) diùide *f*, (*more distant*) dùinteachd *f invar*

reserve *v* (*book seat &c*) glèidh *vt*

reserved *adj & past part* **1** glèidhte, (*copyright*) **all rights ~** na còraichean *fpl* uile glèidhte; **2** (*of persons: reticent &c*) diùid, sàmhach, (*more distant*) fad' às, dùinte

reservoir *n* loch-tasgaidh *m*

reside *v* còmhnaich *vi*, fuirich *vi*

residence *n* **1** (*abstr*) còmhnaidh *f*, **~ permit** cead *m* còmhnaidh *gen*; **2** (*con*) àite-còmhnaidh *m*, àite-fuirich *m*, dachaigh *f invar*

resident *n* neach-còmhnaidh *m* (*pl* luchd-còmhnaidh *m sing coll*)

residue *n* fuidheall *&* fuigheall *m*, iarmad *m*, **he got his pick of it, I got the ~** fhuair esan a roghainn *mf* dheth, fhuair mise am fuidheall

resolute *adj* **1** (*persevering, undaunted, determined*) gramail *&* greimeil, misneachail, suidhichte; **2** (*bold &c*) dàna

resolution *n* **1** (*of character*) misneach *f*, misneachd *f invar*; **2** (*~ of problem &c*) fuasgladh *m*; **3** (*aim, intention, also admin &c*) rùn *m*, **pass/adopt a ~** gabh *vi* ri rùn

resolve *n* rùn *m* (suidhichte)

resolve *v* **1** (*to do something*) cuir *vt* roimhe (*&c*), rùnaich *vi*, **they ~ed to build a house** chuir iad romhpa taigh *m* a thogail; **2** (*~ difficulty, situation &c*) fuasgail *vt*, rèitich *vt*

resource *n* **1** (*admin &c: esp equipment, materials &c*) goireas *m*, stòras *m*, **~ centre** ionad-ghoireasan *m*, **natural ~s** stòrasan nàdarra(ch), **renewable ~** stòras leantainneach; **2** (*admin &c: esp fin ~s*) ionmhas *m sing*

resourceful *adj* innleachdach, tionnsgalach

resourcefulness *n* innleachd *f*, tionnsgal *m*, tionnsgalachd *f invar*

respect *n* meas *m*, urram *m*, onair *f*, **I have a great deal of ~ for her** tha meas mòr agam oirre, **worthy of ~** airidh air urram, urramach, measail, **mark of ~** comharradh *m* urraim *gen*

respect *v* thoir urram *m*, thoir meas *m*, *(with prep* do)

respectable, respected *adj* measail

respectful *adj* modhail, cùirteil, sìobhalta

respiration *m* analachadh *m*

respite *n* *(from pain, suffering)* faothachadh & faochadh *m*, **he experienced some ~** thàinig *vi* faothachadh air

respond *v* freagair *vt*

response *n* freagairt *f*

responsibility *n* uallach *m*, cùram *m*, dleastanas *m*, **they charged me with the ~ for the journey** chuir iad orm uallach an turais, **it's your ~** is ann oirbhse a tha an t-uallach, **under Donald's ~** air cùram Dhòmhnaill

responsible *adj* **1** *(in charge)* an urra (**for** ri), **I was ~ for the Post Office** bha mi an urra ri Oifis *f* a' Phuist, **they made me ~ for the journey** chuir iad orm uallach *m* an turais; **2** *(the cause of or reason for something)* coireach (**for** ri), **there's not a soul on the street today, who's/what's ~ for that?** chan eil duine beò air an t-sràid *f* dat an-diugh; cò/dè as *(for* a is*)* coireach ri sin?, **James was ~ for it** is e Seumas a bu choireach ris

rest[1] *n* fois *f*, tàmh *m*, **take a ~** gabh fois, *also (fam)* leig d' *(&c)* anail *f*, *(esp of dead)* **they are at ~ now** tha iad aig fois/nan tàmh a-nise; **2** *in expr* **come to ~** *(on a surface)* laigh *vi*; **3** *(~ in music)* tosd *m invar*

rest[2] *n* **1** *(others, (the) other people)* **the ~** càch *pron*, an fheadhainn *f sing* eile, **she did better than the ~** rinn i na b' fheàrr na càch, **like the ~** coltach ri càch/ris an fheadhainn eile; **2** *(other things)* **the ~** an còrr *m invar*, **will you take the ~?** an gabh thu an còrr?; **3** *(remainder, residue)* fuidheall & fuigheall *m*

rest *v* gabh fois *f*, *(fam)* leig d' *(&c)* anail *f*

restaurant *n* taigh-bìdh *m*

restrain *v* caisg *vt*, bac *vt*, cuir casg *m* *(with prep* air*)*, ceannsaich *vt*

restraint *n* bacadh *m*, casg *m*, casgadh *m*

restrict *v* *(limit)* cuingealaich *vt*, cuibhrich *vt*, *(to* gu*)*, **a speech ~ed to five minutes** òraid *f* air a cuingealachadh/air a cuibhreachadh ri còig mionaidean *fpl*

result *n* *(of action &c)* toradh *m*, buil *f*, èifeachd *f invar*, **the ~(s) of your behaviour** toradh do dhol-a-mach *m invar*, **as a ~ of that** mar thoradh air sin, **exam ~** toradh deuchainn *f gen*

retailing *n* meanbh-reic *m*

retain *v* glèidh *vt*, cùm *vt* (air ais)

retard *v* cuir maille *(with prep* air *or* ann*)*, maillich *vt*

retch *v* rùchd *vi*

retching *n* rùchd *m*, rùchdail *f*

retire *v* 1 (*for night*) rach *vi* a laighe *mf invar*, rach *vi* don leapaidh *f*; 2 (*from work*) leig dheth (*&c*) obair *f*/dreuchd *f*, **I'll ~ next year** leigidh mi dhìom m' obair/mo dhreuchd an ath-bhliadhna *f*

retirement *n* cluaineas *m*, **come out of ~** thig *vi* air ais bho chluaineas, **~ pension** peinnsean *m* cluaineis *gen*

retract *v* thoir *vt* air ais, tarraing *vt* air ais

retrospect *n* ath-bheachd *m*

return *n* tilleadh *m*, **~ journey** turas-tillidh *m*

return *v* 1 (*as vi*) till *vi*, **~ing home** a' tilleadh dhachaigh *adv*; 2 (*as vt*, **~ to owner** *&c*) cuir *vt* air ais, thoir *vt* air ais

reveal *v* 1 (*objects*) leig *vt* ris, nochd *vt*, seall *vt*, **~ing her knees** a' leigeil a glùinean *mfpl* ris; 2 (*facts*) foillsich *vt*

revelation *n* (*of facts*) foillseachadh *m*

revenge *n* dìoghaltas *m*

revenue *n* teachd-a-steach *m invar*

reverence *n* urram *m*

reverend *adj* urramach, (*of minister*) **the Reverend William Campbell** an t-Urramach Uilleam Caimbeul

review *n* 1 (*critique of book*) lèirmheas *m invar* (**of** air); 2 (*study, investigation*) sgrùdadh *m*, rannsachadh *m*, (**of** air); 3 (*reappraisal &c*) ath-sgrùdadh *m*, ath-bheachdachadh *m*, (**of** air)

review *v* 1 (*book*) dèan leirmheas *m invar* (*with prep* air); 2 (*study, investigate*) sgrùd *vt*, rannsaich *vt*; 3 (*reappraise &c*) ath-bheachdaich *vi* (*with prep* air), ath-sgrùd *vt*

revile *v* màb *vt*, càin *vt*

revise *n* 1 (*for exam &c*) ath-sgrùd *vt*; 2 (*go back on*) atharraich *vt*, **I've ~d my opinion on that** tha mi air mo bheachd *m* atharrachadh air sin

revival *n* 1 (*general*) ath-bheòthachadh *m*; 2 (*relig ~*) dùsgadh *m*

revive *v* ath-bheòthaich *vt*

revolt *n* ar-a-mach *m invar* (**against** an aghaidh, *with gen*)

revolt *v* èirich *vi* (suas), dèan ar-a-mach *m invar*, (**against** an aghaidh, *with gen*)

revolver *n* daga *&* dag *m*

reward *n* duais *f*

rheumatism *n* (*used with art*) an lòinidh *mf invar*

rhyme *n* co-fhuaim *m*

rhyme *v* dèan co-fhuaim *m* (**with** le *or* ri)

ribbon *n* rioban *m*

rice *n* rus *m*

rich *adj* 1 (*wealthy*) beartach, saidhbhir; 2 (*of soil*) torach

riches *n* beartas *m*, saidhbhreas *m*, ionmhas *m*, stòras *m*, maoin *f*

rick *n* cruach *f*, (*small*) cruachan *m*, coc *&* goc *m*, ruc(a) *m*

rid *adj & adv* 1 saor (**of** o), **we're ~ of them at last!** tha sinn saor uapa mu dheireadh thall!; 2 *in expr* **get ~ of** faigh cuidhteas *m* (*with or without* *prep* de), (*less trad*) faigh clior is, **we got ~ of the bad lodgers** fhuair sinn cuidhteas (de)/fhuair sinn clior is na droch lòisdearan *mpl*

rid *v, in expr* ~ **oneself** (*&c*) faigh cuidhteas *m* (*with or without prep* de), (*less trad*) faigh clior is, **we ~ ourselves of the bad lodgers** fhuair sinn cuidhteas (de)/fhuair sinn clior is na droch lòisdearan *mpl*

riddle *n* (*puzzle &c*) tòimhseachan *m*

riddle *v* (*grain &c*) criathraich *vt*

ride *n* (*on vehicle*) cuairt *f*, **we had a ~ on a bus** ghabh sinn cuairt air bus *m*

ride *v* **1** (*esp horse*) marcaich *vi*; **2** (*on vehicle*) siubhail *vi* (**on** air)

rider *n* marcaiche *m*

ridge *n* **1** (*topog*) druim *m*; **2** (*agric, hist: ~ of land for cultivation*) iomair(e) *f*, imire *m*, (*in the form of a 'lazybed'*) feannag *f*

ridge-pole *n* maide-droma *m*, maide-mullaich *m*

ridicule *n* fanaid *f*, bùrt *m*

ridicule *v* dèan fanaid *f* (*with prep* air)

ridiculous *adj* (*person, situation*) amaideach, gun chiall *f*

riding *n* (*of horse*) marcachadh *m*, marcachd *f invar*, ~ **school** sgoil-mharcachd *f*

rifle *n* raidhfil *f*

rifle *v* rannsaich *vt*

rig[1] *n* (*agric, hist: ridge of land for cultivation*) iomair(e) *f*, imire *m*, (*in the form of a 'lazybed'*) feannag *f*

rig[2] *n* **1** (*equipment &c*) uidheam *f sing coll*, acainn *f sing coll*; **2** *in expr* **oil ~** crann-ola *m*

rig out *v* (*equip with machinery &c*) uidheamaich *vt*, beartaich *vt*

rigging *n* uidheam *f sing coll*, acainn *f sing coll*

right *adj* **1** (*opposite of* left) deas, (*less usu*) ceart, **my ~ hand** mo làmh dheas, **on the ~ hand side** air an làimh dheis (*dat*); **2** (*correct*) ceart, **the answers are ~** tha na freagairtean *fpl* ceart, **absolutely ~**, **as ~ as can be** cho ceart ri ceart, ~ **angle** ceart-uilinn *f*, **put ~** cuir *vt* ceart, ceartaich *vt*; **3** *in exprs* **standing up for what is ~** a' seasamh na còrach (*gen of* còir *f*), **he repaid it, as was only ~** dh'ath-dhìol e e, mar bu chòir

right *adv, in exprs* ~ **in the middle of the town** ann an teis-meadhan *m* a' bhaile, ann an ceart-mheadhan *m* a' bhaile, **the ~ Reverend William Campbell** am Fìor Urramach Uilleam Caimbeul, **~!**, ~ **then!** ceart ma-thà!

right *n* **1** (*opposite of* left) an làmh dheas, **on the ~** air an làimh dheis (*dat*); **2** (*justice &c*) còir *f*, ceartas *m*, ceart *m*, **standing up for ~** a' seasamh na còrach (*gen of* còir *f*), (*prov*) **might before ~** thèid neart *m* thar ceart; **3** (*moral or legal entitlement*) còir *f*, dlighe *f invar*, dleas *m*, **you've no ~ to do that** chan eil còir agad sin a dhèanamh, ~ **of entry/access** còir inntrigidh *m gen*, **human ~s** còraichean daonna, (*copyright statement*) **all ~s reserved** na còraichean uile glèidhte

righteous *adj* ionraic, dìreach

righteousness *n* ionracas *m*

rightful *adj* dligheach

rightly *adv* **1** (*in accordance with morality &c*) mar bu chòir, **he returned the money, (quite) ~,** chuir/thug e an t-airgead air ais, mar bu chòir; **2** *in expr* **if I remember ~** mas math mo chuimhne *f invar*

rigid *adj* **1** (*lit*) rag, cruaidh; **2** (*fig: of person: in opinions, attitudes &c*) rag-bharaileach, rag-mhuinealach

rigidity *n* raige *f invar*

rim *n* oir *f*, bile *f*, iomall *m*

ring *n* **1** cearcall *m*, **dancing in a ~** a' dannsadh ann an cearcall; **2** (*for finger*) fàinne *mf*, **wedding ~** fàinne-pòsaidh, fainne-pòsta, **engagement ~** fàinne-gealladh-pòsaidh; **3** *in expr* **~ finger** mac-an-aba *m*

ringlet *n* dual *m*, bachlag *f*, camag *f*

ring-road *n* cuairt-rathad *m*

rinse *v* sgol *vt*

rip *n* reubadh *m*

rip *v* reub *vt*, srac *vt*

ripe *adj* abaich

ripen *v* abaich *vti*

ripeness *n* abaichead *m*

rise *n* **1** (*topog: slope*) leathad *m*, bruthach *mf*, **we climbed a slight ~** dhìrich sinn leathad/bruthach beag; **2** (*promotion, increment*) àrdachadh *m*, **a pay ~** àrdachadh pàighidh (*gen of* pàigheadh *m*); **3** (*teasing, vexing*) *in expr* **take a ~ out of** farranaich *vt*, tarraing *vi* (*with prep* à)

rise *v* **1** (*phys*) èirich *vi*, **he rose to his feet/to a standing position** dh'èirich e na sheasamh *m*, **she rose early in the morning** dh'èirich i tràth sa mhadainn *f*; **2** (*become higher, lit or fig*) rach *vi* an àirde *f invar*, **prices/costs are rising** tha prìsean/cosgaisean *fpl* a' dol an àirde; **3** (*rebel*) **~ (up)** èirich suas, dèan ar-a-mach *m invar*, (**against** an aghaidh *with gen*)

risk *n* cunnart *m*, **at ~** ann an cunnart, **put at ~** cuir *vt* an cunnart

risky *adj* **1** cunnartach, (*usu stronger*) gàbhaidh; **2** (*of precarious business venture &c*) cugallach

rival *n* (*in business, sport &c*) farpaiseach *m*

rivalry *n* còmhstri *f*, farpais *f*

road *n* rathad *m*, **main ~** rathad mòr, **single/double track ~** rathad singilte/dùbailte, **~ accident** tubaist *f* rathaid *gen*, **the ~ home** an rathad dhachaigh *adv*

roar *n* beuc *m*, ràn *m*

roar *v* beuc *vi*, ràn *vi*, (*esp of animals*) nuallaich *vi*

roaring *n* beucadh *m*, rànail *m invar*, rànaich *f*

roast *adj & past part* ròsda & ròsta

roast *v* ròist & ròsd *vt*

roasted *adj & past part* ròsda & ròsta

rob *v* creach *vti*, spùill & spùinn *vti*

robber *n* mèirleach *m*, spùinneadair *m*, gadaiche *m*

robe *n* (*ceremonial*) èideadh *m*

robin *n* brù-dhearg *m*

robust *adj* (*of persons*) calma, tapaidh, rùdanach

rock *n* 1 (*the material & a ~*) creag *f*; 2 (*pillar of ~*) carragh *f*; 3 (*esp a ~ by the sea*) carraig *f*

rock *v* 1 (*as vi: seas, ship, trees &c*) tulg *vi*, luaisg *vi*; 2 (*as vt*) tulg *vt*, **~ the cradle** tulg a' chreathail; 3 *in expr* **~ to sleep** tàlaidh *vt*

rocket *n* rocaid *f*

rocking *n* luasgan *m*

rocking-chair *n* sèithear-tulgaidh *m*

rocky *adj* creagach

roe-buck *n* boc-earba *m*

roe-deer *n* earb *f*

roll *v* 1 (*seas, ship &c*) tulg *vi*, luaisg *vi*; 2 (*as vi, of ball, wheel; as vt, ~ pastry, cigarette &c*) roilig *vti*; 3 (*material &c*) **~ (up)** paisg *vt*, fill *vt*; 4 (*sleeves*) **~ up** tru(i)s *vt*, **he ~ed up his sleeves** thruis e a mhuilchinnean *mpl*

ROM *n* (*IT*) *abbrev* **read only memory** cuimhne bhuan

Roman *adj & n* 1 Ròmanach *m*; 2 *in expr* **~ Catholic** Caitligeach *m & adj*

romance *n* 1 (*romantic novel*) ròlaist *m*, nobhail *f* romansach; 2 (*love affair*) leannanachd *f invar*

Romania *n* Romàinia *f*

Romanian *n & adj* Romàinianach *m*

roof *n* mullach *m*, ceann *m*

roof-tree *n* maide-droma *m*, maide-mullaich *m*

rook *n* ròcais *f*

room *n* 1 (*space*) rùm *m*, **there was no ~ in the boat** cha robh rùm sa bhàta *m*; 2 (*apartment*) seòmar *m*, rùm *m*

root *n* (*lit & fig*) freumh *m*, **tree ~** freumh-craoibhe *m*, **he went off to the islands, in search of his ~s** thug e na h-eileanan *mpl* air, an tòir air a fhreumhaichean

rope *n* ròp(a) *m*

rosary *n* conaire *f*, paidirean *m*

rose *n* ròs *m*

rot *n* grodadh *m*, lobhadh *m*

rot *v* grod *vi*, lobh *vi*

rotate *v* 1 (*as vi*) rach *vi* *irreg* mun cuairt; 2 (*as vt*) cuir *vt* mun cuairt, cuir car *m* (*with prep* air); 3 (*~ crops &c*) cuartaich *vt*

rotted, rotten *adj* grod, lobhte, *in expr* **go rotten** lobh *vi*

rottenness *n* lobhadh *m*

rough *adj* 1 (*to the touch*) garbh, **~ material** stuth garbh; 2 (*fig*) garbh, **a ~ night** oidhche gharbh; 3 (*hairy, shaggy*) molach, fionnach; 4 (*uncouth, violent &c*) borb, garg

roughness *n* gairbhe *f invar*, gairbhead *m*

round *adj* cruinn

round *adv* timcheall, mun cuairt *&* mu chuairt, **the picture on the telly was going ~ and ~** bha dealbh *mf* an telly *m* a' dol timcheall, timcheall, **pass ~ the biscuits** cuir timcheall na briosgaidean *fpl*, **the cold's going ~** tha an cnatan a' dol mun cuairt

round *n* cuairt *f*, **the postman's ~** cuairt a' phosta, **a ~ of golf** cuairt-ghoilf *f*

round *prep* **1** timcheall (*with gen*), timcheall (*with prep* air), mun cuairt (*with prep* air), **we'll go ~ the loch** thèid sinn timcheall an locha, **there are salesmen going ~ the town** tha luchd-reic *m sing coll* a' dol timcheall a' bhaile, **they built houses ~ his garden** thog iad taighean *mpl* timcheall air a' ghàrradh *m* aige, **are there any shops ~ here?** a bheil bùithtean *mfpl* timcheall air an seo?, **all ~ her** fada mun cuairt oirre; **2** (*esp of garment &c*) mu (*takes the dat*), **~ me** umam(sa), **~ you** (*sing*) umad(sa), **~ him/it** (*m*) uime(-san), **~ her/it** (*f*) uimpe(se), **~ us** umainn(e), **~ you** (*pl*) umaibh(se), **~ them** umpa(san), **put your coat ~ you** cuir umad do chota *m*, **a bandage ~ his head** bann *m* mu cheann *m*

round up *v* (*livestock &c*) cruinnich *vt*, tionail *vt*, tru(i)s *vt*

roundabout *adj, in expr* **we went/took a ~ way** (*ie a detour*) ghabh sinn bealach *m*

roundabout *n* (*at road junction, also in playpark &c*) timcheallan *m*

roundness *n* cruinne *mf*, cruinnead *m*

rouse *v* **1** (*from sleep*) dùisg *vti*, mosgail *vti*; **2** (*arouse emotions, courage &c*) brod *vt*, brosnaich *vt*, misnich *vt*; **3** *in excl* **~ yourself!** tog ort!

rout *n* (*military &c*) rua(i)g *f*, ruith *f*

route *n* rathad *m*, slighe *f*, **they took another ~** ghabh iad rathad eile, **I didn't know the ~** cha robh mi eòlach air an t-slighe, **en ~** air an t-slighe

routine *adj* gnàthach

routine *n* gnàth-chùrsa *m*

row[1] *n* **1** (*din*) gleadhraich *f*, othail *f*, faram *m*; **2** (*quarrel, squabble*) trod *m*, tuasaid *f*; **3** *in exprs* **they had a ~** chaidh iad thar a chèile, **give a ~ to** càin *vt*

row[2] *n* **1** (*line, succession &c*) sreath *mf*; **2** *in expr* **in a ~** (*ie in succession*) an sreath *mf* a chèile, an ceann *m* a chèile, an dèidh a chèile, **three accidents in a ~** trì tubaistean *fpl* an sreath a chèile/an ceann a chèile/ an dèidh a chèile

row[1] *v* (*boat*) iomair *vti*

row[2] *v* (*quarrel*) connsaich *vi*, troid *vi*

rowan *n* caorann *mf*

rowdy *adj* ùpraideach, gleadhrach

rowing *n* (*boat*) iomradh *m*, **good at ~** math air iomradh

royal *adj* rìoghail

royalties *npl* (*for book &c*) dleas *m sing* ùghdair *m gen*

royalty *n* **1** rìoghalachd *f invar*

rubber *n* rubair *m*, **~ band** crios-rubair *m*

rubbish *n* **1** (*household &c refuse*) sgudal *m*, (*less usu*) fuighleach *m*; **2** (*objects of little worth or value*) sgudal *m*, truileis *f invar*, treal(l)aich *f*; **3** (*fam, one's odds & ends, possessions*) treal(l)aich *f*, **put that ~ of mine on the floor and sit down** cuir an treallaich sin agam air an làr *m* agus dèan suidhe *m*; **4** (*foolish or inaccurate remarks, opinions &c*) sgudal *m*, **it's a load of ~!** 's e tòrr *m* sgudail *gen* a th' ann!/a tha 'n sin!

rucksack *n* màileid-droma *f*, poca-droma *m*

ruddy *adj* ruiteach

rude *adj* mì-mhodhail, mì-shìobhalta

rugged *adj* garbh, **a ~ land** tìr *mf* gharbh

ruin *n* **1** (*~ or ~s of building*) tobhta *f sing*, làrach *f sing*; **2** (*fin ~*) bris(t)eadh *m*

ruin *v* **1** creach *vt*, sgrios *vt*, mill *vt*; **2** (*child &c: spoil*) mill *vt*, **they're ~ing that boy** tha iad a' milleadh a' bhalaich ud; **3** (*fin*) bris(t) *vt*

ruination *n* **1** creach *f*, sgrios *m*, milleadh *m*; **2** (*fin*) bris(t)eadh *m*

ruinous *adj* **1** (*causing ruin*) sgriosail, millteach; **2** (*of building*) a' tuiteam sìos, a' tuiteam às a chèile

rule[1] *n* **1** (*authority*) ceannsal *m*, smachd *m invar*, reachd *m invar*, **under his enemy's ~** fo cheannsal/smachd/reachd a nàmhaid *m*; **2** (*a ~, ordinance &c*) riaghailt *f*, (*less usu*) reachd *m invar*

rule[2] *n* (*for measuring*) rùilear *m*

rule *v* **1** (*govern a country &c*) riaghail *vti*; **2** (*issue order, ordain &c*) reachdaich *vi*, òrdaich *vi*

ruler[1] *n* (*head of state &c*) riaghladair *m*

ruler[2] *n* (*for measuring*) rùilear *m*

Rum *n* Rùm, Eilean *m* Rù(i)m, Eilean Ruma

rum *n* ruma *m*

rumble, rumbling *n* **1** torman *m*; **2** (*of intestines*) rùchdail *f*

ruminate *v* **1** (*cows &c*) cnàmh a' chìr; **2** (*humans: think over &c*) cnuas & cnuasaich *vi* (**on, about** air)

rummage *v* ruamhair *vi*, rùraich *vi*, rannsaich *vi*, sporghail *vi*

rumour *n* fathann *m*, **~s are going around** tha fathannan a' dol timcheall

run *n* **1** ruith *f*, **they went away at a ~** dh'fhalbh iad nan ruith; **2** *in exprs* **he was on the ~** bha e fon choill *f invar*, **out of the common/ordinary ~ of things** às a' chumantas *m invar*

run *v* **1** ruith *vti*, **she ran two miles yesterday** ruith i dà mhìle *mf sing* an-dè, **the train's/the water's not ~ning** chan eil an trèana/an t-uisge a' ruith; **2** (*misc exprs*) **~ out** (*of supplies &c: come to an end*) ruith *vi* a-mach (**of** à), **the sugar ran out** ruith an siùcar a-mach, **we ran out of sugar** ruith sinn a-mach à siùcar *m*, **~ out** (*of liquids: flow*) sruth *vi*, ruith *vi*, sil *vi*, **~ away** (*flee*) teich *vi*, tàrr às, *also* tàir às, **the soldiers ran away** theich na saighdearan *mpl*, thàir na saighdearan às, **~ over** (*overflow*) cuir *vi* thairis

rung *n* rong *f*, rongas *m*

running *n* ruith *f*, **I like ~** is toigh leam a bhith a' ruith

runny *adj* (*liquids, foods &c*) tana

runway *n* (*airport &c*) raon-laighe *m*

rural *adj* dùthchail

rush, rushes *n*(*pl*) (*ie the plant*) luachair *f sing coll*

rush *n* 1 (*haste, hurry*) cabhag *f*, **we're in a ~** tha cabhag oirnn, **he finished it in a ~** chuir e crìoch *f* air ann an cabhaig (*dat*); **2** (*hurried gait*) dian-ruith *&* deann-ruith *f*, **he left in a ~** dh'fhalbh e na dhian-ruith

rush *v* **1** (*carry out action &c hurriedly*) *expr by the appropriate verb followed by* na (*&c*) d(h)ian-ruith *m*, *or* ann an cabhaig (*dat of* cabhag *f*), *or* gu cabhagach, **they ~ed home** chaidh iad dhachaigh nan dian-ruith, **they ~ed their dinner** ghabh iad an dìnnear *f* ann an cabhaig/gu cabhagach; **2** (*cause to ~*) cuir cabhag *f* (*with prep* air), **she ~ed the pupils at the end of the morning** chuir i cabhag air na sgoilearan aig deireadh *m* na maidne

Russia *n* Ruisia *f*, an Ruis *f*

Russian[1] *n & adj* Ruiseanach *m*

Russian[2] *n* (*lang*) Ruiseanais *f invar*

rust *n* meirg *f*

rust *v* meirg *vti*, meirgich *vti*

rustproof *adj* meirg-dhìonach

rusty *adj* meirgeach

rut *n* (*in ground*) clais *f*, sgrìob *f*

rut, rutting *n* (*of deer*) dàmhair *f*

rutting *adj* **1** (*of deer*) dàireach; **2** *in expr* **~ time/season** dàmhair *f*

rye *n* seagal *m*

S

sack *n* poca *m*, sac *m*

sack *v* **1** (*ransack &c*) rannsaich *vt*, creach *vt*; **2** (*dismiss from job*) cuir *vt* à dreuchd *f*

sacred *adj* naomh, coisrigte

sacrifice *n* (*relig*) ìobairt *f*

sacrifice *v* (*relig*) ìobair *vt*

sad *adj* brònach, muladach, truagh, dubhach, cianail, **that's ~!** is truagh sin!, **I'm ~** tha mi brònach/muladach, tha mulad orm, (*more trad*) tha mi fo bhròn *m*/fo mhulad *m*

saddle *n* dìollaid *&* diallaid *f*

sadness *n* bròn *m*, mulad *m*, cianalas *m*

safe *adj* **1** (*building, place of refuge &c*) dìonach, tèarainte; **2** (*person*) sàbhailte; **3** *in expr* **~ and sound** slàn is fallain, (*more trad*) gu slàn fallain

safeguard *n* tèarmann *m*, dìon *m*

safeguard *v* dìon *vt*

safety *n* tèarainteachd *f invar*, sàbhailteachd *f* invar, **in ~** an tèarainteachd, **~ equipment** uidheam *f sing coll* sàbhailteachd

sailor *n* seòladair *m*, maraiche *m*, **he's a ~** tha e na sheòladair, *also* tha e aig muir *mf*/aig fairge *f*

saint *n* naomh *m*

saintliness *n* naomhachd *f invar*

saintly *adj* naomh

salary *n* tuarasdal *&* tuarastal *mf*

sale *n* **1** reic *m invar*, **it's not for ~** chan eil e ri reic; **2** (*esp of livestock*) fèill *f*, **lamb ~** fèill-uan *f*

salesperson neach-reic *m* (*pl* luchd-reic *m sing coll*)

saliva *n* seile *m invar*

sallow *adj* odhar, lachdann

salmon *n* bradan *m sing & coll*

salt *n* salann *m*, **a grain of ~** gràinnean *m* salainn *gen*

saltire *n* (*heraldry &c*) crann *m*, **the Saltire** An Crann

salutation *n* fàilte *f*

salute *n* fàilte *f*, (*bagpipe music*) **Chisholm's ~** Fàilte an t-Siosalaich

salute *v* fàiltich *vt*

same *adj* **1** ceart (*precedes the noun*), (*more emph*) ceudna, dearbh (*precedes the noun, which it lenites where possible*), fhèin, **at the ~ time** aig a' cheart àm *m*, **the ~ amount/quantity** a' cheart uimhir *f invar*, a' cheart uiread *m invar*, **the (very) ~ man** an duine ceudna, an dearbh dhuine, *also* an aon duine, **the (very) ~ man I saw yesterday** an duine fhèin a chunna mi an-dè

same *n* **1** (*similar, identical*) ionann, co-ionann (*used with v* is), **you and I are**

not the ~ chan ionann thusa 's mise, **it wasn't the** ~ **when we were young** cha b' ionann nuair a bha sinn òg; **2** *in expr* **the** ~ **as** ionann is/agus, co-ionann ri, **Y is the** ~ **as X** is ionann Y is/agus X, tha Y co-ionnan ri X, **'burn' and 'uisge' are the** ~ **as each other** tha burn is/agus uisge co-ionann ri chèile; **3** *in expr* (**give me** *&c*) **the** ~ **again** (thoir dhomh *&c*) uimhir *f invar* eile, (thoir dhomh *&c*) uiread *m invar* eile

sample *n* eisimpleir *m*, taghadh *m*, samhla *m*

sanctity *n* naomhachd *f invar*

sanctuary *n* (*abstr & con*) tèarmann *m*, comraich *f*

sand *n* gainmheach *f*

sandal *n* cuaran *m*

sandpaper *n* pàipear-gainmhich *m*

sandwich *n* pìos *m*, (*more trad*) ceapaire *m*

sandy *adj* gainmheil

sanity *n* ciall *f*, rian *m*, reusan *m*, **I nearly lost my** ~ cha mhòr nach deach mi às mo chiall/mo rian, cha mhòr nach do chaill mi mo rian

sap *n* **1** (*of tree*) snodhach *m*, sùgh *m*; **2** (*fig: essence, vigour*) brìgh *f invar*

sarcasm *n* gearradh *m*, searbhas *m*

sarcastic *adj* geur, searbh

sardonic *adj* searbh

satchel *n* màileid *f*

satellite *n* saideal *m*

satisfaction *n* toileachadh *m*, sàsachadh *m*.

satisfied *adj & past part* riaraichte, sàsaichte, toilichte

satisfy *v* riaraich *vt*, sàsaich *vt*, toilich *vt*, foghain *vi* (*with prep* le)

Saturday *n* Disathairne *m invar*

sauce *n* **1** (*for food*) leannra *m*, (*less trad*) sabhs *m*; **2** (*fam: cheek*) aghaidh *f*, bathais *f*

saucer *n* sàsar *m*, flat *m*

saunter *v* sràidearaich *vi*

sausage *n* isbean *m*

savant *n* eòlaiche *m*

save *v* **1** (~ *from danger or other difficulty*) sàbhail *vt*, teasairg & teasraig *vt*, **they were ~d by a lifeboat** chaidh an sàbhaladh/an teasrgainn le bàta-teasargainn *m*, **it's the visitors who ~d the island** is e an luchd-tadhail *m sing coll* a theasairg an t-eilean; **2** (*spiritually: convert &c*) tèarainn *vt*, sàbhail *vt*, ~ **the heathens** tèarainn na pàganaich *mpl*; **3** (*preserve, keep safe*) glèidh *vt*, **God will** ~ **us** glèidhidh Dia sinn; **4** (*money: put aside*) sàbhail *vt*, glèidh *vt*, cuir *vt* mu seach; **5** (*money: economise*) caomhain *vt*

saved *adj & past part* sàbhailte

savings *n* sàbhaladh *m*, tasgadh *m*

sawdust *n* min-sàibh *f*

say *v* abair *vti irreg*, can *vti def*, **what are you ~ing?** dè a tha thu ag ràdh?,

what did you ~? dè a thu(bha)irt thu?, **~ it again** can a-rithist e, **as they ~** mar a chanas iad, **what do you ~ in Gaelic for 'spade'?** dè a chanas sibh sa Ghàidhlig *f* ri 'spade'?, *also* dè a' Ghàidhlig a th' air 'spade'?

saying *n* seanfhacal *m*, facal *m*, (*less usu*) ràdh *m invar*, **'blood is thicker than water' is a ~** is e seanfhacal a th' ann an 'is tighe fuil *f* na bùrn *m*'

scab *n* sgreab *f*, càrr *& *càir *f*

scale[1] *n* (*of fish, reptile &c*) lann *f*

scale[2] *n* **1** (*range, sequence*) raon *m*, sreath *mf*, **~ of temperature** raon teodhachd *f invar*; **2** (*mus*) sgàla *f*; **3** (*in drawings &c: proportion*) sgèile *f*, tomhas *m*, **~ drawing** dealbh *mf* sgèile *gen*

scales *n* (*for weighing*) meidh *f*, cothrom *m*

scallop *n* creachan *m*, **~ shell** slige *f* chreachain *gen*

scalpel *n* sgian *f* lèigh *m gen*

scandalous *adj* tàmailteach, maslach

Scandinavia *n* Lochlann *f*

Scandinavian *n & adj* Lochlannach *m*

scant *adj* gann, tearc

scantness *n* gainne *f invar*, gainnead *m invar*, teirce *f invar*

scanty *adj* **1** gann, tearc; **2** (*hair, crop &c*) gann, tana; **3** (*garment*) goirid

scar *n* làrach *f*

scarce *adj* gann, tearc

scarcely *adv* **1** (*to a small extent, rarely*) is gann (*with conj* a), cha mhòr (*with conj* gun), **we ~ ever saw him** is gann a chunnaic sinn e, **he ~ uttered two words** is gann a leig e às dà fhacal *m sing*, cha mhòr gun do leig e às dà fhacal; **2** (*esp expr difficulty*) is ann air èiginn *f invar* (*with conj* a), **we ~ made out what she was saying** is ann air èiginn a rinn sinn a-mach dè a bha i ag ràdh, **he ~ opened his eye** is ann air èiginn a dh'fhosgail e a shùil *f*

scarceness, scarcity *n* gainne *f invar*, gainnead *m invar*, teirce *f invar*

scarecrow *n* bodach-ròcais *m*

scare *n* eagal *m*, (*weaker*) clisgeadh *m*, **I had a ~** ghabh mi an t-eagal

scare *v* cuir an t-eagal (*with prep* air), **he ~d her** chuir e an t-eagal oirre

scared *adj & past part* **1** fo eagal *m*, **a ~ man** duine *m* fo eagal *dat*; **2** (*misc exprs*) **I was ~** (*became ~*) thàinig an t-eagal orm, ghabh mi an t-eagal, (*was in a ~ state*) bha an t-eagal orm, **I was ~ stiff/~ to death** bha eagal mo bheatha *f gen* orm, **I never get ~** cha ghabh mi an t-eagal uair sam bith

scarlet *adj* **1** sgàrlaid; **2** *in expr* **~ fever** (*used with art*) am fiabhras dearg

scarlet *n* sgàrlaid *f*

scary *adj* critheanach

scatter *v* sgap *vti*, (*less brusque*) sgaoil *vti*

scatter-brained *adj* guanach, *in expr* **~ girl** guanag *f*

scattered *adj & past part* sgapte

scenery *n* sealladh *m* dùthcha (*gen of* dùthaich *f*)

scent *n* (*pleasant or unpleasant*) fàile & fàileadh *m*, àile *m*, boladh *m*, (*usu pleasant*) boltrach *m*

sceptical *adj* teagmhach

schedule *n* **1** clàr-tìde *m*, clàr-obrach *m*; **2** *in exprs* **ahead of** ~ tràth *adv*, ron mhithich *f invar*, air thoiseach, **behind** ~ fadalach, air dheireadh

scheme *n* **1** sgeama *m*, **housing** ~ sgeama-thaighean *m*; **2** (*plot &c*) innleachd *f*, cuilbheart *f*

scheme *v* dèan innleachd(an) *f(pl)*

scholar *n* **1** (*school pupil & learned adult*) sgoilear *m*; **2** (*learned adult*) eòlaiche *m*

scholarly *adj* sgoilearach

scholarship *n* (*abstr: erudition; also con: bursary &c*) sgoilearachd *f*

school *n* sgoil *f*

schooling *n* sgoil *f*, **we got our** ~ **in Fort William** fhuair sinn ar sgoil anns a' Ghearastan

schoolmaster *n* maighistir-sgoile *m*

schoolmistress *n* ban(a)-mhaighstir-sgoile *f*

schoolteacher *n* tidsear *m*, fear-teagaisg *m*, neach-teagaisg *m* (*pl* luchd-teagaisg *m sing coll*), bean-teagaisg *f*, maighistir-sgoile *m*, ban(a)-mhaighstir-sgoile *f*

science *n* saidheans *m*, eòlas *m*

scientific *adj* saidheansail

scientist *n* neach-saidheans *m* (*pl* luchd-saidheans *m sing coll*), eòlaiche *m*

scoff[1] *v* (*mock &c*) mag *vi*, dèan fanaid *f*, (*with prep* air)

scoff[2] *v* (*way of eating*) glàm & glàmh *vt*

scoffing *adj* (*mocking*) magail

scoffing[1] *n* (*mockery*) magadh *m*

scoffing[2] *n* (~ *of food*) glàm(h)adh *m*

scold *v* càin *vt*, cronaich *vt*

scolding *n* càineadh *m*, cronachadh *m*

scoop *n* ladar *m*, liagh *f*, taoman *m*

scorch *v* dòth *vt*

score[1] *n* (*in wood &c*) sgrìob *f*

score[2] *n* (*twenty*) fichead *m* (*takes the nom sing, ie radical, of the noun*), **three** ~ **years** trì-fichead bliadhna *f*

score[3] *n* (*sports, games*) sgòr *m*, (*more trad*) cunntas *m*

scorn *n* tarcais *f*, tailceas *m*, tàir *f*, dìmeas *m invar*

scorn *v* dèan tarcais *f*, dèan tàir *f*, dèan dìmeas *m invar*, (*all with prep* air), **they ~ed us** rinn iad tarcais/tàir/dìmeas òirnn

scorned *adj & past part* fo dhìmeas *m invar*

scornful *adj* tarcaiseach, tailceasach, tàireil, dìmeasach

Scot *n* Albannach *m*

Scots *n* (*lang*) (a') B(h)eurla Ghallta, Albais *f*

Scotsman *n* Albannach *m*

Scots pine *n* giuthas *m*

Scotswoman *n* ban-Albannach *f*

Scottish *adj* Albannach

scoundrel *n* slaoightire *m*, balgair *m*

scourge *n* **1** (*lit*) sgiùrs(air) *m*; **2** (*fig: destructive events &c*) sgrios *m*, plàigh *f*

scourge *v* sgiùrs *vt*

scowl *n* gruaim *f*, mùig *m*, sgraing *f*

scowl *v* cuir gruaim *f*, cuir mùig *m*, (*with prep* air), **she ~ed** chuir i gruaim/
mùig oirre, **sitting in the corner, ~ing** (*of male person*) na shuidhe anns
a' chòrnair *m*, is gruaim/mùig air

scowling *adj* gruamach

scrap[1] *n* **1** (*small piece*) mìr *m*, bìdeag *f*, criomag *f*; **2** (*left after scrapping
machinery &c*) fuigheall *m*

scrap[2] *n* (*fight*) tuasaid *f*, (*usu more serious*) sabaid *f*

scrap[1] *v* (*fight*) bi *vi irreg* ri tuasaid *f dat*

scrap[2] *v* **1** (*worn-out machinery &c*) bris(t) *vt* suas, cuir *vi* às (*with prep* do);
2 (*plans &c*) leig *vt* seachad

scrape *n* **1** (*scratch &c*) sgrìob *f*; **2** (*tricky situation &c*) (droch) staing *f*, cùil-
chumhang *f*

scrape *v* **1** (*general*) sgrìob *vti*; **2** (*involuntarily: esp skin of hand &c*) rùisg *vt*

scratch *n* sgrìob *f*, sgròb *m*

scratch *v* **1** (*damage*) sgrìob *vt*; **2** (*~ an itch*) tachais *vt*, sgròb *vt*, sgrìob *vt*

scream *n* sgreuch *m*, sgread *m*, sgiamh *m*

scream *v* leig sgread *m* (*with prep* à), sgreuch *vi*, sgread *vi*, sgiamh *vi*, **she
~ed** leig i sgread aiste

scree *n* sgàirneach *f*

screech *n* sgread *m*, sgreuch *m*

screech *v* sgread *vi*, sgreuch *vi*

screen *n* sgàilean *m*

screen *v* sgàil *vt*, sgàilich *vt*, failich *vt*, ceil *vt*

screw *n* sgriubha *mf*, (*more trad*) bithis *f*

screwdriver *n* sgriubhaire *m*

scripture *n* sgriobtair *m*

scrotum *n* clach-bhalg *m*

scrub *v* sgùr *vt*

scruffy *adj* luideach, robach

scruple *n* imcheist *f*, teagamh *m*

scrupulous *adj* **1** (*morally ~*) ionraic, onarach, cogaiseach; **2** (*punctilious &c*)
mion-chùiseach, mionaideach, pongail, cùramach

scrutineer *n* sgrùdair *m*

scrutinise *v* sgrùd *vt*, rannsaich *vt*

scrutiny *n* sgrùdadh *m*, rannsachadh *m*

scullery *n* cùlaist *f*

sculpture *n* **1** (*the action*) snaigheadh *m*; **2** (*the product*) ìomhaigh (shnaighte)

scurf *n* càrr *f*

scurrilous *adj* tuaileasach, sgainnealach, maslach

scythe *n* speal *f*

sea *n* **1** muir *mf*, cuan *m*, fairge *f*, **on land and** ~ air muir 's air tìr *mf*, **go to** ~ rach *vi irreg* gu muir, **he's at** ~ tha e aig muir/aig fairge, ~ **bird** eun-mara *m*, ~ **loch** loch-mara *m*; **2** *in expr (fig)* **all at** ~ troimh-a-chèile, am breisleach *m*

sea-bed *n* grunnd *m* na mara, grinneal *m*

seaboard *n* oirthir *f*

sea-chart cairt-iùil *f*

seafarer *n* maraiche *m*

seagull *n* faoileag *f*

seal[1] *n* (*sea creature*) ròn *m*

seal[2] *n* (*identifying image, also* ~ *on document &c*) seula *m*

seam *n* fuaigheal *m*

seam *v* fuaigh *vt*, fuaigheil *vt*

seaman *n* **1** maraiche *m*, seòladair *m*; **2** *in expr* **he's a** ~ tha e aig muir *mf*

search *n* tòir *f*, lorg *f*, **be in** ~ bi *vi irreg* an tòir *f* (**of** air), lorg *vt*, sir *vt*, **he went to town in** ~ **of his sister** chaidh e dhan bhaile *m* an tòir air a phiuthair *f dat*

search *v* **1** rannsaich *vt*, ~ **the building** rannsaich an togalach; **2** ~ **for** bi *vi irreg* an tòir *f* (*with prep* air), lorg *vt*, sir *vt*

seashore *n* (*esp between high- and low-water mark, esp sandy*) tràigh *f*, (*can be stony/shingly*) cladach *m*

sea-sickness *n* cur *m invar* na mara, tinneas *m* (na) mara

season *n* **1** (*spring &c*) ràith *f*; **2** (*less specific*) tràth *m*, **a word in** ~ (*ie at the appropriate time*) facal *m* na thràth

sea-spray *n* cathadh-mara *m*

seat *n* **1** (*phys*) suidheachan *m*; **2** (*more abstr: place where one sits*) àite-suidhe *m*, **there wasn't a** ~ **to be had** cha robh àite-suidhe ri fhaighinn; **3** *in expr* **take a** ~! dèan suidhe *m*!; **4** (*site of an activity &c*) ionad *m*, **a** ~ **of learning** ionad-sgoilearachd *m*; **5** (*fam: backside*) màs *m*, tòn *f*

sea-trout *n* bànag *f*

sea-voyage *n* turas-mara *m*

seaweed *n* feamainn *f*

secluded *adj* (*place*) falaichte, uaigneach, **a** ~ **glen** gleann falaichte

second *adj* **1** dara *&* dàrna, **the** ~ **day of the month** an dara là den mhìos *mf*, **he was/came** ~/**in** ~ **place** bha e san dara h-àite *m*; **2** *in expr* ~ **sight** an dà shealladh *m*, taibhsearachd *f invar*

second *n* (*clock time*) diog *m*, tiota *m*, (*more loosely*) tiotag *f*, **I'll only be a** ~ cha bhi mi ach diog/tiotag

second *v* cuir taic *f* (*with prep* ri), **I will** ~ **the motion** cuiridh mi taic ris a' ghluasad *m*

secondary *adj* **1** (*subsidiary*) fo- *prefix* (*lenites following cons where possible*), ~

characteristics fo-fheartan *fpl*; **2** (*ed: above primary*) ~ **school** àrd-sgoil *f*, ~ **education** foghlam *m* àrd-sgoile *gen*

second-hand *adj* cleachdte

secrecy *n* dìomhaireachd *f invar*

secret *adj* **1** (*of place*) uaigneach; **2** (*of fact, document &c*) dìomhair

secret *n* cagar *m*, rùn (dìomhair) *m*

secretarial *adj* clèireach

secretary *n* **1** (*clerical grade staff*) clèireach *m*, ban(a)-chlèireach *f*; **2** (*PA*) neach-cuideachaidh *m* pearsanta, ban(a)-chuideachaidh phearsanta *f*; **3** (*political &c office*) rùnaire *m*, ban-rùnaire *f*, **the Secretary of State** Rùnaire na Stàite

secrete¹ *v* (*conceal*) cuir *vt* am falach *m*, falaich *vt*

secrete² *v* (~ *liquids*) sil *vti*, snigh *vti*

secretly *adv* os ìosal *&* os ìseal

section *n* **1** (*esp of objects*) earrann *f*, pàirt *mf*, **a** ~ **of his novel** earrann den nobhail *f* aige, **a** ~ **of the building** earrann/pàirt den togalach *m*; **2** (*group of people, department &c*) roinn *f*, buidheann *mf*, **the secretarial** ~ an roinn chlèireach, **a** ~ **of soldiers** buidheann (de) shaighdearan *mpl*

sector *n* roinn *f*, **the public/private** ~ an roinn phoballach/ phrìobhaideach

secular *adj* saoghalta, talmhaidh

secure *adj* **1** (*safe &c*) tèarainte, dìonach, ~ **hide-out** àite-falaich *m* tèarainte/ dìonach; **2** (*officialy/legally recognised*) tèarainte, ~ **tenure** (*of land &c*) gabhaltas tèarainte, ~ **status for Gaelic** inbhe thèarainte airson na Gàidhlig; **3** (*business &c: fin* ~) urrasach

security *n* tèarainteachd *f invar*, (*IT*) **data** ~ tèarainteachd dàta *m invar*

sediment *n* (*in liquids*) grùid *f*

see *v* **1** faic *vti irreg*, **I can't** ~ **anything at all** chan fhaic mi càil *m invar* sam bith, **it's good to** ~ **you** 's math d' fhaicinn, **I'll be** ~**ing you** bidh mi gad fhaicinn/gur faicinn, **I'll** ~ **you later/again** chì mi fhathast sibh/ thu, **we'll** ~! chì sinn!; **2** (*understand, realise*) faic *vti irreg*, tuig *vti*, is *v irreg def* lèir (*with prep* do), **I** ~ **now!** tha mi a' faicinn/a' tuigsinn a-nis, **he could** ~ **that he was wrong** bu lèir dha gun robh e ceàrr; **3** (*find out, check*) feuch *vi*, faic *vi*, **I'll go and/to** ~ **if the potatoes are done/ready** thèid mi ann feuch a bheil am buntàta *m sing coll* deiseil, **open the door to/and** ~ **if it's still raining** fosgail an doras *m* feuch a bheil an t-uisge ann fhathast; **4** (*be sure to &c*) feuch *vi* (*with conj* gu), ~ **that you're there early** feuch gum bi thu ann ron àm *m*; **5** (*visit*) **come/go to** ~ thig/rach *v irreg* air chèilidh *mf*, tadhail *vi*, (*with prep* air), **we'll come to** ~ **you tomorrow** thig sinn air chèilidh oirbh a-màireach; **6** ~ **to** (*tend to objects &c*) sgeadaich *vt*, cuir *vt* ceart, ~ **to the fire** sgeadaich an teine *m*; **7** (*misc exprs*) **I'll** ~ **to it** nì mise e, **I'll** ~ **you along the road** thèid mi an rathad *m* leat/còmhla riut, **let's** ~ fuirich (ort), **I saw him . . . let's** ~ **. . . yesterday** chunna mi e . . . fuirich (ort) . . . an-dè, ~ **off** (*drive away*) rua(i)g *vt*, cuir *vt* an teicheadh *m* (*with prep* air), **the dog saw off the fox** ruaig an cù am madadh ruadh, chuir an cù teachadh air a' mhadadh ruadh, ~ **off** (*defeat &c*) dèan a' chùis/an gnothach, faigh làmh *f* an uachdair, (*with prep* air), **we saw off the other team** rinn sinn a' chùis/ an gnothach air an sgioba *mf* eile, ~ **red** rach *vi* air bhoile *f invar*

seed *n* sìol *m sing coll*, fras *f sing coll*, **barley** ~ sìol-eòrna *m invar*, **sow** ~ cuir sìol

seek *v* sir *vt*, lorg *vt*

seem *v* **1** (*expr resemblance, or impression given*) bi *vi irreg* coltas *m* (*with gen & prep* air), **he ~s like a decent man** tha coltas *m* duine *m gen* chòir air; **2** *in expr* (*impersonal*) **it ~s** tha e coltach (*with conj gu*), a rèir c(h)oltais (*gen of* coltas *m*), **it ~s that he lost his job** tha e coltach gun do chaill e obair *f*, **it ~s there'll be a storm** a rèir choltais, bidh stoirm *mf* ann; **3** (*expr experience, or impression received*) bi *vi irreg followed by the appropriate adj* (*with prep* do), **the days ~ed long to us** bha na làithean *mpl* fada dhuinn, **it ~ed long/tedious to me** (*more trad*) b' fhada leam e

seemingly *adv* a rèir c(h)oltais (*gen of* coltas *m*)

seer *n* fiosaiche *m*, fàidh *m*

seethe *v* **1** (*water &c*) goil *vi*; **2** (*person:* ~ *with rage*) bi *vi irreg* air bhoile *f invar*, bi *vi irreg* air bhàinidh *f invar*

segregate *v* dealaich *vt* (**from** ri)

segregation *n* dealachadh *m* (**from** ri)

seize *v* glac *vt*, beir *vi*, gabh grèim *m*, (*all with prep* air), greimich *vt* (*with prep* air *or* ri)

seized *adj & past part* glacte

seizure *n* glacadh *m*

seldom *adv* is gann, (*more trad*) is ainneamh, (*with conj* a), **you'll ~ see the likes of him** is gann a chì thu a leithid *f*

select *v* tagh *vt*, roghnaich *vt*, **he ~ed the team** thagh e an sgioba *mf*

selected *adj & past part* air a (*&c*) t(h)aghadh, taghta

selection *n* taghadh *m*, roghainn *m*

-self *reflexive suffix* fhìn, fhèin, **myself** mi fhìn, **yourself** (*sing fam*) thu fhèin, **himself** e fhèin, **herself** i fhèin, **ourselves** sinn fhìn, **yourselves/ yourself** (*pl & sing formal*) sibh fhèin, **themselves** iad fhèin; **he saw himself** chunnaic e e fhèin, **they were washing themselves** bha iad gan nighe fhèin, **take care of yourself** thoir an aire *f invar* ort fhèin, **as for myself** air mo shon fhìn, **Mary herself** Màiri fhèin

self- *reflexive prefix* fèin- (*lenites following cons where possible: see examples below*)

self-government *n* fèin-riaghladh *m*

self-importance *n* fèin-spèis *f*

self-indulgence *n* fèin-mhilleadh *m*

selfish *adj* fèineil, fèin-chùiseach

selfishness *n* fèinealachd *f invar*

selfless *adj* neo-fhèineil

self-love *n* fèin-spèis *f*

self-respect *n* fèin-mheas *m*

self-service *n* fèin-fhrithealadh *m*

self-sufficient *adj* fèin-fhoghainteach

sell *v* reic *vti*, **I've nothing to** ~ chan eil càil *m invar* agam ri reic, ~ **at a good price** reic air deagh phrìs *f*

seller *n* reiceadair *m*

semen *n* sìol *m*, sìol-ginidh *m*

semi(-) *prefix* leth- (*lenites following cons where possible: see examples below*)

semicircle *n* leth-chearchall *m*

semicircular *adj* leth-chearclach

semicolon *n* leth-choilean *m*

semi-detached *adj* leth-dhealaichte

seminar *n* (*business &c*) seiminear *m*, (*more trad*) co-labhairt *f*

semivowel *n* leth-fhoghair *m*

senate *n* seanadh *m*

senator *n* seanadair *m*

send *v* cuir *vt* (**to** gu), ~ **away/off** cuir *vt* air falbh, **I sent you a letter** chuir mi litir *f* thugad, ~ **him word** cuir fios *m* thuige, ~ **for someone** cuir *vi* a dh'iarraidh cuideigin *mf invar*, cuir fios *m* air cuideigin, ~ **for the AA** cuir fios air an AA, ~ **on an errand** cuir *vt* air gnothach *m*

senior *adj* **1** (*first in rank*) prìomh (*precedes the noun & lenites following cons where possible*), ~ **judge** prìomh bhritheamh *m*; **2** (*oldest*) as sine, (*in past & conditional tense*) a bu shine; **3** *in expr* ~ **citizen** seann duine *m*, neach-peinnsein *m* (*pl* luchd-peinnsein *m sing coll*)

sensation *n* (*abstr*) mothachadh *m*, (*abstr & con*) faireachdainn *f*

sense *n* **1** (*understanding, intelligence*) tuigse *f invar*, ciall *f*; **2** (*common* ~) toinisg *f*, ciall *f*; **3** (*esp in pl: one's reason*) rian *m*, ciall *f*, **I nearly went out of my ~s** cha mhòr nach do chaill mi mo rian, theab mi a dhol às mo rian

senseless *adj* **1** (*foolish, meaningless, pointless*) gun chiall *f*, dìomhain, faoin; **2** (*stunned &c*) neo-fhiosrach

sensibility *n* mothachadh *m*

sensible *adj* (*having common sense*) ciallach, tuigseach, toinisgeil

sensitive *adj* **1** mothachail; **2** (*too* ~) bog, maoth; **3** (*touchy*) frionasach; **4** (*of situations: tricky, precarious*) cugallach

sensitivity *n* mothachadh *m*

sensual *adj* feòlmhor, collaidh

sensuality *n* feòlmhorachd *f invar*

sentence *n* **1** (*legal*) binn *f*, breith *f invar*, **give/pronounce** ~ thoir a-mach binn, thoir breith, (**on** air); **2** (*gram*) seantans *mf*, (*more trad*) rosg-rann *f*

sentence *v* **1** thoir a-mach binn *f*, thoir breith *f invar*, (*with prep* air), **he ~d them** thug e a-mach binn orra; **2** *in ezpr* ~ **to death** dìt *vt* gu bàs *m*

sentiment *n* **1** (*feeling*) mothachadh *m*; **2** (*opinion: usu in pl*) beachdan *mpl*, smuaintean *fpl*, **the ~s you expressed** na beachdan a chuir sibh an cèill (*dat of* ciall *f*)

sentimental *adj* (*of person*) maoth-inntinneach

sentinel, sentry *n* fear-faire *m*

separate *adj* **1** (*apart, another*) air leth, fa leth, eile, **in a ~ room** ann an seòmar *m* air leth/fa leth, ann an seòmar eile; **2** (*distinct, independent*) eadar-dhealaichte, (*less strong*) diof(a)rach, **the two questions are completely ~** tha an dà cheist *f sing* gu tur eadar-dhealaichte

separate *v* **1** dealaich *vti* (**from** ri), **he ~d the brothers (from each other)** dhealaich e na bràithrean *mpl* (ri chèile), **death ~d them** dhealaich am bàs iad; **2** (*~ into smaller quantities, portions &c*) roinn *vt*

separation *n* **1** dealachadh *m* (**from** ri); **2** (*of spouses*) sgaradh-pòsaidh *m*

sequence *n* sreath *mf*, ruith *f*

serene *adj* ciùin, socair, (*less usu*) suaimhneach

series *n* sreath *mf*

serious *adj* **1** (*important, weighty*) trom, cudthromach, **~ matters** cuspairean *mpl* troma/cudthromach; **2** (*severe, extreme*) droch, **a ~ crime** droch eucoir *f*; **3** (*persons: ~ minded, earnest*) dùrachdach, (*sober, staid*) stòlda; **4** (*opposite of jesting*) ann an da-rìribh, **I told you I was pregnant, but I wasn't ~!** dh'innis mi dhut gu robh mi trom, ach cha robh mi ann an da-riribh!

serpent *n* nathair *f*

serve *v* **1** fritheil *vi* (*with prep* air), **~ someone** fritheil air cuideigin, **~ at table** fritheil air a' bhòrd *m*, (*more trad*) freastail *vi* don bhòrd; **2** (*dish out food &c*) riaraich *vt*, thoir *vt* seachad; **3** (*do the task in hand &c*) **that will ~** nì sin an gnothach *m*; **4** (*animals mating*) rach *vi irreg* air muin *f* invar (*with gen*), **the bull ~ed the cow** chaidh an tarbh air muin na bà

service *n* **1** freastal *m*, frithealadh *m*, **~ at table** freastal don bhòrd *m*, **~ station, ~ area** stèisean *m*/ionad *m* frithealaidh *gen*; **2** (*helpful action*) seirbheis *f*, **he rendered me a ~** rinn e seirbheis dhomh; **3** (*church, tennis, garage &c*) seirbheis *f*

service *v* **1** (*machinery &c*) gleus *vt*, cùm *vt* air dòigh *f*; **2** (*provide support, supplies &c for*) fritheil *vi* (*with prep* air)

servile *adj* tràilleil

session *n* (*parliament, committee &c*) seisean *m*, **in ~** ann an seisean

set *adj & past part* (*fixed, established*) suidhichte, stèidhichte, **~ procedures** dòighean-obrach *fpl* suidhichte, **~ in his ways** suidhichte na dhòighean *fpl*

set *n* seat(a) *m*

set *v* **1** (*place, position*) suidhich *vt*, socraich *vt*, cuir *vt*, **~ the statue on the column** suidhich/socraich/cuir an ìomhaigh air a' cholbh *m*; **2** *in various exprs with* cuir *vt*, **~ up** cuir *vt* air chois (*dat of* cas *f*), cuir *vt* air bhonn *m*, **she ~ up a business** chuir i gnothach *m* air chois/air bhonn,

~ **apart** cuir *vt* air leth *m invar*, ~ **aside** cuir *vt* an dara taobh *m*, cuir *vt* mu seach, **this ~ me thinking** chuir seo gu smaointeachadh *m* mi, ~ **the cat among the pigeons** cuir an ceòl air feadh na fìdhle; 3 (*of the sun*) laigh *vi*, rach *vi* fodha; 4 (*other misc exprs*) ~ **the house on fire** leig an taigh na theine *m*, cuir teine ris an taigh, ~ **free** fuasgail *vt*, ~ **to/about** teann *vi* (*with prep* ri), crom *vi* (*with prep* air), **he ~ about climbing** theann e ri streap, **she ~ to work** chrom i air an obair *f*, **she ~ off/out** ghabh i an rathad *m*, thog i oirre, **they ~ about each other** ghabh iad dha chèile

settee *n* sòfa *f*, (*more trad*) langasaid *f*

setting *n* (*situation &c*) suidheachadh *m*

settle *v* 1 (*calm, make or become comfortable &c*) socraich *vti*; 2 (*sort, solve*) rèitich *vt*, socraich *vt*, ~ **the matter/dispute** rèitich an gnothach/a' chonnspaid; 3 (*close, finalise*) cuir crìoch *f* (*with prep* air), **that ~s the matter!** tha sin a' cur crìoch air a' chùis *f*!; 4 (*come to rest*) laigh *vi*, **the bird ~d on its nest** laigh an t-eun air a nead *m*; 5 (*esp liquids*) tràigh *vi*; 6 (*inhabit*) tuinich *vi*, **the first race that ~d in America** a' chiad chinneadh *m* a thuinich ann an Ameireagaidh *f*

settled *adj & past part* (*fixed, established*) suidhichte, seasmhach, ~ **in his ways** suidhichte na dhòighean *fpl*

settlement *n* 1 (*habitational: abstr & con*) tuineachadh *m*; 2 (*of dispute &c*) rèiteachadh *m*

settler *n* 1 neach-tuineachaidh *m* (*pl* luchd-tuineachaidh *m sing coll*); 2 *in expr* (*pej*) **white ~** seatlair geal

sever *v* 1 (*cut off*) geàrr *vt* dheth; 2 (*fig: part, separate*) dealaich *vti*, sgar *vti*, (**from** ri)

several *adj* iomadh, ~ **hundred years** iomadh ceud *m* bliadhna *f*

severe *adj* 1 (*person, discipline &c*) cruaidh, teann; 2 (*hard to bear*) goirt, **a ~ trial** deuchainn ghoirt; 3 (*extreme*) droch (*precedes the noun, which it lenites where possible*), ~ **disadvantage** droch anacothrom *m*

sew *v* fuaigh *vti*, fuaigheil *vti*

sewage *n* òtrachas *m*, ~ **works** ionad *m* òtrachais *gen*

sewer *n* sàibhear *m*, giodar *m*

sewing *n* (*abstr & con*) fuaigheal *m*

sewn *adj & past part* fuaighte

sex *n* 1 (*gender*) gnè *f invar*, **the female/male ~** a' ghnè bhoireann/fhireann; 2 (*sexual activity, lovemaking*) feise *f*, (*less usu*) sùgradh *m*, **have ~** faigh muin *f invar*, co-ghin *vi*, cuplaich *vi*, **he had ~ with her** chaidh e air a muin

sexist *adj* gnèitheil

sexual *adj* 1 gnèitheach, gnèitheasach; 2 *in exprs* ~ **equality** co-ionannachd *f* nan gnè *f invar*, ~ **relations/intercourse** feise *f*, ~ **desire** miann *mf*, (*more lustful*) ana-miann *mf*, drùis *f*

shabby *adj* 1 luideach, cearbach, robach; 2 (*conduct &c*) suarach, (*stronger*) tàireil

shackle *n* geimheal *m*

shackle *v* geimhlich *vt*

shade *n* dubhar *m*, sgàil(e) *f*, dubharachd *f invar*, **in the ~ of the walls** fo dhubhar(achd)/sgàil nam ballachan *mpl*

shade *v* duibhrich *vti*

shadow *n* **1** (*shade*) dubhar *m*, sgàil(e) *f*, dubharachd *f invar*, **in the ~ of the walls** fo dhubhar(achd)/sgàil nam ballachan *mpl*; **2** (*thrown ~*) faileas *m*, **her ~ fell on me** laigh a faileas orm

shadowy *adj* faileasach

shady *adj* dubharach

shaggy *adj* molach, ròmach, fionnach, robach

shake *n* (*involuntary*) crith *f*

shake *v* **1** (*deliberately*) crath *vti*, **he shook his head/fist** chrath e a cheann *m*/a dhòrn *m*; **2** (*involuntarily*) bi *vi irreg* air chrith *f*, (*less usu*) crith *vi*, **he was shaking with the fever** bha e air chrith leis an fhiabhras *m*, *in expr* **start to ~** rach *vi* air chrìth; **3** (*surfaces &c*) luaisg *vi*, **the building was shaking** bha an togalach a' luasgadh; **4** *in expr* **~ hands**, beir *vi* air làimh *f dat* (*with prep* air), **he didn't ~ hands with me** cha do rug e air làimh orm

shaking *adj* air chrith *f*, **~ with fever** air chrith leis an fhiabhras *m*

shaking *n* luasgan *m*

shaky *adj* **1** (*lit*) cugallach, critheanach, (*stronger*) tulgach, **~ on his feet** cugallach air a chasan, **~ bridge** drochaid chritheanach; **3** (*fig: dodgy, dubious*) cugallach, **don't get involved in it, it's pretty ~** na gabh gnothach *m* ris, tha e gu math cugallach

shallow *adj* **1** (*lit*) eu-domhainn, (*of water*) tana; **2** (*fig: of person, activity &c*) faoin, dìomhain

shambles *n* bùrach *m*, **in a ~** ann am bùrach

shame *n* **1** nàire *f invar*, masladh *m*, tàmailt *f*, **feel ~** gabh nàire, **without ~** gun nàire, **for ~!** nàire!, **~ on you!** mo nàire ort!; **2** *in exprs* **put to ~** nàraich *vt*, maslaich *vt*, **that's a ~!** tha sin duilich!, (*more trad*) is truagh sin!

shame *v* nàraich *vt*, maslaich *vt*

shame-faced *adj* nàrach

shameful *adj* nàr, maslach, tàmailteach

shameless *adj* gun nàire, ladarna

shaming *n* nàrachadh *m*, maslachadh *m*

shamrock *n* seamrag *f*

shape *n* cruth *m*, cumadh *m*, dealbh & deilbh *mf*, **a stone in the ~ of a horse** clach *f* air chumadh/dhealbh/cruth eich *m gen*, **I made out his ~ in the darkness** rinn mi a-mach a chruth/a chumadh san dorchadas *m*

shape *v* cum *vt*, dealbh *vt*

shapely *adj* cuimir

share *n* **1** cuid *f*, cuibhreann *m*, roinn *f*, **there's your ~** sin agad do chuid-sa (dheth), **a half** ~ leth-chuid; **2** (*fin*) earrann *f*, sèar *m*, ~**s fell today** thuit earrannan/sèaraichean an-diugh

share *v* **1** (~ *something with others*) co-roinn *vt*; **2** (~ *out*) pàirtich *vt*, roinn *vt*, riaraich *vt*

shared *adj & past part* **1** roinnte; **2** (*held or used in common*) coitcheann, ~ **facilities** goireasan *mpl* coitcheann

sharp *adj* **1** geur, ~ **knife** sgian gheur, ~ **eye** sùil gheur, *also* sùil bhiorach, ~ **taste** blas geur; **2** (*pointed*) biorach, **a** ~ **stick** maide biorach; **3** (*mentally* ~) geur/grad/luath na (*&c*) inntinn *f*, eirmseach; **4** (*remarks, tongue &c*) geur, guineach, biorach

sharpen *v* faobharaich *vt*, geuraich *vt*

sharpness *n* gèire *f invar*

shatter *v* **1** (*as vi*) rach *vi irreg* na bloighdean *fpl*; **2** (*as vt*) bloighdich *vt*

shattered *adj & past part* **1** (*lit*) na (*&c*) b(h)loighdean *fpl*; **2** (*fig & fam: exhausted*) seac searbh sgìth

shave *v* beàrr *vt*, lom *vt*

she *pers pron* i, (*emph form*) ise, ~ **saw her** chunnaic i i

sheaf *n* (*of corn*) sguab *f*

shear *v* (*sheep*) rùisg *vt*, lom *vt*

shearing *n* (*of sheep &c*) rùsgadh *m*, lomadh *m*

shears *n* (*ie a pair of* ~) deamhais *mf sing*

shebeen *n* taigh dubh, bothan *m*

shed *n* seada *mf*, bothan *m*

shed *v* dòirt *vt*, ~ **blood** dòirt fuil *f*

sheep *n* (*single* ~) caora *f*, (*pl*) caoraich *fpl*

sheepdog *n* cù-chaorach *m*

sheepfank faing & fang *f*

sheepfold *n* crò(-chaorach) *m*, faing & fang *f*

sheepish *adj* nàrach & nàireach

sheep-shearer *n* lomadair *m*

sheep-tick *n* mial-chaorach *f*

sheet *n* **1** (*for bed*) siot(a) *m*; **2** (*of paper*) duilleag *f*

shelf *n* **1** sgeilp *f*; **2** (*topog: rock* ~) leac *f*, (*esp in sea*) sgeir *f*

shell *n* **1** (*of nuts, eggs*) plaosg *m*, slige *f*; **2** (*of* ~*fish; also artillery* ~) slige *f*, **scallop** ~ slige-chreachain *f*

shell *v* **1** (*nuts, eggs*) rùisg *vt*, plaoisg; **2** (*peas & beans*) plaoisg *vt*

shellfish *n* (*a* ~, *also coll*) maorach *m*

shelter *n* **1** (*esp from elements*) fasgadh *m* (**from** o & bho), ~ **belt** crios fasgaidh *gen*, **take** ~ **from the downpour** gabh fasgadh on dìle *f*; **2** (*esp protective* ~) dìon *m*, **in the** ~ **of the castle** fo dhìon a' chaisteil

shelter *v* **1** (*as vi: take cover &c*) gabh fasgadh *m* (**from** bho/o), **we** ~**ed from the weather** ghabh sinn fasgadh on t-sìde; **2** (*as vt, lit and fig: provide* ~) thoir fasgadh *m* (*with prep* do), (*esp protectively*) dìon *vt*, **the castle** ~**ed us** dhìon an caisteal sinn

sheltered *adj* fasgach, (*esp protectively*) dìonach, **~ spot** bad fasgach

sheltering *adj* fasgach, (*esp protectively*) dìonach, **a ~ wood** coille fhasgach

shepherd *n* cìobair *m*

shepherding *n* cìobaireachd *f invar*

sheriff *n* siorram *m*, **the Sherrif Court** cùirt *f* an t-siorraim

sheriffdom *n* (*hist*) siorramachd *f invar*

shield *n* **1** sgiath *f*, (*trad, hist*) targaid *f*; **2** (*fig*) dìon *m*

shield *v* dìon *vt*

shieling *n* (*hist*) àirigh *f*, (*less usu*) ruighe *mf*, **~ hut/bothy** bothan *m* àirigh

shift *v* caraich *vt*, gluais *vti*, cuir car *m* (*with prep* de)

shifting *adj* **1** (*liable to move*) gluasadach; **2** (*inconstant, liable to change*) caochlaideach, carach, luaineach

shifty *adj* fiar, carach

shilling *n* (*hist*) tastan *m*

shin *n* lurgann *f*, faobhar *m* na lurgainn

shine *n* (*on shoes &c*) lìomh *f*

shine *v* **1** (*as vi: lights &c*) deàlraich *vi*, deàrrs *vi*, **the sun's not shining** chan eil a' ghrian a' deàrrs(ach)adh; **2** (*as vt: ~ shoes &c*) lìomh *vt*

shingle *n* mol *m*, morghan *m*

shining *adj* **1** (*esp lights*) deàlrach; **2** (*~ with polish &c*) lìomharra

shinty *n* iomain *f*, camanachd *f invar*, **we were playing ~** bha sinn ag iomain, *in expr* **~ stick** caman *m*

shiny *adj* **1** (*esp lights*) deàlrach; **2** (*~ with polish &c*) lìomharra, gleansach

ship *n* long *f*, soitheach *m*, bàta (mòr) *m*

shipping *n* loingeas & luingeas *m*, luingearachd *f invar*

shipwreck *n* long-bhris(t)eadh *m*

shirt *n* lèine *f*

shit *v* (*fam/vulg*) cac *vi*

shit(e) *n* (*fam/vulg*) cac *m*, (*fig: fam/vulg, pej*) **it's a load of ~!** 's e tòrr *m* caca gen a th' ann!

shiver *n* crith *f*

shiver *v* bi *vi irreg* air chrith *f*, crith *vi*, **start to ~** rach *vi irreg* air chrith

shivering *adj* air chrith *f*, **~ with cold** air chrith leis an fhuachd *mf*

shivering *n* crith *f*

shock *n* (*through fear or surprise*) clisgeadh *m*, **he gave me a ~** chuir e clisgeadh orm

shocking *adj* oillteil, uabhasach

shoddy *adj* **1** luideach, cearbach, robach; **2** (*workmanship &c*) dearmadach, coma co-dhiù

shoe *n* **1** bròg *f*; **2** (*of horse*) bròg-eich *f*, (*more trad*) crudha *m*

shoe *v* (*horse*) crudhaich *vt*, cuir crudha *m* (*with prep* air)

shoe-lace *n* iall *f* bròige (*gen of* bròg *f*), barrall *m*

shoemaker, shoe-repairer *n* greusaiche *m*

shoot *n* (*of plants &c*) ògan *m*, gas *f*, bachlag *f*

shoot *v* 1 (*with a firearm*) loisg *vti*, tilg *vti*, (**at** air); 2 (~ *a person*) tilg *vi* ann (*&c*), leig peilear *m* ann (*&c*), **he shot her** leig e peilear innte

shooting *n* losgadh *m*, tilgeil *f*

shop *n* bùth *mf*, **fish** ~ bùth èisg (*gen of* iasg *m*), **chemist's** ~ bùth-chungaidh *f*, **craft** ~ bùth chiùird (*gen of* ceàrd *&* cèard *m*), *in expr* **blacksmith's** ~ ceàrdach *f*,

shopkeeper *n* neach-bùtha *m* (*pl* luchd-bùtha *m sing coll*), **the** ~ fear *m* na bùtha, bean *f* na bùtha

shore *n* 1 (*of sea: esp between high- and low-water mark, esp sandy*) tràigh *f*, (*can be stony/shingly*) cladach *m*; 2 (*in opposition to sea*) tìr *mf*, **on** ~ air tìr *mf*

short *adj* 1 goirid, geàrr, ~ **story** sgeulachd ghoirid, **the days are getting** ~ tha na làithean *mpl* a' fàs goirid, **a** ~ **time ago** o chionn ghoirid, **in/after a** ~ **time** an ceann ghoirid, an ùine gheàrr, **in the** ~ **term** sa gheàrr-ùine *f*; 2 (*of person: brusque &c*) aithghearr, cas; 3 *in exprs* **in** ~ **supply** gann, a dhìth, easbhaidheach, **food is** ~/**in** ~ **supply** tha biadh gann/a dhìth, **we won't go** ~ cha teid sinn a dhìth, ~ **cut** bealach goirid, **we took a** ~ **cut** ghabh sinn bealach goirid

shortage *n* cion *nm invar*, dìth *m*, gainne *f*, uireasbhaidh *f*, **the potato** ~ cion/dìth a' bhuntàta *m sing coll*

shortcoming *n* fàillinn *f*, meang *m*

shorten *v* 1 (*as vt*) giorraich *vt*; 2 (*as vi: grow shorter*) rach *vi* an giorrad *m*

shorter *comp adj* giorra, **the days are getting** ~ tha na làithean *mpl* a' fàs nas giorra, *also* tha na làithean a' dol an giorrad *m*

shorthand *n* geàrr-sgrìobhadh *m*

short-legged *adj* geàrr-chasach

shortly *adv* 1 a dh'aithghearr, an ceann ghoirid, (ann) an ùine gheàrr, **she'll be here** ~ bidh i ann a dh'aithghearr; 2 (*brusquely*) gu grad

shortness *n* giorrad *m*

shorts *n* 1 (*trousers*) briogais ghoirid; 2 (*cinema*) filmichean *mpl* goirid

short-sighted *adj* geàrr-sheallach

short-sightedness *n* geàrr-shealladh *m*

shot *n* 1 (*from firearm*) urchair *f*, **I heard a** ~ chuala mi urchair; 2 (*fam: attempt*) oidhirp *f*, ionnsaigh *f*, (**at** air), **he had another** ~ **at it** rinn e oidhirp eile air, *in expr* (*fam*) **I gave it my best** ~ rinn mi mo dhìcheall *m* air; 3 (*ironic*) **a big** ~ duine mòr (cudthromach), **the big** ~s na daoine *mpl* mòra

shotgun *n* gunna-froise *m*

should *auxiliary v* bu (*past of* is *v irreg def*) chòir *f* (*with prep* do), **I** ~ **go/I** ~ **be going** bu chòir dhomh (a bhith a') falbh, **you** ~**n't smoke** cha bu chòir dhut smocadh *m*, **it's not as good as it** ~ **be** chan eil e cho math 's a bu chòir (dha a bhith)

shoulder *n* 1 gualann *&* gualainn *f*, ~ **to** ~ gualainn ri gualainn; 2 *in expr* ~ **blade** cnàimh-slinnein *m*

shout *n* glaodh *m*, iolach *f*, èigh *f*

shout *v* glaodh *vi*, dèan/tog iolach *f*, èigh *or* èibh *vi*

shove *v* **1** (*jostle &c*) put *vt*; **2** (*esp ~ objects*) sàth *vt*, spàrr *vt*, ~ **it into the cupboard** sàth a-steach sa phreas *m* e, ~ **your hand into the sack** spàrr do làmh *f* sa phoca *m*

shovel *n* sluasaid *f*

show *n* **1** (*of art, goods, techniques &c*) taisbeanadh *m*; **2** (*ostentation &c*) spaide *f*

show *v* **1** seall *vt*, nochd *vt*, (**to** do), ~ **me it** seall/nochd dhomh e, *also* leig fhaicinn dhomh e; **2** (*fam: turn up &c*) nochd *vi*, **he didn't ~ (up) before midnight** cha do nochd e (a-staigh) ro mheadhan-oidhche *m*; **3** (*exhibit*) taisbean *&* taisbein *vt*

shower *n* **1** (*of rain*) fras *f*, (*heavier*) meall *m*, meall-uisge *m*; **2** (*bathroom equipment*) frasair *m*, (*the shower one takes*) fras *m*; **3** *in expr* (*fam: group of incompetents*) **what a ~!** abair bumalairean *mpl*!

showery *adj* frasach

showing *adv* ris, **her elbow was ~** bha a h-uileann *f* ris

showy *adj* spaideil, basdalach

shrewd *adj* geur-chùiseach, tuigseach, (*less usu in this sense*) seòlta

shriek *n* sgread *m*, sgreuch *m*

shriek *v* sgread *vi*, sgreuch *vi*

shrill *adj* sgalanta

shrimp *n* carran *m*

shrink *v* lùghdaich *vti*, teannaich *vti*

shrinkage *n* lùghdachadh *m*, teannachadh *m*

shrivel *v* searg *vi*, crìon *vi*

shroud *n* marbhfhaisg *f*

shrub *n* preas *m*, (*less usu*) dos *m*

shrunken *adj & past part* crìon, seargte

shun *v* **1** (*avoid*) seachain *vt*, cùm *vi* (*with prep* o), ~ **her** seachain i, cùm uaipe; **2** (*ostracise &c*) cuir cùl *m* (*with prep* ri)

shut *adj & past part* **1** (*buildings, objects &c*) dùinte; **2** (*fam: rid*) cuidhteas *m* (*with or without prep* de), saor (**of** o), clior (**of** is), **we got ~ of the builders** fhuair sinn cuidhteas an/den luchd-togalaich *m sing coll*, **we're ~ of them at last!** tha sinn saor uapa/tha sinn clior is iad mu dheireadh thall!

shut *v* dùin *vti*, ~ **the door** dùin an doras, **the shop was ~ting** bha a' bhùth *mf* a' dùnadh, **the window ~ with a bang** dhùin an uinneag le brag *m*, (*vulg*) ~ **your gob!** dùin do chab/ghob *m*!

shy *adj* diùid

shy *v* **1** (*horse &c*) thoir uspag *f*; **2** *in expr* **apt to ~** sgeunach

shyness *n* diùide *f invar*, diùideachd *f invar*

sick *adj* **1** (*ill &c*) tinn, euslainteach, (*less usu*) anfhann, *in exprs* ~ **pay** pàigheadh *m* tinneis *m gen*, ~ **leave** fòrladh *m* tinneis *gen*; **2** *in expr* **be ~** (*ie vomit*) dìobhair *vi*, sgeith *vi*; **3** (*fed up &c*) sgìth, (*stronger*) seac searbh sgìth (of de), **I'm ~ and tired/heartily ~ of your carrying-on!** tha mi seac searbh sgìth den dol-a-mach *m invar* agad!

sick *n* **1** (*in pl: ill people*) **the** ~ na h-euslaintich *mpl*; **2** (*vomit*) dìobhairt *m invar*

sick up *v* dìobhair *vt*, tilg *vt*, cuir *vt* a-mach, **the boy sicked up his dinner** dhìobhair/thilg am balach a dhìnnear *f*, chuir am balach a-mach a dhìnnear

sicken *v* **1** (*become sick*) fàs *vi* tinn; **2** (*disgust*) cuir sgreamh *m* (*with prep* air), sgreataich *vt*, **it ~s me** tha e a' cur sgreamha *gen* orm

sickle *n* corran *m*

sickly *adj* (*off colour*) bochd, (*stronger*) tinn, euslainteach

sickness *n* tinneas *m*, gearan *m*, galar *m*, ~ **benefit** sochair *f* tinneis *gen*

side *n* **1** taobh *m*, (*more trad*) leth *m invar*, (*esp of body, hill*) cliatha(i)ch *f*, **there's a pain in my ~** tha pian *f* nam chliathaich, **the lorry struck the ~ of the house** bhuail an làraidh *f* taobh/cliatha(i)ch an taighe *m*, **the west ~** (*of the country &c*) an taobh siar *also* an taobh an iar, **at my ~** rim thaobh, **~ by ~** taobh ri taobh, **put to/on one ~** cuir an dara taobh, *in expr* **~ of the head** lethcheann *m*; **2** (*topog: ~ of hill*) leathad *m*, bruthach *mf*, cliatha(i)ch *f*; **3** (*in dispute &c*) taobh *m*, leth *m invar*, **we took her ~** ghabh sinn a taobh-se, chaidh sinn às a leth, chùm sinn taobh rithe; **4** (*pride*) leòm *f*

side *v in expr* **we ~d with her** ghabh sinn a taobh-se *m*, chaidh sinn às a leth *m invar*, chùm sinn taobh rithe

sideways *adv* an comhair a (*&c*) t(h)aoibh (*gen of* taobh *m*), **the mare fell ~** thuit an làir *f* an comhair a taoibh

siege *n* sèist *mf*, **under ~** fo shèist, **lay ~** cuir sèist (**to** air)

siesta *n* dùsal *m* feasgair *m gen*

sieve *n* criathar *m*

sieve, sift *v* criathraich *vt*

sigh *n* osna *f*, osnadh *m*, osann *m*, (*less usu*) ospag *f*, **heave a ~** leig/dèan osna, osnaich *vi*

sigh *v* leig/dèan osna *f*, osnaich *vi*

sighing *n* osnaich *f*, osnachadh *m*

sight *n* **1** (*eye~*) fradharc & radharc *m*, lèirsinn *f invar*, (*less usu in this sense*) sealladh *m*; **2** (*field of vision*) sealladh *m*, (f)radharc *m*, fianais *f*, **he was/he came in(to) ~** bha/thàinig e an sealladh/san t-sealladh, bha/thàinig e san (fh)radharc/am fianais, **out of ~** à sealladh, às an t-sealladh, às an (fh)radharc, à fianais, **out of my ~!** a-mach às mo shealladh/às m' fhianais!, **we lost ~ of him** chaill sinn sealladh air, **we were in ~ of the island** bha sinn am fianais an eilein; **3** (*view, spectacle*) sealladh *m*, **beautiful ~s** seallaidhean brèagha; **4** *in expr* **second ~** an dà shealladh *m sing*, taibhsearachd *f invar*

sign *n* **1** comharra(dh) *m*, samhla(dh) *m*, **that's a good/bad ~!** is e deagh/droch chomharradh a tha ('n) sin!, **~ of respect** comharradh urraim *m gen*, **'-an' is a ~ of the plural** is e '-an' samhla/comharradh an iolra; **2** (*giving information, directions &c*) soighne *m*, **road ~** soighne-rathaid *m*; **3** (*hint, signal*) sanas *m*, comharra(dh) *m*, **he gave me a ~ with a wink of his eye** thug e sanas dhomh le priobadh *m* a shùla (*gen of* sùil *f*); **4** (*trace &c*) lorg *f*, sgeul *m*, **there's no ~ of it/him** chan eil lorg air, **is there any ~ of Seumas?** a bheil sgeul air Seumas?

sign *v* cuir m' (*&c*) ainm *m* (*with prep* ri), **she ~ed the letters** chuir i a h-ainm ris na litrichean *fpl*

signal *n* sanas *m*, comharra(dh) *m*, **he gave me a ~ with a wink of his eye** thug e sanas dhomh le priobadh *m* a shùla (*gen of* sùil *f*)

signature *n* ainm *m* (sgrìobhte), **append your ~ to the contract enclosed** cuir d' ainm ris a' chùmhnant *m* a tha an cois (na litreach seo)

significance *n* brìgh *f*, ciall *f*, **statements of no ~** briathran *mpl* gun bhrìgh

significant *adj* **1** (*of importance*) cud(th)romach, **a ~ change** atharrachadh cudthromach; **2** (*meaningful*) brìgheil

signify *v* ciallaich *vt*, **what does the new policy ~?** dè a tha am poileasaidh ùr a' ciallachadh?

signpost *n* clàr-seòlaidh *m*, post-seòlaidh *m*, soighne

silence *n* tosd *m invar*, sàmhchair *f*, (*as command*) **~!** tosd!

silent *adj* **1** sàmhach, gun fhuaim *mf*, (*esp of persons*) tosdach, na (*&c*) t(h)osd *m invar*, **they were ~** bha iad nan tosd; **2** (*rendered speechless*) balbh, (*stronger*) bog balbh, **he was ~ in the face of his wife's anger** bha e balbh ro fheirg *f dat* na mnà aige

silk *n* sìoda *m*

silky *adj* sìodach

silliness *n* gòraiche *f invar*, amaideas *m*, faoineas *m*

silly *adj* gòrach, faoin, baoth, **don't be ~!** na bi gòrach!

silt *n* eabar *m*, poll *m*

silver *n* airgead *m*

silver *adj* airgid (*gen of* airgead *m, used adjectivally*)

silversmith *n* ceàrd-airgid *m*

similar *adj* coltach (**to** ri), **all the buildings were ~ (to each other)** bha na togalaichean *mpl* air fad coltach ri chèile

similarity *n* coltas *m*

simile *n* (*Lit &c*) samhla(dh) *m*

simple *adj* **1** (*easy*) furasta, soirbh, sìmplidh, **a ~ job/question** obair/ ceist fhurasda; **2** (*plain, unpretentious*) sìmplidh, **a ~ dwelling** àite-còmhnaidh sìmplidh; **3** (*~-minded*) sìmplidh, baoth

simplicity *n* sìmplidheachd *f invar*

simplify *n* sìmplich *vt*

simultaneous *adj* **1** co-amail; **2** *in expr* **~ translation** eadar-theangachadh *m* mar-aon *adv*

simultaneously *adv* aig an aon àm *m*

sin *n* **1** peacadh *m*, **a mortal** ~ peacadh-bàis, **original** ~ peacadh-gine; **2** (*not necessarily in full rel sense*) ciont(a) *m*

sin *v* peacaich *vi*, (*not nec in full rel sense*) ciontaich *vi*

since *conj* **1** (*causal*) on & bhon (*with conj* a), a chionn is (*with conj* gu), **they put the stock on the hill** ~ **the grazing was good up there** chuir iad an sprèidh *f* dhan mhonadh *m* on a bha/a chionn 's gu robh an t-ionaltradh math shuas an sin; **2** (*time*) o & bho, on & bhon (*with conj* a), **the first letter she's sent me** ~ **I got to know her** a' chiad litir a tha i air a chur thugam bhon a chuir mi eòlas *m* oirre, **it's a long time** ~ **I was at school** 's fhada on a bha mi san sgoil *f*, (*or, with subordinate v in neg*) 's fhada o nach robh mi san sgoil, **it's a long time** ~ **we saw you** is fhada o nach fhaca sinn sibh

since *prep* (*time*) o chionn & bho chionn, **I've been working for him** ~ **a year ago** tha mi ag obair aige bho chionn bliadhna *f*

sincere *adj* dùrachdach, fosgarra

sincerity *n* dùrachd *mf*, treibhdhireas *m*

sincerely *adv* (*corres*) **yours** ~ le dùrachd *mf*, is mise le meas *m invar*

sinew *n* fèith *f*

sinewy *adj* fèitheach

sinful *adj* peacach

sing *v* **1** seinn *vti*, gabh *vt*, **will you** ~ **for us?** an seinn thu dhuinn?, ~ **a song!** gabh òran *m*!; **2** *in expr* ~ **to sleep** tàlaidh *vt*; **3** (*of birds*) ceileir *vi*

singe *v* dòth *vt*

singer *n* seinneadair *m*, ban-seinneadair *f*

single *adj* **1** singilte, ~ **track road** rathad singilte, ~ **bed** leabaidh shingilte; **2** (*unmarried*) singilte, gun phòsadh *m*, **when I was** ~ **and my pocket did jingle** nuair a bha mi singilte 's a bha mo phòca *m* a' gliongadaich; **3** *in exprs* **a** ~ **man** fleasgach *m*, **a** ~ **woman** maighdeann *f*; **4** (*in emph exprs*) aon, **we didn't see a** ~ **person** chan fhaca sinn fiù is aon duine *m*, *also* chan fhaca sinn duine sam bith/duine beò/duine no duine, **every** ~ gach aon, **it rained every** ~ **day** bha an t-uisge ann gach aon là *m*

singular *adj* **1** (*strange*) àraid, neònach, (*stronger*) iongantach, **wasn't that** ~? nach robh sin àraid/neònach?, (*trad*) nach neònach sin?, **a** ~ **occurrence** tachartas *m* iongantach; **2** (*exceptional*) sònraichte, àraidh, **a** ~ **man** duine sònraichte/àraidh; **3** (*gram*) singilte, ~ **noun** ainmear singilte

sink *v* **1** (*levels, liquids*) tràigh *vi*, traogh *vi*, sìolaidh *vi*; **2** (*send/go to the bottom*) cuir *vt* fodha, rach *vi irreg* fodha, ~ **a boat** cuir fodha bàta *m*, **the boat sank** chaidh am bàta fodha

sink *n* (*kitchen &c*) sinc(e) *mf*

sinner *n* peacach *m*

sip *n* drùdhag *f*, balgam *m*

sip *v* gabh drùdhag *f*, gabh balgam *m*, (**of** de)

siren *n* dùdach *mf*, dùdag *f*

sister *n* piuthar *f*, **~-in-law** (*spouse's ~*) piuthar-chèile *f*, (*brother's wife*) bean-bhràthar *f*

sisterhood, sisterliness *n* peathrachas *m*

sit *v* **1** (*be in a sitting position*) bi *vi irreg* na (*&c*) s(h)uidhe *m*, **you were ~ting in the corner** bha thu nad shuidhe sa chòrnair *m*; **2** (*take a seat*) suidh *vi*, dèan suidhe *m*, **he sat in the corner** shuidh e sa chòrnair, **~ down** suidh *vi* sìos, dèan suidhe *m*, **~ (down) beside me** dèan suidhe rim thaobh *m*; **3** (*seat someone*) cuir *vt* na (*&c*) s(h)uidhe, **we sat them (down) in the corner** chuir sinn nan suidhe iad anns a' chòrnair *m*; **4** *in expr* **~ an exam** feuch/suidh deuchainn *f*

site *n* **1** làrach *f*, ionad *m*, **a house ~, a ~ for a house** làrach taighe *m gen*, **Site of Special Scientific Interest** Ionad de Shuim Shònraichte Shaidheansail; **2** (*setting, location, position*) suidheachadh *m*, **a good ~ for a cinema** deagh shuidheachadh airson taigh-dhealbh *m gen*; **3** (*IT*) ionad *m*, làrach *f*, **internet/web ~** làrach-lìn *f*

sitting *n* **1** (*~ of court, parliament &c*) suidhe *m*, seisean *m*; **2** *in expr* **~ room** seòmar suidhe *gen*

situation *n* **1** (*circumstances*) suidheachadh *m*, staid *f*, **our ~ was better after I found work** bha an suidheachadh againn na b' fheàrr an dèidh dhomh obair *f* fhaighinn, **we were in a bad ~ financially** bha sinn ann an droch staid a thaobh airgid *m gen*, **in a (very) difficult ~** ann an droch staing *f*; **2** (*setting, location, position*) suidheachadh *m*, **a good ~ for a cinema** deagh shuidheachadh airson taigh-dhealbh *m gen*; **3** (*post, job*) dreuchd *f*

six *n & num adj* **1** sia; **2** (*idioms*) **~ and half a dozen** bò mhaol odhar agus bò odhar mhaol, **at ~es and sevens** troimh-a-chèile

sixty *n & num adj* trì-fichead

size *n* **1** meud *m invar*, meudachd *f invar*, **the ~ of the house/the field** meud an taighe/an achaidh, **increase in ~** rach *vi irreg* am meud, **the ~ of their debts** meud/meudachd nam fiachan *m* aca, **about the ~ of a pig** mu mheudachd muice (*gen of* muc *f*); **2** (*dimensions*) tomhas *m*, **the ~ of the tractor tyre** tomhas taidhr *f* an tractair

sizeable *adj* tomadach *&* tomaltach, (*more fam*) gu math mòr

skeleton *n* cnàimhneach *m*

sketch *n* sgeidse *f*, **~ book** leabhar *m* sgeidse *gen*

skewer *n* dealg *f*

ski *n* sgith *f*, **~s** sgithean

ski *v* sgithich *vi*

skiing *n* sgitheadh *m*

skilful, skilled *adj* gleusta *&* gleusda, sgileil, teòma, **~ in the handling of weapons** gleusta ann an làimhseachadh *m* nan arm *mpl gen*/nam ball-airm *mpl gen*

skill *n* sgil *m*

skin *n* **1** (*of creatures, humans*) craiceann *m*; **2** (*hide of bovine &c*) seiche *f*, bian *m*, *in expr* **calf** ~ laoighcionn *m*; **3** (*of fruit, vegetables*) plaosg *m*, rùsg *m*

skin *v* **1** (*fruit, vegetables*) rùisg *vt*, plaoisg *vt*; **2** (*animals*) thoir an craiceann *m* (*with prep* de); **3** (*graze &c*) rùisg, **I ~ned my hand** rùisg mi mo làmh *f*; **4** (*peat-bank*) feann *vt*

skinny *adj* **1** (*thin*) caol, tana, seang; **2** (*mean*) spìocach, mosach

skip *n* leum *m*, sùrdag *f*

skip *v* **1** (*small jump*) leum *vi*, dèan sùrdag *f*; **2** (*with rope*) sgiobaig *vi*; **3** (*omit*) rach *vi irreg* thairis (*with prep* air), **we'll ~ the last question** thèid sinn thairis air a' cheist *f* mu dheireadh

skipper *n* (*of boat &c*) sgiobair *m*, caiptean *m*

skipping *n* (*with rope*) sgiobaigeadh *m*

skirt *n* sgiort *f*

skittish *adj* **1** guanach, luaineach, tuainealach, *in expr* ~ **girl** guanag *f*; **2** (*horse &c: mettlesome*) clisgeach, sgeunach

skivvy *n* sgalag *f*

skull *n* claigeann *m*

sky *n* speur *m*, adhar *m*, iarmailt *f*, **up in the** ~ shuas san speur/sna speuran *mpl*/san adhar

skylark *n* uiseag *f*, (*less usu*) topag *f*

slab *n* **1** (*of stone, rock*) leac *f*, *in exp* **slab-like** leacach; **2** (~ *of cake &c*) sgonn *m*

slacken *v* (*fastenings &c*) fuasgail *vt*, lasaich *vt*

slander *n* cùl-chàineadh *m*

slander *v* cùl-chàin *vt*, càin *vt*

slanderous *adj* cùl-chainnteach

slant *n* fiaradh *m*, claonadh *m*, **at a** ~ air fhiaradh

slanting *adj* air fhiaradh, fiar

slap *n* sgailc *f*, sgealp *f*, sgleog *f*

slap *v* sgealp *vt*

slate *n* sglèat *m*

slaughter *n* casgairt *f invar*

slaughter *v* casgair *vt*

slaughterhouse *n* taigh-spadaidh *m*

slave *n* tràill *mf*

slaver *n* ronn *m*, seile *m invar*

slavery *n* tràilleachd *f invar*, tràillealachd *f invar*

slay *v* casgair *vt*, mort *&* murt *vt*, marbh *vt*

sledge *n* slaodan *m*

sleek *adj* slìom

sleep *n* **1** cadal *m*, (*light* ~) dùsal *m*, (*usu deeper*) suain *m*, **go to** ~! thall' a chadal!, dèan cadal!, **peaceful** ~ cadal sàmhach/sèimh, **I didn't get a wink of** ~ cha d'fhuair mi (fiù is) norrag *f* chadail *gen*; **2** *in expr* **sing/ rock to** ~ tàlaidh *vt*

sleep *v* **1** dèan cadal *m*, caidil *vi*, ~ **now/go to sleep now!** dèan cadal a-nis!, thall' a chadal a-nis!, ~ **well!** caidil gu math!; **2** (*be asleep*) bi *vi irreg* na (*&c*) c(h)adal *m*, **we were ~ing** bha sinn nar cadal

sleeping-bag *n* poca *m* cadail *m gen*

sleepless *adj* gun chadal *m*, **a ~ night** oidhche *f* gun chadal

sleepy *adj* **1** cadalach, **a ~ child** pàiste cadalach; **2** *in expr* **I'm** (*&c*) ~ tha an cadal orm (*&c*), *also* tha mi cadalach

sleet *n* flin *&* flinne *m invar*

sleeve *n* muinchill, muinichill *&* muil(i)cheann *m*, **he rolled up his ~s** thruis e a mhuilcheannan

sleigh *n* slaodan *m*

slender *adj* caol, seang

slice *n* (~ *cut from something; also kitchen tool*) sliseag *f*, **fish-~** sliseag-èisg *f*

slide *n* (*in playpark &c, or made on ice*) sleamhnag *f*, sleamhnan *m*

slide *v* (*on slippery surface*) sleamhnaich *vi*

slight *adj* **1** beag, **a ~ cold** cnatan beag, **a ~ mist on the hill** ceò beag air a' mhonadh *m*; **2** (*of person: ~ in build*) beag, tana; **3** (*of little value or merit*) aotrom, (*more pej*) suarach

slight *v* cuir *vt* an suarachas *m*, cuir *vt* air dìmeas *m invar*, cuir *vt* air bheag sùim *f*, dèan dìmeas (*with prep* air)

slightly *adv* beagan, **she left ~ early** dh'fhalbh i beagan ron àm *m*, **it was raining ~** bha beagan uisge *m gen* ann

slim *adj* caol, tana, seang

slim *v* seangaich *vt*, *in expr* **I had to ~** b' fheudar dhomh cudthrom *m* a chall

slime *n* clàbar *m*

slimming *n* seangachadh *m*, call *m* cudthruim *m gen*

slink *v* èalaidh *vi*, siolp *vi*, ~ **off home** èalaidh/siolp dhachaigh, ~ **away** èalaidh/siolp air falbh

slip *n* **1** (*stumble &c*) tuisleadh *m*; **2** (*error*) mearachd *f*, (*less usu*) iomrall *m*; **3** *in expr* ~ **of the tongue** tapag *f*

slip *v* **1** (*stumble*) tuislich *vi*, (*esp on slippery surface*) sleamhnaich *vi*; **2** (*surreptitious movement*) siolp *vi*, èalaidh *vi*, ~ **inside/away** siolp a-steach/air falbh, ~ **off home** èalaidh dhachaigh *adv*; **3** *in expr* **it ~ped my mind** chaidh e às mo chuimhne *f invar*

slipped *adj & past part, in expr* ~ **disc** clàr *m* sgiorrte

slipper *n* slapag *f*

slippery *adj* **1** (*lit*) sleamhainn; **2** (*fig: of person*) carach, fiar

slipshod *adj* (*of workmanship &c*) dearmadach, coma co-dhiù

slippy *adj* sleamhainn

slip-up *n* mearachd *f*

slit *n* sgoltadh *m*

slit *v* sgoilt *&* sgolt *vt*

sliver *n* sgealbag *f*

slogan *n* sluagh-ghairm *f*

slop *v* dòirt *vt*

slope *n* 1 claonadh *m*; 2 (*topog: hill~*) leathad *m*, bruthach *mf*, aodann *m*

slope *v* 1 claon *vti*; 2 (*fam*) ~ **off** èalaidh *vi* air falbh

sloping *adj* claon

sloppy *adj* 1 (*food &c*) tana, ~ **porridge** brochan tana; 2 (*of workmanship &c: careless*) dearmadach, coma co-dhiù; 3 (*in appearance*) cearbach, luideach, robach

slosh *v* (*sound*) plubraich *vi*, plub *vi*

sloth *n* leisg(e) *f*

slothful *adj* leisg, dìomhain

slovenly *adj* luideach, rapach, robach

slow *adj* mall, slaodach, màirnealach

slow, slow down *v* 1 (*go/become slower*) rach *vi irreg* am maille *f invar*; 2 (*make slower*) cuir maille *f invar* (*with prep* air *or* ann)

slowness *n* maille *f invar*

slow-witted *adj* mall na (*&c*) inntinn *f*, (*fam, pej*) tiugh

sludge *n* eabar *m*, poll *m*

slug *n* 1 (*the creature*) seilcheag *f*; 2 (*fam: bullet*) peilear *m*

sluggish *adj* slaodach

slum *n* slum(a) *m*

slumber *n* suain *f*, cadal *m*

slurry *n* giodar *m*

slut *n* (*slatternly woman*) luid *f*, breunag *f*

sly *adj* carach, fiar

smack *n* sgailc *f*, sgealp *f*

smack *v* sgealp *vt*

small *adj* 1 beag, mion- *prefix* (*lenites following cons where possible*), (*very ~*) meanbh, ~ **girl** caileag bheag, ~ **salary** tuarastal beag, ~ **town** baile beag, **cut up** ~ mion-gheàrr *vt*, **theft on a** ~ **scale** mion-bhraide *f*; 2 *in exprs* ~ **change** airgead pronn *m*, ~ **intestine** caolan *m*

smart *adj* 1 (*in dress, appearance &c*) grinn, cuimir, snasail; 2 (*mentally ~*) geur/luath na (*&c*) inntinn *f*, eirmseach, geur-chùiseach, toinisgeil

smash *v* smuais *vt*, smùid *vt*, spealg *vt*, bris *vt* na (*&c*) spealgan *fpl*

smashed *adj & past part* 1 smuaiste, briste, na (*&c*) spealgan *fpl*; 2 (*fam: drunk*) air a (*&c*) p(h)ronnadh, **I was** ~ bha mi air mo phronnadh, *also* bha smùid (mhòr) orm

smashing *adj* (*fam: great, excellent &c*) sgoinneil, taghta, **that's** ~! tha sin sgoinneil/taghta!, (*as excl*) ~! taghta!, *also* math dha-rìribh!

smear *v* smiùr *vt*, smeur *vt*

smell *n* (*pleasant or unpleasant*) àile(adh) & fàile(adh) *m*, boladh *m*, (*usu pleasant*) boltrach *m*, (*bad or foul*) tòchd *m invar*, **it had a bad** ~ bha droch àile (a' tighinn) dheth

smell *v* 1 (*as vt*) fairich *vt*, feuch *vt*, **can you** ~ **the peat reekt?** am fairich thu/am feuch thu ceò *m* na mòna?; **2** (*as vi*) **it ~s** tha fàileadh *m* (a' tighinn) dheth

smiddy *n* ceàrdach *f*

smile *n* faite-gàire *f*, fiamh-ghàire & fiamh a' ghàire *m*, snodha-gàire *m*, (*sly* ~) mìog *f*

smile *v* dèan faite-gàire *f*, dèan fiamh-ghàire *or* fiamh a' ghàire *m*, dèan snodha-gàire *m*

smirk *n* mìog *f*

smite *v* buail *vt*

smith *n* **1** ceàrd & ceàrd *m*, **silver~** ceàrd-airgid *m*, **copper~** ceàrd-copair *m*; **2** (*black~*) gobha *m*

smithy *n* ceàrdach *f*

smoke *n* smùid *f*, ceò *m*, (*usu lighter*) toit *f*, **emit/give out** ~ cuir smùid, **peat** ~ ceò na mòna

smoke *v* **1** (*fire &c*) cuir smùid *f*, smùid *vi*, **the fire's smoking** tha an teine a' cur smùide *gen*; **2** (~ *tobacco*) smoc *vti*, **do you ~?** am bi thu a' smocadh?

smoking *n* (*of cigarettes &c*) smocadh *m*, **no ~**, **~ not allowed** chan fhaodar (*pres habitual passive of* faod *vi def*) smocadh *m*

smoky *adj* ceòthach, toiteach

smooth *adj* (*surface &c*) mìn, rèidh

smoothe *v* dèan *vt* rèidh, dèan *vt* mìn

smoothly *adv, in exprs* **the day passed** ~ chaidh an latha *m* seachad gu socair, *in expr* **we get on/along** ~ **with them** tha sinn rèidh riutha

smother (*fire, person, dissent &c*) mùch *vt*, tùch *vt*, (*person*) tachd *vt*, (*esp fire*) smà(i)l *vt*

smoulder *v* cnàmh-loisg *vi*

smudge *n* smàl *m*

smudge *v* smeur *vt*

smug *adj* toilichte leis (*&c*) fhèin/fhìn, **he says we're** ~ tha e ag ràdh gu bheil sinn toilichte leinn fhìn

smuggler *n* cùl-mhùtaire *m*

smuggling *n* cùl-mhùtaireachd *f invar*

smut *n* **1** (*small dirty mark*) smal *m*, spot *m*; **2** (*suggestive talk*) drabastachd *f invar*, draostachd *f invar*, rabhd *m*

smutty *adj* (*suggestive*) drabasta, draosta

snack *n* srùbag *f*, pìos *m*

snag *n* duilgheadas *m*

snail *n* seilcheag *f*

snake *n* nathair *f*

snappy *adj* **1** (*short-tempered: of people*) aithghearr, cas, (*of dogs & people*) dranndanach; **2** (*of action &c: brisk, prompt*) deas, aithghearr

snare *n* ribe *m*

snarl *v* dèan dranndan *m*, **the dog ~ed** rinn an cù dranndan, *in expr* **apt to** ~ dranndanach

snarl, snarling *n* dranndan *m*, dranndail *f invar*

snatch *v* glac *vt*, beir *vi irreg* (*with prep* air)

sneak *v* èalaidh *vi*, snàig *vi*, siolp *vi*, ~ **off home** èalaidh dhachaigh

sneer *v* dèan fanaid *f* (**at** air)

sneering *n* fanaid *f* (**at** air)

sneeze *n* sreothart *m*

sneeze *v* dèan sreothart *m*

sneezing, sneezing fit *n* sreothartaich *f*

sniff *n* boladh *m* (**at/of** de), **a ~ at/of the cooking pot** boladh den phrais *f*

sniff *v* **1** (*flower &c*) gabh boladh *m* (*with prep* de); **2** *in expr* ~ **at** (*look down on*) dèan tàir *f* (*with prep* air)

snivel *v* smùch *vi*

snooze *n* dùsal *m*, norrag *f*, norrag chadail *f gen*, **take/have a ~** dèan dùsal/norrag

snooze *v* dèan dùsal *m*, gabh norrag *f*

snore *n* srann *f*

snore *v* srann *vi*

snoring *n* srannail *f*, **what a lot of ~ you were doing last night!** dè an t-srannail a bha ort an raoir!

snout *n* soc *m*

snow *n* sneachd *m*

snow *v* cuir (sneachd *m*), **it's ~ing** tha e a' cur (an t-sneachda)

snowdrift *n* cathadh *m*

snowflake *n* bleideag *f* (shneachda *m gen*), pleòdag *f*

snowman *n* bodach-sneachda *m*

snowplough *n* crann-sneachda *m*

snub *v* cuir a (*&c*) c(h)ùl (*with prep* ri), **they ~bed us** chuir iad an cùl rinn

snug *adj* seasgair

so *adv* **1** (*before an adj*) cho, **he was ~ busy!** bha e cho trang!, **I'm not ~ good today** chan eil mi cho math an-diugh, **I'm not ~ young as I was** chan eil mi cho òg agus a bha mi; **2** ~ **many/much** (na h-) uimhir *f invar*, **there were ~ many people there** bha na h-uimhir de dhaoine *mpl* ann, **I had ~ much money** bha uimhir de dh'airgead *m* agam; **3** *in exprs* **and ~ on** 's mar sin (air adhart), **apples, pears, cherries and ~ on** ùbhlan *mpl*, peuran *fpl*, siristean *fpl* 's mar sin, *also* 's a leithid sin, **she said we were lazy, rude, scruffy . . . and ~ on, and ~ on** thuirt i gu robh sinn leisg, mì-mhodhail, luideach . . . 's mar sin air adhart, ~ **far** chun a seo, gu ruige seo, **it hasn't happened ~ far** cha do thachair e chun a seo/gu ruige seo, **you didn't do it! I did ~!** cha do rinn thu e! rinn gu dearbh!, (*excl expr agreement*) **just ~!** direach!, *also* dìreach sin!

so *conj* **1** (*therefore*) mar sin, **I'm tired (and) ~ I'm leaving** tha mi sgìth 's mar sin tha mi a' falbh; **2** (*in order that*) gus an/am, (*neg*) gus nach, airson, (*neg*) airson nach, ~ **(that) he would have some pocket money** gus am biodh airgead-pòcaid *m* aige, ~ **(that) you can find the house** gus an urrainn dhut an taigh a lorg, ~ **(that) she wouldn't be hungry**

gus/airson nach biodh an t-acras oirre, (*in order that, also with the result that*) air dhòigh is, air chor is, (*with conjs* gu, nach), ~ **(that) I wouldn't be impolite** air dhòigh 's nach bithinn mì-mhodhail, **he shut the door ~ (that) I wouldn't get in** dhùin e an doras air dhòigh is/air chor is nach fhaighinn a-steach, **he spoke in a low voice ~ (that) I didn't hear him** bhruidhinn e ann an guth *m* ìosal air dhòigh 's nach cuala mi e

so *pron* **1** (*rendered by repetition of v of foregoing sentence*) **did he wash his hands? I think ~** an do nigh e a làmhan *fpl*? saoilidh mi gun do nigh, **is it gold? I don't think ~** an e òr a th' ann? cha chreid mi gur e

soak *v* **1** drùidh *vi* (*with prep* air), fliuch *vt* (chun na seiche), **the rain ~ed me (to the skin)** dhrùidh an t-uisge orm, **he got ~ed to the skin** chaidh a fhliuch(d)adh chun na seice; **2** (*steep washing &c*) cuir *vt* am bogadh *m*, **she put some clothes to ~** chuir i aodach *m sing coll* am bogadh; **3** *in expr* ~ **up** sùigh & sùgh *vt*, **my coat ~ed up the rain** shùigh mo chòta *m* an t-uisge

soaked, soaking *adj* bog fliuch

soap *n* siabann *m*

soapy *adj* siabannach

sob *n* glug *m* caoinidh *m*

sober *adj* **1** measarra, stuama, stòlda; **2** (*not drunk*) sòbair, stuama

sobriety *n* stuaim *f invar*

soccer *n* ball-coise *m*

sociability *n* conaltradh *m*

sociable *adj* cuideachdail, conaltrach, cèilidheach

social *adj* **1** (*of person*) conaltrach; **2** (*pertaining to society*) sòisealta, ~ **security** tèarainteachd shòisealta, ~ **work** obair shòisealta

socialism *n* sòisealachd *f invar*

socialist *adj* sòisealach

socialist *n* sòisealach *m*

society *n* **1** (*the social community*) comann-sòisealta *m*, sòisealtas *m*, **he turned his back on ~** chuir e a chùl *m* ris a' chomann-sòisealta/ri sòisealtas; **2** (*company*) cuideachd *f*, **he likes the ~ of young people** is toigh leis cuideachd na h-òigridh; **3** (*club, organisation &c*) comann *m*, **The Gaelic Society of Inverness** Comann Gàidhlig Inbhir Nis, **building ~** comann-togalaich *m*

sock *n* socais *f*

socket *n* (*electric*) bun-dealain *m*

sod *n* **1** fòid & fòd *f*, fàl *m*; **2** (*coll*) fòid *f*, **when I'm beneath the ~** nuair a bhios mi fon fhòid *dat*

sod *v* (*swear*) ~ **the lot of them!** taigh *m* na galla dhaibh uile!

sofa *n* langasaid *f*

soft *adj* **1** (*to the touch*) mìn, bog, ~ **material** stuth mìn/bog, (*of book*) ~ **cover** còmhdach bog; **2** (*of character*) bog, maoth; **3** *in expr* ~ **drink** deoch *f* lag

soften *v* maothaich *vti*, bogaich *vti*

software *n* (*IT*) bathar bog, ~ **development** leasachadh *m* bathair buig *gen*

soggy *adj* bog fliuch

soil *n* talamh *m* (*f in gen sing*), ùir *f*

soil *v* salaich *vt*

solace *n* furtachd *f invar*, sòlas *m*, (**for** air), ~ **for his anguish** furtachd air a dhòrainn *f*, *in expr* **bring** ~ furtaich *vi* (*with prep* air), **we will bring you** ~ furtaichidh sinn oirbh

solar *adj* (na) grèine (*gen of* grian *f*), **the Solar System** Rian *m* na Grèine, An Coras-grèine

solder *v* tàth *vt*

soldering iron *n* iarrann *m* tàthaidh *m gen*

soldier *n* saighdear *m*

sole *n* bonn *m*, ~ **of the foot/of the shoe** bonn na coise/na bròige (*gen of* cas *f &* bròg *f*)

solemn *adj* sòlaimte

solicitor *n* neach-lagha *m*, (*male*) fear-lagha *m*, (*female*) bean-lagha *f*, ~**s** luchd-lagha *m sing coll*

solicitude *n* iomagain *f*, imnidh *&* iomnaidh *f*

solid *adj* 1 cruaidh, ~ **fuel** connadh cruaidh; 2 (*sound, durable*) teann, daingeann, ~ **foundation** bunait theann/dhaingeann, ~ **structure** structar daingeann; 2 (*more fig; well-founded, reliable*) tàbhachdach, **a** ~ **business** gnìomhachas tàbhachdach

solidify *v* cruadhaich *vti*

solitary *adj* (*place, person*) uaigneach, aonaranach

solitude *n* uaigneas *m*, aonaranachd *f invar*

soluble *adj* so-leaghte

solution *n* 1 (*in liquid*) leaghadh *m*, eadar-sgaoileadh *m*; 2 (~ *to problem &c*) fuasgladh *m*

solve *v* (*problem, difficulty &c*) fuasgail *vt*, ~ **a crossword** fuasgail tòimhseachan-tarsainn *m*

some *adj* 1 (*not always rendered in Gaelic*) **give me** ~ **money** thoir dhomh airgead *m*, **I could do with** ~ **peace** b' fheàirrde mi sìth *f*; 2 (*a certain amount*) deannan (*with gen*), **he has a nice house and** ~ **money** tha taigh snog agus deannan airgid *m gen* aige; 3 *in expr* ~ **people** feadhainn *f sing coll*, cuid *f sing coll*, ~ **people are in favour, others are against** tha feadhainn/cuid air a shon, tha feadhainn eile/cuid eile na aghaidh

some *pron* (*people*) feadhainn *f sing coll*, cuid *f sing coll*, ~ **are in favour,** ~ **are against** tha feadhainn/cuid air a shon, tha feadhainn eile/cuid eile na aghaidh

some- *prefix* –eigin (*suffix*), *see* **somebody, someday, someone, something, sometime, somewhere**

somebody, someone *pron* cuideigin *mf invar*, duine *m*, ~**'s come in** tha cuideigin air tighinn a-steach, **is there** ~ **there/in?** a bheil duine ann?

someday *adv* latheigin *m invar & adv*

someone *pron see* **somebody**

somersault *n* car *m* a' mhuiltein

something *pron* rudeigin *m invar & pron*, (*less usu*) nitheigin *m invar*, **is ~ wrong?** a bheil rudeigin ceàrr?

sometimes *adv* uaireannan *adv*, air uairean *fpl*, **~ I'm sad, ~ I'm cheerful** uaireannan bidh mi muladach, uaireannan eile bidh mi sunndach

somewhat *adv* rudeigin, rud beag, car, **she was ~ depressed** bha i rudeigin/rud beag sìos na h-inntinn *f*, bha i rudeigin/rud beag ìseal, **~ tired** rud beag/car/rudeigin sgìth

somewhere *adv* ann an àiteigin *m invar*, **I lost it ~** chaill mi ann an àiteigin e

somnolent *adj* cadalach

son *n* mac *m*, **they have two ~s** tha dithis mhac *mpl gen* aca, **the prodigal ~** am mac stròdhail/struidheil

song *n* òran (*in some areas* amhran) *m*, (*less usu*) luinneag *f*, duanag *f*, **sing a ~!** gabh òran!, **waulking ~** òran luadhaidh/luaidh *m gen*

son-in-law *n* cliamhainn *m*

sonorous *adj* ath-fhuaimneach

soon *adv* **1** (*in a short time*) a dh'aithghearr, ann an ùine ghoirid, ann am beagan ùine, **we'll be there ~** bidh sinn ann a dh'aithghearr, **it was ~ finished/over** bha e seachad ann an ùine ghoirid/ann am beagan ùine, **they were ~ lost** ann am/an dèidh beagan ùine bha iad air chall, *also* cha b' fhada gus an robh iad air chall; **2** (*before the usual, set or expected time*) tràth, **we didn't expect you so ~** cha robh dùil *f* againn riut cho tràth, **it's too ~ for ripe apples** tha e ro thràth airson ùbhlan *mpl* abaich; **3** *in expr* **as ~ as** cho luath 's/is/agus (*with conj* a), **as ~ as he arrived the noise stopped** cho luath 's/agus a thàinig e sguir am fuaim *mf*

sooner *adv* **1** nas tràithe (*in past & conditional tenses* na bu tràithe; **2** *in expr* **~ or later** luath no mall, **~ or later that wall will fall down** luath no mall tuitidh am balla sin

soot *n* sùith(e) *m*

soothe *v* ciùinich *vt*, tàlaidh *vt*, (*esp suffering*) faothaich *vt*

soothsayer *n* fiosaiche *m*

sorcerer, sorceress *n* draoidh *m*, ban-draoidh *f*

sorcery *n* draoidheachd *f invar*

sordid *adj* **1** (*morally*) suarach, truaillidh, coirbte; **2** (*phys*) dràbhail, salach, grod, mosach

sore *adj* goirt, **a ~ head** ceann goirt, **my back's ~** tha mo dhruim *m* goirt, **a ~ trial** deuchainn ghoirt

sorrow *adj* bròn *m*, mulad *f*, (*less usu*) tùirse & tùrsa *f invar*

sorrowful *adj* brònach, muladach, tùrsach

sorry *adj* **1** duilich, **I'm ~!** tha mi duilich!, **I'm ~ for myself** tha mi duilich air mo shon fhìn, *also* (*more trad*) tha truas *m* agam rium fhìn; **2** (*causing* *sympathy, regret &c*) truagh, **it was a ~ affair** 's e rud/gnothach truagh a bh' ann; **3** (*unsatisfactory, paltry*) suarach, **a ~ excuse** leisgeul suarach

sort *n* **1** seòrsa *m*, (*less usu*) gnè *f invar*, **all ~s of things** rudan *mpl* de gach seòrsa, **a book of that ~** leabhar *m* den t-seòrsa sin; **2** *in expr* **out of ~s** (*ie grouchy &c*) diombach & diumbach, (*usu of child*) crost(a)

sort *v* **1** (*classify; also ~ post*) seòrsaich *vt*; **2** (*arrange, order, ~ out*) cuir *vt* an òrdugh *m*, òrdaich *vt*, cuir *vt* air dòigh *f*; **3** (*objects: put right, mend*) càirich *vt*, cuir *vt* air ghleus *mf*; **4** (*resolve/~ out situations, relationships &c*) rèitich *vt*; **5** (*tidy*) càirich *vt*, sgioblaich, rèitich *vt*, **~ your bed!** càirich do leabaidh *f!*, **~ your room!**, sgioblaich an rùm *m* agad!

so-so *adj* ach meadhanach (*after verb in neg*), **I'm only ~ today** chan eil mi ach meadhanach an-diugh, **the food was only ~** cha robh am biadh ach meadhanach

soul *n* **1** anam *m*, **body and ~** corp *m* is anam; **2** *in expr* **a (living) ~** duine beò, **there wasn't a (living) ~ on the road** cha robh duine beò air an rathad; **3** (*fam: usu expr sympathy*) creutair *m*, **the poor ~!** an creutair bochd!

sound *adj* **1** (*of persons: ~ in health*) fallain, **safe and ~** slàn is fallain; **2** (*of organisations &c: secure, trustworthy*) tàbhachdach, urrasach, **a ~ business** gnìomhachas tàbhachdach/urrasach; **3** (*of judgement &c: reliable*) earbsach

sound *n* **1** fuaim *mf*, **the ~ of the traffic** fuaim na trafaig, **~ wave** fuaim-thonn *mf*; **2** (*much quieter: usu in neg exprs*) bìd *f*, bìog *f*, **he can't hear a ~** cha chluinn e bìd/bìog, **he didn't utter a ~** cha tuirt e bìd/bìog

soup *n* brot *m*, (*trad*) eanraich *f*

sour *adj* goirt, searbh, geur, **~ milk** bainne goirt

source *n* bun *m*, tùs *m*, **the ~ of evil** bun an uilc (*gen of* olc *m*), (*prov*) **the fear of God is the ~ of (all) wisdom** 's e tùs a' ghliocais eagal *m* Dhè (*gen of* Dia *m*)

south *n & adj* **1** deas *f invar & adj*, **South Uist** Uibhist a Deas, **the South Pole** Am Pòla a Deas, **the ~ of the country** an taobh deas den dùthaich *f*, taobh a deas na dùthcha, **living in/going to the ~** a' fuireach/a' dol mu dheas, **the islands in the ~** na h-eileanan *mpl* mu dheas, **a breeze from the ~** oiteag *f* on deas, **Kinross is ~ of Perth** tha Ceann Rois deas air Peairt; **2** (*the compass direction*) **~** an àird(e) deas

southerly *adj* mu dheas, **~ islands** eileanan *mpl* mu dheas, **he went in a ~ direction** chaidh e mu dheas

southern *adj* deas, mu dheas, **the ~ part of the country** taobh a deas na dùthcha, **in the ~ corner of a wood** anns a' chùil *m* mu dheas de choille *f*, **the ~ isles** na h-eileanan *mpl* mu dheas

southerner *n* deasach *m*

souvenir *n* cuimhneachan *m*

sovereign *n* rìgh *m*

sow *n* cràin *f*, muc *f*

sow *v* **1** (*seed*) cuir *vt*; **2** (~ *dissent, doubt &c*) sgaoil *vt*

sowing *n* **1** (*of seed &c*) cur *m*; **2** (*of dissent, doubt &c*) sgaoileadh *m*

space *n* **1** (*room*) rùm *m*, **there was no ~ in the boat** cha robh rùm sa bhàta *m*; **2** (*opening, gap &c*) beàrn *f*, **a small ~ in the wall** beàrn bheag sa bhalla *m*; **3** (*extra-terrestrial ~*) fànas *m*, **the ~ age** linn *mf* an fhànais, an linn-fànais *mf*

spacecraft, spaceship *n* soitheach-fànais *m*, speur-shoitheach *m*

spacious *adj* rùmail

spade *n* spaid *f*, (*more trad*) caibe *m*

spanner *n* spanair *m*

spar *n* (*joinery &c*) rong *f*, rongas *m*

spare *adj* **1** saor, **~ time** ùine shaor, *also* saor-ùine *f*; **2** (*surplus*) a bharrachd, **~ money** airgead *m* a bharrachd; **3** *in expr* (*machinery &c*) **~ parts**, **~s** pàirtean-càraidh *mfpl*

spare *v* **1** (*from punishment &c*) dèan iochd *f invar* (*with prep* ri), leig *vt* mu sgaoil, fuasgail *vt*, **the emperor ~ed her** rinn an t-ìompaire iochd rithe; **2** *in expr* **if I'm ~d** ma bhios mi air mo chaomhnadh, ma mhaireas (*rel fut of* mair *vi*) mi beò, **I'll see you tomorow, if I'm ~ed** chì mi a-màireach thu, ma bhios mi air mo chaomhnadh

spark *n* **1** sradag *f*, **give off ~s** leig sradagan; **2** (~ *of life, vital* ~) rong *m*, **there's not a ~ of life in her** chan eil rong innte

sparkle *n* drithleann *m*, lainnir *f*

sparkle *v* lainnrich *vi*

sparkling *adj* lainnireach

sparrow *n* gealbhonn *m*

sparse *adj* gann, tana, **~ crop** bàrr gann, **~ hair** falt tana

speak *v* **1** bruidhinn *vti*, (*less usu*) labhair *vi*, (**to** ri), **~ to him** bruidhinn ris, **~ing Gaelic** a' bruidhinn (na) Gàidhlig, **~ing in Gaelic** a' bruidhinn sa Ghàidhlig, *in expr* (*idiom*) **~ing with one voice** a' bruidhinn às beul *m* a chèile; **2** *in expr* **I ~ Gaelic/English** (*&c*) tha Gàidhlig/Beurla (*&c*) agam; **3** (*address*) thoir *vt irreg* seachad òraid *f* (*with prep* do), **tomorrow I'm ~ing to the local history society** a-màireach bidh mi a' toirt seachad òraid *f* don chomann *m* eachdraidh *f* ionadail; **4** *in expr* **broadly/generally ~ing** san fharsaingeachd *f invar*, **broadly/generally ~ing, the roads are good** san fharsaingeachd, tha na rathaidean *mpl* math

speaker *n* **1** (*lecturer &c*) òraidiche *m*, neach-labhairt *m*; **2** *in expr* **native ~** (*of a lang*) fileantach *m*, **the native ~s' class** clas *m* nam fileantach; **3** (*office in parliament*) Labhraiche *m*

spear *n* gath *m*, sleagh *f*

special *adj* àraidh, sònraichte, air leth, **it's a ~ place to/for me** 's e àite *m* àraidh/sònraichte/air leth a th' ann dhomh(sa), **a ~ bottle of wine** botal *m* air leth de fhìon *m*

specialist *n* spèisealaiche *m*

species *n* (*biol*) gnè *f invar*, cineal *m*, seòrsa *m*

specific *adj* àraidh, sònraichte, **it's a ~ car that I'm looking for** is e càr *m* àraidh/sònraichte a tha mi a' sireadh

specifically *adv* a dh'aon ghnothach *m*, a dh'aon rùn *m*, **I wrote the letter ~ to bring the matter to an end** sgrìobh mi an litir *f* a dh'aon ghnothach/ a dh'aon rùn gus/airson a' chùis a thoirt gu ceann *m*

specify *v* sònraich *vt*, comharraich *vt*

specimen *n* sampall *m*

speck *n* smal *m*

speckled *adj* ballach, breac

spectacle *n* sealladh *m*

spectacles *npl* speuclairean *mpl*, glainneachan *fpl*

spectator *n* neach-coimhid *m* (*pl* luchd-coimhid *m sing coll*)

spectre *n* bòcan *m*, taibhse *mf*

speculate *v* **1** (*mentally*) beachdaich *vi* (**about** air); **2** (*fin*) dèan tuairmeas *m* (**on** air)

speculation *n* **1** (*mental*) beachdachadh *m*; **2** (*fin*) tuairmeas *m*

speculative *adj* **1** (*mentally*) beachdachail, baralach; **2** (*fin*) tuairmseach

speech *n* **1** (*in general & abstr sense*) cainnt *f*, labhairt *f invar*, **the faculty of ~** comas *m* cainnte/labhairt *gen*; **2** (*talk, oration*) òraid *f*, **give/make a ~** thoir seachad òraid, dèan òraid; **3** (*lang, gram*) còmhradh *m*, **indirect ~** còmhradh neo-dhìreach

speechless *adj* balbh, (*stronger*) bog balbh

speed *n* **1** luas *m*, luath(a)s *mf*, (*esp of vehicles*) astar *m*, **~ limit** crìoch *f* astair *gen*, **at an incalculable ~** aig astar gun tomhas *m*, **an insane ~** astar gun chiall *f*, **they were going at a good ~** bha astar math aca; **2** (*esp of persons: haste*) deann *f*, (*stronger*) deann-ruith & dian-ruith *f*, **he left at (great) ~** dh'fhalbh e na dheann, **he left at full ~** dh'fhalbh e na dhian-ruith, *also* (*more fam*) dh'fhalbh e aig peilear *m* a bheatha; **3** *in expr* **put on ~** luathaich *vi*

speed *v* **1** dràibhig *vi* ro luath/aig astar *m* ro mhòr; **2** *in expr* **~ up** luathaich *vi*

speedy *adj* luath, cabhagach, (*esp vehicles*) astarach

spell[1] *n* (*enchantment*) geas *f*, seun *m*, ortha *f*, **under a ~** fo gheasaibh (*obs dat pl of geas*)

spell[2] *n* **1** (*of time*) greis *f*, **a ~ of unemployment** greis gun obair *f*, **we were in Skye for a ~** bha sinn greis san Eilean *m* Sgitheanach, bha sinn san Eilean Sgitheanach airson/fad greis, **a ~ at/with the scythe** greis air an speal *f*, **sunny ~** greis ghrèine (*gen of* grian *f*); **2** *in expr* (*esp after prolonged wet weather*) **dry ~** turadh *m*, **what a good dry ~!** is math an turadh (e)!

spell *v* litrich *vt*

spellbound *adj & past part* fo gheasaibh (*obs dat pl of* geas *f: with gen*), **~ by her beauty** fo gheasaibh a bòidhcheid (*gen of* bòidhchead *f*)

spelling *n* litreachadh *m*

spend *v* **1** (*money*) cosg *vt*, caith *vt*; **2** (*time*) cuir *vt* seachad, (*less usu*) caith *vt*, **I spent the holidays in the States** chuir mi seachad na saor-làithean *mpl* sna Stàitean *fpl* (Aonaichte)

spendthrift *adj* caith(t)each, struidheil & stròdhail

spendthrift *n* struidhear *m*

sperm *n* sìol(-ginidh) *m*, *in expr* ~ **cell** cealla-sìl *f*

spew *v* cuir *vti* a-mach, sgeith *vi*, (*fam/vulg*) **I ~ed my guts up** chuir mi a-mach rùchd *m* mo chaolanan *mpl gen*

sphere *n* cruinne *mf*

spherical *adj* cruinn

spice *n* spìosradh *m*

spice *v* (*lit*) spìosraich *vt*, (*lit & fig*) ~ **(up)** piobraich *vt*

spicy *adj* spìosrach

spider *n* damhan-allaidh *m*

spike *n* spìc *f*, bior *m*

spill *v* dòirt *vti*, ~ **blood** doirt fuil *f*

spin *n* **1** (*revolution*) car *m*, **give the wheel a** ~ cuir car den chuibhle *f*; **2** (*drive &c*) cuairt (bheag), **we'll go for a** ~ **in the car** gabhaidh sinn cuairt (bheag) sa chàr *m*

spin *v* cuir car *m* (*with prep* de), ~ **the propeller** cuir car den phropailear *m*

spine *n* **1** (*backbone*) **(the)** ~ cnà(i)mh *m* (an) droma; **2** (*on thistle &c*) bior *m*

spinster *n* boireannach *m* gun phòsadh *m*, (*esp elderly* ~: *fam*) seana-mhaighdeann *f*

spirit *n* **1** (*relig*) spiorad *m*, **the Holy Spirit** An Spiorad Naomh; **2** (*ghostly* ~) taibhse *f*; **3** (*courage &c*) misneach *f*, misneachd *f invar*, smior *m*; **4** (*alcoholic*) ~**s** deoch *f* làidir

spirited *adj* misneachail, smiorail/smearail

spiritual *adj* (*relig*) spioradail, ~ **songs** dàin *mpl* spioradail

spirituality *n* spioradalachd *f invar*

spirtle *n* maide *m* poite *f gen*

spit[1] *n* (*saliva &c*) smugaid *f*

spit[2] *n* (*for cooking*) bior-ròstaidh *m*

spit *v* tilg smugaid *f*

spite *n* gamhlas *m*, tarcais *f*, tailceas *m*

spite *v* dèan tarcais *f* (*with prep* air)

spiteful *adj* gamhlasach, tarcaiseach, tailceasach

spittle *n* smugaid *f*

splash *n* plubraich *f*, plub *m*, **make a** ~ dèan plubraich

splash *v* plubraich *vi*, dèan plubraich *f*, plub *vi*

splendid *adj* gasta & gasda, greadhnach, àlainn, **the soldiers looked** ~ bha na saighdearan a' coimhead gasta, **that was** ~! bha sin gasta/àlainn!, *also* bha sin math dha-rìribh

splendour *n* greadhnachas *m*

split *adj & past part* **1** sgoilte; **2** *in expr* (*fam*) ~ **new** ùr-nodha

split *n* sgàineadh *m*, sgoltadh *m*

split *v* **1** sgoilt *&* sgolt *vti*; **2** ~ **(up)** (*ie divide*) roinn *vt* (**between** air), **the estate was ~ up** bha an oighreachd air a roinn suas, **we ~ it between them** roinn sinn orra e; **3** *in expr* ~ **up** (*ie separate, part*) dealaich *vi* (*with prep* ri), sgar *vti*, **the couple ~ up** dhealaich a' chàraid (phòsta) ri chèile

splosh *v* plubraich, plub

splutter *v* dèan plubraich *f*

spoil *v* **1** (*as vi*) rach *vi irreg* bhuaithe; **2** (*as vt*) mill *vt*; **3** (*indulge child &c*) mill *vt*

spoil, spoils *n* (*plunder &c*) cobhartach *mf*, spùilleadh *&* spùinneadh *m*, creach *f*

spoilt *adj & past part* **1** (*lit, also fig of child, dog &c*) millte; **2** *in expr* ~ **brat** uilleagan *m*

spoke *n* spòg *f*

spokesman *n* fear-labhairt *m*

spokesperson *n* neach-labhairt *m* (*pl* luchd-labhairt *m sing coll*)

sponsor *n* (*of sporting or cultural event &c*) goistidh *m*

sponsorship *n* goistidheachd *f invar*

spool *n* iteachan *m*

spoon *n* spàin *f*

spoonful *n* làn-spàine *m*

sport *n* **1** (*games, also fun &c*) spòrs *f*, **we had some ~ with him/at his expense** bha spòrs againn air, **football's my favourite ~** 's e ball-coise *m* an spòrs as fheàrr leam, **~s complex** ionad-spòrsa *m*; **2** *in expr* **fond of/good at ~** spòrsail

sporting *adj* **1** (*fair*) cothromach, (*idiom*) **a ~ chance** cothrom *m* na Fèinne; **2** (*relating to sport*) spòrsail

sporty *adj* spòrsail

spot *n* **1** (*pimple &c*) guirean *m*, plucan *m*; **2** (*place*) bad *m*, àite *m*, **a sunny ~** bad grianach, **a bonny ~** àite brèagha; **3** (*stain &c*) smal *m*, spot *m*; **4** *in exprs* **beauty ~** (*on face*) ball-maise *m*, (*place to visit*) àite brèagha, **on the ~** (*ie immediately*) anns a' bhad, **she did it on the ~** rinn i anns a' bhad e, *also* rinn i an làrach *f* nam bonn *mpl* e

spot *v* (*see: usu at a distance*) faigh fàire *f* (*with prep* air)

spouse *n* cèile *m invar*

spout *n* **1** (*of pot &c*) feadan *m*; **2** (*jet or flow of liquid*) spùt *m*, steall *f*; **3** (*large waterfall*) spùt *m*

sprain *n* (*of ankle &c*) sgochadh *m*, siachadh *m*

sprain *v* (*ankle &c*) sgoch *vt*, siach *vt*

spray *n* **1** (*device for watering &c*) steallaire *m*; **2** (~ *from sea*) cathadh-mara *m*

spray *v* steall *vti*

spree *n* (*esp drinking* ~) daorach *f*

spread *v* sgaoil *vti*, **she ~ (out) her arms** sgaoil i a gàirdeanan *mpl*, **the rumour ~ through the town** sgaoil am fathann air feadh a' bhaile *m*, **fine views ~ out beneath us** seallaidhean *mpl* brèagha air an sgaoileadh fodhainn

sprightly *adj* lùthmhor, clis, sgairteil, brìghmhor

spring *n* **1** (*leap*) leum *m*; **2** (*of water*) fuaran *m*, tobar *mf*; **3** (*the season*) earrach *m*, **in (the)** ~ as t-earrach; **4** *in expr* ~ **tide** reotha(i)rt *mf*

spring *v* **1** (*leap*) leum *vi*; **2** (*appear; fam*) nochd *vi* (**from** à), **where did you ~ from?** cò às a nochd thu(sa)?; **3** *in exprs* ~ **to mind** thig *vi* na (*&c*) inntinn *f*, thig *vi* na (*&c*) c(h)uimhne *f invar*

sprinkle *v* crath *vt*, ~ **salt on the fish** crath salann *m* air an iasg *m*

sprint *n* deann-ruith *&* dian-ruith *f*

sprout *n* **1** (*on plant*) bachlag *f*; **2** (*veg*) **Brussels ~** buinneag Bhruisealach

sprout *v* (*plant*) cuir a-mach bachlagan *fpl*

spruce *adj* cuimir, snasail, sgiobalta

spruce *n* giuthas *m*, **Norway ~** giuthas Lochlannach

spry *adj* beothail, clis, **a ~ old guy** bodach beothail

spur, spur on *v* **1** (*encourage*) brosnaich *vt*, spreig *vt*, stuig *vt*, piobraich *vt*; **2** (*hurry on*) cuir cabhag *f* (*with prep* air), greas *vt*, brod *vt*

spurt *n* **1** (*of liquid*) steall *f*, stealladh *m*, spùt *m*; **2** (*acceleration*) briosgadh *m*, cabhag *f*, **get/put a ~ on!** dèan cabhag!, *also* greas ort!

spurt *v* (*liquids*) steall *vti*, spùt *vti*

spy *n* **1** brathadair *m*, fear-brathaidh *m*; **2** *in expr* ~ **satellite** saideal *m* brathaidh *m gen*

spying *n* **1** (*espionage*) brathadh *m*; **2** (*eavesdropping on neighbours &c*) farchluais *f*

spy *v* **1** (*engage in espionage*) brath *vi*; **2** (*eavesdrop on neighbours &c*) dèan farchluais *f* (**on** air)

squabble *n* connsachadh *m*, tuasaid *f*, trod *m*

squabble *v* connsaich *vi*, troid *vi*, (**with** ri), **they were squabbling** bha iad a' trod ri chèile

squabbling *n* trod *m*

squad *n* buidheann *mf*, sguad *m*

squalid *adj* **1** dràbhail, robach, grod, mosach; **2** (*action, behaviour*) suarach, tàireil

squall *n* sgal *m*, meall *m*

squalor *n* mosaiche *f invar*

squander *v* caith *vt*

square *adj* **1** (*in shape*) ceàrnach; **2** (*surface area*) ceàrnagach, ~ **metre** meatair ceàrnagach

square *n* (*shape, also* ~ *in town &c*) ceàrnag *f*

squash *v* **1** (*lit*) brùth *vt*, preas *vt*; **2** (*fig: quash, quell*) ceannsaich *vt*, mùch *vt*

squat *n* (*position*) crùban *m*

squat *v* dèan crùban *m*, rach *vi* na (*&c*) c(h)rùban *m*, crùb *vi*, **they ~ted (down)** rinn iad crùban, chaidh iad nan crùban

squeak, squeaking *n* **1** (*of objects rubbing together &c*) dìosgan *m*, dìosgail *f invar*, gìosg *m*; **2** (*of animals &c*) sgiamh (beag)

squeak *v* **1** (*objects rubbing &c*) gìosg *vi*; **2** (*animals &c*) sgiamh *vi*

squeal *n* sgiamh *m*, sgal *m*

squeal *v* sgiamh *vi*, sgal *vi*

squeamish *adj* òrraiseach

squeeze *n* teannachadh *m*, fàisgeadh *m*

squeeze *v* teannaich *vt*, fàisg *vt*, preas *vt*

squint *adj* (*aslant*) claon, fiar, air fhiaradh

squint *n* claonadh *m*, fiaradh *m*, spleuchd *m*

squint *v* seall *vi* claon, seall *vi* fiar, spleuchd *vi*

squirrel *n* feòrag *f*

squirt *n* (*of liquid*) steall *f*, stealladh *m*

squirt *v* steall *vti*

St Kilda *n* Hiort *&* Hirt *f invar*

St Kildan *n & adj* Hiortach, Hirteach *&* Tirteach *m*

stab *n* **1** sàthadh *m*; **2** (*fam: a try, a shot*) oidhirp *f*, ionnsaigh *mf*, (**at** air), **we'll have another ~ at it** bheir/nì sinn oidhirp/ionnsaigh eile air

stab *v* sàth *vti*

stabilise *v* **1** (*as vt*) bunailtich *vt*; **2** (*as vi*) fàs *vi* bunailteach

stability *n* bunailteachd *f invar*, seasmhachd *f invar*

stable *adj* seasmhach, bunailteach

stable *n* stàball *m*

stack *n* (*of corn &c*) cruach *f*, mulan *m*, coc/goc *m*, **small ~** cruachan *m*

stack *v* cruach *vt*, càrn *vt*

stack-yard *n* iodhlann *f*

staff[1] *n* (*employees*) luchd-obrach *m sing coll*, **clerical ~** luchd-obrach clèireachail

staff[2] *n* **1** (*of bishop &c*) bachall *m*; **2** (*music*) cliath *f*

stag *n* (*red deer ~*) damh *m*

stage[1] *n* **1** (*of progress, development, ability &c*) ìre *f invar*; **2** *in expr* **at this ~ in/of my life** aig an ìre *f invar* seo/aig an àm *m* seo de mo bheatha *f*

stage[2] *n* (*theatre &c*) àrd-ùrlar *m*

stagger *v* **1** tuimhsich *vi*, tuislich *vi*; **2** (*fig: surprise*) cuir (mòr-)iongnadh *m* (*with prep* air), **I was ~ed** bha (mòr-)iongnadh orm

stagnant *adj* marbh, **~ water** uisge marbh

staid *adj* stòlda

stain *n* smal *m*, spot *m*, sal *m*

stain *v* **1** dath *vt*; **2** (*accidentally*) fàg smal *m*, fàg spot *m*, (*with prep* air), **it ~ed her dress** dh'fhàg e smal air an dreasa *f* aice

stained *adj & past part* **1** dathte, **~ glass** glainne/gloinne dhathte; **2** (*accidentally*) salaichte

stair *n* **1** (*single step*) ceum *m*; **2** (*single step & staircase, a flight of ~s*) staidhre *f*, staidhir *f*, **she went up the** ~ chaidh i suas an staidhre, **she's up the** ~ tha i shuas an staidhre

staircase, stairs *n* staidhir *f*, staidhre *f*

stake[1] *n* (*for fencing &c*) post *m*, stob *m*, (*more trad*) cipean *m*

stake[2] *n* (*in gambling*) geall *m*

stalk *n* gas *f*

stallion *n* àigeach *m*

stalwart *adj* **1** (*sturdy*) calma, tapaidh, smioral, treun; **2** (*loyal, dependable*) seasmhach, daingeann, dìleas

stamina *n* **1** (*strength*) neart *m*, spionnadh *m*; **2** (*staying power*) cumail-ris *f*, fulang *m*,

stamp *n* (*postage*) stamp(a) *f*

stamp *v* **1** (*letter*) cuir stamp(a) *f* (*with prep* air); **2** (*with foot*) breab *vt*, stamp *vti*, **she ~ed her foot at me** bhreab i a cas *f* rium; **3** *in expr* ~ **out** cuir *vi* às (*with prep* do), ~ **out racism** cuir às do chinealas *m*/ghràin-chinnidh *f*

stance *n* (*phys, moral, philo &c*) seasamh *m*

stand *v* **1** (*rise to one's feet*) seas *vi*, èirich *vi* (na &c s(h)easamh *m*), **the audience stood (up)** sheas an luchd-èisteachd *m sing coll*, **he stood up** sheas e suas, sheas e an-àird, dh'èirich e (na sheasamh); **2** (*be in a standing position*) bi *vi irreg* na (&c) s(h)easamh *m*, **I stood/was ~ing under a tree** bha mi nam sheasamh fo chraoibh *dat*; **3** (*tolerate, bear*) fuiling & fulaing *vti*, (*less trad*) cuir *vi* suas (*with prep* ri), **they had to** ~ **cold and hunger** b' fheudar dhaibh fuachd *mf* is acras *m* fhulang, b' fheudar dhaibh cur suas ri fuachd is acras, **I can't ~ him/it!**, chan fhuiling mi e!; **4** *in expr* ~ **up for** (*ie support*) seas *vt*, **who will ~ up for you?** cò a sheasas thu?

standard *adj* **1** (*usual, normal*) suidhichte, cumanta, gnàthach; **2** (*applicable to all*) coitcheann

standard *n* **1** (*unit of comparison, a criterion*) slat-thomhais *f*; **2** (*level of achievement, ability &c*) ìre *f invar*, inbhe *f*

stand-in *n* (*theatre &c*) neach-ionaid *m*

standing stone *n* tursa *m*, carragh *f*, gallan *m*

standing jump cruinn-leum *m*

stanza *n* rann *mf*

star *n* reul *f*, rionnag *f*, **the pole** ~ an reul-iùil *f*

starch *n* stalc *m*

stare *n* spleuchd *m*

stare *v* spleuchd *vi* (**at** air)

starfish *n* crasgag & crosgag *f*

stark *adj* **1** (*landscape, situation &c*) garbh, cruaidh; **2** *in expr* ~ **naked** dearg rùisgte

starling *n* druid *f*, druideag *f*

start *n* **1** (*in time*) toiseach *m*, tùs *m*, **the ~ of summer** toiseach an t-samhraidh, **he's been working here from/since the (very) ~** tha e ag obair an seo o thùs; **2** (*of a process &c*) tòiseachadh *m*, **a fresh ~** tòiseachadh as ùr, *in expr* **make a fresh ~** tòisich *vi* as ùr; **3** (*shock, fright, nervous reaction*) clisgeadh *m*, uspag *f*, **he gave me a ~** chuir e clisgeadh orm, **he gave a ~** thug e uspag

start *v* **1** tòisich *vi* (*with preps* air *or* ri), teann *vi* (*with prep* ri), **~ singing** tòisich a' seinn, **~ to sing** tòisich air/ri seinn, **he ~ed climbing** theann e ri streap, **~ afresh** tòisich as ùr, (*saying*) **~ing/getting ~ed is a day's work** is e obair *f* latha *m gen* tòiseachadh *m*; **2** (*nervous reaction*) clisg *vi*, thoir uspag *f*, **he ~ed** chlisg e, thug e uspag

startle *v* cuir clisgeadh *m* (*with prep* air), clisg *vt*, **he ~d me** chuir e clisgeadh orm, chlisg e mi

starvation *n* gort & goirt *f*

starve *v* **1** (*as vi: die of starvation*) caochail *vi* leis a' ghoirt *f dat*; **2** (*as vt: deprive of food*) cuir trasg *f*, leig goirt *f*, (*with prep* air), **they ~d me** chuir iad trasg orm, leig iad goirt orm; **3** *in expr* **he ~d them to death** chuir e gu bàs *m* leis a' ghoirt iad

state *n* **1** (*condition*) cor *m*, staid *f*, **the pitiful ~ of the refugees** cor truagh nam fògarrach *mpl*, **~ of emergency** staid èiginneach, **in a bad ~** ann an droch staid; **2** *in expr* **he was in a good ~ of mind** bha e air a (dheagh) dhòigh *m*; **3** (*pol*) stàit *f*, **the French ~** an stàit Fhrangach, stàit na Frainge

state *v* **1** (*feelings, thoughts, ideas &c*) cuir *vt* an cèill (*dat of* ciall *f*), **I will ~ my opinion** cuiridh mi mo bheachd *m* an cèill; **2** (*facts, details &c*) thoir *vt* (seachad), **~ your name** thoir seachad ur n-ainm *m*

stately *adj* stàiteil, **~ gait/pace** ceum *m* stàiteil

statement *n* **1** (*abstr*) cur *m* an cèill (*dat of* ciall *f*); **2** (*esp in pl: utterances, things said*) **~s** briathran *mpl*, **foolish ~s** briathran amaideach, **I don't believe politicians' statements** cha chreid mi briathran luchd-poileataics (*m sing coll*); **3** (*account of events, circumstances &c: verbal or written*) aithris *f*, (*esp formal & written*) aithisg *f*, (*esp for legal purposes*) teisteanas *m*

statesman *n* stàitire *m*

station *n* **1** (*transport, radio &c*) stèisean *m*; **2** (*IT &c*) **work ~** ionad-obrach *m*

stationary *adj* na stad *m*, gun gluasad *m*

stationery *n* pàipearachd *f sing coll*, stuth-sgrìobhaidh *m*

statue *n* ìomhaigh *f*

stature *n* **1** (*height*) àirde *f*; **2** (*build*) dèanamh *m*, togail *f*, meudachd *f*; **3** (*moral, professional &c ~*) inbhe *f*

status *n* inbhe *f*, **~ symbol** comharradh *m* inbhe *gen*

statute *n* reachd *m invar*, riaghailt *f*

statutory *adj* **1** (*in accordance with statutes*) reachdail, dligheach; **2** (*compulsory by law/statute*) reachdail

staunch *adj* seasmhach, daingeann, dìleas, treun, làidir

staunch *v* caisg *vt*

stave *n* (*music*) cliabh *m*

stave off *v* cuir dàil *f* (*with prep* ann *or* air), cùm *vt* air falbh, ~ **the summons** cuir dàil air a' bhàirlinn *f invar*, **in order to ~ hunger** gus an t-acras a chumail air falbh

stay *v* **1** (*remain*) fuirich *vi*, fan *vi*, **you ~ where you are!** fuirich/fan thusa far a bheil thu!; **2** (*dwell*) fuirich *vi*, fan *vi*, gabh còmhnaidh *f*, (in ann an), **we were ~ing in Islay at the time** bha sinn a' fuireach/a' gabhail còmhnaidh ann an Ìle aig an àm *m*, **~ing with Calum** a' fuireach/a' fantainn/a' fantail aig Calum

steadfast *adj* **1** (*loyal*) dìleas; **2** (*steady, enduring*) daingeann, seasmhach

steady *adj* **1** (*of structures &c: firm*) cunbhalach, bunai(l)teach, seasmhach, daingeann, teann; **2** (*of persons*) stòlda, stuama; **3** *as adv in exprs* ~!, ~ **on!**, socair!, **take it ~!/go ~!** air do shocair!, gabh *vi* air do shocair!

steady *v* daingnich *vt*

steak *n* staoig *f*

steal *v* **1** (*as vt*) goid *vt*; **2** (*as vi*) dèan meirle *f invar*, bi *vi irreg* ri goid *f*; **3** *in expr* ~ **away** siolp *vi* air falbh, èalaidh *vi* air falbh

stealing *n* goid *f*, mèirle *&* meirle *f invar*, (*usu more petty*) braid *f*

steam *n* toit *f*, smùid *f*, deatach *f*, ~ **from the pot** toit às a' phoit *f*, *in expr* ~ **boat** bàta-smùide *m*

steam *v* **1** cuir toit *f*, **it was ~ing** bha e a' cur toite *gen*, bha toit a' tighinn às; **2** (*fam: very drunk*) **I was ~ing** bha mi air mo phronnadh/air mo dhalladh

steel *n* stàilinn *f*, cruaidh *f*

steep *adj* cas, **a ~ brae** bruthach c(h)as

steep *v* (*in liquid*) tum *vt*, cuir *vt* am bogadh *m*

steeple *n* stìoball *m*

steer *v* stiùir *vt*

steering-wheel *n* cuibhle-stiùiridh *f*

steersman *n* stiùireadair *m*

stem *n* **1** (*of plant*) gas *f*; **2** (*of boat*) toiseach *m*

stench *n* tòchd *m invar*

step *n* **1** (*pace*) ceum *m*, **take a ~ forward/backward** gabh ceum air adhart/ air ais, ~ **by** ~ ceum air cheum, *also* uidh air n-uidh; **2** (*of stair &c: single* ~) ceum *m*, (*flight of* ~*s*) ceumannan *mpl*, **go up the ~s** rach *vi* suas/dìrich *vt* na ceumannan

step *v* gabh ceum *m*, thoir ceum, ~ **forward** gabh ceum air adhart

step-brother *n* leas-bhràthair *m*

step-child *n* dalta *mf*

step-father *n* oide *m*

step-mother *n* muime *f*

stepping-stone *n* sìnteag *f*

step-sister *n* leas-phiuthar *f*

sterile *adj* **1** (*barren*) seasg, neo-thorach; **2** (*fig: fruitless*) gun toradh *m*, gun fheum *m*, dìomhain, ~ **debate** deasbad *m* gun toradh/gun fheum

stern *n* **1** (*of boat*) deireadh *m*; **2** (*fam: backide*) tòn *f*, màs *m*

stern *adj* **1** (*of discipline, master &c*) cruaidh, teann; **2** (*unsmiling &c*) dùr, gruamach, gnù, mùgach

sternum *n* cliathan *m*

stew *n* **1** stiubha *f*; **2** *in expr* (*fam, fig*) **in a** ~ ann an (droch) staing *f*, ann an cruaidh-chas *m*, ann an èiginn *f invar*

steward *n* **1** (*on estate &c*) maor *m*; **2** (*on boat &c*) stiùbhard *m*; **3** *in expr* **shop** ~ riochdaire *m* aonaidh *m gen*

stewardess *n* bana-stiùbhard *f*

stick *n* bata *m*, maide *m*, (*supple* ~) gad *m*, **walking** ~ bata-coiseachd *m*,

stick *v* **1** (*adhere*) lean *vi* (**to** ri); **2** (*get stuck, caught*) rach *vi* an sàs *m* (**in** ann an), **she stuck in the brambles** chaidh i an sàs anns na drisean *fpl*; **3** (*thrust, push carelessly*) sàth *vt*, ~ **it in the cupboard** sàth a-steach dhan phreas *m* e; **4** *in expr* ~ **at it!** (*persevere*) cùm *vi* ort!, cùm *vi* ris!, lean *vi* ort!

stick-in-the-mud *n* duine *m* lag-chùiseach

sticky *adj* leanailteach

stiff *adj* **1** (*lit*) rag; **2** (*fam: difficult, excessive, harsh*) doirbh, cruaidh, **a** ~ **exam** deuchainn dhoirbh, **a** ~ **sentence** binn chruaidh; **3** *in expr* **I was scared** ~ bha eagal *m* mo bheatha *f* orm

stiffen *v* **1** (*lit*) ragaich *vti*; **2** (*fig: laws, conditions &c*) dèan *vt* nas cruaidhe; **3** (*resolve &c*) daingnich *vt*

stiffness *n* raige *f invar*

stifle *v* **1** (*fire &c*) smà(i)l *vt*, mùch *vt*, tùch *vt*; **2** (*person, life*) mùch *vt*, tachd *vt*; **3** (*uprising, spirit, opposition &c*) mùch *vt*, ceannsaich *vt*

still *adj* **1** (*weather*) ciùin, sàmhach, sèimh, **a** ~ **morning** madainn chiùin; **2** (*motionless*) gun ghluasad *m*, na (*&c*) t(h)àmh, **the trees were** ~ **after the storm** bha na craobhan *fpl* gun ghluasad/nan tàmh an dèidh na stoirme

still *adv* **1** fhathast, **it's** ~ **raining** tha an t-uisge ann fhathast; **2** (*nevertheless*) a dh'aindeoin sin, air a shon sin, co-dhiù, **it's hard, but we'll manage it** ~ tha e doirbh, ach nì sinn an gnothach *m* air a dh'aindeoin sin/air a shon sin/co-dhiù

still *n* poit-dhubh *f*

still *v* ciùinich *vti*, sìthich *vti*, socraich *vti*

stimulate *v* **1** (*phys, emotionally, sexually*) brod *vt*, (*emotionally*) brosnaich *vt*; **2** (*revive, revitalise*) beothaich *vt*

sting *n* (*of wasp &c*) guin *m*, gath *m*

sting *v* guin *vt*, cuir gath *m* (*with prep* ann), **it stung me** ghuin e mi, chuir e gath annam

stinginess *n* spìocaireachd *f invar*

stinging *adj* **1** (*sensations &c*) geur, goirt; **2** (*remarks &c*) guineach, geur

stingy *adj* spìocach, mosach

stink *n* tòchd *m invar*

stint *n* greis *f*, treis *f*, (*shorter*) greiseag *f*, treiseag *f*, (**at** air/aig) **a ~ at the peats** greis air/aig a' mhòine *f*

stipend *n* tuarastal *f*

stipulate *v* sònraich *vt*

stipulation *n* **1** (*abstr*) sònrachadh *m*; **2** (*con: in contracts &c*) cumha *f*, cùmhnant *m*

stir *v* **1** (*phys*) gluais *vi*, caraich *vi*, **down in the forest something ~red** shìos sa choille *f* ghluais rudeigin; **2** (*emotionally*) gluais *vt*, drùidh *vi* (*with prep* air), **the music ~red me** ghluais an ceòl mi, dhrùidh an ceòl orm; **3** (*liquids, food*) cuir car *m* (*with prep* de), **~ the soup** cuir car den bhrot *m*; **4** *in exprs* **~ up** (*enliven &c*) beothaich *vt*, **she ~red up the embers of the fire** bheothaich i èibhleagan an teine, **~ up** (*emotionally, to action &c*) brod *vt*, brosnaich *vt*, (*fam*) **~ your stumps!** tog ort!

stirk *n* gamhainn *m*

stirring *adj* **1** (*to action*) brosnachail; **2** (*emotionally*) gluasadach, drùidhteach

stitch *n* **1** (*needlework*) grèim *m*; **2** (*pain in side*) acaid *f*

stitch *v* fuaigh *vt*, fuaigheil *vt*

stitched *adj & past part* fuaighte

stoat *n* neas *f*, neas mhòr

stob *n* stob *m*, post *m*

stock *n* **1** (*livestock*) stoc *m*, (*esp cattle*) sprèidh *f*, crodh *m*; **2** (*of shop*) bathar *m sing coll*; **3** (*fin*) sèaraichean *mpl*, earrannan *fpl*, **the ~ market** margadh *mf* nan sèaraichean/nan earrannan

stocking *n* stocainn *f*, osan *m*

stolid *adj* dùr, stòlda

stomach *n* stamag *f*, (*less usu*) goile *f*, (*more fam*) balg *m*, broinn *f*, brù *f*, mionach *m*, maodal *m*

stomachful *n* (*lit & fig*) làn *m* a (*&c*) b(h)ronn (*gen of* brù *f*) (**of** de), **I had a ~ of it** fhuair mi làn mo bhronn dheth

stone *n* (*individual ~, ~ in general*) clach *f*, **he threw a ~ at me** thilg e clach orm, **~ walls** ballachan *mpl* cloiche (*gen*), **a memorial ~** clach-chuimhne *f*, *also* carragh-chuimhne *f*, **a plum ~** clach-phlumaise *m*, **precious ~** clach uasal, **the Stone of Destiny** Clach na Cinneamhainn, *also* Clach Sgàin (*ie 'of Scone'*), An Lia-Fàil *f*, *in expr* **pelt with ~s** clach *vt*; **2** (*weight*) clach *f*, **~ of potatoes** clach bhuntàta *m sing coll*; **3** (*slab of ~*) leac *f*, **tomb~**, **grave~** leac-uaighe *f*, **paving-~** leac-ùrlair; **4** *in exprs* **standing ~** gallan *m*, tursa *m*, **~ circle** tursachan *mpl*

stone *v* clach *vt*, tilg clachan *fpl* (*with prep* air)

stonemason *n* clachair *m*

stony *adj* clachach

stool *n* stòl *m*, furm *m*, (*trad*) creapan *m*

stoop *v* crùb *vi*

stop *n* **1** (*abstr*) stad *f*, **they came to a ~** thàinig iad gu stad, **he brought the car to a ~** thug e an càr gu stad, **put a ~ to something** cuir stad air rudeigin, *in expr* **bus ~** àite-stad *m* bus *m gen*; **2** (*typog*) puing *f*, **full ~** stad-phuing *f*

stop *v* **1** (*as vi*) stad *vi*, thig *vi* gu stad *m*, sguir *vi*, **the lorry ~ped** stad an làraidh *f*, thàinig an làraidh gu stad, (*break off work &c*) **we ~ped at noon** sguir sinn aig meadhan-latha *m*; **2** (*as vt*) stad *vt*, thoir *vt* gu stad, cuir stad (*with prep* air), **he ~ped the lorry** stad e an làraidh, thug e an làraidh gu stad, **I'll ~ your carrying-on!** cuiridh mi stad air do dhol-a-mach *m invar*!; **3** (*prevent*) cuir bacadh *m* (*with prep* air), caisg *vt*, cuir casg *m* (*with prep* air), **her parents ~ped them getting married** chuir a pàrantan bacadh air am pòsadh *m*; **4** (*give up, abandon an activity*) leig *vt* (*with prep* de), leig *vt* seachad, sguir *vi* (*with prep* de), **she ~ped work/ working** leig i dhith a h-obair *f*/an obair, **I'm ~ping smoking** tha mi a' sgur de smocadh *m*/a' leigeil seachad smocadh, **~ it!** sguir dheth!; **5** *in expr* **~ up** (*aperture &c*) tachd *vt*, dùin *vt* suas

stopcock *n* goc *m*

stoppage *n* **1** (*cessation of activity*) stad *m*, (*through industrial action*) stailc *f*; **2** (*obstruction, blockage*) bacadh *m*, dùnadh *m*

storage *n* stòradh *m*

store *n* **1** (*repository &c*) ionad-tasgaidh *m*, tasgaidh *f*, stòr *m*; **2** (*shop*) bùth *mf*, **go to the ~ for me** thalla don bhùth dhomh; **3** (*hoard, accumulation, of objects, knowledge &c*) stòr *m*

store *v* **1** stò(i)r *vt*, (*esp in museums &c*) taisg *vt*; **2** *in expr* **~ away** cuir *vt* air an spàrr *m*

storehouse *n* ionad-tasgaidh *m*

storey *n* lobht(a) *m*

storm *n* stoirm *f*, doineann *f*, gailleann *f*

stormy *adj* (*of weather*) stoirmeil, doineannach, gailleanach, gailbheach

story *n* **1** (*fictional*) sgeulachd *f*, **short ~** sgeulachd ghoirid; **2** (*can be factual: when fictional, often trad in content*) sgeul *m*, **a ~ about Finn** sgeul air Fionn, **the ~ of my life** sgeul mo bheatha *f gen*; **3** (*usu verbal, often humorous*) stòiridh & stòraidh *m*, naidheachd *f*

story-teller *n* sgeulaiche *m*, (*of trad stories*) seanchaidh *m*

stout *adj* **1** (*brave, enduring*) treun, **~ heroes** gaisgich threuna *mpl*; **2** (*plump &c*) reamhar, sultmhor

stove *n* stòbh(a) *f*

stow *v* **1** (*store, conserve*) taisg *vt*, glèidh *vt*; **2** (*put/tidy away*) cuir *vt* (air falbh), **~ it in the cupboard** cuir (air falbh) dhan phreas *m* e

straddle *v* rach *vi irreg* casa-gobhlach, bi *vi irreg* casa-gobhlach, rach *vi irreg* gobhlachan, (*all with prep* air), **he ~d the chair** chaidh e casa-gobhlach/ chaidh e gobhlachan air a' chathair *f*, **he was straddling the chair** bha e casa-gobhlach air a' chathair

straggle *v* bi *vi irreg* air dheireadh

straggler *n* slaodaire *m*, neach *m* (a tha &c) air dheireadh

straight *adj* **1** dìreach, ~ **line** loidhne dhìreach; **2** (*honest, trustworthy*) dìreach, ceart, onarach; **3** (*idiom*) **I gave it to her** ~ thuirt mi rithe/ dh'innis mi dhi an clàr *m* a h-aodainn *m* e

straighten *v* dìrich *vti*

strain *n* **1** (*tension: on rope &c*) teannachadh *m*; **2** (*from phys effort*) spàirn *f*; **3** (*psych* ~) uallach *m*, **under a** ~ fo uallach

strain *v* **1** (*put* ~ *on rope &c*) teannaich *vt*; **2** (*make phys effort*) dèan spàirn (mhòr), **he had to** ~ **to lift the barrel** b' fheudar dha spàirn mhòr a dhèanamh gus am baraille a thogail/mun togadh e am baraille; **3** (~ *liquids*) sìolaidh *vt*

strainer *n* **1** (*for liquids*) sìol(t)achan *m*; **2** (*tensioner*) teannaire *m*

strait *n* caol *m*, caolas *m*

straits *npl* (*ie difficulties*) droch staing *f*, cruaidh-chàs *m*, èiginn *f invar*, **in dire** ~ ann an droch staing, ann an cruaidh-chàs, ann an èiginn

strand[1] *n* (*seashore*) tràigh *f*

strand[2] *n* (*of material; also of argument &c*) dual *m*

strange *adj* **1** (*odd, unusual, surprising &c*) neònach, annasach, (*stronger*) iongantach; **2** (*unfamiliar*) coimheach

stranger *n* coigreach *m*, srainnsear *m*, coimheach *m*

strangle mùch *vt*, tachd *vt*

strangulation *n* mùchadh *m*, tachdadh *m*

strap *n* iall *f*

strapping *n* (*physique*) tomadach & tomaltach, calma

stratagem *n* cuilbheart *f*, innleachd *f*

strategy *n* roimh-innleachd *f*

strath *n* srath *m*

straw *n* **1** connlach *f sing coll*; **2** (*for drinking*) sràbh *m*

stray *adj* (*lost, wandering &c*) air seachran *m*, air iomrall *m*, *in exprs* ~ **animal** ainmhidh-seachrain *m*, ~ **dog** cù-fuadain *m* (*gen of* seachran & fuadan *m*, *used adjectivally*)

stray *v* (*phys or morally*) rach *vi* air seachran *m*, rach *vi* air iomrall *m*

straying *n* dol *m invar* air seachran *m*, dol air iomrall *m*

streak *n* stiall *f*, srian *f*

streak *v* stiall *vt*

stream *n* sruth *m*, (*often more precipitous*) allt *m*, (*small* ~) sruthan *m*, alltan *m*, (*large* ~) abhainn *f*

stream *v* ruith *vi*, sruth *vi*, sil *vi*

street *n* sràid *f*

strength *n* **1** neart *m*, spionnadh *m*, lùth & lùths *m*, brìgh & brìogh *f invar*, **at the height of his/her** ~ an treun *f invar* a neirt *gen*, aig àird *f* a neirt; **2** (*pol, military* ~) cumhachd *mf invar*, neart *m*

strengthen *v* **1** (*esp phys*) neartaich *vt*; **2** (~ *structure, buildings, beliefs, intentions &c*) daingnich *vt*

strenuous *adj* saothrachail

stress *n* **1** (*emphasis*) cudthrom & cuideam *m*, **lay ~ on punctuality** leig cudthrom air pongalachd *f invar*; **2** (*psych ~*) uallach *m*, **under ~** fo uallach; **3** (*lang*) cudthrom & cuideam *m*, **the ~ comes on the first syllable** thig an cudthrom air a' chiad lide *m*

stress *v* (*emphasise*) leig cudthrom (mòr) (*with prep* air), **~ punctuality** leig cudthrom air pongalachd *f invar*

stretch *n* (*phys*) sìneadh *m*

stretch *v* sìn *vti*, **the rope is ~ing** tha an ròpa *m* a' sìneadh, **she ~ed (out) her left leg** shìn i a-mach a cas chlì

stretched *adj & past part* sìnte, **~ (out) on the ground** sìnte air an làr *m*, *also* na (&c) s(h)ìneadh air an làr

strew *v* sgaoil *vt*, sgap *vt*, **they ~ed flowers on the ground** sgaoil iad flùraichean *mpl* air an làr *m*

strict *adj* (*of person, discipline &c*) cruaidh, teann

stride *n* ceum *m*, (*longer*) sìnteag *f*, **a ~ forward** ceum air adhart, **we quickened our ~** luathaich sinn ar ceum

strife *n* strì *f*, còmhstri *f*

strike *n* (*industrial &c*) stailc *f*

strike *v* **1** (*hit*) buail *vt*; **2** (*industry &c*) rach *vi irreg* air stailc *f*; **3** (*impress*) drùidh (*with prep* air), **I was struck by her beauty** dhrùidh a bòidhchead *f* orm; **4** (*occur to*) thig *vi* a-steach (*with prep* air), **it struck me that he was a liar** thàinig e a-steach orm gun robh e na bhreugaire *m*; **5** *in expr* **~ up a tune** tog fonn *m*

striking *adj* drùidhteach

string *n* **1** sreang *f*; **2** (*of musical instrument*) teud *m*

string *v* **1** (*violin &c*) cuir teud *m* (*with prep* air); **2** *in expr* **~ two words together** cuir dà fhacal *m sing* an ceann *m* a chèile

stringency *n* teanntachd *f invar*

stringent *adj* teann

strip *n* (*of material &c*) stiall *f*

strip *v* (*body &c*) rùisg *vt*, lom *vt*

stripe *n* stiall *f*

stripe *v* stiall *vt*

striped *adj* stiallach

stripling *n* òganach *m*, òigear *m*

stripped *adj & past part* rùisgte

strive *v* **1** (*contend &c*) strì *vi* (**with/against** ri); **2** (*make great effort*) dèan spàirn *f* (**to** gus)

stroke *n* **1** (*blow*) buille *f*, (*less usu*) beum *m*; **2** (*sport*) buille *f*; **3** (*med*) stròc *m*

stroke *v* **1** (*dog &c*) slìob & slìog *vt*; **2** (*persons, affectionately or amorously*) cnèadaich & cniadaich *vt*

stroll *n* cuairt *f*, car *m*, **I'll take a ~ outside** gabhaidh mi cuairt a-muigh

stroll *v* gabh cuairt *f*, coisich *vi* gu socrach, coisich air ceum socrach

strong *adj* **1** (*phys*) làidir, neartmhor, lùthmhor, (*can be with overtones of bravery*) treun; **2** *in expr* ~ **drink** deoch-làidir *f*

stronghold *n* daingneach *f*, (*trad*) dùn *m*

strop *n* iall *f*

structural *adj* structarail

structure *n* structair *m*

struggle *n* **1** (*abstr & con*) strì *f*, spàirn *f*, (*con*) gleac *m*, (**with**, **against** ri); **2** (*in aid of something, to achieve something*) iomairt *f*

struggle *v* strì *vi*, gleac *vi*, (**with**, **against** ri)

strut *v* spai(s)dirich *vi*

stubborn *adj* **1** (*obstinate*) rag, dùr, (*stronger*) rag-mhuinealach; **2** (*tenacious*) diorrasach

stuck *adj & past part* an sàs *m*, **he was/got ~ in the mud** bha e/chaidh e an sàs sa pholl *m*, **get ~ into the work** rach *vi* an sàs anns an obair *f*, *also* crom *vi* air an obair

stud *n* (*of horses*) greigh *f*

student *n* oileanach *m*, **mature ~** oileanach inbheach, **part time ~** oileanach pàirt-ùine

studies *npl* foghlam *m*, cùrsa *m* foghlaim *m gen*, **she was neglecting her ~** bha i a' leigeil a' chùrsa foghlaim aice air dhearmad *m*

study *n* **1** (*learning*) ionnsachadh *m*; **2** (*investigation of a topic*) rannsachadh *m*, sgrùdadh *m*; **3** (*room*) seòmar-leughaidh *m*

study *v* **1** (*learn a particular subject &c*) ionnsaich *vt*, **~ing Gaelic** ag ionnsachadh na Gàidhlig; **2** (*investigate, research*) rannsaich *vt*, sgrùd *vt*, dèan rannsachadh/sgrùdadh *m* (*with prep* air)

stuff *n* **1** (*material &c*) stuth *m*, (*trad*) cungaidh *f*, (*fam*) **that's good ~!** 's e stuth math a tha sin!; **2** (*fam: assorted possessions &c*) treal(l)aich *f*, **tidy up your ~** sgioblaich do threallaich

stuff *v* **1** lìon *vt*; **2** (*push roughly*) sàth *vt*, dinn *vti*, (**into** a-steach do)

stumble *n* tuisleadh *m*

stumble *v* tuislich *vi*

stumbling-block *n* cnap-starra(dh) *m*

stump *n* ploc *m*, stoc *m*

stun *v* cuir *vt* na (*&c*) t(h)uaineal *m*

stunt *n* cleas *m*

stupid *adj* **1** (*unintelligent*) gòrach, baoghalta, (*more fam*) tiugh; **2** (*silly*) gòrach, amaideach, baoth, faoin, **don't be ~!** na bi (cho) gòrach!

stupidity *n* **1** (*lack of intelligence*) gòraiche *f invar*, baoghaltachd *f invar*; **2** (*silliness*) gòraiche *f invar*, amaideas *m*, faoineas *m*

stupor *n* tuaineal *m*

sturdiness *n* tapachd *f invar*

sturdy *adj* (*phys*) calma, (*phys & morally*) tapaidh, **a ~ handsome man** duine calma gasta

sty *n* (*agric*) fail *f*

style *n* **1** stoidhle *f*, **I like his ~!** is toigh leam an stoidhl' (a th') aige, **there's a ponderous ~ about his writing** tha stoidhle throm air a chuid *f* sgrìobhaidh *m gen*; **2** (*mode of doing things*) modh *mf*, (*more trad*) nòs *m*, **the traditional ~** (*esp of singing*) an seann nòs

sub- *prefix*, fo-, *eg* **subconscious** *adj* fo-mhothachail, **subtitle(s)** *n* fo-thiotal(an) *m*, **sub-contract** *v* fo-chunnraich *vt*

sub-committee *n* fo-chomataidh *f*

subconscious *adj* **1** fo-mhothachail; **2** (*in Freudian sense*) fo-inntinneil

subconscious *n* fo-inntinn *f*

subdivide *v* fo-roinn *vt*

subdue *v* **1** (*people*) ceannsaich *vt*, cuir *vt* fo smachd *f*; **2** (*spirit, uprising &c*) mùch *vt*,

subject *n* **1** (*ed*) cuspair *m*, **a core ~** prìomh chuspair, **my favourite ~** an cuspair as fheàrr leam; **2** (*~ matter &c*) cuspair *m*, **the ~ of our conversation** cuspair a' chòmhraidh againn, **the ~ of his novel/talk** cuspair na nobhail(e)/na h-òraid(e) aige; **3** (*of monarchy &c*) ìochdaran *m*; **4** (*gram*) cùisear *m*, suibseig *f*

subjection *n* **1** (*abstr: the state or condition*) ceannsal *m*, smachd *m invar*; **2** (*con: the action*) ceannsachadh *m*

subjugate *v* cuir *vt* fo smachd *f*, smachdaich *vt*, ceannsaich *vt*

subjugation *n* **1** (*abstr: the state or condition*) ceannsal *m*, smachd *m invar*; **2** (*con: the action*) ceannsachadh *m*

submerge *v* tum *vt*, cuir *vt* fodha

submission *n* gèilleadh *m*, strìochdadh *m*, gèill *f*

submissive *adj* macanta, umha(i)l

submissiveness *n* ùmhlachd *f invar*

submit *v* **1** (*as vi: give in &c*) gèill *vi*, strìochd *vi*, (**to do**); **2** (*as vt: present, hand in &c*) cuir *vt* a-steach, **~ a proposal** cuir a-steach moladh *m*

subordinate *n* ìochdaran *m*

subscription *n* (*to magazine &c*) fo-sgrìobhadh *m*

subsection *n* fo-earrann *f*

subside *v* **1** laigh *vi*, lùghdaich *vi*, rach *vi* sìos, socraich *vi*, sìolaidh *vi*, **the wind's subsiding** tha a' ghaoth a' laighe; **2** (*esp liquids*) tràigh *vi*, sìolaidh *vi*, **the floods ~d** thràigh na tuiltean *fpl*

subsidence *n* fo-thuiteam *m*

subsidy *n* tabhartas *m*, subsadaidh *m*

subsistence *n* teachd-an-tìr *m*, bith-beò *mf* **~ allowance** cuibhreann *m* teachd-an-tìr *gen*, **~ agriculture** tuathanachas bith-beò *gen*

subsoil *n* fo-thalamh *m*, fo-ùir *f*

substance *n* **1** (*abstr*) brìgh *f*, susbaint *f*, **a book without ~** leabhar *m* gun bhrìgh; **2** (*material, matter*) stuth *m*, **explosive ~** stuth sgailceanta

substantial *adj* **1** (*sound, solid*) tàbhachdach, **a ~ business** gnìomhachas tàbhachdach; **2** (*~ in bulk*) tomadach *&* tomaltach

substantiate *v* dearbh *vt*

substitute *n* (*sport &c*) neach-ionaid *m* (*pl* luchd-ionaid *m sing coll*)

substitute *v* cuir *vt* an àite *m* (*with gen*), ~ **X for Y** cuir X an àite Y

subterfuge *f* cuilbheart *f*, innleachd *f*

subterranean *adj* fon talamh *mf*

subtitle(s) *n* fo-thiotal(an) *m*(*pl*)

subtitle *v* cuir fo-thiotalan *mpl* (*with prep* air)

subtle *adj* (*mentally*) geur-chùiseach, innleachdach

subtract *v* thoir *vt* air falbh (**from** bho)

suburb *n* iomall-baile *m*

subway *n* fo-rathad *m*, fo-shlighe *f*,

succeed *v* 1 (*follow*) lean *vt*, thig *vi* an dèidh (*with gen*); 2 (*thrive &c*) soirbhich *vi*, also as *vi* impersonal with prep le, **the business ~ed** shoirbhich an gnìomhachas, **we ~ed totally** shoirbhich leinn uile gu lèir

success *n* 1 buaidh *f*; 2 (*esp material*) soirbheachas *m*

successful *adj* soirbheachail

succession *n* 1 (*series, sequence &c*) sreath *mf*, **a ~ of ministers preached there** shearmonaich sreath de mhinistearan *mpl* an sin; 2 *in expr* **in ~** an ceann *m* a chèile, an sreath *mf* a chèile, an dèidh a chèile, fear *m* mu seach, tè *f* mu seach, **three accidents in ~** trì tubaistean *fpl* an ceann a chèile/an sreath a chèile, **the Ministers resigned in ~** thug na Ministearan *mpl* suas an dreuchd *f* an ceann a chèile/fear mu seach

succinct *adj* (*report, document &c*) cuimir

such *adj* 1 den leithid *f*, den t-seòrsa *m*, (*follows the noun*), **you shouldn't read ~ trash!** cha bu chòir dhut truileis *f invar* den t-seòrsa (sin)/den leithid (sin) a leughadh; 2 *in expr* **in ~ a way (that)** air dhòigh *f* is, air chor *m* is, (*with conjs* gun, nach), **in ~ a way that I couldn't get in** air dhòigh/air chor is nach b' urrainn dhomh faighinn a-steach

such *pron* a leithid *f*, samhail *m*, **I saw ~ a thing as that once** chunnaic mi a leithid sin (a rud *m*) aon turas *m*, **I knew ~ a man** bha mi eòlach air a leithid de dhuine *m*, **~ as her never existed** cha robh a leithid/a samhail ann a-riamh, a leithid cha robh a-riamh ann

such *adv* 1 *in expr* **~ a lot** na h-uimhir *f invar*, na h-uiread *m invar*, (**of** de), **there were ~ a lot of people there** bha na h-uimhir/na h-uiread de dhaoine *mpl* ann; 2 *in excl* **~ a** with *adj & n*, abair, **~ a kind man!** abair duine caoibhneil!

suck *v* deoghail *vti*, sùgh *vti*

suction *n* deoghal *m*, sùghadh *m*

sudden *adj* grad, obann, gun fhiosta, **~ noise** fuaim *mf* ghrad/obann/gun fhiosta

suddenly *adv* gu grad, gu h-obann, gun fhiosta, **he rose ~** dh'èirich e gu grad/gu h-obann/gun fhiosta

suddenness *n* graide *f*, graidead *m*

suet *n* geir *f*

suffer *v* fuiling *&* fulaing *vti*, **he didn't ~ when he was ill** cha do dh'fhuiling e nuair a bha e tinn, **they had to ~ cold and hunger** b' fheudar dhaibh fuachd *mf* is acras *m* fhulang

suffering *n (mental or phys)* cràdh *m*, fulang *m*, fulangas *m*

suffice *v* foghain *vi*, **will that ~?** am foghain sin?

sufficiency *n* leòr *f invar*, fòghnadh *m*

sufficient *adj & n* gu leòr, na dh'fhòghnas, **~ time** ùine *f* gu leòr, **have you got ~?** a bheil gu leòr agad?, **is that ~?** am foghain sin?

suffocate mùch *vt*

suffocation *n* mùchadh *m*

suffrage *n* còir-bhòtaidh *f*, guth-bhòtaidh *m*

sugar *n* siùcar *m*

suggest *v* mol *vt*

suggestion *n* moladh *m*

suicide *n* fèin-mhort *& fèin-mhurt *m*

suit *n (of clothes)* deise *f*, *(less usu)* culaidh(-aodaich) *f*, trusgan *m*

suit *v* freagair *vi (with prep* air *&* do), thig *vi (with prep* do *&* ri), **that hat doesn't ~ you!** chan eil an ad sin a' freagairt ort!, **it doesn't ~ me to be unoccupied/idle** cha fhreagair dhomh a bhith nam thàmh, **how's the job ~ing you?** ciamar a tha an obair a' freagairt dhut?/a' tighinn riut?

suitable *adj* freagarrach, *(less usu)* iomchaidh *& iomchuidh, **the house wasn't ~ for him** cha robh an taigh *m* freagarrach dha, **a place ~ for swimming** àite freagarrach airson snàimh *m gen*

suitcase *n* ceus *m*, màileid *f*

sulk *n* gruaim *f*, mùig *m*

sulk *v* cuir gruaim *f*/mùig *m (with prep* air), **he ~ed/began to ~** chuir e gruaim/mùig air

sulkiness *n* gruaim *f*, mùig *m*

sulking, sulky, sullen *adj* gruamach, mùgach

sully *v* truaill *vt*, salaich *vt*, cuir smal *m (with prep* air)

sulphur *n* pronnasg *m*

sulphurous *adj* pronnasgail

sultry *adj (weather)* bruthainneach, bruicheil

sum *n* sùim *f*, **a ~ of money** sùim airgid *m*, **we did ~s at school** rinn sinn suimeannan anns an sgoil *f*

summarise *v* thoir geàrr-chunntas *m (with prep* air)

summary *adj (brief, brusque)* aithghearr, bras

summary *n* geàrr-chunntas *m* (**of** air)

summer *n* samhradh *m*, **~ school** sgoil-shamhraidh *f*

summit *n* 1 mullach *m*, bàrr *m*, **~ of the mountain** mullach na beinne; 2 *in expr* **~ meeting** *n* coinneamh *f* nan ceannardan *mpl*, àrd-choinneamh *f*

summon *v* gairm *vt*, cuir *vi* a' dh'iarraidh, cuir fios *m (with prep* air)

summons *n* 1 gairm *f*; 2 *(legal)* sumanadh *m*, *(more trad)* bàirlinn *f invar*

summons *v (legal)* sumain *vt*

sumph *n* amadan *m*, òinseach *f*

sumptuous *adj* sòghail

sun *n* grian *f*, **the ~'s rays** gathan *mpl* na grèine, **eclipse of the ~** dubhadh *m* na grèine

sunbathe *v* gabh a' ghrian

sunbeam *n* gath-grèine *f*

sunburn *n* losgadh-grèine *m*

Sunday *n* 1 (*trad used by Catholic communities*) Didòmhnaich *m invar*; 2 (*trad used by Protestant communities*) Là *m* na Sàbaid

sunder *v* 1 (*of persons: part, separate*) dealaich *vt* (**from** ri); 2 (*of objects: split &c*) sgàin *vti*

sundial *n* uaireadair-grèine *m*

sundry *adj* 1 (*assorted*) de gach seòrsa *m*, de dh'iomadach seòrsa, measgaichte *adj*, ~ **objects** rudan *mpl* de gach seòrsa/de dh'iomadach seòrsa; 2 (*various*) caochladh *m* (*with gen pl*), iomadach *adj* (*precedes the noun which is in nom sing/radical case*), **in ~ places** ann an caochladh àiteachan, ann an iomadach àite

sunflower *n* neòinean-grèine *m*

sunlight *n* solas *m* (na) grèine

sunny *adj* 1 grianach, **a ~ spot** bad grianach; 2 *in expr* ~ **interval/spell** greis *f* ghrèine (*gen of* grian *f*)

sunrise *n* èirigh *f* (na) grèine

sunset *n* dol-fodha *m* (na) grèine, laighe *mf invar* (na) grèine

sunshade *n* sgàilean-grèine *m*

sunstroke *n* beum-grèine *m*

sunwise *adj* deiseal (*the opposite of this is* tuathal)

superannuation *n* peinnseanachadh *m*

Super-Ego *n*, **the ~** an Sàr-Fhèin *m*

supercilious *adj* àrdanach

superficial *adj* uachdarach, eu-domhainn

superfluous *adj* thar a' chòrr, iomarcach

superior *adj* 1 (*in rank*) uachdarach; 2 (~ *in quality*) (n)as fheàrr, (*in past & conditional tenses*) (n)a b' fheàrr)

superior *n* (*in rank*) uachdaran *m*

supernatural *adj* os-nàdarra(ch)

supersonic *adj* thar-astar-fuaim

superstition *n* saobh-chràbhadh *m*

superstitious *adj* saobh-chràbhach

supervise *v* cùm sùil *f* (*with prep* air), stiùir *vt*

supper *n* suipeir *f*

supple *adj* sùbailte, lùbach

supplier *n* solaraiche *m*

supplies *n* (*esp foodstuff*) lòn *m*

supply *n* 1 (*abstr*) solar *m*; 2 (*more con*) *in expr* **there was a good ~ of meat**

bha an fheòil pàilt, bha feòil gu leòr ann/againn (&c); **3** *in expr* **in short** ~ gann, a dhìth, **food was in short** ~ bha biadh *m* gann/a dhìth

supply *v* solaraich *vt*

support *n* (*lit or fig*) taic(e) *f*, tacsa *m*, **financial** ~ taic-airgid *m*

support *v* **1** (*assist, back*) cùm taic *f* (*with prep* ri), thoir taic (*with prep* do), seas *vt*, **who will** ~ **you?** cò a chumas taic riut?, cò a sheasas thu?; **2** (*side with*) cùm taobh *m* (*with prep* ri), gabh taobh, **we ~ed her** chùm sinn taobh rithe, ghabh sinn a taobh; **3** (*maintain*) cùm *vt* suas, **I've a family to** ~ tha teaghlach *m* agam ri chumail suas

supporter *n* fear-taice *m*, neach-taice *m* (*pl* luchd-taice *m sing coll*)

supporting, supportive *adj* taiceil

suppose *v* saoil *vi*, **I** ~ **they'll be on the train** saoilidh mi gum bi iad air an trèana *f*, **I** ~ **you're right** saoilidh mi gu bheil thu ceart

suppress *v* (*emotions, rising &c*) mùch *vt*, ceannsaich *vt*, cùm *vt* fodha

supreme *adj* àrd- *prefix*, sàr- *prefix*, prìomh (*precedes the noun, which it lenites where possible*), ~ **power** àrd-chumhachd *f*

sure *adj* **1** cinnteach, deimhinn(e) & deimhinnte, (*of* às), **are you** ~ **she'll come?** a bheil thu cinnteach gun tig i?, **it'll rain, I'm** ~ (*of it*) bidh an t-uisge *m* ann, tha mi cinnteach/deimhinnt' às; **2** (*in statement of agreement, or certainty*) expressed by creid *vi* & double neg, **I'll be drunk tonight! I'm** ~ **you will!** bidh mi air an daorach *f* a-nochd! cha chreid mi nach bi!, **I'm** ~ **he'll be at the game tonight** cha chreid mi nach bi e aig a' ghèam a-nochd; **3** (*reliable &c*) earbsach, seasmhach

surety *n* (*esp in fin matters*) urras *m* (**for** air), *in expr* **stand (as)** ~ **for someone** rach *vi* an urras air cuideigin

surface *n* uachdar *m*, bàrr *m*, **on the** ~ **of the earth/the waves** air uachdar *m* na talmhainn/nan tonn *mpl*

surface *v* thig *vi* an uachdar *m*

surfeit *n* sàth *m*, leòr *f invar*, cus *m*, **we got a** ~ **of it** fhuair sinn ar sàth/ar leòr dheth, **a** ~ **of wine** cus fiona *m gen*

surge *v* brùchd *vi* (**out of** a-mach à), **they ~d out of the hall** bhrùchd iad a-mach às an talla *m*

surgeon *n* làmh-lèigh *m*

surgery *n* **1** (*the discipline*) làmh-leigheas *m*; **2** (*surgical intervention*) obair-lèigh *f*; **3** (*the place*) lèigh-lann *f* (dotair *m gen*), **a dental** ~ ionad *m* fiaclaire *m gen*; **4** (~ *of politician &c*) freasdal-lann *f*

surly *adj* gruamach, mùgach, gnù, iargalt(a)

surname *n* sloinneadh *m*, (*less usu*) cinneadh *m*, **what's your ~?** dè an sloinneadh a th' agaibh/a th' oirbh?, *also* dè an fhin' a th' agaibh

surplus *n* còrr *m*, (*excessive*) cus *m*, **our guests have eaten, give the** ~ **to the neighbours** tha ar n-aoighean *mpl* air ithe, thoir an còrr do na nàbaidhean *mpl*, **a** ~ **of talking** cus bruidhne (*gen of* bruidhinn *f*)

surprise *n* **1** iongnadh *m*, (*stronger*) mòr-iongnadh *m*, iongnantas *m*; **2** *in expr* **she took us by** ~ thàinig i òirnn gun fhiosta

surprise *v* **1** cuir iongnadh *m* (*with prep* air), **she ~d us** chuir i iongnadh oirnn; **2** (*by arriving unexpectedly*) **she ~d us** thàinig i òirnn gun fhiosta

surprised *adj & past part, in expr* **I was ~** ghabh mi iongantas *m*/iongnadh *m*

surprising *adj* iongantach, **that's not ~** (*trad*) chan iongnadh *m* sin

surrender *n* gèilleadh *m*, strìochdadh *m*, (**to** do)

surrender *v* gèill *vi*, strìochd *vi*, (**to** do)

surround *v* **1** cuartaich & cuairtich *vt*, iadh & iath *vt*; **2** *in expr* **the house was completely ~ed by woods** bha an taigh air a chuairteachadh ceithir thimcheall le coilltean *fpl*, *also* bha coilltean fada mun cuairt air an taigh

survey *n* **1** (*of land &c*) tomhas *m*, (*less trad*) suirbhidh *m*, **the Ordnance Survey** an Suirbhidh Òrdanais; **2** (*a study, investigation &c*) sgrùdadh *m*, rannsachadh *m*; **3** (*~ in form of questionnaire &c*) suirbhidh *m*, **postal ~** suirbhidh tron phost *m*

survey *v* **1** (*land &c*) tomhais *vt*; **2** (*study, investigate &c*) sgrùd *vt*, rannsaich *vt*, dèan sgrùdadh/rannsachadh *m* (*with prep* air)

surveyor *n* fear-tomhais *m*, neach-tomhais *m* (*pl* luchd-tomhais *m sing coll*)

survive *v* thig *vi* beò, mair *vi* beò, (**on** air), cùm beò, **if I ~** ma thig mi às beò, ma mhaireas mi beò, **I can't ~ on that!** cha tig mi beò air sin!, **how are you? I'm surviving** ciamar a tha thu? tha mi beò fhathast/tha mi a' cumail beò

suspect *adj* fo amharas *m*

suspect *n* neach *m* fo amharas *m*

suspect *v* bi *vi irreg* amharas *m* (*with prep* aig), **I ~ that these figures are wrong** tha amharas agam gu bheil na figearan *mpl* seo ceàrr

suspend *v* **1** (*phys*) croch *vt*; **2** (*put in abeyance*) cuir dàil *f* (*with prep* ann), **~ the work** cuir dàil air an obair *f*; **3** (*relieve of duties*) cuir *vt* à dreuchd *f*

suspension *n* crochadh *m*, *in expr* **~ bridge** drochaid-chrochaidh *f*

suspicion *n* amharas *m*

suspicious *adj* amharasach (**of** à)

sustain *v* (*feed &c*) cùm *vt* suas, beathaich *vt*

sustenance *n* lòn *m*, beathachadh *m*

swagger *v* spai(s)dirich *vi*

swallow[1] *n* (*of liquid*) balgam *m*, (*more copious*) steallag *f*

swallow[2] *n* (*bird*) gobhlan-gaoithe *m*

swallow *v* sluig & slug *vti*

swallowing *n* slugadh *m*

swamp *n* boglach *f*, fèith(e) *f*, bog *m*

swan *n* eala *f*

swarm *n* sgaoth *m*

swarm *v* sgaothaich *vi*

swarthy *adj* (*of persons*) ciar, lachdann

sway *v* luaisg *vi*, tulg *vi*

swear *n* mionn *mf*, bòid *f*

swear *v* 1 (*legal &c*) mionnaich *vti*; 2 *in exprs* ~ **an oath** thoir mionnan *m*, *also* mionnaich/gabh bòid *f*, **will you ~ to it?** an toir thu d' fhacal *m* air?; 3 (*curse &c*) mionnaich *vi*

swearing *n* 1 (*of legal oath &c*) mionnachadh *m*; 2 (*cursing, bad language*) droch-chainnt *f*, mionnachadh *m*, guidheachan *mpl*

sweat *n* fallas *m*, ~ **gland** fàireag-fhallais *f*

sweat *v* bi *v irreg* fallas (*with prep* air), cuir fallas (*with prep* de), **I'm ~ing** tha fallas orm, tha mi a' cur fallas dhìom, *also* tha mi nam fhallas

sweaty *adj* fallasach

sweep *v* sguab *vti*

sweet *adj* 1 (*tastes*) milis; 2 (*smells*) cùbhraidh; 3 (*sounds, music*) binn

sweet *n* 1 (*dessert*) mìlsean *m*; 2 (*sweetie*) suiteas *m*, ~s suiteis *mpl*, siùcairean *mpl*, rudan *mpl* milis

sweeten *v* mìlsich *vt*

sweetheart *n* leannan *m*

sweetness *n* mìlseachd *f invar*

swell *v* at *vi*, sèid *vi*, (*less usu*) bòc *vi*

swelling *v* at *m*, bòcadh *m*

swift *adj* 1 (*of movement*) luath, siubhlach; 2 (*of person: ~ in performing tasks &c*) clis, deas, ealamh; 3 (*sudden*) grad

swim *v* snàmh *vi*, **I like to ~** is toigh leam a bhith a' snàmh

swimmer *n* snàmhaiche *m*

swimming *n* snàmh *m*

swing *n* 1 (*child's ~*) dreallag *f*; 2 (*in voting habits &c*) gluasad *m*

swing *v* (*in wind &c*) luaisg *vi*, tulg *vi*

Swiss *adj* Eilbheiseach

switch[1] *n* (*elec*) suidse *f*

switch[2] *n* (*supple stick*) gad *m*

switch *v* 1 (*lights &c*) ~ **on** cuir *vt* air, ~ **off** cuir *vt* às/dheth; 2 (*exchange, ~ round*) cuir *vt* an àite *m* a chèile, **she ~ed the glasses round** chuir i na glainneachan *fpl* an àite a chèile

switchboard *n* suids-chlàr *m*

swoon *n* neul *m*, laigse *f*

swoon *v* rach *vi* an neul *m*, rach *vi* an laigse *f*, fannaich *vi*, fanntaich *vi*

sword *n* claidheamh *m*, **two-handed** ~ claidheamh dà-làimh, claidheamh mòr

swordsman *n* claidheamhair *m*

syllable *n* 1 (*lit*) lide *m*; 2 (*loosely*) bìog *f*, bìd *m*, smid *f*, *esp in expr* **they** (*&c*) **didn't utter a ~** cha tuirt iad (*&c*) bìog/smid

syllabus *n* clàr-oideachais *m*, clàr-oideachaidh *m*

symbol *n* 1 comharra(dh) *m*, **status ~** comharradh-inbhe *m*; 2 (*Lit &c*) samhla *m*

symbolic, symbolical *adj* samhlachail

symbolise *v* riochdaich *vt*, samhlaich *vt*

symbolism *n* samhlachas *m*

symmetrical *adj* cothromaichte

symmetry *n* co-chothromachd *f invar*

sympathetic *adj* co-fhulangach, mothachail, co-mhothachail, tuigseach

sympathise *v* co-fhuiling *vi*, co-mhothaich *vi*

sympathy *n* co-fhulangas *m*, co-mhothachadh *m*, tuigse *f invar*

symposium *n* co-labhairt *f*

symptom *n* comharra(dh) *m*

synopsis *n* giorrachadh *m*, geàrr-chunntas *m*

synthetic *adj* fuadain

syphon *n* lìonadair *m*

syringe *n* steallair(e) *m*

system *n* **1** (*order*) riaghailt *f*, rian *m*; **2** (*mechanisms, procedures &c*) siostam *m*, modh *mf*, dòigh *f*, **~ of government** siostam riaghlaidh *m gen*, modh-riaghlaidh *m*; **3** *in expr* **public address ~** glaodhaire *m*

systematic(al) *adj* riaghailteach, òrdail

T

table *n* **1** bòrd *m*; **2** (*in book &c*) clàr *m*, **~ of contents** clàr-innse *m*

tacit *adj* tosdach, **~ approval** aonta tosdach

taciturn *adj* tosdach, dùinte, (*through shyness*) diùid

tack[1] *n* (*sailing*) gabhail *mf*, taca *f*

tack[2] *n* (*small nail*) tacaid *f*

tacket *n* tacaid *f*

tackle *n* (*gear, equipment*) uidheam *f sing coll*, acainn *f sing coll*

tackle *v* thoir ionnsaigh *f*, thoir oidhirp *f*, (*with prep* air), rach *vi* an sàs *m* (*with prep* ann an), **tomorrow we'll ~ Sgùrr Alasdair** a-maireach bheir sinn ionnsaigh/oidhirp air Sgùrr *m* Alasdair *gen*, **she ~d her new job full of optimism** chaidh i an sàs san obair *f* ùr aice 's i làn dòchais *m gen*

tactic *n* innleachd *m*

tactical *adj* innleachdach

tadpole *n* ceann-pholan *m*, ceann-simid *m*

tail *n* earball *m*, **a dog wagging its ~** cù *m* (is e) a' crathadh earbaill *gen*, **forked ~** earball gobhlach

tailor *n* tàillear *m*

taint *v* **1** (*sully*) truaill *vt*, salaich *vt*; **2** (*flavour*) thoir droch bhlas *m* (**to** do)

take *v* **1** gabh *vti*, **~ place** gabh àite *m*, *also* tachair *vi*, **~ leave** gabh cead *m invar* (**of** de), **~ in** (*ie comprise, include, also* ~ **in** *mentally*) gabh *vt* a-steach, **~ in hand**, **~ on** (*work &c*) gabh *vt* os làimh (*dat of* làmh *f*), **~ pity** gabh truas *m* (**on** de & ri), (*food &c*) **will you ~ a cup of tea?** an gabh thu cupan *m* tì?, **~ counsel/advice** gabh comhairle *f*, **~ a rest/ break** gabh fois *f*, **~ things easily** gabh air a (*&c*) s(h)ocair *f*, *in expr* (*excl*) **~ it easy!** socair! *or* air do shocair!, **~ a stroll/walk** gabh cuairt *f*, **she took to her bed** ghabh i ris an leabaidh *f*, **~ advantage of X** (*not nec unfairly*) gabh cothrom *m* air X, **~ (unfair) advantage of X** gabh brath *m* air X, **the hall will ~ 300 (people)** gabhaidh an talla trì ceud (duine); **2** thoir *vt*, **~ it to him** thoir dha e, **~ away** thoir air falbh, **I'll ~ a trip to Glasgow** bheir mi sgrìob *f* do Ghlaschu, **~ a look** thoir sùil *f* (**at** air), **~ care (of yourself)** thoir an aire (ort fhèin), **~ yourself off!** thoir do chasan *fpl* leat!, *also* tog ort!, **they took to their heels** thug iad na buinn (*pl of* bonn *m*) asta, **she took herself off to America** thug i Ameireagaidh *f* oirre, *also* thog i oirre gu Ameireagaidh; **3** *misc exprs* **~ a breather!** leig d' anail *f*!, **~ a photograph** tog dealbh *mf*, (*in family &c*) **~ after someone** rach *vi* ri taobh cuideigin *mf*, **~ an exam** feuch deuchainn *f*, **~ my hand** beir *vi* air mo làimh (*dat of* làmh *f*), **~ to someone** teòdh *vi* ri cuideigin *m*, **~ your coat off** cuir *vt* dhìot do chòta *m*, **~ part** gabh pàirt *mf* (**in** ann), compàirtich *vi*, **~ (Holy) Communion** comanaich *vi*, **~ on** (*workers*) fastaich & fastaidh *vt*, **~ in** (*ie understand*) tuig *vt*, (*ie deceive*) meall *vt*

taken in *adj & past part* (*deceived*) meallta

tale *n* sgeulachd *f*, (*esp trad* ~) sgeul *m*

talent *n* tàlann *m*

talented *adj* tàlantach, ealanta

talk *n* **1** (*abstr*) bruidhinn *f*; **2** (*conversation*) còmhradh *m*, **we had a** ~ rinn sinn còmhradh (beag), *also* (*more fam*) chuir sinn ar cinn *mpl* còmhla, **a bit of a** ~ còmhradh beag, bonn *m* còmhraidh *gen*; **3** (*address, speech*) òraid *f*, **give a** ~ thoir *vt* seachad òraid, dèan *vt* òraid, (**to** do)

talk *v* **1** bruidhinn *vi*, (*less usu*) labhair *vi*, (**to** ri); **2** (*converse*) dèan còmhradh *m*; **3** *in exprs* ~**ing of this and that** a' còmhradh a-null 's a-nall, *also* a' cnàmh na cìre, **the minister was** ~**ing away** bha am ministear a' cur dheth

talkative *adj* còmhraiteach, bruidhneach, (*more pej*) beulach, cabach, gabach

talking *n* bruidhinn *f*, (*less usu*) labhairt *f*

tall *adj* (*people, buildings &c*) àrd, (*of people, less usu*) fad(a), **a** ~ **woman/ building** boireannach/togalach *m* àrd, **a** ~ **lanky woman** boireannach fada caol

talon *n* spu(i)r *m*, ìne *f*

tame *adj* **1** (*animal &c*) calla & callda, solt; **2** (*insipid, unexciting*) gun bhrìgh *f*, gun smior *m*, **his speech was** ~ bha an òraid *f* aige gun bhrìgh

tame *v* callaich *vt*, ceannsaich *vt*

tamper *v* **1** bean *vi*, buin *vi*, (**with** do *or* ri), **don't** ~ **with the radio** na bean ris an rèidio *m*; **2** (*more maliciously*) ~ **with** mill *vt*

tan *v* **1** (*leather*) cairt & cart *vt*; **2** (*sunbathe*) gabh a' ghrian

tangible *adj* beanailteach

tank[1] *n* (*for water &c*) amar *m*

tank[2] *n* (*warfare*) tanca *f*

tanker *n* tancair *m*, **oil** ~ tancair ola *f gen*

tanning *n* (*leather*) cartadh *m*

tannoy *n* glaodhaire *m*

tap[1] *n* (*plumbing*) tap *mf*, goc *m*

tap[2] *n* (*light blow*) cnag *f*

tape *n* teip *f*, **measuring** ~ teip-thomhais *f*, **recording** ~ teip-chlàraidh *f*, **did you hear their new** ~? an cuala tu an teip ùr aca?

tar *n* teàrr *f*, bìth *f*

tardy *adj* **1** (*late*) fadalach; **2** (*slow*) mall, màirnealach, (*less usu*) athaiseach

targe, target *n* targaid *f*

target *n* **1** (*archery &c*) targaid *f*, cuspair *m*; **2** *in expr* (*publicity &c*) ~ **audience** luchd-amais *m sing coll*

tariff *n* clàr-phrìsean *m*

tart *adj* **1** (*tastes*) geur, searbh; **2** (*remarks &c*) geur, searbh, guineach

tartan *n* breacan *m*

tartan *adj* breacanach, tartanach, ~ **cloth/clothing** aodach breacanach/ tartanach

task *n* **1** obair *f*, pìos *m* obrach (*gen of* obair *f*), gnìomh *m*, gnothach *m* **the ~ before us** an obair/an gnìomh/an gnothach a tha romhainn, **~ force** buidheann *f* ghnìomha *gen*; **2** *in expr* **take to ~** thoir achmhasan *m* (*with prep* do), **I must take them to ~** feumaidh mi achmhasan a thoirt dhaibh

taste *m* **1** (*flavour*) blas *m*, **the ~ of honey** blas na meala (*gen of* mil *f*); **2** (*small quantity*) blasad *m*, **a ~ of honey** blasad meala; **3** (*artistic &c discernment*) tuigse *f invar* (a thaobh ealaine *f gen &c*)

taste *v* **1** (*as vt*) blais *vt*, feuch *vt*, **~ this beer** blais/feuch an leann *m* a tha seo; **2** (*as vi*) *in exprs* **it doesn't ~ of anything** chan eil blas *m* (sam bith/ idir) air, **it ~s of paint** tha blas a' pheanta air, **cake tasting of honey** cèic *f* air blas na meala (*gen of* mil *f*)

tasteless *adj* mì-bhlasta, gun bhlas *m*

tasty *adj* blasta, (*stronger*) blasmhor

tatter *n* luideag *f*, cearb *f*, **the curtains are in ~s** tha na cùirtearan *mpl* nan luideagan

tattered *adj & past part* luideach, cearbach, nan (*&c*) luideagan *fpl*, reubte

tatty *adj* luideach, cearbach

taunt *n* magadh *m*

taunt *v* mag *vi* (*with prep* air), **they were ~ing her** bha iad a' magadh oirre

taut *adj* teann

tavern *n* taigh-òsta *m*

tawdry *adj* suarach

tawny *adj* lachdann, odhar, ciar

tax *n* cìs *f*, càin *f*, **~ avoidance** seachnadh *m* cìse *gen*, **~ cut** gearradh *m* cìse *gen*, **~ rate** ìre *f* cìse *gen*

tax *v* **1** (*cause to pay tax*) cuir/leag càin *f* (*with prep* air), **~ the population** cuir càin air an t-sluagh *m*; **2** (*levy tax on goods &c*) cuir cìs *f* (*with prep* air), **~ tobacco** cuir cìs air tombaca *m*

taxable *adj* cìs-bhuailteach

taxation *n* cìs *f*, càin *f*

taxi *n* tagsaidh *m*

tea *n* **1** (*drink*) tì *f invar*, teatha *f invar*, **a cup of ~** cupa *m* tì *gen*; **2** (*meal*) biadh *m* feasgair *f gen*

teach *v* teagaisg *vti*, ionnsaich *vti*, (**to** do), **my grandfather taught me what wisdom I have** theagaisg mo sheanair *m* dhomh na tha agam de ghliocas *m*, **~ maths** teagaisg matamataig *m*, **~ boys** teagaisg gillean *mpl*, **~ boys maths/~ maths to boys** teagaisg matamataig do ghillean

teacher *n* fear-teagaisg *m*, neach-teagaisg *m*, bean-teagaisg *f*, tidsear *m*, maighistir-sgoile *m*, ban(a)-mhaighistir-sgoile *f*, **~s** luchd-teagaisg *m sing coll*

teaching *n* teagasg *m*, (*less usu*) oileanachadh *m*, **the ~ staff** an luchd-teagaisg *m sing coll*

team *n* buidheann *mf*, (*esp sport*) sgioba *mf*, **research** ~ buidheann-rannsachaidh, **football** ~ sgioba ball-coise *m gen*

tear *n* reubadh *m*, sracadh *m*

tear *v* **1** (*lacerate &c*) reub *vt*, srac *vt*; **2** (*snatch*) spìon *vt* (**from** à), ~ **it (away) from him** spìon às e; **3** (*rush &c*) falbh (*&c*) na (*&c*) d(h)ian-ruith *f*, **she tore out of the house** dh'fhàg i an taigh *m* na dian-ruith, *also* dh'fhàg i an taigh aig peilear *m* a beatha *f gen*

tear *n* sracadh *m*

tear, teardrop *n* deur *m*

tearful *adj* deurach

tease *v* tarraing *vi* (*with prep* à), farranaich *vt*, **he's teasing the other boy** tha e a' tarraing às a' bhalach *m* eile

teat *n* sine *f*

tea-towel *n* tubhailte-shoithichean *f*

technical *adj* teignigeach, teicneolach

technician *n* teicneolaiche *m*

technique *n* dòigh(-obrach) *f*, alt *m*

technological *adj* teicneolach

technologist *n* teicneolaiche *m*

technology *n* teicneolas *m*, (*IT*) **information** ~ teicneolas fiosrachaidh *m gen*

tedious *adj* fadalach, liosda, màirnealach

tedium *n* fadachd *f invar*, fadal *m*, fadalachd *f invar*, liosdachd *f invar*

teem *v* cuir *vi* thairis (**with** le), **the woods ~ed/were ~ing with creatures of every kind** bha na coilltean *fpl* a' cur thairis le creutairean *mpl* de gach seòrsa *m*

teenager *n* (*of either sex*) deugaire *m*

teens *npl* deugan *mpl*

telephone *n* fòn *mf*, **I was talking to him on the** ~ bha mi a' bruidhinn ris air a' fòn, **what's your** ~ **number?** dè an àireamh-fòn *f* a th' agad?

telephone *v* cuir fòn *mf*, fòn *vi*, fònaig *vi*, (*all with prep* gu), **he ~d her** chuir e fòn thuice, dh'fhòn e thuice

telescope *n* prosbaig *mf*

television *n* telebhisean *m*, *used with & without art*, **I saw a good programme on (the)** ~ chunnaic mi prògram math air an telebhisean, ~ **licence** cead *m* telebhisein *gen*

tell *v* **1** (*command*) òrdaich *vi* (*with prep* do), **they told me to shut the gates** dh'òrdaich iad dhomh / (*less formal*) thuirt iad rium na geataichean *mpl* a dhùnadh; **2** (*recount, relate*) innis *vti*, ~ **me about it!** innis dhomh mu dheidhinn!, ~ **a story** innis sgeulachd *f*, **I'll** ~ **what I know (about it)** innsidh mi na tha a (*for* de) dh'fhios *m* agam (air), **to** ~ **(you) the truth, I don't know** leis an fhìrinn innse, chan eil fhios am

temper *n* **1** nàdar *m*, **bad** ~ droch nàdar; **2** *in expr* **in a bad** ~ diombach *&* diumbach, crost(a) *&* crosda

temperament *n* mèinn *f*, nàdar *m*

temperance *n* stuamachd *f invar*

temperate *adj* (*of people*) measarra, stuama, (*of weather*) sèimh

temperature *n* teodhachd *f invar*

tempest *n* doineann *f*, gailleann *f*

tempestuous *adj* gailbheach, doineannach

temple[1] *n* (*relig*) teampall *m*

temple[2] *n* (*anat*) lethcheann *m*

temporal *adj* aimsireil, talmhaidh, saoghalta

temporary *adj* sealach, ~ **accommodation** àite-còmhnaidh sealach

tempt *v* buair *vt*, meall *vt*, (*with milder overtones*) tàlaidh *vt*, **the devil/evil one ~ed me** bhuair/mheall an diabhal *m* mi, ~ **the customers back** tàlaidh an luchd-ceannach *m sing coll* air ais

temptation *n* buaireadh *m*, mealladh *m*

ten *n & adj* 1 deich; 2 (*of people*) deichnear *mf invar* (*with gen pl*), ~ **sons** deichnear mhac

tenacious *adj* dìorrasach

tenacity *n* dìorrasachd *f invar*

tenancy *n* gabhaltas *m*

tenant *n* màladair *m*

tend[1] *v* (*care for*) eiridnich *vt*, ~ **the sick/ill** eiridnich na h-euslaintich *mpl*

tend[2] *v* 1 (*be liable to*) bi *vi irreg* buailteach, bi dual(t)ach, (*with infinitive of verb or with prep* air), **he ~s to be mean** tha e dualach/buailteach a bhith spìocach, **she ~s to spend money** tha i dualach/buailteach airgead *m* a chosg, **we ~ to get tired** tha sinn buailteach air fàs sgìth; 2 (*habit, routine*) *in expr* ~ **to** mar as trice bi *vi irreg, with participial construction*, **we ~ to get up very late on Sunday** mar as trice, bidh sinn ag èirigh glè anmoch (air) Là *m* na Sàbaid

tendency *n* 1 (*trend*) aomadh *m*, **economic** ~ aomadh eaconomach; 2 (*propensity*) *in expr* **he** (*&c*) **has a** ~ **to complain** (*&c*) tha e (*&c*) buailteach/dual(t)ach a bhith a' gearan (*&c*)

tender *adj* (*phys or emotionally*) maoth, (*emotionally*) bog, **a ~ heart** cridhe bog

tender *n* (*commerce &c: offer*) tairgse *f*

tender *v* (*commerce &c: offer*) tairg *vti*

tendril *n* ògan *m*

tense *n* (*gram*) tràth *m*, **the present** ~ an tràth làthaireach, **the past (preterite)** ~ an tràth caithte, **the imperfect** ~ an tràth neo-choileanta, **the perfect** ~ an tràth coileanta, **the future** ~ an tràth teachdail, **the conditional** ~ an tràth cumhach

tense *adj* 1 (*phys*) teann, rag; 2 (*emotionally, nervously*) nearbhach, clisgeach, frionasach

tense *v* teannaich *vti*

tension *n* 1 (*esp phys*) teannachadh *m*; 2 (*emotional, nervous*) frionas *m*

tent *n* teanta *f*, (*large*) pàillean *m*, (*larger still*) puball & pùball *m*

tenth *adj* deicheamh

tenure *n* gabhaltas *m*

tepid *adj* (*lit & fig*) leth-fhuar, flodach, ~ **soup** brot *m* leth-fhuar, **the relationship between us had become** ~ bha an dàimh *mf invar* a bha eadarainn air fàs leth-fhuar

term[1] *n* **1** (*condition*) cumha *f*, **the ~s of the contract** cumhachan a' chùmhnaint; **2** (*terminology*) briathar *m*, **what/which** ~ **do you use for 'ministerial'?** cò am briathar a th' agaibh air 'ministerial'?, **technical ~s** briathran teicneolach/teignigeach; **3** (*in relationships*) *in exprs* **be on good ~s with someone** bi *vi irreg* rèidh ri cuideigin, **they are on bad ~s** tha iad troimh-chèile/thar a chèile, *also* chan eil iad a' tarraing ro mhath

term[2] *n* (*period*) teirm *f*, **the autumn** ~ teirm an fhoghair, **his** ~ **of office** teirm na dreuchd aige

terminal *n* (*IT*) ceann-obrach *m*

terminate *v* cuir crìoch *f* (*with prep* air), thoir *vt* gu crìch (*dat*), ~ **a lease** cuir crìoch air gabhail *mf*

terminology *n* **1** (*abstr*) briathrachas *m*; **2** (*con: in form of lexicon &c*) briathrachan *m*

terminus *n* ceann-uidhe *m*

terra firma *n* tìr *mf*

terrible *adj* (*with full or attenuated meaning*) eagalach, uabhasach, sgriosail, **it was just** ~! bha e dìreach eagalach/uabhasach/sgriosail!

terribly *adv* **1** uabhasach, anabarrach, eagalach, ~ **good** uabhasach/anabarrach math, *also* uabhasach fhèin math; **2** *in exprs* **how did it go? it went absolutely** ~! ciamar a chaidh dhuibh? cha deach(aigh) ach gu dubh dona!, **things are** ~ **busy just now** tha cùisean *fpl* garbh dripeil an-dràsta

terrier *n* abhag *f*

terrify *v* cuir oillt *f*, cuir eagal mòr, (*with prep* air), oilltich *vt*

territory *n* dùthaich *f*, tìr *mf*, **the Mackay** ~ Dùthaich MhicAoidh *m sing gen*

terror *n* uamhann & uabhann *m*, oillt *f*, uabhas *m*

terse *adj* aithghearr, **a** ~ **reply** freagairt *f* aithghearr

tertiary *adj in expr* ~ **education** foghlam *m* (aig) àrd-ìre *f invar*

test *n* **1** dearbhadh *m*, deuchainn *f*, **~s on a new car** dearbhaidhean air càr *m* ùr, **put to the** ~ cuir *vt* gu deuchainn, dearbh *vt*; **2** (*ed*) deuchainn *f*, **entrance** ~ deuchainn-inntrigidh *f*

test *v* cuir *vt* gu deuchainn *f*, dearbh *vt*, **they ~ed the new machines** chuir iad na h-innealan *mpl* ùra gu deuchainn

testament *n* (*legal &c, Bibl*) tiomnadh *m*, **the Old Testament** An Seann Tiomnadh, **the New Testament** An Tiomnadh Nuadh

testicle *n* magairle *mf*, clach *f*

testify *v* thoir fianais *f*

testimonial *n* teisteanas *m*

testimony *n* fianais *f*, teisteanas *m*, dearbhadh *m*

testy, tetchy *adj* frionasach, cas

tether *n* feist(e) *f*, teadhair *f*, *in exprs* ~ **post** cipean *m*, (*calque*) **at the end of my** ~ aig ceann *m* mo theadhrach *gen*

text *n* **1** teacsa *f*; **2** (*of sermon &c*) ceann-teagaisg *m*

textual *adj* teacsail

than *conj* **1** na, **they are older** ~ **me** tha iad nas sine na mise; **2** *in expr* **more** ~ còrr is, barrachd air, **more** ~ **twenty miles** còrr is/barrachd air fichead *m* mìle *mf sing*, **more** ~ **Mary has** barrachd air na tha aig Màiri

thank *v* **1** thoir taing *f* (*with prep* do), **I want to** ~ **you** tha mi airson taing a thoirt dhut/dhuibh; **2** *in exprs* ~ **you!** tapadh leat/leibh!, (*less usu*) taing dhut/dhuibh!, ~ **you very much!** mòran taing!, ceud taing!

thankful *adj* taingeil, buidheach

thanks *n* taing *f*, **many** ~!, ~ **a lot!** mòran taing!, **give** ~ thoir taing (**to** do)

that *adj* sin, a tha 'n sin, (*usu more distant or remote*) ud, ~ **book** an leabhar sin/ud, an leabhar a tha 'n sin, (*as adv*) **it wasn't** ~ **good** cha robh e cho math sin

that *rel pron* a, (*in neg*) nach, **the drink** ~ **I drank** an deoch *f* a dh'òl mi, **the film** ~ **I didn't see** am film nach fhaca mi

that *pron* sin, (*usu more distant or remote*) siud, **what's** ~? dè a tha sin/siud?, ~**'s my house** sin an taigh agam, ~**'s the point** is e sin an rud/a' chùis, ~ **is my hope**, ~**'s what I hope** 's e sin mo dhòchas *m*, ~**'s a lot of money** 's e airgead mòr a tha sin, **it wasn't as good as** ~! cha robh e cho math sin!, **are you tired? I am** ~! a bheil thu sgìth? tha mi sin! (*also* 's mi a tha!), ~**'s it!** sin e!

that *conj* **1** gu, gun, (*before b, f, m & p*) gum, (*neg*) nach & (*with v* is) gur, **it's certain/definite** ~ **she's lost** 's cinnteach gu bheil i air chall, **I'm glad** ~ **you came** tha mi toilichte gun tàinig sibh, **they said** ~ **they weren't ready** thuirt iad nach robh iad deiseil, **is it gold? I don't think** ~ **it is** an e òr a th' ann? cha chreid mi gur e; **2** *in expr* **so** ~ (*ie with the intention* ~), gus am, gus an, (*neg*) gus nach, **so** ~ **he would have some pocket money** gus am biodh airgead-pòcaid *m* aige, **so that you can find the house** gus an urrainn dhut an taigh *m* a lorg, **so** ~ **she wouldn't be hungry** gus nach biodh an t-acras oirre; **3** *in expr* **so** ~ (*ie with the result* ~, *also, with the intention* ~) air dhòigh *f* is, air chor *m* is, (*with conjs* gu, gun, gum, (*neg*) nach), **she didn't lock the door so** ~ **I could get in** cha do ghlas i an doras *m* air dhòigh/air chor 's gum (b' urrainn dhomh) faighinn a-steach, **he spoke in a low voice, so** ~ **I didn't hear him** bhruidhinn e ann an guth *m* ìosal, air dhòigh/air chor is nach cuala mi e

thatch *n* tughadh *m*

thatch *v* tugh *vt*

thaw *n* aiteamh *m*

thaw *v* leagh *vti*

the *definite art* **1** *masc sing: nom & acc* an, am, an t-, *gen & dat* an, a', an t-; **2** *fem sing: nom & acc* an, a', an t-, *gen* na, na h-, *dat* an, a', an t-; **3** *pl, both genders: nom & acc* na, na h-, *gen* nan, nam, *dat* na, na h- (*see table on p. 422*)

theatre *n* taigh-cluiche *m*

theft *n* goid *f*, mèirle *&* meirle *f invar*

them *pron mpl & fpl* iad, (*emph form*) iadsan

theme *n* **1** cuspair *m*, **the ~ of her talk** cuspair na h-òraid aice; **2** (*mus*) ùrlar *m*

themselves *reflexive pron* iad-fhèin, *for examples of use see* **myself**

then *adv* **1** (*at that time*) aig an àm *m* sin, **I was young ~**, bha mi òg aig an àm sin; **2** (*next*) an uair sin, **he read the paper and ~ he went to bed** leugh e am pàipear(-naidheachd) 's an uair sin chaidh e a chadal *m*/ don leabaidh *f*; **3** (*in that case*) ma-thà *&* ma-tà, **the door's open! close it ~!** tha an doras fosgailte! dùin e ma-tà!, **right ~!** ceart ma-thà!

theologian *n* diadhaire *m*

theology *n* diadhachd *f invar*

theory *n* **1** (*principles*) teòiridh *f*, **in ~** a rèir teòiridh *gen*; **2** (*a surmise &c*) beachd *m*, beachd-smuain *m*

therapist *n* leasaiche *m*, teiripiche *m*, **speech ~** leasaiche-cainnt *m*

there *adv* **1** an sin, sin, (*usu more distant or remote*) an siud, (*more emph*) ann an sin, ann an siud, **I was born ~** rugadh mi an sin, **where's my book? it's ~/~ it is** càit a bheil an leabhar *m* agam? sin e, **what are you doing ~?** dè a tha thu a' dèanamh ann an sin?; **2** (**over**) **~** (*usu expr position*) thall (an sin), **here and ~** thall 's a-bhos, an siud 's an seo, **over ~ in America** (*&c*) ann an Ameireagaidh *f* (*&c*) thall, **what are they doing over ~?** dè a tha iad a' dèanamh thall an sin?; **3** (*present*) ann, an làthair *f*, **I knew those who were ~** bha mi eòlach air na bha ann/na bha an làthair

there *pron* **1** (*expressed by the v irreg* bi, *& a prep phrase*) **~'s a man at the door** tha duine *m* aig an doras *m*, **~'s not a lot of peace in the world** chan eil mòran sìthe *f gen* san t-saoghal *m*; **2** (*expressed by the v irreg* bi *& a prep pron*) **~'s a strike** tha stailc *f* ann, **~ was no petrol** cha robh peatrail *m* ann, **~'s nothing to be done** chan eil dad *m invar* ri dhèanamh, *also* chan eil cothrom *m* air; **3** (*expressed by the v irreg* bi *& a verbal expr*) **~'s something happening** tha rudeigin a' tachairt

therefore *adv* a chionn sin, air sgàth sin, mar sin, do bhrìgh sin, uime sin, **we've no money, ~ we've no food** chan eil airgead *m* againn, (agus) mar sin/air sgàth sin chan eil biadh *m* againn

thereupon *adv* le sin, leis a sin, **the bar closed, ~ he went home** dhùin am bar, (is) leis a sin chaidh e dhachaigh

thermometer *n* teas-mheidh *f*, tomhas-teas *m*

these *pron, see* **this**

thesis *n* tràchdas *m*

they *pron mpl & fpl* iad, (*emph forms*) iadsan, iad fhèin

thick *adj* **1** (*phys*) tiugh; **2** (*of trees, hair, vegetation &c: dense*) dlùth, dòmhail
    & dùmhail; **3** (*mentally: fam*) tiugh

thicket *n* doire *mf*, bad *m*

thickness *n* tighead *m*

thickset *adj* tomadach & tomaltach

thief *n* gadaiche *m*, mèirleach & meirleach *m*

thieve *v* goid *vti*, dèan meirle *f invar*, (*usu more petty*) dèan braid *f*

thieving *n* goid *f*, mèirle & meirle *f invar*, (*usu more petty*) braid *f*, **are you
    still at your ~?** a bheil thu ri goid fhathast?

thigh *n* sliasaid *f*, (*less usu*) leis *f*

thimble *n* meuran *m*

thin *adj* **1** (*of persons*) caol, tana, seang; **2** (*of substances: ~ in consistency*) lom,
    tana, **~ porridge** brochan *m* lom/tana; **3** (*of trees, hair &c: sparse*) tana,
    gann, lom

thin *v* (*crops &c*) tanaich *vt*

thing *n* **1** (*object*) rud *m*, nì *m*, **a stone is a ~** 's e rud a tha ann an clach *f*; **2**
    (*more fam & general*) càil *m invar*, sian & sìon *m*, dad *m invar*, **what's in
    the cupboard? not a ~** dè a th' anns a' phreas *m*? chan eil càil/sian/
    dad; **3** (*matter, affair &c*) cùis *f*, rud *m*, **~s are pretty busy just now**
    tha cùisean gu math dripeil an-dràsda, **their divorce was a bad ~** 's e
    droch rud a bh' anns an dealachadh-phòsaidh *m* aca; **4** (*point at issue*)
    cùis *f*, gnothach *m*, **did he steal it or didn't he? that's the ~** an do ghoid
    e e no nach do ghoid? 's e sin a' chùis/an gnothach; **5** *in exprs* **first ~ in
    the morning** a' chiad char *m* sa mhadainn *f*, **I haven't heard a ~ about
    him** cha chuala mi guth *m* mu dheidhinn

think *v* **1** (*consider, contemplate: philosopher &c*) beachd-smaoin(t)ich *vi*,
    beachdaich *vi*, (*less rigorously*) smaoin(t)ich *vi*, cnuas & cnuasaich *vi*,
    meòmhraich & meamhraich *vi*, (**about** air), **he set me ~ing** chuir e gu
    smaointeachadh *m* mi; **2** (*be of the opinion*) creid *vi*, saoil *vi*, bi *vi irreg*
    den bheachd *m*, **I ~ that you are right** tha mi a' creidsinn/saoilidh
    mi/tha mi den bheachd gu bheil sibh ceart; **3** *in exprs* **I ~ it good** (*&c*)
    (*trad*) is math (*&c*) leam e, **~ over** cnuas & cnuasaich *vi* (*with prep* air),
    ~ over what happened cnuasaich air na thachair

thinking *n* **1** (*the process, faculty, activity*) smaoin(t)eachadh *m*, beachdachadh
    m; **2** (*rationale*) feallsanachd *f*, **the ~ behind the proposals** feallsanachd
    nam molaidhean *mpl*

think-tank *n* buidheann-bheachdachaidh *f*

thinning *adj* tana, **~ hair** falt tana

third *n* trian *m invar*, **I lost two ~s of my savings** chaill mi dà thrian de
    mo shàbhaladh *m*

third *num adj* **1** treas, **the ~ (day) of the month** an treas là *m* den mhìos *mf*;
    2 *in expr* (*insurance &c*) **~ party** an treas neach *m*

thirst *n* pathadh *m*, (*stronger*) tart *m*, ìota(dh) *m*

thirsty *adj* **1** pàiteach, (*stronger*) tartmhor, ìotmhor, **a ~ dog** cù pàiteach; **2** *in exprs* **I was/I grew ~** bha/thàinig am pathadh orm

thirteenth *num adj* treas deug, **the ~ (day) of the month** an treas là *m* deug den mhìos *mf*

thirty *num & adj* deich ar (*for* thar) fhichead, fichead 's a deich, (*in alternative numbering system*) trithead *m*

this, these *pron* **1** seo, **who's this?** cò (a) tha seo?, **this is my wife, and these are the boys** seo a' bhean agam, agus seo na gillean; **2** (*as demonstrative adjective*) seo, *also* a tha seo, **this boy** am balach (a tha) seo, **this one** (*m*) am fear (a tha) seo, (*f*) an tè (a tha) seo, **these ones** an fheadhainn *f sing coll* (a tha) seo, iad seo, **these (ones) are going home** tha an fheadhainn seo/iad seo a' dol dhachaigh

thistle *n* cluaran *m*, fòghnan *m*, gìogan *m*

thither *adv* **1** ann, a-null, **I'm going ~** tha mi a' dol ann/a-null; **2** *in expr* **hither and ~** thall 's a-bhos, a-null 's a nall

thong *n* iall *f*

thorax *n* cliabh *m*

thorn *n* **1** (*the plant*) droigheann *m*; **2** (*the prickle*) dealg *f*, bior *m*

thorny *adj* **1** (*lit*) droighneach; **2** (*fig: tricky, sensitive &c*) duilich. doirbh, **a ~ problem** duilgheadas doirbh/duilich

thorough *adj* **1** (*of person*) pongail, dìcheallach, dealasach; **2** (*of job of work &c*) mionaideach, mion- *prefix*, **a ~ enquiry/study** sgrùdadh mionaideach, **~ knowledge/acquaintance** mion-eòlas *m* (**of/with** air); **3** (*out and out, utter*) dearg (*precedes n*), gu c(h)ùl *m* (*follows the n*), **a ~ fool** dearg amadan *m*, amadan gu chùl, **a ~ scoundrel** dearg slaoightear *m*, slaoightear gu chùl

thoroughfare *n* tro-shlighe *f*

though *adv* ge-tà *&* ged-thà, **I was at the fank all day, I'm not tired ~** bha mi aig an fhaing *f dat* fad an là *m gen*, chan eil mi sgìth ge-tà

though *conj* ged, **~ he wasn't ill** ged nach robh e tinn, **she didn't stop ~ she was exhausted** cha do sguir i ged a bha i claoidhte

thought *n* **1** (*the process, faculty, activity*) smaointeachadh *m*, beachdachadh *m*; **2** (*a ~*) smuain *&* smaoin *f*, (*can be more rigorous ~*) beachd *m*, beachd-smuain *m*, **melancholy ~s** smuaintean dubhach, **~s on the coming war** smuaintean/beachdan/beachd-smuaintean air a' chogadh *m* a tha romhainn; **3** (*interest, concern*) for *m invar* (**for** air), **he had no ~ for anything but his own affairs** cha robh for aige ach air a ghnothaichean *mpl* fhèin

thoughtful *adj* **1** (*pensive &c*) smuainteachail; **2** (*considerate*) tuigseach, suimeil

thousand *n* mìle *m* (*followed by nom sing ie radical*)

thrash *v* slac *&* slaic *vt*

thrashing *n* slacadh *m*

thrawn *adj* rag, dùr, (*stronger*) rag-mhuinealach

thread *n* **1** (*single ~*) snàthainn *m*; **2** (*coll*) snàth *m sing coll*

threadbare *adj* lom, **a ~ coat** còta *m* lom

threat *n* maoidheadh *m*, bagairt *f*, bagradh *m*, **a ~ of war** bagairt cogaidh *m gen*

threaten *v* maoidh *vi*, bagair *vi*, (*with prep* air), **he was ~ing me** bha e a' maoidheadh/a' bagairt orm

three *num adj* **1** trì; **2** (*of people*) triùir *mf invar* (*with gen pl*), **~ brothers** triùir bhràithrean (*gen pl of* bràthair *m*)

threefold, three-ply *adj* trì-fillte

threesome *n* triùir *mf invar* (*with gen pl*)

thresh *v* buail *vti*, **~ing the corn** a' bualadh an arbhair *m sing gen*

threshold *n* stairs(n)each *f*

thrifty *adj* **1** cùramach (a thaobh airgid *m*), glèidhteach; **2** *in expr* **be ~ (with)** caomhain *vti*

thrill *n* gaoir *f*, **give a ~** cuir gaoir (**to** air)

thrill *v* cuir gaoir *f* (*with prep* air)

thrilling *adj* gaoireil

thrive *v* **1** soirbhich *vi*, **the business ~d** shoirbhich an gnìomhachas; **2** soirbhich *vi* (*as impersonal v, with prep* le), **he ~d** shoirbhich leis

throat *n* **1** amha(i)ch *f*, sgòrnan *m*; **2** *in expr* **I set them at each other's ~s** chuir mi aig ugannan *mpl* a chèile iad, chuir mi thar a chèile iad

throb *n* (*esp of heart*) plosg *m*

throb *v* (*esp heart*) plosg *vi*, dèan plosgartaich *f*, (*less severe*) plap *vi*

throbbing *n* (*esp of heart*) plosgadh *m*, plosgartaich *f*

throne *n* rìgh-chathair *f*

throng *n* sluagh mòr, mòr-shluagh *m*

throng *v* rach (*&c*) *vi* nan (*&c*) ceudan *mpl*/nam (*&c*) mìltean *mpl*/nan (*&c*) dròbh(an) *m(pl)*, **we ~ed to the meeting** chaidh/thàinig sinn dhan choinneimh *f* nar ceudan/nar mìltean/nar dròbh

throttle *v* mùch *vt*, tachd *vt*

through *adv* **1** (*fam: finished &c*) deiseil, (*less usu*) ullamh, deas, (**with** de), **are you ~?** a bheil thu deiseil?, **they aren't ~ with the phone yet** chan eil iad deiseil den fòn *mf* fhathast, **they were ~ asking questions** bha iad ullamh de cheasnachadh *m*; **2** *in expr* **~ and ~** gu c(h)ùl *m*, **a Gael/ Highlander ~ and ~** Gàidheal *m* gu chùl

through *prep* tro & troimh (*takes dat, & lenites following cons where possible*), *with art* tron, **~ me** tromham(sa), **~ you** (*sing*) tromhad(sa), **~ him, ~ it** (*m*) troimhe(san), **~ her, ~ it** (*f*) troimhpe(se), **~ us** tromhainn(e), **~ you** (*pl*) tromhaibh(se), **~ them** tromhpa(san), **~ a glass darkly** dorcha tro ghlainne *f*, **they came ~ the wood** thàinig iad tron choille *f*

throw *n* tilgeadh *m*

throw *v* **1** tilg *vt*, caith *vt*, (**at** air), **he threw it at me** thilg e orm e, **don't ~ stones!** na tilg clachan *fpl*!; **2** *in exprs* **~ away** tilg *vt* air falbh, **~ down** (*ie*

demolish, fell) leag *vt* (gu làr *m*), ~ **up** tilg (suas) *vti*, dìobhair *vti*, sgeith
vti, **he threw up his dinner** thilg e suas a dhìnnear *f*

thrush *n* (*the bird*) smeòrach *f*

thrust *n* 1 sàthadh *m*, **a ~ of the knife** sàthadh na sgeine; 2 (*fig: essence,
'drift'*) brìgh *f invar*, comhair *m*, **the ~ of his argument** brìgh na
h-argamaid(e) aige

thrust *v* 1 sàth *vti*, spàrr *vt*, (**in/into** (a-steach) do), ~ **your hand into the
sack** sàth/spàrr do làmh *f* a-steach don phoca *m*, *in expr* **he ~ the knife
into him/it** shàth e an sgian *f* ann; 2 *in expr* (*fig*) ~ **upon** spàrr *vt* (*with
prep* air), **the new law was ~ upon us** chaidh an lagh *m* ùr a sparradh
òirnn

thumb *n* òrdag *f*

thump *n* buille *f* (dhùirn, *gen of* dòrn *m*)

thump *v* dòrn *vt*, slac & slaic *vt*

thunder *v* tàirneanaich & tàirnich *vi*

thunder *n* tàirneanach *m*

Thursday *n* Diardaoin *m invar*

thus *adv* air an dòigh *f* seo, air an dòigh a leanas, (*less formal*) mar seo,
open the packet ~ fosgail a' phacaid air an dòigh seo/air an dòigh a
leanas/mar seo

thwart *v* cuir bacadh *m*, cuir stad *m*, (*with prep* air), **we ~ed his schemes**
chuir sinn bacadh/stad air a chuid *f* innleachdan *fpl gen*

tick[1] *n* (*marking &c*) strìochag *f*

tick[2] *n* 1 (*sound of clock*) diog *m*; 2 (*instant*) diog *m*, tiota *m*, (*dimin*) tiotan *m*,
tiotag *f*, **I'll be with you in a ~** bidh mi agaibh/leibh ann an diog/ann
an tiotag

tick[3] *n* (*the parasite*) mial *f*, **sheep-~** mial-chaorach *f*

ticket *n* ticead *f*, tiocaid *f*, ticeard *f*

tickle *v* diogail *vti*

ticklish *adj* diogalach, ciogailteach

tide *n* 1 seòl-mara *m*, tràigh *f*, **there's a big ~ today** tha tràigh mhòr ann
an-diugh; 2 (*usu with art*) **the ~** an tìde *mf*, an tìde-mhara *mf*, **the ~'s
against us** tha an tìde(-mhara) nar n-aghaidh; 3 *in exprs* **high ~** muir-
làn *m*, làn-mhara *m*, **spring-~** reothart *f*, **neap ~** con(n)traigh *f*, **the ~
came in** lìon *vi* am muir

tidings *n* naidheachdan *fpl*, (*more fam*) sgeul *m*, guth *m*, ~ **from the
battlefield** naidheachdan on bhlàr *m*, **are there any ~ of Iain?** a bheil
sgeul/guth air Iain?

tidy *adj* 1 (*of person, figure: well turned-out; also of objects: trim, well-made &c*)
cuimir, grinn, sgiobalta, snasail, snasmhor; 2 (*of room, space, objects &c;
neat, not untidy*) sgiobalta, (*less usu*) cunbhalach

tidy *v* sgioblaich *vt*, òrdaich *vt*, cuir *vt* an òrdugh *m*, cuir *vt* air dòigh *f*,
rèitich *vt*

tie *n* 1 (*necktie*) taidh *f*; 2 (*for fastening, securing*) ceangal *m*, bann *m*; 3 (*link(s)* *of relationship, friendship*) dàimh *mf invar*, càirdeas *m*, **the ~s between the two families** an dàimh/an càirdeas eadar an dà theaghlach *m sing*

tie *v* ceangail *vt* (**to** ri), ~ **together** ceangail *vt* ri chèile

tier *n* sreath *m*, **two ~s of government** dà shreath de riaghaltas *m*

ties *n* (*of kinship, friendship*) dàimh *mf invar*, càirdeas *m* (*see* tie *n* 3)

tight *adj* 1 (*lit*) teann, **a ~ rope** ròpa teann; 2 (*leaving little leeway*) teann, **a ~ budget/timescale** buidseat *m*/raon-ama *m* teann; 3 (*in short supply &c*) gann, **money's ~ this month** tha (an t-) airgead gann air a' mhìos *mf* seo; 4 *in expr* (*fig*) **a ~ corner** cruaidh-chàs *m*, cùil-chumhang *f*, cruadal *m*, staing *f*

tighten *v* teannaich *vti*

tightening *n* teannachadh *m*

tile *n* leac *f*, (*smaller*) leacag *f*

till *conj* gus an, gus am, (*neg*) gus nach, **I won't get the meal ready ~ you come home** cha deasaich mi am biadh gus an tig thu dhachaigh, **I'll earn money ~ we've got enough of it** cosnaidh mi airgead *m* gus am bi gu leòr againn dheth, **keep it ~ you don't need it** cùm e gus nach bi feum *m* agad air

till *prep* gu & gus (*with dat*), gu ruige (*with nom*), **we'll wait/stay ~ six o'clock** fanaidh sinn gu sia uairean *fpl*, **I can't keep/save it ~ tomorrow** chan urrainn dhomh a ghleidheadh gu(s) a-màireach, **we'll be busy ~ New Year** bidh sinn trang gu ruige a' Bhliadhna Ur

till *v* àitich *vt*, obraich *vt*, ~ **the soil/land/ground** àitich/oibrich am fearann

tiller *n* 1 (*of boat*) failm *f*, ailm *f*; 2 (~ *of land*) fear-àitich *m*

tilt[1] *n* (*slant*) claonadh *m*, fiaradh *m*

tilt[2] *n*, *in expr* **at full ~** na (*&c*) d(h)ian-ruith *f*, (*more fam*) aig peilear *m* a (*&c*) b(h)eatha *f gen*, **they left at full ~** dh'fhalbh iad nan dian-ruith/aig peilear am beatha

tilt *v* claon *vi*, aom *vi*, rach *vi* air fhiaradh *m*

tilted, tilting *adjs* air fhiaradh *m*

timber *n* fiodh *m*, **a ~ house** taigh-fiodha *m*

time *n* 1 (*the abstr phenomenon*) tìm *f*; 2 (*clock ~*) uair *f*, **what ~ is it?** dè an uair a tha e?, **at this ~** aig an uair seo; 3 (~ *as it is lived/experienced*) tìde *f*, ùine *f*, (**the**) ~'s **passing** tha an tìde a' dol seachad, **spend ~** cuir seachad tìde/ùine, **all the ~** fad na tìde, fad na h-ùine, **plenty of ~** tìde/ùine gu leòr, **a waste of ~** call *m* ùine *gen*, **an hour's ~** uair a (*for* de) thìde, **about ~ too!** bha a thìde aige!, **he took his ~** thug e fada gu leòr!, **in ~** (*ie eventually*) ri tìde, ri ùine; 4 (*specific moments or periods of* ~) àm *m*, linn *mf*, rè *f invar*, **at this ~** aig an àm seo, **at the ~ of the Great War** aig àm a' Chogaidh Mhòir, **she was poorly at the ~** bha i bochd aig an àm, **from ~ to ~** bho àm gu àm, **at ~s he's naughty and at other ~s he's good** aig amannan bidh e crosta agus aig amannan eile bidh e glè mhath, **olden ~s** na laitheachan *mpl*/an t-àm a dh'fhalbh,

these modern ~s na h-amannan ùra seo, **in our ancestors'** ~ ri linn ar sinnsirean *mpl gen*, **in my grandfather's** ~ ri linn/an rè mo sheanar *m gen*; **5** (*an appointed or appropriate ~*) àm *m*, (*less usu*) tràth *m*, **she arrived before** ~ thàinig i ron àm, **it's** ~ **for us to leave** tha an t-àm againn falbh, **it's high ~/not before** ~ tha an t-àm ann, **meal** ~ tràth-bìdh *m*, **prayer** ~ tràth-ùrnaigh *m*, **a word at the right** ~ facal *m* na thràth; **6** (*a period or stretch of ~*) ùine *f*, greis *f*, treis *f*, (*less usu*) tamall *m*, (*shorter*) ùine ghoirid, greiseag *f*, treiseag *f*, (*less usu*) tacan *m*, **for a** ~ airson greis, car uair, **after a** ~ an ceann greise/tamaill, **a short** ~ **before that** ùine ghoirid roimhe sin; **7** (*occasion, repetition*) uair *f*, turas *m*, **I was there one** ~ bha mi ann aon uair/aon turas, **any** ~ uair sam bith, **many ~s, many a** ~ iomadach uair, iomadh uair, ~ **and** ~ **again** uair is uair, **the first** ~ **I saw her** a' chiad uair a chunna mi i, **at ~s** uaireannan, air uairean, **the last** ~ an turas mu dheireadh; **8** *in exprs* **some** ~ uaireigin *m & adv*, **I'll see you some** ~ chì mi uaireigin thu, **some** ~ **or other** uair no uaireigin

timely, timeous *adj* mithich, an deagh àm *m*, tràthail
timepiece *n* uaireadair *m*
times *adv* (*arith &c*) uiread *m invar*, air iomadachadh (*with prep* le), **two** ~ **two** a dhà uiread a dhà, a dhà air iomadachadh le a dhà
timescale *n* raon-ama *m*
timetable *n* clàr-tìde *m*, clàr-ama *m*
timid *adj* **1** (*shy, bashful*) diùid, nàrach, màlda; **2** (*jumpy, nervous*) clisgeach; **3** (*fearful*) meata, (*usu stronger*) gealtach
timidity *n* **1** (*shyness*) diùide *f invar*, nàire *f invar*; **2** (*fearfulness*) meatachd *f invar*, (*stronger*) gealtachd *f invar*
tin *n* **1** (*the metal*) staoin *f*; **2** (*can for drinks, food &c*) cana *m*, canastair *m*
tinge *n* **1** fiamh *m*, dath *m*; **2** (*esp of complexion*) fiamh *m*, tuar *m*
tinker *n* ceàrd *& cèard *m*
tinkle *v* dèan gliong *m*, dèan gliongartaich *f invar*
tinkling *n* gliong *m*, gliongartaich *f invar*
tint *n* **1** fiamh *m*, dath *m*; **2** (*esp of complexion*) fiamh *m*, tuar *m*
tiny *adj* crìon, (*less usu, & used mainly as prefixes*) meanbh, mion
tip *n* (*slender end of anything*) bàrr *m*, **on the** ~ **of my tongue** air bàrr mo theangaidh *f gen*
tippler *n* pòitear *m*, misgear *m*
tippling *n* pòitearachd *f invar*
tipsy *adj* air leth-mhisg *f*
tiptoe *n* corra-biod *m invar*, **on** ~ air a (*&c*) c(h)orra-biod
tire *v* **1** sgìthich *vti*; **2** (*as vi*) fàs *vi* sgìth; **3** *in expr* ~ **out** claoidh *vt*
tired *adj & past part* **1** sgìth; **2** *in exprs* ~ **out** claoidhte, ~ **of** sgìth de, **sick and** ~ **of** seac searbh sgìth de
tiresome *adj* frionasach, sàrachail
tissue *n* stuth *m*

title *n* (*book &c ~, rank &c*) tiotal *m*

tittle-tattle *n* goileam *m*, gobaireachd *&* gabaireachd *f invar*

tizzy *n*, *in expr* **in a ~** troimh-a-chèile, am breisleach *m*

to *conj* **1** (*in order ~*) gus, airson, **she bought a broom ~ clean the house** cheannaich i sguab *f* gus/airson an taigh *m* a ghlanadh, **he found a job ~ get some money** fhuair e obair *f* gus/airson airgead *m* fhaighinn, **come ~ see me** thig gam fhaicinn; **2** *in expr* **he came home ~ eat** thàinig e dhachaigh gu (a) bhiadh *m*

to *prep* **1** gu *&* gus, *when followed by art,* thun *&* chun (*with gen*), **~ me** thugam(sa) *&* chugam(sa), **~ you** (*sing*) thugad(sa) *&* chugad(sa), **~ him, ~ it** (*m*) thuige(san) *&* chuige(san), **~ her, ~ it** (*f*) thuice(se) *&* chuice(se), **~ us** thugainn(ne) *&* chugainn(ne), **~ you** (*pl & polite sing*) thugaibh(se) *&* chugaibh(se), **~ them** thuca(san) *&* chuca(san), **he went ~** (*esp to the outskirts of, as far as*) **Glasgow** chaidh e gu Glaschu, **I'll send a book ~ her** cuiridh mi leabhar *m* thuice, **we went ~ the gate** chaidh sinn chun a' gheata *m*; **2** do (*takes the dat, lenites following cons where possible*), **~ me** dhomh(sa), **~ you** (*sing fam*) dhu(i)t(sa), **~ him/ it** (*m*) dha(san), **~ her/it** (*f*) dhi(se), **~ us** dhuinn(e), **~ you** (*pl & sing polite*) dhuibh(se), **~ them** dhaibh(san), **give it ~ Iain** thoir do dh'Iain e, **tell it ~ Mary** innis do Mhàiri e, **he's a good friend ~ me** tha e na dheagh charaid *m* dhomh, **what happened ~ you?** dè a thachair dhut?, **he went ~** (*ie into*) **Glasgow** chaidh e do/a Ghlaschu, **I'll go ~ (the) church** thèid mi don (*or* dhan) eaglais *f*, **a trip ~ the islands** sgriob/ cuairt *f* do (*or* dha) na h-eileanan *mpl*; **3** (*with compass directions*) mu, **he went ~ the south** chaidh e mu dheas; **4** (*expr that something is or needs to be done*) ri, **I've lots ~ do** tha mòran agam ri dhèanamh, **that house is ~ be sold** tha an taigh *m* sin ri reic, **they deserve ~ be praised** tha iad rim moladh *m*; **5** (*when equivalent to part of the English infinitive*) a (*followed by the verbal noun, which is lenited where possible*), **I'm going ~ swim** tha mi a' dol a shnàmh, **you ought not ~ hit your brother** cha bu chòir dhut do bhràthair a bhualadh

toad *n* muile-mhàg *f*

toast *n* (*drink*) deoch-slàinte *f*

tobacco *n* tombaca *m*

today *adv* an-diugh

toe *n* òrdag *f*, òrdag-choise *f*, **the big ~** an òrdag mhòr

together *adv* **1** còmhla, le chèile, **living ~** a' fuireach còmhla (ri chèile), a' fuireach le chèile, **they left ~** dh'fhalbh iad còmhla (ri chèile); **2** *in exprs* **~ with** còmhla ri, **she left ~ with the others** dh'fhalbh i còmhla ri càch *pron*, **join ~** ceangail *vt* (ri chèile), **come ~** (*congregate, unite*) thig *vi* còmhla, coinnich *vi*, cruinnich *vi*, **bring ~** cruinnich *vt*, **pulling/ working ~** (*idiom*) a' tarraing air an aon ràmh *m*, **string/put two words ~** cuir dà fhacal *m* an ceann a chèile/an altaibh (*obs dat pl of* alt *m*) a chèile *m gen*

toil *n* saothair *f*, obair chruaidh

toil *v* saothraich *vi*, bi *vi irreg* ag obair *f* gu cruaidh

toilet *n*, (*public or private*) taigh-beag *m*, (*public*) goireasan *mpl*

tolerable *adj* meadhanach math

tolerably *adv* meadhanach math, **you only did ~ well** cha do rinn thu ach meadhanach math

tolerance *n* ceadachas *m*

tolerant *adj* ceadach

tolerate *v* fuiling *vt*, cuir *vi* suas (*with prep* le *or* ri)

tomb *n* uaigh *f*, tuam *m*

tombstone *n* leac *f* uaighe *f gen*

tomcat *n* cat fireann

ton *n* tonna & tunna *m*

tongs *n* (*pair of ~*) clobha *m sing*

tongue *n* **1** teanga *f*, **on the tip of my ~** air bàrr *m* mo theangaidh *gen*; **2** *in expr* **slip of the ~** tapag *f*; **3** (*language*) cànain *f*, cànan *m*, **the ~ of the Gaels** cànan nan Gàidheal

tonne *n* tunna *m*

too *adv* (*ie also*) cuideachd, **has Ewan left? yes, and Iain ~** an do dh'fhalbh Eòghann? dh'fhalbh, agus Iain cuideachd

too *adv* **1** (*to an excessive extent*) ro (*lenites following adj where possible*), **it's ~ late to go for a walk** tha e ro anmoch airson cuairt *f* a ghabhail, **~ keen on drink** ro dhèidheil air an deoch *f*; **2** *in expr* **~ much** cus *m* (*with gen*), tuilleadh *m* 's a' chòir *f*, **~ much talking** cus bruidhne (*gen of* bruidhinn *f*), **I ate ~ much** dh'ith mi cus, **here's some ironing for you, I've too much already!** seo iarnaigeadh *m* dhut, tha tuilleadh 's a' chòir dheth agam mar a tha!

tool *n* inneal *m*, ball-acfhainn *m*

tooth *n* fiacail *f*, **wisdom ~** fiacail-forais *f*, **false teeth** fiaclan-fuadain *fpl*, **~ of a saw** fiacail sàibh *m gen*

toothache *n* dèideadh *m* (*used with art*), **I've got (the) ~** tha an dèideadh orm

toothbrush *n* bruis-fhiaclan *f*

toothed *adj* fiaclach

toothpaste *n* uachdar-fhiaclan *m*

toothy *adj* fiaclach

top *adj* **1** (*phys*) as àirde, **the ~ floor** an lobht' *m* as àirde; **2** (*best, foremost &c*) as fheàrr, prìomh (*precedes the noun, which is lenited where possible*)

top *n* **1** bàrr *m*, mullach *m*, ceann *m* as àirde, **~ of the milk** bàrr a' bhainne, **the ~ of a tree** bàrr craoibhe *f gen*, **the ~ of a mountain** mullach beinne *f gen*, **~ of the ladder** mullach an àraidh, *also* ceann shuas an àraidh, **a great stone with a bird on ~ of it** clach mhòr is eun *m* air a mullach; **2** *in exprs* **on ~ of** air muin *f invar* (*with gen*), **she put on a blouse and on ~ of that a jacket** chuir i blobhs *m* oirre agus air muin sin seacaid *f*, **he**

was singing at the ~ of his voice bha e a' seinn (aig) àird *f* a chlaiginn (*gen of* claigeann *m*)

top *v* (*beat, cap*) thoir bàrr *m* (*with prep* air), **that ~s everything I ever saw!** tha sin a' toirt bàrr air a h-uile càil *m invar* a chunna mi a-riamh!

topic *n* cuspair *m*

topography *n* cumadh-tìre *m*

topsy-turvy *adj* bun-os-cionn, troimh-a-chèile

torch *n* leus *m*, lòchran *m*

torment *n* (*mental/emotional*) dòrainn *f*, (*mental/emotional or phys*) cràdh *m*

torment *v* (*mentally/emotionally or phys*) cràidh *vt*, sàraich *vt*, (*weaker*) pian *vt*, **my conscience was ~ing me** bha mo chogais *f* gam chràdh/gam shàrachadh

torrent *n* **1** (*watercourse &c*) bras-shruth *m*, dòrtadh *m*; **2** (*downpour*) dìle *f*, dìle bhàthte

torso *n* com *m*

tortuous *adj* (*road, river, argument &c*) lùbach

torture *n* (*mental or phys*) cràdh *m*, (*weaker*) pianadh *m*, **put to ~** cuir *vt* an cràdh

torture *v* (*esp phys*) cuir *vt* an cràdh *m*, ciùrr *vt*, (*mentally or phys*) cràidh *vt*, (*weaker*) pian *vt*

Tory *adj* Tòraidheach, **the ~ Party** am Pàrtaidh Tòraidheach

Tory *n* Tòraidh *m*

toss *n, in expr* (*fam*) **I don't give a ~ for X** cha toir mi ho-ro-gheallaidh *m invar* air X

toss *v* **1** (*as vi: seas, ship, trees &c*) tulg *vi*, luaisg *vi*; **2** (*as vt: throw*) tilg *vt*, **~ the caber** tilg an cabar; **3** *in expr* **~ a coin** cuir crainn (*pl of* crann *m*), **they ~ed a coin to see who would pay** chuir iad crainn feuch cò a phàigheadh

total *adj* **1** iomlan, uile-gu-lèir, **~ cost** cosgais *f* iomlan/uile-gu-lèir; **2** (*utter, complete*) dearg (*precedes the noun, which it lenites where possible*), gu c(h)ùl *m* (*follows the noun*), **a ~ fool** dearg amadan *m*, amadan gu chùl

total *n* (*result of addition*) sùim *f*, iomlan *m*

totally *adv* gu tur, (gu) buileach, gu h-iomlan, uile-gu-lèir, **the two things are ~ different** tha an dà rud *m sing* gu tur eadar-dhealaichte/(gu) buileach eadar-dhealaichte, **I'll defeat him ~** nì mi an gnothach *m* air gu buileach/gu h-iomlan, **we succeeded ~** shoirbhich *vi impersonal* leinn uile-gu-lèir/gu h-iomlan/gu buileach

touch *v* **1** (*phys*) bean *vi* (*with prep* ri *or* do), làimhsich *vt*, **don't ~ the pictures** na bean ris na dealbhan *mfpl, also* na teirig faisg air na dealbhan; **2** (*fig, have to do with &c*) bean *vi* (*with prep* ri), buin *vi* (*with prep* do *or* ri), gabh gnothach *m* (*with prep* ri), **it's a dodgy business, don't ~ it** 's e gnothach cugallach a th' ann, na bean ris/na buin dha/na buin ris/na gabh gnothach ris idir; **3** (*~ emotionally*) gluais *vti*, drùidh *vt* (*with prep* air), **the song ~ed them** ghluais an t-òran iad, dhrùidh an t-òran orra, *also* bha buaidh mhòr aig an òran orra; **4** *in expr* ~ **on/upon** (*ie mention, refer to*) thoir iomradh *m*, thoir tarraing *f*, (*with prep* air), **in his talk he ~ed upon the state of the economy** anns an òraid aige thug e iomradh/tarraing air staid *f* an eaconomaidh

touching *adj* (*emotionally affecting*) gluasadach, drùidhteach

touchy *adj* frionasach, frithearra

tough *adj* **1** (*of persons*) cruaidh, fulangach, buan; **2** (*materials, food &c*) righinn

toughen *v* rìghnich *vti*

toughness *n* **1** (*of persons*) cruas *m*, fulang *m*, fulangas *m*; **2** (*of materials, food &c*) rìghnead *m*

tour *n* cuairt *f*, turas *m*, ~ **to the islands** cuairt/turas do na h-eileanan *mpl*

tourism *n* turasachd *f invar*

tourist *n* neach-turais *m*, ~s luchd-turais *m sing coll*, ~ **office** oifis *f* turasachd *f invar*, **the Scottish Tourist Board** Bòrd *m* Turasachd *f invar* na h-Alba

towards *prep* **1** (*when followed by a noun*) a dh'ionnsaigh (*with gen*), chun & thun (*with gen*), ~ **the town(ship)** a dh'ionnsaigh a' bhaile, chun/thun a' bhaile; **2** (*when followed by a pers pron*) a dh'ionnsaigh, ~ **me** dham ionnsaigh, ~ **you** (*fam sing*) dhad ionnsaigh, ~ **him/it** (*m*) dha ionnsaigh, ~ **her/it** (*f*) dha h-ionnsaigh, ~ **us** dhar n-ionnsaigh, ~ **you** (*pl or formal sing*) dhur n-ionnsaigh, ~ **them** dhan ionnsaigh, **the boy was running ~ her** bha am balach a' ruith dha h-ionnsaigh

towel *n* tubhailte *f*, searbhadair *m*

tower *n* tùr *m*, turaid *f*

town *n* baile *m*, (*bigger*) baile mòr, **market** ~ baile-margaidh *m*, ~ **hall** talla-baile *m*, **the ~ hall** talla *m* a' bhaile

township *n* baile *m* (croitearachd *f*), **the ~ clerk** clàrc *m* a' bhaile

toy *n* dèideag *f*

trace *n* **1** lorg *f*, làrach *f*, sgeul *m*, **it didn't leave a ~** cha do dh'fhàg e lorg/làrach, **there's no ~ of it** chan eil lorg/sgeul air; **2** (*idiom*) **there was (absolutely) no ~ of Murdo** sgeul no fathann *m* cha robh air Murchadh

trace *v* faigh lorg *f* (*with prep* air), lorg *vt*, **the police ~ed them** fhuair am poileas lorg orra

track *n* **1** (*path &c*) ceum *m*, frith-rathad *m*, ùtraid *f*; **2** (*often with more abstr connotations: route*) slighe *f*, **a ~less wilderness** fàsach *m* gun slighe; **3** (~ *left by person, animal, object*) lorg *f*, **on the ~ of the deer** air lorg an fhèidh (*gen of* fiadh *m*)

track, track down *v* faigh lorg *f* (*with prep* air), **the police ~ed him down** fhuair am polas lorg air

tract *n* (*pamphlet &c*) tràchd *mf*

tractable *adj* soitheamh, (*excessively so*) socharach

tractor *n* tractar *m*

trade *n* **1** (*a craft*) ceàird *f*, ~(s) **union** aonadh-ceàird & aonadh-ciuird *m*;

2 (*commercial exchange*) malairt *f*, ceannachd *f invar*, ceannach *m*, **engage in ~** dèan malairt, malairtich *vi*

trade *v* dèan malairt *f*, malairtich *vi*

trader *n* neach-malairt *m* (*pl* luchd-malairt *m sing coll*), marsanta *m*, ceannaiche *m*

tradesman *n* **1** (*practitioner of a trade*) fear-ceàirde *m*; **2** (*retailer, merchant &c*) marsanta *m*, ceannaiche *m*

trading *n* ceannachd *f invar*, ceannach *m*, malairt *f*

tradition *n* **1** (*cultural heritage: in terms of one's descent/ancestry*) dualchas *m*, (*or the place one belongs to*) dùthchas *m*; **2** (*oral ~: esp song & story*) beul-aithris *f invar*, (*oral ~: esp trad lore & learning*) beul-oideachas *m*, beul-oideas *m*

traditional *adj* tradaiseanta, dualchasach, **~ music** ceòl *m* tradaiseanta/dualchasach

tradition-bearer *n* seanchaidh *m*

traffic *n* (*road &c*) trafaig *f*

tragic *adj* dòrainneach, mìcheanta, **a ~ story** sgeulachd dhòrainneach

trail *n* (*~ left by person, animal*) lorg *f*, **on the ~ of the deer** air lorg an fhèidh (*gen of* fiadh *m*)

trailer *n* (*transport*) slaodair *m*

train *n* (*railway, tube*) trèan(a) *f*, **I missed the ~** chaill mi an trèana, **express ~** luath-thrèana *f*

train *v* **1** (*sport, ed &c*) trèan *vti*; **2** (*teach a trade &c*) teagaisg *vt*, oileanaich *vt*

trained *adj* ionnsaichte, uidheamaichte

training *n* **1** (*sport, ed*) trèanadh *m*; **2** (*ed, for trade &c*) teagasg *m*, oileanachadh *m*, uidheamachadh *m*

trait *n* (*of character*) fea(i)rt *m*

traitor *n* brathadair *m*

trample *v* saltair *vt*

trance *n* neul *m*, **go into a ~** rach *vi* an neul

tranquil *adj* ciùin, sàmhach, sìtheil, sèimh

tranquility *n* ciùineas *m*, sàmhchair *f*, sìth *f*, fois *f*

tranquilizer *n* tàmhadair *n*

transact *v* dèan *vt*, **~ business** dèan gnothach *m* (**with** ri)

transgress *v* **1** ciontaich *vi*; **2** (*usu in relig sense*) peacaich *vi*

transgression *n* **1** ciont(a) *m*; **2** (*in relig sense: abstr & con*) peacachadh *m*, peacadh *m*

transient, transitory *adj* diombuan, siùbhlach

translate *v* eadar-theangaich *vti* (**into** gu), cuir *vt* (*with prep* air), **~ into English** eadar-theangaich gu Beurla *f invar*, **~ English into Gaelic** cuir Gàidhlig *f* air Beurla

translation *n* (*abstr & con*) eadar-theangachadh *m*

translator *n* eadar-theangair *m*

transmission *n* craobh-sgaoileadh *m*, craoladh *m*

translucent *adj* trìd-shoillseach

transmit *v* craobh-sgaoil *vti*

transmitter *n* crann-sgaoilidh *m*

transparent *adj* trìd-shoilleir

transport *n* **1** (*general*) còmhdhail *f*; **2** (*for people: travel from place to place*) siubhal *m*, **means/modes of** ~ dòighean *fpl* siubhail *gen*; **3** (*for goods &c: carriage from place to place*) giùlan *m*, (*less usu*) iomchar *m*

transport *v* giùlain *vt*, (*less usu*) iomchair *vt*

trap *n* ribe *mf*

trap *v* rib *vt*, glac *vt*

trapped *adj & past part* glacte, an sàs *m*

trappings *n* uidheam *f coll*, acainn *f coll*

trash *n* treal(l)aich *f*, truileis *f invar*, (*more worthless*) sgudal *m*

travel *n* siubhal *m*, *in exprs* ~ **agency** bùth-turais *mf*, ~ **centre** ionad *m* siubhail *gen*

travel *v* siubhail *vi*, (*also as vt, rather trad, eg*) ~**ling (over) the moor** a' siubhal na mòintich/na mòinteach, (*less usu*) triall *vi*

traveller *n* neach-siubhail *m*, ~**s** luchd-siubhail *m sing coll*

travelling *adj* siubhail (*gen of* siubhal *m, used adjectivally*), ~ **bank** banca *m* siubhail

trawler *n* tràlair *m*

tray *n* sgàl *m*

treachery *n* brathadh *m*, cealgaireachd *f invar*

tread *v* (*as grapes &c*) saltair *vt*

treason *n* brathadh *m*

treasure *n* ionmhas *m*, ulaidh *f*, tasgaidh *m*

treasurer *n* ionmhasair *m*

treasury *n* (*department of government*) roinn *f* an ionmhais *m*

treat *v* **1** (*behave towards*) làimhsich *vt*, gnàthaich *vt*, dèilig *vi* (*with prep* ri), **he ~ed his wife badly** is dona a làimhsich e/a ghnàthaich e a' bhean aige, **how does he ~ the customers?** ciamar a bhios e a' dèiligeadh ris an luchd-ceannaich *m sing coll*; **2** (*med*) leighis *vt*

treatise *n* tràchd *mf*, tràchdas *m*

treatment *n* **1** (*way of behaving towards someone*) làimhseachadh *m*, gnàthachadh *m*; **2** (*med*) leigheas *m*

treaty *n* co-chòrdadh *m*, cunnradh *m*

treble *adj* trìobailte

tree *n* **1** craobh *f*, **fruit** ~ craobh mheas *gen*, **oak** ~ craobh-dharaich; **2** (*now usu in names of trees only*) crann *m*, *eg* **fig** ~ crann-fìogais *m*, **olive** ~ crann-ola *m*

tremble *n* crith *f*

tremble *v* bi *vi irreg* air chrith *f*, crith *vi*, **he was trembling** bha e air chrith, **start to** ~ rach *vi irreg* air chrith

trembling *adj* air chrith *f*, ~ **with fear** air chrith leis an eagal *m*

tremendous *adj* **1** (*in size*) uabhasach mòr; **2** (*in quality*) uabhasach (fhèin) math, (*more fam*) taghta

tremor *n* crith *f*

trench *n* clais *f*, treinnse *f*

trend *n* aomadh *m*, **economic ~** aomadh eaconomach

trespass *n* (*on land*) briseadh *m* chrìochan *fpl gen*

trespass *v* (*on land*) bris crìochan *fpl*

trews *n* triubhas *m*

tri- *prefix* trì-, *eg* **triangle** *n* trì-cheàrnag *f*, **trilingual** *adj* trì-chànanach, **tripartite** *adj* trì-phàirteach

trial *n* **1** dearbhadh *m*, **~s on a new car** dearbhaidhean air càr *m* ùr; **2** (*ordeal*) deuchainn *f*, **my mother's illness was a ~ for me** bha tinneas *m* mo mhàthair *f gen* na dheuchainn dhomh

triangle *n* trì-cheàrnag *f*, triantan *m*

triangular *adj* trì-cheàrnach, triantanach

tribe *n* treubh *f*, cinneadh *m*, fine *f*

tribulation *n* trioblaid *f*, deuchainn *m*

tribute *n* moladh *m*, *in expr* **pay ~ to** mol *vt*

trick *n* **1** (*usu playful*) cleas *m*, (*can be less playful*) car *m*, (*more elaborate & serious: a plot &c*) cuilbheart *f*, **play a ~** dèan cleas (**on** air), thoir an car (**on** à), **they played a ~ on me** rinn iad cleas orm, thug iad an car asam; **2** *in expr* (*fam*) **that'll do the ~!** nì sin an gnothach!, nì sin a' chùis!

trick *v* meall *vt*, (*can be less serious*) thoir an car *m* (*with prep* à), **they ~ed her** thug iad an car aiste

trickle *n* sileadh (beag)

trickle *v* sil *vi*

trifling *adj* crìon, suarach

trilingual *adj* trì-chànanach

trim *adj* cuimir, sgiobalta, snasail, snasmhor

trim *n* gleus *mf*, **in good ~** air ghleus

trip[1] *n* (*journey*) turas *m*, cuairt *f*, sgrìob *f*, **~ to the islands** turas/cuairt/ sgrìob do na h-eileanan *mpl*

trip[2] *n* (*stumble*) tuisleadh *m*, sgiorradh *m*

trip *v* (*stumble*) tuislich *vi*

triple *adj* trì-fillte, tribilte

triumph *n* buaidh *f*

triumphant *adj* buadhmhor

trivial *adj* **1** (*pointless, empty*) faoin, dìomhain; **2** (*without significance*) crìon, suarach

troop *n* **1** (*of soldiers &c*) buidheann *mf*, cuideachd *f*; **2** (*of actors*) còmhlan *m*

Tropic of Cancer *n* Tropaig *f* Chansar

Tropic of Capricorn *n* Tropaig *f* Chapricorn

tropical *adj* tropaigeach

trot *n* trotan *m*

trot *v* dèan trotan *m*

trotting *n* trotan *m*

trouble *n* **1** (*inconvenience, bother, worry*) dragh *m*, **I don't want to put you to any** ~ chan eil mi airson dragh a chur oirbh; **2** (*misfortune, difficulties &c*) trioblaid *f*, duilgheadasan *mpl*, (*droch*) staing *f*, (*can be more serious*) èiginn *f invar*, ~ **came upon us** thàinig trioblaid òirnn, **the loss of my job was the start of our ~s** b' e call *m* m' obrach *f gen* toiseach *m* ar trioblaidean, **I'm in** ~ tha mi ann an droch staing, tha mi nam èiginn, tha mi ann an èiginn, **an aeroplane in** ~ **above the airport** itealan *m* ann an èiginn os cionn a' phuirt-adhair *m*; **3** (*effort, putting oneself out*) saothair *f*, **it's not worth the/your** ~ chan fhiach dhut do shaothair; **4** (*disturbance, disorder, unrest*) aimhreit *f*, buaireas *m*

trouble *v* **1** (*inconvenience*) cuir dragh *m* (*with prep* air), (*more fam*) bodraig *vt*, **I don't want to** ~ **you** chan eil mi airson dragh a chur oirbh/airson ur bodraigeadh; **2** (*harass, vex*) sàraich *vt*, **they were ~d with/by debts/ bad neighbours** bha iad air an sàrachadh le fiachan *mpl*/le droch nàbaidhean *mpl*; **3** (*disturb, upset*) buair *vt*, **the bad news ~d me greatly** bhuair an drochd naidheachd *f* mi gu mòr; **4** (*take the* ~, *make the effort, fam*) bodraig *vi*; **5** *in expr* **what's troubling you?** dè (a) tha a' gabhail riut?, dè (a) tha a' cur ort?

troubled *adj* **1** (*anxious*) fo iomagain *f*, fo chùram *m*; **2** (*vexed, harassed*) air a (*&c*) s(h)àrachadh; **3** (*upset*) air a (*&c*) b(h)uaireadh, air a (*&c*) t(h)àmailteachadh

troublesome *adj* (*person, situation*) draghail, buaireasach

trounce *v* (*sport*) dèan an gnothach/a' chùis (*with prep* air), **we ~d them this time!** rinn sinn an gnothach/a' chùis orra an turas seo!

troupe *n* còmhlan *m*, ~ **of actors** còmhlan de dh'actairean *mpl*

trousers *n* (*also a pair of* ~) briogais *f*, triubhas *m*

trout *n* breac *m*

truce *n* fosadh *m*, **call/declare a** ~ gairm fosadh

truck[1] *n* (*transport*) làraidh *f*

truck[2] *n* (*dealings &c*), **have** ~ bean *vi* (**with** ri), buin *vi* (**with** do *or* ri), gabh gnothach *m* (**with** ri), **have no** ~ **with them** na bean riutha, na buin dhaibh/riutha, na gabh gnothach riutha, *also* cùm *vi* bhuapa

true *adj* **1** (*factual, accurate, truthful*) fìor, fìrinneach, **the rumour/story is** ~ tha am fathann/an sgeul *f* fìor, **a true account of what happened** cunntas fìrinneach air na thachair; **2** (*genuine, authentic, real*) fìor (*precedes the noun, which it lenites where possible*), (*of person*) gu c(h)ùl *m*, ~ **gold** fìor òr *m*, **a** ~ **Scot** fìor Albannach *m*, Albannach gu chùl; **3** (*loyal*) dìleas

truly *adv* fìor (*lenites a following adj where possible*), **the food was** ~ **good** bha am biadh fìor mhath

trumpet *n* trombaid *f*

trunk *n* **1** (*of human body*) com *m*; **2** (*of elephant &c*) sròn *f*; **3** (*luggage &c*) ciste *f*; **4** (*of tree*) stoc *m*, bun *m* craoibhe (*gen of* craobh *f*)

trust *n* **1** earbsa *f invar*, creideas *m*, **put one's ~ in something** cuir earbsa ann an rudeigin *m*; **2** (*legal, fin, business: a ~*) urras *m*, **set up a ~** stèidhich urras, **a ~ fund** ciste-urrais *f*

trust *v* **1** thoir creideas *m* (*with prep* do), earb *vti* (*with prep* à), **do you ~ me? no!** an toir thu creideas dhomh? cha toir!, *also* a bheil earbsa agad annam/asam? chan eil!, **they didn't ~ their neighbours** cha robh iad ag earbsadh às na nàbaidhean *mpl* aca, cha robh earbsa aca às na nàbaidhean aca; **2** *in expr* **~ in** cuir earbsa *f invar* (*with prep* ann), **~ in providence** cuir earbsa anns an fhreastal

trusting *adj* earbsach

trustworthy *adj* (*person, business &c*) earbsach

trusty *adj* dìleas

truth *n* **1** fìrinn *f*, **to tell (you) the ~/ to tell, I don't know** leis an fhìrinn innse, chan eil fhios am; **2** *in expr* **he's telling the ~** 's e an fhìrinn a th' aige

truthful *adj* fìrinneach

try *n* **1** (*attempt*) oidhirp *f* (**at** air), **he had another ~ at it** thug e/rinn e oidhirp eile air; **2** *in expr* **give it a ~** (*ie sample it*) feuch e, feuch *vi* ris

try *v* **1** feuch *vti* (**to** ri), **I'll ~ to open the door** feuchaidh mi ris an doras fhosgladh, **they tried to lift us** dh'fheuch iad ri ar togail *f*, **~ it (out)** (*ie sample it*) feuch ris, **~ this beer** feuch an leann *m* a tha seo, **~ to be there early** feuch gum bi sibh ann ron àm *m*, **be good! I'll ~** bi math! feuchaidh mi; **2** (*~ out, test &c*) cuir *vt* gu deuchainn *f*, dearbh *vt*, **they tried out the new machines** chuir iad na h-innealan *mpl* ùra gu deuchainn

trying *adj* deuchainneach

tube *n* (*small*) feadan *m*, (*of various sizes*) pìob *f*

tuberculosis *n* (*used with the art*) a' chaitheamh

tuck up *v* (*garment*) tru(i)s *vt*, **her petticoats were tucked up** bha na còtaichean-bàna *mpl* aice air an trusadh

Tuesday *m* Dimàirt *m invar*

tug *n* tarraing *f*

tug *v* tarraing *vti* (**at** air)

tuition *n* teagasg *m*, (*less usu*) oideachas *m*

tumble *n* tuiteam *m*

tumble *v* **1** (*as vi*) tuit *vi*, **he ~d to the ground** thuit e gu làr *m*; **2** (*as vt*) leag *vt*, **he ~d him to the ground** leag e gu làr *m* e

tumour *n* at *m*

tumult *n* ùpraid *f*, iorghail *f*, othail *f*

tumultuous *adj* ùpraideach, iorghaileach

tune *n* **1** (*air, melody*) port *m*, fonn *m*, **strike up a ~ on the fiddle** gabh port air an fhidhill (*dat of* fidheall *f*), **a song to the tune 'The Thistle of**

Scotland' òran *m* air fonn 'Fòghnan na h-Alba', **raise a ~** tog fonn; **2** (*correct tuning*) gleus *mf*, **in ~** air ghleus

tune *v* (*musical instrument, machine &c*) gleus *vt*, cuir *vt* air ghleus *mf*

tuned *adj & past part* air ghleus *mf*

tuneful *adj* ceòlmhor, fonnmhor, binn

tuning *n* (*the pitch*) gleus *mf*, (*the action*) cur *m* air ghleus

tuning-fork *n* gobhal-gleusaidh *m*

tup *n* reithe *m*, rùda/rùta *m*

turbulence *n* **1** (*unruliness &c*) gairge *f invar*, aimhreit *f*, buaireas *m*; **2** (*of sea &c*) luaisgeachd *f invar*, tulgadh *m*

turbulent *adj* **1** (*of people, situations &c: unruly, troublesome*) garg, aimhreiteach, buaireasach; **2** (*of seas, flight &c*) luaisgeach, tulgach

turd *n* tudan *&* tùdan *m*

turf *n* **1** (*a single ~*) fàl *m*, sgrath *f*, ceap *m*, ploc *m*; **2** (*coll & individual*) fòid *&* fòd *f*, **when I'm beneath the ~** nuair a bhios mi fon fhòid *dat*

Turk *n* Turcach *m*

Turkey *n, used with art*, An Tuirc *f*

turkey *n* eun-Frangach *m*, cearc-Fhrangach *f*

Turkish *adj* Turcach

turn *n* **1** (*circular movement*) car *m*, tionndadh *m*, **give the wheel a ~** cuir car den chuibhle *f*, **a turn of the wheel** car/tionndadh den chuibhle; **2** (*stroll*) car *m*, cuairt *f*, **I'll take a ~ outside** bheir/gabhaidh mi car/cuairt a-muigh; **3** (*in games, queue &c*) cuairt *f*; **4** (*deviation*) tionndadh *m*, **a ~ to the left** tionndadh chun na làimh chlì; **5** *in expr* **in ~** mu seach, fear *m* mu seach, tè *f* mu seach, **they each spent a while in ~ in the kitchen** thug iad greis *f* mu seach anns a' chidsin *m*, **they went in ~ through the door** fear mu seach/tè mu seach, chaidh iad tron doras *m*, **she picked up the cards in ~** thog i na càirtean *fpl* tè mu seach

turn *v* **1** tionndaidh *vti*, (*as vi*) (*phys & fig*) **the tide's ~ing** tha an tìde-mara *f* a' tionndadh, **whom could he ~ to?** cò ris a thionndadh e?, **he ~ed against me** thionndaidh e nam aghaidh, **the lead ~ed to gold** thionndaidh an luaidhe *mf invar* na h-òr/gu òr *m*, (*as vt*) **she didn't ~ her head** cha do thionndaidh i a ceann *m*, **~ the steering wheel** tionndaidh a' chuibhle(-stiùiridh) *f*, *also* cuir car *m* den chuibhle(-stiùiridh), **~ the mirror to the wall** tionndaidh an sgàthan *m* ris a' bhalla *m*; **2** cuir *vti*, **I ~ed my back to/on him** chuir mi mo chùl *m* ris, **~ over** cuir *vt* thairis, **~ them away** cuir air falbh iad, **he ~ed against me** chuir *vi* e nam aghaidh; **3** *misc exprs* **~ out** (*ie happen, 'go'*), tachair *vi*, rach *vi irreg*, (*both can be used impersonally*) **as it ~ed out** mar a thachair (e), **how did it ~ out (for you)?** ciamar a chaidh dhut?, **~ up** (*appear, arrive &c*) nochd *vi*, tionndaidh *vi* suas, tionndaidh *vi* an-àird', **he didn't ~ up last night** cha do nochd e/cha do thionndaidh e suas a-raoir, **she ~ed up** (*ie at the house*) **unexpectedly** thàinig i a-steach gun dùil againn rithe/gun fhiosta *m*

turret *n* turaid *f*

tussle *n* tuasaid *f*

tut tut! *excl* ud ud!

tweed *n* clò *m*, **Harris ~** An Clò Mòr, An Clò Hearach

tweezers *n* greimiche *m*

twelfth *adj* dara-deug, **the ~ day** an dara là *m* deug

twelve *n & adj* **1** d(h)à-dheug, **~ o'clock** dà uair *f* dheug; **2** *(fam)* dusan *m*, **~ years old** dusan bliadhna *f sing* a *(for* de*)* dh'aois *f*

twentieth *adj* ficheadamh

twenty *num* fichead *m*, *takes the nom sing (radical) of the noun*, **~ pence/years** fichead sgillinn/bliadhna *f*

twice *adv* **1** *(repetitions)* dà uair *f*, dà thuras *m*, **we did it ~** rinn sinn dà uair/dà thuras e, **once or ~** uair no dhà; **2** *(quantity)* **~ as much** a dhà uiread *m invar* (*as* agus/is), **give me ~ as much as Màiri has** thoir dhomh a dhà uiread agus a tha aig Màiri

twig *v* *(understand)* tuig *vti*

twilight *n* *(morning or evening)* eadar-sholas *m*, camhana(i)ch *f*, **morning ~** camhana(i)ch an latha, bris(t)eadh *m* an latha, **evening ~** camhana(i)ch na h-oidhche, *also* duibhre *f invar*

twin *n* leth-aon *m*, leth-chàraid *f*, **a pair of ~s** càraid *f sing coll*

twine *v* toinn *vti*

twinkle *v* priob *vi*

twinkling *n* *(lit & fig)* priobadh *m*, *in expr (fig)* **in the ~ of an eye** ann am priobadh na sùla

twist *n* car *m*, snìomh *m*, toinneamh *m*

twist *v* snìomh *vt*, dualaich *vt*, toinn *vti*

twisted *adj & past part* snìomhte, toinnte

twitter *v* ceilearaich *vi*

two *n & adj* **1** d(h)à (*takes the dat, lenites a following noun where possible*), **~ dogs** dà chù *m*, **~ stones** dà chloich *f*, **a time or ~** uair no dhà; **2** (*usu used of people only: with gen pl of following noun*) dithis *f*, **there were ~ people at the table** bha dithis aig a' bhòrd *m*, **~ soldiers** dithis shàighdearan *mpl gen*, **they came in ~s** thàinig iad nan dithisean, **the ~ of you** an dithis agaibh; **3** (*as prefix*) dà-, *eg* **~-eyed** *adj* dà-shùileach, **~-tier** *adj* dà-shreathach, **~-legged** *adj* dà-chasach

twosome *n* dithis *f* (*cf previous entry, rubric* 2)

two-tier *adj* dà-shreathach

type[1] *n* (*kind &c*) seòrsa *m*, gnè *f invar*

type[2] *n* (*printing &c*) clò *m*

type *v* clò-sgrìobh *vti*

typed *adj & past part* clò-sgrìobhte

typescript *n* clò-sgrìobhadh *m*, clò-sgrìobhainn *f*

typewriter *n* clò-sgrìobhadair *m*

typical *adj* **1** (*representative*) samhlachail, àbhaisteach; **2** (*of person:*

characteristic, in character) dual(t)ach (**of** do), **it's ~ of you to tell lies** tha e dualtach dhut a bhith ag innse bhreugan *fpl gen*

typist *n* clò-sgrìobhaiche *m*

tyrannical *adj* aintighearnail

tyranny *n* aintighearnas *m*

tyrant *n* aintighearn(a) *m*

tyre *n* taidhr *f*

U

udder *n* ùth *m*

ugliness *n* gràndachd *&* granndachd *f invar*

ugly *adj* grànda *&* grannda

uileann pipes *n* pìob-uilne *f*

ulcer *n* neasgaid *f*

ultimate *adj* deireannach, mu dheireadh

ultimately *adv* aig a' cheann *m* thall

umbilical *adj* imleagach

umbilicus *n* imleag *f*

umbrage *n*, *(idiom)* **take ~ at something** gabh rudeigin anns an t-sròin *(dat of* sròn *f)*

umbrella *n* sgàilean-uisge *m*

un- *prefix* **1** eu- *prefix, eg* **unlikely** *adj* eu-coltach; **2** mì- *prefix, eg* **unfortunate** *adj* mì-fhortanach; **3** neo- *prefix, eg* **unusual** *adj* neo-àbhaisteach; **4** ain- *prefix, eg* **unwilling** *adj* aindeònach; **5** ana- *prefix, eg* **unfairness** *n* ana-cothrom *f*; **6** *the neg idea of* **un-** *is also rendered by* gun *followed by a noun or verbal noun, eg* **unemployed** *adj* gun obair *f*, **unsolved** *adj* gun fhuasgladh *m*; **7** *the prefix* do- *indicates that something cannot be done, eg* **uncountable** *adj* do-àireamh, **ungovernable** *adj* do-riaghlaidh; **8** *dictionaries give very many examples of words beginning with the prefixes listed above, and a good number are given below, but it is often more natural in Gaelic to use instead a verbal construction in the negative, or a noun constr with* gun *– the next entry below exemplifies this*

unable *adj* **1** eu-comasach; **2 I was ~ to lift it** cha robh e comasach dhomh a thogail, cha b' urrainn dhomh a thogail, **~ to move** gun lùth *m*, **~ to speak** gun chainnt *f*

unaccustomed *adj* neo-chleachdte (**to** ri)

unadventurous *adj* lag-chùiseach

unanimity *n* aon-inntinn *f*

unanimous *adj* aon-inntinneach, aon-ghuthach, aon-toileach

unasked *adj* gun iarraidh *m*, **come ~** thig *vi irreg* gun iarraidh

unassuming *adj* iriosal *&* ìriseal

unattainable *adj* do-ruigsinn

unavoidable *adj* do-sheachanta

unceasing, unceasingly *adj & adv* gun sgur *m*

uncertain *adj* mì-chinnteach

uncertainty *n* teagamh *m*, mì-chinnt *f*

uncivil *adj* mì-shìobhalta

uncle *n* (*on mother's side*) bràthair *m* màthar *f gen*, (*on father's side*) bràthair athar *m gen*

unclothed *adj* lomnochd, rùisgte, (*less usu*) lom

uncommon *adj* neo-chumanta, tearc

unconcerned *adj* coma

unconditional *adj* gun chumhachan *fpl*, ~ **surrender** geilleadh *m* gun chumhachan

uncountable *adj* do-àireamh

uncouth *adj* borb, garbh, gràisgeil

uncouthness *n* gràisgealachd *f invar*

uncultivated *adj* fàs, bàn, ~ **ground** talamh fàs/bàn

undecided *adj & past part* ann an iomadh-chomhairle *f*, eadar dhà lionn *m sing*, ~ **as to what I would do** ann an iomadh-chomhairle dè a dhèanainn

under- *prefix* **1** (*referring to lower phys level &c*) fo-, *eg* **underpass** *n* fo-rathad *m*, fo-shlighe *f*, **underclothes** *npl* fo-aodach *m*; **2** (*expr subordination*) fo-, iar-, **Under-Secretary of State** Fo-rùnaire *m* na Stàite, **under-clerk** iar-chlèireach *m*, **under-gamekeeper** iar-gheamair *m*; *see also examples below*

under *prep* **1** fo (*lenites following noun where possible & takes the dat*), ~ **me** fodham(sa), ~ **you** (*sing fam*) fodhad(sa), ~ **him**, ~ **it** (*m*) fodha(san), ~ **her**, ~ **it** (*f*) foidhpe(se) *or* foipe(se), ~ **us** fodhainn(e), ~ **you** (*pl or sing formal*) fodhaibh(se), ~ **them** fòdhpa(san) *or* fòpa(san), ~ **the surface** fon uachdar *m*, ~ **a tree** fo chraoibh *f*, ~ **an obligation** fo chomain *f* (**to** aig), ~ **control** fo smachd *m invar*, ~ **a spell** fo gheasaibh (*obs dat pl of* geas *f*); **2** (*adv usage*) **the boat went** ~ chaidh am bàta fodha

underclothes *npl* fo-aodach *m sing coll*

underdeveloped *adj* dì-leasaichte

undergo *v* **1** (*endure &c*) fuiling *& fulaing vt*, ~ **hardship** fuiling cruadal *m*; **2** *in expr* ~ **surgery** rach *vi* fo obair-lèigh *f*

undergraduate *n* fo-cheumnaiche *m*

underground *adj* fo-thalamh

undergrowth *n* fo-fhàs *m*

underhand *adj* cealgach, os ìosal *& os* ìseal

underline *v* **1** (*lit*) cuir loidhne *f* (*with prep* fo); **2** (*fig: confirm, emphasise*) comharraich *vt*, leig cudthrom *m* (*with prep* air), daingnich *vt*

underling *n* ìochdaran *m*

underpants *n* drathais *& drathars f invar*

underpass *n* fo-rathad *m*, fo-shlighe *f*

under-secretary *n* (*clerical grade*) iar-chlèireach *m*, (*government office*) fo-rùnaire *m*

understand *v* tuig *vti*, lean *vti*, **are you ~ing me?** a bheil sibh gam thuigsinn/gam leantainn?

understanding *adj* tuigseach, mothachail, **an ~ friend** caraid tuigseach

understanding *n* **1** (*the mental faculty or capacity; also sympathetic* ~) tuigse *f invar*; **2** (*good sense, judgement, intelligence*) ciall *f*, toinisg *f*, tùr *m*; **3** (*agreement between parties*) còrdadh *m*, **we had an ~ about that** bha còrdadh againn/eadarainn mu dheidhinn sin, **reach/come to an ~** thig *vi* gu còrdadh

undertake *v* **1** (*take on*) gabh *vt* os làimh (*dat of* làmh *f*); **2** (*guarantee, promise to do something*) geall *vi*

undertaker *n* neach-adhlacaidh *m* (*pl* luchd-adhlacaidh *m sing coll*)

undertaking *n* **1** (*project &c*) gnothach *m*; **2** (*commitment, assurance &c*) gealladh *m*

underwear *n* fo-aodach *m sing coll*

undo *v* **1** neo-dhèan *vt*; **2** (*untie &c*) fuasgail *vt*, lasaich *vt*, ~ **a knot/a shoelace** fuasgail snaidhm *m*/barrall *m*

undoubtedly *adv* gun teagamh *m* (sam bith)

undress *v* **1** (*as vt*) rùisg *vt*; **2** (*as vi*) cuir dheth (*&c*) a (*&c*) c(h)uid *f* aodaich *m gen*, **we ~ed** chuir sinn dhinn ar cuid aodaich

undressed *adj* lomnochd, rùisgte

unease *n* an-shocair *f*, imcheist *f*

uneasy *adj* anshocrach, an-fhoiseil, fo imcheist *f*

unemployed *adj* gun obair *f*, gun chosnadh *m*

unemployment *n* cion-cosnaidh *m*, ~ **benefit** sochair *f* cion-cosnaidh, (*fam*) dòil *m invar*

unenterprising *adj* lag-chùiseach

unequal *adj* neo-ionann

unexpected *adj*, **unexpectedly** *adv*, gun dùil *f* ris (*&c*), gun sùil *f* ris (*&c*), gun fhiosta, **an ~ visit** cèilidh *mf* ris nach robh dùil/sùil , **he arrived ~ly** thàinig e gun dùil/sùil againn (*&c*) ris, thàinig e gun fhiosta (dhuinn *&c*)

unfair *adj* mì-chothromach

unfairness *n* ana-cothrom *m*, mì-chothrom *m*

unfaithful *adj* neo-dhìleas

unfamiliar *adj* coimheach

unfashionable *adj* neo-fhasanta

unfavourable *adj* neo-fhàbharach

unfeeling *adj* fuar, neo-mhothachail

unfeigned *adj* fìor, neo-chealgach

unfit *adj* **1** (*in health*) euslainteach, (*less usu*) anfhann; **2** *in expr* **he's ~ for the job** (*through lack of ability &c*) chan eil e aig ìre *f invar* na h-obrach, (*more fam: calque*) chan eil e suas ris an obair *f*

unfold *v* sgaoil *vti*, fosgail *vti*

unforeseen *adj* gun dùil *f*, gun sùil *f*, **an ~ occurrence** tachartas *m* ris nach robh dùil/sùil (againn *&c*)

unfortunate *adj* mì-fhortanach, mì-shealbhach

unfounded *adj* (*claim &c*) gun bhunait *mf*

unfriendly *adj* neo-chàirdeil

unfruitful *adj* neo-tharbhach, neo-thorach

unfurl *v* sgaoil *vti*, fosgail *vti*

ungainly *adj* cearbach

ungodly *adj* neo-dhiadhaidh

ungovernable *adj* do-riaghlaidh

ungrateful *adj* mì-thaingeil, mì-bhuidheach

unhappiness *n* mì-shonas *m*

unhappy *adj* mì-shona, mì-thoilichte

unhealthy *adj* **1** (*in poor health*) tinn, euslainteach, (*less usu; infirm*) anfhann; **2** (*bad for health*) mì-fhallain, (*more fam*) dona (dhut &c)

unholy *adj* **1** (*not holy*) mì-naomh; **2** (*satanic &c*) diabhlaidh

unhurt *adj* slàn, slàn is fallain

unification *n* co-aonachadh *m*

unified *adj & past part* (co-)aonaichte

uniform *adj* cunbhalach, aon-fhillte

uniform *n* èideadh *m*, deise *f*

unify *v* co-aonaich *vt*

unilateral *adj* aon-taobhach

unimportant *adj* gun chudthrom *m*, gun bhrìgh *f*, neo-chudthromach

uninjured *adj* slàn, slàn is fallain

unintelligent *adj* neo-thoinisgeil

unintelligible *adj* do-thuigsinn

uninteresting *adj* liosda, tioram, neo-inntinneach

uninterrupted *adj* (*ie continual*) gun stad *m*, gun sgur *m*, leanailteach, leantainneach

uninvited *adj & adv* gun iarraidh *m*, **come ~** thig *vi* gun iarraidh

union *n* aonadh *m*

unique *adj* gun samhail *m*, gun seis(e) *m*, air leth

unit *n* (*team, organisation &c*) aonad *f*, **development ~** aonad-leasachaidh *f*

unitary *adj* aonadach

unite *v* **1** (*join*) ceangail *vt*, co-cheangail *vt*, (**to/with** ri), aonaich *vti*; **2** (*join together, cooperate*) thig *vi* còmhla

united *adj & past part* aonaichte, **the United Nations** Na Dùthchannan *fpl* Aonaichte, **the United States** Na Stàitean *fpl* Aonaichte

unity *n* aonachd *f invar*

universal *adj* (*common to all*) coitcheann, uile-choitcheann, **~ suffrage** còir-bhòtaidh choitcheann

universe *n* **1** (*used with art*) an domhan, an cruinne-cè *mf*, A' Chruitheachd; **2** *in expr* **the King/Lord of the Universe** (*ie the Deity*) Rìgh *m* nan Dùl (*gen pl of* dùil *f*)

university *n* oilthigh *m*, **Glasgow University** Oilthigh Ghlaschu *gen*, **the Open University** An t-Oilthigh Fosgailte, **she's at ~** tha i aig an oilthigh

unjust *adj* mì-cheart, ana-ceart

unkempt *adj* luideach, cearbach, robach

unkind *adj* neo-choibhneil

unkindness *n* neo-choibhneas *m*

unknowable *adj* do-aithnichte

unknown *adj* 1 neo-aithnichte; 2 *in exprs* ~ **to** (*ie without someone's knowledge*) gun fhios *m* (*with prep* do *or* aig), ~ **to Mary, he sold the house** gun fhios do Mhàiri/gun fhios aig Màiri, reic e an taigh *m*; 3 *in expr* **a book/man** (*&c*) ~ **to me** (*ie that I have no knowledge of*) leabhar/duine *m* (*&c*) nach eil mi eòlach air/air nach eil mi eòlach

unlawful *adj* mì-laghail

unless *conj* 1 *can be expressed by the conjs* ach *&* mur(a), **I won't go ~ you're agreeable/in favour** cha tèid mi ann ach ma tha thusa air a shon, cha tèid mi ann mura bheil thusa air a shon; 2 *note also the cumbersome construction* **he wouldn't be satisfied ~ I went with him** chan fhòghnadh leis gun mise dhol còmhla ris

unlicensed *adj* gun cheadachd *f invar*

unlike, unlikely *adj* eu-coltach

unlimited *adj* neo-chrìochnach

unload *v* falmhaich *vt*, aotromaich *vt*

unlucky *adj* mì-shealbhach, mì-fhortanach

unmanageable *adj* do-stiùiridh, do-cheannsachaidh

unmanly *adj* neo-fhearail

unnecessary *adj* neo-riatanach

unobtrusive *adj* neo-fhollaiseach

unoccupied *adj* fàs, falamh

unofficial *adj* neo-oifigeil

unpaid *adj* 1 (*bill &c*) neo-dhìolta; 2 (*worker &c*) gun phàigheadh *m*, gun tuarastal *m*

unparalleled *adj* gun choimeas *f*

unpleasant *adj* mì-thaitneach, mì-chàilear

unpolluted *adj* neo-thruaillidh

unprepared *adj* neo-ullamh, gun ullachadh *m*

unproductive *adj* neo-tharbhach

unprofitable *adj* (*esp fin*) neo-bhuannachdail, (*more generally*) neo-tharbhach

unprotected *adj* neo-thèarainte

unrecognised *adj* neo-aithnichte

unreasonable *adj* mì-reusanta

unreliable *adj* neo-earbsach, cugallach, **the world is ~** (*trad*) is cugallach an saoghal

unresolved *adj* gun fhuasgladh *m*, **an ~ problem/question** ceist *f* gun fhuasgladh

unripe *adj* an-abaich

unrivalled *adj* gun seis(e) *m*, gun choimeas *m*

unruliness *n* gairge *f invar*, aimhreit *f*, buaireas *m*

unruly *adj* (*people*) garg, aimhreiteach, buaireasach, ùpraideach

unsafe *adj* mì-shàbhailte

unsaleable *adj* do-reicte

unsavoury *adj* mì-bhlasta

unselfish *adj* neo-fhèineil

unsettled *adj* neo-shuidhichte

unsheathe *v* (*sword &c*) rùisg *vt*

unskilled *adj* neo-ealanta, neo-uidheamaichte

unsociable *adj* neo-chuideachdail

unsolved *adj* gun fhuasgladh *m*, **an ~ problem/question** ceist *f* gun fhuasgladh

unsound *adj* neo-fhallain

unsparingly *adv* gun chaomhnadh *m*

unspeakable *adj* do-labhairt

unstable *adj* neo-sheasmhach, critheanach, cugallach

unsteady *adj* critheanach, cugallach, tulgach, **~ on his feet** cugallach air a chasan *fpl*

unsuitable *adj* mì-fhreagarrach, neo-iomchaidh

untidy *adj* **1** (*of places, objects*) mì-sgiobalta, troimh-a-chèile; **2** (*esp of person's appearance*) cearbach, luideach, robach

untie *v* fuasgail *vt*, **~ a knot/a shoelace** fuasgail snaidhm *m*/barrall *m*

until *conj* gus an, gus am, (*neg*) gus nach, **I won't get the meal ready ~ you come home** cha deasaich mi am biadh gus an tig thu dhachaigh, **I'll earn money ~ we've got enough of it** coisnidh mi airgead *m* gus am bi gu leòr againn dheth, **keep it ~ you don't need it any more** cùm e gus nach bi an còrr feum *m* agad air

until *prep* **1** gu & gus (*with dat*), **we'll wait/stay ~ six o'clock** fanaidh sinn gu sia uairean *fpl*, **I can't keep/save it ~ tomorrow** chan urrainn dhomh a ghleidheadh gu(s) a-màireach; **2** (*up ~*) gu ruige (*with nom*), **we'll be busy ~ New Year** bidh sinn trang gu ruige a' Bhliadhna Ùr

untimely *adj* neo-thràthail

untruth *n* breug *f*

untruthful *adj* breugach

unusual *adj* **1** neo-àbhaisteach, neo-chumanta; **2** (*novel*) annasach

unwell *adj* tinn, (*more fam*) bochd

unwilling *adj* **1** leisg, aindeònach; **2** *in expr* **I am ~ to sell it** (*&c*) chan eil mi deònach (air) a reic *m invar* (*&c*), is leisg leam a reic (*&c*)

unwillingly *adv* an aghaidh a (*&c*) t(h)oil *f gen*, **I stood up ~** sheas mi (suas) an aghaidh mo thoil

up *adv* & *prep* **1** (*expr position*) shuas, **there's a plane ~ there** tha plèana *mf* shuas an sin, **she's ~ the stair** tha i shuas an staidhre *f*; **2** (*expr movement: from point of view of person(s) away from whom the movement is made*) suas, **she went ~** chaidh i suas, **she went ~ the stair/the street** chaidh i suas an staidhre/an t-sràid; **3** (*expr movement: from point of view of person(s) towards whom the movement is made*) a-nìos (*lit 'from below'*), **come ~ to us!** thig *vi* a-nìos thugainn!; **4** (*misc idioma & exprs*) **~ the hill/slope** ris a' bhruthaich *mf*, **get ~** (*from bed, sitting position &c*)

èirich *vi* (suas), **I got ~ late yesterday** dh'èirich mi anmoch an-dè, (*more colloquially*) bha mi fada gun èirigh *f* an-dè, **stand** ~ seas *vi*, seas *vi* suas, seas *vi* an àird, èirich *vi* (na *&c* s(h)easamh *m*), **we stood** ~ sheas sinn (suas/an àird), dh'èirich sinn nar seasamh, **rise** ~ (*rebel &c*) èirich *vi* suas, ~ **and about** air chois (*dat of* cas *f*), **keep it ~!** cùm *vi* ort!, **don't give ~!** cùm *vi* ris!, **grow** ~ (*ie mature*) thig *vi* gu inbhe *f*, **grow ~!** na bi cho leanabail!, **dry** ~ (*ie wither*) crìon *vti*, **hurry** ~! (ie be quick) greas ort/(*pl*) greasaibh oirbh!, dèan/dèanaibh cabhag *f*, **is he ~ to the job?** a bheil e aig ìre *f* na h-obrach?, (*also*) a bheil e suas ris an obair?, **what are you ~ to?** dè a tha sibh ris?, (*fam*) **what's ~?** dè a tha ceàrr (ort *&c*)?, **put ~ a notice** cuir suas sanas *m*, cuir sanas an àirde, **wake ~** dùisg *vti*, **shut ~!** dùin do bheul *m*!

up *prep in expr* ~ **to** (*of movement* ~ *as far as*; *of time* ~ *until*) chun *&* thun (*with gen*), gu ruige (*with nom*), **we went ~ to the gate** chaidh sinn chun a' gheata *m*, **the floods came (right) ~ to the house** thàinig na tuiltean *fpl* gu ruige an taigh, **it hasn't happened ~ to now** cha do thachair e chun a seo/gu ruige seo, **we'll be busy (right) ~ to New Year** bidh sinn trang gu ruige a' Bhliadhna Ùr

upkeep *n* **1** cumail *f* suas; **2** (*of livestock &c*) beathachadh *m*

uphill *adv* ris a' bruthaich *mf dat*

uphold *v* cùm *vt* suas

upland *n* aonach *m*, monadh *m*, (*esp in place-names*) bràigh *m*, uachdar *m*

uplifting *adj* brosnachail, a thogas an cridhe *m*

upon *prep* **1** (*lit & fig*) air, ~ **the table** air a' bhòrd, **we came ~ him on the hill** thachair *vi* e òirnn/thachair sinn air anns a' mhonadh *m*, **it is incumbent ~ you** tha e mar fhiachaibh (*obs dat pl of* fiach *m*) oirbh; **2** (*in addition to*) thar (*with gen*), **thousands ~ thousands** mìltean *mpl* thar mhìltean

upper *adj* **1** (*lit & fig*) uachdrach, (*politics, law court &c*) **the ~ chamber** an seòmar uachdrach, (*of river*) ~ **reaches** cùrsa *m* uachdrach; **2** *in exprs* ~ **lip** beul-uachdair *m*, **get the ~ hand** faigh làmh *f* an uachdair, dèan an gnothach *m*, dèan a' chùis *f*, (**of/over** air), **we got the ~ hand over them** fhuair sinn làmh an uachdair orra, rinn sinn an gnothach/a' chùis orra

upright *adj* **1** (*phys & morally*) dìreach, **stand ~** seas *vi* dìreach; **2** (*morally*) onarach, ceart, ionraic, **an ~ man** duine dìreach/onarach/ceart/ionraic

uproar *n* ùpraid *f*, gleadhar *m*, othail *f*, iorghail *f*

uproarious *adj* ùpraideach

upset *v* **1** (*knock over, overturn*) leag *vt*, cuir *vt* bun-os-cionn; **2** (*put objects, situations &c into disarray*) cuir *vt* troimh-a-chèile; **3** (~ *someone emotionally*) buair *vt*, cuir *vt* troimh-a-chèile, **the news ~ us** chuir an naidheachd *f* troimh-a-chèile sinn, bhuair an naidheachd sinn

upsetting *adj* (*of situations &c*) buaireasach, frionasach

upside down *adj* bun-os-cionn

upstairs *adv* **1** (*expr motion*) suas an staidhre *f dat*, **they went** ~ chaidh iad suas an staidhre; **2** (*expr position*) shuas an staidhre, **they're** ~ tha iad shuas an staidhre

upstream *adv* (*expr motion*) ris an t-sruth *f dat*, **she went** ~ chaidh i ris an t-sruth

up-to-date *adj* ùr-nodha

upturn *n* (*in fortunes, economy &c*) car math

urban *adj* bailteil, ~ **development** leasachadh bailteil, ~ **sprawl** sgaoileadh bailteil

urbane *adj* suairc(e)

urbanity *n* suairceas *m*

urge *v* **1** (~ *to do something*) cuir impidh *m*/ìmpidh *f* (*with prep* air), spreig *vt*, stuig *vt*, coitich *vt*, **they** ~**d me to give up my job/to retire** chuir iad impidh/ìmpidh orm mo dhreuchd *f* a leigeil dhìom; **2** ~ **on** (*encourage*) brosnaich *vt*, piobraich *vt*, (*hurry on, drive on*) greas *vt*, (*esp livestock*) iomain *vt*

urgency *n* deifir *f*, cabhag *f*

urgent *adj* deifireach, cabhagach

urging *n* impidh *m &* ìmpidh *f*, spreigeadh *m*

urinate *v* dèan mùn *m*, mùin *vi*

urination *n* mùn *m*, dèanamh *m* mùin *m gen*

urine *n* mùn *m*, fual *m*

usage *n* (*custom, habit &c*) cleachdadh *m*, àbhaist *f*, nòs *m*, gnàth(s) *m*

use *n* **1** (*utilisation*) feum *m*, **make** ~ **of** cuir *vt* gu feum, dèan feum (*with prep* de), **we made** ~ **of it** chuir sinn gu feum e, rinn sinn feum dheth; **2** (*value, usefulness*) feum *m*, (*occas*) math *m*, **this machine's no** ~ chan eil feum (sam bith) anns an inneal *m* seo, **what's the** ~ **of talking?** dè am feum a bhith a' bruidhinn?, dè am math a bhith a' bruidhinn?

use *v* **1** cleachd *vt*, dèan feum *m* (*with prep* de), ~ **a hammer** cleachd òrd *m*; **2** (*expr habitual situation in the past*) cleachd *vi*, **I** ~**d to be bad-tempered** chleachd mi a bhith droch-nàdarrach, **it's not as cold as it** ~**d to be** chan eil e cho fuar agus a chleachd e a bhith, *also* chan eil e cho fuar 's a b' àbhaist

used *adj & past part* **1** cleachdte, ~ **car** càr cleachdte; **2** (*accustomed*) cleachdte (**to ri**), **I'm not** ~ **to it** chan eil mi cleachdte ris; **3** *in expr* **get** ~ **to it!** cleachd thu fhèin ris!

useful *adj* **1** feumail, **a** ~ **book** leabhar feumail; **2** *in expr* **be** ~ dèan feum *m* (**to do**), **scissors would be** ~ **just now** dhèanadh siosar *mf sing* feum an-dràsta, bhiodh siosar feumail an-dràsta

useless *adj* gun fheum *m*, **a** ~ **man/job** duine *m*/obair *f* gun fheum

user *n* neach-cleachdaidh *m*, ~**s** luchd-cleachdaidh *m sing coll*

usual *adj* àbhaisteach, cumanta, gnàthach

usually *adv* mar as trice, an cumantas *m*, am bitheantas *m*

uterus *n* machlag *f*

utilise *v* cleachd *vt*, cuir *vt* gu feum *m*, dèan feum (*with prep* de)

utility *n* **1** (*abstr*) feum *m*, feumalachd *f invar*; **2** (*con: water, electricity &c companies*) *in expr* **the ~ industries** na gnìomhachasan-seirbheis *mpl*

utter *adj* dearg (*precedes the noun, which it lenites where possible*), gu c(h)ùl *m*, **an ~ fool** dearg amadan *m*, amadan gu chùl

utter *v* abair *vt irreg*, can *vt def*, cuir *vt* an cèill (*gen of* ciall *f*)

utterly *adv* **1** gu tùr, gu h-iomlan, gu buileach, uile-gu-lèir, air fad, **~ different** gu tùr eadar-dhealaichte, **they were ~ destroyed** chaidh an sgrios *m* gu h-iomlan/gu buileach/uile-gu-lèir/air fad; **2** (*idiomatic uses with* dearg *&* dubh) **she's ~ spoilt** tha i air a dearg mhilleadh, **~ naked** dearg rùisgte, **he's ~ lazy** tha e leisg agus dubh leisg

u-turn *n* car *m* iomlan

uvula *n* cìoch *f* an t-sluigein

V

vacancy *n* dreuchd *f*/àite *m* (*&c*) ri lìonadh

vacant *adj* **1** (*of site &c*) falamh, bàn; **2** (*of job vacancy &c*) ri lìonadh

vacuous *adj* faoin

vacuum *n* falmhachd *f invar*

vagina *n* faighean *m*, pit *f*

vague *adj* neo-phongail, neo-shoilleir

vain *adj* **1** (*futile*) faoin, dìomhain, **the ~ endeavours of mankind** oidhirpean *fpl* faoin/dìomhain mhic-an-duine *m gen*; **2** (*conceited &c*) mòr às (*&c*) fhèin/fhìn, mòrchuiseach, **I'm not ~** chan eil mi mòr asam fhìn

valid *adj* èifeachdach, tàbhachdach, **a ~ driving licence** cead-dràibhidh *m* èifeachdach

validate *v* dearbh *vt*

valley *n* gleann *m*, (*small, narrow*) glac *m*

valour *n* gaisge *f invar*, gaisgeachd *f invar*

valuable *adj* luachmhor, prìseil

valuation *n* luachachadh *m*, meas *m*

value *n* **1** luach *m invar*, (*esp in neg exprs*) fiù *m invar*, **what's its ~?** dè an luach a th' ann?, **it's of no ~** tha e gun fhiù, *also* chan fhiach e; **2** *in expr* **is this of ~ to/for you? no** an fhiach *vi* seo dhut? chan fhiach

value *v* **1** (*estimate value of*) luachaich *vt*, meas *vt*; **2** (*prize*) cuir luach *m invar* (*with prep* air)

valued *adj* measail

valueless *adj* gun fhiù *m invar*, gun luach *m invar*

valve *n* cìochag *f*

vandal *n* milltear *m*

vanguard *n* toiseach *m*, **the ~ of the army** toiseach an airm

vanity *n* **1** (*futility*) faoineas *m*, dìomhanas *m*, (*Bibl*) **~ of vanities** dìomhanas nan dìomhanas; **2** (*conceit &c*) mòrchuis *f*

vapour *n* deatach *f*, smùid *f*, **emit/give out ~** cuir deatach

variable *adj* caochlaideach

variation *n* atharrachadh *m*

variety *n* **1** (*abstr*) caochladh *m*, **a ~ of** caochladh (*with gen pl*), **a ~ of occupations** caochladh dhreuchdan *fpl gen*; **2** (*sort, kind, genus*) seòrsa *m*, gnè *f*

various *adj* caochladh *m* (*with gen pl*), **in ~ places** ann an caochladh àiteachan *mpl gen*

varnish *n* falaid *m*

varnish *v* falaidich *vt*

vary *v* atharraich *vti*

vat *n* dabhach *f*

vault *n* (*architecture*) crùisle *m*

veal *n* laoigh-fheòil *f*

veer *v* claon *vi*

vegetable, vegetables *n* glasraich *f invar, sing & coll*

vehemence *n* dèineas *m*

vehement *adj* dian

vehicle *n* carbad *m*

vein *n* cuisle *f, (less usu)* fèith *f*

velocity *n* luas *&* luaths *m*, astar *m*

velvet *n* meileabhaid *f*

vendor *n* reiceadair *m*

venerable *adj* urramach

vengeance *n* dìoghaltas *m*

vennel *n* caol-shràid *f*

venom *n (fig & lit)* nimh *&* neimh *m, (lit)* puinnsean *m*

venomous *adj (fig & lit)* nimheil, *(lit)* puinnseanach, puinnseanta

venture *n (business &c)* iomairt *f*

verb *n* gnìomhair *m*, **regular ~s** gnìomhairean riaghailteach, **irregular ~s** gnìomhairean neo-riaghailteach

verbal *adj* beòil *(gen of* beul *m, used adjectivally)*, **a ~ agreement** còrdadh *m* beòil

verbatim *adj & adv* facal *m* air an fhacal

verbose *adj* faclach, briathrach

verdict *n* breith *f invar*

verge *n* **1** oir *f*, iomall *m*, crìoch *f*, **the ~ of the wood** oir/iomall na coille; **2** *(at roadside)* fàl *f*

verify *v* dearbh *vt*

vernacular *n* cainnt *f* (na) dùthcha, cainnt dhùthchasach

versatile *adj* iol-chomasach

versatility *n* iol-chomas *m*

verse *n* **1** *(poetry)* bàrdachd *f invar*, rann *m*, dànachd *f invar*; **2** *(esp contrasted with prose)* rann *m*, **prose and ~** rosg *m* is rann; **3** *(a single ~)* rann *m*; **4** in *expr* **free ~** saor-rannaigheachd *f invar*

versification *n* rannaigheachd *f invar*

vertical *adj* dìreach

very *adv* **1** glè, fìor, *(stronger)* ro, *(all lenite a following cons where possible)*, **~ old** glè shean, **~ quickly** glè luath, **the food was ~ good** bha am biadh fìor mhath, **the ~ Reverend William Campbell** An Ro-urramach/Am Fìor urramach Uilleam Caimbeul; **2** in *expr* **~ ... indeed** cianail fhèin, uabhasach fhèin, **~ good indeed** cianail fhèin math; **3** *(exact, identical)* dearbh, ceart, ceudna, fhèin, **the ~ man!** an dearbh dhuine! *m*, an ceart duine!, an duine ceudna!, an duine fhèin!, **the ~ thing I needed** an dearbh rud *m* a bha dhìth orm; **4** *(even)* fhèin, **I lost the ~ lace out of my shoe** chaill mi am barall fhèin às mo bhròig *(dat of* bròg *f)*

vessel *n* **1** *(sailing ~)* soitheach *m*, long *&* lung *f*, bàta *m*; **2** *(dish)* soitheach *m*

vest *n* fo-lèine *f*, peitean *m*

vestige *n* lorg *f*, **there's no ~ of it** chan eil lorg air

vet *n* bheat *n*, (*more trad*) lighiche-bheathaichean *m*, lighiche-sprèidh *m*

vet *v* sgrùd *vt*

veto[1] *n* bhèato *m*

veto[2] *n* dèan bhèato *m* (*with prep* air)

vex *v* sàraich *vt*, claoidh *vt*, farranaich *vt*

vexing *adj* (*situations &c*) frionasach, leamh, **they're constantly asking me ~ questions** bidh iad a' cur cheistean *fpl gen* frionasach orm fad na h-ùine

vice[1] *n* **1** (*immorality, wickedness*) aingidheachd *f invar*; **2** (*undesirable trait or habit*) droch-ghnàths *m*, droch-bheus *f*, droch-bheart *f*

vice[2] *n* (*clamp*) teanchair & teannachair *m*

vice- *prefix* iar- (*lenites following cons where possible*), *eg* **vice-president** iar-cheann-suidhe *m*, **vice-chairman** iar-chathraiche *m*, iar-fhear-cathrach *m*

vice versa *adv*, **(and) ~** agus a chaochladh *m*, **he gave her a present, and ~** thug e tiodhlac *m* dhi, agus a chaochladh

vicious *adj* **1** aingidh; **2** (*hurtful &c*) guineach, nìmheil, **~ criticism** càineadh guineach/nìmheil; **3** (*phys violent*) brùideil, **a ~ beating** slacadh brùideil

victim *n* (*of accident*) leòinteach *m*

victor *n* buadhaiche *m*, buadhair *m*

victory *n* buaidh *f*

video *n* bhideo *f*

view *n* **1** (*attractive scenery &c*) sealladh *m*, sealladh dùthcha (*gen of* dùthaich *f*), **beautiful ~s** seallaidhean brèagha; **2** (*a field of vision*) fradharc & radharc *m*, sealladh *m*, fianais *f*, **come into ~** thig *vi* san (fh)radharc, thig an sealladh *or* san t-sealladh, thig am fianais; **3** (*opinion*) beachd *m*, **I take the ~ that . . .** tha mi den bheachd gu . . . , **that is not my ~!** chan e sin mo bheachd-sa!; **4** *in exprs* **in ~ of** (*ie considering*) a' cur san aireamh *f* (*followed by gen*), leis mar a bha (*followed by noun*), **in ~ of the rent, we took the house** a' cur san aireamh am màl/leis mar a bha am màl, ghabh sinn an taigh *m*, **point of ~** sealladh *m*, **it's an improvement from the point of ~ that the costs will be lower** is e leasachadh *m* a th' ann bhon t-sealladh 's gum bi na cosgaisean *fpl* nas ìsle, (*or more simply*) is e leasachadh a th' ann a-thaobh 's gum bi na cosgaisean nas ìsle

viewer *n* (*TV &c*) neach-coimhid *m*, **~s** luchd-coimhid *m sing coll*

vigilance *n* furachas *m*

vigilant *adj* furachail

vigorous *adj* **1** (*phys*) lùthmhor, brìghmhor, sgairteil; **2** (*in argument, discussion &c*) sgairteil, **a ~ exposition of his views** mìneachadh *m* sgairteil de na beachdan *mpl* aige

vigour *n* **1** (*phys*) lùth & lùths *m*, neart *m*, sgairt *f*; **2** (*intellectual*) sgairt *f*

vile *adj* **1** (*disgusting &c*) gràineil, grànda & grànnda; **2** (*abject*) dìblidh

vilify *v* màb *vt*, dubh-chàin *vt*

vine *n* crann-fìona *m*, fìonnan *m*

vinegar *n* fìon-geur *m*

violence *n* fòirneart *m*, ainneart *m*

violent *adj* brùideil

violin *n* fidheall *f*, **a tune on the** ~ port *m* air an fhidhill *dat*

violinist *n* fìdhlear *m*

viper *n* nathair-nimhe *f*

virgin *n* òigh *f*, ainnir *f*, maighdeann *f*

virginal *adj* òigheil

virginity *n* (*phys & abstr*) maighdeannas *m*

virtue *n* **1** (*moral conduct*) subhailc *f*, deagh-bheus *f*; **2** (*Lit: inherent quality, value*) brìgh *f invar*, **a food without** ~ biadh *m* gun bhrìgh; **3** *in expr* **by** ~ **of** do bhrìgh, air sgàth, a chionn, (*all with gen*), **she got the job by** ~ **of her qualifications** fhuair i an obair *f* do bhrìgh/air sgàth nan teisteanan *mpl* (a bh') aice

virtuous *adj* (*of moral conduct*) subhailceach, deagh-bheusach

virulent *adj* nimheil

visible *adj* ri f(h)aicinn, ris, faicsinneach, lèirsinneach, **there was nothing** ~ cha robh càil *m invar* ri fhaicinn, **her elbow was** ~ bha a h-uileann ris

vision *n* **1** (*eyesight*) fradharc & radharc *m*, lèirsinn *f invar*); **2** (*foresight &c*) lèirsinn *f invar*; **3** (*supernatural dream &c*) aisling *f*

visit *n* **1** (*esp to a person*} tadhal *m*, cèilidh *mf*, **pay X a** ~ cuir cèilidh air X, *also* tadhail *vi* air X; **2** (*to a place*) turas *m*, sgrìob *f*, (**to do**), **a** ~ **to Uist** turas/sgrìob do dh'Uibhist, **on a** ~ air turas

visit *v* **1** (~ *people*) tadhail *vi*, rach *vi* a chèilidh, rach air chèilidh *mf*, (*all with prep* air), **~ing my parents** a' tadhal air mo phàrantan *mpl*, ~ **friends** tadhail air caraidean *mpl*, rach a/air chèilidh air caraidean; **2** (~ *places*) rach *vi* air turas *m* (*with prep* gu), **we ~ed the Isle of Man** chaidh sinn air turas gu Eilean Mhanainn, *also* bha turas againn gu Eilean Mhannain

visitor *n* **1** neach-tadhail *m* (*pl* luchd-tadhail *m sing coll*); **2** (*holidaymaker &c*) fear-turais *m*, neach-turais *m* (*pl* luchd-turais *m sing coll*)

vital *adj* **1** (*lively &c*) beothail, brìghmhor, lùthmhor; **2** *in expr* ~ **spark** rong *f*; **3** (*indispensable*) riatanach, deatamach, ro-chud(th)romach

vitality *n* beothalachd *f invar*

vivacious *adj* beothail, meanmnach

vivacity *n* beothalachd *f invar*, meanmna *m*

vocabulary *n* **1** (*abstr*) faclan *mpl*, briathran *mpl*; **2** (*con: in book form &c*) faclair *m*, briathrachan *m*

vocation *n* **1** (*esp a calling, eg the church*) gairm *f*; **2** (*occupation*) dreuchd *f*

vocational *adj* dreuchdail, ~ **training** oideachas dreuchdail

vocative *adj* (*gram*) gairmeach, **the ~ case** an tuiseal gairmeach

voice *n* **1** guth *m*, **in a low ~** ann an guth ìosal/ìseal; **2** *in expr* **singing at the top of my ~** a' seinn *vi* (aig) àrd mo chlaiginn (*gen of* claigeann *m*); **3** (*gram*) guth *m*, **the passive ~** an guth fulangach

voice *v* cuir *vt* an cèill (*gen of* ciall *f*), **she ~d her own anxiety** chuir i an cèill a h-iomagain *f* fhèin

void *n* fal(a)mhachd *f invar*, fànas *m*, fàsalachd *f invar*

volatile *adj* caochlaideach

volcanic *adj*, bholcànach

volcano *n* bholcàno *m*, beinn-theine *f*

volume *n* (*capacity*) tomhas-lìonaidh *m*

voluntary *adj* saor-thoileach

volunteer *n* saor-thoileach *m*

vomit *n* dìobhairt *mf invar*

vomit *v* dìobhair *vti*, sgeith *vti*, cuir *vti* a-mach

vomiting *n* dìobhairt *mf invar*, sgeith *m*

voracious *adj* craosach, geòcach, gionach

vote *v* **1** bhòt *vi* (**for** airson); **2** *in expr* **~ into office** tagh *vt*

voter *n* neach-bhòtaidh *m* (*pl* luchd-bhòtaidh *m sing coll*)

voting *n* bhòtadh *m*, **~ rights** còraichean *fpl* bhòtaidh *gen*

vouch *v* rach *vi* an urras *m* (**for** air), **~ for someone** rach an urras air cuideigin *mf invar*

voucher *n* cùpon *m*

vow *n* gealladh *m*, bòid *f*

vow *v* geall *vti*, thoir gealladh *m*, gabh bòid *f*, bòidich *vi*, **he ~ed he wouldn't do it again** gheall e nach dèanadh e a-rithist e

vowel *n* fuaimreag *f*

voyage *n* turas-mara *m*, bhòids(e) *f*

vulgar *adj* **1** (*uncouth &c*) gràisgeil, garbh, borb; **2** (*indecent*) draosta, drabasta; **3** (*belonging to the people*) coitcheann, cumanta, **~ tongue** cainnt choitcheann/chumanta

vulgarity *n* **1** (*uncouthness*) gràisgealachd *f invar*; **2** (*indecency*) draostachd *f invar*, drabastachd *f invar*

vulnerable *adj* so-leònte

vulva pit *f*

W

wafer *n* sliseag *f*

wag *v* **1** (*as vi*) bog *vi*, **the dog's tail was ~ging** bha earball a' choin a' bogadh; **2** (*as vt*) crath *vt*, **a dog ~ging his tail** cù *m* (is e) a' crathadh earbaill *m gen*

wage, wages *n* tuarastal *f*, pàigheadh *m*, (*less usu*) duais *f*, cosnadh *m*

wage *v* dèan *vt*, **~ war** dèan cogadh *m*

wager *n* geall *m*, **put/lay/place a ~** cuir geall (**on** air)

wager *v* **1** (*lit*) cuir geall *m* (**on** air); **2** (*fig*) cuir *vi* an geall *m*, rach *vi irreg* an urras *m* (*with conj* gu/nach), **I'll ~ he won't come** cuiridh mi an geall nach tig e, thèid mi an urras nach tig e

wail *v* caoin *vi*, guil *vi*

waist *n* meadhan *m*

waistcoat *n* peitean *m*

wait *v* **1** fuirich *vi*, feith *vi*, (**for** ri), **you ~ here!** fuirich thusa an seo!, **I was ~ing for you** bha mi a' fuireach riut/a' feitheamh riut, **~ a minute!** fuirich mionaid *f!*, **~ing for the bus** a' feitheamh ris a' bhus *m*; **2** *in expr* **the bus was ~ing** bha am bus na stad *m*; **3** (*serve*) freastail *vi* (*with prep* air), fritheil *vi* (**on** air), **~ at table** freastail don bhòrd *m*, **~ on the guests** fritheil air na h-aoighean *mpl*

waiter *n* gille-frithealaidh *m*

waiting list *n* liosta-feitheimh *f*

waitress *n* caileag-fhrithealaidh *f*

wake, waken *v* **1** dùisg *vti*, **I wakened/woke (up) at six** dhùisg mi aig (a) sia, **~ me (up)/~ me in two hours** dùisg mi an ceann dà uair *f gen* a (*for* de) thìde *f*; **2** *in excl* **~ up!** dùisg!/dùisgibh!, (*to slow or sleepy person*) crath dhìot an cadal!

wakened *adj & past part* na (*&c*) d(h)ùisg, na (*&c*) d(h)ùsgadh

walk *n* cuairt *f*, **go for/take a ~** gabh cuairt/rach *vi irreg* air chuairt

walk *v* **1** coisich *vi*, **I ~ed along/on/onwards** choisich mi romham; **2** (*as opposed to driving/riding*) rach *vi irreg* de chois (*dat of* cas *f*), **I'll ~ there** thèid mi ann dhem chois, *also* 's e coiseachd *f invar* a nì mi (ann)

walker *n* coisiche *m*

walking *n* coiseachd *f invar*, **~ stick** bata *m* coiseachd *gen*

wall *n* **1** (*esp defensive or fortified*) mùr *m*; **2** (*usu inner or outer ~ of building, but occas freestanding*) balla *m*; **3** (*freestanding ~, eg of garden*) gàrradh & gàradh *m*

wallpaper *n* pàipear-balla *m*

walnut *n* **1** cnò Fhrangach *f*, gall-chnò *f*; **2** (*~ tree*) crann *m* ghall-chnò *gen*

walrus *n* each-mara *m*

wan *adj* glas-neulach

wand *n* slat *f*, slatag *f*

wander *v* **1** (*travel far & wide, at random, or like an exile*) rach *vi irreg* air fhuadan *m*, bi *vi irreg* air fhuadan, (*more trad*) rach/bi air allaban *m*; **2** (*get lost, stray*) rach *vi irreg* air seachran *m*, rach *vi* air iomrall *m*; **3** *in expr* **you made me ~ from the point** chuir thu às mo ghabhail *mf* mi

wandering *adj* **1** (*lost, astray*) air iomrall *m*, air seachran *m*; **2** (*like an exile, a traveller*) air fhuadan *m*, air allaban *m*

wandering *n* **1** (*when lost, astray*) seachran *m*, iomrall *m*; **2** (*like an exile, a traveller*) fuadan *m*, allaban *m*

want *n* **1** (*lack*) dìth *m*, cion *m invar*, uireasbhaidh *f*, easbhaidh *f*; **2** (*poverty*) bochdainn *f*, (*less usu*) ainnis *f*

want *v* **1** (*require, wish for*) iarr *vt*, (*more fam*) bi *vi* airson (*with gen*), **do you ~ a/some coffee?** a bheil thu ag iarraidh cofaidh *m*?, **the children ~ed me to buy a kitten** bha a' chlann ag iarraidh orm piseag *f* a cheannach, **I don't ~ you to be on your own** chan eil mi airson gum bi thu nad aonar *mf*; **2** (*require, look for*) sir *vt*, **the company ~s workers** tha a' chompanaidh a' sireadh luchd-obrach *m sing coll*; **3** (*in shop &c*) **what do you ~?** dè tha a dhìth *m* oirbh?, **I ~ a coat** tha còta *m* a dhìth orm; **4** (*lack, need*) bi *vi irreg* a dhìth, bi a dh'easbhaaidh *f*, (*with prep* air), **what do they ~ (for)?** dè a tha a dhìth/a dh'easbhaidh orra?; **5** (*like, wish*) togair *vi* (*often used in relative fut tense*), **we'll go on holiday, if you ~** thèid sinn air laithean-saora *mpl*, ma thogras tu

wanting *adj* a dhìth *m*, a dh'easbhaidh *f*, easbhaidheach, **food is ~** tha biadh *m* a dhìth

war *n* cogadh *m*, **the First (World) War** a' Chiad Chogadh, An Cogadh Mòr, **make/wage ~** dèan cogadh, **on a ~ footing** air ghleus *mf* cogaidh *gen*

warble *v* ceileir *vi*

warcry *n* gairm-chogaidh *f*, sluagh-ghairm *f*

wardrobe *n* preas-aodaich *m*

warehouse *n* batharnach *m*

wares *n* bathar *m sing coll*, **selling their ~** a' reic an cuid *f* bathair *gen*

warfare *n* cogadh *m*

warlike *adj* **1** (*as term of praise*) cathach; **2** (*more pej: belligerent &c*) cogach

warm *adj* **1** (*of weather, objects*) blàth, **it's ~ today** tha i blàth an-diugh, **~ milk** bainne blàth; **2** (*of people, emotions, atmosphere*) blàth, cridheil, càirdeil, **a ~ welcome** fàilte chridheil

warm *v* **1** teasaich *vt*, teòdh *vt*, blàthaich *vt*, **~ (up) the soup** teasaich am brot; **2** (*fig: emotionally*) teòth *vi* (**to** ri), **~ to someone** teòdh ri cuideigin *mf invar*

war-memorial *n* cuimhneachan-cogaidh *m*

warm-hearted *adj* blàth-chridheach

warming *n* teasachadh *m*, blàthachadh *m*, teòdhadh *m*, **global ~** blàthachadh na cruinne *mf*

warmth *n* **1** (*lit*) blàths *m*; **2** (*of people, emotions, atmosphere*) blàths *m*, cridhealas *m*

warn *v* thoir rabhadh *m* (*with prep* do), earalaich *vt*, (**about/against** air), **they ~ed me about/against her** thug iad rabhadh dhomh oirre

warning *n* rabhadh *m*, earalachadh *m*, **a ~ bell** clag-rabhaidh *m*

warrant *n* **1** (*guarantee*) bar(r)antas *m*, urras *m*; **2** (*authorisation*) bar(r)antas *m*, **building ~** barrantas-togail *m*, **arrest ~** barrantas-glacaidh *m*

warrior *n* **1** fear-cogaidh *m* (*pl* luchd-cogaidh *m sing coll*); **2** (*as trad term of praise*) gaisgeach *m*, laoch *m*, curaidh *m*, seud *m*

warship *n* long-chogaidh *f*

wart *n* foinne *m*

wary *adj* **1** (*alert*) faiceallach, cùramach; **2** (*mistrustful*) amharasach, teagmhach

wash *v* nigh *vt*, ionnlaid *vt*, **~ the baby** nigh an leanabh *m*, **I was ~ing** bha mi gam nighe fhìn

washbasin *n* mias-ionnlaid *f*

washer[1] *n* (*for screw or bolt*) cearclan *m*

washer[2] *n* (*for clothes*) nigheadair *m*

washhouse *n* taigh-nighe *m*

washing *n* (*abstr*) nighe *m invar*, ionnlad *m*; (*con: a batch of washing*) nigheadaireachd *f invar*

washing-machine *n* nigheadair *m*, inneal-nighe *m*, inneal-nigheadaireachd *m*

wasp *n* speach *f*, **~'s sting** gath *f* speacha *gen*

waste *adj* fàs, **~ ground** talamh fàs

waste *n* **1** call *m*, cosg *m invar*, **a ~ of time/money** call/cosg ùine *f gen*/ airgid *m gen*; **2** (*refuse*) sgudal *m*, **~ collection/disposal** togail *f*/ glanadh *m* sgudail *gen*

waste *v* (*esp money*) caith *vt*, cosg *vt*, struidh *vt*

wasteful *adj* caith(t)each, struidheil

waster *n* struidhear *m*

watch[1] *n* **1** (*abstr: guard*) faire *f*, caithris *f invar*, **keep ~** dèan/cùm faire, **the night ~** faire na h-oidhche, caithris (na h-oidhche); **2** (*con: ie the people on ~*) luchd-faire *m sing coll*, freiceadan *m sing coll*, **a (single) ~/a member of the ~** fear-faire *m*; **3** *in expr* **The Black Watch** Am Freiceadan Dubh

watch[2] *n* (*timepiece*) uaireadair *m*

watch *v* coimhead *vt*, **~ a film/TV** coimhead film *m*/an TBh *m*

watcher *n* neach-coimhid *m* (*pl* luchd-coimhid *m sing coll*)

watchful *adj* furachail

watchfulness *n* furachas *m*

watchman *n* fear-faire *m*, fear-coimhid *m*

water *n* **1** uisge *m*, (*esp in Lewis Gaelic*) bùrn *m*, **a drink of ~** deoch *f* uisge *gen*, **fresh ~** (*ie as opposed to salt ~*) fìor-uisge, **~ mill** muileann-uisge *mf*; **2** *in expr* **pass ~** dèan mùn *m*, mùin *vi*

water *v* uisgich *vt*

waterfall *n* eas *m*, leum-uisge *m*, linne *f*, spùt *m*

waterfowl *n & npl* eun-uisge *m*, *pl* eòin-uisge

watering can *n* peile-frasaidh *m*

waterproof *adj* dìonach, uisge-dhìonach

watershed *n* druim-uisge *m*

watertight *adj* (*house, boat &c*) uisge-dhìonach, **wind and ~** dìonach

waterway *n* slighe-uisge *f*

watery *adj* uisgeach

waulk *v* luaidh *vti*

waulking *n* luadhadh *m*, **~ songs** òrain *mpl* luadhaidh & òrain luaidh *gen*

wave *n* (*in sea, physics &c*) tonn *mf*, **~-power** cumhachd *mf invar* tuinne (*gen of* tonn), **sound ~** fuaim-thonn *mf*, **heat ~** teas-tonn *mf*

wave *v* **1** (*oscillate &c*) luaisg *vi*, tulg *vi*; **2** (*signal with the hand*) smèid *vi*, crath a (*&c*) làmh(an) *f(pl)*, (**to/at** ri), **they were waving to her** bha iad a' smèideadh rithe/a' crathadh an làmhan rithe

wax *n* cèir *f*

waxen, waxy *adj* cèireach

way *n* **1** (*route, road*) rathad *m*, (*sometimes with more abstr sense*) slighe *f*, **the ~ home** an rathad dhachaigh, **they went that ~** chaidh iad an rathad sin, ghabh iad an t-slighe sin, **we met them on the ~** thachair sinn riutha air an rathad/air an t-slighe, **give ~** gèill slighe, **right of ~** còir-slighe *f*, **~ out** (*ie exit*) slighe dol *m* a-mach, (**~** *out via a door*) doras *m* dol *m* a-mach; **2** (*direction*) taobh *m*, rathad *m*, **they're coming this ~** tha iad a' tighinn an taobh/an rathad seo; **3** (*distance*) astar *m*, **a long ~ fada** *adj*, **that's a fair/a long ~!** 's e astar mòr/math a tha sin!, 's fhada sin!, **a long ~ away** fad' air falbh; **4** (**~** *of doing something*) dòigh *f*, modh *f*, seòl *m*, **do it (in) this ~** dèan air an dòigh seo e, **in a particular ~** air mhodh àraidh, **~ of life** dòigh-beatha *f*; **5** *in expr* (*fam*) **there's no ~ that will work!** chan obraich sin idir idir!, chan eil dòigh gun obraich sin; **6** (*custom(s) &c*) dòigh *f*, **they aren't used to our ~s** chan eil iad cleachdte ris na dòighean againn; **7** *in exprs* **~ out** (*ie escape*) dol-às *m invar*, **there was no ~ out for us now except . . .** cha robh dol-às againn a-nis ach . . ., **that's the ~ it is!** is ann mar sin a tha (e)!

weak *adj* **1** (*phys*) lag, (*faint*) fann, (*less usu*) lapach, **~ from hunger** lag/fann leis an acras *m*, **a ~ voice** guth fann; **2** (*emotionally*) bog, meata, maoth, gun smior *m*

weaken *v* lagaich *vti*, (*less usu*) fannaich *vti*

weakening *n* lagachadh *m*, fàillinn *f*

weak-minded *adj* lag na (*&c*) inntinn *f*

weakness *n* laigse *f*

wealth *n* beartas & beairteas *m*, saidhbhreas *m*, ionmhas *m*, stòras *m*, (*less usu*) maoin *f*

wealthy *adj* beartach & beairteach, saidhbhir

weapon *n* ball-airm *m*

wear *n* **1** (*abstr*) caitheamh *f*; **2** (*con: apparel*) aodach *m*, **evening** ~ aodach-feasgair *m*

wear *v* **1** (*clothes*) cuir *vt* (*with prep* air *or, more trad,* mu), ~ **your coat today** cuir (ort) do chòta *m* an-diugh; **2** *in expr* **a man** ~**ing a suit** fear *m* is deise *f* air

wear out *v* **1** (*clothing &c*) caith *vt*; **2** (*of people: exhaust, weary*) claoidh *vt*, sgìthich *vt*

weariness *n* **1** (*through fatigue*) sgìths & sgìos *f invar*, claoidheadh *m*, claoidh *f invar*; **2** (*through tedium &c*) fadachd *f invar*, fadal *m*

weary *adj* **1** (*through fatigue*) sgìth, claoidhte, (*esp through stress, worry &c*) sàraichte, **grow** ~ fàs *vi* sgìth; **2** (*causing weariness*) cian, **a** ~ **road** rathad cian; **3 grow** ~ (*esp through tedium*) gabh fadachd *f invar*

weary *v* claoidh *vt*, sgìthich *vt*, (*esp by harassment, pressure &c*) sàraich *vt*

wearying *adj* sgìtheil

weasel *n* neas (bheag)

weather *n* **1** aimsir *f*, sìde (*also less usu* tìde) *f*, **bad** ~ droch aimsir/shìde, **unsettled** ~ sìde chaochlaideach, ~ **forecast** tuairmse *f* (na) sìde, (*a spell of*) **dry/fine/fair** ~ (*following rain*) turadh *m*; **2** *in expr* **appalling/terrible/atrocious** ~ sìde nan seachd sian(tan) *fpl*

weather-beaten *adj* (*complexion &c*) air dath *m* nan sian *fpl*

weathercock *n* coileach-gaoithe *m*

weave *v* figh *vti*

weaver *n* breabadair *m*, figheadair *m*

weaving *n* fighe *mf invar*, breabadaireachd *f invar*, ~ **loom** beart-fhighe *f*

web *n* **1** lìon *m*, **spider's** ~ lìon damhain-allaidh *m gen*; **2** (*IT*) *usu with art,* **the** ~ an t-eadar-lìon, ~ **site** ionad *m* eadar-lìn *gen*, làrach-lìn *f*

wed *adj & past part* pòsta, **newly** ~ nuadh-phòsta, **newly** ~**s** càraid *f* nuadh-phòsta, **get** ~ pòs *vi*

wedder *n* mult & molt *m*

wedding *n* banais *f*, ~ **reception** cuirm *f* bainnse *gen*, *in expr* ~ **ring** fàinne-pòsaidh *mf*, fàinne-pòst(a) *mf*

wedge *n* geinn *m*

wedlock *n* pòsadh *m*

Wednesday *n* Diciadain *m invar*

wee *adj* **1** beag, **a** ~ **boy** balach beag; **2** *in expr* **a** ~ **bit** (*adv*) caran *m*, rud beag, **a** ~ **bit tired** caran sgìth, rud beag sgìth

weed *n* luibh *mf*, lus *m*

week *n* seachdain *f*, **a** ~ **today** seachdain an-diugh

weekend *n* deireadh-seachdain *m*, **at the** ~ aig deireadh na seachdaine

weekly *adj* seachdaineach, seachdaineil, (*adv*) a h-uile seachdain *f*

weep *v* caoin *vi*, guil *vi*, gail *vi*, (~ *vigorously*) ràn *vi*

weeping *n* caoineadh *m*, gul *m*, gal *m*, (*usu vigorous*) rànail *m invar*, rànaich *f invar*

weigh *v* **1** (*as vt*) cothromaich *vt*, cuideamaich *vt*; **2** (*as vi*) **what's it** ~? dè an cudthrom a tha ann?, **it ~s a kilogram** tha cileagram *m* de chudthrom *m* ann; **3** (*mentally*) **~ (up)** beachdaich *vi*, gabh beachd *m*, (*with prep* air), **~ing up the situation** a' beachdachadh/a' gabhail beachd air an t-suidheachadh *m*

weight *n* cudthrom *m*, **a kilogram in ~** cileagram *m* de chudthrom, **I had to put on ~** b' fheudar dhomh cudthrom a chur orm

weighty *adj* cudthromach, trom, **~ matters** cuspairean *mpl* cudthromach/ troma

weird *adj* neònach

welcome *adj* **1** (*as excl*) **~!** fàilte *f* oirbh/ort!, **~ to my house!** fàilte *f* oirbh/ ort don taigh *m* agam!, **they bid us ~** chuir iad fàilte òirnn; **2** (*after expr of thanks, appreciation &c*) **you're ~** is/'s e do bheatha *f*, is/'s ur beatha, **thank you very much! you're ~** mòran taing! 's e do bheatha/ur beatha

welcome *n* fàilte *f*, gabhail *mf*, **we got a hearty/lukewarm ~** fhuair sinn fàilte chridheil/leth-fhuar, **what sort of a ~ did you get?** dè an seòrsa fàilte a fhuair sibh?

welcome *v* cuir fàilte *f* (*with prep* air), fàiltich *vt*, **they ~ed us** chuir iad fàilte òirnn

welcoming *adj* fàilteachail, fàilteach

weld *v* tàth *vt*

welfare *n* **1** (*material & psychological circumstances*} cor *m*, **he became anxious about the ~ of the refugees** ghabh e cùram *m* mu chor nam fògarrach *mpl gen*; **2** (*social security, benefits &c*) sochair (shòisealta), **~ state** stàit *f* shochairean *gen pl*

well *adj* gu math, fallain, slàn, **I'm ~, thank you** tha (mi) gu math, tapadh leat, **he's not a ~ man** chan e duine fallain a th' ann (dheth)

well *adv* **1** gu math, **she did the work ~** 's ann gu math a rinn i an obair; **2** (*in Gaelic constructions with air plus the verbal noun*) deagh, **it's ~ made/done** tha e air a dheagh dhèanamh, *also* tha e air a dhèanamh gu math; **3** (*other idioms & exprs*) **~ done!** math thu-fhèin!, nach math a rinn thu!, **he's ~ off** tha e glè mhath dheth, **as ~ as** (*ie in addition to*) cho math ri, a thuilleadh air, a bharrachd air, **we have two flats as ~ as the house** tha dà lobhta *m* againn cho math ris/a thuilleadh air/a bharrachd air an taigh *m*, **we get on (very) ~ (with each other)** tha sinn gu math mòr aig a chèile, tha sinn rèidh ri chèile, tha sinn a' tarraing glè mhath

well *n* tobar *mf*, fuaran *m*, **wishing ~** tobar-miann *mf*

well-behaved *adj* beusach, modhail, sìobhalta

wellbeing *n* (*material & psychological circumstances*} cor *m*, math *m*, **he became anxious about the ~ of the refugees** ghabh e cùram *m* mu chor nam fògarrach *mpl gen*

well-built *adj* **1** (*of person: sturdy &c*) tomadach, tapaidh, calma; **2** (*of building*) air a dheagh thogail

well-informed *adj* fiosrach (**about** air)

wellington (boot) *n* bòtann *m*

well-known *adj* ainmeil, (*esp persons*) iomraiteach

well-liked *adj* mòr-thaitneach, mòr-chòrdte

well-mannered *adj* modhail

well-ordered *adj* dòigheil, òrdail, riaghailteach

well-timed *adj* an deagh àm *m*

Welsh *adj* Cuimreach

Welshman *n* Cuimreach *m*

west *adj* siar *adj*, an iar *f invar*, **the ~ wind** a' ghaoth an iar, **the ~ coast/~ side (of the country)** an taobh an iar, an taobh siar

west *adv* an iar *f invar*, **we're going ~** tha sinn a' dol an iar, **~ of the island** an iar air an eilean *m*, siar air an eilean

west *n* iar *f invar*, **the ~** (*ie compass direction*) an àird *f* an iar, **the ~** (*ie location*) an taobh an iar *or* an taobh siar, **breezes from the ~** oiteagan *fpl* on iar

westerly *adj* on iar *f invar*, **a ~ wind** gaoth *f* on iar

western *adj* siar *adj*, an iar *adv*, **the Western Isles** Na h-Eileanan *mpl* an Iar *or* Na h-Eileanan Siar

westward(s) *adv* an iar, chun an iar, chun na h-àirde an iar, **going ~** a' dol (chun) an iar

wet *adj* fliuch, **a ~ day** là fliuch, **I'm ~ through/soaking ~** tha mi bog fliuch

wet *v* 1 fliuch *vt*, **the water overflowed, ~ting everything** chuir an t-uisge thairis, a' fliuchadh a h-uile càil *m invar*, (*fam*) **~ your whistle!** fliuch do ribheid *f*!; 2 *in expr* **he ~ himself** chaill e a mhùn *m*

wether *n* mult *&* molt *m*

whale *n* muc-mhara *f*

what *inter pron* dè, **~'s your name?** dè an t-ainm a th' oirbh?, **~'s happening?** dè a tha a' tachairt?, **~'s the good/use of talking!** dè am math a bhith a' bruidhinn!, **~ do you think?** dè do bheachd *m* (air)?, **I don't know ~ I'll do** chan eil fhios agam (gu) dè a nì mi; 2 *in expr* **~ (did you say)?** b' àill leat/leibh?, (*less polite*) dè an rud *m*?; 3 (*esp when* '*what*' *could be replaced in Eng by* '*which*') cò, **~ books do you like best?** cò na leabhraichean *mpl* as fheàrr leat?; 4 *in exprs* **~ for?** carson?, **~ did you do that for?** carson a rinn thu sin?, **~ a** (*followed by a noun*) abair (*imperative of* abair *vti irreg*), *eg* **~ a fool!** abair amadan *m*!, **~ a mess!** abair bùrach *m*!

what *rel pron* na, **I gave him ~ I had** thug mi dha na bha agam, **they lost ~ food they had** chaill iad na bha aca de bhiadh *m*

whatever *pron* 1 (*envisaging multiple possibilities*) ge b' e *with the appropriate pron, usu* dè, **~ I did there, I don't remember it** ge b' e dè a rinn mi (ann) an sin, chan eil cuimhne *f* agam air, **~ the weather may be like** ge b' e dè an aimsir/an t-sìde a bhios ann; 2 (*as object of main verb*) càil *m invar* sam bith *f invar*, rud *m* sam bith, nì *m* sam bith, *also* càil (*&c*)

air bith, **you will get** ~ **you want** gheibh thu càil/rud/nì sam bith a thogras tu; 3 (*emph for* **what**) dè fon ghrèin (*dat sing of* grian *f*), dè air an t-saoghal, ~ **do you mean?** dè fon ghrèin/dè air an t-saoghal a tha thu a' ciallachadh?, (*trad*) gu dè as ciall dhut?

wheat *n* cruithneachd *&* cruineachd *f invar*

wheel *n* cuibhle *f*, (*more trad, less usu*) roth *mf*

wheelchair *n* cathair-chuibhle *f*, sèithear-cuibhle *m*

wheeled *adj* rothach

wheesht! *excl* ist!, *pl* istibh! *&* eist!, *pl* eistibh!, tosd!

whelk *n* faochag *f*

whelp *n* cuilean *m*

when *adv* (*inter*) cuine (*before a vowel* cuin), ~ **was that?** cuin a bha sin?, **I don't know** ~ **it was** chan eil fhios *m* am cuin a bha e

when *conj* (*non-inter*) an uair a *&* nuair a, **give me it** ~ **you've finished with it** thoir dhomh e an uair a bhios tu deiseil dheth

whenever *pron* 1 (*where there is doubt about the time of occurrence &c*) ge b' e cuin(e), ~ **it happened, I don't remember it** ge b' e cuin a thachair e, chan eil cuimhne *f* agam air,; 2 (*where the time of occurrence is unimportant or undefined*) uair *f* sam bith, **come and see us** ~ **you like** thig gar faicinn *f invar* uair sam bith a thogras tu; 3 (*emph for* **when**) cuin air bith, ~ **did you say that?** cuin air bith a thuirt thu sin?

where *adv* 1 (*inter*) càite (*before a vowel* càit), ~**'s Iain?** càit a bheil Iain?; 2 *in expr* ~ . . . **from?** cò às . . . ?, ~ **are you from?** cò às a tha thu?, ~ **did he** (*emph*) **spring from?** cò às a nochd esan?

where *conj* (*non-inter*) far a, **you'll find it** ~ **you left it** gheibh thu e far na (*for* far an do) dh'fhàg thu e

wherever *pron* 1 (*where there is doubt about the place of occurrence &c*) ge b' e càit(e), ~ **it happened, I don't remember it** ge b' e càit a thachair e, chan eil cuimhne *f* agam air; 2 (*where the place of occurrence is unimportant or undefined*) àite *m* sam bith, **we'll go** ~ **the sun's shining** thèid sin do àite sam bith far a bheil a' ghrian a' deàrrsadh; 3 (*emph for* **where**) càit air bith, ~ **did you see that?** càit air bith a chunna tu sin?

whereupon *adv* (is) leis (a) sin, **the bar closed,** ~ **he went home** dhùin am bàr, is leis a sin chaidh e dhachaigh

whether *conj* co aca, co-dhiù, **I don't care** ~ **you come or not** tha mi coma co aca/co dhiù an tig thu no nach tig

which *pron* cò, ~ **books do you like best?** cò na leabhraichean *mpl* as fheàrr leat?, **I'm not sure** ~ **of them I'll marry** chan eil mi cinnteach cò aca a phòsas mi

while *conj* fhad is a, ~ **she was in France she learnt French** fhad 's a bha i anns an Fhraing dh'ionnsaich i an Fhraingis

while *n* greis *f*, treis *f*, tamall *m*, tràth *m*, (*short* ~) greiseag *f*, treiseag *f*, tacan *m*, **for a** ~ fad greis/tamaill, airson greis/tamaill, *also* car uair *f*, **a** ~ **ago** o chionn ghreis/tamaill

while *v in expr* ~ **away time** cuir seachad ùine *f* (gu dìomhain)

whim *n* saobh-smuain *m*

whimper *n* sgiùgan *m*

whimper *v* dèan sgiùgan *m*

whinny *n* sitir *f*

whinny *v* dèan sitir *f*

whin(s) *n* conasg *m sing & coll*

whip *n* cuip *f*

whip *v* cuip *vt*, (*less usu*) sgiùrs *vt*

whipping *n* cuipeadh *m*

whisky *n* uisge-beatha *m*, (*nickname*) mac-na-bracha *m*

whisper *n* cagar *m*

whisper *v* cagair *vti*

whispering *n* cagar *m*, cagarsaich *f*

whistle *n* **1** (*the noise*) fead *f*; **2** (*the instrument: penny ~, Irish ~*) feadag *f*, fideag *f*, **he played a tune on the ~** ghabh e port *m* air an fheadaig *dat*; **3** *in expr* (*fam*) **wet your ~!** fliuch do ribheid *f*!

whistle *v* **1** (*a single whistle*) dèan fead *f*, leig fead (*with prep* à), **I ~d** rinn mi fead, leig mi fead asam; **2** (*more continuous whistling*) fead *vi*, **the wee boy was whistling** bha am balach beag a' feadail

whistling *n* **1** fead *f*, **the ~ of the wind** fead na gaoithe; **2** (*continuous, with the mouth*) feadaireachd *f invar*, feadalaich *f invar*, feadarsaich *f invar*

white *adj* **1** (*general*) geal, **black and ~** dubh is geal, **~ wine** fìon geal; **2** (*esp of hair, & of colouring of humans & animals*) bàn, (*trad*) fionn, **the ~ dog/ horse** an cù/an t-each bàn

white *n* **1** geal *m*, **the ~ of the eye** geal na sùla; **2** *in expr* **the ~ of an egg** gealagan *m*

whiten *v* gealaich *vti*

whiteness *n* gile *f invar*, gilead *m*

whiting *n* cuidhteag *f*

who *inter pron* cò, **~'s he?** cò esan?, **~ did it?** cò a rinn e?, **I don't know ~ it is** chan eil fhios *m* agam cò a th' ann

who *rel pron* a, (*in neg sentence*) nach, **the man ~ sang and the woman ~ wasn't listening to him** am fear *m* a sheinn agus an tè *f* nach robh ag èisdeachd ris

whoever *pron* **1** (*where there is doubt about the identity of the person*) ge b' e cò, **~ did it, I don't remember it** ge b' e cò a rinn e, chan eil cuimhne *f* agam air; **2** (*where the identity of the person is unimportant or undefined*) duine *m* sam bith, **we'll welcome ~ comes to the house** cuiridh sinn fàilte *f* air duine sam bith a thig dhan taigh *m*; **3** (*emph for* **who**) cò air bith, cò fon ghrèin (*dat sing of* grian *f*), **~ told you that?** cò air bith/cò fon ghrèin a dh'innis sin dhut?

whole *adj* **1** (*an object, period &c in its entirety*) gu lèir, air fad, uile, **the ~ army was captured** chaidh an t-arm gu lèir/air fad/uile an sàs *m*,

a ~ month mìos *mf* gu lèir/air fad, **they ravaged the ~ country** sgrios iad an dùthaich *f* air fad/gu lèir; **2** (*intact, undivided*) slàn, iomlan, **the (standing) stone isn't ~** chan eil an tursa slàn/iomlan, **a ~ word** facal slàn, **a ~ number** àireamh shlàn; **3** (*of periods of time*) fad (*with the gen*), **the ~ time** fad na h-ùine, **I was poor my ~ life** bha mi bochd fad mo bheatha *f gen*, **I'll be up the ~ night** bidh mi air mo chois (*gen of* cas *f*) fad na h-oidhche

whole *n* **1** *used with art,* an t-iomlan *m,* **do you want the ~ of it?** a bheil thu ag iarraidh an t-iomlan (dheth)?; **2** *in expr* **on the ~** san fharsaingeachd *f invar,* **on the ~ the majority are against him** san fharsaingeachd tha a' mhòr-chuid na aghaidh

wholeness *n* slàine *f invar*

wholesome *adj* slàn, fallain, **~ food** biadh slàn/fallain

whooping-cough *n* (*used with art*) an triuthach *f*

why *inter adv* carson, **~ did he leave?** carson a dh'fhalbh e?, **~ isn't Màiri at work? don't ask ~** carson nach eil Màiri ag obair? na faighnich carson

wicked *adj* olc, (*less usu*) aingidh

wickedness *n* olc *m,* donas *m,* (*less usu*) aingidheachd *f invar*

widdershins *adj* tuathal

wide *adj* farsaing, leathann, **far and ~** fad is farsaing

widen *v* leudaich *vti*

widened *adj* leudaichte

widow *n* ban(n)trach *f*

widower *n* ban(n)trach *m*

widowhood *n* banntrachas *m*

width *n* farsaingeachd *f invar,* leud *m*

wield *v* (*tool, weapon &c*) làimhsich *vt,* iomair *vt*

wife *n* **1** bean *f,* bean-phòsta *f,* **my ~** a' bhean agam; **2** *in expr* (*fam*) **the ~** a' chailleach

wife, wifie *n* (*fam*) cailleach *f,* **the hen ~** cailleach nan cearc *fpl*

wig *n* gruag-bhrèige *f*

wild *adj* **1** (*not domesticated*) fiadhaich, **~ goat** gobhar fhiadhaich; **2** (*weather, landscape &c*) garbh, **a ~ night** oidhche gharbh, **~ country** tìr *mf* gharbh; **3** (*unruly, turbulent*) garbh, garg, borb, **a ~ people** sluagh garbh/garg/borb; **4** (*fam: angry*) fiadhaich, **I was ~ after what he said to me** (*fam*) bha mi fiadhaich an dèidh na thuirt e rium; **5** (*fam: hard-living, hard-drinking &c*) fiadhaich, garbh, **he's a ~ man, right enough!** 's e duine fiadhaich/garbh a th' ann dheth, ceart gu leòr!; **6** *in expr* **~ and woolly** molach

wildcat *n* cat fiadhaich

wilderness *n* fàsach *mf,* (*less usu*) dìthreabh *f*

wildness *n* gairbhe *f invar,* gairbhead *m,* gairge *f invar,* buirbe *f invar*

wile *n* cuilbheart *f,* innleachd *f,* car *m*

wilful *adj* ceann-làidir, rag, rag-mhuinealach, dùr

will *n* **1** toil *f*, **God's** ~ toil Dhè (*gen of* Dia *m*), (*prov*) **where there's a** ~ **there's a way** far am bi toil, bidh gnìomh *m*; **2** (*for making legacy*) tiomnadh *m*, **he didn't make a** ~ cha do rinn e tiomnadh

willing *adj* deònach, èasgaidh, toileach, **they're not** ~ **to do it** chan eil iad deònach (air) a dhèanamh, chan eil iad èasgaidh/toileach a dhèanamh

willingly *adv* a dheòin, ~ **or not/or otherwise**, ~ **or un**~ a dheòin no a dh'aindeoin

willingness *n* deòin *f*

willow *n* seileach *m*

willy-nilly *adv* a dheòin no a dh'aindeoin

wily *adj* carach, fiar, seòlta, (*less usu*) caon

win *v* **1** (*as vt*) coisinn *vt*, faigh *vt irreg*, buannaich *vt*, ~ **fame/glory** coisinn/ buannaich cliù *m invar*, ~ **a prize** coisinn/faigh/buannaich duais *f*; **2** (*as vi: in battle, race, competition &c*) buannaich *vi*, buinnig & buintig *vi*, **we won** bhuannaich sinn, (*fam: eg to someone working at a task*) **are you ~ning?** a bheil thu a' buintig?; **3** *in expr* ~ **to** (*ie reach*) buannaich *vt*, **we won to the village at dusk** bhuannaich sinn am baile am beul *m* na h-oidhche

wind *n* **1** gaoth *f*, **the west** ~ gaoth an iar, **a breath of** ~ oiteag *f*, ospag *f*; **2** (*intestinal* ~) *used with art*, a' ghaoth

wind *v* toinn *vt*

windfall *n* turchairt *f*

winding *adj* (*road, river &c*) lùbach

winding-sheet *n* marbhfhaisg *f*

windmill *n* muileann-gaoithe *mf*

window *n* **1** uinneag *f*, **look out of the** ~ coimhead *vi* a-mach air an uinneig (*dat*), ~ **bars** cliath-uinneige *f*; **2** *in expr* ~ **pane** lòsan *m*

windowsill *n* oir *f* (na h-)uinneige

windsock *n* muincheann-gaoithe *m*

windy *adj* **1** gaothach, **a** ~ **day** latha gaothach; **2** *in expr* **it's** ~ **today** tha gaoth *f* ann an-diugh

wine *n* fìon *m*, **red/white** ~ fìon dearg/geal

wing *n* **1** sgiath *f*; **2** *in expr* **on the** ~ air iteig (*dat of* iteag *f*)

wink *n* **1** priobadh *m* (na sùla); **2** *in expr* ~ **of sleep** norrag *f* chadail *m gen*, **I didn't get a** ~ **of sleep** cha d'fhuair mi norrag chadail

wink *v* priob *vi*, (*less usu*) caog *vi*

winkle *n* faochag *f*

winner *n* buannaiche *m*

winter *n* geamhradh *m*

wintry *adj* geamhrachail

wipe *v* suath *vt*, siab *vt*

wiper *n* siabair *m*

wire *n* uèir *f*, **barbed** ~ uèir-bhiorach

wisdom *n* gliocas *m*

wise *adj* glic

wish *n* **1** (*a* ~ *to achieve, acquire &c something, an ambition*) miann *mf*, rùn *m*, togradh *m*, (*less usu*) dèidh *f*; **2** (~ *directed towards others*) guidhe *mf*, **a good/ill** ~ deagh/droch ghuidhe, (*a good* ~, *a greeting*) dùrachd *m*, (*corres &c*) **with best ~es** leis gach deagh dhùrachd

wish *v* **1** (*desire something,* ~ *for something*) miannaich *vt*, rùnaich *vt*; **2** (~ *that something were the case*) is miann leis (*&c*), bu mhiann leis (*&c*), **I** ~ **I could win a prize in the lottery** bu mhiann leam gum faighinn duais *f* sa chrannchur *m*; **3** (*often used as vi in rel fut tense*) togair *vi*, **we'll go on holiday, if you** ~ thèid sinn air làithean-saora *mpl*, ma thogras tu, **just as you** ~ dìreach mar a thogras sibh; **4** (*directing a good or bad* ~ *at someone*) guidh *vt* (*with preps* air & do), **I** ~ **a curse on him** guidhidh mi mallachd *f* air, **~ing him a Happy Christmas** a' guidhe Nollaig Chridheil dha, **I** ~ **you health and happiness** (*trad*) guidheam (*present imperative*) slàint' *f* is sonas *m* dhut

wishing well *n* tobar *mf* miann *mf gen*

wisp *n* (*esp of straw, hay*) sop *m*

wit *n* **1** (*witty humour*) eirmse *f*; **2** (*common sense*) toinisg *f*, ciall *f*; **3** (*usu in pl: mind, sanity*) ~**s** ciall *f*, rian *m*, reusan *m*, **he lost his ~s** chaill e a chiall, **she was at her ~s' end** bha i gu bhith às a ciall

witch *n* **1** bana-bhuidseach *f*; **2** *in expr* **old** ~ (*pej*) cailleach *f*

witchcraft *n* buidseachas *m*

with *prep* **1** (*accompanying, in the company of*) còmhla ri, le (*takes the dat; before the art,* leis), (*less usu, more trad*) cuide ri, mar ri, maille ri, **I went** ~ **the others** chaidh mi ann còmhla ri càch *pron*, **where's Eilidh?** ~ **the old folks** càit a bheil Eilidh? còmhla ris na seann daoine *mpl*, ~ **compliments** le deagh dhùrachd *m*, *Note: the use of* le/leis *for this sense of* **with** *when referring to people is not always considered to be good style;* **2** (*by means of*) le (*takes the dat: before the art,* leis), **he hit it** ~ **a hammer/~ the hammer** bhuail e e le òrd/leis an òrd; **3** (*expr direction, esp in the exprs*) (**going &c**) ~ **the slope/~ the current** (a' dol *&c*) leis a' bhruthaich *mf*/leis an t-sruth *m*; **4** (*as a consequence of*) leis, **I can't see you** ~ **it being so dark** chan fhaic mi thu leis cho dorch 's a tha e

withdraw *v* tarraing *vti* air ais, thoir *vt* air ais

withdrawn *adj* (*of persons*) fad às, dùinte

wither *v* crìon *vti*, searg *vti*

withered *adj & past part* crìon, seargte

withhold *v* cùm *vt* air ais

without *prep* gun (*takes dat, aspirates/lenites following cons except for d, n & t*), ~ **peace/rest** gun fhois *f*, ~ **delay** gun dàil *f*, **she bought it** ~ **my knowledge/~ me knowing** cheannaich i e gun fhios *m* dhomhsa

withstand *v* **1** (*resist*) seas *vi* (*with prep* ri); **2** (*bear, tolerate*) fuiling & fulaing *vt*

witness *n* **1** (*abstr*) fianais *f*, **bear ~ thoir** fianais; **2** (*con: a ~ at scene of crime, at trial &c*) fear-fianais *m*, neach-fianais *m* (*pl* luchd-fianais *m sing coll*)

witness *v* **1** faic *vt*, bi *vi irreg* na (*&c*) f(h)ear-fianais *m*; **2** (*legal: ~ a document &c*) dèan fianais *f* (*with prep* do)

witty *adj* eirmseach

wizard *n* buidseach *m*, draoidh *m*

wizardry *n* draoidheachd *f invar*

wizened *adj* crìon

wobbly *adj* cugallach, **~ table** bòrd cugallach

woe *n* **1** (*grief*) bròn *m*, mulad *f*; **2** (*grief & misfortune*) dòlas *m*, truaighe *f*; **3** *in excls &c* **~ is me!** an dòlas!, mo thruaighe!, mo sgrios *m*!, **~ to/~ betide** (*trad*) is mairg *adj* (*with rel pron* a), **~ to/~ betide anyone who would come near him** (*trad*) is mairg a thigeadh faisg air

woeful *adj* brònach, muladach, truagh

wolf *n* madadh-allaidh *m*, (*less usu*) faol *m*

woman *n* boireannach *m*, tè *f*, (*less usu*) bean *f*, **women on the left please!** boireannaich air an làimh *f dat* chlì mas e ur toil *m* e!, **the ~ who sang** am boireannach/an tè a sheinn, **the ~ of the house** bean an taighe *m*, **an old ~** seann bhoireannach, (*fam*) cailleach *f*, (*of one's wife*) **the/my old ~** (*fam*) a' chailleach

womanly *adj* banail

womb *n* machlag *f*, brù *f*, broinn *f*

wonder *n* iongnadh *m*, (*stronger*) iongantas *m*, mìorbhail *f*, **no ~ he's pleased!** chan iongnadh gu bheil e toilichte!

wonderful *adj* iongantach, mìorbhaileach

wood *n* **1** (*the material: ~ in general, ~ not worked*) fiodh *m*, **put ~ on the fire** cuir fiodh air an teine *m*; **2** (*usu for shaped or worked ~*) maide *m*; **3** (*a group of trees*) coille *f*, (*small ~*) doire *mf*; **4** *in expr* **pine ~** giùthsach *f*

woodcock *n* coileach-coille *m*

woodcutter *n* coillear *m*, geàrradair-fiodha *m*

wooden *adj* fiodha (*gen sing of* fiodh *m*), **a ~ house** taigh *m* fiodha

wood-louse *n* reudan *m*

wool *n* clòimh *f*, olann *f*

woollen *adj* de chlòimh *f*

woolly *adj* **1** clòimheach, ollach; **2** (*of unkempt human hair*) **(wild and) ~** molach, ròmach; **3** (*of thinking &c*) ceòthach

word *n* **1** (*written or spoken*) facal *m*, **'eaglais' is a feminine ~** is e facal boireann a tha ann an 'eaglais', **she said a ~ or two/a few ~s in Gaelic** thubhairt i facal no dhà anns a' Ghàidhlig *f*, **we didn't speak a ~ of Gaelic on the ferry** cha do bhruidhinn sinn facal Gàidhlig air a' bhàt'-aiseig *m*, **~ for ~** facal air an fhacal; **2** (*esp in pl, statements, pronouncements &c*) briathran (*pl of* briathar *m*), **foolish/sensible ~s** briathran amaideach/ciallach, **don't believe politicians' ~s** na creid briathran luchd-poileataics *m sing coll*; **3** (*promise, ~ of honour*) facal *m*,

will you give me your ~ (on it)? an toir thu dhomh d' fhacal (air)?;
4 (*information, news*) fios *m*, guth *m*, sgeul *m*, **we sent him** ~ chuir
sinn fios thuige, **is there any** ~ **of Mary?** a bheil fios/sgeul air Màiri?,
I didn't hear a ~ **about her** cha chuala mi guth mu deidhinn; 5 (*esp in
neg sentences: a sound, a syllable &c*) bìd *f*, bìog *f*, smid *f*, **he didn't say a**
~ cha duirt e bìd/bìog/smid, **he didn't hear a** ~ cha chuala e bìd/bìog;
6 *in exprs* (IT) ~ **processor** facladair *m*, ~ **processing** facladaireachd *f*
invar

wordy *adj* faclach, briathrach

work *n* 1 (*abstr & con*) obair *f*, (*usu more abstr*) cosnadh *m*, **I've got** ~ **to do**
tha obair agam ri dhèanamh, **hard** ~ obair chruaidh, **out of** ~ a-mach à
dh'obair, gun obair, gun chosnadh; 2 (*the product of* ~) obair *f*, **needle**~
obair-ghrèis *f*, **handi**~ obair-làimhe *f*; 3 (IT) ~ **station** ionad-obrach *m*

work *v* 1 (*as vi*) obraich *occas* oibrich *vi*, **the washer isn't** ~**ing** chan eil an
t-inneal-nighe ag obrachadh, **we tried to play a trick on her but it
didn't** ~ dh'fheuch sinn car *m* a chur aiste ach cha do dh'obraich e; 2
(*as vt*) obraich *vt*, ~ **a machine** obraich inneal *m*, ~ **land/a croft** obraich
fearann *m*/croit *f*, *also* àitich fearann/croit; 3 (*to be at* ~) bi *vi irreg* ag
obair, **he's** ~**ing today** tha e ag obair an-diugh; 4 (*to have* ~) bi *vi irreg*
obair (*with prep* aig), **are you** ~**ing just now?** a bheil obair agad an-
dràsta?

worker *n* 1 fear-obrach *m*, neach-obrach *m*, oibriche *m*, ~**s** luchd-obrach
or luchd-oibre *m sing coll*, **fellow** ~ co-oibriche *m*; 2 *in expr* **forestry** ~
coillear *m*

workforce *n* luchd-obrach *or* luchd-oibre *m sing coll*

working party *n* buidheann-obrach *mf*

workman *n* oibriche *m*, fear-obrach *m*

workshop *n* bùth-obrach *mf*

world *n* 1 (*esp the* ~ *as man's abode, and as opposed to heaven*) saoghal *m*;
2 (*esp the* ~ *as the physical globe, the planet*) cruinne *mf* (*used with art:
m in nom sing, f in gen sing*), **the** ~ an cruinne, **the end(s) of the** ~
crìoch *f* na cruinne, (*sport*) **the World Cup** Cuach *f* na Cruinne; 3 (*a
particular sphere of activity*) saoghal *m*, **the business** ~/**the** ~ **of business**
saoghal a' ghnìomhachais *m*; 4 *in expr* (*emph*) **where in the** ~ càit air an
t-saoghal, **where in the** ~ **are they going?** càit air an t-saoghal a bheil
iad a' dol?

worldly *adj* 1 (*as opposed to heavenly, spiritual &c*) saoghalta, talmhaidh;
2 *in exprs* ~ **goods/wealth** maoin *f*, **my** ~ **possessions/goods** (*trad*) mo
chuid *f* den t-saoghal *m*

worm *n* boiteag *f*, cnuimh *f*

worn *adj & past part* 1 caithte; 2 (*of clothing, fabrics: threadbare &c*) lom, **a** ~
coat còta *m* lom; 3 *in expr* ~ **out** (*of objects*) caithte, (*of living creatures:
exhausted &c*) claoidhte

worried *adj* 1 fo chùram *m*, draghail, fo iomagain *f*, iomagaineach, (**about**

mu), **she was** ~ bha i fo chùram/fo iomagain, *also* bha uallach *m* oirre; **2** *in expr* **become** ~ gabh uallach, gabh/dèan dragh *m*; **3** (~ *in a nervy, niggly way*) frionasach

worry *n* **1** dragh *m*, uallach *m*, **lack of money is causing me** ~ tha dìth *m* airgid *m gen* a' dèanamh dragh dhomh; **2** *in expr* **prone to** ~ cùramach

worry *v* **1** (*as vi: be worried, begin to worry*) gabh dragh *m*, dèan dragh *m*, gabh uallach *m*, **don't** ~**!** na dèan dragh!, *also* dad ort!, coma leat!, na gabh ort!; **2** (*as vt: cause worry*) cuir dragh *m* (*with prep* air), dèan dragh (*with prep* do), ~ **someone** cuir dragh air cuideigin, dèan dragh do chuideigin, **lack of money is** ~**ing me** tha dìth *m* airgid *m gen* a' dèanamh dragh dhomh; **3** *in expr* **it didn't** ~ **me in the least** cha do chuir e suas no sìos mi (*fam*)

worrying *adj* (*person, situation*) draghail, iomagaineach, imcheisteach

worse *comp adj* **1** nas miosa, (*in past tense*) na bu mhiosa, **the father is wicked but the son is** ~ tha an t-athair olc ach tha am mac nas miosa, **get/become** ~ fàs *vi* nas miosa, *also* rach *vi irreg* am miosad *f*; **2** *in expr* **the** ~ miste & misde (*with v irreg & def* is), **I am the** ~ **for it** is miste mi e, **you'd be none the** ~ **for a dram** cha bu mhiste sibh drama *m*

worship *n* adhradh *m*

worship *v* dèan/thoir adhradh *m* (*with prep* do)

worst *superlative adj* **1** as miosa, (*in past tense*) a bu mhiosa, **you were the** ~ is tusa a bu mhiosa, **the** ~ **man/one** am fear as miosa; **2** *in exprs* **the** ~ **of** diù *m invar* (*with gen*), **the** ~ **of jobs/professions** diù nan dreuchdan *fpl*, **at** ~ aig a' char *m* as miosa, **we'll only spend four pounds at** ~ cha chosg sinn ach ceithir notaichean *fpl* aig a' char as miosa

worth *adj* fiach *adj*, fiù *adj*, (*with v* is), luach *m invar*, **one more time? it's not** ~ **it!** aon uair *f* eile? chan fhiach e!, **a thing** ~ **seeing** rud *m* as fhiach fhaicinn *f invar*, **is this** ~ **anything to/for you? no!** an fhiach seo dhut? chan fhiach!, **for what it's** ~ airson na 's fhiach e, **it's not** ~ **our while/** ~ **our effort** chan fhiach dhuinn ar saothair *f*, **what's it** ~ dè a luach?, **it's not** ~ **10p** chan fhiù e deich sgillinn *f*

worth *n* fiach *m*, **give me two pounds'** ~ **of it** thoir dhomh fiach dà nota *f* dheth

worthless *adj* **1** (*without value*) gun fhiù *m invar*, gun luach *m invar*; **2** (*of no use*) gun fheum *m*

worthwhile *adj* fiach *adj*, with *v irreg & def* is (*to/for* do), **is it** ~ **for us?** an fhiach e dhuinn?, an fhiach dhuinn ar saothair *f*?

worthy *adj* **1** airidh, toillteanach, (*of* air), ~ **of a kiss** airidh/toillteanach air pòg *f*; **2** (*decent*) còir, **a** ~ **man** duine còir

wound *n* (*phys or emotional*) leòn *m*, (*less usu*) lot *m*, creuchd *f*

wound *v* (*phys or emotionally*) leòn *vt*, (*less usu*) lot *vt*, creuchd *vt*

wounded *adj* **1** leònta & leònte; **2** *in expr* **the** ~ na leòintich *mpl*

wounding *adj* (*remarks &c*) guineach

woven *adj & past part* fighte

wrangle *n* conas *m*

wrangle *v* connsaich *vi*, connspaid *vi*

wrangling *n* connspaid *f*

wrangling *adj* connspaideach

wrap *v* **1** (*envelope &c*) suain *vt*; **2** ~ **(up)** (*parcel &c*) paisg *vt*, fill *vt*

wrapping *n* pasgadh *m*

wrath *n* fearg *f*

wrathful *adj* feargach

wreathe *v* toinn *vt*

wreck *n* (*of ship*) long-bhriseadh *m*

wreck *v* **1** sgrios *vt*, mill *vt*; **2** (*fig:* ~ *someone's plan &c*) mill *vt*

wren *n* dreathan-donn *m*

wrestle *v* gleac *vi* (**with, against** ri)

wretch *n* **1** (*poverty-stricken, unfortunate &c person*) truaghan *m*; **2** (*despicable &c person*) duine suarach, duine tàireil

wretched *adj* **1** (*pitiable*) truagh, ~ **poverty** bochdainn thruagh, ~ **person/ creature** truaghan *m*; **2** (*despicable &*) suarach, tàireil

wring *v* fàisg *vt*

wrinkle *n* preas & preasadh *m*, preasag *f*, (*less usu*) roc *f*

wrinkle *v* preas *vt*

wrinkled, wrinkly *adj* preasach

wrist *n* caol *m* an dùirn (*gen of* dòrn *m*), **my** ~ caol mo dhùirn

writ *n* sgrìobhainn-chùirte *f*

write *v* **1** sgrìobh *vti* (**to** gu), **she wrote me a letter** sgrìobh i litir *f* thugam, **he** ~**s poetry** bidh e a' sgrìobhadh bàrdachd *f invar*; **2** *in expr* ~ **off debts** cuir fiachan *mpl* às a' chunntas *m*

writer *n* **1** sgrìobhadair *m*, sgrìobhaiche *m*; **2** *in expr* **writer-in-residence** filidh *m*, **writer-in-residence at Sabhal Mòr Ostaig** filidh aig Sabhal Mòr Ostaig

writing *n* sgrìobhadh *m*, (*hand~*) làmh-sgrìobhadh *m*

wrong *adj* **1** (*of statements, opinions &c: incorrect, inappropriate*) ceàrr, mearachdach, iomrallach, **a** ~ **answer** freagairt cheàrr, **you are** ~! tha thu ceàrr!, **the** ~ **train** an trèana cheàrr, **far** ~ fada ceàrr; **2** (*morally* ~) eucorach, (*stronger*) olc, ~ **actions** gnìomhan *mpl* eucorach

wrong *adv* **1** (*not as it should be, awry*) ceàrr, tuathail, **there's something** ~ **with my back/my radio** tha rudeigin ceàrr air mo dhruim *m*/air an rèidio *m* agam; **2** *in expr* **what's** ~ **with you**? dè a tha a' gabhail riut?, dè a tha thu a' gearan?; **3** *in expr* **go** ~ (*ie make a mistake*) rach *vi* air iomrall *m*; **4** *in expr* **go** ~ (*morally*) rach *vi* air iomrall *m*, rach *vi* air seachran *m*

wrong *n* eucoir *f*, coire *f*

wrong *v* dèan eucoir *f* (*with prep* air), **they** ~**ed me** rinn iad eucoir orm

wrongful *adj* eucorach

wynd *n* caol-shràid *f*

X

x-ray *n* x-gath *m*, gath-x *m*, ~ **therapy** leigheas *m* x-gath
xenophobia *n* gall-ghamhlas *m*
Xmas *n* (*usu used with definite art*) An Nollaig *f*, ~ **time** àm *m* na Nollaig(e),
    Merry ~! Nollaig Chridheil!
xylophone *n* saidhleafon *m*

Y

yacht *n* sgoth-long *f*, (*less trad*) gheat *f*
yard[1] *n* **1** (*enclosed space*) cùirt *f*; **2** (*school play area &c*) raon-cluiche *m*;
    3 (*agric: for corn, straw &c*) iodhlann *f*
yard[2] *n* (*unit of measurement*) slat *f*
yardstick *n* (*lit & fig: ie criterion &c*) slat-thomhais *f*
yawl *n* geòla *f*
yawn *n* mèaran *&* mèanan *m*
yawn *v* dèan mèaranaich/mèananaich *f*, **you're ~ing a lot today!** 's ann ort
    a tha a' mhèaranaich an-diugh!
yawning *n* mèaranaich *&* mèananaich *f*
year *n* bliadhna *f*, **four ~s old** ceithir bliadhna a dh'aois, **leap ~** bliadhna-
    leum *f*, (*advs*) **this ~** am bliadhna, **next ~** an ath-bhliadhna, **last ~** an-
    uiridh, **the ~ before last** a' bhon-uiridh
yearling *adj* bliadhnach
yearling *n* bliadhnach *m*
yearly *adj* bliadhnail
yearning *n* fadachd *f invar*, fadal *m* (**for** ri)
yeast *n* beirm *f*
yell *n* sgairt *f*, glaodh *m*, ràn *m*, (*esp shrill & sudden*) sgal *m*, sgiamh *m*
yell *v* dèan sgairt *f*, glaodh *vi*, ràn *vi*, (*esp shrilly & suddenly*) sgal *vi*, sgiamh
    vi
yelling *n* sgreuchail *f invar*, rànail *m invar*, rànaich *f invar*, sgaladh *m*
yellow *adj* buidhe, **the Yellow Pages** Na Duilleagan *fpl* Buidhe
yes *adv* **1** (*as affirmative response*) *rendered by repetition of the main verb used in*
    the question, **are you tired?** ~ a bheil thu sgìth? thà, **did you believe it?**
    ~ an do chreid thu e? chreid, **will you go?** ~ an tèid thu ann? thèid, **did**
    you see him? ~ am faca tu e? chunnaic; **2** (*as a non-affirmative response*
    to a statement, or on being addressed &c) seadh *adv* (*v irreg & def* is, *plus*
    obs neuter pron eadh), **Iain! ~?** Iain! Seadh?, **I saw Màiri yesterday. ~?**
    Chunna mi Màiri an-dè. Seadh? **I was in the bar. The bar? The bar**
    in the village. Oh yes. Bha mi anns a' bhàr. Am bar? Am bar anns a'
    bhaile. Oh seadh, seadh

yesterday *adv* an-dè

yet *adv* **1** fhathast, **the rain hasn't stopped** ~ cha do sguir an t-uisge fhathast, **is breakfast ready? not** ~ a bheil a' bhracaist deiseil? chan eil fhathast, **we'll get the better of it/crack it** ~ nì sinn a' chùis air fhathast; **2** *in expr* **the bus (&c) hasn't come (&c)** ~ tha am bus (&c) gun tighinn (&c) fhathast

yet *conj* ach, ge-tà, air a shon sin, **they got engaged, ~ they didn't get married** thug iad gealladh-pòsaidh *m* dha chèile, ach cha do phòs iad/cha do phòs iad ge-tà/cha do phòs iad air a shon sin

yew *n* (*wood & tree*) iubhar *m*, (*tree*) craobh-iubhair *f*

yield *n* (*of crops, investment &c*) toradh *m*

yield *v* **1** (*submit*) gèill *vi*, strìochd *vi*, (**to** do); **2** (*as vt*) thoir *vt* suas (**to** do), **he ~ed his power** thug e suas a chumhachd *mf invar*; **3** (*give, provide*) thoir *vt* seachad, **this investment ~s five per cent** bidh an tasgadh seo a' toirt seachad còig sa cheud *m*, *also* 's e toradh *m* an tasgaidh seo còig sa cheud

yielding *adj* (*of ground &c*) bog, tais; (*of person, character*) sochar, meata

yielding *n* gèilleadh *m*, strìochdadh *m*

yobbish *adj* gràisgeil

yobbishness *n* gràisgealachd *f invar*

yoke *n* cuing *f*, (*also fig*) **beneath the tyrant's** ~ fo chuing an aintighearna

yolk *n* buidheagan *m*

yon, yonder *adj* ud, ann an siud, ~ **house** an taigh ud, an taigh ann an siud

yonder *adv* **1** an siud, ann an siud; **2** *in expr* **over** ~ thall, thall an siud, **over ~ in America** ann an Ameireagaidh *f* thall, thall an Ameireagaidh, **it's raining over** ~ tha e a' sileadh thall an siud

you *pers pron* (*sing fam*) thu, (*pl & formal sing*) sibh, (*emph*) thusa, sibhse & thu-fhèin, sibh-fhèin, **I'm well, how are ~?** tha mi gu math, ciamar a tha thu-fhèin/sibh-fhèin?, **good for ~!** 's math thu fhèin!, (*Note Gaelic constr with poss adj & verbal noun eg*) **it's good to see ~** is math d' fhaicinn/ur faicinn

young *adj* **1** òg, **a ~ girl** caileag *f* òg, **a ~ man** duine *m* òg, *also* gille *m*, òganach *m*, ~ **people/folk** *n* daoine *mpl* òga, *also* òigridh *f sing coll invar*; **2** *in exprs* **my ~ days** làithean *mpl* m' òige *f invar*, ~ **love** gaol *m* na h-òige,

young *n* **1** (~ *of animals, birds*) àl *m*; **2** *in expr* **the** ~ (*ie young people*) na daoine *mpl* òga

youngster *n* (*male*) òganach *m*, (*of either sex*) òigear *m*, ~**s** òigridh *f sing coll invar*

your *poss adj* **1** (*sing, fam*) do (*lenites following cons where possible*), (*pl & formal sing*) ur, bhur, ~ **parents** do phàrantan *mpl or* ur pàrantan, **get ~ breath back!** leig d' anail *f*! *or* leigibh ur n-anail; **2** *also expressed by prep prons* agad (*sing, fam*) & agaibh (*pl & formal sing*), *appended to the* *noun*, ~ **house** an taigh *m* agad/agaibh; *Note that as a general rule the poss adjs* mo, do, *&c tend to be used in preference to* agam, agad *&c where the connection with the object concerned is more intimate*

yours *poss pron* **1** (*sing, fam*) leat(sa), (*pl & formal sing*) leibh(se), **is it ~?** an ann leatsa/leibhse a tha e?; **2** (*in corres*) **~s sincerely** le dùrachd *m*, is mise le meas *m invar*

yourself *reflexive pron* (*sing, fam*) thu-fhèin, (*pl & formal sing*) sibh-fhèin, **take care of ~** thoir an aire ort fhèin, thoiribh an aire oirbh fhèin; *for further examples cf* **myself**

youth *n* (*abstr*) **1** òige *f invar*, **the days of my ~** làithean *mpl* m' òige; **2** (*young male person*) **a ~** òigear *m*, òganach *m*, gille *m*; **3** (*coll: young people*) òigridh *f sing coll invar*, **the ~ of today/today's ~** òigridh an là an-diugh, **a ~ club/group** buidheann *mf* òigridh

Z

zeal *n* dìoghras *m*, dealas *m*, eud & iad *m invar*
zealous *adj* dealasach, dùrachdach, dìcheallach
zero *n* neoni *f invar*
zestful *adj* brìghmhor
zinc *n* si(o)nc *m*
zone *n* sòn *m*
zoo *n* sutha *f*

The Forms of the Gaelic Article

	Singular		Plural
	Masculine	**Feminine**	**Both Genders**
Nom & Acc	**an** (*before consonants, exc b, f, m, p*) **am** (*before b, f, m, p*) **an t-** (*before a vowel*)	**an** (*before a vowel or fh, d, l, n, r or t*) **a'** (*before bh, ch, gh, mh, ph*) **an t-** (*before s followed by l, n, r, or by a vowel*)	**na** **na h-** (*before a vowel*)
e.g.	an taigh, **an sìol**, an sruth **am** bodach, **am** fraoch an t-eilean	an ite, an fhras a' chraobh. **a'** ghaoth an t-sìde, **an t-sròn**	**na** caileagan **na h-òrain**
Gen	**an** **a'** } *Same as Nom Feminine* **an t-**	**na** **na h-** (*before a vowel*)	**nan** **nam** (*before b, f, m, p*)
e.g.	an eilean, an taighe, an fhraoich a' bhodaich **an t-sìl**, **an t-sruith**	na gaoithe, **na craoibhe**, **na sròine** **na h-ite**	nan taighean, **nan** òran **nam** bodach
Dat	**an** **a'** } *Same as Nom Feminine* **an t-**	**an** **a'** } *Same as Nom Feminine* **an t-**	**na** **na h-** } *Same as Nom Plural*
e.g.	an eilean, an taigh, an fhraoch a' bhodach **an t-sìol**, **an t-sruth**	an tràigh a' ghaoith, a' chraoibh **an t-sùil**, **an t-slait**, **an t-sròin**	**na** caileagan **na h-òrain**

Note: In the Dative Singular, for both genders, after a preposition ending in a vowel the article is shortened to **'n** or **'n t-**, and combined with the preposition. E.g: **don** bhùth, **on** taigh, **bhon t-**sìol, **tron** choille, **fon t-**sruth, **mun** bhòrd.